VOLUME A:
ANTIQUITY AND THE MID

MW00999741

# THE WESTERN
# EXPERIENCE

VOLUME A:
ANTIQUITY AND THE MIDDLE AGES

# THE WESTERN EXPERIENCE

*EIGHTH EDITION*

MORTIMER CHAMBERS
*University of California, Los Angeles*

BARBARA HANAWALT
*The Ohio State University*

THEODORE K. RABB
*Princeton University*

ISSER WOLOCH
*Columbia University*

RAYMOND GREW
*University of Michigan*

Boston   Burr Ridge, IL   Dubuque, IA   Madison, WI   New York   San Francisco   St. Louis
Bangkok   Bogotá   Caracas   Kuala Lumpur   Lisbon   London   Madrid   Mexico City
Milan   Montreal   New Delhi   Santiago   Seoul   Singapore   Sydney   Taipei   Toronto

# McGraw-Hill Higher Education ⅋

*A Division of The* **McGraw-Hill** *Companies*

THE WESTERN EXPERIENCE VOLUME A: ANTIQUITY AND THE MIDDLE AGES
Published by McGraw-Hill, a business unit of The McGraw-Hill Companies, Inc., 1221 Avenue of the Americas, New York, NY, 10020. Copyright © 2003, 1999, 1995, 1991, 1987, 1983, 1979, 1974 by The McGraw-Hill Companies, Inc. All rights reserved. No part of this publication may be reproduced or distributed in any form or by any means, or stored in a database or retrieval system, without the prior written consent of The McGraw-Hill Companies, Inc., including, but not limited to, in any network or other electronic storage or transmission, or broadcast for distance learning.

1 2 3 4 5 6 7 8 9 0 DOW/DOW 0 9 8 7 6 5 4 3 2

ISBN 0-07-249377-1

Vice president and editor-in-chief: *Thalia Dorwick*
Executive editor: *Lyn Uhl*
Sponsoring editor: *Monica Eckman*
Editorial coordinator: *Angela Kao*
Marketing manager: *Janise Fry*
Media technology producer: *Ginger Warner*
Senior project manager: *Jean Hamilton*
Senior production supervisor: *Lori Koetters*
Freelance design coordinator: *Gino Cieslik*
Senior supplement producer: *Rose M. Range*
Photo research coordinator: *Ira C. Roberts*
Photo researcher: *PhotoSearch, Inc.*
Cover Design: *Gino Cieslik*
Typeface: *10/12 Palatino*
Compositor: *GAC Indianapolis*
Printer: *R. R. Donnelley*

**Library of Congress Control Number: 2002107630**

www.mhhe.com

# About the Authors

**Mortimer Chambers** is Professor of History at the University of California at Los Angeles. He was a Rhodes scholar from 1949 to 1952 and received an M.A. from Wadham College, Oxford, in 1955 after obtaining his doctorate from Harvard University in 1954. He has taught at Harvard University (1954–1955) and the University of Chicago (1955–1958). He was Visiting Professor at the University of British Columbia in 1958, the State University of New York at Buffalo in 1971, the University of Freiburg (Germany) in 1974, and Vassar College in 1988. A specialist in Greek and Roman history, he is coauthor of *Aristotle's History of Athenian Democracy* (1962), editor of a series of essays entitled *The Fall of Rome* (1963), and author of *Georg Busolt: His Career in His Letters* (1990) and of *Staat der Athener*, a German translation and commentary to Aristotle's *Constitution of the Athenians* (1990). He has edited Greek texts of the latter work (1986) and of the *Hellenica Oxyrhynchia* (1993). He has contributed articles to the *American Historical Review and Classical Philology* as well as to other journals, both in America and in Europe. He is also an editor of *Historia*, the international journal of ancient history.

**Barbara Hanawalt** is the King George III Chair of British History at The Ohio State University and the author of numerous books and articles on the social and cultural history of the Middle Ages. Her publications include *The Middle Ages: An Illustrated History* (1999), *'Of Good and Ill Repute': Gender and Social Control in Medieval England* (1998), *Growing Up in Medieval London: The Experience of Childhood in History* (1993), *The Ties That Bound: Peasant Life in Medieval England* (1986), and *Crime and Conflict in English Communities, 1300–1348* (1979). She received her M.A. in 1964 and her Ph.D. in 1970, both from the University of Michigan. She has served as president of the Social Science History Association and has been on the Council of the American Historical Association and the Medieval Academy of America. She is currently second vice president of the Medieval Academy of America. She was an NEH fellow (1997–1998), a fellow of the Guggenheim Foundation (1998–1999), an ALCS Fellow in 1975–1976, a fellow at the National Humanities Center (1997–1998), a fellow at the Wissenschaftskolleg in Berlin (1990–1991), a member of the School of Historical Research at the Institute for Advanced Study, and a senior research fellow at the Newberry Library in 1979–1980.

**Theodore K. Rabb** is Professor of History at Princeton University. He received his Ph.D. from Princeton, and subsequently taught at Stanford, Northwestern, Harvard, and Johns Hopkins universities. He is the author of numerous articles and reviews in journals such as *The New York Times*, and the *Times Literary Supplement*, and he has been editor of *The Journal of Interdisciplinary*

*History* since its foundation. Among his books are *The Struggle for Stability in Early Modern Europe* (1975), *Renaissance Lives* (1993), and *Jacobean Gentleman* (1999). He has won awards from the Guggenheim Foundation, the National Endowment for the Humanities, the American Historical Association and The National Council for Historical Education. He was the principal historian for the PBS series, *Renaissance,* which was nominated for an Emmy.

**Isser Woloch** is Moore Collegiate Professor of History at Columbia University. He received his Ph.D. (1965) from Princeton University in the field of eighteenth- and nineteenth-century European history. He has taught at Indiana University and at the University of California at Los Angeles where, in 1967, he received a Distinguished Teaching Citation. He has been a fellow of the ACLS, the National Endowment for the Humanities, the Guggenheim Foundation, and the Institute for Advanced Study at Princeton. His publications include *Jacobin Legacy: The Democratic Movement under the Directory* (1970), *The Peasantry in the Old Regime: Conditions and Protests* (1970), *The French Veteran from the Revolution to the Restoration* (1979), *Eighteenth-Century Europe: Tradition and Progress, 1715–1789* (1982), *The New Regime: Transformations of the French Civic Order, 1789–1820s* (1994), *Revolution and the Meanings of Freedom in the Nineteenth Century* (1996), and *Napoleon and His Collaborators: The Making of a Dictatorship* (2001).

**Raymond Grew** is Professor of History Emeritus at the University of Michigan. He has also taught at Brandeis University, Princeton University, and at the Écoles des Hautes Études en Sciences Sociales in Paris. He earned both his M.A. and Ph.D. from Harvard University in the field of modern European history. He has been a Fulbright Fellow to Italy and a Fulbright Travelling Fellow to Italy and to France, a Guggenheim Fellow, and a Fellow of the National Endowment for the Humanities. In 1962 he received the Chester Higby Prize from the American Historical Association, and in 1963 the Italian government awarded him the Unitá d'Italia Prize; in 1992 he received the David Pinkney Prize of the Society for French Historical Studies and in 2000 a citation for career achievement from the Society for Italian Historical Studies. He has twice served as national chair of the Council for European Studies, was for many years the editor of the international quarterly, *Comparative Studies in Society and History,* and is one of the directors of the Global History Group. His recent publications include essays on historical comparison, global history, Catholicism in the nineteenth-century, fundamentalism, and Italian culture and politics. His books include *A Sterner Plan for Italian Unity* (1963), *Crises of Development in Europe and the United States* (1978), *School, State, and Society: The Growth of Elementary Schooling in Nineteenth-Century France* (1991), with Patrick J. Harrigan, and two edited volumes: *Food in Global History* (1999) and *The Construction of Minorities* (2001).

This book is dedicated
to the memory of David Herlihy
whose erudition and judgment
were central to its creation
and whose friendship and example
continue to inspire
his coauthors.

# Brief Contents

# Contents

## Chapter 1

## THE FIRST CIVILIZATIONS 3

## Chapter 2

## THE FORMING OF GREEK CIVILIZATION 37

## Chapter 3

# CLASSICAL AND HELLENISTIC GREECE 73

## Chapter 4

# THE ROMAN REPUBLIC 103

*Chapter 5*

## THE EMPIRE AND CHRISTIANITY  137

*Chapter 6*

## THE MAKING OF WESTERN EUROPE  177

*Chapter 7*

## THE EMPIRES OF THE EARLY MIDDLE AGES (800–1000): CREATION AND EROSION  209

*Chapter 8*

# Restoration of an Ordered Society 247

*Chapter 9*

# The Flowering of Medieval Civilization 289

*Chapter 10*

## THE URBAN ECONOMY AND THE CONSOLIDATION OF STATES 329

*Chapter 11*

## BREAKDOWN AND RENEWAL IN AN AGE OF PLAGUE 341

*Chapter 12*

## TRADITION AND CHANGE IN EUROPEAN CULTURE, 1300—1500 401

# Maps

# Boxes

## PRIMARY SOURCE BOXES

## HISTORICAL ISSUES BOXES

## CHRONOLOGICAL BOXES

# Preface

When this book was originally conceived, the authors who came together shared several concerns. First, several of us were very active in what was then the newly growing field of social history, and we wanted a textbook that would introduce students to these exciting issues and ways of thinking about history. Secondly, we wanted the textbook not merely to set forth information but to serve as an example of historical writing. That means we cared a lot about the quality of the writing itself and also that we wanted the chapters to be examples of a historical essay that set up a historical problem and developed arguments about that problem using historical evidence. Thirdly, we recognized that for American students the *Western Civilization* textbook needed to provide an overview of that civilization, giving students an introduction to the major achievements in Western thought, art, and science as well as the historical context for understanding them. And lastly, we were determined that our book would treat all these various aspects of history—politics, culture, economics, etc.—in an integrated way. Too many books, we felt, dealt with these topics separately, even in separate chapters, and we sought to demonstrate and exemplify the connections. To that end, *The Western Experience* is designed to provide an analytical and reasonably comprehensive account of the contexts within which, and the processes by which, European society and civilization evolved. Now in the eighth edition, this book has evolved with the strength of prior revisions, including the seventh edition's entire rewriting and reordering of the six chapters that cover the Middle Ages.

To continue that evolution, the eighth edition includes substantially revised selected chapters to make difficult concepts more understandable and to remove material that interfered with the general flow of the text. We have worked conscientiously to make the text more readily comprehensible for the student readers, while preserving an analytical framework and the latest historiographical information.

## Features of *The Western Experience*, Eighth Edition

Each generation of students brings different experiences, interests, and training into the classroom—changes that are important to the teaching-learning process. The students we teach have taught us what engages or confuses them, what impression of European history they bring to college, and what they can be expected to take from a survey course. Current political, social, and cultural events also shape what we teach and how we teach. Our experience as teachers and the helpful comments of scores of other teachers have led to a rewriting and reordering throughout the book as we have sought to make it clearer and more accessible without sacrificing our initial goal of writing a reasonably sophisticated, interpretive, and analytic history.

Among the changes that we have made in this edition to clarify the text is the use of a **color-coded thematic grid** in each chapter. This enables students and teachers to pick out which of the seven themes are developed in each chapter. A teacher can aid the students to follow through the themes, such as changes in gender roles, the economy, or warfare in various periods. Such a grid makes comparative questions easier to address and permits students to trace different responses to historical change over time. The grid also helps teachers to plan lectures and lessons and coordinate them with supplementary books or audio and visual materials in the course.

The **maps** in *The Western Experience* are already much admired by instructors and much copied in other textbooks. In the eighth edition students will be able to use a URL link to the same maps in an interactive format on the website for the text. The URL location of the website will be available in the book, so that students can have immediate access to the map they wish to work on.

To encourage students to move beyond rote learning of historical "facts" and to think broadly about history, the authors have added **"Questions for Further Thought"** at the end of each chapter. These are too broad to be exam questions; instead they are meant to be questions that stimulate the students to think about history and social, political, and economic forces. Some are comparative, some require students to draw on knowledge of a previous chapter, some ask about the role of great leaders in politics, and some ask about how the less famous people living at the time perceived the events surrounding them.

The Online Learning Center can be accessed through the McGraw-Hill Higher Education website. The Online Learning Center contains a Student Center, Instructor Center, and an Information Center. The features included in the Online Learning Center are PowerPoint presentations, quizzes, flash cards, audio pronunciation, a new "Who am I?" game, and map and chronology exercises. The integration of the Online Learning Center as an instructional component makes teaching and learning with *The Western Experience* much more accessible and enjoyable.

## ◆ INCORPORATION OF RECENT HISTORIOGRAPHY

For us the greatest pleasure in a revision lies in the challenge of absorbing and then incorporating the latest developments in **historical understanding.** From its first edition, this book included more of the results of quantitative and social history than most general textbooks of European history, an obvious reflection of our own research. Each subsequent edition provided an occasion to incorporate current methods and new knowledge, a challenge that required reconsidering paragraphs, sections, and whole chapters in the light of new theories and new research, sometimes literally reconceptualizing part of the past. That evolution continues with this edition.

We have taken into account recent work in all aspects of history, including economic, intellectual, cultural, demographic, and diplomatic history as well as social and political history. Most striking of all are the new perspectives that arise from work in **gender studies and cultural studies,** which we have sought to incorporate in this text.

## ◆ A BALANCED, INTERPRETIVE, AND FLEXIBLE APPROACH

At the same time, we recognize that the professional scholar's preference for new perspectives over familiar ones makes a distinction that students may not share. For them, the latest **interpretations** need to be integrated with established **understandings and controversies,** with the history of people and events that are part of our cultural lore. We recognize that a textbook should provide a coherent presentation of the basic information from which students can begin to form their historical understanding. We believe this information must be part of an interpretive history but also that its readers—teachers, students, and general readers—should be free to use it in many different ways and in conjunction with their own areas of special knowledge and their own interests and curiosity.

### ◆ OVERARCHING THEMES

Throughout this book, from the treatment of the earliest civilizations to the discussion of the present, we pursue certain key themes. These seven themes constitute a set of categories by which societies and historical change can be analyzed.

(1) *Social structure* is one theme. In early chapters, social structure involves how the land was settled, divided among its inhabitants, and put to use. Later discussions of how property is held must include corporate, communal, and individual ownership, then investment banking and companies that sell shares. Similarly, in each era we treat the division of labor, noting whether workers are slave or free, male or female, and when there are recognized specialists in fighting or crafts or trade. The chapters covering the Ancient world, the Middle Ages, and the early modern period explore social hierarchies that include nobles, clergy, commoners, and slaves or serfs; the treatments of the French Revolution, the Industrial Revolution, and twentieth-century societies analyze modern social classes.

(2) Another theme we analyze throughout this book is what used to be called the *body politic*. Each era contains discussions of how political power is acquired and used and of the political structures that result. Students learn about the role of law from ancient codes to the present, as well as problems of order, and the formation of governments, including why government functions have increased and political participation of the population has changed.

(3) From cultivation in the plains of the Tigris and Euphrates to the global economy, we follow changes in the organization of production and in the impact of *technology*. We note how goods are distributed, and we observe patterns of trade as avenues of cultural exchange in addition to wealth. We look at the changing economic role of governments and the impact of economic theories.

(4) The *evolution of the family and changing gender roles* are topics fundamental to every historical period. Families give form to daily life and kinship structures. The history of demography, migration, and work is also a history of the family. The family has always been a central focus of social organization and religion, as well as the principal instrument by which societies assign specific practices, roles, and values to women and men. Gender roles have changed from era to era, differing according to social class and between rural and urban societies. Observing gender roles across time, the student discovers that social, political, economic, and cultural history are always interrelated; that the present is related to the past; and that social change brings gains and losses rather than evolution in a straight line—three lessons all history courses teach.

(5) No history of Europe could fail to pay attention to *war*, which, for most polities, has been their most demanding activity. Warfare has strained whatever resources were available from ancient times to the present, leading governments to invent new ways to extract wealth and mobilize support. War has built and undermined states, stimulated science and consumed technology, made heroes and restructured nobility, schooling, and social services. Glorified in European culture and often condemned, war in every era has affected the lives of all its peoples. This historical significance, more than specific battles, is one of the themes of *The Western Experience*.

(6) *Religion* has been basic to the human experience, and our textbook explores the different religious institutions and experiences that societies developed. Religion affects and is affected by all the themes we address, creating community and causing conflict, shaping intellectual and daily life, providing the experiences that bind individual lives and society within a common system of meaning.

(7) For authors of a general history, no decision is more difficult than the space devoted to *cultural expression*. In this respect, as elsewhere, we have striven for a balance between high and popular culture. We present as clearly and concisely as possible the most important formal ideas, philosophies, and ideologies of each era. We emphasize concepts of recognized importance in the general

history of ideas and those concepts that illuminate behavior and discourse in a given period. We pay particular attention to developments in science that we believe are related to important intellectual, economic, and social trends. Popular culture appears both in specific sections and throughout the book. We want to place popular culture within its social and historical context but not make the gulf too wide between popular and high or formal culture. Finally, we write about many of the great works of literature, art, architecture, and music. Because of the difficulties of selection we have tried to emphasize works that are cultural expressions of their time, but that also have been influential over the ages and around the globe.

Attention to these seven themes occasions problems of organization and selection. We could have structured this book around a series of topical essays, perhaps repeating the series of themes for each of the standard chronological divisions of European history. Instead, we chose to preserve a narrative flow that emphasizes interrelationships and historical context. We wanted each chapter to stand as an interpretive historical essay, with a beginning and conclusion. As a result, the themes emerge repeatedly within discussions of a significant event, an influential institution, an individual life, or a whole period of time. Or they may intersect in a single institution or historical trend. Nevertheless, readers can follow any one of these themes across time and use that theme as a measure of change and a way to assess the differences and similarities between societies.

### ◆ STRONG COVERAGE OF SOCIAL HISTORY

To discuss history thematically is to think comparatively and to employ categories of social history that in the last generation have greatly affected historical understanding. The impulse behind social history was not new. As early as the eighteenth century many historians called for a history that was more than chronology, more than an account of kings and battles. Closer to our own time, Virginia Woolf asked why there was not a history of ordinary people rather than kings and monarchs. Although in the nineteenth century historical studies gave primary place to politics, diplomacy, and war (using evidence from official documents newly accessible in state archives), the substantial changes brought about by the Industrial Revolution and colonialism led historians to begin to look at economic and social history. Intense interest in social history came in the 1960s and 1970s when the academic world opened its doors to students from the working class and the availability of computers and large data sets made it possible to trace the life patterns and accomplishments of workers, minorities, and women. But even those working with qualitative sources documented the daily life in ancient Rome or Renaissance Florence or old New York as reflected in styles of dress, housing, diet, and so on. Historical museums and popular magazines featured this "pots and pans history," which was appealing in its concreteness but tended (like the collections of interesting objects that it resembled) to lack a theoretical basis. Historians writing the history of those who were often illiterate have found abundant sources to bring the lives of ordinary people into our understanding of a society beyond the tiny minority who were the powerful, rich, and educated (and who left behind the fullest and most accessible records of their activities). The ordinary people now have a place within a larger interpretive framework, borrowing from the social sciences, especially anthropology, sociology, economics, and political science. Still an arena of active and significant research, social history has also expanded, strengthened by new work on the history of women. With the development of a stronger theoretical sense, these interests have grown into gender studies that give a fresh new dimension to familiar historical issues. Social history has changed in another way, too, shifting away from explanations that gave priority to social structure and material factors and toward cultural studies.

### ◆ CHRONOLOGICAL/CONCEPTUAL ORGANIZATION AND PERIODIZATION

These developments in social history, which have greatly expanded the range of evidence and issues that historians must consider, have changed our ideas of periodization. The mainstay for organizing historical knowledge has been the rise and fall of dynasties, the formation of states, and the occurrence of wars and revolutions. But we all know that people did not wake up on the morning after the war between Sparta and Athens, or Waterloo, or even the Second World War to find their family structures and basic economic needs radically altered because a balance of political power or a change of dynasty had occurred. The periodization most appropriate for describing changes in culture and ideas, economic production, or science and technology is often quite different, and changes in everyday life and popular culture often occur on a still different scale. We have sought a compromise for *The Western Experience*. It maintains the traditional chronological sequence of the introductory European history course. At the same time, insofar as each chapter is an interpretive essay, the information it contains illustrates arguments to describe a period of European history. For all these reasons, chapters also have topical emphases, and sometimes a cluster of chapters is required to treat a given era.

# Pedagogical Features of the Eighth Edition

The eighth edition of *The Western Experience* continues the precedent of earlier editions with its high-quality book production, and the inclusion of full color, clearly focused maps, and a highly accessible format. This edition offers more than 100 maps and 400 illustrations, each with an explanatory caption that enhances the text coverage. It features a variety of pedagogical devices to help students tackle the content without sacrificing subtlety of interpretation or trying to escape the fact that history is complex.

## ◆ COLOR CODED GRID OF SEVEN THEMES

Positioned at the start of every chapter, this grid highlights the seven themes developed in each chapter.

| CHAPTER 28. THE GREAT TWENTIETH-CENTURY CRISIS | | | | | | | |
|---|---|---|---|---|---|---|---|
| | Social Structure | Body Politic | Changes in the Organization of Production and in the Impact of Technology | Evolution of Family and Changing Gender Roles | War | Religion | Cultural Expression |
| I. TWO SUCCESSFUL REVOLUTIONS | ▓ | ▓ | ▓ | ▓ | ▓ | ▓ | |
| II. THE DISTINCTIVE CULTURE OF THE TWENTIETH CENTURY | | | ▓ | | | | █ |
| III. THE RETREAT FROM DEMOCRACY | | ▓ | ▓ | | | | █ |
| IV. NAZI GERMANY AND THE U.S.S.R. | ▓ | | ▓ | | | | |
| V. THE DEMOCRACIES' WEAK RESPONSE | ▓ | ▓ | | | | | █ |

## ◆ PRIMARY SOURCE BOXES

These excerpts from primary sources are designed to illustrate or supplement points made in the text, to provide some flavor of the issues under discussion, and to allow beginning students some of that independence of judgment that comes from a careful reading of historical sources.

## OEDIPUS' SELF-MUTILATION

◆

*In Sophocles' tragedy* King Oedipus, *Jocasta, the mother of Oedipus, hangs herself after learning that she has married her own son. An attendant then narrates what follows. (Those he "should never have seen" are the daughters Oedipus fathered by his mother-wife.)*

"We saw a knotted pendulum, a noose,
A strangled woman swinging before our eyes.
The King saw too, and with heart-rending groans
Untied the rope, and laid her on the ground.
But worse was yet to see. Her dress was pinned
With golden brooches, which the King snatched out
And thrust, from full arm's length, into his eyes—
Eyes that should see no longer his shame, his guilt,
No longer see those they should never have seen,
Nor see, unseeing, those he had longed to see,
Henceforth seeing nothing but night . . . To this wild
tune

He pierced his eyeballs time and time again,
Till bloody tears ran down his beard—not drops
But in full spate a whole cascade descending
In drenching cataracts of scarlet rain.
Thus two have sinned; and on two heads, not one—
On man and wife—falls mingled punishment.
Their old long happiness of former times
Was happiness earned with justice; but to-day
Calamity, death, ruin, tears, and shame,
All ills that there are names for—all are here."

From E. F. Watling (tr.), Sophocles, *The Three Theban Plays*, Penguin Classics, 1971, pp. 60–61.

### ◆ HISTORICAL ISSUES BOXES

These boxes explain major controversies over historical interpretations so that students can see how historical understanding is constructed. They encourage students to participate in these debates and formulate their own positions.

## TWO VIEWS OF COLUMBUS

◆

*The following two passages suggest the enormous differences that have arisen in interpretations of the career of Christopher Columbus. The first, by Samuel Eliot Morison, a historian and a noted sailor, represents the traditional view of the explorer's achievements that held sway until recent years.*

1. "Columbus had a Hellenic sense of wonder at the new and strange, combined with an artist's appreciation of natural beauty. Moreover, Columbus had a deep conviction of the sovereignty and the infinite wisdom of God, which enhanced all his triumphs. One only wishes that the Admiral might have been afforded the sense of fulfillment that would have come from foreseeing all that flowed from his discoveries. The whole history of the Americas stems from the Four Voyages of Columbus, and as the Greek city-states looked back to the deathless gods as their founders, so today a score of independent nations unite in homage to Christopher the stouthearted son of Genoa, who carried Christian civilization across the Ocean Sea."

From S. E. Morison, *Admiral of the Ocean Sea: A Life of Christopher Columbus* (Boston: Little, Brown, 1942), pp. 670–671.

2. "For all his navigational skill, about which the salty types make such a fuss, and all his fortuitous headings, Admiral Colón [Christopher Columbus] could be a wretched mariner. The four voyages, properly seen, quite apart from bravery, are replete with lubberly mistakes, misconceived sailing plans, foolish disregard of elementary maintenance, and stubborn neglect of basic safety—all characterized by the assertion of human superiority over the natural realm. Almost every time Colón went wrong, it was because he had refused to bend to the inevitabilities of tide and wind and reef or, more arrogantly still, had not bothered to learn about them.

From Kirkpatrick Sale, *The Conquest of Paradise: Christopher Columbus and the Columbian Legacy* (New York: Knopf, 1990), pp. 209–210, 362.

#### ◆ MORE HEADING LEVELS

We have given particular attention to adding more descriptive content guides, such as the consistent use of three levels of headings. We believe these will help students identify specific topics for purposes of study and review as well as give a clear outline of a chapter's argument.

#### ◆ CHRONOLOGICAL CHARTS

Nearly every chapter employs charts and chronological tables that outline the unfolding of major events and social processes and serve as a convenient reference for students.

## *Chronology*

### AN OVERVIEW OF EVENTS
#### *CA. 7000–486*

(ALL DATES B.C.*)

| | |
|---|---|
| ca. 8000 | First permanent villages in Near East. |
| ca. 3000 | Formation of cities in Sumer; unification of Upper and Lower Egypt. |
| ca. 1900 | Hebrews begin immigration into Palestine. |
| 1792–1750 | Hammurabi unifies Babylonia and issues his law code. |
| ca. 1595 | Sack of Babylon by Hittites. |
| ca. 1570–1085 | Egyptian Empire (New Kingdom). |
| ca. 1400–1200 | High point of Hittite kingdom. |
| ca. 1230 | Exodus of Israelites from Egypt and their invasion of Canaan. |
| ca. 900–612 | Assyrian conquests. |
| 559–530 | Cyrus founds Persian Empire. |
| 522–486 | Rule of Darius in Persia. |

*Some historians use an alternative system of dating: B.C.E. (Before the Common Era) and C.E. (Common Era).

## Available Formats

To provide an alternative to the full-length hardcover edition, *The Western Experience*, Eighth Edition, is available in two-volume and three-volume paperbound editions. Volume I includes chapters 1 through 17 and covers material through the eighteenth century. Volume II includes chapters 15 through 30 and the Epilogue, and covers material since the sixteenth century. Volume A includes chapters 1 through 12, Antiquity and the Middle Ages; Volume B includes chapters 11 through 21, The Early Modern Era; and Volume C includes chapters 19 through 30 and the Epilogue, The Modern Era. The page numbering and cross-references in these editions remain the same as in the hardcover text.

## Ancillary Instructional Materials

McGraw-Hill offers instructors and students a wide variety of ancillary materials to accompany *The Western Experience*. These supplements listed here may accompany *The Western Experience*. Please contact your local McGraw-Hill representative for details concerning policies, prices, and availability, as some restrictions may apply.

#### ◆ FOR THE STUDENT

*Student Study Guide/Workbook with Map Exercises, Volumes I and II:* Includes the following features for each chapter: chapter outlines, chronological diagrams, four kinds of exercises—map exercises, exercises in document analysis, exercises that reinforce the book's important overarching themes, exercises in matching important terms with significant individuals—and essay topics requiring analysis and speculation.

New Multimedia Supplements for the Student:

- *The Online Learning Center:* A fully interactive, book-specific website featuring links to chapter- and topic-appropriate sites on the World Wide Web, and a guide to using the Internet. Some outstanding tools included on the site:
  - Chapter outlines

- Interactive "drag and drop" exercises ask students to match up significant individuals and key terms with the correct identifications.
- An audio function helps students pronounce difficult terms.
- Self-tests offer students a chance to find out in what areas they need more study.
- Essay questions
- Map exercises are also included.
- Links with exercises
- New animated maps

### ◆ FOR THE INSTRUCTOR

An integrated instructional package is available in either print or electronic format.

*Instructor's Manual/Test Bank:* This fully revised and expanded manual includes chapter summaries, lecture and discussion topics, and lists of additional teaching resources such as recommended films, novels, and websites. In addition, the test bank for the seventh edition of *The Western Experience* includes more questions than ever before. Types of questions include multiple choice, identification, sentence completion, essay (both factual and interpretive), and critical thinking exercises (such as map analysis or source analysis questions).

*Computerized Test Bank:* A computerized test bank is available in Windows or Mac formats.

*Overhead Transparency Acetates:* This expanded full-color transparency package includes all the maps and chronological charts in the text.

*The Instructor's Resource CD-ROM:* Allows instructors to create their own classroom presentation using resources provided by McGraw-Hill. Instructors may also customize their presentations by adding slides or other electronic resources. In addition, this CD allows instructors access to all their instructional materials (including the test bank) in one integrated instructional package. The IRCD includes the following resources: a PowerPoint slide show, electronic overhead transparencies (maps and chronological charts from the text), the instructor's manual (with hyperlinks to appropriate maps and timelines to help the instructor build lecture presentations), and the test bank.

*The Online Learning Center:* Available to the instructor and includes the Instructor's Manual and PowerPoint slides in addition to students' resources.

## Acknowledgments
◆

*Manuscript Reviewers and Consultants, eighth edition:* Sig Sutterlin, Indian Hills Community College; John Tanner, Palomar College; Fred Murphy, Western Kentucky University; Guangquin Xu, Northwest Arkansas Community College; Tyler Blethen, West Carolina University; Gunar Freibergs, Los Angeles Valley College; Neil Heyman, San Diego State University; Laura Pintar, Loyola University; Vickie Cook, Pima Community College; Owen Bradley, University of Tennessee; Elizabeth McCrank, Boston University; Mary DeCredico, U.S. Naval Academy; Richard Cole, Luther College; Ron Goldberg, Thomas Nelson Community College; Thomas Rowland, University of Wisconsin-Oshkosh; Dan Brown, Moorpark College; Charles Steen, University of New Mexico; George Monahan, Suffolk Community College; Anne Quartararo, U.S. Naval Academy; Edrene Stephens McKay, Northwest Arkansas Community College; Valentina Tikoff, DePaul University.

*Manuscript Reviewers and Consultants, seventh edition:* Frank Baglione, Tallahassee Community College; Paul Goodwin, University of Connecticut; Robert Herzstein, University of South Carolina; Carla M. Joy, Red Rocks Community College; Kathleen Kamerick, University of Iowa; Carol Bresnahan Menning, University of Toledo; Eileen Moore, University of Alabama at Birmingham; Frederick Murphy, Western Kentucky University; Michael Myers, University of Notre Dame; Robert B. Patterson, University of South Carolina at Columbia; Peter Pierson, Santa Clara University; Alan Schaffer, Clemson University; Marc Schwarz, University of New Hampshire; Charles R. Sullivan, University of Dallas; Jack Thacker, Western Kentucky University; Bruce L. Venarde, University of Pittsburgh.

*Manuscript Reviewers and Consultants, sixth edition:* S. Scott Bartchy, University of California, Los Angeles; Thomas Blomquist, Northern Illinois

University; Nancy Ellenberger, United States Naval Academy; Steven Epstein, University of Colorado at Boulder; Laura Gellott, University of Wisconsin at Parkside; Barbara Hanawalt, University of Minnesota; Drew Harrington, Western Kentucky University; Lisa Lane, Mira Costa College; William Matthews, S.U.N.Y. at Potsdam; Carol Bresnahan Menning, University of Toledo; Sandra Norman, Florida Atlantic University; Peter Pierson, Santa Clara University; Linda Piper, University of Georgia; Philip Racine, Wofford College; Eileen Soldwedel, Edmonds Community College; John Sweets, University of Kansas; Richard Wagner, Des Moines Area Community College.

*Focus Group Reviewers from Spring 1992:* Michael DeMichele, University of Scranton; Nancy Ellenberger, United States Naval Academy; Drew Harrington, Western Kentucky University; William Matthews, S.U.N.Y. at Potsdam.

We would like to thank Lyn Uhl, Monica Eckman, and Angela Kao of McGraw-Hill for their considerable efforts in bringing this edition to fruition.

# *Introduction*

Everyone uses history. We use it to define who we are and to connect our personal experience to the collective memory of the groups to which we belong, including a particular region, nation, and culture. We invoke the past to explain our hopes and ambitions and to justify our fears and conflicts. The Charter of the United Nations, like the American Declaration of Independence, is based on a view of history. When workers strike or armies march, they cite the lessons of their history. Because history is so important to us psychologically and intellectually, historical understanding is always shifting and often controversial.

Historical knowledge is cumulative. Historians may ask many of the same questions about different periods of history or raise new questions or issues; they integrate the answers and historical knowledge grows. The study of history cannot be a subjective exercise in which all opinions are equally valid. Regardless of the impetus for a particular historical question, the answer to it stands until overturned by better evidence. We now know more about the past than ever before, and we understand it as the people we study could not. Unlike them, we know the outcome of their history; we can apply methods they did not have, and often we have evidence they never saw.

Humans have always found pleasure in the reciting and reading of history. The poems about the fall of Troy or the histories of Herodotus and Thucydides entertained the ancient Greeks. The biographies of great men and women, dramatic accounts of important events, colorful tales of earlier times can be fascinating in themselves. Through these encounters with history we experience the common concerns of all people; and through the study of European history, we come to appreciate the ideals and conflicts, the failures and accidents, the social needs and human choices that formed the Western world in which we live. Knowing the historical context also enriches our appreciation for the achievements of European culture, enabling us to see its art, science, ideas, and politics in relationship to real people, specific interests, and burning issues.

We think of Europe's history as the history of Western civilization, but the very concept of a Western civilization is itself the result of history. The Greeks gave the names east and west to the points on the horizon at which the sun rises and sets. Because the Persian Empire and India lay to their east, the Greeks labeled their own continent, which they called Europe, the west. The distinction between Western civilization and others, while frequently ethnocentric, arbitrary, and exaggerated, was reinforced by the many encounters that Europeans had with other peoples and civilizations. The view that the Western civilization is all one can be easily challenged in every respect save its cultural tradition.

*The Western Experience* gives primary attention to a small part of the world and thus honors that cultural tradition. The concentration on Europe nevertheless includes important examples of city and of rural life; of empires and monarchies and republics; of life before and after industrialization; of societies in which labor was organized through markets, serfdom, and slavery; of cultures little concerned with science and of ones that used changing scientific knowledge; of non-Christian religions and of all the major forms of Christianity in action.

Throughout this book, from the treatment of the earliest civilizations to the discussion of the present, certain themes are pursued. These seven themes constitute a set of categories by which societies and historical change can be analyzed: social structure, the body politic, changes in the organization of production and in the impact of technology, the evolution of the family and changing gender roles, war, religion, and cultural expression. The themes are developed more fully in the Preface. These themes help readers integrate the narrative of events with a deeper understanding of how societies and individuals responded to changing circumstances. By following through the themes in the text, readers will have a basis of comparison of historical responses to politics, the economy, family and gender roles, war, religion, and culture. The themes are a constant of human history, but each period, sometimes each generation, had different responses to them. Readers of this book will find many ways to enrich their understanding of history. It introduces historical methods; it provides a framework for what they already know about Western society; and it challenges preconceptions about the past, about how societies are organized, and about how people behave. Historical study is an integrative enterprise that must take into account long-term trends and specific moments, social structure and individual actions.

A college course alone cannot create an educated citizen. Nor is history the only path to integrated knowledge. Western history is not the only history a person should know, nor is an introductory survey necessarily the best way to learn it. Yet, as readers consider and then challenge interpretations offered in this text, they will exercise critical and analytical skills. They can begin to overcome the parochialism that attributes importance only to the present. To learn to think critically about historical evidence and know how to formulate an argument on the bases of this evidence is to experience the study of history as one of the vital intellectual activities by which we come to know who and where we are.

*Mortimer Chambers*
*Barbara Hanawalt*
*Theodore K. Rabb*
*Isser Woloch*
*Raymond Grew*

▲ GREAT HALL OF BULLS, LASCAUX CAVES
**An example of animals depicted in a prehistoric cave painting.**
Musée des Antiquités St. Germain en Laye/Dagli Orti/The Art Archive

## Chapter 1

# THE FIRST CIVILIZATIONS

The subject of this book is the Western experience—that is, the history of European civilization, which is the civilization of modern Europe and America. Yet we do not begin with the mainland of present-day Europe, for our civilization traces its origins to earlier ones in Mesopotamia and around the Mediterranean Sea. Human beings began to abandon a nomadic existence and live in settled agricultural villages about 8000 B.C. This change in human lifestyle points to some of the themes that will run through this book—for example, the rise of technology to contain rivers and to survey and map areas for farming, or the art of cutting and assembling huge stones to build walls and pyramids.

By about 3000 B.C. humans had created settlements of some size along the banks of the Tigris, Euphrates, Nile, and Indus rivers. People's efforts to build a better life transformed the agricultural villages into something we can recognize as cities—having a scale and pattern crucial for the development of civilization. In these valleys, types of behavior and institutions first appeared that have persisted, in varying forms, throughout all periods of Western civilization.

Powerful kingdoms and great empires, centered on sizable cities, gradually arose in Mesopotamia and in Egypt. Their achievement of literacy and their many written records; their long-distance trade; their invention of increasingly ingenious tools, utensils, vehicles, and weapons; their development of monumental architecture and representative art; and their advances in medicine, astronomy, and mathematics marked the change from primitive life and constituted civilization.

| CHAPTER 1. THE FIRST CIVILIZATIONS | Social Structure | Body Politic | Changes in the Organization of Production and in the Impact of Technology | Evolution of Family and Changing Gender Roles | War | Religion | Cultural Expression |
|---|---|---|---|---|---|---|---|
| I. THE EARLIEST HUMANS | | | | | | | |
| II. THE FIRST CIVILIZATIONS IN MESOPOTAMIA | | | | | | | |
| III. EGYPT | | | | | | | |
| IV. PALESTINE | | | | | | | |
| V. THE NEAR EASTERN STATES | | | | | | | |

# I. The Earliest Humans

Our first task as we try to grasp historical chronology is to gain a sense of the overwhelmingly long period that we call "prehistory." The astronomer Carl Sagan reckoned that, if the entire history of the universe were plotted out over the span of one year, everything that we usually think of as European history—the subject of this book—would have taken place in the last two or three minutes of the year.

All human beings are members of the species *Homo sapiens* ("thinking human being"), which evolved, according to present evidence, about 400,000 years ago. The immediate predecessor was *Homo erectus*, which may have emerged as long ago as 1.5 million years. Back in time beyond Homo erectus is an area of doubt and controversy. There is growing support for the theory that humanity originated, in the form of *Homo habilis*, roughly "skillful human being," in east Africa about 2 million years ago. As to mankind's emigration from Africa, recent excavations in the nation of Georgia (part of the former Soviet Union) have discovered two skulls that are considered the most ancient human remains outside Africa. They date to about 1.7 million years ago and suggest that people emigrated when they became carnivorous and had to expand their territory in search of meat; they also show that the emigration must have been under way by this time.

As historians seek to understand earliest mankind, they must remember that there is no *inevitable* pattern of development in social groups. Hunter-gatherers can remain such indefinitely, and small farming communities may never turn into anything else.[1] But there seem to be certain patterns through which many societies have developed and out of which civilization arose.

At least in the part of the world treated in this book, humanity did change from people who gathered and hunted food wherever they could into farmers in small villages. This change led in turn to an increase in population and the forming of larger, long-lived towns.

## ◆ HUMAN BEINGS AS FOOD GATHERERS

Human beings have always had to try to come to terms with their environment. For the greatest part of their time on earth, they have struggled simply to hunt and gather food. Only at a later stage did people live in stable settlements—first villages, then cities.

*Labor in Early Communities*  In all observed societies, labor is divided on the basis of sex. In the earliest societies, both hunting and gathering food were the means of survival. Current research suggests that women may have done most of the gathering as well as caring for the young. If hunting animals required longer expeditions, we may guess that men usually performed this duty. Even

---

[1] A point convincingly made by Johnson and Earle, p. 6 (see recommended readings at end of chapter).

later, as agriculture became the basis of the economy, modern research suggests that women must have continued their domestic tasks, such as cooking and tending children.

We can surely guess that quarrels of some kind broke out between societies. One hunting band, for example, might have had to turn aside the claims of another band to certain territory. In such clashes, we may guess that men assumed leadership through their strength and thus created a division of roles based on sex that gave them dominance of their communities. One result of this social division has been a comparative lack of information about the role of women in history; the reconstruction of this role, the restoring of women to history, has been a leading theme of historical research in the present generation.

*The Old Stone Age*   The period during which people gathered food is often called the Old Stone Age, or Paleolithic Age, and ranges from the beginning of human history to about 11,000 B.C. Even in this early period, some human beings developed a remarkably sophisticated kind of painting, the earliest demonstration of the role of artistic creation as another theme in the history of civilization. The most striking creations known from food-gathering societies are a series of cave paintings that survive at their finest in Lascaux in France and Altamira in Spain (28,000–22,000 B.C.). Most of the paintings show wild animals, enemies of human beings and yet part of their essential support. The paintings may have a quasi-religious meaning as symbolic attempts to gain power over the quarry; scars on the walls suggest that people threw spears at the painted animals, as if to imitate killing them. If so, the cave paintings provide our earliest evidence for one of the main themes of history: the attempt to communicate with forces outside human control through symbolic action, art, and thought—that is, through religion and ritual acts.

◆ HUMAN BEINGS AS FOOD PRODUCERS

*The Discovery of Agriculture*   About 11,000 B.C., according to recent research, there occurred the most important event in all human history: People turned from hunting animals and gathering food to producing food from the earth. This event, the

rise of agriculture, is called the Neolithic Revolution and introduced the Neolithic Age, or New Stone Age.[2] The word *revolution* usually implies dramatic action over a short time, which was in no way true of this one. Yet revolution it was, for it made possible the feeding of larger populations. The rise of agriculture gave continuity to human existence and demanded long-term planning and the practice of new skills and specialties. Those people not needed in agriculture could engage in hunting (for this skill was still needed), weaving, pottery, metalwork, and trade. Agriculture, once mastered, became another enduring theme throughout history and has always been the largest single factor in the economy of the world. Indeed, increasing the food supply was the imperative step to be taken on the path to cities and civilization.

*Patterns in Population*   But *why* did this revolution take place? What caused people to turn from the pattern of roaming the countryside that had lasted hundreds of thousands of years? The driving force was probably an inevitable increase in population. As mankind multiplied in the later, or "upper," Paleolithic Age, it became imperative to develop a continuous food supply and to have a secure reserve over the whole year. But traditional foraging might not guarantee such a supply. As people hunted animals, they inevitably made their prey scarcer. Even gathering fruit and grains required ever longer journeys. Therefore farming became a necessity. People grew grain in the summer and stored it in winter, but not all single families could be certain of enough food at all times. Storage of food became a task for the community, and this led to social cooperation, which in turn required social control—an approach to political organization and government.

Moreover, when people invested labor in their settlements and began to depend on land, protecting and even expanding their territory became of immense importance. Therefore one effect of the agricultural revolution was the impetus to gain control over territory—sometimes through negotiation, but sometimes through war. War is

---

[2]The Mesolithic (Middle Stone) Age, beginning around 8000 B.C., was limited to northwestern Europe.

another of the constantly recurring themes of Western civilization. The reasons for making war will vary considerably through the centuries, and the tools of war will become ever more sophisticated; but the willingness to seize a weapon, shed other people's blood, and risk one's own life to gain or to protect territory descends from the earliest permanent human settlements.

## ◆ EARLY NEAR EASTERN VILLAGES

***The First Settlements***   The Neolithic Revolution first occurred probably in the hills of what is now southern Turkey and northern Iraq, especially in the Zagros hills east of the Tigris River. But, again, why was *this* region the cradle of agriculture? Historians have concluded that only this location held a sufficient supply of animals for domestication along with the needed vegetables and cereals. The earliest known settlements, dating from about 9000 B.C., were unwalled and unfortified, and their people lived in simple huts. About 8000 B.C. the first somewhat larger villages appeared. The oldest seem to have been Jericho and Jarmo, but even these were still small settlements; by about 8000 B.C. Jericho may have had 2,000–3,000 people. The population of Jarmo, settled about 7000 B.C., is estimated at about 150, crowded into twenty to twenty-five houses of baked clay.

***Invention, Travel, Trade***   As villages became permanent, they also became more versatile in their inventions; our first evidence of pottery, for example, comes from what is now Syria and dates from about 8000 B.C. This invention allowed the storage of food and sustained the population in periods when hunting and gathering were more difficult. Another invention, the art of weaving, was practiced in Anatolia, now within modern Turkey, by about 7000 B.C. and provided both new occupations and new resources for a village.

About this time, too, people began to travel in crude rafts and in carts with wheels. Potters gradually learned to fashion their wares on the surface of a turning wheel, and thus could make in minutes what had previously taken hours; and the pot, the raft, and the wheel combined to provide the means to transport grain and other goods. Thus arose another institution of all later societies: the mutually profitable exchange of goods in

*Chronology*

## AN OVERVIEW OF EVENTS

*CA. 7000–486*

(ALL DATES B.C.*)

| | |
|---|---|
| **ca. 8000** | First permanent villages in Near East. |
| **ca. 3000** | Formation of cities in Sumer; unification of Upper and Lower Egypt. |
| **ca. 1900** | Hebrews begin immigration into Palestine. |
| **1792–1750** | Hammurabi unifies Babylonia and issues his law code. |
| **ca. 1595** | Sack of Babylon by Hittites. |
| **ca. 1570–1085** | Egyptian Empire (New Kingdom). |
| **ca. 1400–1200** | High point of Hittite kingdom. |
| **ca. 1230** | Exodus of Israelites from Egypt and their invasion of Canaan. |
| **ca. 900–612** | Assyrian conquests. |
| **559–530** | Cyrus founds Persian Empire. |
| **522–486** | Rule of Darius in Persia. |

*Some historians use an alternative system of dating: B.C.E. (Before the Common Era) and C.E. (Common Era).

trade, pursued by people skilled enough to make a living at it. Some archaeologists have suggested that a number of towns were formed not for the sake of local agriculture but to serve as trading centers. Trade needs safe routes and a guarantee of safety for traders, which in turn require some kind of political protection, mutual understanding between communities, and control.

***Agricultural Communities***   The early farmers were naturally much concerned with fertility. When people feared that their own efforts might not solve life's problems, they turned to divine powers for help. These societies therefore sought to communicate with goddesses in the form of statuettes of unmistakable earth-mothers with large buttocks and breasts, whose fertile bodies, it was hoped, would make the soil productive. Such figures also signify the importance of human mothers, for the villages flourished only if women produced and sustained each new generation.

So by stages there arose agrarian communities with communal gods, domesticated animals, simple technologies and economies, and some regulation of social behavior. Yet we must remember how painfully slow was the transition from nomadic hunters to food-producing villagers. And still another 4,000–5,000 years were to separate such agricultural villages from the first civilizations.

# II. The First Civilizations in Mesopotamia

History has been called an argument without end. It is still not definitely clear where civilization began, but the region of Mesopotamia has at least some claim as the cradle of civilization. The historian can point to the forming of cities, as distinct from farming towns, in this region, and Mesopotamia was also home to one of the two earliest systems of writing. From these beginnings arose two of the earliest civilizations, those of Sumer and of Babylonia. Both have left behind them written documents that are priceless sources for the thoughts and practices of these societies.

## ◆ THE EMERGENCE OF CIVILIZATION

We may define civilization as a social organization with more complex rules than those that guided dwellers in caves or the earliest farmers. In a civilization, there are more sophisticated divisions of authority and labor, including duties, powers, and skills that pass down within certain families. A sensational excavation in A.D. 2000 at the site of Tell Hamoukar, in modern Syria, has revealed that people were living there by about 4000 B.C. and that they developed the earliest known civilization at this site about 3700 B.C. (the ancient name of the city has not yet been found). Among the signs of civilization found here are monumental architecture and seals used, perhaps by officials, to stamp valuable goods. Further knowledge of this site must await more excavation.

*The Beginnings of Government*   The establishment of firm authority requires the acceptance by both governors and the governed of their status; we shall see this balance throughout history, but we shall also observe its collapse when conflict leads to the replacement of one governing group by another. Rulers, however named, often arise from among the heads of powerful families. But there may be other sources of political strength. Seeking social order, people give authority to a man or woman who seems to have some special quality of leadership or ability.

An equally essential part of the social cement, in all periods of civilization, has been law, formally accepted codes of behavior, as distinct from the simple customs of a village. Law may develop slowly, but eventually it is recorded in detailed law codes, which tell us how societies controlled their people. Such codes can also tell us about ethical values, divisions between citizens, and social structure.

There is tension, in any civilization, between control and freedom. Law codes not only control people but are also a way of restraining one citizen from interfering with another. Such restraint in turn guarantees some liberties, and law exists partly to make us more free. The constant discussion and refinement of law is another permanent theme of our history.

*The Power of Cities*   Cities are larger and therefore stronger than villages; they have the power to dominate the hinterland and its inhabitants. In many early civilizations, one society even enslaved parts of another society. Slavery, though deplorable in modern eyes, allowed the enslavers more varied occupations by freeing them from the mundane requirements of existence. As people began to use their freedom, however obtained, to pursue special skills, some gained a reputation for religious knowledge and became the state's communicators with divine powers; and such is the strength of religious belief that these priests could form a class of advisers whom even kings could not ignore.

Other citizens used their new freedom to develop new arts and crafts. Along with improved techniques of pottery, weaving, and domestication of animals, a major step forward took place when workers discovered how to blend other

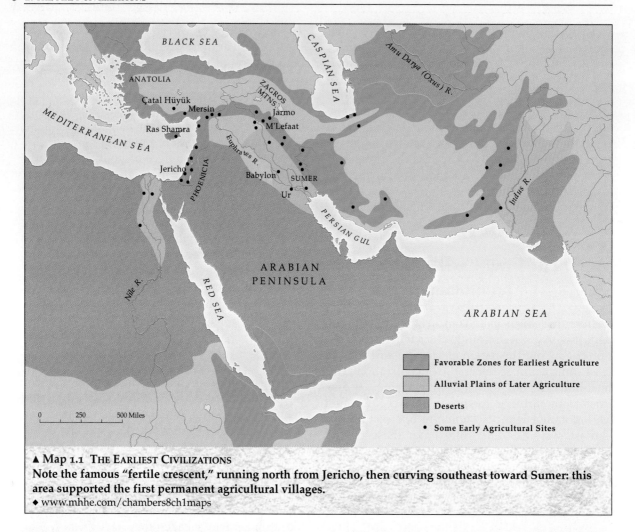

▲ **Map 1.1  THE EARLIEST CIVILIZATIONS**
**Note the famous "fertile crescent," running north from Jericho, then curving southeast toward Sumer: this area supported the first permanent agricultural villages.**
◆ www.mhhe.com/chambers8ch1maps

metals with copper to fashion bronze, especially for weapons. As the first cities reached significant size, humanity thus entered the Bronze Age, which started about 3000 B.C. and ended between 1200 and 1000 B.C.

### ◆ SUMER

*Cities of Sumer*  Mesopotamia (the "land between the rivers") is a rich alluvial plain created by deposits from the Tigris and Euphrates rivers. At the southern end of this plain, within modern Iraq, arose a civilization with a more advanced scale of development than that of the people of Tell Hamoukar. This took place in the area known as Sumer. Geography both nourished and threatened the Sumerians. The land was fertile, yet the rivers could roar over their banks, carrying away

homes and human lives. Also, the land was open to invasion. Thus survival itself was often uncertain, a fact reflected in a strain of pessimism in Sumerian thought.

The people of Sumer and their language appear to be unrelated to any other known people or language. By about 3000 B.C. Sumer contained a dozen or more city-states—in other words, cities that were each independent of the others, each ruled by its own king (known as the *lugal*) and worshiping its own patron deity, a god that was thought to offer protection to the city. Sumerian religion held that rule by the king was a divine gift to the people and that the king ruled in the service of the gods. Thus religion and government, two of the large themes of civilization, were combined to comfort the people and, at the same time, to organize and control society.

Sumerian cities were much larger than the early farming villages already mentioned. One of them, Uruk, had a population estimated at 50,000 by around 3000 B.C. and a walled circumference of ten miles. The citizens of each city were divided into three classes: nobles and priests, commoners, and slaves. These classifications are the first example of what we shall often meet in history: a recognized, legal division of people into social orders. The king was not considered divine, but rather a servant of the gods. In practical political terms, he held power only so long as he could command support from the powerful priests and nobles.

***The City and Its God*** At the center of a Sumerian city usually stood a ziggurat, a terraced tower built of baked brick and culminating in a temple, probably for the patron god of the city. A ziggurat might be a stupendous structure: The wall surrounding one was some thirty-six feet thick. The

Old Testament contains many echoes from Sumer, and it seems likely that the story in the Bible of the Tower of Babel was ultimately based on the memory of a ziggurat.

In Sumerian culture, the patron god theoretically owned the whole city; but in fact, much of the land was private property, held mainly by powerful men and their families but also by private citizens. Most houses were of a single story and were jammed into narrow streets, but some richer houses had two stories and an open court. The people were monogamous, and women held property and took part in business but did not hold political office.

***Trade and Mathematics*** Geography also forced Sumerians to devise the art of trading. Trade was essential for the growth of Sumerian cities because, despite the region's astonishing fertility, it lacked good timber and stone. Sumerians

▲ A ziggurat from Ur. The stairway leads up to a room in which a god could rest and take his pleasure. The ziggurat formed the core of a temple compound, while around it were storehouses.
Georg Gerster/Comstock

pioneered the art of building in baked brick, but to obtain other materials they had to export such goods as metalwork, a craft at which they became outstanding.

Perhaps to bolster their expertise in the essential art of trading, the Sumerians developed a precise system of mathematical notation. Their system was the sexagesimal, in which the number 60 (*sexaginta* in Latin) is one of the main elements; this system has the advantage of including 3, 10, and 12 as factors. One of the longest-lasting legacies of Mesopotamia to our world is this system: Even today, the foot has 12 inches; the day, twice 12, or 24, hours; the minute and hour, 60 units each; and the circle, 360 degrees.

*Sumerian Writing* Historians have long disputed whether the Sumerians or the Egyptians first developed the art of writing; recent research may show a slight lead in favor of Egypt. In any case, the Sumerians were writing by about 3000 B.C. The most important intellectual tool ever discovered, writing enables people to keep records, codify laws, and transmit knowledge. All the record keeping, libraries, and literature of later times are made possible by this invention. Their script was pictographic: Each sign was originally a stylized picture of the article that the scribe had in mind.

In time, scribes reduced the complexity of the system by simplifying pictures and by combining several pictures into one. In this process of abstraction, the meaning of a sign might change. For example, a crude picture of a star was simplified into four wedge-shaped marks and given the meaning of "god" or "heaven."[3] In another kind of refinement, the Sumerian script became at least partly alphabetic and phonetic rather than remaining purely a system of pictographic writing. Sumerian texts were written on clay tablets by pressing the end of a reed or bone stylus into the wet clay; the resulting wedge-shaped marks are called *cuneiform* (Latin *cuneus*, meaning "wedge"), a name used for all such scripts in whatever language they occur. *Scripts* are not *languages:* They are symbols that can be used to write several

[3]The Sumerian system of writing is excellently described by S. N. Kramer, *The Sumerians*, 1963, pp. 302 ff.

▲ A relief showing the Sumerian hero Gilgamesh holding a conquered lion, from the reign of Sargon II of Assyria, eighth century B.C. The relief shows the long continuation of the Sumerian legend.
Giraudon/Art Resource

languages, as the Latin script is used to write all the languages of western Europe.

***The Epic of Gilgamesh*** Sumerian literature has left us a priceless document, a moderately long and stirring narrative known as the Epic of Gilgamesh. There evidently was a king in Sumer with this name (about 2700 B.C.), but in the epic, Gilgamesh is a great hero and ruler, said to be part man and part god. The woodless geography of Sumer dictates part of the story, as Gilgamesh sets out to recover cedar from northern lands (probably what is now Syria). He travels with his companion Enkidu, who is killed by the storm god, Enlil. Gilgamesh, mourning the loss of his friend and confronted with the near certainty of death, plods on through the world in search of eternal life. He finds the plant that restores youth, but a serpent swallows it while Gilgamesh is bathing. In sorrow he returns home, and the epic ends with his death and funeral.

The epic is profoundly pessimistic and gives us a key to the Sumerian view of the universe. The gods, who created the world, established the standards by which people had to live. The storm god, Enlil, lived in heaven. Normally kind and fatherly, Enlil made the rich soil of Mesopotamia fertile and was credited with designing the plow. At times, however, when Enlil had to carry out the harsh decrees of other gods, he became terrifying.

***The Fate of Humanity in Sumerian Thought*** This fearful alternation between divine favor and divine punishment doubtless reflects the uncertainty bred in the Sumerians by the constant threat of floods. When the rivers overflowed and destroyed the crops, the Sumerians thought the gods had withdrawn their favor, and they rationalized such treatment by assuming that they had somehow offended the gods or failed to observe their requirements.

In Sumerian mythology, humanity was almost completely dependent on the gods. Indeed, Sumerian myth taught that the gods had created people merely to provide slaves for themselves. In another Sumerian epic, *The Creation of Mankind,* Marduk the creator says, "Let him be burdened with the toil of the gods, that they may freely breathe." Other Sumerian myths foreshadow the biblical accounts of eating from the tree of knowledge in paradise and of the flood that covered the earth.

***Sargon of Akkad and the Revival of Ur*** Wars among the cities of Sumer weakened them and prepared the way for the first great warlord of Western history: Sargon, of the area called Akkad, named for a city just north of Babylon. Sargon ruled from 2371 to 2316 B.C.[4] and conquered all Mesopotamia; his kingdom even reached the Mediterranean Sea. From the name Akkad, the language of Sargon is called Akkadian; it is of the Semitic linguistic family and includes both Babylonian and Assyrian. Thus, through Sargon, we meet one of the most important of all groups of peoples in Western civilization, the Semites. The difference between Semites and other peoples of the region—indeed, between most peoples—is linguistic, not "racial." The peoples of the region spoke a number of related languages including Akkadian, Hebrew, and Canaanite. Akkadian, also written in cuneiform, now replaced Sumerian as a spoken language, although Sumerian continued as a written language until about the beginning of the Christian era.

Sargon and his successors ruled from Akkad until about 2230 B.C., when invasion, and perhaps internal dissension, dissolved the Akkadian kingdom. The Sumerians then regained control of southern Mesopotamia and established the so-called Third Dynasty of Ur. The chief ruler of this period was Ur-Nammu (2113–2096 B.C.). He created another practice that we will see again and again in history when he issued the first law code and spelled out regulations and penalties for a broad range of offenses. He also established standard weights and measures, a recognition of the importance of trade to the people of his state. Ur-Nammu's law code is preserved in only fragmentary form, but it is clear that he laid down fines in money rather than calling for physical retribution: "If a man has cut off the foot of another man . . .

---

[4]Dates in early Near Eastern history are in constant revision. For dates in this chapter, we normally rely on the *Cambridge Ancient History,* 3rd ed., 1970–2000.

he shall pay ten shekels . . . If a man has severed with a weapon the bones of another man . . . he shall pay one mina of silver." (Some historians assign this code to his son Shulgi.)

### ◆ THE BABYLONIAN KINGDOM

Ur declined, toward the year 2000 B.C., and was destroyed by neighboring peoples in 2006. A Semitic people called Amorites soon established their own capital at Babylon, within the region known as Babylonia. Hammurabi, the sixth king of the dynasty in Babylon itself, finally succeeded in unifying Mesopotamia under his rule.

*Hammurabi and His Law Code*  Hammurabi (1792–1750 B.C.) is a towering figure whose greatest legacy is the most significant of all the documents written down to this time: a stone column, now in the Louvre Museum in Paris, recording in cuneiform script a long series of legal judgments published under his name. This so-called Code of Hammurabi, like the earlier one of Ur-Nammu, is not a complete constitution or system of law; rather, it is a compilation of those laws and decisions that Hammurabi thought needed restating. Its form is important. The code begins with a preamble, in which the god Marduk declares that he is giving his laws to Hammurabi; this preamble thus validates the laws by assigning them a divine origin.

The code includes 280 sections, much more carefully organized than any earlier one that we know (see "Hammurabi's Law Code," p. 13). Hammurabi has always been considered the primary example of the lawgiver, the man who grasped the organizing power of royal declarations of law; his example was to be followed by many other potentates, whether or not they consciously looked back to the Babylonian model. The sections of the code, like those of Ur-Nammu's code, are all arranged in the form, "If *A* takes place, *B* shall follow," for example, "If a man strikes his father, they shall cut off his hand."

Hammurabi recognized three classes within his society: We follow the historian H. W. F. Saggs[5]

and call them gentleman (one of the landowning families), landless free citizen, and slave. The penalties for various offenses were not uniform; rather, they differed according to the status of the victim. Sometimes the code allowed monetary compensation rather than physical retaliation. For example, "If a man destroys another man's eye, they shall destroy his eye"; but "If a man destroys the eye of another man's slave, he shall pay one half the slave's price." The penalties were severe, to say the least, and the rule of strict retaliation between members of the same class has given us the saying "an eye for an eye, a tooth for a tooth"[6] as a motto for Hammurabi's principles.

*Women and the Family in the Code*  But Hammurabi was not concerned merely with retaliation. Among the most forward-looking provisions in his code were those regarding the family. Hammurabi evidently recognized the vulnerable position of women and children in his society and took care to protect them. If a man's wife became ill, he could marry another woman but had to continue to support the first wife; and she, if she wished, could move out and keep her dowry, that is, the contribution made by her family when she was married. A widower could not spend his dead wife's dowry but had to save it for her sons; and a widow could keep her dowry.

Hammurabi regulated marriage with care, evidently wanting to secure a stable life for future generations. He dealt with breach of promise by decreeing that, if a man had paid a marriage price to his potential father-in-law and then decided not to marry the young woman, the woman's father could keep the marriage price. If a man wanted to divorce a wife who had not produced children, he could do so but had to return her dowry.

*The Code and Society*  The code is not wholly a progressive document. Some decisions in the code reflect a double standard for the sexes. A wife could divorce her husband for adultery and reclaim her dowry, but only if she had been chaste; if not, she was thrown into the river (and, presumably,

---

[5]*Civilization before Greece and Rome*, 1989, p. 44.

[6]This formulation also reaches us through the Bible (Exod. 21:24).

---

## HAMMURABI'S LAW CODE

*Here are some excerpts from the "judgments" laid down by Hammurabi in his famous law code.*

"When Marduk [the patron god of Babylon] sent me to rule the people and to bring help to the country, I established law and justice in the language of the land and promoted the welfare of the people. At that time I decreed:

"1. If a man accuses another man of murder but cannot prove it, the accuser shall be put to death.

"2. If a man bears false witness in a case, or cannot prove his testimony, if that case involves life or death, he shall be put to death.

"22. If a man commits robbery and is captured, he shall be put to death.

"23. If the robber is not captured, the man who has been robbed shall, in the presence of the god, make a list of what he has lost, and the city and the governor of the province where the robbery was committed shall compensate him for his loss.

"138. If a man wants to divorce his wife who has not borne him children, he shall give her money equal to her marriage price and shall repay to her the dowry she brought from her father; and then he may divorce her.

"142. If a woman hates her husband and says, 'You may not possess me,' the city council shall inquire into her case; and if she has been careful and without reproach and her husband has been going about and belittling her, she is not to blame. She may take her dowry and return to her father's house.

"195. If a son strikes his father, they shall cut off his hand.

"196. If a man destroys the eye of another man, they shall destroy his eye.

"197. If he breaks another man's bone, they shall break his bone.

"200. If a man knocks out a tooth of a man of his own rank, they shall knock out his tooth."

From Robert F. Harper (tr.), *The Code of Hammurabi,* Gordon Press, 1904, 1991 (language modified).

---

drowned) along with her lover. Nowhere does the code state that a husband will suffer the same punishment if he has been unfaithful.

At the end of his long document, Hammurabi added a proud epilogue, reading in part, "The great gods called me, and I am the guardian shepherd whose beneficent shadow is cast over my city. In my bosom I carried the people of the land of Sumer and Akkad; I governed them in peace; in my wisdom I sheltered them." He thus combined the power of both law and religious belief to create a civic order for his society.

### ◆ MESOPOTAMIAN CULTURE

Hammurabi's subjects used all manner of commercial records (bills, letters of credit, and the like), and their knowledge of mathematics was amazing. They built on foundations laid by the Sumerians, using the sexagesimal system, with the number 60 as the base. They had multiplication tables, exponents, tables for computing interest, and textbooks with problems for solution.

The Mesopotamians also developed complex systems of astrology (the art of predicting the future from the stars) and astronomy. It is not certain which science inspired the other, but we have both astrological predictions and astronomic observations from the second millennium. The Babylonian calendar had twelve lunar months and thus had only 354 days, but astronomers learned how to regularize the year by adding a month at certain intervals. When the Hebrews and Greeks wanted to order time through a calendar, they learned the method from the Babylonians. In fact, the calendars of both Jerusalem and Athens were also lunar, with 354 days and a month added from time to time.

## III. Egypt

---

The early cities of Mesopotamia had turbulent histories, falling now to one warlord, now to another. The kingdom of Egypt, by contrast, achieved a nearly incredible permanence. The

▶ **Top: The ceremonial palette of King Narmer is a symbolic representation of the unification of Upper and Lower Egypt. This side of the palette shows the king, wearing the white crown of Upper Egypt, smashing the head of an enemy. The god Horus, in the form of a falcon, holds a rope attached to a captive of Lower Egypt, a region symbolized by six papyrus plants.**

▶ **Bottom: On this side of the palette King Narmer has completed his conquest of Lower Egypt and wears the red crown of that kingdom. He is reviewing the bodies of decapitated victims. The exotic beasts with necks intertwined may symbolize the unity of the two Egypts.**
Hirmer Fotoarchiv

basic element in the long history of Egyptian civilization is the Nile River. The Nile overflows its banks each summer, reviving the land with fresh water and depositing a thick layer of alluvial soil for cultivation. Only this yearly flood protected the early Egyptians from starvation.

The geography of Egypt must also have played a part in the social organization of the state. In

▲ **An example of a hieroglyph. The man on the left says (reading from right to left), "Seize [it] well." The worker on the right replies (from top to bottom), "I will do as you wish." From the tomb of Ptahhotep (Old Kingdom, Dynasty V. ca. 2565–2423 B.C.).**

effect, Egyptians could live only along the Nile and could not withdraw into any kind of interior. Moreover, the need to live close to the river isolated Egypt from other peoples and allowed a long, generally unbroken development. The climate is usually equable, and the river was a friend, not the potential enemy that it was in Sumer.

These conditions allowed the kings to control their subjects through governors and, if need be, with troops up and down the river. The narrow bed of the Nile as it flows down to the Mediterranean Sea is almost a metaphor for the highly "vertical" structure of Egyptian society. Egyptians must have thought that the regularity of their agricultural life was a gift from the gods. The kings and their servants saw to the maintenance of religion, and the faith of Egypt was a large factor in the strength and longevity of their society.

### ◆ THE OLD AND MIDDLE KINGDOMS

***Unification of Egypt and Its Kings***  Historians treat Egyptian history in three periods: the Old, Middle, and New Kingdoms. These periods in turn are divided into some thirty-one groups of kings, or dynasties. Early Egypt was divided into two regions, Upper Egypt (the Nile Valley) and Lower Egypt (the river delta, where the water spreads into a shape like the Greek letter delta). A king, Menes (also known as Narmer), who lived about 3100 B.C., unified Upper and Lower Egypt and established a capital at Memphis. By the beginning of the Old Kingdom (about 2700 B.C.), the land had been consolidated under the strong central power of the king, who enjoyed a supremacy that we can hardly imagine today. The king (he was not called *pharaoh* until the New Kingdom, which began about 1570 B.C.) was the owner of all

Egypt and was considered a god as well. The whole economy was a royal monopoly; serving the king was a hierarchy of officials, ranging from governors of provinces down through local mayors and tax collectors. Artisans, peasants, and servants, all working for the king, nourished the whole system.

The supreme monuments of the Old Kingdom are the three immense pyramids, tombs for kings, built at Giza (now within the city of Cairo) between 2600 and 2500 B.C. These staggering feats of engineering dwarf any other monuments from any age. The Egyptians were the unchallenged masters in cutting and manipulating stone. They fitted the tremendous blocks in the pyramids together with nearly perfect tightness. Building such a pyramid may well have been the chief activity of the king during his rule. The ability to move and arrange such huge weights was a sign of an omnipotent ruler.

*Religion*    The king was seen as a god—specifically, the incarnation of the god Horus, who is represented in art as a falcon. Here Egypt differs from the Mesopotamian kingdoms, in which the ruler was not considered divine. Thus Egypt offers another example of the political power of re-

▲ THE PYRAMIDS OF GIZA. **Left to right, the pyramid of Menkaure, Khefre, and Khufu (the "Great" pyramid).**
Henning Bock/AKG London

ligion in organizing early societies. Other gods, who occupied lesser positions in Egyptian religion, appeared in a variety of forms, often as animals, and in origin were probably deities of the villages up and down the Nile. The Egyptians believed in a pleasant life after death, in which people would perform their usual tasks but with more success. The king, already a god, would become a greater god; soothsayers, priests, and administrators would hold even higher positions. For everyone who had lived a good life, there would be delights such as boating and duck hunting.

In Egyptian mythology, the god who ruled over the dead was Osiris, originally a god of fertility. Myths taught that he had given Egypt its laws and shown the people how to prosper. Legend also told that he was murdered by his treacherous brother and his body cut into fragments, which his loving wife and sister, Isis, reassembled, thus resurrecting him. Osiris' son, Horus, was identified with the king, who was, as we have said, considered the incarnation of Horus on earth and the center of the world.

In harmony with their expectation of survival beyond death, the Egyptians made careful preparations for the physical needs of the afterlife, especially by placing favored possessions, such as jewelry and wine cups, into a tomb and embalming and making mummies of the dead. Statues sat in the tombs of kings as receptacles for their spirits in case their bodies should be destroyed.

*Maat*    The Egyptians recognized an abstract ethical quality called *maat*, which Egyptologists translate roughly as "right order." *Maat* existed if everything was in the order that the gods had ordained. *Maat* was a kind of primeval and cosmic harmonizing force that arranged all created things in the right relationships. All ancient societies valued order—most of them had a monarchic system that naturally prized discipline—but the notion of *maat* seems to show a new way of advocating moral behavior. When a society can give a name to the abstract idea of right order, a subtler kind of thinking is taking place. Right order would, indeed, help to hold Egyptian society together. The king maintained *maat* and acted in accordance with it; he could not, therefore, be evil or act wrongly. Thus *maat* illustrates another

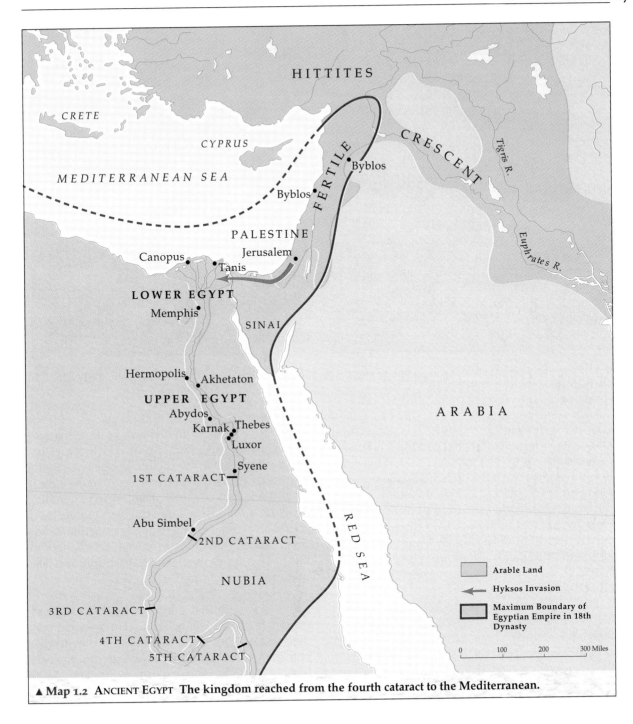

▲ **Map 1.2  Ancient Egypt  The kingdom reached from the fourth cataract to the Mediterranean.**

frequent use of religion throughout history: as a carefully crafted tool to promote and maintain social order and political control. Egyptian religion also taught that Osiris, ruler of the next world, judged human beings and decided whether the dead truly deserved admission to the hereafter.

At a later period Osiris is shown in art accompanied by 42 judges, who weigh the merits of the deceased against the demands of *maat*. The Egyptian judgment of the dead may be the earliest example of the need and reward for ethical conduct in life.

▲ **An Egyptian papyrus showing an antelope and a lion in a game of chess; a playful scene from daily life.**
The British Museum.

*Writing*  Egyptians developed a form of writing known as *hieroglyphs* ("sacred carvings"). The indispensable key to the Egyptian past has been the Rosetta stone, discovered when Napoleon occupied part of Egypt in A.D. 1798. This stone, now in the British Museum, contains a partly preserved hieroglyphic text along with a translation in the cursive Egyptian script that evolved from hieroglyphs and another translation in Greek, a known language that offered a way of deciphering the other two.

Like the cuneiform script of Mesopotamia, hieroglyphs began as pictorial signs. Recent research has suggested that writing in Egypt began as early as about 3200 B.C. If so, Egypt could claim the prize as the society that invented writing, a little ahead of Sumer. Hieroglyphs sometimes use merely a picture of the object represented; for example, a small oval represents "mouth." But at some point the scribes decided to use the pictures as phonetic signs; thus *ra* continued to mean "mouth" but was also used for the sound of the consonant *r*. Fully developed hieroglyphs, like Sumerian cuneiform, are therefore a combination of pictograms and phonetic signs.

*Papyrus*  The Egyptians made writing material from the papyrus plants (from which comes our word *paper*) that grew in abundance in the Nile. The reeds of the plant were placed crosswise in layers, then soaked, pressed, and dried to produce sheets and rolls. Because of the dry climate, thousands of papyri have survived in legible condition; most papyri come from the New Kingdom, but in later times much Greek literature was also preserved on papyri.

*Literature and Instructions*  Egyptians developed a rich, lively literature. Their works, like their art, are full of mythology and the afterlife, and their hymns to various deities, poems celebrating the king's victory over death, and stories about the gods all reflect the serene Egyptian confidence in the beneficence of divine powers. Various texts, collectively known as the *Book of the Dead*, provide charms and other methods of ensuring a successful transition to the other world.

Success in this world appears as the central concern of another literary genre, appropriately known as "instructions" or "instructions in wisdom." These books, in which a wise man gives advice about how to get ahead in the world, offer a key to Egyptian social attitudes, especially the supreme position of the king. The writers counsel discretion and loyalty:

> If you are a man of note sitting in the council of your lord, fix your heart upon what is good. Be silent—this is better than flowers. Speak only if you can unravel the difficulty . . . to speak is harder than any other work. . . . Bend your back to him that is over you, your superior in the king's administration. So will your house endure with its substance, and your pay be duly awarded. To resist him that is set in authority is evil.[7]

*Love Poetry* We also have Egyptian love poetry: "I love to go to the pond to bathe in your presence, so I may let you see my beauty in my tunic of finest royal linen, when it is wet." And there are meditations, songs, ghost stories, and fables of all kinds. In fact, not until the Greeks did the ancient world have another literature with variety and beauty equal to that of Egypt.

*Mathematics and Medicine* The Egyptians were pioneers in applied science. The need for careful planting in the silt deposits of the Nile forced them to master arithmetic, geometry, and the art of surveying; an unusually rich overflow might wipe out the boundaries between plots of land, and when this happened the land had to be remeasured.

Medicine in Egypt depended largely on driving out demons from the body. The Egyptians believed that a separate god ruled over each organ and limb, and treatment consisted largely in finding the right chant to appease the appropriate deity and then delivering it in the right tone of voice. Sometimes a sorcerer simply threatened a demon by promising to invoke the aid of the gods if it did not depart at once.

*An Approach to Diseases* But medicine was not based entirely on magic. We have recipes for toothache, for depression, for constipation, and much more. The Edwin Smith Papyrus, a treatise on surgery, discusses some forty-eight medical problems, classified according to the various parts of the body. Whenever possible, the author gives a diagnosis and suggests a treatment through surgery. A verdict is often given in one of three forms—"An ailment that I will treat," "An ailment with which I will contend," or "An ailment not to be treated"—probably according to whether the prognosis was favorable, uncertain, or unfavorable. This text is a witness to the birth of a kind of inquiry that transcends haphazard

▲ **Queen Hatshepsut of Egypt (1503–1482 B.C.), history's first female ruler, pictured as a sphinx, which was a divine animal. Surrounding her face are a lion's mane and a ceremonial false beard.**
The Metropolitan Museum of Art, Rogers Fund, 1931 (31.3.166).

---

[7]Adolf Erman, *The Ancient Egyptians: A Sourcebook of Their Writings*, 1966, pp. 61–62 (language modified).

folk medicine. Such maturing and broadening of knowledge independent of magic characterize the civilizing process throughout history.

### ◆ THE NEW KINGDOM

*The Invasion of the Hyksos*  A major disaster struck Egypt about 1630 B.C., the invasion of the Hyksos (the name means roughly "rulers of foreign lands"). Historians are still not certain who these invaders were, but they were probably a group of western Asiatic peoples from Syria and Palestine. Part of their success was due to their use of the horse-drawn chariot in war. They seized and controlled mainly the region of the delta, but by about 1522 B.C. Egyptian warriors from Thebes had counterattacked and had driven the Hyksos from the delta and back into their homeland. The period following their expulsion is called the New Kingdom or the Egyptian Empire.

*The Eighteenth Dynasty*  During the Eighteenth Dynasty the rulers in Thebes, now called *pharaohs*, strengthened the power of the central government over the nobles and organized Egypt into a military state. They enlarged their domain by invading Asia (campaigning in what is roughly modern Syria), where they clashed above all with another kingdom known as Mitanni.

*Hatshepsut (1503–1482 B.C.)*  Within the Eighteenth Dynasty there reigned the most powerful female ruler of ancient times, Hatshepsut. This dynamic woman seized power and in 1503 B.C. had herself crowned king of Egypt, representing this act as the will of the god Amon. It was an act of breathtaking audacity in a social system in which men had always held the absolute power of monarch. Perhaps to emphasize her right to rule as king, she had herself portrayed as a sphinx with a beard.

▲ Akhnaton and Nefertiti in a familial scene hold three of their children while the sun-disk blesses and cherishes them. The style of art (round bellies, slender bodies, elongated jaws) is typical of the Amarna period.
M. Büsing/Bildarchiv Preussischer Kulturbesitz.

Hatshepsut wanted to be remembered above all as a builder, the restorer of Egypt. "I have repaired," she proclaimed on inscribed walls, "what was destroyed by the Hyksos; I have raised up what was in pieces ever since the Asiatics had been in the Delta, overthrowing what had been made." Her great temple tomb in the Nile valley is among the most majestic of temples in Egypt.

*Thutmose III (1504–1450 B.C.)* Thutmose III, Hatshepsut's successor, became Egypt's greatest military leader. He made seventeen expeditions into Asia and expanded the empire as far as the Euphrates River. He proudly recorded his victory over Mitanni (about 1465 B.C.). His successors, exploiting these conquests, grew rich on the tribute paid by subject peoples. With this economic power the Egyptians expanded their trade, honored their gods with more temples, and continued working the rich copper mines in the Sinai peninsula.

*Akhnaton's Religious Reform* After the conquests of Thutmose III, a dramatic conflict of religions took place in the New Kingdom. This struggle arose from a contest between the pharaoh and certain priests and nobles, as each party strove to make its own god the supreme one. Thus the apparent religious battle—not for the last time in history—was, in reality, a political one. Although this battle was but one event during the centuries of the New Kingdom, the reforming aims of one side in this conflict have fascinated modern observers.

Early in his reign, King Amenhotep IV (1379–1362 B.C.) began to oppose the worship of Amen-Re, for centuries the traditional god of Thebes, and sponsored the worship of the *aton,* the physical disk, or circle, of the sun. Supported by his wife, Nefertiti, Amenhotep appears to have been trying to overcome the influence of priests and bureaucrats in Thebes. To advertise the new faith among his people, he changed his own name to Akhnaton, meaning "he who serves Aton." He moved his capital from Thebes to a completely new city called Akhetaton, "the horizon of Aton" (a village called El Amarna today), where he built a temple to Aton. He composed a soaring hymn in praise of Aton, hailing him as the creator of the world—an account of creation comparable to

those of the Sumerians and the Israelites.[8] Doubtless through his desire, art of the Amarna period became realistic; the king was shown with a pot belly and elongated head and jaw, and this style reached into portraits of common people as well.

There is evidence that Akhnaton fought the worship of other gods, and some historians have gone so far as to call him the first monotheist. But such a conception is anachronistic and overlooks how Aton was worshiped: The royal family alone worshiped the god, while the Egyptian people were expected to continue to worship the pharaoh himself. Artistic scenes show priests and nobles in attitudes of reverence, but they are addressing their prayers to the pharaoh, not directly to Aton.

*The Reaction against Akhnaton* The more conservative priests, and probably most Egyptians, continued to worship Amen-Re, and Akhnaton's religious reform ended with his death. The next pharaoh changed his name from Tutankhaton to Tutankhamen, thus indicating that Amen-Re, the older chief deity, was again in favor. The royal court moved back to Thebes, and the city named for Aton, Akhetaton, was abandoned and destroyed. Akhnaton's name was savagely hacked off monuments and king lists, and he was now known as "the criminal of Akhetaton." The young king Tutankhamen reigned for only nine years and was buried with dazzling splendor. His tomb, discovered in A.D. 1922 intact with all its treasures, is one of the most stunning finds in the history of Egyptology.

*Ramses II (1294–1227 B.C.)* In the Nineteenth Dynasty, the New Kingdom emerged from the period of religious conflict with renewed strength and was led by ambitious pharaohs, the most famous of whom was Ramses II. He fought a major, though inconclusive, battle with the Hittite kingdom of Asia Minor in 1290 B.C., at Kadesh in Palestine and carried on the war until 1274 B.C. At this time the two kingdoms signed a peace treaty;[9]

---

[8]Strong resemblances have been seen between this hymn and Psalm 104. See J. A. Wilson, *The Culture of Ancient Egypt,* 1951, p. 227.

[9]Both the Hittite and Egyptian texts of this document are translated in J. B. Pritchard (ed.), *Ancient Near Eastern Texts Relating to the Old Testament,* 1969, pp. 199–203.

▲ **Syrian subjects presenting tribute to the pharaoh of Egypt on a wall painting at Thebes in the period of the empire.**
C. M. Dixon/British Museum

this may have been the world's first nonagression pact and brings forth another of the themes that run through history, namely diplomacy and negotiation between states.

Ramses II devoted much of Egypt's wealth to amazing building projects. At Karnak, for example, he completed an enormous hall of columns sacred to Amen-Re, who had now fully regained his old position. Ramses' supreme achievement as a builder is the colossal temple that he had carved out of the rocky cliffs along the Nile at Abu Simbel. In front of the temple sit four 65-foot high statues of the king. The building of the Aswan Dam by the modern Egyptians would have drowned the temple and its statues beneath the water of an artificial lake; but an international group of engineers preserved Ramses' desire to be remembered for all time by cutting the outer monuments free and raising them above the level of the water.

### ◆ A VIEW OF EGYPTIAN SOCIETY

***Administration and Slavery***   In antiquity, communication by ship was greatly superior to overland transportation in animal-drawn carts

because of the greater speed and economy of sailing. The Nile therefore imposed a natural administrative unity on Egypt. The kings secured their power through the help of ministers and advisers, especially the class of priests, while a complex bureaucracy carried out the routine work of government and saw to the economy, which was a royal monopoly with the exception of marketing the simplest household products.

Slaves existed, but the economic difference between free citizens and slaves was not always vast. Both classes worked the fields, labored on the pyramids, and were indeed the ultimate economic basis for the regime, although their own lives changed little from one generation to another.

***Education***   For all its controls, the Egyptian hierarchy did allow youths to enter and rise through education. The kings and their gods needed all manner of scribes, treasurers, and functionaries, and Egyptian children might learn the art of writing in a school run by a temple or a palace or even from a private teacher in a village. They normally studied from age four to age sixteen and could then enter the army or the royal service. Scribes were also needed for the arts of medicine and architecture and for the priesthoods; most priests were men, but some were women.

***Women and the Family*** Men and women viewed marriage as most desirable and often married as teenagers. The desire for children was universal as insurance against the future. One wise man of the Eighteenth Dynasty advised, "Take a wife when you are young, so that she might give you a son. Happy is the man with a large family, for he is respected on account of his children." On marriage, a woman obtained the title "mistress of the house," and the house and its management were her responsibilities. Agricultural work was by far the main occupation of Egyptians, and women participated in the task; they also went shopping, a fact noted with surprise by the Greek historian Herodotus on his visit to Egypt.

Most women were peasants with little education, but they had certain powers not granted, for example, to women of Israelite or Greco-Roman societies. Most remarkably, in view of the critical importance of ownership of land in Egypt, land passed down from mother to daughter; probably, it has been said, because it is always clear who one's mother is, while paternity can be uncertain. Likewise, men commonly identified themselves by citing the name of their mother, not of their father.

***Women and Occupations*** This method of passing on property meant that women could own and manage both land and other property. Thus a woman did not have to turn her property over to her husband at the time of marriage. Women could also initiate legal action, buy and sell property, and execute wills. But women were legally equal to men only within their own class. Most women were peasants and shared the daily work of planting crops, picking fruit, and carrying baskets; above all, they had to produce children.

Men normally held the important positions in the state and the bureaucracy (again the amazing position of the queen Hatshepsut should be remembered). Below this level of political influence, women performed tasks like overseeing weavers, singers, and cooks; some were treasurers in private businesses. A respected occupation was that of midwife, and midwives delivered most Egyptian babies. A great many women were singers,

dancers, and professional mourners at funerals. Among higher positions open to women were priesthoods, often including priestesses who chanted or played instruments in temples.

Women were buried along with their men, sharing in the elegance of the tomb according to the rank of their husbands. Privileged women could be given in death a profusion of jewels, necklaces, and other ornaments.

***The Permanence of Egypt*** We must not overlook the turmoil within Egyptian history: the invasion of the Hyksos, wars in Asia, the collapse of the New Kingdom, and its conquest by Assyria and then by Persia (see "Dates in Egyptian History"). Yet there remains the awesome *permanence* of Egypt: No other state, in the history of the nations we call Western, ever survived so long. On the whole, over the span of some thirty centuries, life flowed predictably, like the Nile, making severe demands but bringing the material for a well-earned reward.

# IV. Palestine

We have already discussed the Semitic societies of Babylonia and Assyria and turn now to Semites in the area of Palestine. They include the Phoenicians, who were famous as sailors and explorers; they also developed a simple alphabet that became the mother of all the scripts of Europe. Even more important to the Western experience was the society of Israel, which gave the Western world its greatest book—the Bible.

## ◆ CANAANITES AND PHOENICIANS

The region of Palestine was originally inhabited by a group of Semitic tribes known as the Canaanites, among whose cities were Jericho and Jerusalem. By about 1200 B.C. the Canaanites had settled mainly in Phoenicia, a narrow region along the Mediterranean Sea (roughly modern Lebanon). The Phoenicians drew part of their culture from the Mesopotamian and Egyptian states nearby, but they were also brilliant innovators.

***The Phoenician Alphabet*** Their outstanding contribution was a simplified alphabet with twenty-two characters that was later adopted by

Egyptian (hieroglyphs)

Akkadian (cuneiform)

Phoenician

ΔΑΡΕΙΟΣ ΕΙΜΙ

Greek

▲ **Several translations of "I am Darius," in Phoenician, Akkadian, hieroglyph, and Greek.**

the Greeks and became the ancestor of Western alphabets. The political and social importance of this invention is impossible to overstate. It ended the long period during which people had to learn thousands of pictorial symbols to be reasonably literate and writing was a mysterious art known to only a few. Especially in the hands of the Greeks, writing brought a knowledge of law codes and historical records within the intellectual reach of ordinary citizens and led to reevaluation of the past and a critical spirit about received tradition.

*Phoenician Exploration*    The Phoenicians lacked the military power to create an empire, but they influenced other cultures, especially through trade on both land and sea. They established trading posts or colonies far from Palestine, the most famous of which was Carthage, a powerful city on the north coast of Africa that controlled parts of North Africa and Spain. The Greek historian Herodotus records that some Phoenicians for the first time sailed completely around Africa.

Among the Phoenician articles of trade was a reddish dye that the ancients called *purple;* cloth dyed in this color became a luxury and has remained a mark of royalty or eminence. The Phoenicians' wide explorations made them masters of the sea, and because of their sailing ability they provided the navy for the Persian Empire.

They and other Canaanite peoples had thus developed a high urban civilization by the time the Israelites began their invasion of the Palestinian coast.

## ◆ HEBREW SOCIETY AND THE BIBLE

South of Phoenicia is the region of Palestine that today is known as Israel, also settled in antiquity by speakers of the Semitic Hebrew language. The Hebrew Bible, or Old Testament, provides a continuous record of how this people viewed its past, but before historians can use the narratives and chronicles of the Jewish and Christian sacred books as a source, they must take a stand on the credibility of the documents. Scholars in the nineteenth century questioned whether the Old Testament contained unchallengeable, divinely revealed truth. Archaeology in recent years has often confirmed the Bible, at least in questions of geography and topography, but literal accuracy is not, after all, the central issue to the historian. Religious traditions of any society, whether or not they are strictly verifiable, can instruct us about a society, just as do law codes and lists of kings.

The Israelite chroniclers concentrated on a single god and on humanity's relationship to him. This great theme, varied in countless ways, fuses the Old Testament into a story about one god and the history of his chosen people. Unlike

Mesopotamian epics, the Bible deals with real people and real times; it combines ethics, poetry, and history into the most influential book in the Western tradition.

***The Early Hebrews and Moses*** Hebrew tradition tells that a nomadic tribe led by Abraham migrated into Palestine from the east. A probable date for this movement is about 1900 B.C. His grandson, Jacob, is said to have organized the settlers into twelve tribes under the leadership of his twelve sons. Jacob himself also took the name Israel (meaning "God strove" or "God ruled"), and this name is also used for the people.[10] Israel was therefore a tribal society, unlike the urban society of Sumer or the unified monarchy of Egypt.

***Egypt and the Exodus*** Some Israelite tribes settled in Canaan. Others migrated to Egypt, according to the Bible to escape a severe famine, although immigration into Egypt had long been allowed. They remained there, but evidently suffered such harsh conditions that they determined to return to their homeland. Their return took place probably about 1240–1230 B.C., in the "exodus" (see "The Salvation of Israel," p. 26). At their head was Moses, who led them across the Sinai peninsula during a period of general unrest in the Near East. Their return was the critical formative event in their history. Moses organized the tribes of Israel and some neighboring Canaanites into a confederation bound by a covenant to the god he named YHWH (by convention, we write this word Yahweh; in English it later became Jehovah) and placed all the people in Yahweh's service. Moses proclaimed the new covenant between God and his people on Mount Sinai, in the wastes of the desert. According to the Old Testament Book of Exodus, he received his instructions directly from Yahweh. These instructions, a document of the greatest historical interest, include the Ten Commandments, in which Yahweh issues the terse order, "Thou shalt have no other gods before me." That is, the Commandments do not deny the existence of other gods; rather, they insist that Yahweh

be worshiped as the supreme one (such a doctrine is known as henotheism). So far as we can tell, this was the first time that any people in Western civilization accepted one god above all others.

But *why* did Israel accept one god as the highest, in contrast to the rest of the ancient world, in which families of deities were the rule? Was Moses perhaps influenced by Akhnaton's worship of Aton as the supreme god? We do not know, but we may guess that Moses saw the need to unify his people so that they would be strong enough to regain their home in Palestine; and what could forge a stronger bond than having the whole people swear allegiance to one god above all?

Moses also laid down a code of laws, which, unlike earlier codes, is a series of laws prescribing ethically right conduct. Far more than other ancient codes, this one respects people over property, lays down protection for the oppressed, and insists on respect for parents. This code appears to be the first intervention of religion into the private behavior of human beings. The historical reality of Moses, the fact that his laws are connected with the experience of a people, and the power of the ethical concerns of that people have given the faith of Israel an immediacy to which Sumerian or Egyptian religion could hardly pretend.

***Israel and Its Society*** Early Israelite society was clearly father-dominated through the patriarchs and God, whom they considered their supreme father. This structure led to a patriarchal family and shaped the legal status of women. Marriage occurs through purchase throughout the Old Testament, and a daughter might be bestowed on a man as a kind of salary, as in the moving story of Jacob and Rachel. Jacob loved Rachel dearly, and this is the point of the story, but he worked seven years to gain her in lieu of the purchase price (Gen. 29). Sometimes women were awarded as prizes for military success.

Some women did indeed rise above such a level of dependence on the family, and their heroism is all the greater. For example, the book of Ruth tells the story of Naomi, a woman of Bethlehem who moved to Moab (east of the river Jordan and the Dead Sea). When she planned to return to Bethlehem, her loving Moabite daughter-in-law Ruth refused her orders to remain behind. Ruth toils faithfully in the field and meets Naomi's relative Boaz, whom she marries. Her grandson is Jesse

---

[10]The book of Genesis (32, 35) gives two versions of how Jacob changed his name. In the first, he wrestles with an angel, who then designates him as he who "strove with God and with humans"; in the second, God appears to him and tells him that his name shall be Israel.

## THE SALVATION OF ISRAEL

*The Old Testament book of Exodus narrates the escape of the Israelites from Egypt and preserves the hymn of praise sung by Moses and his people after they reached the holy land. The poem celebrates the strength of God and his generosity in saving Israel. It also shows that Israel saw itself as having a special compact with God.*

"I will sing to the Lord, for he has triumphed gloriously; the horse and his rider he has thrown into the sea. The Lord is my strength and my song, and he has become my salvation; this is my God, and I will praise him, my father's God, and I will exalt him. The Lord is a man of war; the Lord is his name. Pharaoh's chariots and his host he cast into the sea; and his picked officers are sunk in the Red Sea. The floods cover them; they went down into the depths like a stone. Thy right hand, O Lord, glorious in power, thy right hand, O Lord, shatters the enemy. . . . Thou hast led in thy steadfast love the people whom thou has redeemed, thou hast guided them by thy strength to thy holy abode . . . the sanctuary, O Lord, which thou hast made for thy abode, the sanctuary, O Lord, which thy hands have established. The Lord will reign for ever and ever."

From Exodus, 15, Revised Standard Version of the *Bible*, National Council of Churches of Christ, 1946, 1952, 1971.

and her great-grandson is David, who became King of Israel and whom Christians consider an ancestor of Jesus (Matthew 1). Again, there is the strong figure of Deborah. The book of Judges (5) preserves her hymn of praise to God, which many scholars consider the oldest passage in the Bible. She was also one of the judges, leaders of the villages of Israel before there was a united kingdom, and is said to have served forty years.

*The Israelite Monarchy*  By a series of attacks on Canaanite cities and by covenants made with other tribes, the Israelites established themselves in Palestine. About 1230 B.C. they invaded Canaanite territory in a campaign aimed at expansion. Biblical stories say that Joshua, the successor of Moses, led the tribes of Israel across the Jordan River and followed God's instructions to take the Canaanite city of Jericho by siege. Many modern scholars would modify the biblical account and assume a more gradual process of occupation.

During the years of the conquest of Canaan, Israel still lacked a central government. The "judges" managed to reunite the people in periods of crisis, but the tribes then habitually drifted apart. They were also under pressure from the Philistines, a warlike people living along the coast of Palestine. According to the Bible, the people finally demanded a king, evidently wanting to imitate the practice of the Canaanites and also as protection against the Philistines: "We will have a king over us; then we shall be like other nations, with a king to govern us, to lead us out to war and fight our battles" (1 Sam. 8:20). The first king was Saul (1020?–1000?). His successor, David (1000?–961?), captured Jerusalem and made it Israel's capital. The entire nation now took the name Israel, and during his reign David extended the kingdom to its farthest boundaries. He conquered the neighboring kingdoms of Edom, Moab, Ammon, and Zobah; in modern terms, his domain included modern Israel, Lebanon, much of Jordan, and part of Syria even north of Damascus.

*Solomon*  Solomon, David's son and successor (961?–922?), was famed for his wisdom. Like all great kings of the period, Solomon was a builder. He left behind him the physical memorial that symbolized the faith of Israel through the centuries—the Temple in Jerusalem. But the temple could not compare in size with his magnificent palace and citadel, whose stables, according to tradition, housed twelve thousand horses.

Solomon's autocratic rule and extravagance caused resentment among his people, who were heavily taxed to pay for his palace and army. After his death the kingdom split into two parts. The northern half, centered on the ancient town of Shechem, retained the name of Israel; the southern half, ruled from Jerusalem, was now called Judah. Weakened by internal quarrels, the northern kingdom of Israel was conquered in 722 B.C. by the

## JEREMIAH REPROACHES ISRAEL

*The people of Israel discovered henotheism, but to maintain it was not easy. The prophet Jeremiah warned his people that they were backsliding into worshiping false gods such as Baal, rather than retaining allegiance to the one true God.*

"The Lord said to me, 'There is revolt among the men of Judah and the inhabitants of Jerusalem. They have turned back to the iniquities of their forefathers, who refused to hear my words; they have gone after other gods to serve them; the house of Israel and the house of Judah have broken my covenant which I made with their fathers. Therefore, thus says the Lord, Behold, I am bringing evil upon them which they cannot escape; though they cry to me, I will not listen to them. . . . The Lord once called

you, "A green olive tree, fair with goodly fruit"; but with the roar of a great tempest he will set fire to it, and its branches will be consumed. The Lord of hosts, who planted you, has pronounced evil against you, because of the evil which the house of Israel and the house of Judah have done, provoking me to anger by burning incense to Baal.'"

From Jeremiah, 11, Revised Standard Version of the *Bible*, National Council of Churches of Christ, 1946, 1952, 1971.

---

Assyrians to the northeast, who deported much of the population into Babylonia.

***The Dissolution of Israel***   Judah was now the only Israelite kingdom. The Greeks called this people *Ioudaioi*, from which comes the name Jews. Judah also fell in 586 B.C. to the Neo-Babylonian Kingdom ruled by Nebuchadnezzar. The captives were deported to Babylon, in the so-called Babylonian captivity, but later in the same century they were allowed by King Cyrus of Persia to trickle back into Palestine. In general the Jews became pawns of the various forces that ruled Palestine until A.D. 1948, when a revived Jewish state—the republic of Israel—took its place among sovereign nations.

***The Faith and the Prophets***   Judaism was also shaped by a few resolute critics, known as the prophets: men of the people, tradesmen, and preachers, such as Amos, Micah, Hosea, Jeremiah, and Isaiah. These prophets were not kings and had no military power that could make the people listen to their message. The most authoritative prophet had been Moses, and all successors looked back to him for guidance. The later prophets spoke one general message: Israel was becoming corrupt and only a rigid moral reform could save it. Worship of Yahweh had sometimes been blended with that of the gods, or Baalim, of the Canaanites. Luxury, promiscuity, and extravagance were weakening the discipline of Israelite society (see "Jeremiah Reproaches Israel"). Perhaps most important, they

warned that worship of Yahweh had become, for many, only a matter of form and ritual. They insisted that their people should put their faith in God and live in a just and righteous manner.

But even as they denounced the prevalent wickedness, the prophets promised that God would forgive Israel if the people repented and that he would further prove his love to Israel by sending a Messiah. The word *Messiah* (*mashiah* in Hebrew) means a person or even a thing possessing a divine power or purpose; referring to people, it came to mean one "anointed" by God to perform a special mission. From about 200 B.C. onward, Jewish thought held that a king would some day appear, a descendant of David, who would restore the power and glory of Israel on earth. The famous Dead Sea Scrolls (discussed in chapter 5), ranging in date from the second century B.C. through the first century A.D., often speak of the awaited Messiah. Christians, too, developed their theory of a Messiah, who would return to rule on earth over all humanity: To them, the "anointed one" (*ho christós* in Greek) is Jesus, but to Jews, the hero is still unborn or unknown.

***The Preservation of the Faith***   Another event that strengthened Judaism was the organization of the sacred writings. Ezra, who wrote about 445 B.C., is the prototype of a new kind of spiritual leader—the scribe and scholar. He collected and published the first five books of the Old Testament (the Pentateuch); later scholars collected the

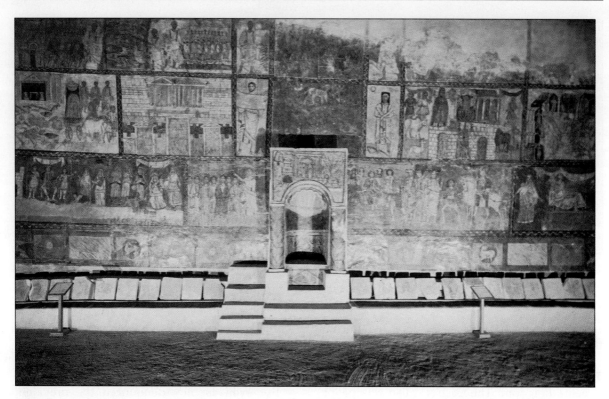

▲ **An extreme rarity, the only example of frescoes in a Jewish synagogue showing scenes from the Bible. From Dura Europus, ca. A.D. 239; now in a museum at Damascus.** Princeton University Press/Art Resource.

books of the prophets. The Temple in Jerusalem, destroyed during the Neo-Babylonian invasion, had been rebuilt during the sixth century B.C. and, in the absence of a free Jewish state, assumed even greater importance as the nucleus of the faith. It fell once more, in A.D. 70, this time to the Romans, who destroyed it. But part of the western wall of the outer court survived, and at this site the Jews were permitted to gather and pray.

#### ◆ THE JEWISH LEGACY

The Jews are the only society originating in the ancient Near East whose social and religious traditions have continued to influence modern European civilization. For reasons that no one can fully explain, adversity has never broken the Jewish spirit, and over many centuries the Jews have persisted as a society even without an independent state. Their faith provided the most persuasive answer to the problem that also troubled their neighbors—the nature of the relationship between humanity and God.

To Israel, there was only one supreme god; unlike the gods of the pagans, he was an exclusive and intolerant one. He judged severely, but he was also prepared to forgive those who sincerely regretted wrong behavior. He had created the world but stood outside the world; he had no association with the world of nature and never appeared as an animal or in any other form. Above all, he was a god for everyone, not just for nobles, priests, and kings. Christianity, the religion of medieval and modern Europe, and Islam, the chief religion of the Near East, are both children of Judaism and have drawn on the morality and ethics of the older faith.

## V. The Near Eastern States

A series of general disruptions about 1250 to 1150 B.C. left no state dominant for the next few centuries until the Assyrians began their conquests. They became the first people to accomplish a political unification of large parts of the Near East (see map 1.3). The Persians, the next great imperialists of this region, built on foundations laid by the Assyrians and ruled with an administrative skill that only the Roman Empire would equal in ancient times. The Persians also developed a widely accepted religion, Zoroastrianism, some of whose doctrines persisted long after the Persian Empire had disappeared.

## ◆ THE ASSYRIAN STATE

*The Assyrians* The Assyrians were descended from Semitic nomads who had entered northern Mesopotamia about 2500 B.C. and founded the city of Ashur, named after their chief god. From this name comes the designation *Assyrian* for the people. Their language was a Semitic dialect closely resembling that of the Babylonians, and they wrote in the cuneiform script that had originated in Sumer and had remained in general use.

*Assyrian Conquests* About 900 B.C. the Assyrians began their most important period of conquest and expansion. They became masters of the upper reaches of Mesopotamia, and their territory included Babylonia to the south, the cities of Palestine to the west, and northern Egypt. By the middle of the seventh century B.C. their dominion embraced most of the Near East.

If any one concept could characterize Assyrian society, it would be militarism. The army was especially dominant and efficient. In administering their empire, the Assyrians faced a greater challenge than any earlier state in absorbing large kingdoms such as Egypt and Babylonia. They ruled with a degree of control unknown in any of the earlier conglomerates.

*Assyrian Rule* The Assyrian kings exacted heavy payments of tribute as the price of leaving the conquered territories in peace. Some peoples, such as the inhabitants of Judah, escaped further burdens, but other less independent peoples had to accept a vizier, or governor, serving the king. In some cases the imperial government deported subject peoples who might prove troublesome— for example, those inhabitants of Israel who were dispersed within the Assyrian domain. Assyrian armies stationed in the provinces were a further guarantee of stability. We must also record that

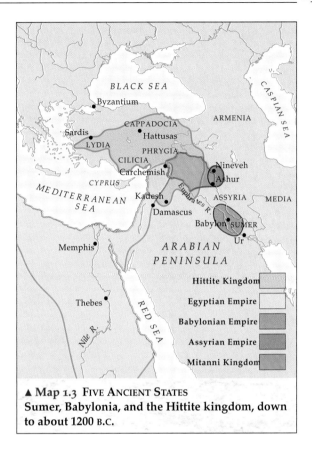

▲ **Map 1.3** FIVE ANCIENT STATES
**Sumer, Babylonia, and the Hittite kingdom, down to about 1200 B.C.**

Assyrian kings took pride in their brutal treatment of enemies and victims. Certainly, brutality has always existed in war, but the boast of one king is repellent:

> 3000 of their combat troops I felled with weapons.
> . . . Many of the captives taken from them I burned
> in a fire. Many I took alive; from some (of these)
> I cut off their hands to the wrist, from others I cut
> off their noses, ears, and fingers; I put out the eyes
> of many of the soldiers. . . . I burnt their young men
> and women to death.[11]

Language became another means of unifying the Assyrian domain; the Semitic language known as Aramaic (originally spoken by the Aramaeans, who controlled parts of Mesopotamia from about 1100 to about 900 B.C.) was ultimately spoken everywhere in lands dominated by Assyria. It later became the common tongue of the Near East and was the official language of the

---

[11]From H. W. F. Saggs, *The Might That Was Assyria*, 1984, p. 261.

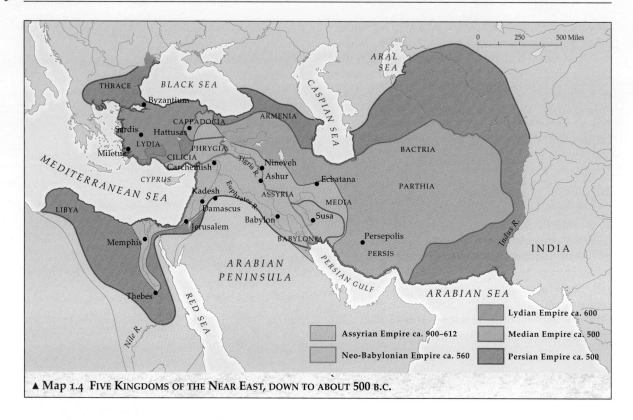

▲ **Map 1.4** FIVE KINGDOMS OF THE NEAR EAST, DOWN TO ABOUT 500 B.C.

Persian Empire. In Palestine, Aramaic was spoken by the Jews, including Jesus.

***Assyrian Art and Writings*** For all their harsh militarism and their brutal rule over their conquered subjects, the Assyrians created magnificent works of art. Much of the wealth extracted from the empire was spent on glorifications of the king and his conquests. Most notable are the reliefs cut on the palace walls at Nineveh, the capital, and elsewhere. The last powerful Assyrian king, Ashurbanipal (668–627 B.C.), also created a library of cuneiform texts. The largest single group of these texts covers omens, divination, or observations of the stars, because Assyrian kings relied heavily on omens and their interpretation by priests to guide royal policy.

It is hardly surprising that the subjects of the Assyrians watched for any chance to rebel. Finally, in 612 B.C., a combination of forces led by Babylonians captured Nineveh, and the Assyrian empire collapsed. Within a few years Assyria was reduced to a primitive state of nonurbanized living. Greek explorers 200 years later found it only sparsely populated.

◆ THE CHALDEANS AND THE MEDES

The Assyrian Empire gave way to two successor states: the Chaldean, or Neo-Babylonian, Kingdom and the Kingdom of the Medes. The Chaldeans, the dominant tribe within a new kingdom based on Babylon, were the most learned astronomers of antiquity. They kept minute records of eclipses, charted a plan of the heavens, and calculated the length of the year mathematically. Their discoveries were passed on to the Greeks and Romans and influenced all medieval and modern astronomy.

Babylon, the capital of the Neo-Babylonian Kingdom, was notorious as a center of luxury and wealth. Nebuchadnezzar (604–562 B.C.), the most famous king of the Chaldean dynasty, built lavish temples to the gods and is said to have constructed a terraced roof garden known as the Hanging Gardens, which was considered one of the Seven Wonders of the ancient world. It was he who captured Jerusalem in 586 B.C., destroyed the city and its holy temple, and scattered thousands of Jews within Babylonia, a tragedy recorded by the prophet Jeremiah.

*The Iranians*    Down to this point we have met the Sumerians, the Egyptians, and some Semite peoples. We come now to a people who spoke an Indo-European language, the Iranians. No documents have been found in the original Indo-European language, but from this language almost all the modern languages of Europe descend. Germanic languages including English, Greek, Latin, Romance languages, Slavic languages including Russian, and the languages of India, Pakistan, and Iran all belong to this family. Perhaps about 6000–5000 B.C. the Indo-European peoples began a slow dispersion across Europe and parts of Asia. Some of them finally settled on the Indian subcontinent, while others moved westward into Greece, Italy, central Europe, and Asia Minor.

A new people, the Iranians, appeared, another branch of the family that spoke Indo-European languages. Two noteworthy Iranian societies were the Medes and the Persians. The Medes, living in the area of Media to the east of Mesopotamia, formed a coherent kingdom about 625 B.C., and they took part in the capture of Nineveh in 612 B.C. We know little of their society because no written documents from Media have yet been found.

Their neighbors, the Persians, lived in the same general area and eventually subdued the Medes. Yet the Medes had enough prestige to be named first in official documents in which both Medes and Persians are mentioned. The Greeks, too, used *Medes* (Medoi) as the term embracing both Medes and Persians, and they called their two wars with the Persian Empire the *Medic* wars.

### ◆ THE PERSIAN EMPIRE

*Cyrus (559–530 B.C.)*    The Persians proceeded to form the largest, most efficient state down to their time. The founder of the Persian Empire was King Cyrus. His actions show him as a determined imperialist, and his first conquest was his victory over Media, to the north, in 550 B.C. A few years later Cyrus led his forces into western Asia Minor and conquered the kingdom of Lydia. This advance brought the Persian Empire westward as far as the Aegean Sea, which separates Asia Minor from Greece, and set the stage for a direct clash between the vast empire of the Near East and the new culture of the Greeks; but this clash was not to come for another two generations.

To secure the southern flank of his growing empire, Cyrus led his forces against the neo-Babylonian empire and captured Babylon. The inhabitants evidently welcomed him, for they offered little resistance. Their judgment was sound; Cyrus treated the city with moderation, not

◄ An Assyrian relief showing Ashurbanipal's soldiers attacking a city. Some soldiers swim to the attack; others scale the walls with ladders while defenders fall from the ramparts.
Hirmer Fotoarchiv.

▲ Part of the Bisitun inscription in Iran, showing
King Darius of Persia (522–486 B.C.) receiving the
submission of rebels. Carved in three languages, this
inscription provided the key to deciphering
cuneiform writing.
Photography by Dr. G. G. Cameron, The University of
Pennsylvania (Neg ANEP Plate 462).

sacking it as an Assyrian conqueror might have
done. In fact, his administration was marked by a
notable toleration of the customs and religions of
the people he brought under his control. We have
seen that he allowed as many as 40,000 refugees
from Judah to return to their homeland.

*Cambyses and Egypt*  Cyrus' successor, Cambyses
(530–522 B.C.), made the third conquest that completed the Persian Empire: He conquered Egypt

in 525 B.C., and the rich valley of the Nile remained under Persian rule until Alexander the
Great captured it in 332 B.C.

*Darius (522–486 B.C.)*  The most skillful administrator of the Persian Empire was Darius. He left
behind a superb monument—a proud summary
of his reign written in three languages (Old Persian, Akkadian, Elamite). Carved under a relief
showing Darius and some of his captives, this text
survives high on the face of a rock at Bisitun in
Iran. In a series of paragraphs, each beginning
"Saith Darius the king," he records his conquests,
including that of Babylon, and the defeat and mu-
tilation of his enemies. He also clarifies that he is
the only source of law: "As was said by me, thus it
was done." The tone and physical setting of this
grandiose monument confirm the lofty position of
the king in the Persian state. A later inscription on
his tomb also proclaimed his devotion to justice:
"I am a friend to right, not to wrong. Whoever
does harm, I punish him according to the damage
he has done." This statement reminds us of the insistence on restitution built into Hammurabi's
code and shows how some Near Eastern kings,
for all their unchallengeable power, tried to earn a
reputation for fairness.

*The Administration of the Empire*  Darius divided his empire into some twenty satrapies, or
provinces, each ruled by a satrap ("protector of
the realm"). The king, naturally, was the supreme
head of the state, but the satraps had a high degree of independence; they dispensed justice, designed foreign policy, and were in charge of
finance. Each satrap, for example, was responsible
for collecting an assigned amount of revenue from
his province. This system of delegating authority
became the model for the Roman Empire when it
expanded Rome's domain outside Italy.

The Greek historian Herodotus, writing in the
fifth century B.C., mentions with admiration the
Persian system of roads begun by Cyrus and perfected by Darius. A great highway ran across the
empire from the capital at Susa westward to
Sardis in Lydia, a distance of more than one thousand miles. The first long highway built anywhere, this road served trade and commerce and
also bound the far-flung empire together.

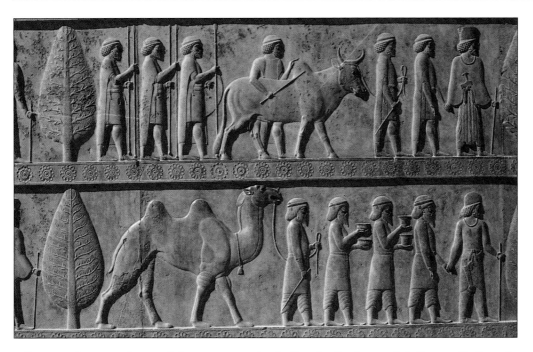

▲ Two panels on a staircase of the great reception hall at the Persian capital, Persepolis. In each panel an official leads a messenger whose followers bear tribute for the king of Persia.
George Holton/Photo Researchers

***Some Features of Persian Rule***   The Persian kings ruled their immense empire from several capital cities, of which Susa and Persepolis were the most famous. The king was the absolute and supreme ruler. His word was law, and he was surrounded with pomp and ceremony; his isolation from his subjects contributed to his reputation for awesome power, which went far to establish the aura of magnificence that has colored monarchy in the Roman Empire and the subsequent kingdoms of Europe.

***Royal Persian Women***   Mothers of the king of Persia had privileges uncommon in the Near Eastern kingdoms.[12] "Mother of the king" and "wife of the king" were technical terms, and the king's mother had direct access to the monarch. She had no formal political power but could intervene, even with the all-powerful king, for the sake of members of her family. The king's wife ranked below his mother and formed, with his mother, the center of the royal court. She could possess large holdings of land and treasure, riches beyond the dreams of any influential Greek woman.

***Zoroaster***   The Persian king was never considered divine, but he often served as a priest and claimed to have received his authority from the god of the Persians, Ahura Mazda. The prophet who formed the Persian faith was Zoroaster (also known as Zarathustra). We are not sure of the date of his life and work, but a number of historians think he lived about 600 B.C. or soon after.

Zoroaster was not considered divine; rather, he taught that the supreme god, Ahura Mazda, a god of light, had created the world and directed the heavens and seasons. The Persian conception of God as creator of the world, and of light and darkness, seems to have influenced Judaism to some degree. Within the book of the prophet Isaiah, God says, "I form light and create darkness. . . . I made the earth, and created humankind upon it; it was my hands that stretched out the heavens" (ch. 45).

***The Dualist Religion of Persia***   Around Ahura Mazda gathered good deities such as "Truth," "Righteous Thought," "Devotion," and so on,

---

[12]For these facts, see M. Brosius, *Women in Ancient Persia,* 1996, pp. 21–31.

whose ideals humanity should follow. But the Persian faith taught that Ahura was opposed by Ahriman, a wholly evil spirit—a devil, in fact. Thus Zoroaster taught a dualist religion, that is, one with two divine forces, although only Ahura is the true god whose message we are to hear. A concern with the devil was to expand greatly in the New Testament. Another similarity to Christian thought is found in Zoroaster's proclamation that, after thousands of years, a day of judgment will see the final triumph of good, and those people who have followed Ahura in morally good lives will gain paradise, while the rest will suffer in the realm of endless night. Zoroaster also rejected such ancient practices as the sacrifice of animals. The faith he taught demanded recognition of the one good spirit and a life of devotion to Ahura's ideals. His noble thought far outlasted the Persian Empire and still has followers today in Iran and in India.

In this chapter we have observed several historical themes. The rise of agriculture, which enabled humanity to live in permanent villages, led to the expansion of such villages into cities. In the cities, civilization arose with more ingenious tools that led to monumental architecture. Trade and its companion, writing, emerged. Monarchy became and remained the form of government, and rulers issued law codes to control their societies.

## SUMMARY

◆

The mighty legacy of the ancient Near Eastern societies—including the art of writing, monumental architecture, the development of pottery and weaponry—also influenced the development of their neighbors, the Greeks. The Greeks further learned from the older societies the use of coinage, the measurement of time, and forms of diplomacy. They added to this heritage a radical individualism and a passion for logical argument; their policies and institutions have influenced our own, even more directly and profoundly than those of the Near East, as will be apparent when we turn to the Mediterranean and the peoples of Greece.

## QUESTIONS FOR FURTHER THOUGHT

◆

**1. This chapter has looked at religious practices in several societies. How does the religion of Israel resemble some other religions? How does it differ from them?**

**2. In the forming of societies, which contributes more, intellectual skills or the dominance and administration of a strong government?**

## RECOMMENDED READING

◆

**Sources**

Lichtheim, Miriam. *Ancient Egyptian Literature: A Book of Readings.* 3 vols. 1973–1980. Excellent gathering of original sources in modern translation.

Metzger, B. M., and M. D. Coogan (eds.). *The Oxford Companion to the Bible.* 1993. Best general introduction to the Bible.

*The New Oxford Annotated Bible.* 1991. The New Revised Standard Version, with helpful annotation throughout.

Pritchard, James B. (ed.). *Ancient Near Eastern Texts Relating to the Old Testament.* 1969. More than the title implies; a wide-ranging collection of cuneiform and hieroglyphic texts on many subjects, with brief commentaries by eminent scholars.

Sandars N. K. (tr.). *The Epic of Gilgamesh,* 1972. The great Sumerian epic, in a highly readable translation with informative introduction.

**Studies**

Albright, William Foxwell. *The Biblical Period from Abraham to Ezra*. 1963. A brief history of Israel from a giant in the field.

*The Cambridge Ancient History*. 3d ed. 12 vols. 1970–2000. The standard history of the ancient world; chapters by numerous scholars, with large bibliographies.

Childe, V. Gordon. *What Happened in History*. 1985. Compact but profound analysis of history by a great anthropologist.

Crawford, H. *Sumer and the Sumerians*. 1991. A new history of the earliest civilization.

Dandamaev, Muhammad A. *A Political History of the Achaemenid Empire*. 1990. The Persian empire and its organization.

Ehrenberg, Margaret. *Women in Prehistory*. 1989. On women's roles in the rise of agriculture and in the early cities.

Frankfort, Henri. *The Birth of Civilization in the Near East*. 1956. A comparison of early Mesopotamian and Egyptian history.

Frye, Richard N. *History of Ancient Iran*. 1984. All-inclusive history of Persia.

Gardiner, Sir Alan. *Egypt of the Pharaohs*. 1969. A detailed political narrative.

Gimbutas, Marija. *The Goddesses and Gods of Old Europe, 6500–3500 B.C.: Myths and Cult Images*. 1984. Challenging work that argues for a matriarchal structure in earliest Europe that gave way to male domination.

Grimal, Nicolas. *A History of Ancient Egypt*. 1992. A recent complete history in one volume.

Hallo, William W. *Origins: The Ancient Near Eastern Origins of Some Modern Western Institutions*. 1996. Excellent example of the comparative method in history.

Hallo, William W., and William K. Simpson. *The Ancient Near East: A History*. 2d ed. 1998. American textbook survey of Mesopotamian/Egyptian history.

Johnson, Allen W. and Timothy Earle. *The Evolution of Human Societies: From Foraging Group to Agrarian State*. 2d ed. 2000. Anthropological study that allows deductions about developments in earliest times.

Kemp, Barry J. *Ancient Egypt: Anatomy of a Civilization*. 1989. Social and intellectual history.

Kramer, Samuel Noah. *The Sumerians: Their History, Culture, and Character*. 1963. Full portrait of Sumerian society by a leading authority.

Lamberg-Karlovsky, C. C., and Jeremy A. Sabloff. *Ancient Civilizations: The Near East and Mesoamerica*. 1979. Good coverage of the agricultural revolution, tools, early cities.

Læssøe, Jørgen. *People of Ancient Assyria, Their Inscriptions and Correspondence*. 1963. Good collection of original Assyrian texts.

Lerner, Gerda. *The Creation of Patriarchy*. 1986. Studies, from a feminist perspective, the rise of the social system in which men assume roles of command and leadership.

Meyers, Carol L. *Rediscovering Eve: Ancient Israelite Women in Context*. 1988. Women in Israelite society and in the Bible, with attention to folk customs.

Oates, Joan. *Babylon*. 1979. A survey for the nonspecialist.

Redford, Donald B. *Akhenaten: The Heretic King*. 1984. Highly readable study of this king in historical setting.

Reeves, Nicholas, and Richard H. Wilkinson. *The Complete Valley of the Kings: Tombs and Treasures of Egypt's Greatest Pharaohs*. 1996. A stunning photographic record of Egyptian architecture.

Robins, G. *Women in Ancient Egypt*. 1993. Well-illustrated treatment.

Roux, Georges. *Ancient Iraq*. 3d ed. 1992. Detailed, readable survey of ancient Mesopotamia.

Saggs, H. W. F. *Civilization before Greece and Rome*. 1989. Chapters on law, trade, religion, and so on; not a continuous narrative.

———. *Everyday Life in Babylonia and Assyria*. Rev. ed. 1987.

———. *The Greatness That Was Babylon*. 1988. General history of Mesopotamia; good survey of everyday life.

———. *The Might That Was Assyria*. 1984. Sympathetic portrait of this militaristic society.

Shanks, Hershel (ed.). *Ancient Israel: From Abraham to the Roman Destruction of the Temple*. Rev. ed. 1999. Eight chapters by experts, forming a concise modern history.

Wilson, John A. *The Culture of Ancient Egypt*. 1951. A timeless classic, superb for the history of ideas.

▲ **A magnificent mask of gold foil, found pressed on the face of a ruler of Mycenae, ca. 1500 B.C. This is one of the first Europeans on whose faces we can look.**
Nimatallah/Art Resource, NY

# Chapter 2

# THE FORMING OF GREEK CIVILIZATION

Greek civilization has been praised by our own more than any other for its creativity, its artistic genius, its intellectual daring. It created forms of thought and expression that have been imitated ever since: philosophy, drama, epic poetry, and history. It also assigned a leading role to reason, debate, and logical argument. This civilization honored personal heroism and independence, and its literature is the oldest one with many individually known writers.

In Greece, for the first time, we see another theme that runs through Western civilization: a body politic, a political system with laws fashioned by the people and with guaranteed participation for citizens. The Greeks developed a civic culture that broke with the Near Eastern traditions of monarchy. They lived in independent communities, or city-states. These cities were normally dominated by an upper class of some kind, but even this structure extended power beyond the all-powerful ruler of older civilizations.

Citizens of Greek city-states took pride in their temples, their civic traditions, the qualities of their own state, their participation in its life. In Athens the government was a democracy in which the male citizens themselves, not their representatives, made political decisions directly. This democracy allowed no role for women, foreigners, or slaves. Sparta, Athens' leading rival, chose by contrast a severe, authoritarian form of rule and was the only Greek state to retain monarchy after it had vanished in all others.

These two states led Greece into its most brilliant victories in war, the defeat of forces twice sent from the vast Persian Empire. They also became the nuclei of alliances that followed this triumph with tragedy, as their rivalry escalated into the long, destructive Peloponnesian War.

| CHAPTER 2. THE FORMING OF GREEK CIVILIZATION | | | | | | | |
|---|---|---|---|---|---|---|---|
| | Social Structure | Body Politic | Changes in the Organization of Production and in the Impact of Technology | Evolution of Family and Changing Gender Roles | War | Religion | Cultural Expression |
| I. CRETE AND EARLY GREECE | ▓ | | | ▓ | | ▓ | |
| II. THE GREEK RENAISSANCE | ▓ | ▓ | | | | ▓ | ███ |
| III. THE POLIS | ▓ | ▓ | ▓ | | ▓ | | ███ |
| IV. THE CHALLENGE OF PERSIA | | | | | ▓ | | |
| V. THE WARS OF THE FIFTH CENTURY | | ▓ | | | ▓ | | |

# I. Crete and Early Greece (ca. 3000–1100 B.C.)

The first important society in the Greek world developed on the island of Crete, just south of the Aegean Sea. The people of Crete were not Greek and probably came from western Asia Minor well before 3000 B.C. They traded with the nearby Greeks and left their influence in art, in religion, and in a system of writing. They were followed in history by a number of cities in Greece governed by monarchs. The most imposing such city was Mycenae, where tombs have disclosed stunning works of art. Greek legend also tells of a war against Troy in which Mycenae was the leading Greek power.

### ◆ CRETAN CIVILIZATION

We have no reliable historical narratives about early Cretan civilization. Therefore we must rely on archaeological evidence, found especially in a magnificent villa at Knossos. The historian must recognize that archaeological evidence often calls for much conjecture in its interpretation. The villa is known as the Palace of Minos; the civilization of Crete is thus often called Minoan.

***King Minos and His Palace***   Greek legend told of the Minotaur ("Minos-bull"), a monster that lived

in a labyrinth (surely a memory of the complex palace) and devoured girls and boys sent to it as tribute. The myth suggests that Greeks had at least a dim recollection of a ruler called Minos, and the historian Thucydides tells of Minos, the powerful king who "cleared the seas of piracy, captured islands, and placed his sons in control over them."

Other palaces on Crete exist, but none is so elegant as that at Knossos. For our knowledge of the palace, and much of Cretan culture generally, we must thank (Sir) Arthur Evans, a wealthy Englishman who began to excavate at Knossos in 1900 and spent some forty years at his task: he named the palace the Palace of Minos and restored much of it, including its colorful wall paintings.

The Palace of Minos was built over a period of about 700 years from ca. 2200 to ca. 1500 B.C. It was an extensive structure, with a vast eastern courtyard, an impressive grand staircase leading to upper rooms, and many wings and storage chambers. The palace even had a plumbing system with water running through fitted clay pipes.

The walls of the palace at Knossos were decorated with frescoes showing the Cretans' delight in nature. Gardens, birds, and animals are vividly portrayed, and one spectacular painting shows young men vaulting over the horns of a bull. The absence of walls around the palace suggests that Minoan civilization was essentially peaceful.

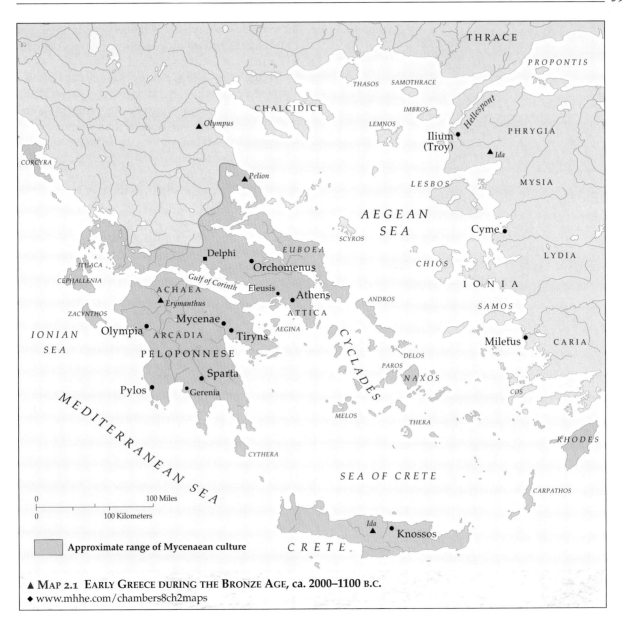

▲ **MAP 2.1  EARLY GREECE DURING THE BRONZE AGE, ca. 2000–1100 B.C.**
◆ www.mhhe.com/chambers8ch2maps

*Cretan Society and the Roles of Women*  Knossos was clearly the wealthiest of the Cretan cities, and the king was served by an efficient bureaucracy. The rulers were probably men; one wall painting shows a man, often identified as a priest or king, leading an animal to some kind of ceremony. Women were respected in this society, and jeweled ladies in elegant gowns appear in Minoan wall paintings.

Some historians have argued that women on Crete had actual political power in a system of matriarchy, or rule by women. This theory descends from a book published in 1861 by a Swiss scholar, Johann Bachofen, who theorized that early societies worshiped a goddess called the Great Mother, Mother Goddess, or Earth Goddess. Only over time, the theory holds, did men wrest political power away from women. Statuettes of women are known from Crete, holding snakes or grain in their hands and thus dominating nature. This much need not surprise us, since the earth is a noun of the feminine gender in many languages and is clearly the mother of all crops. But these facts fall short of proving the existence of a true

matriarchy on Crete; it is better simply to accept that these figurines probably represent goddesses of nature.

On the other hand, paintings found at Knossos show women in elegant coiffures, dressed in splendid robes and wearing dramatic makeup. Their faces show no hint of hard labor; these women, at least, enjoyed an upper-class lifestyle, whether or not they had political influence.

*A Cretan Empire?*  Much of the wealth of Crete came from trade, and Cretan pottery has been found far and wide throughout the Mediterranean world. About a dozen sites in the Greek world, probably trading posts, are called *Minoa*, obviously named after Minos. But we cannot speak of a true Cretan empire with political control of wide areas like the dominions of Assyria or

▼ **Roman wall painting, showing Theseus having killed the Minotaur; he is surrounded by grateful Athenian children, whom he has saved from possibly being devoured by the half-man, half-beast monster.**
Scala/Art Resource, NY

▲ **This marble statuette of a goddess is a product of the Cycladic culture (named for its home in the Cyclades Islands of Greece), which preceded the coming of the Greeks. Carved ca. 2800 to 2300 B.C., the statuette represents the early emphasis on female rather than male gods. Neolithic art preferred abstraction to Paleolithic realism and points the way toward later abstract thought. In the twentieth century, artists like Brancusi and Mondrian returned to this type of noble, elegant simplicity.**
© British Museum.

◀ A wall painting from Knossos, showing athletes vaulting over the horns of a bull. The figure at the right will catch the leaper in the center. The location of this painting in the palace suggests that the sport was a kind of ceremony. The bull may represent raw nature being tamed in this agricultural society.
Erich Lessing/Art Resource, NY

Persia, for Crete lacked the population to conquer and permanently subdue overseas possessions.

#### ◆ CRETE AND THE GREEKS

Minoan civilization reached its height between 1550 and 1400 B.C. Greek art of this period shows Minoan influence, and at least two Greek goddesses, Athena and Artemis, were probably adopted from Crete.

*Cretan Writing* The Minoans also had interchange with the Greeks through writing. Clay tablets have been found at Knossos in two similar scripts, called Linear A and Linear B. Both scripts are syllabic: Each symbol represents a sound, such as *ko,* rather than a letter of an alphabet. The language written in Linear A, the older script (used ca. 1700–1500 B.C.), has not yet been deciphered; but Linear B, the younger of the two scripts (used ca. 1450–1400 B.C.), has been deciphered as an early form of Greek. The decipherment was the work of a brilliant English architect, Michael Ventris, not a professional classical scholar. He achieved this feat in 1952 and tragically died in a motoring accident in 1956. The tablets contain inventories, rosters, and records of all kinds, listing footstools, helmets, vessels, seeds, and the like. They thus show that the rulers on Crete governed through fairly elaborate bureaucracies.

That these Linear B tablets were written in a form of Greek is a startling discovery, for it shows

▼ Throne room at Palace of Knossos.
Bridgeman Art Library

▲ A "marine style" vase by a Greek artist, about 1500 B.C., clearly imitating Cretan models. Sea creatures were often used in Minoan pottery in a free, naturalistic style.
C. M. Dixon

▲ A large vase from Crete in the Late Minoan II style, ca. 1450 to 1400 B.C., when Cretan art came under Greek influence and became more disciplined and geometric. Note the double ax motif; found in the palace at Knossos.
C. M. Dixon

that the Greeks, who at this time had not developed writing of their own, learned to write their language in a Cretan script. Their presence on Crete during this period suggests that Greeks had come to dominate Knossos, perhaps through outright military seizure. Probably the only Greek community that could have done this was that of Mycenae.

***The Collapse of Cretan Civilization***   About 1380 B.C., a catastrophe, whose causes are uncertain, engulfed Knossos and other Cretan cities; several of the stately palaces were burned or destroyed. A massive earthquake shook the island at this time, but the disaster may also have been connected with a quarrel or rebellion against Greek rule.

Some historians have tried to link the collapse of Knossos with a tremendous earthquake on the island of Thera (or Santorini) about seventy-five miles north of Crete. This earthquake is now dated to about 1625 B.C. It must have done damage on Crete, but the exact relationship, if any, between this natural disaster and the destruction of Knossos remains unclear.

## ◆ MYCENAEAN CIVILIZATION
### (ca. 1600–1100 B.C.)

The Greeks, the people who spoke and imported the Greek language, began to settle in Greece about 2000 B.C., arriving from the Balkan areas to the north; they were members of the general family of Indo-Europeans who had started to migrate into Europe at an uncertain time, perhaps around 5000 B.C. (see chapter 1, p. 31). They called themselves Hellenes and their country Hellas; the Greeks still use these names, and only in West European languages are they called *Greeks*, a name given them by the Romans.

▲ **A tablet in Greek, written in the Linear B script, from Pylos, about 1200 B.C. Note that each line contains a brief listing, probably items from an inventory, followed by a number. Such tablets reveal a complex bureaucracy within the monarchy at Pylos during the Mycenaean Age.**
C. M. Dixon

*The City of Mycenae* Geography divides Greece into many small valleys and forced the Greeks to develop independent communities with kings, but without the direction—or oppression—of a central ruler like a pharaoh. By about 1600 B.C., the Greeks had created wealthy, fortified cities, among which the most prominent was Mycenae, a huge citadel built on a hill in the Peloponnese. The years from 1600 to 1100 B.C. are therefore often called the Mycenaean Age.

*The Work of Heinrich Schliemann* Another pioneer of archaeology, the German Heinrich Schliemann, is mainly responsible for the rediscovery of Mycenae. Arriving here in 1876, he discovered six graves, probably those of a ruling dynasty, containing gold masks and ornaments of stunning workmanship. The graves at Mycenae have given us a glimpse of the wealth and artistic accomplishments of this city. They contained such luxuries as masks of gold foil that were pressed on the

faces of the dead and a complete burial suit of gold foil wrapped around a child, as well as swords, knives, and hundreds of gold ornaments. Tablets written in Linear B, attesting a palace bureaucracy, have been found at Mycenae and other sites of the Mycenaean Age.

*The Zenith of Mycenaean Power and the Trojan War* Between 1400 and 1200 B.C., Mycenae reached the height of its prosperity and created the most imposing monuments in Bronze Age Greece. A mighty decorated gateway with a relief of lions carved over it, known as the Lion Gate,

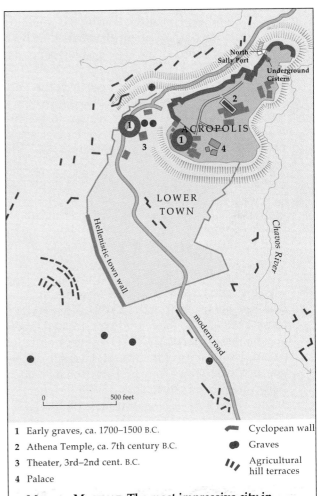

1 Early graves, ca. 1700–1500 B.C.
2 Athena Temple, ca. 7th century B.C.
3 Theater, 3rd–2nd cent. B.C.
4 Palace

Cyclopean wall
Graves
Agricultural hill terraces

▲ MAP 2.2 MYCENAE **The most impressive city in Bronze Age Greece, Mycenae, was first settled on its citadel. As the population expanded, a lower town developed, also surrounded by a wall. Outside the walls were terraced agricultural plots.**

formed the entrance to the walled citadel. Some rulers were buried in immense vaulted beehive-shaped tombs, of which the grandest and best preserved is the so-called Treasury of Atreus, named by archaeologists for the legendary father of King Agamemnon; but we do not really know which ruler or rulers were buried here.

Each city of the Mycenaean Age was probably independent under its own king. The only time these cities appear to have united was during the war against Troy, a rich city of obscure ethnic origin in Asia Minor near the Dardanelles. The evident wealth of the city must have offered a tempting prey to pirates and looters. Such was probably the real cause of the war against Troy, but Greek legend explained the war by the romantic story in Homer's *Iliad* about the seduction by a Trojan prince of Helen, the wife of a king of Sparta.

***The Troy of Homer***   Because Homer is the only source recording the Greek attack on Troy, we must proceed with caution if we are to believe that there really was such a war, for Homer was a poet, not a historian. Still, excavations at Troy have revealed several layers of building, among which one layer, called Troy VII A, was destroyed by some invaders about 1250 B.C., and this layer may well be the Troy that Homer says the Greeks attacked; some historians, however, would favor Troy VI, the preceding city.

***The Decline of Mycenae***   The war against Troy was the last great feat of the Mycenaean Age. Between about 1300 and 1200 B.C., marauders, called sea-peoples, made trade by sea so dangerous that the export of Mycenaean pottery virtually ended. The identity of these warriors is still uncertain, but their homes were probably somewhere in Asia Minor. Even more significant to the collapse of the Mycenaean Age was a series of attacks by land, lasting roughly from 1200 to 1100 B.C.; around 1100 B.C., Mycenae itself was overrun, though not obliterated. This invasion by land was probably the work of a later wave of Greeks who spoke the Doric dialect of the Greek language. Between about 1200 and 1100 B.C., these Greeks made their way southward from central Greece and settled mainly in the Peloponnese, especially in Corinth and Sparta, which became the most important cities in which Doric Greek was spoken.

▲ Picture of elegant little set of scales found in a Mycenean grave, used to weigh out gold in the next world, 16th c. B.C.
National Archaeological Museum, Athens, Greece

***The Dark Age***   The period 1100–800 B.C. is called the Dark Age of Greece, because throughout the area there was sharp cultural decline: less elegant pottery, simple burials, no massive buildings. Even the art of writing in Linear B vanished, perhaps because the more learned class was killed off, or perhaps because the economy was so weakened that the keeping of records became pointless. Nor do we have written sources about the period. But the decline was not a total collapse. Farming, weaving, making pottery, the Greek language in spoken form, and other skills survived.

The invasions of the twelfth century B.C., in which the Dorian Greeks played at least a part, ended forever the domination of the palace-centered kings. The shattering of the monarchic pattern of the Mycenaean Age may even have been liberating. If these monarchies had survived, Greece might have developed as Egypt and Asia Minor did, with centralized rule and priests who interpreted religion in ways that justified kingship. Self-government in Greece might have been delayed for centuries, if it appeared at all.

## II. The Greek Renaissance (ca. 800–600 B.C.)

◆

It is really the historian who is in the dark during the Greek Dark Age. At least near the end of this period, there must have been a revival of confidence and a nourishing of civic life.

▲ The "Lion Gate," the entrance to the citadel at Mycenae, built about 1350 B.C. Two lionesses stand guard over the city; note the depth of the entranceway and the width of the threshold. In early civilizations, power could be demonstrated by moving enormous stones.
Michael Holford Photographs

With the passing of time, Greek culture revived after the Dark Age and entered a period of extraordinary artistic and intellectual vitality. Poetry and art broke new frontiers; the economy expanded, partly through overseas colonization; and the *polis,* or independent city-state, emerged. Historians borrow a term from a later period and call this movement the Greek Renaissance.

## ◆ GREEK RELIGION

The Greeks brought with them, during their earliest immigration around 2000 B.C., the worship of some of their gods, above all Zeus, the sky god, whose name is Indo-European; his counterparts are Dyaus in early India, Jupiter in Rome, and Tiu in Norse myths. Other gods were adapted from other regions: Apollo, the sun god, from western Asia Minor; Aphrodite, goddess of love, from Cyprus; Athena, goddess of wisdom, and Artemis, the hunter goddess, from Crete. At a much later stage, Greeks adopted some Egyptian gods (Isis, for example), but there is no solid evidence for the belief, recently put forth, that they received all or even many of their gods from Egypt (see "The Debate over Black Athena," p. 48).[1]

*The Relationship of Greeks to Their Gods*   Greek gods are not the remote, transcendent deities of Mesopotamian peoples. They intervene in human affairs, they assist their favorites, and they are anthropomorphic: That is, they are humanlike superbeings, differing from people only in their physical perfection and immortality. Even Mount Olympus, their legendary home, is an actual mountain in northern Greece.

---

[1]Herodotus, the first historian, writing around 440 B.C., does say this, but he was perhaps so impressed with the antiquity of Egypt and with the resemblance of gods in the two cultures that he drew this false conclusion.

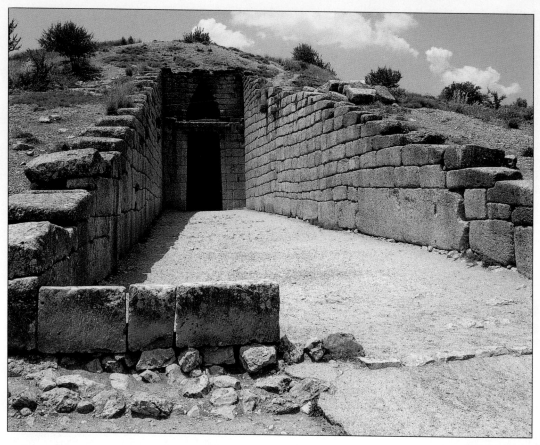

▲ The most spectacular tomb at Mycenae, the "Treasury of Atreus," built in beehive style about 1300 B.C. The long entrance alley and the tomb itself are almost perfectly preserved.
Michael Holford Photographs

The Greeks never developed a code of behavior prescribed by religion, as Israel did. Some acts, such as killing a parent or leaving a relative unburied, were obviously wrong, as were offenses against generally accepted conduct, such as betraying a friend. If people became too arrogant, Nemesis, an avenging force, would sweep down on them and destroy them. But on the whole, Greek religion had no spirit of evil and scarcely any demanding spirits of good.

The gods were viewed as generally benevolent, but they had to be appeased through offerings and suitable ceremonies. The most remarkable feature of Greek religion—especially in contrast to monarchies of Egypt and Mesopotamia—was that the Greeks had priests and priestesses for their temples and smaller shrines but no priestly class that intervened in politics. To put it simply, the Greeks had no church. The societies all around

▼ The "warrior vase" from Mycenae, showing armed warriors departing for battle; at the left, a woman waves her farewell.
C. M. Dixon

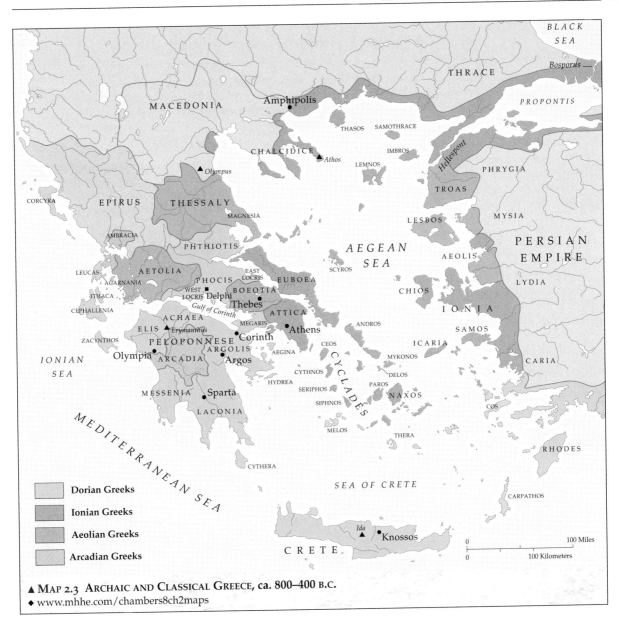

▲ **MAP 2.3 ARCHAIC AND CLASSICAL GREECE, ca. 800–400 B.C.**
◆ www.mhhe.com/chambers8ch2maps

Greece seem to have needed priestly hierarchies to interpret religion and sacred lore. Only thus could they be sure that they were not offending divine powers.

*Forms of Worship* Why the Greeks felt they could worship without such a hierarchy we do not know, but the reason must be connected to the independence of the six to seven hundred individual Greek city-states. There was no king, pharaoh, or emperor who had the power to install such a system. Religion and civic life were inter-twined, and the beautiful temples all over Greece were built by decision of the governing power, but not at the orders of priests or viziers.

Most gods were common to all Greeks, and their worship is a sign of a Panhellenic culture that arose during the Greek Renaissance. Each locality, while recognizing the several gods generally, could have its own patron. For example, various gods had temples in Athens, but Athena was accepted as the protecting goddess of the city. Zeus, though worshiped everywhere as the chief god, was the main local deity at Olympia. Apollo

# The Debate over Black Athena

◆

*Martin Bernal, in* Black Athena, *has set forth the challenging thesis that Greek civilization and even much of the Greek language rest on cultural borrowings from Egypt and the Levant from about 2100 to about 1100 B.C. Bernal also holds that anti-Semitic nineteenth-century scholars deliberately concealed the contribution of Egypt and the Phoenicians. This excerpt, in Bernal's words, summarizes his thesis.*

"The scheme I propose is that while there seems to have been more or less continuous Near Eastern influence on the Aegean over this millennium, its intensity varied considerably at different periods. The first "peak" of which we have any trace was the 21st century. It was then that Egypt recovered from the breakdown of the First Intermediate Period, and the so-called Middle Kingdom was established by the new 11th Dynasty. This not only reunited Egypt but attacked the Levant and is known from archaeological evidence to have had wide-ranging contacts further afield, certainly including Crete and possibly the mainland. . . . It is generally agreed that the Greek language was formed during the 17th and 16th centuries B.C. Its Indo-European structure and basic lexicon are combined with a non-Indo-European vocabulary of sophistication. I am convinced that much of the latter can be plausibly derived from Egyptian and West Semitic. This would fit very well with a long period of domination by Egypto-Semitic conquerors. . . . [I] discuss some of the equations made between specific Greek and Egyptian divinities and rituals, and the general belief that the Egyptian were the earlier forms and that Egyptian religion was the original one."

From Martin Bernal, *Black Athena*, Vol. 1, Rutgers University Press, 1987, pp. 17–23, abridged.

*Mary R. Lefkowitz and Guy MacLean Rogers, professors of classics at Wellesley College, have edited a 500-page volume,* Black Athena Revisited, *in which 24 scholars give their reactions to Bernal's theories. The following is one excerpt from the discussion.*

"No expert in the field doubts that there was a Greek cultural debt to the ancient Near East. The real questions are: How large was the debt? Was it massive, as Bernal claims? Was it limited to the Egyptians and the Phoenicians? . . .

"All of the contributors agree that the early Greeks got their alphabet from the Phoenicians; but little else. Indeed, in terms of language, the evidence that Bernal has presented thus far for the influence of Egyptian or Phoenician on ancient Greek has failed to meet any of the standard tests which are required for the proof of extensive influence. . . .

"Similarly, in the area of religion, Egyptian and Canaanite deities were never worshiped on Greek soil in their indigenous forms. . . .

"Archaeologists, linguists, historians, and literary critics have the gravest reservations about the scholarly methods used in *Black Athena*. Archaeologists cite a constant misconstruing of facts and conclusions and misinterpretation of such archaeological evidence as there is. . . . Linguists see Bernal's methods as little more than a series of assertive guesses, often bordering on the fantastic."

From Guy MacLean Rogers, *Black Athena Revisited*, University of North Carolina Press, 1996, pp. 449–452, abridged.

was the chief god at Delphi and supposedly inspired the oracle, a woman who gave guidance to inquirers after payment of a fee. New research supports the ancient tradition that she inhaled vapors from a chasm.

This woman, or the priests who interpreted her answers, was careful to express these answers in ambiguous language, so that the oracle could be justified no matter what happened. The historian Herodotus reports that, when King Croesus of Lydia asked whether he should invade Persia, he was told that "if Croesus crosses the Halys River [the frontier of Persia], he will destroy a mighty kingdom." He took this to be encouraging, attacked Persia—and destroyed his own kingdom.

The Greek faith in this oracle is another sign of growing common identity among the Greeks. Though never more than a small village, Delphi was adorned with treasure houses built by the various cities to house the gifts they dedicated to Apollo when seeking his guidance.

## ◆ PUBLIC GAMES

Another sign of a growing community among Greeks is the founding of Panhellenic athletic games in 776 B.C. This date is commonly agreed to mark the beginning of the "historic" period of Greek civilization: broadly speaking, the period when writing began and we begin to have fairly solid dates for events.

The first games were held at Olympia, in the Peloponnese, and were dedicated to Zeus; thus, from the beginning the games were connected with religion and demonstrate that religion can have wide uses in a community. But they were also a way of celebrating human perfection and heroism, an aspiration typical of Greek civilization. Originally, the Olympics featured only foot races and wrestling, but gradually they came to include horse and chariot races, boxing, javelin throwing, and other events. Only the winner gained a prize, an olive wreath, but victory also brought rich awards from one's city and lifelong glory; the modern myth of the "amateur athlete" was unknown to the Greeks. In imitation of the Olympics, other cities founded games, and there was eventually one set of Panhellenic games (that is, open to all Greeks) each year, as well as games in many individual cities. The games also give us some of our dates in the archaic period, for the Greeks themselves used the Olympic games especially as chronological reference points.

## ◆ COLONIZATION (CA. 750–550 B.C.)

The growth in population during the Dark Age probably strained the natural resources in Greece, especially the limited farming land, and finally drove the Greeks into foreign colonization. In effect, the mainland Greeks, starting around 750 B.C., tried to relieve social tension by exporting their surplus population. They colonized vigorously from ca. 750 to ca. 550 B.C., and by the end of this period Greeks were spread throughout the Mediterranean. Wherever they went, they settled on the edge of the sea, never far inland. Colonies, when founded, were wholly independent cities, and among them are some of the great ports of modern Europe: Byzantium (today Istanbul in Turkey), Naples, Marseilles, and Syracuse.

This expansion overseas led to a revival of trade after the stagnation of the Dark Age. The Greeks now had access to a greater food supply, above all grain from southern Italy and the Black Sea. Trade brought prosperity to many Greek cities and, even more important, spread Greek civilization throughout the Mediterranean.

## ◆ THE ALPHABET

*Origin of the Alphabet* The Greeks apparently lapsed into illiteracy when the Linear B script vanished, soon after 1200 B.C.; but by about 750 B.C. their trade had brought them to Palestine and into contact with the Phoenicians, who used a Semitic script called the alphabet. This alphabet had only twenty-two characters, but their precision and versatility made this script far easier to master than pictorial cuneiform scripts (see p. 10). Fortunately for the future of European literacy, the

▼ A comparison of Greek and Phoenician alphabets.

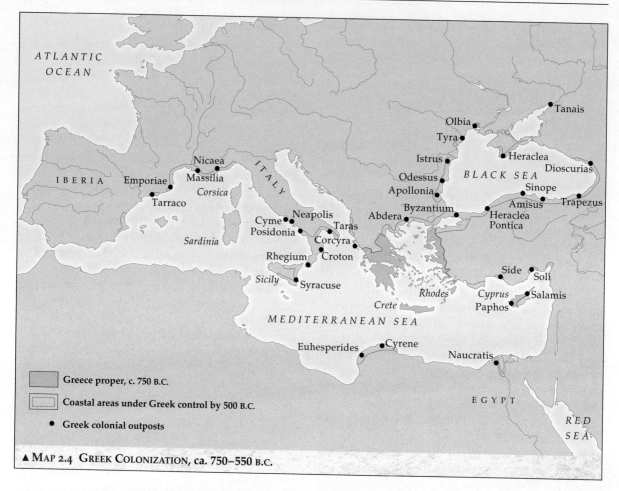

ATLANTIC
OCEAN

IBERIA   Emporiae
Tarraco

Nicaea
Massilia
Corsica

Sardinia

ITALY

Cyme   Neapolis
Posidonia   Taras
Corcyra
Rhegium   Croton
Sicily
Syracuse

Euhesperides   Cyrene

MEDITERRANEAN SEA

Crete

Rhodes

Olbia
Tyra
Istrus
Odessus
Apollonia
Abdera   Byzantium

BLACK SEA

Heraclea
Dioscurias
Sinope
Amisus   Trapezus
Heraclea
Pontica

Tanais

Side   Soli
Cyprus   Salamis
Paphos

Naucratis

EGYPT

RED
SEA

▢ Greece proper, c. 750 B.C.

▢ Coastal areas under Greek control by 500 B.C.

• Greek colonial outposts

▲ **Map 2.4  Greek Colonization, ca. 750–550 B.C.**

Greeks adopted the alphabet and gave even greater precision to their script by changing some of the characters, which were all consonants, to vowels.

Two versions of the Greek alphabet developed. A Western version made its way to Cumae, a Greek town in Italy, and then to the Etruscans, the people in Italy who then controlled Rome. They passed it on to the Romans, who turned it into the alphabet used throughout the Western world. The Eastern version became the standard alphabet in Greece itself. Much later, many letters of the Greek alphabet were used in the Cyrillic script of Russian and other Slavic languages. Thus large parts of the world today use one or another derivative of the Phoenician alphabet in the form it was received from the Greeks.

**The Alphabet and Greek Life**  The Greeks first used the alphabet in public for the proclamation of laws, which ordinary people could read and

grasp; information could circulate more rapidly, with dynamic consequences for political life. Later, from about 500 B.C., especially in Athens, people began to publish all kinds of public decisions and records on prominently displayed stone inscriptions; these were not simply boastful monuments to a king's victories but were documents enabling citizens to understand, criticize, and control the activities of the state.

### ◆ ARCHAIC LITERATURE

**The Homeric Epics**  The greatest literary creations of the Greek Renaissance are the epic poems about the glorious heroes who had supposedly led the war against Troy. The supreme achievements of this poetic tradition are two epics ascribed to Homer, the *Iliad* and the *Odyssey*. The *Iliad* is a portrait—in rolling, majestic verse—of a warrior aristocracy in which greatness in combat is the highest virtue.

The chief hero is the proud warrior Achilles, who withdraws from the siege of Troy when his concubine is taken from him; he then allows his friend Patroclus to wear his armor in combat and, after Patroclus is killed by the Trojan hero Hector, avenges his friend's death by killing Hector in a scene of savage power. The gods take sides with their favorites, but the *Iliad* is essentially a poem about men and women.

The *Odyssey,* by contrast, celebrates cleverness rather than sheer military prowess. Its hero, Odysseus, makes his way home after the Trojan War through dozens of adventures that test his skill and tenacity and that enable Homer to explore human character and behavior in widely different situations. Eventually Odysseus reaches his home, the island of Ithaca, and drives off a band of suitors who are wooing his faithful wife Penelope.

▼ **An Etruscan vase (about 520 B.C.), with a scene from Greek literature. Odysseus and his men escape from the Cyclops, Polyphemus, by putting out his only eye (Homer's *Odyssey*, Book 9). This scene is found on several other vases from Greece.**
Michael Holford Photographs

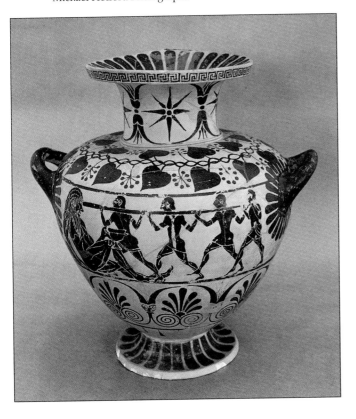

*The Homeric Question* These epics were probably first recited at feasts by traveling bards, but over the years they became known to all through presentation at festivals and finally through study in schools. We have no idea who wrote these great epics. This is the famous "Homeric question." Neither ancient Greeks nor modern scholars have been able to prove whether a person named Homer really lived, whether the epics are the work of one writer or several, and whether they were originally composed orally or in writing.

It is clear, however, that the texts we have date from long after the Trojan War of ca. 1250 B.C. Most scholars date the poems to around 750 B.C., and this disparity raises the question of how any knowledge of the war could have been preserved. The traditions were evidently passed down through the centuries. The poems themselves were probably composed orally, recited for generations, and written down later, after the Greeks had become fluent in the art of writing. In any case, Homer remained the chief inspiration for Greek literature in all periods.

*Hesiod* Homer never speaks in the first person (except to invoke the Muses to inspire him), but his successors began to express their own thoughts and feelings and to create a literature of intensely frank self-expression. The first major post-Homeric poet was Hesiod of Boeotia (in central Greece), whose *Works and Days* dates from around 700 B.C. Hesiod was a farmer, and his poem is a farmer's almanac, celebrating agriculture and, in the "days" of the title, telling the reader when to plow and plant. The poem also contains a bitter attack on the injustice of aristocratic landlords ("gift-devouring rulers") toward their peasants.

In his other surviving poem, the *Theogony,* Hesiod recounts the genealogy of the various gods. He narrates frankly the bloody rise of Zeus to supreme divine power. The god Cronus had castrated his own father, Uranus, to gain rule over the world and had killed his own children except Zeus, who escaped. After a long struggle, Zeus won the final battle and became the supreme god. This conflict resembles similar sagas in Hittite literature, in which gods kill and mutilate one another. But the difference in the Greek conception is that the supremacy of Zeus is seen not just as

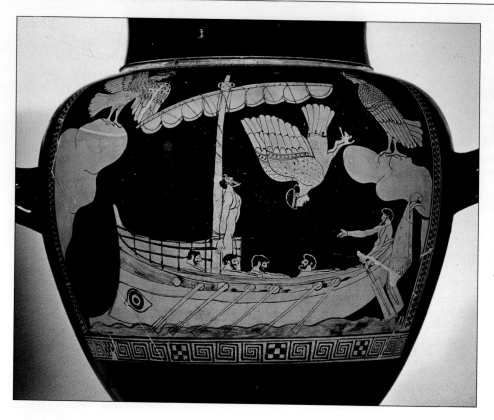

◄ A superb red-figure vase (the figures are left in the natural red of the clay), illustrating a scene from Homer's *Odyssey,* Book 12. Odysseus, bound to the mast of his ship, listens to the song of the Siren, who guides him into troubled waters; by the Siren Painter, about 490 to 480 B.C.
Michael Holford / © British Museum

another act of vengeance but as a fulfillment of the proper divine order.

*Archilochus*    About 650 B.C. Greek poets began to work with more personal themes. Archilochus of Paros has left us brief poems of brilliant vigor and audacity, written as bursts of self-revelation, a typically Greek kind of literature that has no predecessors in the ancient Eastern cultures. He was a traveler, a man of action, and a mercenary soldier who fell in battle. He criticizes traditional forms of chivalry and can be cynical about supposed aristocratic conduct. He boasts, for example, that he once threw away his shield to save his life and laughs off this unmilitary act: "Never mind, I'll buy another one just as good." His love poetry can be astonishingly frank. In one poem he tenderly yet passionately describes his seduction of a girl, including his own sexual fulfillment.

*Sappho*    The most intense and subtle poet of the age was Sappho of the island of Lesbos (about 600 B.C.). We have only one complete poem from her pen and many short quotations (see "Sappho's Love Poetry," p. 53). In her poetry she writes about an association of young women, but it is not certain precisely what kind of group this was. They worshiped Aphrodite and the Muses, minor goddesses who inspired poetry and other arts.

The most tantalizing question, to which the surviving fragments of her work supply no exact answer, is what kind of experiences the group shared. Sappho was a widow and apparently taught the girls poetry, dance, music, and elegant dress as preparation for marriage. Sometimes she sings of the beauty of the girls, sometimes of her pain when one leaves the circle (probably to marry) or is unresponsive to her affection. At other times she speaks frankly of the pleasures of love, and there is little question that she shared physical love with some of the girls. But, unlike Archilochus, she does not boast of her sexuality or of her conquests; rather, she writes of shared experience and love felt mutually. In its exact evocation of emotion, its inventive images, its individuality, her poetry reveals a writer of the highest originality and power. One exquisite poem, in four short lines, expresses loneliness in heart-breaking simplicity:

## SAPPHO'S LOVE POETRY

*The poetry of Sappho of Lesbos is amazingly sensitive and original. This short excerpt from a poem frankly acknowledges her need for love.*

"You have come, and done,
And I was waiting for you

*The following is addressed to a young woman.*

"He seems to be a god, that man
Facing you, who leans to be close,
Smiles, and, alert and glad, listens
To your mellow voice.

"And quickens in love at your laughter
That stings my breasts, jolts my heart
If I dare the shock of a glance.
I cannot speak,

"My tongue sticks to my dry mouth,
Thin fire spreads beneath my skin,

To temper the red desire
That burned my heart."

My eyes cannot see and my aching ears
Roar in their labyrinths.

"Chill sweat slides down my body,
I shake, I turn greener than grass,
I am neither living nor dead and cry
From the narrow between.

"But endure, even this grief of love."

From Guy Davenport (tr.), *7 Greeks*, New Directions, 1995.

---

The moon has set,
so have the Pleiades; it is midnight.
The hour goes past,
but I lie alone.

# III. The Polis

"The human being," said the Greek philosopher Aristotle, "is a political creature." By this he probably meant that humans normally want to live within a community of people sharing cultural traditions and common citizenship. The Greek city, at its largest, had about 40,000 adult male citizens. Originally, monarchs ruled, as they did at Mycenae, but over the years most cities reached at least an approach to government by a body of citizens. In their cities, the Greeks created architecture, dramas, and philosophic writings that are still worshiped and imitated.

### ◆ ORGANIZATION AND GOVERNMENT

For the social and political history of Western civilization, the most important event in the Greek Renaissance was the emergence, soon after 800 B.C., of the independent city-state, the *polis* (plural, *poleis*). Physically, the polis had a central inhabited area (the *astu*), often surrounding a citadel called the *acropolis* ("high city"). Over time, the acropolis came to be reserved for temples, shrines, treasuries, and other official buildings. Within the astu, the nucleus of the city, the people dwelt in closely packed houses, each normally built on more than one level, without internal staircases but with the rooms opening to a courtyard. A wall usually surrounded the astu; outside it, but still part of the polis, were suburbs and fields. Those who owned land might live in the urban center and walk or ride a donkey to their land. Or they might live in smaller villages, which were still legally part of the polis.

*General Structure of the Polis*   Greek cities usually had a large open space, the *agora*, that served as a main public square and civic center. Although used as a public market, the agora was always a sacred place and, like the acropolis, it housed temples and official buildings. In Athens, the agora was also the site of trials, of buildings containing laws and other documents, and of many free-standing inscriptions on marble recording further public business.

In a Greek polis, only male citizens could vote, pass on their property through wills, and generally participate in civic life. Females did not vote but, like men, were protected against seizure and violence. Outside this group, and without civic rights, were slaves and resident aliens. No citizen of a polis had rights in any other polis; thus poleis were both cities and small states.

*Population of the Poleis*   When Greeks referred to the size of the citizen body, they reckoned only adult males, and by this measure the poleis ranged from a few hundred citizens to tens of thousands. Athens, the largest, had between thirty-five and forty-five thousand citizens; if to this we add the estimated number of women, children, resident foreigners, and slaves, the total population of Athens and the outlying villages, which were also part of the polis, was between two and three hundred thousand (the whole region is known as Attica). Sparta, by contrast, probably had an adult male population of no more than twelve thousand.

*Origins of Self-Government*   Despite considerable diversity within the six to seven hundred poleis, one development seems to have been common to all those poleis that we know anything about, namely, the growth of some kind of self-government by the male citizens. The major social problem that Greek poleis solved was how to harness the energies of all the citizens in support of a city rather than allow the rivalries inherent in such crowded quarters to erupt into civil war. In many poleis (Corinth, for example), oligarchy (a system in which a small number of citizens governed) held sway, while other cities, especially Athens, developed control of affairs by the masses.

Evolution toward self-government is rare in history, and the various forms of self-government that arose in Greece may, like the Greeks' lack of a priestly class, be the result of topography and the scale of their towns. In a small state, locked within a ring of hills, no monarch could long remain a remote, transcendent figure like the rulers of Eastern kingdoms. Homer attests that the Greeks of the Mycenaean era had kings, but by about 700 B.C. they had vanished—though we can seldom say precisely how—in nearly all poleis. Sparta, the

most authoritarian Greek state, was an exception and retained a system with two kings, each descended from a royal family, ruling together. The Spartans apparently felt safer in a system in which one king could act as a control over the other.

*Hoplites and Society*   The wealthier classes—using the term loosely, we may call them aristocrats, but there was no hereditary nobility—must have governed, if Homer is to be believed, through assemblies that originated as the armed forces of the poleis. But as populations increased and armies came to include citizens outside the circle of the elite, the upper classes could no longer ignore the wishes of others. In particular, Greek infantry soldiers, called hoplites (Greek *hopla*, arms), may have been an impetus toward self-government, because numbers of armed citizens could more effectively demand a say in political decisions. It is significant that the first Greek legal codes defining citizens' rights were published soon after the disappearance of kings, within the seventh century B.C.—evidence that the populace was no longer willing to accept direction from the wealthy.

*Tyrants and Tyranny*   Also in the seventh century we hear of the first popular leaders who united the masses and overturned the rule of the old aristocracy. These men installed themselves as "tyrants" (the Greek word *tyrannos* meant an autocrat who ruled without strict legal foundation, not necessarily a cruel oppressor). The tyrants, though certainly no sponsors of democracy, did help to undermine rule by the traditional aristocracy and in a way opened the path to self-government. They sometimes built grandiose temples and other public works to beautify their cities and ensure the support of the people. Some sponsored industry and trade of their city's products overseas. Most saw to the buildup of armies, doubtless for their own security. On the whole, tyrants forced progress within their cities and helped lead the cities away from the rule of the older aristocratic class.

*Greek Armies*   In the period of the Greek Renaissance we also see the formation of the armies that were to make the Greeks supreme in battle against their neighbors. Infantry soldiers, or hoplites, were grouped into the formation called the phalanx. This was a close-packed formation of men, usually eight deep. A soldier carried a shield on his left arm and protected his right side by standing close to his neighbor's shield. The weapons were either swords or, especially in the fourth century B.C., long spears. The phalanx became a formidable instrument in battle, especially when moving forward to attack.

As the ranks pushed forward, one adversary or the other would give way. Once the front ranks of either side were broken, the Greeks normally broke off the battle, for they lacked the manpower to sustain huge casualties. Infantry soldiers had to provide their own equipment. This meant that they were men of the middle class, and many historians have concluded that solidarity among the hoplites contributed to the growth of political consciousness and pointed the way to a greater degree of self-government.

### ◆ THE ECONOMY OF THE POLEIS (CA. 700–400 B.C.)

*A Modest Lifestyle*   The poleis were sufficiently similar to allow a general picture of their economy. The basic activity was agriculture, but in many areas of Greece the soil is thin and rocky, not suited to raising grain or pasturing animals. A shortage of food was therefore a constant threat to economic stability. Some states, as we have seen, drained away part of their excess population through colonization and imported grain from areas on the fringe of the Greek world.

All Greek dwellings were modest, and sanitation was primitive, although the Athenians had a main drain under their central market. Grain, and occasionally fish, were staples of the diet; meat was usually reserved for festival days. Breakfast, if taken at all, was a lump of bread dipped in olive oil, which also served as fuel for lamps and even as a kind of soap. Sugar was unknown; the only sweetening agent was honey. With few luxuries available, Greeks could subsist on small incomes. Fishing and farming were suspended in winter, so Greeks had considerable leisure time, which they spent mainly in public places, as is still true today.

*Coinage and Public Expenses*   The development of an economy based on coinage was slow. Coinage itself began in the kingdom of Lydia, in western Asia Minor, about 600 B.C. or a little later. Soon the Greeks began to use coins, but at first they played little part in daily trade: The smallest coin was usually a drachma, said to have been at that time the price of a sheep. In the fifth century the use of coinage expanded rapidly, as fractions of the drachma came into use. Taxation in poleis paid for the upkeep of walls, drains, roads, harbors, and the like, though Greeks had little grasp of the mechanics of public finance. There were no permanent military treasuries until the 300s B.C., a surprising fact since the cities were so often at war. Infantry soldiers had to arm themselves, but they were paid at the expense of the state. When large projects such as public buildings and maintenance of ships were planned, the expenses were assigned to citizens who were judged capable of bearing the cost.

*Use of Slave Labor*   A great social-economic historian, M. I. Finley, once asked the challenging question: Was Greek civilization based on slave labor? Undeniably, slave owners had freedom to pursue civic affairs. Many Greeks looked down on manual labor as beneath their dignity, and it was usually the task of poor citizens or slaves. The troubling institution of slavery was accepted by all ancient societies and was justified by philosophers like Aristotle, who asserted that nature had divided humanity into natural masters and natural slaves—the latter including all "barbarians," that is, non-Greeks. Nor did anyone in antiquity ever recommend abolishing slavery on the ground that it was morally wrong: The only criticism of it was the occasional warning to manage it efficiently.

Greeks commonly obtained slaves through conquest of other territory, though kidnapping and even the sale of children added to recruitment. An ordinary slave might cost about 150 drachmas, roughly four months' pay for a laborer, but a highly skilled one could cost much more.

*Industry*   Greece, unlike Rome, did not use gangs of slaves in agriculture, and industry was rarely more than household craft. The only industries in which slaves worked together in large numbers were mining and stone quarrying, where conditions were atrocious. These industries and domestic service were the only tasks always assigned to slaves. In a unique exception to this rule, Athens had a police force composed of three hundred slaves from Scythia. The Athenian writer Xenophon said, "A man buys a slave to have a companion at work." Potters, shoemakers, and stonecutters might have a slave or two, though a few larger workshops are known: One shield maker, for example, had 120 slaves.

The availability of slaves and the prejudice against manual labor may explain why some slaves worked, along with citizens, on the building of the Parthenon in Athens and were paid the same as free men—one drachma a day, about the same wage paid to soldiers and sailors—and it partly explains the lack of inventions among the Greeks that could have made industry more productive.

## ◆ SPARTA AND ATHENS (ca. 700–500 B.C.)

We know little about the internal workings of most poleis, and the two we know best, Sparta and Athens, were not typical; but their importance requires detailed discussion.

***Early Sparta***   Sparta, the most influential of all the Dorian states, chose to solve its problem of overpopulation by conquering Messenia, the territory to its west, in a war usually dated 736 to 716 B.C. Many, probably most, of the Messenians were then enslaved. Only males of demonstrably pure Spartan descent could be full citizens, and they were each given an allotment of land to be worked for them by the enslaved Messenians, who were known as *helots*. They were public slaves, with no rights whatever, but they differed from other slaves in Greece in that they could not be bought and sold. Spartan landowners spent their lives in constant military training in order to maintain control over the helots, who outnumbered them by about seven to one.

Around 650 B.C. the Messenians tried to rebel, but the uprising failed, and the Spartans responded by making their army more invincible and their state even more rigid. The new arrangements, attributed to a lawgiver named Lycurgus, date from about 600 B.C. The identity of Lycurgus was obscure even in antiquity, though such a man apparently lived around 800 B.C., and many historians believe that Spartan reformers of around 600 B.C. ascribed their system to him in order to give it the appearance of ancient authority.

***Sparta's Government***   In the Spartan regime, oligarchy, or rule by a small number, was tempered with some measure of democracy. The public assembly included all males over the age of thirty, who elected a council of twenty-eight elders over age sixty to serve for life and to plan business for the assembly. The assembly also chose five *ephors* ("overseers") each year; they received foreign delegates, summoned the assembly to meet, and in general acted as a check on the power of the kings. When proposals came before the assembly, voting was limited to yes or no, without debate. As a further safeguard against too much popular control, the ephors and council could simply dismiss the assembly if, in their opinion, it made the wrong choice. Thus, the limited democracy of Sparta yielded to its ultimate faith in oligarchy. To Greek political philosophers, Sparta was a superb example of a "mixed" constitution, in which the kings represented the element of monarchy, the council, oligarchy, and the citizenry, a kind of democracy.

For a time Sparta tried to dominate some other Peloponnesian states by outright conquest. But by around 560 B.C. this policy had failed, and about 530 B.C. the Spartans sought strength through alliance rather than warfare by forming an alliance, known as the Peloponnesian League, with their neighbors. The league is one of the earliest examples of alliance in the Greek world and is a rare instance of the Greeks' transcending the normal exclusiveness of city-state politics. The Spartans led the league but did not wholly control it, and action required approval of the member states.

***Men and Women in Spartan Society***   The Spartan male dedicated most of his life, from age seven through age sixty, to soldiering. The warriors lived and trained together, and their discipline could be sadistic. As tests of their courage and resourcefulness, young men were taught to steal if necessary, to go without food and shelter, even at times to kill a helot.

Spartan women also had a lifestyle that other Greeks found extraordinary. Again the military commitments of the state played a role in shaping social practices, for the girls trained in games in order to become physically strong mothers. Spartan men, living with one another, seldom visited their wives, and if a marriage was childless, a woman could bear a child by a man other than her husband. These customs were meant to ensure enough manpower for the army and to focus loyalty on the state, not on the individual family.

*Spartan Isolationism* Spartans were cut off from the other Greeks by two mountain ranges, and they traded little with other people, even adopting an intrinsically worthless iron currency to maintain their isolation.

Their lifestyle was one of extreme austerity. They rarely traveled, did not welcome visits by foreigners, and deliberately shielded themselves from new ideas that might have inspired intellectual pursuits such as philosophy or historical writing. Their short, abrupt speech is usually called "laconic" from the name of the plain where they lived, Laconia.

Though they did make fine pottery, at least until about 525 B.C., when the art declined, their military regime left little time for or interest in the arts. Thus the isolation of Sparta from other Greeks was both geographic and psychological, but it reflected the deliberate choice of the people.

*Early Athens* The city of Athens also had expansionist beginnings, extending its domain by about 700 B.C. to include the whole plain of Attica. It was a large polis with widespread trading interests, and its political currents were strong and turbulent. As the people experimented again and again with their constitution, their political history became the most varied of all the city-states of Greece.

Athens, like other states, once had kings; but the monarchy ended in 683 B.C. (we do not know exactly how), and the city was managed by three (later nine) *archons,* or administrators, elected annually by an assembly in which all adult male citizens could vote. After their year in office, the nine archons moved permanently into a council called the Areopagus, which eventually numbered about

▲ An Attic kouros, or young man, in the "severe" style, about 510 B.C. The figure is one of ideal physical perfection, typical of the humanity-centered aesthetics of Greece.
Nimatallah/Art Resource, NY

three hundred men. Because it comprised senior men with permanent membership, the Areopagus was probably more influential than the board of archons in setting public policy.

*Draco and Homicide Law*  Our first information about a reform in Athens after the monarchy is dated around 621 B.C. when Draco, an otherwise unknown statesman, codified the law on homicide, apparently distinguishing between voluntary and involuntary homicide. This reform was a large step forward, for early societies often looked on any kind of homicide as defiling the community in the eyes of the gods. This reform was also another in the series of law codes that established a recognized basis for justice and did away with forcing citizens to rely on the dictates of tribal elders.

*Crisis in the Athenian Economy*  An economic crisis in the 500s B.C. forced Athens into far-reaching social changes, the likes of which no Greek state had ever seen. As often happens in history, economic conditions demanded a social response. Down to about 600 B.C. the Athenian economy was trying to do the impossible, namely, feed the growing population of Attica from its own limited area; this strategy caused a nearly desperate social and economic crisis. Some farmers had evidently borrowed food from others who were better off and had gone so deeply into debt in the form of grain that they had lost their own land and had even fallen into slavery by pledging their bodies as security for more food.

Their frustration might have exploded into violent revolution had the Athenians not found a rational solution by giving (probably in the 570s) powers of arbitration to Solon, who had been archon in 594 B.C.[2] He was a poet and statesman whose courageous, compassionate work has made him a towering figure in Greek history, indeed in the history of civilization.

---

[2]That Solon was archon in 594 B.C. is fairly certain, and most historians follow ancient sources in dating his reforms to this year as well. But the assumed linkage between his archonship and his reforms was probably only an inference drawn in antiquity, and there is good reason to think that the reforms took place in the 570s; see C. Hignett, *A History of the Athenian Constitution*, 1952, p. 316.

*Solon and Economic Reform*  Aware that the poor farmers could probably never repay their debts, Solon took the daring step of canceling all agricultural debts and forbade further borrowing against the body. At one stroke the enslaved men were free, but the land they had lost probably remained in the hands of its new owners, who were thus compensated for the cancellation of debt. This legislation left many families without land and made them seek work elsewhere, but the crucial fact was that Solon had prevented civil war. Such arbitration by a private citizen without an army to fight with is heretofore unknown in history.

Because an economic crisis had threatened the community and brought him to power, Solon determined to transform the economy of Athens. He decreed that no product from the soil could be exported except olive oil; by this means he forced the Athenians to cultivate olive trees, which they could grow more successfully than grain. He also changed the commercial weights used by the Athenians, making them the same as those more widely used in Greece, a reform that brought Athens into a wider circle of trade.

*Solon's Political Reforms*  Solon now seized the opportunity to reform the Athenian state with the aim of breaking the grip of the wealthy and those with eminent family backgrounds on public office. He therefore divided all Athenian citizens into four classes based on their income from farmland and allowed members of the two highest classes to hold office. The significance of this reform is that men could improve their status economically and thus achieve positions of leadership regardless of their ancestry.

Solon also created a court of appeal, the Heliaea, somehow drawn from the people, but our sources tell us little of how it worked. His chief contribution was to see the common people as a group with grievances and to take bold steps to help them. He thus pointed the state toward eventual democracy, but he did not want to go too far and by no means gave the masses supreme power; in his own poetry he declared, "I gave the people just enough privilege and no more." Nor did his legislation, humane though it was, wholly end the agricultural problem; freeing farmers

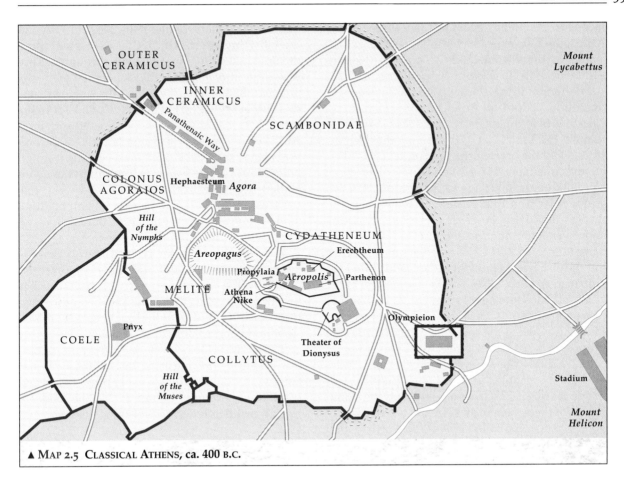

▲ MAP 2.5 CLASSICAL ATHENS, ca. 400 B.C.

from servitude was not the same as guaranteeing them enough to eat, and the agony of those peasants who had lost their land continued.

**The Tyrant Pisistratus** Pisistratus, a popular Athenian military leader supported by poorer farmers from the hill country in eastern Attica, saw his chance in this turmoil. In 561 B.C. he and his followers seized power; though twice driven out, he returned in 546 with a mercenary army to gain permanent control and ruled from that year until his death in 528.

Pisistratus fits well the pattern of the Greek tyrants sketched earlier. He rewarded his supporters with grants of land, surely taken from the estates of landowning aristocrats who had opposed him, thus completing the work of Solon, who lacked the power and probably the will to redistribute land. And like many another "big city boss," he saw to a splendid program of public works. He built temples to Athena and Zeus and established a yearly festival to the god Dionysus. By encouraging dramatic contests at this festival, he opened the way for the development of Athenian tragedy in the next century.

He ruled by cloaking his despotic power in legal form. The assembly still chose archons, but from trusted men picked by the tyrant himself. The legal facade was actually one of his chief contributions, for the Athenians now became familiar with democratic procedures, which gave them experience with the working of real democracy when it came into existence at the end of the sixth century.

**Cleisthenes and Demokratia** Pisistratus' son, Hippias, ruled securely until 514 B.C., when a conspiracy frightened him into using terror as a means to maintain his control. He forced many Athenians into exile, including Cleisthenes, the leader of the Alcmaeonids, a powerful family. While in exile in Delphi, Cleisthenes and his supporters enlisted the help of the Spartans to overthrow Hippias. According to Herodotus, Cleisthenes and his family had spent lavishly to rebuild the temple at Delphi, and the Delphic priests had the oracle urge the Spartans to "liberate the Athenians." Moreover, Hippias had given his daughter in marriage to the son of a Persian vassal ruler, and this move may have looked to the Spartans like a dangerous act that could bring about Persian influence over Greece. In any case, a Spartan force led by the king Cleomenes drove out the Pisistratid family in 510 B.C. and ended the Athenian tyranny.

Cleisthenes returned to his native city and in 508—perhaps to secure his own political supremacy—carried the social revolution further by proposing a scheme whereby the masses would actually direct the state. The Greek word *demos* means "the people," but in Greek political language it also means "the masses," and the domination of the Athenian state by the whole mass of voters came to be called *demokratia*. Participation extended only to the adult male citizens of Athens, for women, aliens, and slaves did not vote; but this system was by far the closest to a democracy that had ever existed.

Cleisthenes anchored his system in popular support by a stroke of genius: He created a council of five hundred members (called the *boulé*) to prepare business for the assembly; all male citizens above age thirty were eligible to serve in it for a year. In later times (and perhaps from the beginning, though our sources do not say so) councillors were chosen by drawing lots, and no man could serve more than twice. There was a fair chance that every eligible Athenian would be chosen to serve during his lifetime, and this widespread participation in the council ensured that the people would want to maintain the new regime. Within about fifty years this new council came to surpass in political power the old Areopagus council, which continued to exist.

**The End of Regional Factions in Athens** Our sources tell us that the Athenians were loosely divided into three groups in Attica: those who lived in the central plain, or along the coast, or "beyond the hills" in eastern Attica. Cleisthenes set out to break up these regional factions through a complex system of building blocks. Every man was now enrolled as a citizen within the single village, or *deme*, in which he lived, and which kept registers of its citizens. These villages throughout Attica were then grouped into ten tribes, so composed that each tribe contained citizens from all parts of Attica. The council's five hundred men included fifty men from each tribe and were, like the tribes, automatically a cross section of Athenian citizens. Thus within the council, too, no local faction could dominate.

As a result, when the council met to prepare business for the assembly, no single region could dominate the discussion. Each of the ten tribes fought as a unit in the army, and here, too, men from all over Attica, not from a single region, stood together in each tribal regiment.

The sovereign body was, as before, the assembly, including all adult male citizens, whether landowners or not. The assembly passed laws and resolutions brought before it by the council, elected magistrates, voted for or against war, and

▲ Athenians used sherds of pottery, called ostraka, to vote men out of town for ten years. The sherd at the lower left bears the name Hippokrates; the others are directed against Themistocles, son of Neocles.
Scala/Art Resource, NY

accepted alliances with other states. Unfortunately, as a democratic assembly, it was vulnerable to being misled or corrupted by unscrupulous politicians. Sometimes it gave way to disastrous or vindictive decisions.

***The Use of the Lot in Elections*** After passing his reforms in 508 B.C., Cleisthenes vanishes from our sources, but the Athenians continued to refine his system, especially through the use of the lot. In 487 B.C. they began to choose their nine annual archons, the executive committee, by drawing lots from a slate of candidates. Later, in the fifth and fourth centuries, all manner of officials, such as public auditors and managers of public land and mines, were so chosen. The theory behind this practice held that many men were equally honest and capable of serving in a democracy and choosing officials by lot reduced corruption and angry competition in the process of selection.

Choosing civic officials by lot greatly diminished the prestige of such positions and caused the most ambitious men not to bother to seek them. As a result, political power shifted to the ten generals, who were elected annually and could be reelected. From this point onward, the great Athenian politicians competed for the position of general.

***Ostracism*** Also in 487 B.C., for the first time, a man was expelled from Athens for ten years by the process of ostracism. In this colorful procedure, the whole people could vote once a year to expel any man whom they considered potentially dangerous. They voted by scratching a name on *ostraka,* or potsherds. If the total number of votes was six thousand or more, the "winner" had to depart Attica for ten years; but neither his property nor his family suffered any penalty. Aristotle attributed the practice to Cleisthenes himself, but this statement remains controversial.

## *Chronology*

### CHRONOLOGY OF THE PERSIAN WARS

(ALL DATES B.C.)

| | |
|---|---|
| **499,** autumn | Greek cities of Ionia in Asia Minor revolt from Persian Empire. |
| **498** | Athens and Eretria (on island of Euboea) take part in burning Sardis in Persian Empire. |
| **496** | Persians besiege Miletus, the leading city in the revolt. |
| **494** | Fall of Miletus. |
| **493** | End of Ionian revolt. |
| **492,** spring | Persian expedition to northern Greece suffers heavy losses in storms. |
| **490,** mid-August | Battle of Marathon near Athens; Persians defeated. |
| **486,** November | Death of King Darius of Persia; accession of Xerxes. |
| **484,** spring–**480,** spring | Xerxes prepares for new invasion of Greece. |
| **480,** spring | Persian army sets out from Sardis. |
| **480,** late August | Battles of Thermopylae and Artemisium. |
| **480,** late September | Battle of Salamis. |
| **479,** early August | Battle of Plataea. |
| **479,** mid-August | Battle of Mycale on coast of Asia Minor (according to Herodotus, fought on the same day as Plataea). |

## IV. The Challenge of Persia

By the beginning of the "classical" period of Greek history, lasting from about 500 to 323 B.C., the Greek states had reached the political form they would retain for more than two centuries. But almost at once they faced their supreme challenge, a clash with the great Persian Empire. In two brief but intensely dangerous wars, they turned the Persian armies back. Their morale was heightened because they were fighting for their own land, and the poet Aeschylus, in his play *The Persians,* records their battle cry: "Now the struggle is about everything." Daring and even trickery played their parts in the remarkable victory.

▲ MAP 2.6 THE FIRST PERSIAN WAR, 490 B.C.

### ◆ THE INVASION UNDER DARIUS AND MARATHON (490 B.C.)

King Darius of Persia (r. 522–486 B.C.) had expanded his empire throughout Asia Minor, including the Greek cities in the region called Ionia, on the west coast. Some of these Greeks sought their liberty from Persian control in 499 B.C. in the "Ionian revolt." The rebels obtained a promise of help from the Athenians, who sent them twenty warships. The historian Herodotus declares that "these ships turned out to be the beginning of trouble for both Greeks and non-Greeks," since they led directly to the two Persian wars. The revolt collapsed in 493 B.C., and Darius now proposed to invade Greece itself, largely for the sake of revenge against Athens, which had helped the rebels in the burning of Sardis, one of his cities.

After a brief campaign in 492, he sent a fleet across the Aegean in 490. The Persians first

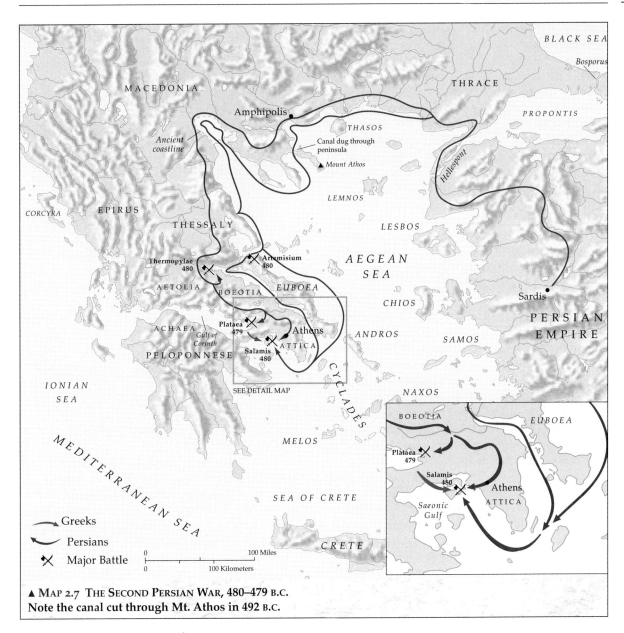

▲ MAP 2.7 THE SECOND PERSIAN WAR, 480–479 B.C.
**Note the canal cut through Mt. Athos in 492 B.C.**

attacked Eretria, on the island of Euboea, and then landed in Attica on the beach at Marathon, a village north of Athens. The Athenian infantry routed them in a brilliant victory and even marched back to Athens in time to ward off a Persian naval attack. A later legend told of an Athenian, Eucles, who ran back to Athens in his armor with the good news; he cried out, "Hail, we rejoice," and dropped dead (the origin of the marathon race). The Athenians never forgot this immortal feat of arms; they lost only 192 men, whose burial mound still stands at Marathon, and the Persians lost about 6,400.

## ◆ THE SECOND PERSIAN WAR
### (480–479 B.C.)

***Preparations for War*** To avenge this defeat, Darius' son, Xerxes (486–465 B.C.), readied a huge force and swore that this time there would be no mistake. Fortunately for Greece and Europe, the Athenians were guided by a shrewd strategist, Themistocles. In 483 B.C., seeing the Persian menace on the horizon, he had persuaded the Athenians to use some newly found veins of silver in their mines to increase greatly the size of their fleet.

With this money they raised the number of their ships to two hundred. These ships were the famous triremes, on which nearly two hundred men rowed, seated in three banks. So swift and strong were these ships that they became, in effect, missiles, capable of smashing and disabling the enemy's ships. By thus greatly multiplying the striking power of one man, the trireme became the naval equivalent of the phalanx, in which hundreds of men could strike together on land.

***The Invasion of 480 and Thermopylae*** Early in 480 some thirty Greek states, also fearing annihilation, formed a military alliance and entrusted to the Spartans command on both land and sea. A few months later Xerxes began his march toward Greece with a force of perhaps sixty thousand men and six hundred ships, in a grandiose amphibious invasion of Europe. The first Greek force sent out in 480 against the Persians was defeated at the pass of Thermopylae in central Greece. The Spartan king in command, Leonidas, dismissed many of his allies, with the result that the Spartans defended the pass almost alone in a stand always remembered for its heroism. A poet, in two simple, grave lines on a stone, immortalized the heroism of the three hundred Spartans and their king who fell there: "Stranger, tell the Spartans that we lie here, faithful to their orders." At the same time, a sea battle at nearby Artemisium was inconclusive.

***Themistocles and the Victory at Salamis*** As the Persian forces continued southward, the Athenians abandoned Athens and the Persians burned the city down. This burning was a reply to the actions of the Athenians and other Greeks, who had burned the Persian city of Sardis in the Ionian revolt in 498. In this nearly desperate situation, Themistocles devised a brilliant trick. He sent a slave to the Persian king with a false message: Themistocles wished him well and advised him that, if he attacked the Greek fleet with his own at

▲ **Themistocles, the great Athenian strategist, was ostracized about 472 B.C. This ostrakon, cast against him, says, "Themistocles, son of Neocles, let him depart"** *(ITO).*
American School of Classical Studies at Athens: Agora Excavations.

once, he would win the decisive battle practically without a blow.

The Persians were taken in by the ruse and sent their ships into the narrows between Athens and the island of Salamis, where the Greek fleet, lying in wait, utterly defeated them. His navy shattered, Xerxes, who had watched the battle from a height, abandoned Greece and marched back toward the Dardanelles (see "'They Have a Master Called Law,'" p. 65).

***The Battle of Plataea (479 B.C.)*** Yet the Persians could still have won the war, for a large Persian army remained in central Greece. The reckoning with this force came in a battle in 479 B.C., at the village of Plataea. Once more a Greek army, under the Spartan general Pausanias, crushed the Persians; out of perhaps fifty thousand Persians, only a few thousand survived.

The Greeks won a further battle at Mycale on the shore of Asia Minor in 479. The Ionian Greeks now proclaimed their freedom and thus completed the work of throwing off Persian control that they had begun twenty years earlier. Thus

## "They Have a Master Called Law"

*As King Xerxes leads his army into Greece in 480 b.c., he asks a former king of Sparta, who is accompanying him, whether the Greeks will really fight against the Persians.*

"Now, Demaratus, I will ask you what I want to know. You are a Greek and one from no minor or weak city. So now tell me, will the Greeks stand and fight me?" Demaratus replied, "Your Majesty, shall I tell you the truth, or say what you want to hear?" The king ordered him to tell the truth, saying that he would respect him no less for doing so.

"Your Majesty," he said, "I am not speaking about all of them, only about the Spartans. First, I say they will never accept conditions from you that would enslave Greece; second, that they will fight you in battle even if all the other Greeks join your side."

Xerxes said, "Demaratus, let's look at it in all logic: why should a thousand, or ten thousand, or fifty thousand men, if they are all free and not ruled by a single master, stand up against such an army as mine? If they were ruled by one man, like my

subjects, I suppose they might, out of fear, show more bravery than usual and, driven into battle by the lash, go up against a bigger force; but if allowed their freedom, they wouldn't do either one."

Demaratus said, "Your Majesty, I knew from the beginning that if I spoke the truth you wouldn't like my message, but, since you ordered me to do so, I told you about the Spartans. They are free men, but not wholly free: They have a master called Law, whom they fear far more than your soldiers fear you. And his orders are always the same—they must not run away from any army no matter how big, but must stand in their formation and either conquer or die. But, your Majesty, may your wishes be fulfilled."

From *Herodotus*, book VII, M. H. Chambers (tr.).

the Greeks crowned the most brilliant victory in the history of their civilization.

# V. The Wars of the Fifth Century (479–404 b.c.)

After a brief period of cooperation, the two leading Greek cities, Athens and Sparta, led their allies into the long, tragic war that fatally weakened the Greek poleis.

## ◆ THE ATHENIAN EMPIRE

The victorious Greeks continued the war against Persia in 479 and 478 b.c., liberating, for example, the Greek city of Byzantium on the Bosporus from Persian control. But in 478 Sparta returned to its perennial isolationism and withdrew from the alliance that had been formed to oppose Persia. In response, many of the newly liberated Greek states met on the island of Delos in 478 and formed an alliance, known as the Delian League, to continue the war and take further vengeance on

Persia. Athens was recognized as head of the league and determined which members should supply ships to the common navy and which members should contribute money.

The military campaigns, often fought under the command of the Athenian general Cimon, were successful until the warfare between Greeks and Persians ended about 450. Meanwhile, Athenian control of the league had become stricter through the years. Sometimes Athens forcibly prevented members from withdrawing from the league; sometimes it stationed garrisons or governors in the supposedly independent member states. Athenian domination became unmistakable in 454, when the league transferred its treasury from Delos to Athens. The cash contributions were now nothing but tribute to Athens, and the alliance of equals had become an Athenian empire.

## ◆ THE AGE OF PERICLES

*The Golden Age of Athens* The leading statesman in the period of the Athenian empire was Pericles (490?–429 b.c.), an aristocrat from a wealthy family who had the support of the common people. Now that the archonship was no longer a position for an ambitious man, Pericles held only the post of general, to which he was reelected from 443 to 429. He was a powerful orator and a highly competent general and was renowned for his personal honesty; moreover, his policies generally favored the common people.

He won them over by establishing pay for Athenian jurors and for those who served in the council. These measures not only supported the people but worked to assure the fullest possible participation in government by all citizens. In 447 B.C. he proposed that the Athenians restore the damage done by the Persian invasion of 480 and rebuild the temples on the Acropolis.

Between 447 and 432 B.C. they built for their goddess Athena the most nearly perfect of all Greek temples, the Parthenon. Inside it was a statue of Athena bearing more than a ton of gold. It was the work of the sculptor Phidias, who probably directed the reliefs on the temple as well. They also built a magnificent gateway to the Acropolis. These public works both beautified the city and served the political aim of providing work for the people.

Moreover, Pericles' lifetime coincided with the zenith of Athenian literature, when Athenian drama, especially, reached its highest development in the plays of Sophocles (a friend of Pericles) and Euripides. (On drama see further chapter 3, p. 81.) So brilliant was this era, and so strongly marked by his leadership, that historians often call the era from 450 to 429 the Age of Pericles. His political dominance drew praise from the historian Thucydides because "he controlled the masses, rather than let them control him. . . . Though the state was a democracy in name, in fact it was ruled by the most prominent man."[3]

### The Athenian Judicial System

The expansion of the empire must have been one of the causes of the development of the Athenian judicial system. Juries were chosen by lot and comprised two to five hundred or even more citizens drawn from all classes. There was no detailed body of civil or criminal law, and in trials there was no judge,

merely a magistrate to keep order. Juries had wide powers of interpretation without the possibility of appeal from their decision. Nor were there professional attorneys, although a man facing trial could pay a clever rhetorician to write a courtroom speech for him. Juries heard all manner of cases with the exception of homicides, which were tried by the Areopagus council (see p. 57). Critics of this system saw it as too democratic, but it expressed the spirit of the Greek state: that the average citizen could and should play a part in governing the city.

### ◆ THE PELOPONNESIAN WAR (431–404 B.C.)

"Historical laws" are difficult to establish and dangerous to use, but the observation of the British historian Lord Acton is hard to resist: "Power tends to corrupt." The Athenian empire, which had emerged out of the heroic victory in the Persian Wars, became more and more dominating over its subject states—its former allies. This movement and the resentment that it caused brought about the long war that sealed the doom of the Greek city-states. By far the longest and most dramatic of all collisions in Greek history, the Peloponnesian War also received an immortal analysis from the greatest of ancient historians, Thucydides of Athens (ca. 455–ca. 395 B.C.).

*The Outbreak of War* In the 430s aggressive action by Athens convinced the allies of Sparta that they must declare a preventive war on Athens. First, in 435 Corinth, an ally of Sparta, went to war with one of its colonies, Corcyra (today the main city on the island of Corfu). The quarrel threatened to become Panhellenic when Corcyra appealed for help to Athens in 433. Despite the warning of ambassadors from Corinth that any assistance would make war inevitable, the Athenians signed an alliance with Corcyra and actually fought with their new allies in a naval battle against Corinth.

Second, also in 433, the Athenians ordered the town of Potidaea, in northern Greece, to demolish its walls, send hostages to Athens, and banish its magistrates. Though Potidaea was a member of the Athenian empire, these demands infuriated the allies of Sparta, especially Corinth. The allies

[3]Thucydides 2.65.

▲ **A portion of the frieze within the Athenian Parthenon, showing officials carrying the robe that will be presented to Athena. On the right, gods sit in conversation, awaiting the procession; note that they are portrayed as larger than the human beings.**
Hirmer Fotoarchiv

demanded a meeting of the Peloponnesian League (see p. 56) and voted to declare war on the Athenians and their allies.

*The Opposing States* Thucydides gives his opinion that these events were only the immediate, incidental causes of the war: "The truest cause, though the least talked about openly, was that the growth of Athenian power frightened the Spartans and finally compelled them to go to war."[4] This judgment seems accurate, for neither the affair of Corcyra nor that of Potidaea threatened the Spartans directly; more menacing was the general disturbance of the balance of power caused by Athenian boldness.

This war, known as the Peloponnesian War, opposed two kinds of states. Sparta, though the head of the Peloponnesian League, controlled no empire and maintained itself through its own resources. Athens relied on its empire to provide grain for its people and tribute to pay for its navy. Sparta had the strongest army in Greece, and Athens was the chief naval power.

*The Archidamian War (431–421 B.C.)* The first ten years of the war are called the Archidamian War, so named for Archidamus, one of the kings of Sparta when the war began. Fighting opened in 431 B.C. but was inconclusive for several years. Sparta sought to break Athenian morale by invading Attica annually, ravaging farms, and then departing for the Peloponnesian harvest. But the Athenians withdrew behind their "long walls" that reached down to their harbor until the enemy left, and Pericles refused to allow the Athenian infantry to challenge Sparta on the field. Instead, the Athenians launched raids by sea against coastal towns in the Peloponnese, but these raids left Sparta untouched. Far more damaging to Athens than the Spartan invasions was a devastating plague (not yet identified with any known disease) that attacked the Athenians, packed inside their walls, in 430 and later years. The plague took thousands of lives within the crowded, unsanitary city; Thucydides survived it and has left us a horrifying description of its effects on the body.

Unfortunately for Athens' effectiveness in the war, Pericles died in 429 B.C. None of his successors could maintain his stable leadership, and

[4]Thucydides 1.23.

▲ **A Roman copy of an idealized portrait of Pericles, the leading Athenian statesman of his time. The helmet symbolizes his position as commander.**
Scala/Art Resource, NY

some were unscrupulous demagogues playing only for their own temporary power. In the 420s both sides achieved certain successes, but the casualties that all parties suffered in the next few years made them ready to end, or at least suspend, the war. A peace treaty, supposed to last for fifty years, and making Athens and Sparta allies, was signed in 421 B.C. It is called the Peace of Nicias for the Athenian general who led the negotiations.

*The "Suspicious Truce" (421–415 B.C.) and the Affair of Melos*   At this point the Greeks could have turned their backs on war, for both Athens and Sparta had shown courage and neither had gained a decisive advantage. Thucydides called the next few years a time of suspicious truce, but

during this period one event demands attention, the brutal subjugation of the small island of Melos by the Athenians in 416.

The Athenians sailed up to this neutral island and commanded the Melians to join the Athenian empire. Thucydides describes the negotiations in a brilliant passage, called the Melian Dialogue, in which envoys on each side argue their cases. It is by no means clear how he could have known what was said by either side, and this dialogue is probably based on his own conjectures. In any case, the Melians protest that they are so few in number that they cannot in any way threaten the Athenians, to which the Athenians reply that it is precisely their weakness that makes them dangerous: If the Athenians allow so small a state to remain neutral, this will show weakness in the Athenians themselves and may tempt their subjects to rebel.

In the Dialogue the Athenians brush aside all arguments based on morality and justice and finally seize the island, kill most of the adult men (probably two to three thousand), and sell the women and children as slaves. Without explicitly stating any moral conclusion, Thucydides shows the Athenians giving way to the corrupting influence of war; as he says in another passage, "War teaches men to be violent."[5]

*The Syracusan Expedition*   In 415 B.C. another occasion for war arose. The people of Segesta, a city in Sicily, appealed to Athens for help in a war they were fighting against Syracuse, the leading power on that island. In commenting on the death of Pericles, Thucydides noted that his successors were often lesser men of poor judgment. It was so now, as Alcibiades, a talented young political leader of enormous ambition and—as it later turned out—few scruples, persuaded the Athenian assembly, against the advice of the Athenian general Nicias, to raise a large fleet and attack Syracuse, with him as one of the generals. This campaign in effect reopened the Peloponnesian War despite the peace treaty of 421 B.C.

Thucydides makes it clear that a quick, resolute attack might well have succeeded, but the Athenians failed to strike when they had a clear advantage. One event that blunted the Athenian attack

[5]Thucydides 3.82.

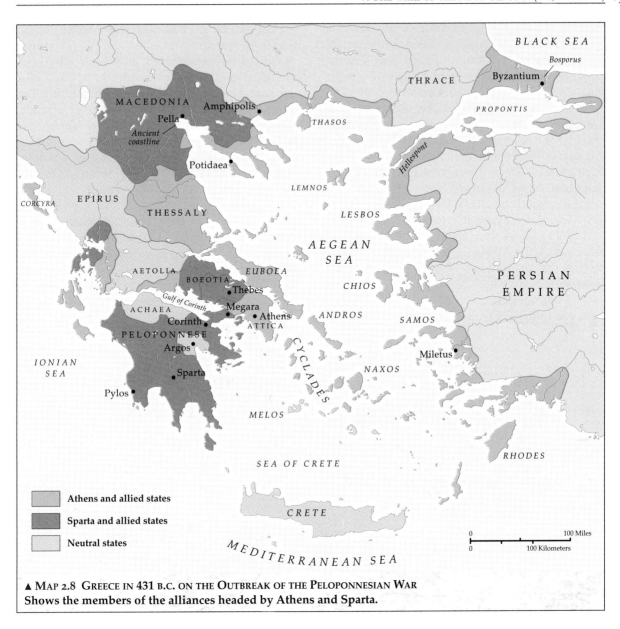

▲ **MAP 2.8  GREECE IN 431 B.C. ON THE OUTBREAK OF THE PELOPONNESIAN WAR** Shows the members of the alliances headed by Athens and Sparta.

was the loss of Alcibiades. He was recalled to Athens to stand trial on two scandalous charges: that he had been part of a gang of rowdies that had mutilated small statues of the god Hermes and that he and his friends had mocked some religious ceremonies known as mysteries. Fearing that his political enemies would be able to secure his conviction, he defected to Sparta and advised them how to fight the Athenians. His defection left Nicias, who had opposed the campaign from the start, in command.

In Syracuse, the Athenians finally decided to break off the campaign, but they lost a critical battle in the harbor and could not sail away. Trying to retreat toward the interior of the island, they were cut off and decimated. Those who survived this calamity were imprisoned in terrible conditions in a quarry at Syracuse; as Thucydides grimly says, "Few out of many returned home."[6]

[6]Thucydides 7.87.

***Athens Defeated*** The disaster in Sicily led to many defections among Athens' subjects, but Sparta still could not strike the final blow. The war dragged on for another eight years until, in 405 B.C., the Spartan admiral Lysander captured the Athenian fleet at a spot called Aegospotami, in the Dardanelles. Athens, now unable to bring grain through the straits, had to surrender in desperate hunger in 404. It abandoned its empire and, as a guarantee for the future and a symbol of humiliation, had to pull down the "long walls" that had protected the population during the war. Sparta proclaimed this event, in language often used by victors in war, as the "liberation of Greece" and imposed on the Athenians a cruel regime (known as the Thirty Tyrants). Pro-Spartan and anti-Spartan factions assailed one another during the rule of this hated clique, with atrocities and murders committed on both sides. After eight months

the Spartan king, Pausanias, restored the democracy in 403 B.C.

Athens never regained its former power, although democracy survived for long years after the war. The quality of political leadership had declined after the death of Pericles, as Thucydides observed. Several times when the war could have ended, ambitious politicians raised support for rash ventures that ended in disaster, of which the Sicilian expedition was only the most notable.

Looking back at the fifth century B.C., we can see that, in interstate politics, the Greek poleis made little constructive use of their brilliant victory over the invaders from Persia. Freed of a foreign enemy, they divided themselves into two blocs that turned against one another and, like characters in a Greek tragedy, involved themselves in the catastrophe of the Peloponnesian War.

## SUMMARY

◆

The Athenians lost their empire, which had made them the richest polis in Greek history. Sparta, persuaded by its allies to go to war in 431, had shattered the Athenian empire, but this empire had been no threat whatever to Sparta's isolated life within the protecting mountains of the Peloponnese. The losses in manpower had been heavy on both sides, but Sparta could less easily sustain these losses because of its smaller population, and in the fourth century it could put fewer and fewer troops in the field.

Besides these losses, there now came a failure of will, a spirit of pessimism and disillusion among Athenian intellectuals. Such a collapse of civic morale all but destroyed the sense of community that was the very heart of the polis. Self-centered individualism replaced the willing cooperation between citizens. Many thought uncontrolled democracy had led to social decline and military disaster, and they contrasted the discipline of Sparta, the victor, with the frequent chaos of Athenian policy. Thucydides often speaks critically of "the masses" and "the rabble," and similar ideas run through the work of Plato and other philosophers, who asked what had gone wrong with democracy and what system should replace it.

## QUESTIONS FOR FURTHER THOUGHT

◆

**1. There was no single ruler of ancient Greece, as there was in Egypt. If there had been such a ruler, how might Greek history and society have been different?**

**2. In what ways would you have liked to live in ancient Greece? What features of Greek life would you have found undesirable?**

# RECOMMENDED READING

◆

## Sources

Herodotus. *The Histories*. Robin Waterfield (tr.). 1998. A new translation with precise notes by Carolyn Dewald.

Homer. *The Iliad*. Robert Fagles (tr.). 1990. A stirring translation in verse.

———. *The Odyssey*. Robert Fagles (tr.). 1996. A worthy companion to Fagles' *Iliad*.

Thucydides. *The Peloponnesian War*. Rex Warner (tr.). 1972. The masterpiece of Greek historical writing.

———. *The Landmark Thucydides*. Robert B. Strassler (ed.). 1996. The Crawley translation, older but still a classic, with many helpful maps, notes, and appendixes.

## Studies

Boardman, John. *Greek Art*. 1973. One of many books by this great authority.

Boardman, John, et al. (eds.). *The Oxford History of Greece and the Hellenistic World*. Sixteen chapters by leading authorities on topics like art, literature, religion, and history.

Burkert, Walter. *Greek Religion*. 1987. By the most original and profound expert of our times.

———. *The Orientalizing Revolution*. 1992. Brief but close-packed study of Eastern influence on Greek art, religion, and culture.

Burn, A. R. *Persia and the Greeks: The Defence of the West, c. 546–478 B.C.* 2d ed. 1984. Accurate narrative of the Persian Wars.

Chadwick, John. *The Decipherment of Linear B*. 2d ed. 1970. Study of the Cretan scripts, with notes on the method of decipherment.

Drews, Robert. *The Coming of the Greeks*. 1988. Important on the arrival of the Greeks and movement of Indo-European peoples.

———. *The End of the Bronze Age: Changes in Warfare and the Catastrophe, ca. 1200 B.C.* 1993. Suggests that Mediterranean cities fell as chariot warfare gave way to massed infantry attacks.

Ehrenberg, Victor. *From Solon to Socrates*. 1968. Standard textbook on the central period of Greek history, with good references to sources.

Fantham, Elaine, et al. *Women in the Classical World*. 1994. Chapters on women in both Greece and Rome. Many good illustrations.

Finley, M. I. *The World of Odysseus*. 2d ed. 1977. Brilliant discussion of the historical material in Homer, both Iliad and Odyssey.

Flacelière, Robert. *Daily Life in Greece at the Time of Pericles*. 1965. Social and economic history of Greek life.

Forrest, W. G. *A History of Sparta, 950–192 B.C.* 1980. Brief history of Sparta, taking the story down through the state's collapse.

Garlan, Yvon. *Slavery in Ancient Greece*. Rev. ed. 1988. Thorough treatment of this institution.

Green, Peter. *The Greco-Persian Wars*. 1996. Modern, accurate narrative of the two Persian Wars.

Guthrie, W. K. C. *A History of Greek Philosophy*. 6 vols. 1962–1981. Encyclopedic history, brilliant and sensitive.

Hansen, Mogens Herman. *The Athenian Democracy in the Age of Demosthenes: Structure, Principles, and Ideology*. 1991. History of the democracy with careful attention to how it functioned.

Kagan, Donald. *The Archidamian War*. 1974. Detailed history of the first part of the Peloponnesian War (followed by two other volumes).

Keuls, Eva C. *The Reign of the Phallus*. 2d ed. 1993. Brilliant but one-sided work arguing that females were severely restrained in classical Greece; many illustrations.

Lawrence, A. W. *Greek Architecture*. 1987. Introductory survey of temples and private buildings.

Lazenby, J. F. *The Spartan Army*. 1985. History and operation of the Spartan army.

Lenardon, Robert J. *The Saga of Themistocles*. 1978. Readable, sound study of the great strategist.

MacDowell, Douglas M. *The Law in Classical Athens*. 1978. Good discussion of all aspects.

Morrison, J. S., and J. F. Coates. *The Athenian Trireme: The History and Reconstruction of an Ancient Greek Warship*. 1986. Essential treatment, solving at last the problem of how the Greek trireme was built.

Page, Denys L. *History and the Homeric Iliad*. 2d ed. 1966. Especially good on Near Eastern connections with the epic.

Patterson, Cynthia B. *The Family in Greek History*. 1998. The most recent study.

Pomeroy, Sarah B. *Goddesses, Whores, Wives, and Slaves*. 1975. The pioneering work that opened the modern study of women in the ancient world; includes chapters on Rome.

Renault, Mary. *The King Must Die*. 1958. An evocative historical novel set in the mythical time of Theseus.

Sealey, Raphael. *Women and Law in Classical Greece*. 1990. Carries the discussion beyond Athens into other Greek societies.

Wycherley, R. E. *How the Greeks Built Cities*. 1976. Greek town planning with description of major urban public buildings.

▲ A superb statue of the god Apollo from the west pediment of the Temple of Zeus at Olympia. In a commanding gesture, the god controls a centaur and symbolically brings Hellenic rationality to bear over an undisciplined universe. The statue combines the power and dignity of a god with the ideal perfection of a human being.
Erich Lessing/Art Resource, NY

# CLASSICAL AND HELLENISTIC GREECE

The Peloponnesian War left the two main Greek political alliances, those built around Athens and Sparta, weak and demoralized. The war thus prepared the way for the conquest of Greece in the next century by the Macedonian king Philip II. His son, Alexander the Great, went on to conquer Egypt, Persia, and vast stretches of Asia Minor.

Despite the tumultuous conditions of Greek politics—and perhaps because of the uncertainties and upheavals—the fifth and fourth centuries witnessed an extraordinary flowering of intellectual and artistic achievement. This burst of creative energy was concentrated in time and space to a degree that was unprecedented in history and, some would argue, has never been duplicated. The theme that runs through Greek civilization now became the inquiry into philosophy and analytical thought. In these years the Greeks wrote their greatest tragic dramas; they invented historical writing; and philosophers probed virtually every phase of human existence. Within society, the classical structure of the family and the several roles of women now become visible.

During the last decades of the fourth century, the Greeks, having lost the world of the independent polis, embraced the larger world of Alexander's empire, which brought them into contact with other peoples. There followed a series of intellectual experiments, especially in science and technology, art and literature, philosophy and religion. The Greek language took deeper roots in the Near East and ultimately became the language for the Christian New Testament.

| CHAPTER 3. CLASSICAL AND HELLENISTIC GREECE | | | | | | | |
|---|---|---|---|---|---|---|---|
| | Social Structure | Body Politic | Changes in the Organization of Production and in the Impact of Technology | Evolution of Family and Changing Gender Roles | War | Religion | Cultural Expression |
| I. CLASSICAL GREEK CULTURE | ▓ | ▓ | | ▓ | | ▓ | ▓ |
| II. THE RISE OF MACEDONIA | | ▓ | | | ▓ | | |
| III. THE HELLENISTIC AGE | | ▓ | ▓ | | | ▓ | ▓ |

# I. Classical Greek Culture
## (ca. 500–323 B.C.)

In less than two centuries, Greek society went through a profound intellectual transformation, apparent above all in literature, philosophy, drama, and historical writing. In all these spheres, reasoned argument became supreme. This cultural trait was hardly to be found among their older eastern neighbors. This era was one of Athenian preeminence, and the study of this "golden age" inevitably focuses on Athens.

## ◆ GREEK PHILOSOPHY

***The Inspiration for Philosophic Thought*** The supreme intellectual invention of the Greeks is the special search for knowledge called philosophy—the attempt to use reason to discover why things are as they are. Philosophy is born when people are no longer satisfied with supernatural and mythical explanations of the world or of human behavior. It is hard to say just why Greeks gradually became skeptical about the accounts that they inherited in their own mythology, but around 600 B.C. they began to suspect that there was an order in the universe beyond manipulation by the gods—and that human beings could discover it.

Life in Greek poleis was conducive to argument and debate, and such conditions encouraged rational inquiry and even dispute. And philosophy, like drama and history, became a means to analyze and understand change and upheaval. Yet philosophy never turned its back on religion.

The earliest philosophers were seeking nothing less than a cosmic plan, a divine world order.

***The Beginnings of Philosophy in Miletus*** The first Greek philosophers lived in the city of Miletus, a prominent trading center on the western shore of Asia Minor in the region of Ionia. Its citizens had direct contact with the ideas and achievements of the Near East, and these intellectual currents must have helped form the city as a center of thought. Soon after 600 B.C., certain Milesians were discovering a world of speculation in an apparently simple yet profoundly radical question: What exists? They sought their answer in some single primal element. One philosopher, Thales, for example, taught that everything in the whole universe was made of water, a notion that echoes Babylonian myths of a primeval flood. He may have reasoned that water is found in several states—as ice, as mist, and as water itself. Moreover, all the first civilizations—Sumer, Egypt, Babylonia—were nourished by great rivers.

The hypothesis of Thales inspired various replies. For example, one of his pupils, Anaximander of Miletus, held (probably about 560 B.C.) that the origin of everything was an infinite body of matter, which he called "the boundless." A whirling motion within the boundless divided its substance into the hot, which rose to form the heavens, and the cold, which sank and assumed form in the earth and the air surrounding it. A further separation into wet and dry created the oceans and the land. Human beings, he thought, had emerged from the sea; in this way he expressed a primitive theory of evolution. This

▲ An Attic red-figure vase (about 470 b.c.), showing scenes from a school. At left, a master teaches a boy to play the lyre; at right, a boy learns to recite poetry from a scroll held by a master while another master supervises the class.

Johannes Laurentius, 1992/Bildarchiv Preussischer Kulturbesitz

theory points toward a common later classification of all matter into four elements: earth, air, fire, and water. Moreover, he said, all things will pass away into that from which they came: Thus—a dark but clearly religious statement—will they "pay the penalty for their wrongdoing according to the ordinance of time."

*Pythagoras and Numbers*  Among the theories proposed to explain the order or substance of all things were those of Pythagoras of Samos (around 530 b.c.), who developed a strikingly different theory to explain the structure of the world. He saw the key to all existence in mathematics and approached the universe through the study of numbers. He discovered the harmonic intervals within the musical scale and stated the Pythagorean theorem in geometry about the area based on the sides of a right triangle. Pythagoras went on to say that all objects are similar to numbers, by

which he probably meant that objects always contain a numerically balanced arrangement of parts. He lacked, of course, the experimental methods of modern physicists; yet his theory is remarkably similar to the modern discoveries of mathematical relationships within all things, including even the genetic code in our bodies.

*The Atomic Theory*  Yet another way of looking at the universe came from Leucippus and his contemporary, Democritus of Abdera, about 450 b.c. They saw the world as made up of invisibly small particles, or atoms (*a-toma* in Greek, meaning "things that cannot be divided"), which come together and cohere at random. Death, according to this theory, leads simply to the redistribution of the atoms that make up our body and soul and thus need hold no terror for humanity. The validity of the atomic theory was eventually to be recognized in the modern era. It is another example of the ability of Greek theorists to hit part of the scientific truth, even though they could not prove it in laboratories.

***The Sophists*** Around 450 B.C. philosophers turned away from speculations about the structure of the universe and toward the study of human beings and the ways they led their lives. The first Greeks to undertake this study were those commonly known as Sophists (*sophistés* in Greek means "expert" or "learned man"). They came to Athens from various places and challenged nearly all accepted beliefs. One of the early Sophists, Protagoras, declared that "man is the measure" of everything; that is, human beings and their perceptions are the only measure of whether a thing exists at all. The very existence of the gods, whom people cannot really perceive, is only an undemonstrable assumption. From such a statement it is only a short step to the belief that it is almost impossible to know anything; in the absence of objective knowledge, the only recourse is to make your way through the world by coolly exploiting to your own advantage any situation you encounter.

The Sophists also drew an important distinction between human customs on the one hand and the law of nature on the other. Thus they argued that what was made or designed by people was arbitrary and inferior; what existed naturally was immutable and proper. This argument called into question all accepted rules of good behavior. Freed of moral constraints, the Sophists suggested that intellectual activity was valuable only in helping one succeed in life. They accepted pupils and said they could train these pupils for success in any calling, since in every line of work there are problems to be solved through reasoning. They taught the art of rhetoric, persuasive speech making that could be used to sway an assembly or to defend oneself in court. Their pupils, they implied, could gain power by analyzing the mechanics of politics and by using the skills the Sophists taught them.

***Socrates of Athens*** The main critic of the Sophists was Socrates (469–399 B.C.). He was active during the intellectually dynamic period before and during the Peloponnesian War. Socrates faulted the Sophists for taking pay for teaching,

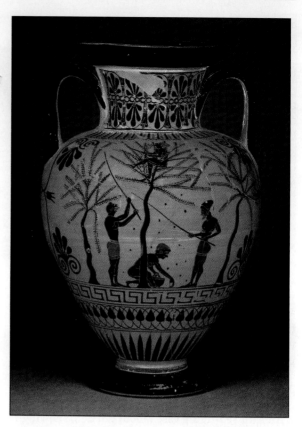

▲ The olive was one of the basic crops in Greek agriculture. In this black-figure vase (the figures are painted black while the background is the natural red of the clay), two men knock olives off a tree at harvest time, while another climbs the branches and a boy gathers the fruit.
British Museum (PS227411)

yet failing to recognize moral absolutes and teach ethically right behavior. In the course of his critique, Socrates transformed philosophy into an inquiry about the moral responsibility of people. His basic questions were not, What is the world made of and how does it operate? but rather, What is right action and how can I know it is right? His mission was to persuade the young men of Athens to examine their lives in the pursuit of moral truth, for "the unexamined life is not worth living."

His technique was to engage his pupils in a dialogue of questions and answers and to refute, correct, and guide them by this "Socratic" method to the right answers. He held that no man is wise who cannot give a logical account of his actions and that knowledge will point to the morally right choices; this belief led to his statement that "knowledge is virtue," one of several Socratic theses that seem paradoxical, for even ignorant men may be virtuous. Another such paradox is his statement that he was the wisest of men because he knew that he knew nothing. It was through ironic statements like these that he made people think critically and thus discover moral truths. The Roman orator and essayist Cicero said that Socrates had brought philosophy down from the heavens and placed it in the cities of the world.

*Socrates' Trial and Death* Socrates had political critics, for he was the tutor of several Athenians who had opposed democracy during the last years of the Peloponnesian War. One, Critias, was a member of a pro-Spartan oligarchy known as the Thirty Tyrants, who ruled Athens after the war. Alcibiades, who joined the Spartan side during the war, was another of his followers. As a result, Socrates was suspected of sympathy with the enemies of Athenian democracy, and in 399 B.C. he was brought to trial on charges of "worshiping strange gods and corrupting the youth"—a way of implying that Socrates had connections with enemies of the democratic state.

One can understand why Athenian jurors, who had just regained their democratic constitution from a short-lived oligarchy that fell in 403, would have wanted to punish anyone who had collaborated with the oligarchs. But there is little reason to think that Socrates was disloyal to the state. Nevertheless, persuaded by Socrates' enemies and acting in misguided patriotism, the jury convicted him. He proposed as his penalty a fine of 100 drachmas, which was about two months' pay, thus not a trifling sum; but when he also ironically requested the honor of dining rights at the town hall, the jury reacted in anger by voting for the death penalty (see "Socrates Is Sentenced to Death," p. 78).

Socrates accepted his fate and declined to seek exile. Perhaps he thought that life outside his polis, at age seventy, offered little pleasure. He may also have wanted to show his young followers that the duty of a good man was to obey the laws of the state. He drank a cup of poison with simple courage.

*Plato: What Is Reality?* Our knowledge of Socrates' thought comes mainly from the writings of his most famous pupil, Plato (428–347 B.C.), for Socrates wrote nothing. Plato continued Socrates' investigation of moral conduct by writing a series of complex and profound philosophical books, mainly in the form of dialogues in which Socrates is the main speaker. In these works, Plato went far beyond the ironic paradoxes proposed by Socrates and sought truth through a subtle process of reasoning and inquiry that modern readers still endlessly discuss and probe.

Plato made his greatest impact on the future of philosophy with his theory of knowledge. Socrates' answer to the question, How can I know what is right? was simply that one must listen to one's conscience. Such reliance on the inner voice within each human being did not satisfy Plato, who believed that we must go beyond the evidence of our senses to find ultimate reality and truth. Moreover, Socrates thought that everyone could recognize and practice right behavior; but Plato believed that moral goodness was restricted to the elite who could master it through philosophic study. He developed and taught his theories in his school in Athens called the Academy.

*The Republic* According to Plato, we see objects as real, but in fact they are only poor reflections of ideal models, or "forms," which are eternal, perfect originals of any given object or notion.[1] In his *Republic,* Plato illustrates our lack of true perception with a famous metaphor. Imagine men sitting in a cave, facing a wall, with a fire behind them. As others carry objects through the cave, in front of the fire, the men see only vague shadows of the objects and therefore cannot make out the reality. Everything that we see is like these imprecise shadows; so what we see as justice, for example, is nothing but an approximation of the true "form" of justice. Only through long training in philosophy can we learn how to perceive and understand the true ideal forms, which exist outside our world.

Plato presents this thesis in several dialogues, of which the most widely read is *The Republic.*

---

[1]Plato used the Greek word *idéa,* which means an image that one can see. Thus "form" is a better translation than the English "idea," even though the latter is widely used.

## SOCRATES IS SENTENCED TO DEATH

*Plato's version of Socrates' words to the jury that sentenced him to death:*

"You too, gentlemen of the jury, must look forward to death with confidence, and fix your minds on this one belief, which is certain: that nothing can harm a good man either in life or after death, and his fortunes are not a matter of indifference to the gods. This present experience of mine has not come about mechanically; I am quite clear that the time had come when it was better for me to die and to be released from my distractions. . . . For my own part I bear no grudge at all against those who condemned me and accused me, although it was not with this kind intention that they did so, but because they thought they were hurting me. . . . However, I ask them to grant me one favor. When my sons grow up, gentlemen, if you think that they are putting money or anything else before goodness, take your revenge by plaguing them as I plagued you; and if they fancy themselves for no reason, you must scold them just as I scolded you, for neglecting the important things and thinking that they are good for something when they are good for nothing. If you do this, I shall have had justice at your hands, both I myself and my children.

Now it is time that we were going, I to die and you to live; but which of us has the happier prospect is unknown to anyone but God."

From Hugh Tredennick (tr.), Plato, *The Last Days of Socrates,* Penguin Classics, 1954, 1972, 1980, p. 76.

---

Like other Athenian intellectuals, Plato opposed democracy as a political system dominated by emotion rather than logic. His repudiation of democracy intensified when a jury was persuaded to condemn Socrates to death, even though he had served the state as a soldier and had committed no crime. Socrates is the main speaker in the *Republic,* and in the work's long debate over the right form of state he expresses severe criticisms of democracy as a volatile, unpredictable, and ineffective system. Yet it is by no means certain that these opinions were really those of the historical Socrates. It is probable that Plato was the real antidemocrat and that he put these opinions into the mouth of Socrates for dramatic purposes. Whatever its source, Plato's denunciation of broad participation by the people in governing has remained a challenge to political theorists ever since.

***Plato's Ideal State***    Looking back at the death of his teacher at the hands of a popular court, Plato sought to demonstrate that people without a philosophical education should never exercise political power. Their chief disqualification was that they had no grasp of reality, because they were unable to perceive the forms.

Government should therefore be in the hands of men who had received an education in philosophy. This ruling elite would see to it that "every-

one will do his proper task." In Plato's preferred system, a second class, warriors, would defend the state; a third class, workers, would produce the needed material goods. Plato sums up his conception of good government in an epigram: "The state will be ruled well when philosophers become kings and kings become philosophers."[2]

Like other visions of a perfect state, Plato's *Republic* has had little effect on actual constitutions, but it remains the most widely read philosophical book of all time. Its analyses probe nearly every problem of philosophy, from statesmanship to the nature of perception, the power of language, and psychology. Many threads run through the book, but one above all: the question, What is justice? As we have seen, the issue of justice was central to Greek thought and also to the debates in the history of Thucydides. Indeed, it recurs throughout the whole fifth century. That the pupil of Socrates, who had seen his teacher condemned in what he considered a brutal distortion of justice, should have been obsessed by this question emphasizes the degree to which Plato was a product of the Athenian society of his time.

***Aristotle: Form and Matter***    Plato had a pupil of equal genius, Aristotle (384–322 B.C.), who was for a time the teacher of Alexander the Great of Mace-

---

[2]Plato, *Republic,* 473 c.

◄ An Attic relief, showing the goddess Athena leaning on her spear and gazing at a tablet, perhaps a list of men fallen in battle. If so, this would justify the name often given to this relief, the "Mourning Athena." Acropolis Museum, Athens

donia. Aristotle founded a school within a grove in Athens called the Lyceum. His investigations, in which he was assisted by his pupils in Athens between 336 and 322 B.C., embraced all fields of learning known to the ancients, including logic, metaphysics, astronomy, biology, physics, politics, and poetry.

Aristotle departed from Plato's theory of an ideal reality that cannot be perceived by the senses. Rather, he saw reality as consisting of both form and matter. In this way, he turned his pupils to empirical sciences, the study of what can be seen to exist. He also had an overall theory of the world of nature. For Aristotle each object has a purpose as part of a grand design of the universe. "Nature does nothing by accident," he said. The task of the philosopher is to study these individual objects to discover their purpose; then he may ultimately be able to determine a general pattern.

***Aristotle and the State*** Like Plato, Aristotle wanted to design the best state. In one of his works, the *Politics,* he classified the types of polit-

ical constitutions in the Greek world and distinguished three basic forms: monarchy, aristocracy, and moderate democracy. He warned that monarchy can turn into tyranny; aristocracy, into oligarchy; and moderate democracy, into radical democracy, or anarchy.

Of the three uncorrupted forms, Aristotle expressed a preference for moderate democracy—one in which the masses do not exercise too much power. The chief end of government, in his view, is a good life for both the individual and the community as a whole. This idea is an extension of the view expressed in his *Ethics,* that happiness is the greatest good of the individual. To achieve this end, people must seek moderation, often called the Golden Mean: a compromise between extremes of excessive pleasure and ascetic denial—a goal that reflected the Greek principle of harmony and balance in all things.

***Aristotle's Physical Theories*** Aristotle's conception of the universe remained influential in scientific speculation for two thousand years. By 350

▼ The so-called Temple of Concord from Agrigento, Sicily. Superb example of a fifth-century Doric temple. The stone was of inferior quality and was originally covered with stucco, still visible on some columns.
John Snyder/Corbis Stock Market

B.C. philosophers generally recognized four elements: earth, air, fire, and water. Aristotle gave the elements purpose and movement. Air and fire, he said, naturally move upward; and earth and water, downward. He explained movement by saying that elements seek their natural place. Thus, a stone falls because it seeks to return to the earth. It also seeks to be at rest; all motion is therefore involuntary and unnatural and must be accounted for by an outside force.

To the four elements Aristotle added a fifth, ether, the material of which the stars are made. He explained that the stars move in a natural circular motion, and outside the whole universe there exists an eternal "prime mover," which imparts movement to all the other parts. This prime mover, or God as Aristotle finally designates him, does not move or change; God is a kind of divine thought or mind that sets the whole universe in motion.

***Aristotle and the World of Nature*** Among the most original and fascinating of all Aristotle's works are his writings on biology, which are based on extensive firsthand observation. In the *Generation of Animals*, he studies the birth and reproduction of animals, birds, fish, insects, and human beings. In the *Parts of Animals*, he discusses the functions of the various parts of the body.

Aristotle believed that nature, the creator of living things, designed every part with a specific function. Thus, for example, the lion and wolf were given no vertebrae in the neck because nature intended that they should have rigid necks for charging their prey. Such explanations are called *teleological* (from the Greek word *telos*, meaning "aim, goal"), and they remained influential for many centuries. Even more influential was Aristotle's effort to classify all that he observed in separate categories. His organizing principles remained the basis for the study of nature until the scientific revolution of the seventeenth century.

#### ◆ GREEK TRAGEDY

One of the most lasting achievements of the fifth century B.C. was the creation and perfection of a new literary and theatrical form, tragedy. Greek dramas were written in the most sublime poetry since Homer, and they first appeared in Athens, at religious festivals honoring the god Dionysus. At these celebrations, also marked by dancing and revelry, dramatic performances addressed increasingly profound moral issues.

***Themes in Greek Tragedy*** The writers of tragedies derived most of their plots from tales of gods and heroes in Greek mythology; therefore drama never lost its close connection with religion. Their central themes include questions fundamental to all religions: What is humanity's relationship to the gods? What is justice? And if the gods are just, why do they allow people to suffer? That tragic drama arose at this time and in this place may be the result of the new confidence of the Athenians following their victory over Persia and the founding of the Athenian empire. Their inspiration may also have derived from their awareness of how short-lived triumphs can be. Greek tragedy relentlessly pursued its main theme—that worldly success can lead to arrogance, and arrogance to folly. Destruction, often sent by the gods as punishment, can be the inevitable result.

***The Production of Plays*** In the fifth century these dramas were performed before audiences of as many as fifteen thousand people of all classes, often during religious festivals. The plays not only moved and inspired but also provided an education in ethics for citizens, who were gripped by the complex debates over which persons were acting justly and which ones should suffer retribution for moral error and crime. Just as philosophy explored the subject of ethical responsibility and right conduct, so do the dramas—but with far greater emotional power. Greek tragedies are still performed and filmed, and they continue to inspire operas, plays, and ballets more than two thousand years after their creation.

***Aeschylus: Fate and Revenge*** Playwrights presented dramas in sets of three, accompanied by a comic playlet known as a satyr play (probably meant to relieve the heavy emotion of the main drama). Only one such "trilogy" has survived: the *Oresteia*, the tragedy of Orestes, the son of Agamemnon, by Aeschylus, which was produced in 458 B.C. Its central theme is the nature of justice, which Aeschylus explores in a tale of multiple murders and vengeance. Agamemnon, the leader of the war against Troy, found his fleet becalmed and had to sacrifice his daughter to revive the winds so that he could fulfill his oath to make war on Troy. On his return, his wife, Clytemnestra, kills him and is in turn killed by her son, Orestes, who is finally tried and acquitted in an Athenian court presided over by the goddess Athena. The cycle of retribution runs its course as the themes of fate and revenge focus on the family, all developed through majestic poetry and intense emotion.

### Sophocles: When Is Civil Disobedience Justified?

Sophocles wrote mainly during the Peloponnesian War of 431–404 B.C. He changed the form of drama by adding a third actor (Aeschylus never had more than two actors on the stage at any time) in order to concentrate more on the interplay of characters and the larger issues of society that they explore. He also shows a greater interest in personality than does Aeschylus.

His *Oedipus the King* is perhaps the most nearly perfect specimen of surviving Greek tragedy; its central concern is the relationship of the individual and the polis. The play is about Oedipus, the revered king of Thebes, who has unknowingly committed the terrible crimes of killing his father and marrying his mother. As the play opens, some unknown offense has brought a plague on his people. Oedipus orders a search to discover the person who has caused this pollution. As the search narrows with terrifying logic to Oedipus himself, he discovers that his crimes of patricide and incest, though unintentional, have disturbed the order of the universe and his polis in particular. The only remedy is for him to serve justice and atone for his offenses. When the truth emerges, Oedipus' wife-mother hangs herself and Oedipus, in a frenzy of remorse and humiliation, plunges the brooches from her robe into his eyes and begins a life of wandering as a blind outcast; the once powerful monarch is now a broken, homeless fugitive (see "Oedipus' Self-Mutilation," p. 83).

Sophocles' *Antigone* continues the saga of Oedipus' family as his daughter Antigone grapples with another dilemma about justice. One of her brothers has been killed while attacking his own city, Thebes. Antigone wants to give him a traditional burial despite his traitorous actions, but the ruler of Thebes forbids such honor for an outlaw. Antigone must therefore decide which laws to obey—those of the gods or those laid down by a man.

Antigone defies the ruler by burying her brother and thus willingly goes to prison, where she hangs herself in heroic loyalty to her beliefs. The play, like most Greek tragedies, raises moral questions that still resonate: When is civil disobedience justified, and is it our duty to resist laws that we consider wrong?

### Euripides: Psychology and Human Destiny

The Athenian poet Euripides, a contemporary of Sophocles, emphasized above all the psychology of his characters. Reacting to the violence of his times, he throws his characters back on their own searing passions. They forge their own fates, alienated from their societies. As a result, we see in Euripides how the workings of the mind and emotions shape a person's destiny. His intense, even fanatical, characters determine the course of events by their own often savage deeds. Compared with Aeschylus and Sophocles, Euripides seems less confident in a divine moral order. In this uncertainty, he reflects the wavering spirit of his age.

In Euripides' *Medea*, for example, Jason, Medea's husband, has deserted her for a princess of Corinth. Driven by overwhelming emotion to take revenge, Medea kills the Corinthian girl and then turns on her own children. As love and hatred battle within her, she weeps over her children but, despite a momentary weakening of will, completes her vengeance and kills them. The powerful woman has found her own way of dealing with the terrors of the world. We should note that she is not punished for her horrible crime, as probably would have happened in a tragedy of Aeschylus or Sophocles.

## ◆ GREEK COMEDY: ARISTOPHANES

Comedy abandoned these serious themes and satirized contemporary situations and people in the real world. Almost the only comedies that have come down to us are those written by the Athenian Aristophanes, a younger contemporary of Sophocles and Euripides. Again and again he emphasized the ridiculous in individual lives as well as in society at large. Aristophanes used fantasy and burlesque to satirize the Peloponnesian

## OEDIPUS' SELF-MUTILATION
◆

*In Sophocles' tragedy King Oedipus, Jocasta, the mother of Oedipus, hangs herself after learning that she has married her own son. An attendant then narrates what follows. (Those he "should never have seen" are the daughters Oedipus fathered by his mother-wife.)*

"We saw a knotted pendulum, a noose,
A strangled woman swinging before our eyes.
The King saw too, and with heart-rending groans
Untied the rope, and laid her on the ground.
But worse was yet to see. Her dress was pinned
With golden brooches, which the King snatched out
And thrust, from full arm's length, into his eyes—
Eyes that should see no longer his shame, his guilt,
No longer see those they should never have seen,
Nor see, unseeing, those he had longed to see,
Henceforth seeing nothing but night . . . To this wild tune

He pierced his eyeballs time and time again,
Till bloody tears ran down his beard—not drops
But in full spate a whole cascade descending
In drenching cataracts of scarlet rain.
Thus two have sinned; and on two heads, not one—
On man and wife—falls mingled punishment.
Their old long happiness of former times
Was happiness earned with justice; but to-day
Calamity, death, ruin, tears, and shame,
All ills that there are names for—all are here."

From E. F. Watling (tr.), Sophocles, *The Three Theban Plays,* Penguin Classics, 1971, pp. 60–61.

---

War, political leaders, intellectuals—including Socrates—and the failings of democracy. Whatever his political motives in writing his satires, they sometimes exposed the folly of human behavior more devastatingly than the tragedies did. And they were particularly cutting in their depiction of the absurdities of arrogant persons in Athenian society.

The earliest of Aristophanes' eleven surviving plays is *The Acharnians* (425 B.C.), an antiwar comedy from the early years of the Peloponnesian War (Acharnae was an Athenian village). Aristophanes continued his antiwar theme in other plays, notably *Lysistrata,* which he wrote after the disastrous Athenian expedition to Syracuse. In this comedy the women of Athens, despairing of any other means of ending the long war, go on a sex strike that humiliates their blustering menfolk, and they succeed in enlisting the other women of Greece in their cause.

Aristophanes reserved some of his sharpest attacks for the democratic leaders who succeeded Pericles. In *The Knights* (424 B.C.) a general tries to persuade an ignorant sausage-seller to unseat Cleon, one of those leaders:

*Sausage-Seller:* Tell me this, how can I, a sausage-seller, be a big man like that?

*General:* The easiest thing in the world. You've got all the qualifications: low birth, marketplace training, insolence.

*Sausage-Seller:* I don't think I deserve it.

*General:* Not deserve it? It looks to me as if you've got too good a conscience. Was your father a gentleman?

*Sausage-Seller:* By the gods, no! My folks were scoundrels.

*General:* Lucky man! What a good start you've got for public life!

*Sausage-Seller:* But I can hardly read.

*General:* The only trouble is that you know anything. To be a leader of the people isn't for learned men, or honest men, but for the ignorant and vile. Don't miss the golden opportunity.[3]

### ◆ HISTORICAL WRITING

Drama is one way of examining the human condition; writing history is another. The constant wars in the fifth century B.C. prompted some men to

---

[3]From L. S. Stavrianos, *Epic of Man to 1500,* 1970.

seek to explain why war was their perpetual companion. They looked to the past to understand what causes war and how people behave during conflict. In so doing, they invented a new literary form: history.

*Herodotus: Father of History*   Herodotus, a Greek from Asia Minor and a contemporary of Sophocles, is rightly called the "Father of History," for he was the first to write a sustained narrative of political events, in his case, the Greek victory over Persia. Yet his narrative was no mere chronicle, for he laid down forever the historian's main question: Why do events happen? Again, Herodotus understood that a major war could also be a clash between two differing cultures. He therefore began by trying to learn the history of the Persian Empire in order to explain its pressure on Europe.

The most impressive dimension of his work is his demonstration that all the cultures of the ancient world were interconnected. Using travelers' tales, interviews, and oral tradition, much as a modern anthropologist does, Herodotus described the character and outlook of the several peoples of the Near East. He also reduced centuries of Near Eastern history into order, chronicling the dynasties and successions from one monarch to another. He did this without the help of any earlier narrative, and the structure he gave to the history of the Persian Empire has not been shaken. He explained the growth of the Persian Empire as the work of powerful, ambitious monarchs, constantly striving for a larger realm. In the end, Herodotus shows his Greek heritage with his verdict that the Greek victory in the Persian Wars was the inevitable triumph of a free society over a despotic one. He also brings the supernatural into his work through dreams, omens, and oracles, and he declared that the Athenians—"next to the gods"—were mainly responsible for the Greek victory.

*Thucydides: Analysis of War*   Greek historians "published" their work by giving readings, perhaps also allowing copies to be made. Thucydides, a younger contemporary of Herodotus, is said to have heard Herodotus read, and this experience may have inspired him when, as a participant in the Peloponnesian War, he decided to write its history. He did not live to finish his work,

▲ Roman wall paintings often show scenes from Greek drama and mythology; this painting shows Medea, in Euripides' play, about to kill her children. "My friends, I am resolved to act, to slay my children quickly and depart from this land." Naples, Archeological Museum. Photo, © Luciano Pedicini

which breaks off in 411, seven years before the end of the war. Thucydides has a narrower theme than Herodotus, for he concentrates on a limited period and area.

Yet he is the more profound inquirer into causation, he weighs evidence more carefully, and he analyzes more keenly the motives of statesmen and warriors. He offers far fewer anecdotes than Herodotus; wit and humor are totally absent. His entire first book, out of the eight that make up his history, explores the causes, both immediate and long-term, for the outbreak of the war. Thucydides brings to bear on events the kind of logical and unemotional analysis that philosophers developed in the late fifth century. Throughout his work he presents a series of speeches and debates about various issues and decisions in order to lay bare the motives of the participants. The speakers are usually contemptuous of moral principles, and arguments based on justice and mercy, if brought up at all, are ruthlessly swept aside by whichever person or force has the upper hand. It is by no means clear that Thucydides himself rejected compassion, but he presents the whole war as a cold pursuit of power. It was by such rigorous analysis that he brought order out of the cruelties and disruptions of his age.

In Thucydides' view, the Athenian state was in good order under Pericles because he could control the Athenian people. His political successors, by contrast, allowed the masses to influence decisions, with tragic consequences for Athens, including above all the expedition to Sicily in 415 B.C. Thucydides combines accuracy and concentration on detail with descriptive powers that rival those of the dramatists, particularly when he brings a scene of horror to life. No reader can avoid feeling a chill over the clinical description of the plague that attacked Athens in 430 B.C. or the shattering defeat of the proud armada that sailed against Syracuse. He is the undisputed master among ancient historians, and for gripping narrative power and philosophical breadth he remains unsurpassed (see "Thucydides: The Melian Dialogue," p. 86).

#### ◆ THE FAMILY IN CLASSICAL GREECE

***Recovering Greek Attitudes*** Greek society assigned certain roles to people according to their sex. Men were the rulers and leaders, and in no Greek state did women vote or hold offices, with the exception of certain priesthoods. They were, however, citizens and so could not be violated or sold into slavery.

Thus, roughly half the citizens of Greek poleis must have been women, but to reconstruct their place in Greek society is not easy, mainly because nearly all our sources were written by men. Probably there was no single view of women in Greek society, as we can see from our oldest source, the Homeric poems. In the *Iliad*, the story opens as Achilles and Agamemnon quarrel over a concubine who is nothing but a sexual slave, while the Trojan hero Hector honors and cherishes his wife, Andromache; equally, in Homer's *Odyssey* Pene-

lope, the wife of the absent Odysseus, is an admired model of wisdom and fidelity.

As we look from the idealized figures of Homer to the women of the polis, we see a much less benign attitude toward women. Certainly

▼ An Attic kouros, or young man, called the Kritios boy, leaning on one foot; shows a movement away from the severe toward a more natural style.
Hirmer Fotoarchiv

# THUCYDIDES: THE MELIAN DIALOGUE

*In 416 B.C., the Athenians mercilessly inform the people of the small island of Melos that they must join the Athenian empire. Thucydides presents the cold logic of their demand.*

*Athenians:* We will use no fine phrases saying, for example, that we have a right to our empire because we defeated the Persians, or that we have come against you now because of the injuries you have done us. And we ask you not to imagine that you will influence us by saying that you have never done us any harm. You know as well as we do that the strong do what they have the power to do and the weak accept what they have to accept.

*Melians:* So you would not agree to our being neutral, friends instead of enemies, but allies of neither side?

*Athenians:* No, because it is not so much your hostility that injures us; rather, if we were on friendly terms with you, our subjects would regard that as a sign of weakness in us, whereas your hatred is evidence of our power.

*Melians:* We trust that the gods will give us fortune as good as yours, because we are standing for what is right against what is wrong.

*Athenians:* Our opinion of the gods and our knowledge of men lead us to conclude that it is a general and necessary law of nature to rule wherever one can. This is not a law that we made ourselves, nor were we the first to act upon it when it was made. We found it already in existence, and we shall leave it to exist forever. We are merely acting in accordance with it, and we know that you or anybody else with the same power as ours would be acting in precisely the same way.

From Rex Warner (tr.), Thucydides, *The Peloponnesian War*, Penguin Classics, 1954, 1980, pp. 403–404 abridged.

---

there was no equality between the sexes. A woman was always under the control of her *kyrios,* or master—at first her father, then her husband, then her father again if she became divorced or widowed. Her father gave her in marriage with a dowry, normally at about age fifteen, to a man perhaps ten to fifteen years her senior. Xenophon describes the education of a young wife in obedience and household skills, and the picture is like the training of a young animal (see "The Training of a Wife," p. 87).

*Women and Property* A wife's main duty, apart from managing the household, was to provide a male heir in order to maintain the family's hold over its property. In Athens, if the family had no male heir, the property came to a daughter, but she held it only temporarily. In this respect Athenian women were far less privileged than, for example, Egyptian women. The heiress must then be married to the nearest available male relative, thus preventing the property from passing from the family. Yet the duty of women to provide heirs did not cause Greeks to think of a woman as a mere breeding machine. On the contrary, the power, possessed only by women, to bear children seems to have made them objects not only to be cherished but also to be feared.

*Restrictions in Women's Lives* Widows and heiresses had to be given new husbands in order to maintain control of property within the family. Since women could thus be transferred from one husband to another, Greeks were not sure about their fidelity; adultery by women was a grave threat because it could bring outsiders into the family and threaten the preservation of property within the correct line. It is always clear who a child's mother is, but doubts can exist about the identity of a father. Such suspicions may partly account for some passages by Greek poets and philosophers in which women are viewed as undisciplined, emotionally unstable, and sexually inexhaustible. By contrast, infidelity in men was looked on as permissible.

To preserve a woman's fidelity, the door of the home was considered her proper frontier, but such restrictions were not possible for families without servants; yet even when women did go out, they were normally accompanied by a handmaiden, a slave, or a relative. The statesman Pericles, in a speech given him by Thucydides, says

## THE TRAINING OF A WIFE

*The Athenian writer-soldier Xenophon wrote a work in which one Ischomachus explains how he trained his wife in her duties. He instructs her as follows.*

"Your duty will be to remain indoors and send out those servants whose work is outside, and superintend those who are to work indoors, and to receive the incomings, and distribute so much of them as must be spent, and watch over so much as is to be kept in store, and take care that the sum laid by for a year be not spent in a month. And when wool is brought to you, you must see that cloaks are made for those that want them. You must see too that the dry corn [i.e., grain] is in good condition for making food. You will have to see that any servant who is ill is cared for.

"There are other duties peculiar to you that are pleasant to perform. It is delightful to teach spin-ning to a maid who had no knowledge of it when you received her; to take in hand a girl who is ignorant of housekeeping and service; to have the power of rewarding the discreet and useful members of your household, and of punishing anyone who turns out to be a rogue. The better partner you prove to me and the better housewife to our children, the greater will be the honour paid to you in our home."

From E. C. Marchant, (tr.), *Xenophon,* Vol. 4, Harvard University Press, 1979, pp. 7. 35–42 abridged.

that the most honored woman is she who is least talked about in society.

Some Greek thinkers were able to rise above such a limiting view of a woman's place. Plato, in his *Republic,* recommended that women share in education with men, although he stopped short of what we would call a truly liberal attitude to sexual equality.

***The Power of Women in Myth*** In several ways, then, men could feel uncertain about their control over women. If we have rightly understood some of this uncertainty, we may be near to understanding why women of Greek drama such as Clytemnestra, Antigone, and Medea are such powerful characters, far stronger and more dangerous than the men in Greek plays. Again, in mythology the "furies," who could drive people mad, were female; Greeks tried to appease them by calling them the "kindly ones." Female too were the powers called Nemesis and Ate, which brought punishing destruction on those who became too arrogant and self-confident; so were the three Fates who spun out the thread of life and cut it off at the end.

***Men, Women, and Sex*** Men, unlike women, were allowed to find sex where they liked. Ele-gant single women were paid companions at men's social affairs; the most famous courtesan of all, Aspasia, had a long affair with the statesman Pericles and bore him a son. Only these women could participate in the refined intellectual life of the city. Poorer women worked, for example, as seamstresses, nurses, or sellers in the market. Prostitutes, who were normally slaves or foreigners, were not difficult to find; a man might have sex with a slave whom he owned. Homosexuality between men was tolerated and is often illustrated in ribald scenes on Greek pottery.

Yet we must not expect perfect consistency where such emotions are at play. By modern Western standards, and even some ancient ones, Greek women suffered severe restrictions. On the other hand, women whose households had slaves may have had to work less than many women in modern emancipated societies. Our museums contain copious statues of beautiful Greek maidens. And many of the most revered deities are women: Athena, who was respected for her warlike nature and never had lovers in myth, was also the protecting goddess to the Athenians, who held her in affection and built for her one of the world's architectural masterpieces, the Parthenon. Aphrodite, who could involve human beings in ruin through sexual passion, was treasured as the model of ideal beauty and was so portrayed in hundreds of statues.

It is impossible to estimate in scientific terms the emotional love between Greek men and women. The recommendation of Plutarch, that a man should sleep with his wife three times a month, suggests that love played only a modest part in marriage. On the other hand, gravestones from many poleis show the affection in which some women were held; typically, a woman is seated, members of her family stand nearby, and a son or her husband takes her hand in a quiet farewell.

## II. The Rise of Macedonia

The Peloponnesian War had caused terrible losses in manpower for the Greek city-states. Instead of the needed healing period, there followed decades of interstate warfare—the perennial tragedy of Greece—that further weakened the poleis. These battles opened the way for an old kingdom from the north of Greece, Macedonia, to become the leading power in the Greek world. Moreover, the Macedonian king Alexander the Great drove the Greek language and many features of Greek culture deeply into Asia Minor and Egypt.

▼ The "Getty Bronze," a fourth-century statue in a soft, relaxed style. Surviving bronze statues from Greece are rare.
Collection of the J. Paul Getty Museum, Malibu, California (77.AB.30)

### ◆ THE DECLINE OF THE INDEPENDENT POLEIS

Athens had lost the Peloponnesian War and Sparta had imposed on the Athenians a puppet regime, known as the Thirty Tyrants, in 404 B.C.; but within a few months popular opposition swept this group away. As the Athenians sought to regain power, they revived their naval league in 394 B.C., though with many fewer members than it had had in the fifth century. But their arrogance had not subsided. Despite their promises to respect the independence of the league's members, the Athenians began to demand tribute from them as they had done under the Delian League. Rebellions followed, and this second league collapsed about 355 B.C.

By now there were no longer only two dominant cities in Greece. The polis of Thebes was becoming an important power, siding now with Athens, now with Sparta, in a series of never-ending quarrels. There was no clear trend in these struggles except that the constant intrigue and war, spanning several decades, drained the energies of all the antagonists. In 371 B.C. the brilliant Theban general Epaminondas won a victory over Sparta and thus finally exploded the long-held belief in Greece that the Spartan infantry was invincible. The Thebans liberated Sparta's slaves, the

▲ **Map 3.1  Macedonia under Philip II, 359–336 B.C.**

helots, and helped them to found their own city, called Messene, in the Peloponnese.

The Spartans thus lost much of their territory and many of the slaves who had worked their land. A shortage of manpower accelerated the decline in Sparta's strength. Aristotle informs us about 335 B.C. that Spartan armies in the field had fewer than one thousand men, rather than the four or five thousand who had gone into battle during the wars of the fifth century. Epaminondas himself died in another battle near Sparta in 362

B.C., and no comparable leader in any polis took his place. The era of independent city-states was all but over, doomed by the constant wars of the fourth century.

## ◆ PHILIP II OF MACEDONIA

*The Rise of Philip*  Macedonia, a kingdom in northern Greece, emerged as a leading power under an ambitious, resourceful king, Philip II, who reigned between 359 and 336 B.C. With shrewd political skill Philip developed his kingdom, built up a powerful army, and planned a program of conquest.

Using both aggression and diplomacy, Philip added poleis and large territories to his kingdom and extended his influence into central Greece. The great Athenian orator Demosthenes (384–322 B.C.), in a series of fiery speeches called "Philippics," beginning in 351, called on his countrymen to recognize the danger from Macedonia and prepare to make war against it. But by the time the Athenians responded, it was too late to halt the Macedonian advance.

***Philip's Victory and Death***   Philip won a decisive battle against Athens and several other poleis at Chaeronea in 338 B.C. All the city-states of southern Greece, except isolated Sparta, now lay at his mercy. He could have devastated many of them, including Athens, but his sense of tactics warned him not to do so. Instead, he gathered the more important poleis into an obedient alliance called the League of Corinth, which recognized Philip as its leader and agreed to follow him in his next project, an invasion of Persia.

But before Philip could open his Persian war, he was murdered in 336 B.C. by one of his officers who apparently had a personal quarrel with the king. Some historians have wondered whether Philip's wife or his son, Alexander, may have been involved in a plot to kill Philip and put Alexander on the throne; but tempting as such speculations may be, the sources do not give them clear support.

## ◆ ALEXANDER THE GREAT

The empire built by Philip now passed to his son, Alexander III (r. 336–323 B.C.), known as Alexander the Great, and never has a young warrior prince made more effective use of his opportunities. During his brief reign Alexander created the largest empire the ancient world had known and, more than any other man, became responsible for the eastward expansion of the Greek world.

***Alexander's Invasion of Persia***   In the next year, 335, a rumor of Alexander's death caused a democratic revolution in the city of Thebes. Alexander marched on Thebes and sacked it with the utmost

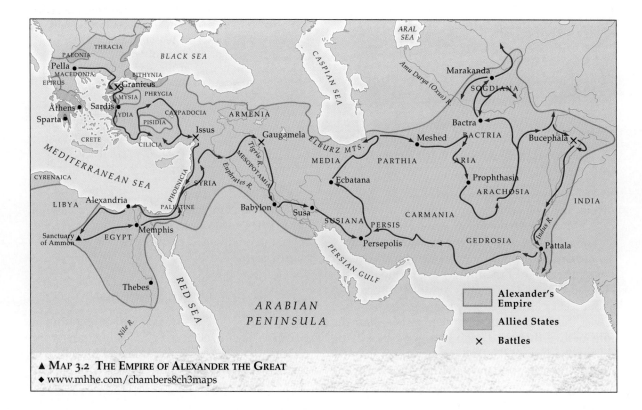

▲ **Map 3.2** **The Empire of Alexander the Great**
◆ www.mhhe.com/chambers8ch3maps

▲ The Venus of Cyrene in Rome (early third century B.C.), a most elegant, graceful depiction of ideal female beauty.
Scala/Art Resource, NY

brutality, destroying every building except temples and the house of the poet Pindar. Having thus warned the Greek cities against any further rebellions, Alexander began the invasion of the

Persian Empire. The Persia that he attacked was a much weaker state than the one that had conquered Babylon or the one that Xerxes had led against the Greeks in 480 B.C. Intrigue and disloyalty had weakened the administration of the empire. Moreover, the king, Darius III, had to rely on Greek mercenary soldiers as the one disciplined element in his infantry, for native troops were mainly untrained. The weakness of Persia helps explain Alexander's success, but in no way does it diminish his reputation as one of the supreme generals in history. His campaigns were astonishing combinations of physical courage, strategic insight, and superb leadership.

*Alexander in Egypt*   Alexander swept the Persians away from the coast of Asia Minor and in 332 B.C. drove them out of Egypt, a land they had held for two centuries. The Egyptians welcomed him as a liberator and recognized him as their pharaoh. He appointed two Egyptians to administer the country, along with a Greek to manage the finances; he was to follow this pattern of dividing power throughout his reign.

▼ The head of Alexander the Great in heroic profile; the obverse of a silver coin issued by Lysimachus, one of Alexander's bodyguards, who after his master's death became king of Thrace.
Gift of Mrs. George M. Brett. Courtesy, Museum of Fine Arts, Boston. Reproduced with permission. © 2001 Museum of Fine Arts, Boston. All Rights Reserved.

▲ A scene from the magnificent "Alexander Sarcophagus" found at Sidon, now in the Archaeological Museum, Istanbul; fourth century B.C. Alexander, left, is shown hunting, accompanied by a Persian. Although we have no reason to think Alexander was ever buried in this sarcophagus, the scene symbolizes Alexander's heroism and virility and calls attention to his conquest of the Persian Empire.
C. M. Dixon

While he was in Egypt (also in 332), Alexander founded the city of Alexandria. He intended this city to serve as a link between Macedonia and the valley of the Nile, and he had it laid out in the grid pattern typical of Greek city planning. Although he did not live to see it, Alexandria remained one of the conqueror's most enduring legacies: a great metropolis throughout history.

*Victories and Death of Alexander* In the next season, 331 B.C., Alexander fought Darius III at Gaugamela, winning a complete victory that guaranteed he would face little further opposition in Persia. Darius III was murdered by disloyal officers in 330 B.C., and Alexander assumed the title of king of Persia. Again he followed his policy of placing some areas in the control of natives: Babylonia, for example, was given to a Persian named Mazaeus.

The expedition had now achieved its professed aim; yet Alexander, for whom conquest was self-expression, continued to make war. During the next few years he campaigned as far east as India, where he crossed the Indus River (see map 3.2), and finally, in 326 B.C., he began his march back. But at Babylon in 323 B.C., he caught a fever after a bout of heavy drinking, and within a few days he died, not yet thirty-three.

*The Reputation of Alexander* Alexander is a figure of such stature and power that he defies easy interpretation, and even today radically different biographies are written about this most famous man in Greek history. Part of our difficulty is that our best narrative source for his life, the Greek historian Arrian, lived four centuries after Alexander's death, and Arrian, for all his merits, was not the kind of probing historian who might have given us a rounded psychological portrait of the king. Yet it is clear that along with Alexander's courage and drive, perhaps as their necessary accompaniment, came a personality sometimes barely containing a raging animal. He ordered the execution of a number of his friends for supposedly being aware of conspiracies against him; another friend he murdered himself in a sudden fury. On the other hand, Arrian tells the moving story of Alexander's pouring a cup of water, offered him by his parched troops, into the desert because he refused to drink if his men could not.

Nor do we know just what Alexander was trying to accomplish. There is little reason to believe the popular myth that he hoped to conquer the world. His goal may have been a stable empire that would maintain his vast conquests, but if so he failed, for he had designated no successor and the empire disintegrated on his death.

*Alexander's Rule*   Alexander established democratic regimes in the Greek states in Asia Minor that he had freed from Persian rule. But he also established some policies that brought Persians and their ways into his regime. We have seen that he used Persians as administrators. He also had young Persians trained in Macedonian style and even enrolled them within Macedonian regiments. These measures were intended to strengthen his empire by enlisting support from natives. Some historians have gone further and have declared that Alexander had a vision of the unity of the human race and was trying to establish an empire in which different peoples would live in harmony as within one family, but this view is widely, and rightly, rejected as sentimental and too idealistic.

Other historians focus on his acts of cruelty and vindictiveness and see him as a paranoiac tyrant. In any case, no portrait of him should overlook his patronage of scholarship, which extended even to his bringing scientists and geographers with him as he invaded Persia. His foundation, Alexandria, became the intellectual center of the next age. However we interpret Alexander, he has remained the prototype of a world conqueror. Some of his successors sought to maintain his memory by putting his portrait on their own coins, and even Roman emperors issued

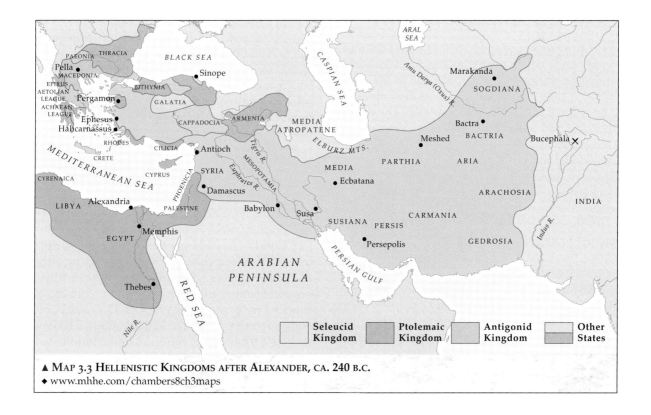

▲ MAP 3.3 HELLENISTIC KINGDOMS AFTER ALEXANDER, CA. 240 B.C.
◆ www.mhhe.com/chambers8ch3maps

medallions portraying him, as if to borrow his glory and power for their often threatened reigns.

# III. The Hellenistic Age
# (323–30 B.C.)

The Classical Age of Greek civilization began about 500 B.C. and ended in 323 B.C., with the death of Alexander the Great. The next period, the Hellenistic Age, began with that event and extended to the death of Cleopatra VII of Egypt in 30 B.C. During this period the Greeks carried their culture throughout the Near East in the movement known as Hellenization. Broadly speaking, Hellenization refers to the increasing use of the Greek language and customs among non-Greeks. This movement had begun well before the death of Alexander, but his invasion of the Persian Empire gave a decided stimulus to such a widespread acceptance of Greek culture. The Greeks in turn received legacies, especially in religion, from the peoples whom they met in this age.

## ◆ THE DISSOLUTION OF ALEXANDER'S EMPIRE

*New Kingdoms* Alexander's empire was shattered almost at once after his death, as his generals seized various parts for themselves. By about 275 B.C., after years of warfare and diplomatic intrigue, three large kingdoms emerged. These were the kingdom of Macedonia and its territories in Greece; Syria, formed by the Macedonian Seleucus; and Egypt, governed by the Macedonian Ptolemy and his successors. A fourth kingdom was formed about 260 around the city of Pergamum in western Asia Minor (see map 3.3).

In the Hellenistic kingdoms the richer classes gained more and more influence, but they sometimes used their wealth to endow spectacular temples and other buildings and to sponsor games and festivals. We may guess that they were acting partly to indulge in prideful display, partly to gain favorable public opinion. In Athens, for instance, Attalus II of Pergamum (r.[4] 158–138)

---

[1]The letter *r.* before a date or series of dates stands for "reigned."

donated a magnificent stoa, or colonnaded building, that was rebuilt in A.D. 1956.

*Kingdoms and Leagues* The subsequent history of these kingdoms is one of continual warfare until they were all eventually absorbed by the Roman Republic. The king of Macedonia controlled northern Greece. The poleis in the south retained their autonomy, and some of them formed defensive leagues to protect their independence from the monarchy. The most influential were the Aetolian League in western Greece and the Achaean League on the northern coast of the Peloponnese.

These leagues tried to strengthen themselves by awarding citizenship in the league to all citizens of their member cities; but this principle of confederation for mutual security arrived too late in Greek history to take firm root before Greece fell to the expanding Roman Republic. As to the Egyptians and inhabitants of the Near East, they had long seen their rulers as divine or semidivine beings, and the Hellenistic kings in these areas exploited this tendency and established themselves as absolute monarchs who owned the kingdom.

*Hellenistic Rulers* Remarkably, considering the military roots of these kingdoms, the Hellenistic Age witnessed the reemergence of women as rulers. Their power first became evident in Macedonia, where Olympias, the mother of Alexander, was a more important political figure than any other woman in classical Greece. The most famous and skillful of all Hellenistic queens was Cleopatra of Egypt, who manipulated such Roman military leaders as Julius Caesar and Mark Antony to the advantage of her kingdom.

Hellenistic monarchs ruled through strong armies and large bureaucracies, and their systems of taxation were extremely efficient. Certain products, such as oil in Egypt, were royal monopolies and could be traded only at official prices. Greeks usually held the chief public offices in the army and bureaucracy, and rulers did allow some democratic institutions, such as a town council, to function in Near Eastern cities, but the autonomy of these cities was limited to local affairs. The king collected tribute from the cities and controlled all foreign policy, and he alone granted and could cancel such rights of self-government as the cities enjoyed.

## ◆ ECONOMIC LIFE

*Agriculture and Industry* One of the sharpest contrasts between the classical and Hellenistic worlds was the scale of economic activity. In classical Greece, farmers worked small plots of land, and industry and commerce were ventures of small entrepreneurs. In the Hellenistic states of Egypt and the Seleucid kingdom, vast estates predominated. Industry and trade operated throughout the Near East on a larger scale than ever before in the ancient world, requiring the services of bankers and other financial agents.

The Hellenistic world prospered as ambitious Greeks, emigrating from their homeland to make their fortunes, brought new vigor to the economies of Egypt and the Near East. They introduced new crops and new techniques in agriculture to make production more efficient. For example, Greeks had long cultivated vines, and they now enhanced the wines of Egypt. At the same time, they improved and extended the irrigation system and could thus devote more acreage to pasturing animals, which provided leather and cloth for the people and horses for the cavalry.

*Trade and Finance* The growth of long-distance trade was even more remarkable. The Hellenistic rulers encouraged these efforts by establishing a sound money system, building roads and canals, and clearing the seas of pirates. Traders ventured eastward to India and, in the west, beyond the Mediterranean to the Atlantic coasts of Africa and Europe.

Unfortunately, the resulting prosperity was not evenly distributed. Rulers and members of the upper classes (usually Greek) amassed great fortunes, but little of this wealth filtered down to the small farmers and laborers. This great disparity between rich and poor led to increasing social conflict.

*Hellenistic Cities* Agriculture remained the major industry in the vast lands of the new kingdoms, but it was in the numerous Greek cities founded by Alexander and his successors that the civilization that we call Hellenistic took form. Most of these new cities were in western Asia, in the Seleucid kingdom. Alexander had founded the brilliant city of Alexandria, in Egypt, but the Ptolemies who ruled Egypt did not follow his example by founding many cities. They considered a docile, rustic civilization far easier to control than citizens of a politically active urban society.

Some Hellenistic cities were magnificently ornate and spectacular. Besides their political institutions the Greeks brought from their homeland many of the amenities of polis life—temples, theaters, gymnasiums, and other public buildings. Pergamum, an outstanding example of city planning, contained a stupendous altar to Zeus, a renowned library, and a theater high above the main city with a superb view. The city may have had as many as one hundred thousand inhabitants (under the Roman Empire its population was about two hundred thousand), while Alexandria, the largest of all, had at least a half million people.

Local families in the upper classes copied Greek ways and sent their children to Greek schools. Moreover, a version of Greek, *koiné* ("common") Greek, became an international tongue. Now, for the first time, people could travel to virtually any city in the Mediterranean world and make themselves understood.

## ◆ LITERATURE, ART, AND SCIENCE

*Libraries and Scholars* The most significant literary achievements in the Hellenistic Age were in the field of scholarship. The kings of Egypt took pride in constructing a huge library in Alexandria that probably contained, by 200 b.c., a half million papyrus rolls. Along with the library, they built the Museum, a kind of research institute, where literary, historical, and scientific studies flourished, each employing its own experts. One of the main interests of literary scholars in Alexandria was the literature of the classical period, and among their achievements was the standardization of the Greek text of Homer. By comparing the many versions that had been handed down in manuscripts over the centuries, scholars were able to establish the text on which modern versions of Homer are based.

The specialization of scholars was characteristic of the growing professionalism of the age. Whereas the citizen of fifth-century Athens could be a farmer, a politician, and a soldier at the same

▲ Panels from the altar to Zeus at Pergamum, in the Pergamon-Museum, Berlin, showing gods in combat with giants. Greek art preferred abstraction to reality, and such scenes probably represent the triumph of Greek civilization over non-Greek peoples. The violence and dramatizing are in the "baroque" tradition of Hellenistic art of the second century B.C.
C. M. Dixon

time, now each of these roles was filled by a professional. The army consisted of professional soldiers, while professional bureaucrats ran the government.

*A New Spirit in Art* Hellenistic rulers also wanted to glorify their cities and provided generous subsidies for art and architecture. The architecture of the age sometimes emphasized size and grandeur, as compared with the simplicity and human scale of classical architecture. Thus, the Altar of Zeus from Pergamum, now in Berlin, included a great stairway, flanked by a frieze four hundred feet long. The figures on the frieze, typical of Hellenistic sculpture, are carved in high relief, with an almost extravagant drama and emotionalism that make them seem to burst out of the background. Hellenistic sculpture also differed from that of the classical period through its devotion to realism. Instead of creating figures of ideal perfection, artists now showed individuality in faces and bodies (see picture of bronze statue of boxer), even depicting physical imperfection or frank ugliness.

*Hellenistic Science*   Advances in the field of science drew strength from the cross-fertilization of cultures in the Hellenistic Age. The Greeks had long speculated about the nature of the universe, and the Near East had an even longer scientific tradition, particularly in the fields of astronomy and mathematics. After Alexander's conquests joined the two cultures, other conditions favored scientific advance: the increased professionalism of the age, the use of Greek as an international language, and the facilities of the Museum in Alexandria. The result was a golden age of science that was not surpassed until the seventeenth century.

*Euclid's Geometric Theorems*   Unlike their eastern neighbors, Greeks had a strong desire for theoretical understanding, even beyond the solving of immediate mathematical and engineering problems. Their work in the realm of theory descends from their skill in philosophic debate.

In mathematics, Euclid (about 300 B.C.) compiled a textbook that is still the basis for the study of plane geometry. Some of his theorems were already known, and others (for example, his demonstration that nonparallel lines must meet somewhere) may seem obvious. His accomplishment was to construct a succession of elegant proofs for these theorems, each based on earlier proofs, starting with the simple proposition that the shortest distance between two points is a straight line. The analytical method of his proofs is a characteristic of Greek thought, for Greek

▲ **Bronze statue of a boxer from Rome, second century B.C. Greek sculptors had abandoned statues of ideal beauty and were now experimenting with scenes of frank realism. Note the boxer's battered face and bandaged hands.**
Scala/Art Resource, NY

philosophers believed that knowing something entailed being able to prove it. The restatement of Euclid's theorems through the study of geometry in schools around the world has made him perhaps the most widely read Greek author.

*Archimedes: Advanced Mathematics and Engineering*   The greatest mathematician of antiquity—indeed, one of the greatest ever, in the class of Newton and Einstein—was Archimedes of

Syracuse, who also lived during the Hellenistic era (287?–212 B.C.). He calculated the value of *pi* (the ratio between the circumference and diameter of a circle); he developed a system for expressing immensely large numbers, by using 100 million as the base (as we use 10); and he discovered the ratio between the volumes of a cylinder and a sphere within it, namely, 3:2. In a testament to his love of theoretical knowledge, he wanted this proportion engraved on his tombstone.

Archimedes was also a pioneer in physics; he demonstrated that a floating body will sink in a liquid only to the point at which it displaces its own weight. He understood the principle of using the lever for lifting massive weights and is said to have proclaimed, "Give me a place where I can stand and I will lift the earth" (that is, standing outside the earth entirely and with a long enough lever). He also invented the water screw, still used for irrigation in Egypt. As the Romans besieged Syracuse in 212 B.C., he devised engines to fight them off; but, tragically, he was murdered by a Roman soldier as the city fell—while he sat drawing a mathematical figure in the sand.

***Aristarchus and the Orbit of the Earth***   About 250 B.C., Aristarchus, an astronomer and mathematician, advanced a heliocentric theory of the movement of the planets. The view that the earth revolves around the sun was not new, but Aristarchus refined it by stating that the earth revolves on its own axis while it, together with the other planets, circles the sun. Not until the sixteenth century did astronomers prove the soundness of Aristarchus' system; meanwhile, the Greek astronomic tradition continued to follow an older geocentric theory, which held that the earth was the center of the solar system and that the sun revolved around it. The false geocentric theory was, however, the basis for the most important Hellenistic text on astronomy, the *Almagest* of Ptolemy of Alexandria (about A.D. 140). This book systematized the Greek study of astronomy and remained the accepted text on the subject for more than one thousand years.

***Other Mathematical Discoveries***   Hellenistic scientists also made important advances in the realm of measurements. Hipparchus calculated the length of the average lunar month to within one second of today's accepted figure. Eratosthenes about 225 B.C. computed the circumference of the earth to be about twenty-eight thousand miles, only three thousand miles more than the actual figure. Other scientists worked out the division of time into hours, minutes, and seconds and of circles into degrees, minutes, and seconds.

## ◆ PHILOSOPHY AND RELIGION

***Philosophies of Comfort***   The change in lifestyle from the relative security of the polis to the increasing uncertainties of a larger world shifted the direction of Greek philosophy. Plato and Aristotle had been philosophers of the polis in the sense that they were concerned with the individual's role in the intimate world of the city-state; the ideal state in their theories would have only a few thousand citizens. But when the city-state came to be governed by a large kingdom headed by a remote ruler, individual men and women could hardly influence its policies even though they were caught up in its wars and its many changes of fortune.

Moreover, the large Hellenistic cities lacked the cohesiveness, the sense of belonging among citizens, that had made the classical poleis internally united. In such conditions, philosophers sought means of accommodation with the larger Hellenistic world that was shaping their lives. They tried to provide people with guidance in their personal lives and were less concerned about the nature of the political framework. Thus, the two most important schools of Hellenistic philosophy, Epicureanism and Stoicism, were philosophies designed to provide comfort and reassurance for the individual human being.

***Epicurus and Atomism***   Epicurus, who taught in Athens during the generation after Alexander, believed that people should strive above all for tranquillity, which he sought to provide through the atomic theory of Democritus. Our bodies and souls, Epicurus taught, are made up of atoms that cohere only for our lifetimes. When we die, the atoms will be redistributed into the universe again, and nothing of us will remain behind to suffer any desire for the life we have lost. Because death therefore holds no terrors, we should concern ourselves only with leading pleasurable lives, above all avoiding physical and mental pain. Sensuality, gluttony, and passionate love, in

Epicurus' view, are equally unrewarding, since they may lead to disappointment and pain. Thus, the wise person withdraws from the world to study philosophy and enjoy the companionship of a few friends. Some later Epicureans came close to advocating an almost heedless pursuit of pleasure, but such was not the message of Epicurus, whose philosophy was intended as a powerful antidote to anxiety and suffering.

***Zeno and the Universe of Stoicism***   A different approach to life's problems was that of a contemporary of Epicurus—namely, Zeno of Cyprus—who founded a philosophical school known as Stoicism, so named because he taught his pupils in a building in Athens called the Stoa. Zeno was a man of Semitic ancestry, and the fact that he taught at Athens is a notable example of the mixing of cultures that took place in the Hellenistic age. A later Stoic, Chrysippus, stated Stoicism in its best-known form: One must act in accordance with nature, choosing one's actions with attention to reason. Such a program will lead one to virtue. A successful life includes pleasure; good health is desirable, provided one uses it in the pursuit of virtue. If one acts in accordance with nature, one cannot be other than happy.

To Stoics, the universe was wholly created and held together by a force sometimes called fire, sometimes *pneuma* or "breath." At certain intervals, the universe is destroyed by fire, but it is born again, and we are reborn with it. Because a single divine plan governs the universe, to find happiness one must act in harmony with this plan. One should be patient in adversity, for adversity is a necessary part of the divine plan and one can do nothing to change it. By cultivating a sense of duty and self-discipline, people can learn to accept their fate; they will then become immune to earthly anxieties and will achieve inner freedom and tranquillity.

***Ethical Duties of the Stoics***   The Stoics did not advocate withdrawal from the world, for they believed that all people, as rational beings, belong to one family. Moreover, to ensure justice for all, the rational person should discover his or her place in the world and consider it a duty to participate in public affairs.

The Stoics advanced ideas that were to have a profound influence on later Western history, espe-

cially as they were interpreted in the Roman and Christian visions of civilization: the concept that all humanity is part of a universal family; the virtues of tolerance; and the need for self-discipline, public service, and compassion for the less fortunate members of the human race. Stoicism is thus part of a great intellectual revolution that led some thinkers to consider similarities among humans more important than differences.

Again, while most earlier Greeks had accepted without question the institution of slavery, the Stoics believed that the practice of exploiting others corrupted the owner (the slave could endure bondage by achieving inner freedom). Stoicism became the most influential philosophy among the educated of the Hellenistic Age and achieved great influence among the Romans, who adopted with conviction the ideals of discipline and fulfillment of public and private duty.

***New Religions***   The search for meaning in life preoccupied all levels of Hellenistic society, but none so painfully as the great masses of the poor. The answers of philosophy were addressed to an intellectual elite: wealthy scholars, as it were, meditating in the study. But the poor—lacking the education, leisure, and detachment for such a pursuit—looked elsewhere for spiritual and emotional sustenance in their daily encounters with the problems of life. For many, religion answered their need for escape and consolation.

Among the new religious practices were the Near Eastern mystery cults that had some features in common as a result of the frequent intermingling of cultures in the cosmopolitan Near East. They are called mystery cults because they centered on the worship of a savior whose death and resurrection would redeem the sins of humanity; their rituals were secret, known only to the participants, and were elaborate, often wildly emotional; and they nourished hope by promising an afterlife that would compensate for the rigors of life on earth. One of the most popular mystery cults was the worship of the Egyptian deities Isis and Osiris. In Egyptian mythology, Osiris had been murdered and dismembered but was reassembled and saved by Isis, his devoted wife; he then became the god of the underworld. Thus, the myth suggested that its followers might also attain salvation and life after death.

# SUMMARY

All these political, scientific, and intellectual explorations were parts of the legacy of Alexander, the Macedonian who brought Greek civilization and the Greek language into the world beyond the Mediterranean Sea. Greek was to be the language in which the New Testament was written, and therefore some historians have also seen his campaigns as preparing the way for Christianity and have even called Christianity his most important legacy. Be this as it may, the Greeks and Macedonians could not maintain permanent control over the remains of Alexander's empire. Not Greece but Rome became the uniting force that passed the legacy of classical civilization to medieval and then to modern Europe.

# QUESTIONS FOR FURTHER THOUGHT

**1. The Greeks invented historical writing. In looking at the past, what are the most important questions a historian should ask?**

**2. The Greek city-states and their system of alliances gave way to the rising power of Macedonia. How might the Greek states have preserved their strength and political power?**

# RECOMMENDED READING

## Sources

Aristotle. *The Athenian Constitution*. P. J. Rhodes (tr.). 1984. The great philosopher's brief history and description of the Athenian state, with helpful commentary.

Arrian. *The Campaigns of Alexander the Great*. Aubrey de Sélincourt (tr.). 1958. Our main source for the life of the great conqueror.

Carey, Christopher (tr.). *Trials from Classical Athens*. 1997. Translations of selected courtroom speeches in Athenian cases.

Demosthenes. *Public Orations*. A. W. Pickard-Cambridge (tr.). 1963. Collects the statesman's orations on public policy, such as his opposition to Philip II.

Grene, David, and Richmond Lattimore (eds.). *The Complete Greek Tragedies*. 9 vols. 1953–1991. The best collection of modern translations.

Lefkowitz, Mary, and Maureen B. Fant. *Women's Life in Greece and Rome: A Source Book in Translation*. 1982. Translated documents and literary excerpts on all features of women's lives.

Plato. *The Republic*. Desmond Lee (tr.). 1974. The central work of Greek philosophy.

Plutarch. *Nine Greek Lives*. Robin Waterfield (tr.). 1998. Biographies of prominent statesmen and commanders, including Pericles and Alexander the Great.

Xenophon. *A History of My Times*. Rex Warner (tr.). 1979. A narrative, often less than profound, of Greek history down to 362 B.C.

## Studies

Bosworth, A. B. *Conquest and Empire: The Reign of Alexander the Great*. 1988. Now the standard treatment of Alexander's life and reign.

Burford, Alison. *Land and Labor in the Greek World*. 1993. Modern treatment of land tenure and agriculture in Greece.

Cawkwell, George. *Philip of Macedon*. 1978. Macedonia before Philip II, father of Alexander, and the expansion of the kingdom.

Dodds, E. R. *The Greeks and the Irrational*. 1951. Brilliant investigation of the Greek mind, showing its irrational and psychological complexity.

Dover, K. J. *Greek Homosexuality*. 1989. Scientific, nonsensational study of this social phenomenon. By today's leading Hellenist.

———. *Greek Popular Morality in the Time of Plato and Aristotle*. 1994. Goes beyond the ethical doctrines of philosophers to discover the values of ordinary Greeks.

Errington, R. Malcolm. *A History of Macedonia*. Catherine Errington (tr.). 1990. Compact one-volume treatment, carrying the story down through Alexander's successors.

Garland, Robert. *The Greek Way of Life: From Conception to Old Age*. 1990. Reconstruction of normal life cycle of Greeks in classical and Hellenistic age.

Golden, Mark. *Children and Childhood in Classical Athens*. 1990. Groundbreaking study of how children interacted with adults.

Green, Peter. *Alexander to Actium: The Historical Evolution of the Hellenistic Age*. 1990. The most comprehensive historical and cultural survey; a colossal study.

Hammond, N. G. L. *The Macedonian State: The Origins, Institutions, and History*. 1989. By the leading expert on Macedonia of the last half century.

Just, Roger. *Women in Athenian Law and Life*. 1989. Brief, admirably up-to-date treatment of marriage, inheritance, freedom and seclusion, and more.

Kitto, H. D. F. *Greek Tragedy: A Literary Study*. 1969. Probably still the best general book on one of the supreme achievements of the Greeks, written without literary jargon.

Lacey, W. K. *The Family in Classical Greece*. 1984. Survey of the family in Greek world, especially in Athens and Sparta.

Lloyd, G. E. R. *Aristotle: The Growth and Structure of His Thought*. 1968. Good survey of all areas of Aristotle's philosophy.

Long, A. A. *Hellenistic Philosophy: Stoics, Epicureans, Sceptics*. 2d ed. 1986. Readable survey of the postclassical Greek philosophers.

Osborne, Robin. *Classical Landscape with Figures: The Ancient Greek City and Its Countryside*. 1987. How the countryside influenced the development of the Greek city.

Parker, Robert. *Miasma: Pollution and Purification in Early Greek Religion*. 1990. Important study of pollution concerning birth, death, crime, and disease, and its purification.

Pickard-Cambridge, A. W. *The Dramatic Festivals of Athens*. 2d ed. by John Gould and David M. Lewis. 1968. Detailed description of dramatic festivals, costumes, and much more.

Pomeroy, Sarah B. *Women in Hellenistic Egypt*. 1989. Especially good on the status of women in this society.

Rowe, C. J. *Plato*. 1984. Modern introduction with ample bibliography.

Sansone, David. *Greek Athletics and the Genesis of Sport*. 1988. On the place and history of games in Greek society.

Sinclair, R. K. *Democracy and Participation in Athens*. 1988. On the opportunities for average citizens to share in running the Athenian state.

Stockton, David L. *The Classical Athenian Democracy*. 1990. Comprehensive description of the working of the state, not excessively technical.

Tarn, W. W. *Alexander the Great*. 1979. Beautifully written biography by the leading Alexander scholar of his day, sometimes giving way to hero worship.

Travlos, John. *Pictorial Dictionary of Ancient Athens*. 1980. Precise locations of and essays on all major buildings and sites in Athens.

Vlastos, Gregory. *Socrates: Ironist and Moral Philosopher*. 1991. Most important recent study of style and significance of Socrates' thought.

Walbank, F. W. *The Hellenistic World*. 1982. The best brief survey of the period.

White, K. D. *Greek and Roman Technology*. 1984. Describes entire range of classical technology.

Wood, Ellen Meiksins. *Peasant-Citizen and Slave: The Foundations of Athenian Democracy*. Rev. ed. 1989. Argues that Athenian agriculture was managed more by free peasants than slaves.

▲ "Noble" Romans, those whose ancestors had been consuls, had the right to have masks representing them carried in funeral processions. This republican noble of about 30 B.C. shows the masks of two of his ancestors.
Scala/Art Resource, NY

# THE ROMAN REPUBLIC

*T*he Greeks flourished in small, intensely competitive communities, but the Romans formed a huge, long-lived empire. The Greek historian Polybius, who lived many years in Rome, has left us his analysis of Rome's successful policy. Drawing on theories of Aristotle, he praised Rome for its mixed constitution. He saw the element of monarchy in the two Roman consuls. The Roman Senate represented oligarchy, or the rule of a few. And the Roman common people supplied the element of democracy. The state, he thought, so long as it was balanced on these three supports, could not fail to prosper and expand.

The history of Rome brings to the fore another of the themes that run through the Western experience: the use of warfare as a deliberately chosen instrument of policy. Sometimes Rome got its way through diplomacy, but when this failed the military machine did not. An army is not a democracy but a body governed by a few experienced men—in fact, an oligarchy.

The Romans exploited the family as a force, a weapon, in society. Political power was based on the strength of a man's family and on the alliances he formed with other families. The state united first the Italian peninsula, then the whole Mediterranean basin. Finally, the Romans came to know a culture that they recognized as superior to their own: that of Greece. The poet Horace said that "Greece, once captured, conquered its captor," as Greek literature and art inspired those of Rome.

In the process of domination, a series of warlords became so powerful that, through their rivalry, they destroyed the republic and the political freedom that Rome had achieved. The response was the formation of an even more powerful autocracy, from which Europe was to descend: the Roman Empire.

| CHAPTER 4. THE ROMAN REPUBLIC | | | | | | | |
|---|---|---|---|---|---|---|---|
| | Social Structure | Body Politic | Changes in the Organization of Production and in the Impact of Technology | Evolution of Family and Changing Gender Roles | War | Religion | Cultural Expression |
| I. THE UNIFICATION OF ITALY | ▓ | ▓ | | ▓ | ▓ | ▓ | |
| II. THE AGE OF MEDITERRANEAN CONQUEST | ▓ | | | | ▓ | | |
| III. THE ROMAN REVOLUTION | | ▓ | ▓ | ▓ | | | |
| IV. THE END OF THE ROMAN REPUBLIC | | ▓ | | | ▓ | | |
| V. THE FOUNDING OF THE ROMAN EMPIRE | | ▓ | | | | ▓ | |

# I. The Unification of Italy (to 264 B.C.)

The inhabitants of Italy greatly outnumbered those of Greece in antiquity. Unlike the Greeks, they became unified under the leadership of a single city, Rome. This movement required centuries, and during this period Rome itself was transformed from a monarchy into a republic with a solid constitution. Families were not only the binding force of the household but became the building blocks of political power. Guided by the Roman Senate, the city expanded its territory until the whole peninsula of Italy was under Roman control.

## ◆ THE GEOGRAPHY OF ITALY

Italy is not, like Greece, divided into many small valleys or islands. The main geographic feature is the Apennine range, which runs diagonally across Italy in the north and then turns southward to bisect the peninsula. North of the Apennines, the Po River flows through a large, fertile valley that was for centuries the home of Celtic peoples known as Gauls. The hills of Italy, unlike those of Greece, are gentle enough for pasturing. The landscape is of unsurpassed beauty; some of the best Roman poetry—by Virgil, Horace, and Catullus—hymns the delights of the land and the pleasure of farming. But the geography of Italy could also be a challenge. The mountains divide the land into sections and made the task of unifying Italy a long and arduous one.

## ◆ EARLY ROME

The legends about the founding of Rome by Aeneas, a Trojan hero who reached Italy after the Trojan war, or by Romulus and Remus (two mythical sons of the war god Mars) are myths, so we must depend on archaeology to recover early Roman history. Pottery finds suggest that the site of Rome, along the Tiber River in the plain of Latium, was inhabited as early as 1400 B.C. Ancient scholars relied on myths to date the "founding" of Rome in 753 B.C. We need not take this date seriously as the moment at which Rome came into existence, but there must have been considerable habitation in the area by that time, especially on the seven hills that surround the city. About 625 B.C. the settlers drained the marshes below the hills and built a central marketplace, the Forum. This area was to be forever the center of Roman history.

***Etruscan Origins***  Besides the Romans themselves, two other peoples laid the basis for Roman

▲ **This sarcophagus is from a late sixth-century Etruscan tomb. The reclining couple on the lid reflects the influence of Greek art on the style of the Etruscans.**
Alinari/Art Source, NY

history. The first were the Etruscans, who actually dominated early Rome from about 625 to 509 B.C. The name *Roma* is Etruscan, and at least some of the kings of Rome, as their names show, were Etruscans. The origin of the Etruscans themselves is obscure and has provoked a famous controversy. Some ancient sources say that they were a native European people, but the Greek historian Herodotus asserts that they arrived from Asia Minor. In any case, the Etruscans appeared in Italy soon after 800 B.C., in the region north of the Tiber River known as Etruria (their name is preserved in modern Tuscany). Their language is still mostly undeciphered even though thousands of short Etruscan inscriptions exist.

The Etruscans had a technologically advanced culture and traded with Greeks and Phoenicians; Greek vases, especially, have been found in Etruscan tombs, and Etruscan art largely imitates that of the Greeks. They also bequeathed to the Romans the technique of building temples, and they introduced the worship of a triad of gods (Juno, Minerva, Jupiter) and the custom of examining the innards of animals to foretell the future.

*Greek Influence* The second non-Roman people who helped shape Roman culture were the Greeks. Beginning about 750 B.C., they established some 50 poleis in southern Italy and on the island of Sicily. So numerous were the Greek cities in southern Italy that the Romans called this region *Magna Graecia* ("Great Greece") and thus gave us the name *Greeks* for the people who have always called themselves Hellenes.[1]

Greek culture from these colonies influenced the Etruscans and, in turn, the Romans. For example, from the village of Cumae, the oldest Greek colony in Italy, the Etruscans learned the Western version of the Greek alphabet and passed it on to Rome; it became the basis for the alphabet used throughout the Western world. And virtually all Roman literature is inspired by Greek models.

[1]The name *Graikoi* (*Graeci*, or Greeks) was sometimes used, according to Aristotle (*Meteorology* 352) and other sources, for the people generally called Hellenes. The name probably comes from one or more villages in central Greece called Graia; one such place is mentioned in Homer (*Iliad* 2.498).

▲ The art of Etruscan tombs often showed dancing and banqueting in the afterlife. This fifth-century painting, from the Tomb of the Lionesses at Tarquinia, shows two dancers with jugs of wine.
Scala/Art Resource, NY

*The Founding of the Roman Republic*   About 500 B.C. (the Romans reckoned the date as 509) Rome freed itself of its last Etruscan king and established a republican form of government. Roman tradition held that the brother of the last Etruscan king, Tarquinius Superbus, raped a noble matron named Lucretia, who killed herself in shame. This event led to an uprising against the arrogant ruler and to a republican government. The uprising was supposedly led by one Brutus, who became leader of the new state; centuries later, his descendant, Marcus Brutus, was one of the assassins of Julius Caesar and was also seen as a liberator. This legend, true or not, shows why the Romans hated the name *rex* (king) and why they insisted on divisions of power in every phase of their constitution. After the founding of the Republic, the Etruscans gradually declined as a power until they were finally absorbed by the Romans in the fourth century.

## ◆ THE EARLY CONSTITUTION

A large part of the history of the Roman Republic concerns the development of its constitution; this was never a written document but rather a set of carefully observed procedures and customs. The Roman system, like that of Sparta, had three major components, which tended to offset and balance one another. The executives were two officers called consuls, who were the supreme civil and military magistrates. On occasion the Romans appointed a man as "dictator," whose authority surpassed that of the consuls, but his office was limited to six months. There was also an advisory body of elder statesmen called the Senate.

Finally, there were assemblies that included all adult male citizens.

***The Assemblies***   The consuls were elected annually by the Assembly of the Centuries (or Comitia Centuriata), which was made up of the entire army divided, in theory, into 193 groups of 100 men each; in this assembly the wealthier citizens voted first and could determine the result if most of them voted the same way. This arrangement illustrates the hierarchical and conservative instincts of the Roman mind; so does the law providing that, in cases in which the two consuls disagreed, one could block the action of the other, and the consul advocating no action prevailed. Consuls possessed a right known as *imperium,* which gave them the power to command troops and to execute any other assignments they might receive from the Senate.

There were two other assemblies, the more important being the Assembly of Tribes (Comitia Tributa), which was divided into thirty-five large voting blocs called tribes. Membership in a specific tribe was determined by a man's residence. This tribal assembly elected officers who did not command troops and therefore did not have imperium; and these magistrates, known as quaestors and aediles, looked after various financial matters and public works. The other body, actually the oldest of the three, was the Assembly of Curiae (Comitia Curiata), or wards of the city; this assembly met only to validate decisions taken elsewhere and

▼ **This temple in central Rome, from the second century B.C., perhaps dedicated to Portunus, the god of harbors, is a typical Roman temple with a closed room for an image of the god. An altar stood in front. The columns are in the Greek Ionic order, and the temple has a deep basement, common in Etruscan building. Thus the temple unites the three cultures that went into the making of Rome.**
Trëe.

▲ **Many inscriptions, written by professional painters in favor of this or that candidate in elections, have been found on the walls of Pompeii, the city buried in the eruption of A.D. 79.**
Alinari/Art Resource, NY

gradually lost importance. In time, the Assembly of Tribes became the most active of the three assemblies and passed most of Rome's major laws.

*The Senate*    The Senate, which existed in the period of the kings, was the nerve center of the whole state. It did not, in the Republic, pass laws, but it did appoint commanders, assign funds, and generally set public policy. The letters SPQR (standing for "The Senate and the Roman People") were carried on the army's standards and showed the preeminent status of this body. The Roman Senate house, which still stands (rebuilt about A.D. 290) in the Forum, was thus the shrine of Roman power. The senators in the Republic (usually about 300) were men who had held elected offices, and membership was for life. Their solid conservatism acted to restrain hot-headed politicians, and more than once they provided the moral leadership that saw the state through a mil-

itary crisis. Indeed, the word *patres* (fathers) was often used to refer to the Senate.

*The Power of the Family*    Rome had no political parties in the modern sense, but the Senate did have factions, often based on families, that were rivals in the struggle for power. Modern historians have learned how to tell the story of the Republic through the study of the family. Alliances, divorces, marriages, and adoptions could all add to the political power of the family. A larger unit, the *gens* (or clan), included a group of related families consisting of, for example, all Romans whose second name was Cornelius or Aemilius. The great clans and their subdivisions contrived to maintain such firm control over high office that by about 100 B.C. it was rare for any man to reach the consulship who had no previous consul in his family. Such an outsider (for example, the orator Cicero) was referred to as a "new man."

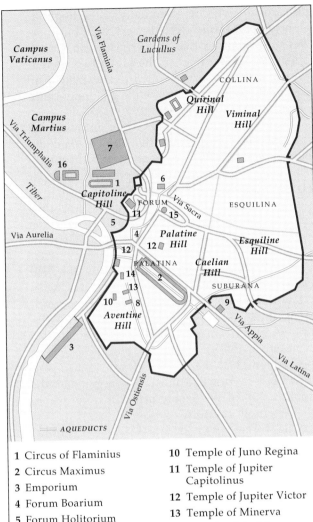

Key to map:

1 Circus of Flaminius
2 Circus Maximus
3 Emporium
4 Forum Boarium
5 Forum Holitorium
6 Comitium
7 Saepta
8 Temple of Diana
9 Temple of Honor and Virtue
10 Temple of Juno Regina
11 Temple of Jupiter Capitolinus
12 Temple of Jupiter Victor
13 Temple of Minerva
14 Temple of the Moon
15 Temple of Vesta
16 Theater of Pompey

▲ MAP 4.1  THE CITY OF ROME IN REPUBLICAN TIMES

*Patron and Client*  Free men of lower standing often attached themselves to an influential citizen and became his clients, while he was their patron. Clients received financial and political support from the patron, whom they in turn followed in political and private life. The size of a man's clientele was an accurate gauge of his power in the state. The Claudian clan is said to have moved to Rome bringing with it a large band of dependents.

The patron-client relationship was recognized in Roman law, which prescribed penalties against a patron who defrauded or mistreated a client.

◆ THE STRUGGLE OF THE ORDERS (494–287 B.C.)

*Patricians and Plebeians*  Within the citizen body, the Romans established a distinction that had no parallel in any Greek state. The patricians, a small number of clans (about five to seven percent of the whole people), were recognized as being socially and legally superior to the vast majority, who were called plebeians. Ancient sources do not explain how the distinction arose; it was probably based on wealth gained from owning land and on the less easily defined criterion of social eminence. Membership in the patrician class was based on birth (or, occasionally, adoption), and originally only patricians could belong to the Senate (the *patres*) and hold office.

The plebeians did win a number of privileges in a long process called the struggle of the orders (or classes). When the struggle ended, the plebeians could point to significant gains, but the great families were still secure in their domination. Indeed, one effect of the struggle of the orders was to make the state an even more efficient machine for conquest: The plebeians could now feel that they had a more favorable position within the system and were thus more willing to fight for their country.

*Concessions to the Plebeians*  The plebeians' first victory in the struggle came in 494 B.C., when they evidently threatened to secede from the state.[2] They now obtained the right to elect annually two men, called tribunes, to represent them; the number eventually rose to ten. The powers of the tribunes reveal the Roman genius for political compromise in the interests of a united state. The patricians evidently recognized that spokesmen for the people were a necessary evil, and oaths were exchanged that made it a religious crime to violate or injure the body of a tribune. The

---

[2]The sources give contradictory dates for, and accounts of, many events in Roman history down to about 280 B.C.; the order adopted here cannot always be proved right in every detail.

"sacrosanctity" of the tribunes allowed them to interfere in any action, since no one could lay hands on them. Out of this protected status arose the famous veto power of the tribunes (sometimes called *intercession*); they could forbid any magistrate from acting and could even arrest consuls. Such power might have threatened to cause anarchy, but in fact, because it reassured the plebeians, it proved to be a stabilizing influence.

Other concessions to the plebeians included the publication of a code of laws, in 450 B.C., on the so-called twelve wooden tablets, and the right, in 445, to intermarry with patricians. Intermarriage created a patrician-plebeian aristocracy that replaced the original one restricted to patricians alone.

**The Licinian-Sextian Laws**   The plebeians won their greatest victory in 367 B.C. Two tribunes, Licinius and Sextius, carried a bill that reserved one consulship every year to a plebeian (there were occasional exceptions, but the principle remained). Their bill also created another office—that of praetor, a kind of assistant consul who also held imperium. His main duty, probably taken away from the consuls, was to be the chief officer

for cases at civil law. Eventually in the Republic eight praetors were elected every year, but there were never more than two consuls at a time. Therefore, as the road to the highest office narrowed, a praetor who wanted to become consul was well advised to observe the generally traditional ways of Roman politics.

The laws of Licinius and Sextius also restricted the amount of public land that any citizen could occupy (the precise acreage allowed is disputed). This measure was supposed to prevent the upper classes from occupying more than a fair share of public land for themselves; but over the years they did precisely this, and the lower orders were often denied their proper amount of farming territory.

**The End of the Struggle of the Orders**   The final concession to the plebeians came in 287 B.C., when a law (the Lex Hortensia)[3] established that decisions of the Assembly of Tribes (or Comitia Tributa, in effect, an assembly of plebeians) were binding on the whole state. Thus the common people now had the absolute legal right to pass laws; but in practice most legislation had the sponsorship of the Senate before it came before the Assembly of Tribes.

The struggle of the orders was a bitter conflict, and only the need to remain united against outside enemies kept it from degenerating into civil war. It led to greater power for the plebeians; but the patrician-plebeian upper class managed to control the changes in the constitution before they could lead to actual direction of affairs by the masses.

## ◆ ROMAN SOCIETY IN THE REPUBLIC

**The Structure of the Roman Family**   The forceful part played by the family in Roman politics was reflected in the organization of the family itself. The Romans accepted direction from the top in most areas of their society, and this kind of structure was built into the family of patricians and plebeians alike. The father of the family, the *paterfamilias*, was the absolute owner of the whole family, which included children, land, other

[3]All Roman laws were named for their proposers, in this case one Hortensius; since *lex* (law) is a feminine noun in Latin, the adjective naming it must end in *-a*.

property, animals, and slaves. So long as he lived, his sons, even if married with their own households, remained in his power. On the death of the father, each of his sons became a *paterfamilias* in his own family. Such a severe system differs from anything known in Greece but has parallels in Israelite society.

*Women in the Early Republic*   The nature of the Roman state, an organization aimed at military defense and expansion, required a constant supply of soldiers. Therefore society designed a role for women that would guarantee the fulfillment of motherhood. Roman legend told that Romulus, the city's mythical founder, led a raid against the Sabines, a neighboring tribe, in which the Romans seized thirty virtuous women to become their wives. This "rape of the Sabines," as it became called, supposedly gave the infant city of Rome a class of strong, loyal women.

▼ **Marble bust of Julius Caesar.**
Archaeological Museum Naples/Dagli Orti/The Archive

Other legends reaffirm the heroic role of women in the early Republic. For example, about 490 a Roman commander, Coriolanus, took sides with a neighboring people in attacking Rome itself. Only the pleas of his wife and his mother persuaded him to halt his troops and lead them away. The legend further says that the women asked the Senate only one reward for their service to the state, namely, to recognize Female Fortune (Fortuna Muliebris) as a goddess and dedicate a temple to her.

*Customs in Marriage*   Despite these tributes to the virtues of Roman women in legend, the early Republic generally kept women in the position of second-class citizens. A young woman normally married at about age fourteen, as in Greece, and was transferred to her new family and lost her right to her native family's property. Her husband was sometimes considerably older and might have been married before, perhaps having lost a wife in childbirth. Wives were legally within the power of their fathers or husbands (again as in ancient Israel), and their chief virtues were considered to be silence and obedience. The sources tell stories about women legally executed by their families for adultery or other offenses.

*Women in the Later Republic*   But this system could not last forever. As Rome became wealthier, the narrow framework of women's lives was loosened, and they began to own significant property. Marriage less often involved the placing of a woman under the absolute power of her husband. The reason for this change was not necessarily a wish to respect women's rights; rather, it was that wealthy families with well-off daughters did not wish to lose control over their property by transferring their wealth out of the family.

Marriages now became less stable, and we find women of prominent families, especially in Rome itself, moving in society and even from husband to husband, with a freedom impossible in Greece. In apparent alarm at the emancipation of women, Marcus Cato, a prominent conservative, spoke in favor of an existing law that forbade women to possess jewelry and wear colored dresses; but his opposition to this luxury tells us that women were doing so in the second century B.C. Despite Cato's dislike of such women's liberation, we do not find in Rome that undercurrent of fear of the mysterious powers of women that can be seen in Greek myth and literature.

***Women and Family Politics***   As in Greece, Roman women could not hold office or vote, but they greatly surpassed Greek women as influences behind the scenes. One especially eminent woman was Cornelia, the daughter of Scipio Africanus, the victorious general in the second Punic War. On the death of her husband she refused all offers of marriage, including one from a king of Egypt, and devoted herself to the education of her twelve children, among whom were the tribunes Tiberius and Gaius Gracchus. She was a woman of high education who maintained a salon and whose letters were praised for their elegant style; indeed, she had a position and prominence unparalleled by that of any woman in classical Greece.

Other women in the Republic also became important as links between powerful families in marriage alliances, which were arranged by fathers, often for the political advantages they could bring with them. One notable such marriage made Julius Caesar the father-in-law of Pompey and cemented the alliance of the two men during Caesar's rise to supreme power. Julia, the daughter of the first emperor, Augustus, was also married to men favored by this emperor in order to continue his family line. The influence of women in politics continued to grow enormously during the Roman Empire, when the long periods of an emperor's reign allowed wives and mothers of rulers to learn and control the levers of power in the imperial court. Yet we must not exaggerate the degree to which Roman women were liberated. In all periods, as in Greece, sarcophagi and tomb reliefs portray men with their wives in conventional poses, and one gravestone for a woman praises her for her domestic virtues: "She was chaste, she was thrifty, she remained at home, she spun wool."

***Religion and Roman Values***   Roman religion consisted largely of forms of worship that upheld Roman tradition. Within the household, the father acted as the priest and led the family in its worship of household gods—for example, Janus, the god protecting the doorway; Vesta, the spirit of the hearth; and household spirits known as Lares and Penates.

◄ A late Republican gravestone showing one Lucius Vibius and his wife and child. Roman realism is evident in the portraiture. The face of the man suggests the determined conservatism that shaped the Roman character during the Republican period.
Scala/Art Resource, NY

Public religion, on the other hand, was closely connected with the interest of the state. Priesthoods were mainly political offices, held only by men. Women were, however, responsible for one of the most important religious duties: It fell to six virgins to maintain the sacred fire of Vesta that guarded the hearth of the state. These Vestal Virgins were held in high honor and lived in a spacious, elegant villa in the Forum; by a remarkable exception, these women were freed of the power of their father.

Roman religion, unlike Greek, often served to maintain conservative old Roman values, such as *pietas* (proper devotion), *dignitas* (the respect that was owed to a good citizen), and *gravitas* (the wish to take things seriously). As to Roman rites, they seem to have been designed mainly to placate the gods, almost to keep them at arm's length, through sacrifices. The Romans believed that their gods would protect them if the gods were shown proper devotion, or *pietas*. The Romans also went to elaborate lengths before declaring war, seeking reasons to believe that the war was just and holy. Eventually some rites hardened into patterns whose original meaning had been forgotten; but so long as the priests did not deviate from routine, the Romans assumed that the gods were satisfied and would not frustrate their enterprises.

*Roman Mythology*   Nearly all of Roman mythology was an adaptation of Greek legend, and Roman gods were often Greek deities with Roman names. The Greek father-god, Zeus, became Iuppiter, or Jupiter; his wife, Hera, became Juno; Athena became Minerva; Hermes became Mercury; and so on. Romans worshiped these gods officially in public and also in the home along with the household deities, these latter being minor gods with no connection to the Greek pantheon. Perhaps because Greek myths often show gods behaving spitefully or immorally, the Romans also created certain uplifting ideals—such as Virtus (manly conduct), Pax (peace), Fides (loyalty), and Pudor (modesty)—and transformed them into gods.

### ◆ EARLY ROMAN LITERATURE

It may seem surprising that it took the Romans centuries to develop a literature. Homeric epic is older than the Greek city-states themselves, but Rome had been independent of the Etruscans for the better part of three centuries before a significant literature emerged. Evidently the Romans needed contact with Greek civilization, which came about during the age of conquest, to stimulate their own literary efforts. After the first Punic War, one Naevius wrote an epic poem about Rome's victory (thus imitating Homer), but it has not survived.

*Comedy*   The earliest preserved Latin literature is the comedies, influenced by the Greeks, of Plautus (250?–184? B.C.) and Terence (190?–159? B.C.). These playwrights imitated Greek New Comedy, as it is called, in which the plays were entirely fiction. The Romans did not approve of Old Comedy, such as the plays of Aristophanes, which savagely lampooned active politicians.

Plautus filled his comedies with stock situations and characters, such as mistaken identities, lecherous old men, and frustrated romances. One of his plays about mistaken identities, the *Menaechmi*, gave Shakespeare the model for his *Comedy of Errors*. Terence wrote comedy in a more refined and delicate style than Plautus. His characters are less earthy, and the humor emerges from more subtle situations or such human foibles as greed.

*Roman Historians: Polybius*   Historical writing, too, began rather late in Rome, around 200 B.C., and the writings of the earliest Roman historians are all lost, surviving only through quotations in other writers. The earliest preserved historical narrative on Rome is from the Greek writer Polybius (200?–118? B.C.). He was deported from Greece as a hostage to Rome in the 160s, where he met many Roman statesmen and became an expert in Roman history. He wrote a general history of the Greco-Roman world from the first Punic War down to his own times, largely to demonstrate the inevitable domination of the Mediterranean by the Romans.

Polybius believed that much of Rome's success in government was due to its well-designed constitution—a commendable mixed form of state that would long maintain Rome's power. He traveled widely and insisted on the need to visit sites in order to grasp the importance of geography to history. His work is analytic and methodical and attempts to revive the high standards of historical writing that Herodotus and Thucydides had established. He is both the most important historian of the Hellenistic Age and the most reliable guide to earlier Roman history.

## ◆ EARLY EXPANSION OF ROME

*Rome's First Conquests*   While the Romans were developing their form of government, they were also expanding their holdings on the Italian peninsula. Sometimes they could use peaceful diplomacy, for example, by making a treaty with neighboring peoples in the plain of Latium. More often they turned to outright military conquest in wars that were clearly long and strenuous. They gained one important victory over the last remaining Etruscan stronghold, the town of Veii, just across the Tiber River, which they took and destroyed in 396 B.C.

*The Invasion by the Gauls*   The period of conquest was not uniformly successful and in fact included one major disaster. In 390 B.C. a marauding tribe of Gauls left their stronghold in the Po valley and captured the city of Rome. The event led to an action that Roman tradition remembered as a heroic deed performed by wealthy Roman women. Rome negotiated a ransom with the Gauls to secure their withdrawal, but only a contribution from women brought the funds up to the full amount demanded. The state honored the women by proclaiming that laudatory orations could be spoken at their funerals. Rome then renewed its policy of expansion, showing the resilience that made it, in the words of the historian Edward Gibbon, "sometimes vanquished in battle, always victorious in war."[4] By the 290s Rome dominated the Italian peninsula as far south as the Greek city-states of Magna Graecia.

*The Roman Army*   No small element in Rome's military victories was the new formation of its army. The Greek phalanx gave way to the system of maniples, or groups of either 60 or 120 men, each commanded by a centurion (roughly a lieutenant in a modern army). The advantage of this system was that the army had both power and versatility, because the maniples could maneuver

independently and could hold together even if the main unit, the legion (6,000 men), lost its formation. About 100 B.C. the maniple was replaced by the cohort (*cohors*), usually a group of 600, but this change was not one of principle, and the cohorts maintained the flexibility of the maniples.

*Pyrrhus Invades Italy*   In the 280s some of the Greek cities of southern Italy, threatened by the growing imperialism of Rome, enlisted Pyrrhus, the king of Epirus (near modern Albania), to save their independence with a campaign against Rome. He brought a large force that included 20 war elephants, a weapon that the Romans had never before confronted. Pyrrhus fought two successful battles in 280 B.C., but at a heavy cost in casualties to his own men (hence the phrase "a Pyrrhic victory"). The Romans again rebounded from defeat, and Pyrrhus abandoned his allies in 275, leaving the Romans free to pursue their conquests. By 265 B.C. Rome controlled the entire Italian peninsula but had not yet mastered the Po valley.

*The Roman Federation*   Rome showed great administrative skill in organizing the conquered communities by establishing different degrees of privilege and responsibility among them. Residents of a few favored communities received the most highly prized status, full Roman citizenship. This status meant that they were on the same legal footing as the Romans; they had the protection of Roman law, they could make legal wills to pass on their property, and they could even hold office in Rome. Members of some other communities became citizens who could not vote but had the right of intermarriage with Romans. At a lower level of privilege were the allied states (*socii*). They enjoyed Rome's protection from other peoples and were also liable to provide troops.

This carefully designed system of confederation enabled the Romans to solve an administrative problem that had frustrated the Greek poleis: how to control a large territory without having to demolish or transform the conqueror's own institutions. Even more important, the creation of this chain of alliances greatly expanded the manpower available to Rome in its progressive domination of the Mediterranean. And as the various communities under Rome's control came more and more to

---

[4]*Decline and Fall of the Roman Empire*, chap. 38.

resemble Rome in social structure, they could climb the rungs up to full Roman citizenship: a powerful stimulus to loyalty that served Rome well in all its conquests.

# II. The Age of Mediterranean Conquest (264–133 B.C.)

Rome had now established its control over the whole Italian peninsula. There followed a period of imperialistic expansion that many historians consider partly involuntary, as Rome became embroiled with other Mediterranean powers. One result, important for the future history of Europe, was the inevitable forming of a system of administering Rome's new territories.

### ◆ THE PUNIC WARS

Rome—by which we now mean not only the ancient city but also the group of peoples in Italy allied with the city—at last had the strength in population to become a world power. The Romans achieved that goal in three wars with Carthage, a city that had been founded by Phoenicians about 700 B.C. and over the next century had established its own Mediterranean empire. By the time Rome had unified the Italian peninsula, Carthage controlled cities in northern Africa, parts of Spain, the islands of Corsica and Sardinia, and much of Sicily. It was beyond comparison the leading naval power in the western Mediterranean and could live off the tribute paid by its possessions. With good reason a German historian called Carthage "the London of antiquity."

*The First Punic War* The first war between Rome and Carthage began in 264 B.C. with a conflict over Messana (modern Messina) in Sicily. It provides a perfect example of how two states can stumble into war. This town was governed by a corps of Italian mercenary soldiers known as Mamertines ("sons of Mars," the Roman god of war). Under threat of conquest by the neighboring city of Syracuse, the Mamertines received troops from Carthage as protectors into their town. Then, when the Carthaginians showed no wish to leave,

## Chronology

### THE ROMAN PROVINCES

The dates when some of the major Roman provinces were legally established. (The actual conquests were sometimes earlier.)

| | |
|---|---|
| 241 B.C. | Most of Sicily (completed in 211). |
| 227 | Corsica and Sardinia, administered as one. |
| 197 | Nearer and Farther Spain. |
| 146 | Macedonia; Africa (former territory of Carthage). |
| 129 | Asia (former territory of Pergamum). |
| ca. 120 | Transalpine Gaul. |
| ca. 81 | Cisalpine Gaul. |
| 62 | Syria. |
| 16–13 | Three Gauls (northern France, formerly conquered by Julius Caesar). |

the Mamertines appealed to Rome to drive them out.

After a hesitant debate, the Romans sent a small force to assist Messana. But, when Carthage replied with more troops of its own, the quarrel escalated into a contest for control of the whole island of Sicily. This was the first of the three Punic Wars, so named from the Latin word *Poeni* for the Phoenicians who had founded Carthage. Roman tenacity finally won this war in 241. In this combat the Romans showed the virtues of which they were most proud—above all determination (*constantia*) and the refusal to be defeated no matter how heavy the casualties. Carthage abandoned Sicily entirely, large parts of the island passed to Rome, and it became the first Roman province (a territory outside Italy controlled by Rome).

In 238 B.C. the Carthaginian garrison on the island of Sardinia rebelled, and the Romans took the opportunity to seize the island. The Carthaginians were also forced to hand over the neighboring island of Corsica, and the two islands, administered together, formed the second Roman province. Carthage was furious over this humiliation, which made a second war with Rome all but inevitable.

***The Second Punic War and Hannibal*** The second of the three wars (219–202 B.C.) was the most critical of all. Carthage, still angry over Rome's seizure of Sardinia and Corsica, sought to build up an empire in southern Spain as some compensation for its losses. In 219 B.C. a quarrel arose over Saguntum, a town in Spain to which Rome had promised protection. The great figure on the Carthaginian side was Hannibal, whose father had made him swear undying hatred of Rome. In 219 he seized Saguntum, thus in effect opening war with Rome. A brilliant and daring strategist, second to almost none in history, he determined to carry the war to the enemy. In autumn 218 he led his army from Spain through the snow across the Alps and down into Italy. He brought with him 37 elephants, the irresistible weapon in ancient war (all but one of them soon died).

Once in Italy Hannibal hoped to arouse the tribes of Gauls in the Po valley and end the alliances of the various peoples with Rome, following which he would conquer Rome itself. Despite his energy, his twofold strategy failed. In 216 B.C. he won a stupendous victory over the Romans at Cannae, in southeastern Italy, which has remained a classic study for strategists ever since; but not even then could he bring about a revolt of the allies. Their loyalty is a testimony to Rome's enlightened statesmanship. At least half of them remained faithful to Rome, and without their help Hannibal's manpower was no match for that of Rome.

***Publius Cornelius Scipio*** While Hannibal was in Italy, the Roman commander Publius Cornelius Scipio, only 26 years old, carried the war into Spain. Scipio was the first man given such a command without having held higher office. He apparently had absolute faith in the favor of the gods and could inspire his men with this conviction. In 209 B.C. he captured the important city of New Carthage and by 206 he controlled most of Spain. In 204 he landed in Africa, near Carthage itself, where his victories brought about the recall of Hannibal from Italy and set the stage for a final clash between these two great generals and their forces. Scipio won the decisive battle in 202, at Zama in North Africa. In honor of the victory, Scipio received the name *Africanus* and proudly added it to his traditional Roman name. Besides

▲ MAP 4.2 ITALY IN 265 B.C., ON THE EVE OF THE PUNIC WARS

paying Rome a huge indemnity, Carthage had to give up all its territory except its immediate surroundings in Africa and was forbidden to raise an army without Roman permission.

Thus the second war ended in a hard-earned victory for Roman perseverance and skill; but a large bill would later have to be paid. Hannibal had laid waste large tracts of farming land in southern Italy and had driven many farmers off their soil. In casualties, too, the cost to Rome had been severe: It is estimated that Roman military manpower fell from about 285,000 in 218 to about 235,000 in 203.

***The Third Punic War*** After the second war, Rome made an alliance with Masinissa, the king of Numidia, just west of Carthage. Over the years

Masinissa began to plunder Carthaginian territory and drove Carthage to the point of armed resistance against him. In Rome a bitterly anti-Carthaginian group was led by Marcus Cato, whose name has become symbolic of narrow intolerance. He and his group argued that Carthage was still dangerous; he constantly urged that it be destroyed. Finally he succeeded in persuading Rome to declare war against Carthage and in making it a campaign of punishment (149–146 B.C.).

Another Scipio, known as Scipio Aemilianus, captured Carthage in 146. The Romans utterly destroyed the city and formally cursed the site (the tale that they poured salt into the soil is only a modern fiction), and the territory became the Roman province called simply Africa. The conquest of the territory formerly held by Carthage in Europe was complete when Rome conquered almost all of Spain by 133 B.C.

### ◆ EXPANSION IN THE EASTERN MEDITERRANEAN

***Wars with Macedonia and Syria*** In the following decades the Romans continued their conquests until they had mastered the whole Mediterranean basin. Historians have long debated whether this policy represented deliberate imperialism or was at least partly accidental. Certainly the first stage was forced on Rome by the king of Macedonia, Philip V (r. 221–179 B.C.). He drew Rome into war by forming an alliance with Hannibal in 215 B.C. and thus opened the gate through which, over centuries, Roman troops and administrators poured as far east as Armenia and changed the course of European history.

During this era Rome also became involved in war with Antiochus III, the Macedonian ruler of Syria, the kingdom founded by Seleucus after the death of Alexander. Roman forces defeated his army at Magnesia in Asia Minor in 190 B.C.—another significant moment in Rome's expansion, as Roman legions left Europe and fought in Asia Minor for the first time.

***Annexation of Greece*** For a time, the Romans tried to stay out of Greek affairs and proclaimed that they were allowing the Greeks freedom. To the Greeks, freedom meant the liberty to do as they liked, but for the Romans it meant behaving as obedient Roman clients. After further quarrels and battles, the Roman Senate realized that outright annexation of the Greek mainland was the only way to secure Rome's interests.

Therefore, in 146 B.C., Macedonia and Greece were combined into a province. This decision brought the Romans into permanent contact with Greek culture, which they passed on over the centuries to Europe. They had already destroyed Carthage, and as they took over Greece their dominance in the Mediterranean could not be denied or reversed. But this domination came at a price. Without the need for unity against outside enemies, Roman society began to lose its cohesiveness; this in turn led to the decline of the Republic.

***The Province of Asia*** Some experienced rulers in the region were shrewd enough to perceive what had happened and began a process of accommodation to Rome. For example, in 133 B.C., the last king of Pergamum died without leaving a successor and the Romans found that he had willed his kingdom to Rome—surely because he had seen that the kingdom of Pergamum could not long survive without Roman protection. Four years later Rome created the province of Asia, based on the territory of Pergamum (see map 4.3). This province possessed great wealth and offered tempting opportunities for a governor of Asia to enrich himself through corruption; the post became highly desirable for ambitious politicians and also brought with it a posting to the pleasant climate of the beautifully built Greek cities.

### ◆ THE NATURE OF ROMAN EXPANSION

***Organization and Force*** Rome's success in its domination of the Mediterranean rested on certain unique historical conditions. Early in its history, events had forced the city to seek defensive alliances. After the expulsion of the Etruscan monarchs, for example, Rome had to unite militarily with its neighbors in the plain of Latium against a possible Etruscan counterattack. Constant wars in the fourth and third centuries, such as the invasion by the Gauls in 390 B.C., further emphasized the need for common security.

The result was a commitment to, and mastery of, military force that proved to be unsurpassed,

**▲ MAP 4.3 THE EXPANSION OF THE ROMAN REPUBLIC, 241–44 B.C.**
◆ www.mhhe.com/chambers8ch4maps

Roman Republic in 241 B.C.

Expansion to 44 B.C.

✕ Battle site

and this military force soon developed into a highly effective and (when necessary) utterly ruthless policy of conquest. Scipio Aemilianus, for example, forced the people of Numantia, in Spain, to surrender in 133 B.C., by reducing them to cannibalism and even cut off the hands of four hundred young men in a neighboring city who had advocated aiding their Spanish brethren. The Senate at home considered Aemilianus' achievements worthy of a triumphal parade, the highest military honor that Romans could bestow on a successful commander.

*Provincial Administration* The Latin word *provincia* means "a duty assigned to a magistrate," and the Romans extended the meaning to denote the various regions that they acquired through conquest. The Senate chose the governors for the various provinces, often giving them the title *pro-*

*consul* ("in place of a consul"). These governors ruled their provinces with absolute power, though they could not violate Roman law or act illegally against Roman citizens. Some provincial governors ruled fairly, but others were notorious for their corruption. From the Roman view, the advantage of the system was its efficiency: Rebellions were not common, and troops stationed in the provinces could maintain control without resorting to massacres.

*Tax Collectors, or* **Publicani**   The provinces furnished financial support for the Roman Republic. Some had to pay tribute in various forms, usually food, while others were assigned a fixed sum of money. In order to obtain these taxes, the state devised a convenient but corruptible system of tax collection. Companies of tax collectors, known as *publicani*, bid for the contracts to collect the taxes of certain provinces, especially Asia. The collectors paid the state a fixed sum in advance and then made their profit by collecting taxes in excess of what they had paid. The governor of the province was supposed to see that the *publicani* did not collect more than a specified sum. Unfortunately, however, the collectors could use their funds as bribes to persuade the governor to overlook their rapacity.[5]

**The Equestrians**   The tax collectors came from a class known as equestrians. The *equites* originally formed the cavalry in Rome's military forces, but over the years the equestrians stopped fighting on horseback and became a social class, roughly the businessmen of Rome. Equestrians did not serve in the Senate. They had to be of high financial standing, and some of them could far outstrip senators in wealth. They held no political offices but formed companies to build roads and aqueducts and to conduct businesses of all kinds.

# III. The Roman Revolution (133–27 b.c.)

The year 133 b.c. saw the final conquest of most of Spain, in the west, and the acquisition of the province of Asia, in the east. This was also the beginning of the Roman revolution, a long political transformation that ended the Roman Republic. Imperialism demanded powerful military commanders, and the selfish rivalry among them burst the bounds of the constitution.

## ◆ SOCIAL CHANGE AND THE GRACCHI

**The Changing World of Italy**   The breakdown of the Roman Republic has been called Hannibal's legacy, for the ravages of years of fighting up and down Italy had brought many farmers to the point of ruin. On the other hand, wealthy citizens had enriched themselves with booty and the spoils of war. The less fortunate had often lost their land or were willing to sell it to these newly wealthy men. There had also been a great increase

---

[5]Cicero, a firm supporter of the *publicani,* called them "the flower of the Roman equestrians, the ornament of the state, and the foundation of the Republic."

---

*Chronology*

# THE ROMAN REVOLUTION

The main landmarks in the Roman revolution were as follows:

| | |
|---|---|
| **133 b.c.** | Tiberius Gracchus elected tribune; is killed in riot. |
| **123–122** | Gaius Gracchus tribune; equestrians gain control of extortion court; Gaius killed. |
| **107** | First consulship of Marius. |
| **91–88** | War with Italian allies. |
| **81–79** | Sulla's dictatorship. |
| **70** | First consulship of Pompey and Crassus. |
| **66** | Pompey given command against Mithridates in Asia. |
| **59** | Julius Caesar consul, receives command in Gaul. |
| **58–50** | Caesar's conquest of Gaul. |
| **49** | Caesar invades Italy, opening of civil war. |
| **44** | Caesar murdered. |
| **31** | Battle of Actium, defeat of Mark Antony. |
| **27** | Supremacy of Octavian, later called Augustus; beginning of Roman Empire. |

in the slave population on Italian soil from prisoners of war, and these slaves depressed the wages paid to private workers.

Often the displaced farmers had little choice but to join the ranks of the permanently unemployed. Their poverty threatened to impede the recruitment of soldiers into the Roman army, for Rome had nothing like a modern war treasury, and only men who had enough money to buy their own armor could be drafted into the legions. Without sufficient recruits, the gains from the conquests might be lost. Moreover, those who could no longer find work lost the spirit of cohesion and loyalty to their society. They became prey to demagogues and many became supporters of this or that warlord. The Senate, which might have provided moral leadership to the state, also showed itself unable to stand firm as the long revolution rolled on.

### Tiberius Gracchus

Two ambitious young Roman statesmen, Tiberius and Gaius Gracchus, moved to solve the problems of those who had lost their land. Their mother, Cornelia, was a well-known daughter of a great family; her father was Publius Cornelius Scipio Africanus, who had won the war against Hannibal. She had married a prominent plebeian politician, Tiberius Gracchus. Because patrician or plebeian status came down through the male line, her sons were plebeian, though descended from the loftiest aristocracy.

Tiberius, the older brother (162–133 B.C.), became tribune in 133 and proposed a bill to the Assembly of Tribes that would assign parcels of publicly owned land to dispossessed farmers. The state would obtain and redistribute such land by enforcing a long-ignored law that limited the amount of public land that anyone could occupy. To serve in the Roman army, a man had to have at least a modest amount of wealth, and Tiberius' aim, a moderate one, was to create prosperous farmers and thus increase the supply of potential recruits for the army. He made the mistake of not submitting his bill for the approval of the Senate before proposing it. Angered at this slight, some senators found another tribune willing to oppose the bill with his veto. Tiberius then persuaded the people to remove that tribune from office. This action was both illegal and dangerous. Once such a step had been taken, what tribune would be safe in the future from an identical threat? But the people followed Tiberius and passed the bill.

### Tiberius Murdered

The distribution of land was in progress when Tiberius decided to run for re-election. This move was a breach of custom, for tribunes held office for only one year. Some of his opponents feared that he might seize permanent leadership of the propertyless and lead them into social revolution. A group of senators, late in 133, took the law into their own hands and provoked a riot in which Tiberius was clubbed to death—an event that gave grim warning of a new intensity in Rome's political struggles. Above all, this action violated the taboo against assassination of a tribune, and this first step, once taken, became easier to repeat. Despite Tiberius' death, the distribution of land continued, and his enemies even took credit for the success of the project.

### Gaius Gracchus

Tiberius' younger brother, Gaius, became tribune ten years later, in 123 B.C. He was the harsher and less compromising of the two plebeians. He remembered that some senators had inspired the murder of his brother, and he wanted to reply with several measures that sought to limit the powers of senators. He proposed, and the people accepted, that the Senate's freedom in assigning governors to provinces should be restricted. One of the most important powers of the Senate was membership in the extortion court, which investigated cases of alleged extortion by provincial governors and tax collectors. The jurors, all senators, were usually not severe in judging governors, who were fellow members of the Senate. Gaius had a bill passed that assigned the seats on this jury to members of the equestrian class.

All tax collectors were equestrians, and it was now they who had the potential to favor members of their group who might be accused and brought to trial for extortion. Gaius' arrangements were later revised, but he was the first to make the extortion court the subject of a bitter political quarrel.

### The Fall and Death of Gaius Gracchus

Gaius had also followed his brother Tiberius in authoring a bill that continued the distribution of public land. It included provisions for the founding of colonies where more citizens could be settled. But he committed a major blunder in proposing to found a colony of Roman citizens on the site of Carthage, the hated enemy in the three Punic wars. This ill-judged action aroused widespread criticism.

Like his brother, Gaius Gracchus came to a violent end. He failed to be elected to a third year as tribune, and his enemies asserted that he and his followers were planning a revolution. The Senate then ordered one of the consuls for the year 121 B.C. to "see to it that the state suffered no harm," thus inviting the consul to use force to suppress the younger Gracchus. This resolution, which was later passed against others whom the Senate wanted to eliminate, was known in Roman politics as the "last decree" (*Senatus consultum ultimum*). When the consul raised up a mob to hunt Gaius down, he had one of his own slaves kill him.

***The Gracchi and History***   The Gracchi had unleashed a whirlwind when they invited the Assembly of Tribes to take a more activist role. It is true that the people had long possessed the right to legislate in this assembly, but they had not always had the will; nor had ambitious tribunes always dared to use such a weapon. But now demagogues began to turn more and more to this assembly to pass bills in favor of their military patrons. From this moment began the slow but sure Roman revolution.

### ◆ THE YEARS OF THE WARLORDS

The Gracchi could not protect themselves from the violence of the Senate because they had no army. But as Roman conquests brought the state into further wars, powerful generals appeared who did have the support of their armies and used it to seize power. Their struggles against one another undermined the republican constitution and the state finally collapsed into dictatorship.

***Marius and a Changed Roman Army***   The first general to play this game was Gaius Marius (157?–86 B.C.), from the countryside near Rome. In Roman terminology, he was a "new man" or *novus homo*, that is, a man none of whose ancestors had been consul. He was a roughneck, of little education, but stalwart and fearless. He is a crucial figure because he changed, radically and forever, the membership of the Roman army and the direction of its loyalty. He gained high prestige by winning a war (111–106 B.C.) against Jugurtha, the king of Numidia in North Africa. Marius had obtained this command after the generals who had been sent out by the Senate had proved incompetent; and Marius showed his hatred for the feeble aristocrats who had thoroughly bungled the campaign.

Marius' reputation grew even more after he drove back an attempted invasion (105–101 B.C.) by some Germanic tribes moving toward northern Italy. Such was his stature in this period that he was consul for five consecutive years and dominated politics from 107 to 100 B.C.

In order to raise large numbers of men for his army, Marius abolished the old requirement that a soldier had to own at least a modest amount of property, and he also accepted volunteers instead of just drafting men for service (the men so enrolled were known as *capite censi*, "enrolled by head count"). As a result, the army came to be composed largely of poor men who served their commander, received booty from him, relied on him as their main patron, and expected him to obtain for them a grant of land that they could farm after they were discharged. Thus Marius converted the army into an instrument for ambitious commanders during the remaining years of the Republic and even throughout the Roman Empire.

***The War with the Italians***   The Italian peoples who were Rome's allies had never been granted Roman citizenship, and in 91 B.C. another reform-minded tribune, Marcus Livius Drusus, tried to carry a bill that would have made them citizens. The Senate declared his law null and void, and Drusus, like the Gracchi, was murdered. At this outrage some of the allies proclaimed themselves independent and opened a war that continued until 88. In the end the Romans negotiated with the Italians and allowed them to acquire citizenship. But the fact that it required a war to obtain this concession shows that both the Roman upper classes—the senators and equestrians—and the Roman masses were still protective of their privileges.

***Sulla the Dictator***   The Italian War made the reputation of another powerful general, Lucius Cornelius Sulla (138?–78 B.C.). He was a man without any scruples, a glutton and sensualist who helped himself to whatever women he liked. In the 80s civil war broke out in Rome over who should obtain the command in a war against Mithridates, the king of Pontus in Asia Minor (r. 120–63 B.C.). One group rallied behind Sulla and his legions, seeing in him the best vehicle for their own ambitions. In 88 he invaded the city of Rome with his supporters—the first but not the last time that Romans themselves marched on and seized the ancient city.

Mithridates had extended his kingdom until it included the Roman province of Asia and even large parts of the Greek mainland. In 88 B.C. he gave orders for the massacre of at least 80,000 Romans and Italians residing in Asia Minor—a testimony to the unpopularity of Roman rule in this province. This massacre could not go unanswered, and Sulla received the command against Mithridates.

Sulla departed for his campaign in 87 B.C., and during his absence Marius and his supporters seized Rome in turn. They conducted a reign of terror, publishing lists ("proscriptions") of those to be killed either with or without "trials" and exhibiting their maimed bodies and even their heads in the streets. But as soon as Sulla was free of his Eastern war, he returned to Italy and once more occupied Rome (November 82). Our sources tell us that he had thousands of his opponents executed and had himself named dictator without limit of time, thus breaking the customary six-month limit for holding that office.

*Sulla's Reforms*   For all Sulla's brutality and self-indulgence, he did have a political program: to reshape the state on strictly authoritarian and conservative lines. Two forces, he thought, had menaced the rigid control over Rome that the Senate should enjoy: the tribunes of the people, who had made the Assembly of Tribes more conscious of its power, and the generals who had used the loyalty of their armies to gain political leverage. To deal with the first of these threats, Sulla forced through a law that blocked tribunes from holding any other office; they also had to wait ten years to be reelected. These measures were meant to discourage any ambitious politicians from seeking this office.

Sulla handled the army commanders through a law that forbade them to leave their provinces or make war outside their borders without instructions from the Senate; thus, no ambitious commander could blunder into a war or make himself into a conqueror. Sulla further established minimum ages at which a man might hold the various offices in a political career (a consul, for example, had to be 42 or older). He also canceled the work of Gaius Gracchus on the jury system; as one might expect from this strict traditionalist, he gave all the seats on the juries back to senators.

Sulla resigned the dictatorship in 79 B.C., a rare act in any supreme ruler, but he evidently thought

▲ **This idealized statue of the first century B.C. shows the ruthless tyrant Cornelius Sulla in the dignified pose of a classical orator.**
Giraudon/Art Resource, NY

he had put the Senate so firmly in control that he was no longer needed; he died in 78. To his enemies he was pitiless, and his executions of Roman citizens were horrifying, but he was also a political strategist. He had done his part for the conservative cause by putting the Senate in charge, but this body proved unable to manage the next generation of warlords.

*The Rise of Pompey* Sulla had used the tool forged by Marius—an army loyal to a commander—and another warlord soon followed his example, namely Gnaeus Pompeius (106–48 B.C.), usually called Pompey. He first gained a reputation in 77 B.C., when he was sent to Spain to end a revolt there. After completing this task, and while his army was still intact, he helped suppress a rebellion of slaves in Italy led by a Thracian slave named Spartacus. This campaign was already under the command of another ambitious Roman, Marcus Licinius Crassus, the richest man of his time. Pompey and Crassus were rivals, but they worked together in suppressing the revolt. No sooner did the slave revolt collapse in 71 B.C. than the joint commanders, Pompey and Crassus, marched their armies to the gates of Rome and demanded both consulships for the year 70. Pompey was legally unqualified for this office, for he was only 36 and had held no previous magistracy. If Crassus, Pompey's rival, had refused to join in this bargain, he might have preserved the Sullan system. But, like him, the Senate also lacked the will to enforce the constitution and resist the two men, and they won election as consuls. This was little short of a coup d'état.

During their consulship Pompey and Crassus canceled several of Sulla's arrangements. They restored to the tribunes their right to propose legislation, and they mixed senators and equestrians in the always controversial juries. At the end of their year in office, both consuls retired without demanding any further appointment—an action that, though at first surprising, was really consistent with Pompey's ambitions. He wanted to be the first man in the state, but he disliked committing himself to open revolution. A modern historian has compared him to Shakespeare's Macbeth: He would not play false and yet would wrongly win.

*Pompey's Military Commands* In 67 B.C. Pompey obtained an extraordinary command to deal with pirates operating in the Mediterranean who were interfering with the grain supply for Rome—a critical matter since the city had to live on grain shipped to its harbor. Pompey fulfilled his orders and cleared the seas in a swift campaign. He also recognized the economic roots of piracy and settled many of the captured pirates on land that they could cultivate in Asia Minor and Greece. Then in 66 B.C. he received through the Tribal Assembly an even more important command in Asia Minor, where Rome was involved in war with Mithridates, Sulla's old enemy, who was still on his throne.

Another Roman general, Lucullus, had practically wiped out Mithridates' forces, so Pompey's campaign was essentially a mopping-up operation. But Pompey took action that had permanent results; he set up a system of client kings, rulers of smaller states whose loyalty to Rome was ensured by the device of "friendship" (*amicitia*). This arrangement was an informal bargain through which Rome would protect local rulers, who paid no taxes to Rome but were expected to assist with manpower and resources when needed. He also captured Syria in 64 B.C.; it became a Roman province in 62 B.C.

*Cicero: Nonmilitary Statesman* During Pompey's absence overseas, Marcus Tullius Cicero (106–43 B.C.) became the chief nonmilitary statesman in Rome. Like Marius, he was a "new man" from the countryside, but unlike Marius, Cicero chose a career in law and administration rather than in the military. His administrative skill won for him each successive political office at the earliest possible legal age. He was genuinely dedicated to compromise and political negotiation and thought that such procedures would establish the combined rule of the two upper classes, the senatorial and equestrian.

Cicero was elected consul for 63 B.C. One of his defeated rivals for the office, Catiline (Lucius Sergius Catilina), formed a conspiracy to take over the city by force. Cicero learned details of this plan and denounced Catiline in four famous speeches (the "Catilinarian" orations). He obtained the Senate's support to execute some of the captured conspirators without trial (a wholly illegal act); Catiline himself died in battle against an army of the state.

Cicero was the most versatile Latin writer of his time, and his polished prose style became the model in Latin for clarity and elegance. He also wrote philosophical treatises. Cicero's treatises do not follow the doctrines of any particular school; he was equally interested in Stoicism, the thought of Plato, and several other schools, and he chose whatever seemed persuasive from Greek writings for his own theories. In *On the Republic,* for example, Cicero accepted the Platonic view that wise leaders ought to govern the state, but he disregarded the more technical aspects of Plato's philosophy.

*Cicero and Other Factions*   Cicero's political speeches are a continuous record of his career and his frustrated ambitions. He enjoyed his political success as a "new man" and sought a place for himself among the upper classes, believing that they should guide the state along established constitutional lines. Unfortunately, most politicians in the later Republic felt little allegiance to the constitution and selfishly followed their own personal advantage. Cicero never became a magnetic leader around whom others gathered. His letters are a frank and often painful record of the compromises forced on him in the treacherous world of Roman politics.

*Pompey Returns to Rome*   When Pompey returned to Rome in 62 B.C. from his Eastern victories, he had two political aims. He wanted the Senate to ratify the arrangements he had made in Asia Minor; and he requested a grant of land for his men. This latter request, as we have seen, was nothing unusual. It reflected the relationship between a general and his troops, which was that of patron and client—one of the oldest traditions in Rome. But some senators, either jealous or fearful of his prestige, combined to frustrate his wishes. This short-term victory practically doomed the Senate and the Republic, for it drove Pompey into a political alliance with Julius Caesar, who proved to have the revolutionary will that Pompey lacked.

## ◆ THE FIRST TRIUMVIRATE

*The Partners and Their Desires*   Gaius Julius Caesar (100–44 B.C.), a descendant of an old patrician family, returned to Rome in 60 B.C. from his post as governor of Spain. Intellectually, he was a brilliant man who wrote elegant, lean Latin. Politically, he is an example of the aristocrat who bases his power on the common people. In this respect he resembles Pericles in Athenian history. Caesar had enemies within the Senate, where many looked on him as a brash upstart or a potential tyrant. They refused his request to be allowed to run for the consulship of 59 in absence and then lead a triumphal parade through the city. Faced with this direct affront to his dignity, Caesar made a political bargain with Pompey. Crassus joined them because he was at odds with some powerful senators over a financial matter. The three formed a coalition known to historians as the First Triumvirate ("body of three men"; it had no official mandate or status). Their united influence at the polls over their clients elected Caesar as one of the consuls for 59. To confirm the bargain in a manner

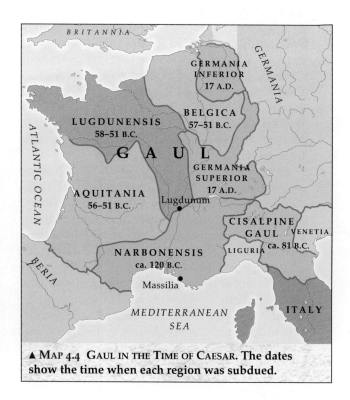

▲ MAP 4.4  GAUL IN THE TIME OF CAESAR. The dates show the time when each region was subdued.

customary in Roman politics, Pompey married Caesar's daughter, Julia.

### Caesar's Consulship and the Gallic War

Caesar's influence secured allotments of land for Pompey's army and the approval of his arrangements in the East. Crassus' financial quarrel was also settled to his satisfaction. Caesar then secured for himself the command over Cisalpine Gaul (the Po valley) and the coast of Illyria for a guaranteed period of five years beginning on March 1, 59 B.C.

About this time the governor of Transalpine Gaul (Provence, in the south of France) died, and the Senate added this province as well to Caesar's command.

Caesar intervened in the politics of the Gallic tribes and opened a series of campaigns that finally brought the whole area of modern France and Belgium under Roman rule. The Romans implanted in Gaul the Latin language (the origin of modern French), Roman technology, and Roman ways in general. Caesar narrated and defended

▼ Perhaps the most spectacular classical monument in Europe, the Pont du Gard was built in the first century A.D. to carry water to Nîmes (ancient Nemausus) in France. The water ran through a trough above the top layer of arches. The aqueduct is an example of the Romans' mastery of hydraulic technology and construction in arches.
Michael Holford Photographs

his actions in his *Commentaries on the Gallic War,* which to this day remains a superb textbook in political-military decision making.

The Gallic War lasted from 58 to 50 B.C. Caesar's two partners in the triumvirate, Pompey and Crassus, were always suspicious of each other, but they maintained fairly good relations and even held a second consulship together in 55. They also had Caesar's command in Gaul renewed for another five years, so that it would not expire until March 1, 49, and they obtained commands for themselves. Crassus went out to Syria, from which he launched a disastrous campaign against the kingdom of Parthia, across the Euphrates River. Here he lost his life in 53 B.C. Pompey was given command over the two provinces of Spain, which he governed through assistants, preferring to remain at the center of power near Rome.

### ◆ THE SUPREMACY OF JULIUS CAESAR

*The Break between Caesar and the Senate*    Caesar's conquest of Gaul greatly enriched the state, but to his enemies it was a cause of dismay. They feared that he might use his victories and his popularity among the people to become another, and perhaps a permanent, Sulla. As protection against Caesar, his enemies in the Senate began to draw Pompey into their camp. Some of them had quarreled with him in the past, but they were willing to gamble that they could eliminate him when they no longer needed him.

As 49 B.C. opened, the Senate met in a state near hysteria. A small band of implacable senators forced through a motion ordering Caesar to lay down his command, even though he was then taking no action beyond remaining in his province of Cisalpine Gaul. The Senate passed a decree establishing martial law (that is, the "last decree," which had been invented for use against Gaius Gracchus) and ordered Pompey to command the armies of Rome against Caesar. The ill-advised Pompey accepted the command; but in doing so he signed his own death warrant and condemned the Republic to extinction in yet another civil war.

*The Attack on the Tribunes of the People*    Finally, the Senate defied the oldest of Roman traditions by threatening the lives of any tribunes who opposed these extreme measures. They thus handed Caesar a superb theme for his own propaganda: He could proclaim that he was defending the rights of the tribunes, of the common people of Rome who had elected them, and of the men in his army who had loyally served in the Gallic wars.

*Caesar's Invasion of Italy*    Caesar saw that his enemies were in effect challenging him to war and decided that he had no course but to fight for his dignity and, as he could now assert, for the people and their sacred tribunes. On about January 11, 49 B.C., he spoke the words, "The die is cast," and crossed the boundary of his province, the small Rubicon River north of Ravenna, thus invading his own country at the head of Roman legions. Yet perhaps his conscience was not wholly clear: The biographer Plutarch records the tale that, on the night before the crossing, he dreamt that he was having sexual relations with his own mother.

Caesar advanced swiftly, and Pompey and his followers had to retreat to Greece; Caesar pursued them and won a decisive battle in 48 B.C. at the town of Pharsalus, in Thessaly. Pompey sought refuge in Egypt, but advisers to the pharaoh realized that Caesar had won the victory and that it was not safe for them to give Pompey protection. As Pompey approached the shore, he was stabbed to death by a former Roman officer of his. His head was cut off and his body thrown into the sea. Caesar followed to Egypt in October 48 B.C. and found that Pompey was dead. He now intervened in a civil war between the young king, Ptolemy XIII, and his sister, the famous Macedonian ruler Cleopatra VII. Caesar arranged that Ptolemy and Cleopatra should share the rule and proceeded to have a long affair with the queen. A boy, called Caesarion (the Little Caesar), was born.[6] Politics played as much a role as love, because Cleopatra's affection guaranteed Roman control over the rich resources of Egypt; Caesar did not follow the usual practice of making Egypt a province but left it as a kingdom to be ruled by Cleopatra and Ptolemy. After other victories Caesar returned to Rome in 46.

---

[6]Scholars have always been uncertain whether Caesar was really the father of this boy.

▲ An arena in El-Djem, Tunisia, imitating the Colosseum in Rome. Built in the second/third century A.D., this arena could seat 50,000 spectators. Wild animals were housed in the long rectangular pit in the center. Roman buildings were widely copied throughout the Empire as other cities sought to identify themselves with the great capital.
Photo Researchers, Inc.

***Caesar's Rule to 44 B.C.*** Caesar now decided to make his rule impregnable and assumed the positions of both dictator and consul. On the model of Sulla, he extended his dictatorship beyond the legal six-month limit; then, in 44, he had himself named dictator for life. He swept aside all restraints on his power that Roman tradition might have imposed and took complete authority to pass laws, declare war, and appoint men to office.

As dictator, Caesar saw to a series of rapid reforms in many areas of Roman life. He raised the membership of the Senate to about nine hundred, packing it with many of his veteran officers. From this time onward the Senate lost its former authority as the bulwark of the state. He scaled down his large army by settling many of his soldiers in newly founded colonies and extended Roman citizenship into some of the provinces. His most lasting reform was one by which we still regulate our lives—the establishment of a calendar based on the old Egyptian reckoning of 365 days, with one day added every fourth year. This "Julian" calendar lasted until 1582, when it was revised by Pope Gregory XIII to our present Gregorian calendar.

## THE MURDER OF JULIUS CAESAR

*The biographer Plutarch, who wrote about A.D. 120, looked back to describe the scene when Caesar was killed, 44 B.C.*

"The place chosen for this murder, where the Senate met on that day, contained a statue of Pompey, one of the adornments for the theater he had built; this made it clear to all that some divine power had guided the deed and summoned it to just that spot. As Caesar entered, the Senate rose as a sign of respect, while those in Brutus' faction came down and stood around his chair. Tillius Cimber seized Caesar's toga with both hands and pulled it down from his neck, which was the signal for the assassination. Casca was the first to strike him in the neck with his sword, but the wound was neither deep nor fatal, and Caesar turned around, grasping and holding the weapon. Those who knew nothing of the plot were terrified and did not dare run away or help Caesar or even utter a sound. But those who came prepared for the murder whipped out their daggers, and Caesar was encircled, so that wherever he turned he met with blows and was surrounded by daggers leveled at his face and eyes and he was grappling with all their hands at once. Everyone was supposed to strike him and have a taste of the murder; even Brutus stabbed him once in the groin. Some say that, as he fought off all the rest, turning his body this way and that and shouting for help, he saw Brutus draw his dagger and pulled his toga down over his head and let himself fall at the base of Pompey's statue, whether by chance or because he was pushed by the assassins. There was blood all around the statue, so that it seemed that Pompey was presiding over the vengeance taken against his enemy, who now lay at his feet and breathed out his life through his wounds. They say he was struck 23 times, and many of the assassins were wounded by one another as they all directed their blows at his body."

Plutarch, *The Life of Caesar*, chap. 66, M. H. Chambers (tr.).

*The Death of Caesar*   The full effect of Caesar's plans was not to be realized, for on March 15, 44 (the date known as the Ides of March), after four years of supremacy, he fell to the daggers of conspirators led by two of his lieutenants, Marcus Brutus and Gaius Cassius. His autocracy had been a grave affront to the upper class; because he had undermined their dignity as members of the governing class, they united against Caesar and carried out the most famous political murder in all history. It is said that Caesar was warned that morning of an imminent conspiracy and that he brushed the warning aside. As the Senate met near a theater built by Pompey, the killers plunged on him; when he recognized his protégé, Marcus Brutus in the group, he said in Greek, "You, too, my boy?" and covered his head with his toga as he fell. His body was carried to the Forum and burned on a rock that still stands in a small temple built to his memory after his death (see "The Murder of Julius Caesar," above).

Caesar's character is baffling and controversial, even as it was to his contemporaries. He was pitiless toward Gauls and Germans, and he enriched himself by selling prisoners of war as slaves; but indifference toward captured foreigners was common in the ancient world. In Rome he showed too little respect for the Senate and republican forms once he became dictator, and for this mistake he paid with his life. On the other hand, in the civil war he was generous enough to dismiss opposing generals whom he had captured, and they lived to fight him another day. Such actions may have rested on cool calculation of their value as propaganda, but they may also show genuine gallantry. No one can question Caesar's fiery leadership. He was wiry and tough, he ignored heat and rain, he swam unfordable rivers, and his troops followed him into Italy with enthusiasm and fought with amazing discipline.

Caesar clearly thought that the old institutions of the Senate and the assemblies were obsolete. "The Republic," he is said to have remarked, "is only a name without body or face, and Sulla did not know the ABCs of politics in resigning his dictatorship."[7] The political weakness of the late Republic largely confirms this harsh evaluation. But in the end Caesar's arrogance was too much for the experienced politicians whom he needed for his administration. His career thus blends triumph and tragedy. He rose to the absolute summit of Roman politics, but in doing so he destroyed both the Roman Republic and himself.

# IV. The End of the Roman Republic

Julius Caesar's dictatorship had all but killed the Roman Republic, but after his death the question still remained whether the republican constitution could be revived. Some politicians tried to restore the republic, and the issue hung in the balance for thirteen years, until Caesar's adopted son, Octavian, eliminated his rival, Mark Antony, and gained supreme control.

## ◆ THE SECOND TRIUMVIRATE

*Antony and Octavian*   Brutus, Cassius, and the other assassins imagined that republican government could be restored with Caesar out of the way. Yet partisans of Caesar commanded armies throughout the Roman world, and they were not men who would meekly surrender their powers to the Senate. One survivor was Marcus Antonius, or Mark Antony, a follower of Caesar and consul for the year 44 B.C. Antony tried to seize for himself the provincial command in Cisalpine Gaul, even though the Senate had already assigned it to another governor for the year 43. The Senate turned on him, with Cicero, now a senior statesman, leading the attack. The state sent an army out to bring Antony to justice, and it must have seemed to many that the old institutions of the Republic had indeed come back to life.

Among the commanders whom the Senate put in action against Antony was a young man of 19—Caesar's grandnephew, whom Caesar adopted in his will. His name, originally Gaius Octavius, became Gaius Julius Caesar Octavianus upon his adoption; modern historians call him Octavian, but he called himself Caesar. He used his name skillfully to win a following among Caesar's former soldiers, but he also played the part of a discreet young supporter of the Senate in its battle against Antony. Cicero, the chief supporter of the old constitution, naively wrote of Octavian after their first meeting, "The young man is completely devoted to me."[8]

*Formation of the Second Triumvirate*   Octavian had been assigned the duty of capturing Antony, but they both recognized that the Senate was really seeking the destruction of the Caesarian faction from which they both derived their political support. If either man were overthrown, the Senate would soon discard the other. Octavian thus calculated his own advantage and turned his back on the duty of attacking Antony. The two Caesarians formed an alliance near Bologna in 43 B.C. They brought into their partnership a lesser commander, Marcus Lepidus; then, following the example of Sulla and others, they invaded Rome and made themselves the military rulers of the ancient capital.

Faced with their armies, the Senate had to acknowledge their leadership, and a tribune proposed a law that turned the state over to their control for a period of five years; their official title was Triumviri (body of three men) "to provide order for the state"—a charge broad enough to supply a legal basis for nearly any action they might wish to take. Thus was formed the Second Triumvirate. In due course they had their collective power renewed for another five years.

Brutus and Cassius, seeing that they did not have popular support, left for the East and in 43 B.C. were given control over all the eastern provinces. But in 42 B.C. the triumvirs eliminated these enemies at the Battle of Philippi in northern Greece. To reward their troops with land, the rulers had already marked out the territory of no fewer than eighteen prosperous towns in Italy. The rule of the Second Triumvirate (43–33 B.C.)

---

[7]Suetonius, *Life of Caesar,* chap. 77.

[8]*Letters to Atticus,* 14.11 (April 25, 44 B.C.).

was thus made secure by the seizure and redistribution of property. A series of "trials" mounted against those who had had the bad luck to be on the losing side provided further security. As in the time of Marius and Sulla, the autocrats brushed aside the traditional guarantees of Roman law as they coldly purged their enemies. The number of the slain was said to be the largest ever. Cicero had placed himself in special danger through a series of orations denouncing Antony (the "Philippics," a term recalling Demosthenes' attacks on Philip II of Macedon; see p. 90). He paid the price and was murdered on Antony's orders in 43 B.C.

#### ◆ OCTAVIAN TRIUMPHANT

***Antony and Cleopatra***    Suspicion now began to grow between the two major partners, Antony and Octavian (Lepidus had been forced into retirement when he tried to take control of Sicily away from Octavian). They now both lusted for supreme power, and Antony did his own cause grave harm by remaining in the East for long periods. On the one hand, he fought a disastrous war against the Parthian kingdom, which had taken certain Roman territories after the death of Crassus in 53. On the other, he carried on a long affair with Cleopatra VII of Egypt. Octavian stayed in Rome and skillfully exploited the rumors that surrounded this romance with Cleopatra. In particular, Octavian falsely asserted that Antony was planning to place this Eastern queen in command of the state.

***Octavian's Victory over Antony***    The final break between the two men came in 32 B.C. Octavian raised a large force from Italy and the western provinces; led by his skillful general Marcus Agrippa, this force defeated Antony in 31 B.C. at Actium, a promontory on the western coast of Greece. Antony shamefully abandoned his men and sailed back to Egypt with Cleopatra, and his army surrendered to Octavian.

The next year Octavian unhurriedly advanced on Alexandria for the reckoning with Antony and Cleopatra. Antony took his own life, and Cleopatra soon did the same—according to the version immortalized in Shakespeare, by letting a poisonous snake bite her. With Cleopatra's death ended the last Macedonian kingdom and,

therefore, the Hellenistic Age, which had begun with the death of Alexander the Great in 323 B.C.

# V. The Founding of the Roman Empire

Those Romans, like Cicero, who had hoped for the restoration of the Republic lost their hopes or their lives. Only one warlord from the Republic, Octavian, had survived the confused years after Julius Caesar. By a supreme political charade, he combined his own autocracy with the restoration of the forms of the Republic. This skillful compromise in effect created the Roman Empire, which he ruled until his death in A.D. 14.

#### ◆ AUGUSTUS AND THE PRINCIPATE

When Octavian returned to Rome in 29 B.C. from his conquest of Egypt, he performed the ceremony of closing the gates of the temple of Janus, the double-headed god who looked both ways; this act symbolized the arrival of a state of peace. His supremacy was beyond challenge. The issue now was whether he would solve the problem that had defeated Caesar: how to rule without seeming to be an autocrat. He achieved this by restoring the appearance—but no more—of republican government. His designated candidates ran for office, and a willing Senate executed only the policies that he favored. Republican structures remained intact, but they were managed by his loyal men. At no time did he announce that he was converting the Republic into an empire. As a result, there is no official beginning for the Roman Empire; the best date is probably 27 B.C., for in that year Octavian laid the foundations of his system.

***Octavian Becomes Augustus***    On January 1, 27 B.C., Octavian appeared in the Roman Senate and announced that the state had returned to peace and that he needed no more extraordinary authority. He resigned his commands and took credit for restoring the Republic. But he arranged that the Senate, full of his loyal creatures, should "voluntarily" give him an enormous provincial command, consisting of Spain, Gaul, and Syria. Most of the legions were concentrated in these provinces; thus Octavian was the legal commander of most of the Roman army. Egypt was handled in a special manner. It was treated as a private possession of Octavian's and managed by his own appointee; therefore it was strictly not one of the Roman provinces.

The older, more pacified provinces (Asia, Africa, Greece, and others) were ruled by governors appointed by the Senate; thus historians speak of "imperial" (governed by the emperor) and "senatorial" provinces. Through this arrangement, Octavian showed respect to the Senate, which Caesar had largely ignored. This is another element in the statesmanship that Octavian was careful to display.

A few days later the Senate met again and conferred on Octavian the name Augustus, meaning "most honored" or "revered." This title brought with it no powers, but its semidivine overtones were useful to Augustus (as we shall now call him) in establishing his supremacy. In 23 B.C. he resigned the consulship but received two additional powers from the Senate. His imperium was extended to cover not only his provinces but the whole Roman world. He also obtained the authority of a tribune (*tribunicia potestas*). As a patrician (by his adoption into Caesar's family), Augustus could not actually be a tribune. Yet his having the "power" of a tribune suggested that he was the patron and defender of the common people of Rome. This power also gave him the legal right to veto any actions and to offer legislation. He was usually called the *princeps*, an old republican word meaning roughly "first citizen," but not an official title. This was another of his skillful pretensions to have restored the Republic. Modern writers often refer to the system that Augustus established as the Principate.

## ◆ AUGUSTUS, THE FIRST ROMAN EMPEROR

*The Administration*   The long reign of Augustus from 27 B.C. to A.D. 14 laid down many abiding features of the Roman Empire. He provided a cash payment from the public treasury to soldiers

▼ The Ara Pacis (Altar of Peace) was built in Rome in 13 B.C. to celebrate the establishment of peace by Augustus. Relatives of the imperial family are portrayed in idealizations of their stations in life rather than in strict Roman realism.
C. M. Dixon

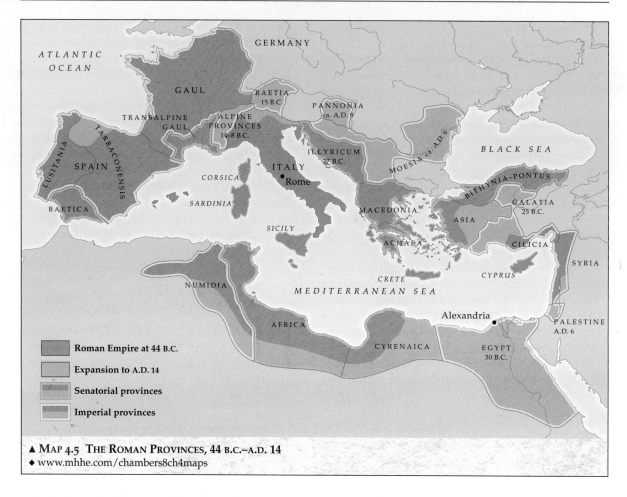

ATLANTIC
OCEAN

GERMANY

GAUL

RAETIA
15 B.C.

PANNONIA
ca. A.D. 9

TRANSALPINE
GAUL

ALPINE
PROVINCES
14–8 B.C.

MOESIA ca. A.D. 6

BLACK SEA

TARRACONENSIS

LUSITANIA

SPAIN

ILLYRICUM
27 B.C.

ITALY
• Rome

CORSICA

BITHYNIA-PONTUS

BAETICA

SARDINIA

MACEDONIA

ASIA

GALATIA
25 B.C.

NUMIDIA

SICILY

ACHAEA

CILICIA

SYRIA

CYPRUS

CRETE

MEDITERRANEAN SEA

Alexandria
•

AFRICA

CYRENAICA

EGYPT
30 B.C.

PALESTINE
A.D. 6

▢ Roman Empire at 44 B.C.

▢ Expansion to A.D. 14

▢ Senatorial provinces

▢ Imperial provinces

▲ MAP 4.5  THE ROMAN PROVINCES, 44 B.C.–A.D. 14
◆ www.mhhe.com/chambers8ch4maps

who had served for twenty years, thus securing the loyalty of the legions to the state, not to their generals. To collect the money, he had to establish a reliable civil service and reform the taxation system, enrolling in effect the whole Roman world. He made the Empire more secure by extending and solidifying the northern frontier (see map 4.5) to reach the Rhine and Danube rivers. His control was all but absolute, but most people were relieved at the ending of the long period of civil war.

He created a permanent fire department and a postal service. He formed a body of soldiers in Rome, the Praetorian Guard. This force of some nine thousand men served as the city's police force and as Augustus' personal bodyguard, but after a few decades it came to play a decisive and violent role in the designation of new emperors.

*The Manipulation of Religion*   Augustus also assumed the office of Pontifex Maximus, or high priest, and made attempts to revive the old Roman religion, probably as a device to promote political stability. He also grasped the possibilities of a ruler-cult. First, he assigned Julius Caesar a place among the Roman gods and built a Temple to the Deified Julius. He also called himself *Divi Filius*, or son of the divine Julius, though he was only the adopted son of Caesar. This verbal trick invited people to imagine that Augustus might some day become divine like Caesar. The poets Virgil and Horace, who wrote at his court, discreetly referred to Augustus as a future deity; and, in fact, Augustus was deified on his death, a political action that was imitated on the deaths of several later emperors who were thought to have ruled well. He also sponsored the building of temples to "Rome and Augustus"—a further suggestion, though not an offensive demand, that the emperor should be worshiped. It also became customary to make an offering to the Genius (protecting spirit) of the emperor.

Part of the religious revival was the rebuilding of scores of temples, but temples were by no means the only Augustan buildings; a famous saying was that "he found Rome made of brick and left it made of marble." The prosperity of the later years of Augustus' rule reflects the general peace that he brought to the Roman world. Freed of the expense of wars, Rome enjoyed a confidence that expressed itself in artistic and literary creativity.

*Legislation, Women, and the Family*   Part of Augustus' program was the revival and maintenance of traditional Roman values. In this effort religion naturally played its part, but he also intervened in the areas of marriage and the family. His proclaimed intention was to restore the old Roman values of chastity and stability within the family, and the historian has little reason to doubt his sincerity. But a more realistic purpose was surely to rebuild the population of Italy after the losses in the civil wars. He therefore awarded special privileges to fathers of three or more children. The Augustan laws even penalized both men and women who did not marry or have children: for example, unmarried persons could not inherit a trust, and childless persons forfeited half their inheritances.

The legal rights of women also advanced under his legislation. Augustus issued strong laws against adultery, and women could now accuse a husband of adultery through a witness. Moreover, freedwomen (that is, former slaves) could now marry any man in Rome with exception of senators, and their children held the rank of citizens. A beautiful monument from the Augustan period, the Altar of Peace (Ara Pacis), prominently displayed women of Augustus' family—the first time that women were shown alongside men in public monumental art. Augustus was probably not working for what we would see as women's liberation, nor did he have the fixed purpose of bringing women's rights up to the level of those enjoyed by men; but these actions were at least a partial result of his work toward the repopulation of Italy.

## SUMMARY

The Roman Republic never gave so much power to the people as the Athenian democracy did. The dominant forces were the great political families, allied through strategic marriages. As success in war created powerful commanders, their rivalry shattered the republican constitution. Augustus was Caesar's adopted son and also his final successor, the last warlord of the Republic. He rose to power in shameless disloyalty and bloodshed. Through his careful control of the army and magistrates, he then gave Rome three decades of healing after the civil wars, and the success of his work is shown by the fact that the state did not relapse into civil war after his death. His personality seems to lack the panache of Caesar, who was invincible in the field and a talented man of letters, but his greatness before history is that he formed the structure from which modern Europe has descended—the Roman Empire.

## QUESTIONS FOR FURTHER THOUGHT

1. What features and conditions of life in Rome were especially conducive to the constant expansion of Rome's territorial holdings?

2. The Roman Republic had a constitution that resembled that of a Greek city-state in many ways, but it collapsed and gave way to one-man rule. How might Roman statesmen and the Senate have preserved the republican constitution?

# RECOMMENDED READING

◆

## Sources

Caesar, Julius. *War Commentaries*. Rex Warner (tr.). 1960 and reprints. An unsurpassed textbook in political-military decision making.

Cicero. *Selected Political Speeches*. Michael Grant (tr.). 1977.

———. *Selected Works*. Michael Grant (tr.). 1960.

Gardner, Jane F., and Thomas Wiedemann (eds.). *The Roman Household: A Sourcebook*. 1991. Translated sources of all kinds on marriage, inheritance, and relations within the family.

Livy. All surviving portions of his history of Rome are in four volumes published by Penguin (various translators). 1965–1982.

Mellor, Ronald (ed.). *The Historians of Ancient Rome: An Anthology of the Major Writings*. 1998. Collection in one volume of long excerpts from the Roman historians.

Plutarch. *Fall of the Roman Republic*. Rex Warner (tr.). 1972. Biographies of Caesar, Pompey, Cicero, and other leading politicians of the Republic.

Polybius. *The Rise of the Roman Empire*. Ian Scott-Kilvert (tr.). 1979. A generous selection from the surviving portions of the historian of Roman imperialism.

Sallust. *Jugurthine War and War with Catiline*. S. A. Handford (tr.). 1963.

Shelton, Jo-Ann (ed.). *As the Romans Did: A Sourcebook in Roman Social History*. 2d ed. 1998. Compilation of many interesting sources, arranged by categories (families, housing, education, and so on).

## Studies

Bradley, Keith R. *Discovering the Roman Family*. 1991. Chapters on child labor, the role of the nurse, divorce, and so on.

Cornell, T. J. *The Beginnings of Rome*. 1995. Extensive narrative of all aspects of the early Republic. Now the best source.

Cornell, T. J., and J. Matthews. *Atlas of the Roman World*. 1982. Historical narrative, well illustrated by excellent maps.

Dixon, Suzanne. *The Roman Family*. 1992. On the development and practices of the family, following her *The Roman Mother*, 1988.

Dupont, Florence. *Daily Life in Ancient Rome*. 1992. On housing, amusements, the economy, the family.

Earl, Douglas. *The Age of Augustus*. 1980. The best survey of political and social life in the Augustan age.

Gardner, Jane F. *Women in Roman Law and Society*. 1986. On the legal position of women and its changes in Roman life.

Habicht, Christian. *Cicero the Politician*. 1990. Admirably concise treatment, placing Cicero within the circle of Roman politicians.

Keaveney, Arthur. *Sulla: The Last Republican*. 1983. Study of Sulla, stressing his program of reform.

Keppie, Lawrence. *The Making of the Roman Army: From Republic to Empire*. 1984. Good history and analysis of the working of the army.

Kleiner, Diana E. E. *Roman Sculpture*. 1992. Complete history and survey of sculpture down to A.D. 330, superbly illustrated.

Meier, Christian. *Caesar*. 1995. The most modern, comprehensive biography of Rome's greatest warrior.

Nicolet, Claude. *The World of the Citizen in Republican Rome*. 1980. On the relation between citizen and state: taxation, military service, membership in assemblies, and so on.

Pallottino, Massimo. *A History of Earliest Italy*. 1991. Culture, economics, and history of the peoples of Italy by a great Etruscologist.

Rawson, Beryl (ed.). *The Family in Ancient Rome*. 1986. Essays on various topics.

Richardson, Lawrence, Jr. *A New Topographical Dictionary of Ancient Rome*. 1992. Lists all known buildings and topographic features; first work to consult on any such question.

Richlin, Amy. *The Garden of Priapus: Sexuality and Aggression in Roman Humor*. 1983. On the often ribald content of Latin literature.

Scullard, H. H. *From the Gracchi to Nero*. 5th ed. 1982. The best textbook narrative of the central period of the Republic and the early Empire.

Seager, Robin. *Pompey: A Political Biography*. 1979. Brief, readable study of the man involved in many central political crises.

Stockton, David. *The Gracchi.* 1979. The best modern study of the two politicians who discovered and used popular support.

Syme, Ronald. *The Roman Revolution.* Originally 1939. The greatest study of the classical world in the last century; brilliant analysis of the collapse of the Republic. For advanced students.

Zanker, Paul. *The Power of Images in the Age of Augustus.* 1988. Architecture, coinage, and other types of art as part of the Augustan program of propaganda.

▲ Gaius Octavius, given the title "Augustus" by the Roman Senate, is
portrayed as ruler and military commander in this idealized statue.
Scala/Art Resource, NY

# THE EMPIRE AND CHRISTIANITY

*T*he history of the Roman Empire is one of amazing continuity. The system of government devised by Augustus and maintained by his successors gave the Empire two centuries of solid prosperity. Historians call this the period of the *Pax Romana,* "the Roman Peace," and the Empire as a system of government remained an ideal in Europe for centuries. In the history of the Empire, one of the main themes is the working of a cohesive political organization. The carefully crafted administration managed the greatest of all ancient Empires, and its remains—stadiums, public baths, marketplaces, temples, official buildings—have inspired imitations down into our own times.

At the beginning of the third century, the Empire entered a period of crisis. Control of the army became the key to power, and emperors and would-be emperors followed one another in confusing succession. When order finally returned during the fourth century, the old Roman Empire was no more. In the East, the Byzantine Empire was formed; in the West, the Empire steadily declined, finally ceasing to be governed by Roman emperors in A.D. 476.

But even as antiquity was passing, ancient peoples were laying the basis for a new form of civilization. A change of religion became the second large historical theme in the Empire, as a new set of beliefs emerged: Christianity, which was destined to transform the life and culture of the Western heirs of the Roman Empire.

| CHAPTER 5. THE EMPIRE AND CHRISTIANITY | | | | | | | |
|---|---|---|---|---|---|---|---|
| | Social Structure | Body Politic | Changes in the Organization of Production and in the Impact of Technology | Evolution of Family and Changing Gender Roles | War | Religion | Cultural Expression |
| I. THE EMPIRE AT ITS HEIGHT | | | | | | | |
| II. THE PERIOD OF CRISIS | | | | | | | |
| III. THE LATE ROMAN EMPIRE | | | | | | | |
| IV. CHRISTIANITY AND ITS EARLY RIVALS | | | | | | | |

# I. The Empire at Its Height

Three unifying elements preserved the Roman Empire that Augustus founded. First was the figure of the emperor, whom all subjects identified as the head of the regime. With some exceptions, the emperors were competent, stable rulers until about A.D. 200. Second were the civil servants and city councils, who collected taxes and maintained urban life. Third was the army, both the ultimate security of the emperor himself and the protector of the frontiers. The three elements supported one another, and the failure of any one of them threatened the other two and thus the fabric of the state (see "Tacitus on the Powers of Augustus," p. 139).

## ◆ THE SUCCESSORS OF AUGUSTUS

*The Julio-Claudian Dynasty*   The first emperor, Augustus, had no male heir. His last wife, Livia, was from the old patrician clan of the Claudians and evidently persuaded him to adopt her son, Tiberius, and to designate Tiberius as his successor. She thus played a leading role in the shaping of the imperial dynasty.

After the death of Augustus in A.D. 14, the Senate recognized Tiberius as ruler and thus confirmed the principle of dynastic succession, establishing the fact that an empire, not a republic, now existed. The dynasty founded by Augustus is known as the Julio-Claudian, because of a complex series of marriages between the Julian and Claudian clans. This dynasty reigned until A.D. 68. Much can be said against the rule of the Julio-Claudians. Tiberius was morbid, suspicious, and vengeful. His successor, Gaius (nicknamed Caligula), suffered from insanity and was murdered by the emperor's bodyguard, known as the Praetorian Guard. Claudius was gullible and was manipulated by his assistants and wives, the last of whom probably poisoned him to secure the throne for her son Nero. Nero ruled with some efficiency for his first five years but then became one of the worst emperors, whose tyranny led to a rebellion in Gaul. When the revolt spread to Rome, he saw that he was doomed and killed himself.

Yet these emperors did maintain, and even expand, the heritage left by Augustus. Claudius, for example, saw to the conquest of southern Britain, which became a Roman province in 47. He established new provinces and founded the city of Cologne in what is now Germany. Moreover, the Empire remained at peace internally, and the provincial administration that Augustus had established continued to function effectively.

*Imperial Administration*   The process of centralization of power in the person of the emperor and away from the Senate continued. Tiberius transferred election of magistrates from the people to the Senate; in effect, those whom he "recommended" were automatically elected. Claudius turned many affairs of state over to his trusted assistants, usually Greeks who had been freed from slavery (thus called *freedmen*), who helped to found the bureaucracy that more and more ran the Empire.

# TACITUS ON THE POWERS OF AUGUSTUS

*The first emperor of Rome, Augustus, maintained that he had restored the Republic after years of civil war. The historian Tacitus, writing about A.D. 120, gave a different evaluation of his work.*

"After Brutus and Cassius were killed, the state had no military force. . . . Even the party of Julius Caesar had no leader left but Augustus, who laid aside the title of Triumvir and called himself a consul. For controlling the people, he contented himself with the rights of a tribune. When he had seduced the army with gifts, the people with distributions of food, and everyone with the pleasure of general calm, he began little by little to increase his authority and to gather to himself the powers of the Senate, the magistrates, and the laws. No one opposed him, since the strongest men had fallen either in battle or through legalized executions, and the rest of the no-

bles, according to who was more ready to accept servitude, were awarded gifts and public offices; since they profited from the new arrangements, they preferred their present security to the previous uncertainties. The provinces, too, accepted this state of affairs, since the former government by the Senate and people was suspect, owing to the struggles among the powerful and the greed of local governors; the protection of the laws had been worthless, because the laws were constantly overturned by violence, intrigue, and finally outright bribery."

From Tacitus, *Annals*, Book 1, ch. 2, M. H. Chambers (tr.).

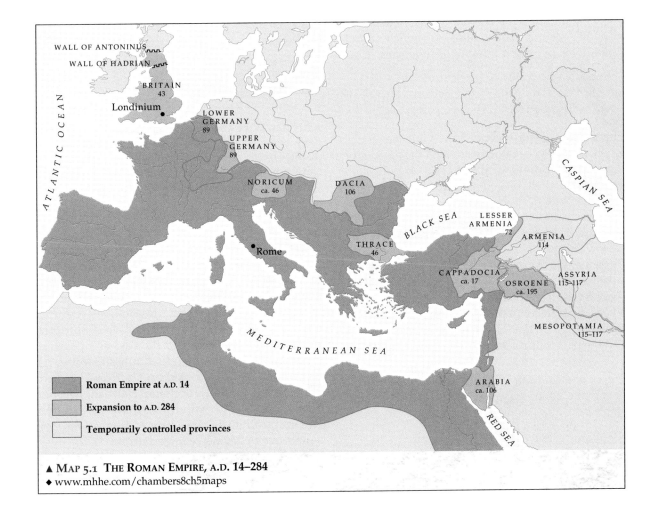

▲ **MAP 5.1  THE ROMAN EMPIRE, A.D. 14–284**
◆ www.mhhe.com/chambers8ch5maps

*Interventions by the Army*   Another factor that weakened senatorial power was the frequent interference in affairs of state by the Praetorian Guard. The Guard first intervened in politics in 41, when it forced the Senate to recognize Claudius as emperor. It did the same for Nero in 54. This repeated invasion of civil authority by the Praetorian Guard was a step on the road toward militarization; within little more than a century, the emperors were to become totally dependent for power on their ability to buy the good will of the soldiery. The army, which had kept the emperors secure, sometimes became a force beyond control.

The military played a significant role in the struggle over the succession after Nero's death in 68, as troops in various quarters of the Empire backed their own candidates for emperor. The year 69 is often called "the year of the four emperors" because in the course of the year four men claimed to be emperor. Vespasian finally stabilized the situation and emerged as sole ruler late in 69. He founded the Flavian dynasty (so called from his second name, Flavius), which lasted through his reign and those of his two sons, Titus and Domitian.

### ◆ THE FIVE GOOD EMPERORS

The Flavian dynasty ended in violence in 96, when a group of senators instigated the murder of the emperor Domitian, Vespasian's despotic son. The Senate then picked a quiet older senator, Nerva (r. 96–98),[1] to be the new emperor. Nerva, who was childless, adopted an experienced military officer, Trajan, and designated him as his successor. The next two emperors, also childless, did the same. This system remained in use for nearly a century: An emperor would choose a qualified successor and adopt him as his son, thus ensuring a peaceful transfer of power. The men thus chosen were so capable that historians have called Nerva and the next four rulers the "five good emperors."

*Trajan and Hadrian*   On the whole, in the period of the five good emperors, the Empire remained stable and even expanded. Trajan was an active

[1]The letter *r.* before a date or series of dates stands for "reigned."

▲ In A.D. 113 the emperor Trajan erected a monumental column to celebrate his war against peoples living across the Danube River. These panels show preparations for the war. Note the figure of the river god at the bottom, under a bridge built for the army.
Trëe.

military emperor and conquered the region of Dacia, north of the Danube River. This was Rome's only permanent conquest north of the Danube and established a permanent home for speakers of Latin; their descendants occupy modern Romania. In 116 Trajan drove the Empire to its farthest extension to the east as he established control over the Tigris-Euphrates valley as far as the head of the Persian Gulf; but he died while trying to return to Rome. Hadrian, his successor, decided to withdraw from this extreme eastern position; he thus changed from a policy of aggressive to defensive imperialism.

Trajan and Hadrian also undertook vast building programs. Trajan erected many structures throughout the Empire. Especially, he built a huge new forum (the Forum of Trajan) in central Rome and placed there an impressive column, which preserves a series of scenes recording episodes in his wars north of the Danube. This new Forum had a large group of buildings—shops, offices, a library—to the east of his column. Hadrian's most famous building project is Hadrian's wall (much of it still stands), built across Britain to protect the frontier between the Roman province of Britain and the areas controlled by Celtic tribes to the north. In Italy, among other projects, he had built an immense luxurious "villa," actually a small town, south of Rome near Tivoli.

Hadrian continued the development of a frank autocracy. Laws now came down straight from the emperor and were known as "decisions" (*constitutiones*). Often the Senate was not even formally invited to approve such laws. He sought advice from an informal council known as the "friends" (*amici*) of the emperor, which included the leading experts in Roman law. One of these, Salvius Julianus, collected the edicts that Roman praetors had issued over the centuries, in an attempt to standardize the procedures of civil law; this action pointed the way toward the great codification of law in the sixth century under the emperor Justinian (see chapter 6). Hadrian's laws, though issued without any pretense of democratic process, were generally fair and humane. They tried to improve the condition of soldiers and slaves and gave women the same rights in court as men.

***Antoninus Pius, Marcus Aurelius*** Hadrian arranged the succession of the next two emperors, Antoninus Pius (r. 138–161) and Marcus Aurelius (r. 161–180), who are the last of the "five good emperors." The rule of Antoninus was peaceful, and under the reign of Marcus Aurelius the Empire

▼ The emperor Hadrian had this famous wall built across Britain to mark off the Roman Empire and keep foreign peoples out.
C. M. Dixon

enjoyed its last years of prosperity. Meanwhile, hostile new peoples were massing to the north and east of the imperial frontiers. In the final years of Marcus' reign, the gathering storm broke in all its fury, and he had to spend years fighting invasions by peoples on the Danube River and in the East.

One campaign was especially disastrous, because the army returning from Asia Minor in the 160s brought with it a devastating plague that spread through much of Europe. This plague must have been one cause of the later weakening of Rome, but the nearly total lack of records prevents our knowing how many died.

Unfortunately, Marcus abandoned the principle of adoption and passed the throne to his worthless son, Commodus (r. 180–192), whose extravagance and cruelty were reminiscent of Nero and Domitian. His murder on the last day of 192 opened a period of terrible instability, to which we shall return (pp. 149–151).

## ◆ ROMAN IMPERIAL CIVILIZATION

**The Economy of the Cities**   The first two centuries of the Empire are often called the "higher" Empire. In this period Italy and the provinces reached a level of prosperity and of flourishing population that Europe would not see again for a thousand years. The results of Roman censuses, which have partially survived, indicate that Italy at the death of Augustus contained about 7.5 million inhabitants. (In about 1500, the earliest date at which we can make a comparable estimate, the same area contained about 10 million people.)

**Cities in the Empire**   In the Western provinces, cities were, for the most part, small; to judge from the area enclosed by Roman walls, most towns contained only a few thousand residents. Yet they usually imitated Rome with temples, markets, arenas, courthouses, and other public buildings and thus displayed an authentic urban character. In the East, cities were often much larger. Alexandria in Egypt is estimated to have had about 400,000 inhabitants; Ephesus in Asia Minor, 200,000; Antioch in Syria, 150,000. The size of the cities in the East is surely one reason why the economy in the Eastern part of the Empire was stronger than that in the Western part.

Largest of all the imperial cities, and a true wonder of the ancient world, was Rome. Estimates of its size generally suggest about 1 million inhabitants. Not until the eighteenth century would European cities again contain such a concentration of people; in the 1780s, for example, Paris held about 600,000 people. Roman civil engineering maintained, even under crowded conditions, acceptable standards of public hygiene and supplied enormous quantities of pure water and food.

**Agriculture**   Agriculture still remained the basic support of the economy, supplying, according to rough estimates, more than 75 percent of the total product of the Empire. One important change in Italian agriculture in the last century of the Republic had been shrinkage in the number of small peasant farms. They gave way to great slave-run estates, called *latifundia,* which generally produced cash crops. The owners of the big *latifundia* were wealthy senators and equestrians, even entrepreneurs from outside the traditional governing classes. Trimalchio, a freed slave who appears as a character in Petronius' novel, the *Satyricon,* boasted that he could ride from Rome to the area near Naples without leaving his own land.

The managers of these vast plantations favored varied forms of agriculture—cultivating vines, olives, and fruit and raising large numbers of cattle, sheep, and goats. Only enough grain was cultivated to feed the resident staff of workers, most of them slaves. The great estates also supplied the cities with building stone, lumber, and firewood; huge quantities of wood were required, for example, to keep the Roman baths at comfortable temperatures. In the view of many historians, extensive deforestation and overgrazing led inevitably to erosion of the land and the loss of fertile topsoil—principal reasons for the economic decline of Roman Italy. Even ancient peoples had the power to injure their environments.

**Economies in the Provinces**   In the provinces, the "Roman peace" favored the development of what had once been backward areas to the point that they threatened Italy's economic leadership. The wine market, for example, passed into the hands of Spanish cultivators in the second century, for Spanish wine rivaled Italian in quality and was

▲ **An arch built by the emperor Trajan at Beneventum. Some panels show sacrifices to the gods, and the whole was intended to commemorate Trajan's generosity to his people. Triumphal and commemorative arches were among the proudest monuments in Rome and have been imitated in many modern cities.**
Nimatallah/Art Resource, NY

cheaper to produce, thanks to lower labor costs. In some areas of industry, too, the provinces began to outrun Italian production.

One of the main Italian industries was pottery, but by about A.D. 50 pottery made in Gaul had replaced Italian pottery even in Italy and had also taken over the market in the provinces and military camps. Thus Rome's success in establishing a commercial network created markets for products from the provinces and eventually contributed to Italy's own economic decline.

*City Life in Italy*   The upper class in Rome lived on a far higher scale, and was more widely separated from the common people, than the rich of Greece. The wealthy had running water tapped into their homes, slaves to tend them hand and foot, and elegant country villas for recreation.

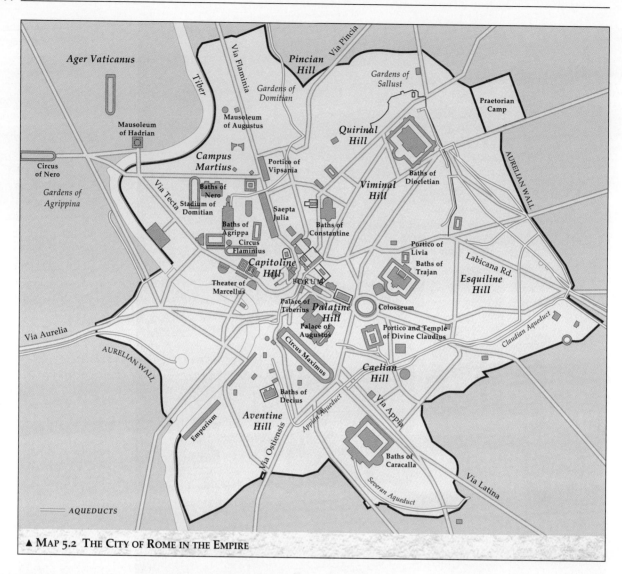

▲ MAP 5.2 THE CITY OF ROME IN THE EMPIRE

Hadrian's villa, or country retreat, near Rome was the size of a small city. These villas approached economic self-sufficiency, because slaves manufactured articles of light industry (clothing, leather goods, domestic utensils) on the farms.

A modern feature of Roman cities was the existence of suburbs and resorts. Pompeii was a commercial town, but its neighbor Herculaneum was a residential suburb. Both towns, buried and thus preserved by the volcanic eruption of Mt. Vesuvius in 79, contain examples of the airy Roman house, built around a central open court, or atrium, and decorated with graceful wall paintings.

***The Working Classes*** The workers of Rome had no such elegant housing, living rather in flimsy and inflammable apartments in high-rise buildings. They often had to plod up a hundred steps or more to their crowded rooms. A bed was the only place for sitting or eating, and the window opened to a noisy street. Rooms lacked running water, but a complex system of aqueducts gave easy access to water outside the home, and Rome always took pride in its enormous, cheap public baths.

There were associations in Rome for every kind of worker: fishermen, engineers, cobblers, silk workers, and so on. Despite their small, crowded apartments, city laborers had working conditions that were beyond the dreams of a Near Eastern peasant. They worked only about six or seven hours a day, and the Roman year contained about

160 holidays, to which the state added from time to time special days of celebration. The modern American actually works longer hours than the ancient Roman, despite our labor-saving devices.

*Social Conditions*   The major amusements for the people during days of leisure were public games, especially chariot races, which brought honor and wealth to the skilled charioteers, in arenas such as the huge Circus Maximus. Besides races, the Romans gave themselves over to brutal contests, which sometimes went on to death, between professional gladiators or between men and animals. The main arena for these spectacles was the grandiose Colosseum, begun by the emperor Vespasian in the 70s. It held about 50,000 spectators, and much of it still stands in central Rome, probably the one monument that most vividly recalls the classical city.

Rome was wealthy enough to support roughly half its population at public expense through free allotments of food, especially grain, which was the most common item in the diet. In the less prosperous years after 200 the cost of these subsidies placed a heavy strain on the Empire's economy.

*The Mixture in Society*   Social mobility became easier under the Empire. For example, some Greeks who had been freed from slavery enjoyed enviable careers as secretaries to emperors or as businessmen. The need for more troops opened new opportunities for provincials, who entered the Roman legions, especially during the second century and later; and even the Senate began to include men born in the provinces. In time the Empire became less "Roman," for in both manpower and economic strength the primacy of Italy was of the past.

▼ **A well-preserved apartment house (second to third century A.D.) in the city of Ostia, which served Rome as a port. The dwelling space is located over shops on the ground floor. The tradition of snack bars everywhere in Rome and Italy is an old one.**
C. M. Dixon

***Women and the Family*** The gains in the status of women continued in the Empire, above all within the families of the ruling elite, who lived in remarkable luxury. But more than this, women in the court of the emperor could even achieve political power comparable to that of such queens in the Hellenistic age as Cleopatra. Livia, the last wife of Augustus, is said to have met with ambassadors of foreign states in the absence of Augustus and to have seen to the advancement of her political favorites. As we have seen, Augustus adopted her son, Tiberius, who became the second emperor of Rome; when Augustus died and was officially proclaimed a god, Livia became the priestess of his cult and received the title Augusta, a parallel to his own name Augustus.

Later in the history of the Julio-Claudian dynasty, Agrippina the Younger, a descendant of Augustus, showed equal political skill in getting her son chosen as the emperor Nero. She married the emperor Claudius, who already had a son from another marriage, and then persuaded Claudius to adopt her son; she probably poisoned Claudius and then obtained the support of the Praetorian Guard for Nero, whom the Senate recognized as emperor. Her influence over Nero in his early years made her almost a co-emperor, and her face appeared on official coins along with his.

The faces of other mothers and wives of emperors were struck on coins, and there were statues to women of the imperial court at many places in the Empire. Of course, not many women could attain such eminence, and the traditional values remained for most women: chastity and deference to the husband, loving care toward the children. In a famous epitaph, a Roman butcher said of his wife,

> She preceded me in death, my one and only, chaste in body,
> loving in spirit, faithful to her faithful husband, always
> cheerful, never neglecting her duty through greed.

***Roman Law*** A complex system of law and procedure was one of the chief cultural contributions of Roman civilization. Roman law had already developed under the Republic, but its further development under the Empire made it even more all-embracing. The Stoic philosophy influenced Roman legal thought, through the idea that the universe is inherently rational and that life should be guided by reason. Moreover, Roman legal thought recognized a kind of natural law, valid for all people, which could be discovered through rational inquiry. At times, especially in periods of crisis, weaker members of society could not always obtain justice; but the overriding social purpose of Roman law was to provide justice rather than simply maintain the stability of the state. As an example, "natural law" denied the legality of slavery.

***The Growth of the Roman Legal System*** The assemblies of the Republic, both that of the Centuries and that of the Tribes (see chapter 4), issued laws mainly on large public issues, such as distributions of land or assignments of military commands overseas. Another influence on the law came from magistrates, especially praetors, who issued edicts that explained the principles by which they would interpret the law during their year in office; these edicts acquired the authority of tradition and ultimately passed into permanent law.

Normally, cases came before a judge, who was a private citizen relying on the advice of other private citizens who were reputed to understand the law but did not actually practice law. These advisers were called jurists (*iurisprudentes* or *iurisconsulti*), and their opinions constantly influenced the growth of the law, especially in the first two centuries of the Empire. They could also rise to high political office. Among the most important jurists were Ulpian, Paulus, and Gaius. They delivered written responses, with authority delegated to them by the emperors, to questions raised by presiding judges and relied mainly on "natural law" for their opinions. Their responses thus shaped Roman laws, even when the laws themselves were issued by emperors as *constitutiones*. They also wrote voluminous commentaries on the law, and their opinions are widely preserved in the final great codification of the law by Justinian in the sixth century.

***Citizens and Noncitizens in Roman Law*** The Romans distinguished their own citizens from the other peoples under their control. Roman citizens were subject to the "civil law" (*ius civile*), or law

◄ **The Sacred Way leads into the Roman Forum through the Arch of Titus, which was erected to celebrate the end of the great Jewish rebellion in A.D. 70. A triumphal procession would enter the Forum through this elegantly placed arch and parade up to the Temple of Jupiter on the Capitoline Hill.**
Trëe

applying to citizens. The number of people subject to this law grew constantly as citizenship was extended to more and more inhabitants. Finally, the emperor Caracalla decreed that all free men and women in the Empire should be citizens, thus subject to the *ius civile.*

Down to the time of this mass grant of Roman citizenship, inhabitants of the Empire who were not citizens had the right to maintain many of their own customs, which came to form the *ius gentium,* or law applying to other nations. These two kinds of law fell, logically enough, to two magistrates for administration, the "urban praetor" (*praetor urbanus*) and the "traveling praetor" (*praetor peregrinus*). But when all free men and women became citizens, the *ius gentium* in this sense was no longer needed.[2]

The Romans' respect for their law is consistent with the remarkable cohesiveness that one sees throughout their society. In war they were often brutal, but then so were many others in all periods of history. Rome's achievement in designing and preserving a system of laws governing the behavior of citizens toward one another has served as a model for much of the law of Western Europe. Codes of law, as we have also observed, are a feature of several other ancient societies, but in richness and complexity the codifications of the late Roman Empire easily surpass all the rest.

*Engineering and Architecture*  The Romans showed brilliance in the fields of engineering and construction. The most enduring monument to Roman civilization is the impressive network of roads found everywhere from Britain to Africa. Originally designed as highways for the rapid movement of legions, these roads became trade routes in more peaceful times and eliminated all barriers to travel.

---

[2]In Roman legal theory, *ius gentium* came to mean a kind of universal law observed by all nations, in effect, a system of law that could be discovered by reason.

From the earliest times the Romans also built aqueducts that converged toward the cities, sloping down and carrying fresh water from the mountains; Rome's imposing system of sewers was constantly flushed by water from the aqueducts. The Romans placed more emphasis on personal cleanliness than did any other civilization until modern times. Several emperors commissioned the building of immense public baths, of which the grandest of all were the Baths of Caracalla at Rome, built in the third century. The English city of Bath is named for the facilities that the Romans built there.

Roman temples, imitating those of the Greeks, were supported by columns, usually in the Corinthian style, crowned with a bell-like acanthus flower. Their temples had large interiors and were often completely walled at the rear, because Romans performed their ceremonies indoors. They were the first to grasp the possibilities of using arches and vaults on a large scale, thus giving their buildings a vastness that the Greeks could not achieve.

### Large Buildings in Concrete

The Romans also invented concrete, which is inexpensive and can be laid by relatively unskilled labor. It can be shaped into forms impossible in marble, and it is lighter in weight and can easily be supported in vaulted buildings. One of its most successful applications is the spacious Pantheon—built in the time of Augustus and then rebuilt under Hadrian—covered by a dome with a striking opening in the center. Sculpture and architecture coincided in triumphal arches, which often bear reliefs depicting the historical event that the arch commemorates.

### Literature in the Empire: Virgil

In Rome, literature was generally the entertainment of the upper classes. In Greece, by contrast, dramas were presented before as many as fifteen thousand spectators, many of them people of the lowest social rank. Augustus, the first emperor, favored several of the most famous Latin poets at his court. Perhaps the leading Latin poet was Virgil (70–19 B.C.). He borrowed from Greek models, as Roman poets often did. His early poems, the *Bucolics* (also called *Eclogues*) and *Georgics*, are polished hymns of praise to the Italian landscape that reflect the style of Theocritus and Hesiod; but the gentle, human spirit of Virgil himself is always present. The best qualities of Virgil appear when he treats civilized emotions—mercy, compassion, and sadness; then his work echoes with a graceful melancholy.

These qualities appear in his patriotic epic, the *Aeneid*, which adopts and transforms materials from Homer. In this work Virgil narrates the wanderings of Aeneas, the Trojan whose descendants were the legendary founders of Rome. Leaving his native city after the fall of Troy, Aeneas reached Carthage and had a romance with its queen, Dido; but his sense of duty compelled him to abandon her in order to reach Italy and fulfill his destiny. Virgil's aim was to sing the glory of Rome and its salvation by Augustus after the civil wars of the late Republic. Virgil knew Augustus, was a favorite at Augustus' court, and at times wrote what could be considered official propaganda.

### Satire: Horace, Juvenal

A contemporary of Virgil's was Horace, whose *Odes*, *Epodes*, and *Satires* examine love, amusement, annoyance, contentment—in short, the feelings of everyday life. He too was well connected with the court of Augustus. Now and then Horace makes an attempt at serious patriotic verse, but these poems are self-conscious and moralizing and do not speak with the real Horatian voice of gentle, amusing irony.

Juvenal, a more pungent satirist than Horace, wrote shortly after A.D. 100. He took as his motto "Indignation inspires my poetry" (*facit indignatio versum*). His poems denounce the excess of pride and elegance in Roman society. His language is colorful, often bitter and obscene. One of his richest and wisest satires concerns the vanity of human wishes. After reviewing the foolishness of human beings, Juvenal gives his advice in a famous epigram: One should pray for "a sound mind in a sound body" (*mens sana in corpore sano*).

### Poetry of Love

There was also a rich literature of sexuality. The poet Ovid (43 B.C.–A.D. 17) wrote a handbook for seduction, *The Art of Love*, and a treatise on love affairs. Perhaps because of his frankly sexual subject matter, Augustus exiled him to a distant town in the Black Sea region: a reminder that the peace and order under the Empire did not always guarantee personal freedom. The poet Propertius (47 B.C.?–2 B.C.?) and others also wrote of their mistresses; and the Greek satirist Lucian (A.D. 120?–185?) has left a racy *Dialogue of the Courtesans.*

***Historians: Livy***   The histories of Rome written during the Republic were usually the work of men directly involved in politics. Under the Empire this situation changed because political contest had almost vanished. It therefore seemed appropriate to look back on the Republic and write a final history of its politics and imperialism. Titus Livius, or Livy, undertook this task during the reign of Augustus, when the decisive political transformation occurred. Livy narrated Roman history from its legendary beginnings until 9 B.C. Because he usually drew on the work of earlier historians, he was sometimes unable to escape the influence of the myths that had clouded the history of the early Republic; thus he is at his best when he uses a good source such as the Greek historian Polybius.

Livy's *Roman History* is a kind of prose epic, filled with patriotism and admiration for the great men who had led Rome when the Republic was conquering the Mediterranean. He also suggests that Rome had declined in moral standards. Livy was the last writer in Latin to attempt a full history of Rome. His work inspired many later writers who looked back at the Republic as the Golden Age of Rome; it was accepted as authoritative until soon after 1800, when historians began to be more skeptical about Roman tradition.

***Tacitus***   The leading Roman historian in intellectual stature was Cornelius Tacitus (55?–120?). His first major work is the *Histories,* in which he treats Roman history from 69, the year of the four emperors, through the death of Domitian in 96, emphasizing the analysis of character. Deeply influenced by satire, the dominant literary form of his age, Tacitus loved to fashion stinging epigrams aimed at members of the governing class, and he treated nearly all his main characters as selfish or corrupt. His disillusioned attitude was partly the result of his being an outsider, probably from southern Gaul; he saw Roman society through the cool eyes of a man from a province who became a senator and even rose to the office of consul.

His most important work is the *Annals,* which covers the reign of the Julio-Claudian emperors from Tiberius through Nero. Tacitus looked back at the early Empire from the vantage point of a later period. Though he said he wrote "without anger or partisanship" (*sine ira et studio*),[3] he found little good to say about the first emperors, and few modern critics would call him impartial. At his best, Tacitus sets a high standard of accuracy, but his wish for accuracy was sometimes at war with his desire to send a moral message about the failings of this or that regime.

# II. The Period of Crisis (192–284)

The Roman Empire, at its height, was in modern language the superpower of the Western world. There was no other state or system that could be called an empire, and certainly none that could challenge or threaten it. But in the third century of our era the Empire faltered and stumbled. The three unifying elements all appeared to be at the end of their strength. Emperors proved to be either weak or corrupt; the civil service was demoralized; and the army was broken up into factions that supported now one emperor, now another. The collapse of these three bulwarks of the state brought the economy crashing to ruin.

## ◆ THE CRISIS OF LEADERSHIP

The centuries of the "Roman peace" ended with the death of the emperor Commodus in 192, and in the following years the political balance shifted to the military. The next generation faced an all but fatal military and political crisis. Wars broke out on the European frontiers, and most emperors could survive only a few years. During the third century, dozens of emperors claimed the throne, but many of these men were really no more than political gamblers or warlords who for a short time purchased the loyalty of their soldiers. Thus two of the stabilizing elements of the Empire—the strong, effective emperor and the disciplined army—began to fall apart.

---

[3]*Annals,* 1.1.

◄ The ancient Greek city Ephesus, on the coast of Turkey, remained prosperous in the Empire. Tiberius Julius Celsus, consul in A.D. 92, endowed this magnificent library, which his son completed about 135.
Comstock

The Roman Senate, which had once been the inspiration and bulwark of the state, now had neither interest nor ability to intervene in affairs of state, while the emperors assumed more and more dictatorial powers and governed through court favorites. The economy of the Empire, too, nearly collapsed during this period, largely because defense costs had risen as raiders plundered the wealth of the Empire on several frontiers. Moreover, the emperors had been supplying the inhabitants of Rome with free food and public games, or "bread and circuses," in the phrase of Juvenal the satirist—a fairly effective means of political domination, but a heavy drain on the economy. Adding to these financial problems was a shortage of silver, on which the imperial currency was based. The emperors resorted to debasing the currency, but this action forced people to hoard what silver they had and actually drove more of the metal out of circulation.

A further problem was the increasing reluctance of people of independent means to hold civic offices, which paid no salary. Moreover, office holders were forced to pay from their own pockets any deficiency in the collection of taxes. Finally, the government had to compel people to take office, a step that pointed to the practice of binding people to their occupations. This in turn led to the collapse of the third crucial element of stability in the state, the efficient administrators and civil servants. Many of the emperors during the century of crisis were men of little leadership; but some of them must have been among the ablest rulers in the history of Rome, for otherwise the Empire would have totally disintegrated.

### ◆ WEAKNESSES IN THE INSTITUTION OF SLAVERY

Like most other ancient states, Rome used slaves widely. The historian's task is not simply to denounce this repugnant system, but to understand its place in Roman society. No earlier society had organized the institution of slavery to such a degree or used slaves in such large numbers. Ancient slavery, unlike slavery in the United States, never comprised members of only one ethnic group. Anyone might have the bad luck to be rounded up and forced into slavery. During the late Republic, the number of available slaves increased dramatically, as Rome overran Greece, Asia Minor, Spain, and Gaul. Julius Caesar reports in his *Gallic War* that he once sold 53,000 Gauls into slavery in a single day. One owner of a large estate mentioned in his will that he owned no fewer than 4,116 slaves. Of the 7.5 million inhabitants of Italy at the death of Augustus, an estimated 3 million were slaves.

The mounting flood of cheap slaves allowed the expansion of the great plantations during the last century of the Roman Republic. In most places slaves were more or less adequately fed. On the other hand, in Sicily they were often turned loose without shelter to feed off the land.

Slaves had a better life in the cities, where they served as artisans, hairdressers, secretaries, and personal servants. Slaves from the East, Greeks in particular, commonly tutored the children of the free classes. Slaves supplied much of the entertainment in ancient society. Girls and boys who could sing, dance, or recite were highly valued; there was also active traffic in beautiful young slaves of both sexes, often for sexual purposes. Gladiators were slaves and reputedly fought harder because of it. If they prevailed over an opponent, they might win their freedom; if they lost, they forfeited nothing more than a miserable existence.

Judged solely as an economic system, ancient slavery offered the Empire certain advantages. It permitted a calculated use of labor in relation to land and capital. But in the long run, the slave system of antiquity also had serious weaknesses, which we must include in the causes for the decline of the Empire in the West. Rome declined in part because its economy could no longer support the army needed to defend the frontiers against invaders. Why was the economy not equal to the task? One principal reason was that the slave system could not resolve two problems that every economy must face: the creation of incentives, to ensure that workers will labor hard and well; and the recruitment of replacements for the aging and the dead. The possibility of being freed provided some incentive to workers, but on the whole the plight of the slave was scarcely to be envied.

Especially in the countryside, the principal incentive that bent slaves to their tasks was the dread of punishment. For this reason, they were best employed in work that required little skill, diligence, or effort. The association of slavery with physical labor drained work of its dignity and dampened interest in technological innovation. And, in the view of most historians, demoralized slaves were poor producers of children, even when they were allowed to marry. Why pass misery down the generations? And conquests ceased

from the time of Hadrian, a fact that threatened the continued supply of slaves.

## ◆ THE PLIGHT OF THE POOR

Within the free population, the spread of the great estates in the last century of the Republic had driven many small cultivators off the land. Many displaced workers drifted to the Roman metropolis, where free bread and circuses purchased their docility. In many provinces, too, rural depopulation and the abandonment of cultivated fields had become a major problem in the centuries after Augustus.

Faced with shrinking numbers of cultivators and taxpayers, the Roman government sought desperately to reclaim and resettle the abandoned fields. For example, Marcus Aurelius initiated a policy of settling foreigners on deserted lands within the Empire. The state also sought to attract free Roman cultivators back to the countryside. The free cultivator who settled on another's land was called a *colonus*, and the institution was called the *colonate*.

***The Poor and the Land*** Roman policy toward the *coloni* and other free cultivators was ambivalent and shifting. In many cases the *colonus* did well, with a light and fixed rent that he paid to the landlord, or *dominus*. He could sell the land he improved or pass it on to his heirs, and he could depart from it at will. But by the fourth century the picture was much worse: The *colonus* was bound to the soil, as were his children after him, and he was subject to the personal jurisdiction of his lord. The long-term interests of society dictated that resettlement within family-owned farms should be encouraged. On the other hand, the hard-pressed government could not overlook any source of revenue, and it often resorted to outrageous fiscal practices. It ruthlessly requisitioned food; it forced settlers to pay the taxes of their absent neighbors; and it subjugated settlers to the authority of their landlords, who could be held responsible for collecting from them services and taxes. By the fourth and fifth centuries, under conditions of devastating fiscal oppression, some peasants preferred to flee the Empire rather than face ruin at home.

# III. The Late Roman Empire

◆

The crisis of the third century came close to a disaster that might have carried the Empire straight to its death. But some of the many emperors, both desperate and determined, managed to hold off invasions on the frontiers. The system designed by Augustus and maintained by his successors proved to have enough resources to weather the storm. As the Empire regained stability, it could not return to the old system in which the Senate provided a measure of guidance and contributed efficient governors. The only promise for the future lay in a strict vertical system. Meanwhile, in the world of faith the old Roman deities commanded less and less devotion, and a change of gods could not be halted or reversed.

## ◆ RESTORATION UNDER DIOCLETIAN

***The Rule of Diocletian (r. 284–305)*** The political crisis of the third century finally ended in 284 when Diocletian, a high army officer, seized the imperial throne. He was from the peasantry of Illyria and was a strong, ruthless man who ruled through an authoritarian bureaucracy. Recognizing that the Empire was too large and too unstable to be directed by one man, Diocletian enlisted three associates to assist him in ruling. The two senior men (Diocletian and Maximian) bore the title Augustus; the two younger (Galerius and Constantius) were known as Caesar. Modern historians call this arrangement the Tetrarchy (rule of four). Each of the four rulers was placed wherever he was needed.

In order to solve the financial crisis, Diocletian had every plot of land taxed at a certain amount, to be paid to the emperor's agents. Trades and professions were also taxed so that the burden would not fall solely on landowners. The cities in the Empire had long had a local council or *curia;* the officials, called *curiales,* were personally responsible for the required tax and had to pay it themselves if they could not collect it from others. Diocletian tried to hold back inflation with a famous Edict on Prices, which fixed maximum prices for nearly all goods and also fixed maximum wages. But natural economic forces led to

▲ **The Tetrarchs (Diocletian and his corulers), shown supporting each other, on a corner of St. Mark's cathedral in Venice: Diocletian and Maximian are on the right; Galerius and Constantius on the left. The heads on the swords are Germanic.**
Michael Holford Photographs

further inflation, and he had to let the edict lapse after a few years.

Diocletian's severe rule stabilized the Empire, though it is hard to find in it much to praise. Many of his practices continued throughout the fourth century, especially his establishment of a despotism that resembled the ancient kingdoms of the Near East in its absolute monarchic rule. All laws came directly from the emperor, and the jurists, who had shaped the growth of law in the first two centuries of the Empire, played no further role. Thus Rome had moved from a "principate," the system of Augustus, to a "dominate" (*dominus,* "master").

***The Accession of Constantine*** Diocletian retired in 305, and soon afterward his system of shared rule broke down. Years of complex intrigue and civil war followed, as several leaders fought for the throne. One of the ruling circle was Constantius, the father of Constantine. When Constantius died in 306, Constantine began to fight for supreme power; in 324 he defeated his last rival and became sole emperor of Rome. Thus forty years after the accession of Diocletian, the Empire once again had a single ruler. In 330 Constantine renamed the old Greek city of Byzantium as New Rome and established it as his capital; popular usage gave it the name Constantinople.

## ◆ CONSTANTINE AND THE BUREAUCRACY

By the end of his reign in 337 Constantine had set the pattern that remained throughout the fourth and later centuries. The whole state was now one rigid structure, almost one massive corporation that brutally discouraged individual initiative.

The economy was in virtual stagnation. Members of all trades and professions were grouped into *corpora,* or corporations, and to change professions was difficult. To make certain that the various day-to-day services would be performed, the state made professions hereditary. A small class of farmers managed to remain independent, but the general trend was toward converting agricultural workers into near slaves. A totally impassable gulf existed between the monarch's court and the common people. Even within the court the emperor stood apart from the rest, surrounded by ceremony. Fourth-century rulers wore expensive cloaks dyed in purple, and courtiers had to kiss a corner of the emperor's robe when approaching the throne. Diadems, the custom of kneeling before the emperor, and other marks of royalty became traditional and have remained so in European monarchies.

## ◆ THE DECLINE OF THE WESTERN EMPIRE

After Constantine's death in 337, the chief administrative question for more than a century was whether one man could be strong enough to rule as

▲ The emperor Constantine tried to increase his glory by commissioning colossal portraits of himself, such as the one in Rome shown here. The original full-length statue was some forty feet tall.
Hirmer Fotoarchiv

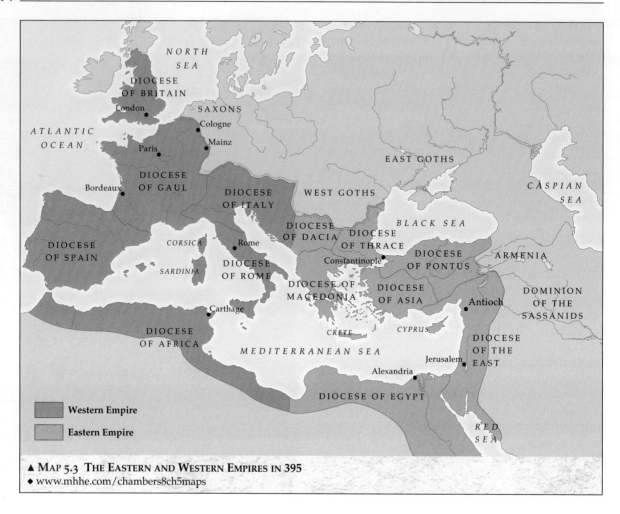

▲ **MAP 5.3  The Eastern and Western Empires in 395**
◆ www.mhhe.com/chambers8ch5maps

sole monarch. For most of the time, this solution proved impossible, and some kind of shared rule became common. On the death of Theodosius in 395, the Empire split into an Eastern half and a Western half, with the dividing line just east of Italy.

In the last centuries of the Empire, society became more and more rigid; it did not, and perhaps could not, allow people to move freely from one class to another. As the central government weakened, local estates, usually called *villas*, became self-sufficient units with hunting lands and workshops that supplied the goods that the local population needed; they therefore became the main economic and political units of the Western Empire. At the same time, trade was declining because of a shortage of new markets and the constant threat of invasions along the frontiers. Moreover, a shortage of labor caused fertile lands to lie fallow and mines to remain unexploited.

*The "Fall" of Rome?*  Such was the background for the dramatic turning point in history that is the end of the Western Empire. The formal end of the Western Empire is traditionally dated to 476, when a Germanic warlord, Odovacar (sometimes Odoacer), deposed the youth whom we call the last Western emperor, Romulus Augustulus, and the Senate resolved not to try to name any further Western emperors. To symbolize the end of the Western emperors, an embassy was sent to Constantinople to surrender the imperial insignia. Modern readers inevitably think of this event in the terminology imposed by the historical masterpiece of Edward Gibbon—that is, as the "decline and fall" of the Empire. But no political structure as large as the Roman Empire really falls like a tree in a forest without further influence or legacy. Moreover, some emperors in Constantinople, notably Justinian in the sixth century, saw

*Chronology*

## THE "FALL" OF ROME

476 is known to all readers of history as the year of the fall of Rome, but the true chronology is more complex.

**393** Theodosius I, ruling in Constantinople, installs his son Honorius as emperor in the West.

**395** Death of Theodosius; the division of the Empire into Eastern and Western parts is maintained.

**423** Death of Honorius in West; other Western emperors continue to be appointed.

**474, June 24** Leo I, emperor in East, appoints Julius Nepos as emperor in West.

**475** Nepos appoints Orestes, a former lieutenant of Attila the Hun, as Master of the Soldiers. Orestes insists that his young son, Romulus Augustus (or Augustulus), be recognized as Western emperor. Nepos flees to Salona in Dalmatia. Romulus is proclaimed emperor in Ravenna on October 31, but the act is without legal force, and Nepos continues to be recognized as official Western emperor.

**476** The German warlord Odovacar (sometimes Odoacer) leads a rebellion against Orestes and kills him, August 28. He deposes Romulus in Ravenna (September 4) and exiles him with a pension to Campania. The Roman Senate sends an embassy to Zeno, the Eastern emperor (r. 474–491), proclaiming no further need for a Western emperor; but Zeno continues to recognize Nepos until his death.

**480, April or May** Nepos is murdered in his villa at Salona.

**ca. 520** Marcellinus, in his Latin *Chronicle* written in Constantinople, states that the Western Empire (*Hesperium imperium*) "perished" with the deposition of Romulus Augustulus in 476, thus establishing this date for the "fall" of Rome.

themselves as the head of the whole traditional Empire, West and East, and tried to reunite the two geographic parts.

***The Survival of the Eastern Empire***   Even though historians take care to speak of the transformation of the Empire rather than of its disappearance, there is no doubt that the Empire in the West did pass away, while the Eastern part, based on Constantinople and called by historians the Byzantine Empire, survived for nearly another thousand years. The problem is to explain why the Western regions could not maintain themselves under a continuous government while no similar dissolution threatened the Eastern portion of the Empire.

***Theories about the Fall***   Some historians have been enticed into trying to state the one great cause for the fall of Rome—and this quest may be impossible. Gibbon, for example, blamed the destructive work of barbarism and religion. But to say that Rome declined because of invasions by Germans, Franks, and Goths only pushes the inquiry back one step: Why were these peoples able to defeat an Empire that had ruled the civilized world for centuries? And why did the Eastern part of the Empire not decline along with the Western?

Some historians suggest that the emperors unintentionally paved the way for the fall of Rome by exterminating possible political rivals in the upper class, thus weakening the group that could have supplied leadership for the state. Others have advanced an economic argument, saying that the Empire was bound to decline because it never really emerged from a domestic economy. But this second theory is hardly convincing, for some societies—admittedly much less complex than the Empire—have existed for many centuries with no more than a domestic economy. If there had been no convulsions and strains in the Empire, the production of goods and food could have continued more or less unchanged. Other historians have proposed exhaustion of the soil and fluctuating cycles of rainfall and drought in order to explain Rome's economic depression, but there is little exact knowledge about the cycles of crops and weather conditions that would indubitably account for the fall of the Empire.

*A Crisis in Manpower*   Still other historians have suggested that the weakness of the Western Empire was due to a shortage of manpower. This explanation does have some merit, because the Eastern cities appear to have been more populous than the Western ones, and thus they had more strength and resilience. The numerical inferiority of the West became even more serious when the villas became self-sufficient units and there was no longer a centralized military system. It was much easier for outsiders to invade the Empire when they met haphazard resistance from local forces. As early as the third century, many Germanic captives and volunteers entered the army, which was scarcely "Roman" in any true sense. The Germanic troops felt little loyalty to Roman tradition and were unwilling to submit to severe discipline. Thus the army—the power base of the Augustan age—sank and pulled the Empire down with it. Also, the relocation of the capital to Constantinople moved the administrative center even farther from the Western provinces and probably accelerated the dissolution of the regions of Italy and Gaul.

*The Routes of Invasion*   But the shortage of manpower was not the only factor in the weakening of the Western Empire. Possibly an even stronger threat was simply the physical geography of Europe. The Western Empire seems to have been far more vulnerable to invasion than the Eastern Empire. Warlike peoples streamed along the Danube valley and through the terrain of Central Europe into the Western provinces, which offered a less hazardous route than the journey south through the difficult mountains of the Balkans, Greece, and Asia Minor into the Eastern Empire.

*Social Conditions and Decline*   Other conditions, too, made the Western Empire less able to resist invasion. In the late second and third centuries the emperors had deliberately increased the prestige of the army and depressed the Senate and the civil service. The creature that they fashioned soon began to rule them, for the armies and their leaders made and unmade emperors at will. The only way to preserve civilian control over the military machine would have been to entrust more responsibility to the Senate and to maintain strong civil servants. But the emperors simply continued along the path of absolute coercion, stifling initiative and making the lower classes apathetic and resentful. These conditions gave citizens only slight motivation to defend their oppressive government; domination by invaders may have seemed not much worse than being in the grip of the Roman state.

We must also consider the large number of holidays and many forms of amusement within the city of Rome: To what degree did such luxuries contribute to the transformation of the Western Empire? There is evidence here and there that the masses in the city gradually lost their feelings of responsibility. For example, in 69, as Tacitus reports, the crowd cheered with pleasure as rival troops fought in the streets for the throne.[4] When the masses no longer had to exert more than minimal effort to survive, they abandoned the discipline and civic cooperation that had created the Empire. The people shunned public office, non-Italians supplied the troops, and appeals for traditional Roman firmness in danger found little response.

*The Role of Christianity*   Finally, historians must take into account the great upheaval in ideas and faith. We cannot express this view in the language of science or statistics, but the new religion, Christianity, may also have weakened the defenses of the Empire. This thesis was first supported by Edward Gibbon, who had rejected the Catholic faith in his own life and scorned Christianity. But even as we recognize Gibbon's prejudices, we must

---

[4]*Histories*, 3.83.

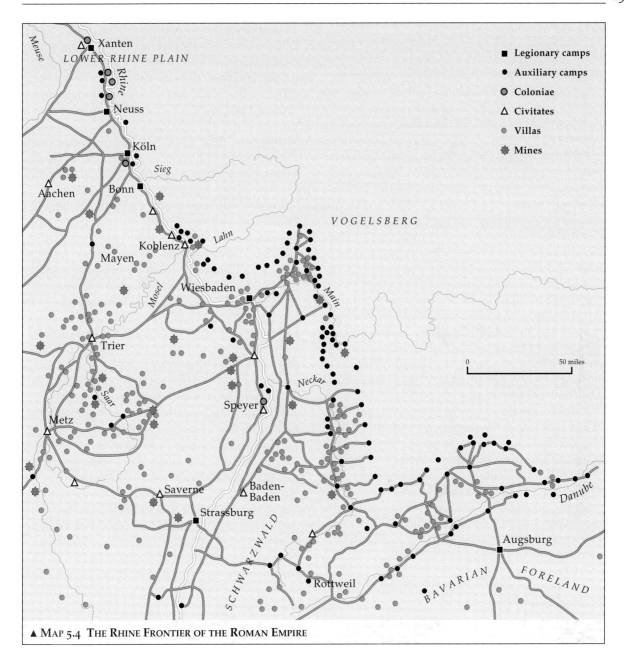

▲ MAP 5.4 THE RHINE FRONTIER OF THE ROMAN EMPIRE

allow that he may have hit a part of the truth. In the Roman scheme the emperors, governors, and administrators stood far above the people, and Roman religion provided little spiritual compensation for a low rank in the world. The Christian faith offered something better: the message that all persons are potentially equal in the eyes of God and may hope for a better afterlife through salvation. As the Western Empire came under constant attack, the increasing number of Christians may have been less than eager to fight to preserve the old system. This spiritual rejection, as we might call it, worked along with the mighty pressures of invasion to cause the "fall" of Rome.

# IV. Christianity and Its Early Rivals

The triumph of Christianity within the Roman Empire was one of the most remarkable cultural revolutions in history—all the more extraordinary because its values were opposed to those of classical thought, which sought the good life in the present world. *Carpe diem,* "Seize the day," said Horace; there is no certainty about tomorrow. But classical values were failing to reach the disadvantaged, the subjugated, the losers. Small wonder that people sought a new meaning for their existence. More than this, Christianity was born into a world alive with religious fervor. Some came from Zoroastrianism with its promise of salvation, some from the Jews, some from mystery religions; and a strain of philosophic thought came from the Stoics. The Jews, especially, contributed zeal. Christians added to this legacy their striving after pure morals and their willingness to welcome everyone, commoner and intellectual alike, into God's world.

Christianity then found its own battles to fight. Martyrs testified for their faith with their lives. Even within the church, some theologians took positions that the established leaders rejected and denounced. A world of debate and interpretation of Christian thought flowed from the pens of the scholars known as Fathers of the Church. Finally the Empire itself adopted Christianity. The victory of the new faith was complete.

## ◆ THE MYSTERY RELIGIONS

One element of a spreading religious ferment under the Empire was the growing popularity of the so-called mysteries, which promised a blessed life after death to those who were initiated into secret (therefore "mysterious") rites. Through these rites, the believer attained a mystical identification with the renewing cycles of nature. The mysteries are generally described in various sources as thrilling, bringing one into another world, carrying one to a summit of emotion and perception.

***The Mysteries of Eleusis*** The oldest and most famous rites were held each fall at Eleusis, a day's walk from Athens. A drama-filled night culminated in the initiate's conviction that he or she would be given a lovely life after death by Demeter, the goddess of grain, just as she caused beautiful new grain to come forth from the apparently dead seed.

***Mithraism*** This hope for survival after death did not bring with it any expectation of a changed moral life, nor did initiation lead to membership in any kind of community of believers or "church," with one notable exception: the religion known as Mithraism. Mithras was originally a Persian god of light and truth and an ally of the good god, Ahura Mazda; he symbolized the daily triumph of life over death by bringing back the sun to the dark heavens. Initiation was open only to men, and Mithraism—with its emphasis on courage, loyalty, self-discipline, and victory— became especially popular in the Roman army.

***Christianity and Mysteries*** When Christians began, around A.D. 30, to proclaim the good news (or "gospel") of the recent death and resurrection of their leader, Jesus of Nazareth,[5] throughout the Empire, many who responded thought they were hearing about the best "mystery" of all: A historical person had conquered death and promised a blessed afterlife to all who believed in him. Yet much early Christian literature was written to teach believers that Christianity was far more than a "mystery." In fact, the historian should not class Christianity among the mystery religions. First, rites in mystery religions were secret, and participation required a period of instruction or purification. The experience, however thrilling, was temporary. Above all, the rituals usually did not lead to forming a community of believers or a church. Christianity, by contrast, demanded that every believer practice love and justice in new communities made up of Jew and Greek, slave and free, male and female, rich and poor, educated and ignorant.

---

[5]"Jesus" was his name. After his death he was called *ho Christós,* "the anointed one," or the Messiah, by his followers. Thus the names "Christ" and "Jesus Christ," though universally used, are not historically accurate, and "Jesus, called the Christ" is cumbersome.

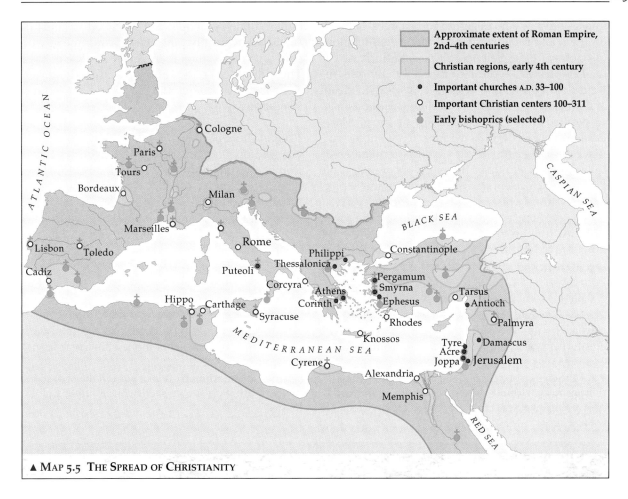

▲ MAP 5.5  THE SPREAD OF CHRISTIANITY

*Characteristics of Christianity*  This new religion hardly looked "religious." Christians had no temples or other holy places, no priests, no ordinary sacrifices, no oracles, no visible gods, no initiations; they made no pilgrimages, did not practice divination, would not venerate the emperor, and challenged the final authority of the father (or oldest male) in family life. No wonder some pagans accused Christians of being atheists who undermined traditional society. The roots of these radical beliefs and practices go back to the long Judaic tradition and its sacred writings. Christians maintained that prophecies in the Hebrew Bible, which in the light of new revelation they began to call the *Old* Testament, had foretold the coming of Jesus as the Messiah, the deliverer of the Jewish people, and the future lord of the world.

Like the Jews, Christians emphasized their god's wish to create a community of men and women who practiced justice and mercy. All the first Christians had been Jews, but they parted company with Jewish tradition by insisting that Jesus' life, his sacrificial death, and his resurrection all meant that God's community had become open to everyone, on absolutely equal terms, from every background.

◆ THE JEWS IN THE ROMAN EMPIRE

*The Jews and Other Powers*  The Jews had been favored subjects of the Persian Empire until Alexander's invasion of the East (334–323 B.C.) swept away Persian rule. In the Hellenistic Age they were governed during the third century B.C. by the Ptolemies of Egypt and then by the Seleucid kings of Syria, who began to force Greek culture on them and finally outlawed the Jewish religion altogether. One Seleucid king, Antiochus IV (r. 175–164 B.C.), defiled the holy Temple in Jerusalem by erecting within it an altar to Zeus and an image of himself. Pious Jewish nationalists responded under the leadership of Judas Maccabaeus with guerrilla warfare. This successful Maccabean Revolt (167–164 B.C.) is remembered today with Hanukkah, the eight-day Festival of Lights, which celebrates the reported miracle of a one-day supply of oil that burned for eight days. After a century of virtual independence, the Jews in Judea (the province created out of the Jewish kingdom of Judah) fell under Rome's control after the arrival in Jerusalem of the Roman general Pompey in 63 B.C.

When Julius Caesar was at war with Pompey in 47 B.C., he had the help of a Jewish force, and he rewarded the Jews with reduced taxes and exemption from military service. The Romans also agreed that Jews could not be called to court on the Sabbath and that they could continue to worship in their synagogues, even in Rome itself. Thus, despite the loss of their century-long freedom, the Jews enjoyed at least some measure of toleration.

***Roman Control over the Jews*** Rome permitted client kings, local rulers who pledged loyalty to Rome, to rule Judea. The most notorious was Herod the Great (r. 40–4 B.C.), hated by most Jews, whom he sought to win over by remodeling the Temple in Jerusalem into one of the wonders of the ancient world. But Herod's son was a weak ruler, and the Romans assumed direct control over Judea through civil servants from Rome; they were usually called procurators, the most famous of whom was Pontius Pilate.

Constant quarrels between the Roman officers and the Jews reached a climax in A.D. 66, when Jerusalem burst into rebellion. This great Jewish

▼ A Mithraeum, or shrine to the savior god Mithras, with benches for worshipers. It was built in the second or third century within a large first-century apartment. On the altar, Mithras is shown sacrificing a bull to Apollo. Above this level was built the church of San Clemente in Rome.
C. M. Dixon

War, as the Romans called it, lasted until 70, when the Romans under the emperor Titus demolished the Temple, except a remnant of the Western Wall, at which Jews were allowed to pray once a year. This portion of wall still stands and is a holy shrine to Jews today. Hoping to retain the favor of the Jews by respecting their god, the Romans did not at first try to eliminate the Jewish faith itself; but they finally did attempt its suppression after another Jewish rebellion (131–135). Nonetheless, Judaism retained its coherence and strength, assuring its people that God would one day send them their redeemer.

*Jewish Factions*   The attractiveness of Hellenistic culture, combined with the insult of Roman occupation, led to a continuing crisis of identity among the Jews. After the Maccabean Revolt, three principal factions arose, each stressing the part of Jewish tradition that it considered most essential for the survival of the Jews as God's people.

First, the landed aristocracy and high priests formed the Sadducees, religious conservatives who rejected belief in an afterlife and in angels because they did not find such teaching in the five Books of Moses (the Pentateuch, called the *Torah* by Jews).

A second faction, the Pharisees, were pious middle-class laypersons who taught the resurrection of the dead, believed in angels, and accepted gentile converts.[6] During the century following the Roman expulsion of the Jews from Jerusalem in 135, the spiritual heirs of the Pharisees, the great rabbis, organized their oral legal traditions, which updated the practice of the Torah, into a book called the Mishnah. This compendium became fundamental for all subsequent Jewish thought and was augmented in the East by an authoritative commentary (the Gemara) to form the Babylonian Talmud, or general body of Jewish tradition. A similar process in the West created the less elaborate Persian Talmud.

*The Essenes*   The third faction was the Essenes, who have drawn the most attention in recent years because of the astonishing discovery of the Dead Sea Scrolls, documents found from 1947 onward in eleven caves near the Dead Sea. Although scholarly debate continues, the consensus is that the writers were ascetic priests who settled at Qumran, fifteen miles into the desert east of Jerusalem, after the Maccabean Revolt; they were evidently protesting against the leadership of the Temple by high priests whom they considered corrupt and unworthy.

These rolls and many fragments of leather have given historians an extraordinary view of the apocalyptic beliefs and strict practices of this protesting faction, which was active from ca. 150 B.C. to A.D. 70. The Essenes were convinced that evil in the world had become so powerful—even prevailing in the Temple—that only a cataclysmic intervention by God, which would soon arrive, could cleanse the world and open the way for righteousness to prevail.

*Doctrines of the Essenes*   A certain "Teacher of Righteousness," the priestly champion of the forces of light, is thought to be the anonymous author of many of the scrolls; his opponent in Jerusalem, who he says serves the powers of darkness, is called the Wicked Priest. The scrolls foresee at least two God-anointed leaders: the Messiah of David (a military commander) and the Messiah of Aaron (a high priest). The writers also predict the return of the "Teacher."

The relations of the Essenes at Qumran to Jesus and the first Christians remain much debated. The Essenes never appear in the Christian Bible, or New Testament. To be sure, in the spectrum of Jewish factions, these two groups could hardly have differed more widely. The Essenes were exclusive, hierarchic, priestly, and withdrawn from society. Jesus and his followers welcomed everyone; they were egalitarian, uninterested in sacrifices in the Temple, and wholly "in the world."

## ◆ ORIGINS OF CHRISTIANITY

*The Person of Jesus*   The modern historical investigation of Jesus of Nazareth has challenged scholars for two centuries. He seems to have been a charismatic Jewish teacher, yet he wrote nothing that we know of. His existence and his execution by the Romans are confirmed by such first- and

---

[6]The Latin word *gentiles* (akin to *gens;* see p. 108) means "foreigners," those born to non-Jewish mothers.

second-century historians as Josephus, Tacitus, and Suetonius.

For details we must sift the writings of early converts, such as Saul of Tarsus (who did not know Jesus) or the authors of the Gospels (the first four books of the New Testament), which focus on Jesus' power over evil forces, his message of hope and moral demands, his healing miracles, and his radical inclusiveness (even lepers were welcomed into the faith). But ancient writers had little interest in presenting his biography in chronological order or in probing his inner life. We know almost nothing about his career as a youth and young adult apart from his being raised a Jew in Galilee;

◄ **The church of Santa Costanza in Rome, built in the early fourth century as a mausoleum for Constantia and Helena, daughters of the emperor Constantine, contains some of the oldest Christian mosaics. This scene from daily life shows workers bringing in the grape harvest.**
Erich Lessing/Art Resource, NY

thus, despite the efforts of many, it is impossible to write a biography of Jesus.

*Jesus as Teacher*   As his followers recalled his career, Jesus was born of a virgin named Mary, who was betrothed but not yet married to a man named Joseph, in the last years of Herod the Great, at a date that modern scholarship sets about 4 B.C. At around age thirty, Jesus went to John the Baptist, an outspoken prophet, to be baptized—that is, to become purified through a ritual washing—and join his apocalyptic movement, which foresaw the coming end of the world. Soon afterward John was imprisoned, and Jesus began a program of itinerant teaching and healing, apparently rejecting John's apocalyptic message by proclaiming instead the "good news" that God's rule had already begun *before* the final judgment. Jesus affirmed the Pharisees' belief in resurrection, yet he urged his disciples to pray that God's will be done here on earth as it is in heaven, that God's kingdom should come to people here. Jesus was, therefore, a man in the tradition of the Hebrew prophets, who brought their message to the people directly.

In the Sermon on the Mount, the summary of Jesus' basic principles recorded in the Gospel of Matthew, Jesus declared that when God rules, the poor, the meek, the pure in heart, the peacemakers, and the justice seekers will be honored. He said too that prayer and piety were matters of personal commitment, not public gestures to win society's acclaim.

*Doctrines of Jesus*   With all other Jews, Jesus believed that God was a gracious, welcoming God. The related questions were: To *whom* is God gracious? and, therefore, Whom must I treat as my neighbor? As Jesus demonstrated by his fellowship at open meals, every person was potentially such a neighbor, especially a person in need.

Jesus' fellowship at meals reached its climax at his last supper at the time of Passover, a Jewish religious holiday. At this meal he urged his disciples to continue a ritual practice in memory of him, using bread and wine to symbolize the gift of his body and the sacrifice of his blood. The early Christians regularly did so, calling this meal the eucharist, or thanksgiving. Jesus' doctrines included the assurance that belief in his message

would bring redemption from sin and salvation with eternal life in the presence of God; above all, he called himself the Son of Man—but also the Son of God, who would sit at God's right hand.

*Jesus' Death*   For the passing of Jesus, only Christian sources give us a narrative, which we cannot compare with others. Christian writers state that the high priests in Jerusalem accused Jesus of blasphemy (he had challenged their authority in the Temple), of pretending to be God's Messiah and a king, and of opposing paying taxes to the Roman emperor. The Roman governor, Pontius Pilate, apparently feared that a riot, led by Jesus' enemies, was about to break out at the Passover. He washed his hands to make himself innocent of Jesus' blood and handed him over to the crowd, which then brought about his crucifixion, a horribly painful form of execution (about A.D. 30).

Jesus' followers became convinced that God raised him from the dead after three days and that this resurrection confirmed the truth of his deeds and words despite his rejection and persecution. The Christians further believed that he ascended bodily into heaven but would return to save his followers and establish his kingdom. Armed with this conviction, they followed the example of Stephen, the first Christian martyr, and began to convert other Jews to their faith.

*Paul and His Mission*   A Pharisee, Saul of Tarsus (in today's southern Turkey), known to us as Paul, became a leader in persecuting Jews who had become Christians. Then, about A.D. 33, on his way to Damascus to organize further persecutions, he saw on the road an apparition of the risen Jesus, who asked him to explain his hatred. Paul realized he had been given a special mission to the gentiles and became Christianity's tireless advocate, traversing the Roman world, organizing Christian communities of both Jews and gentiles, and advising their members through his letters. He was executed in Rome about A.D. 62 while planning a mission to Spain (see map 5.6).

Paul became the best known of all the early Christian teachers. His letters, or epistles, written to give specific guidance to the congregations he founded, were widely circulated and then collected as part of the Christians' authoritative Scriptures. Luke devotes nearly half of the Acts of

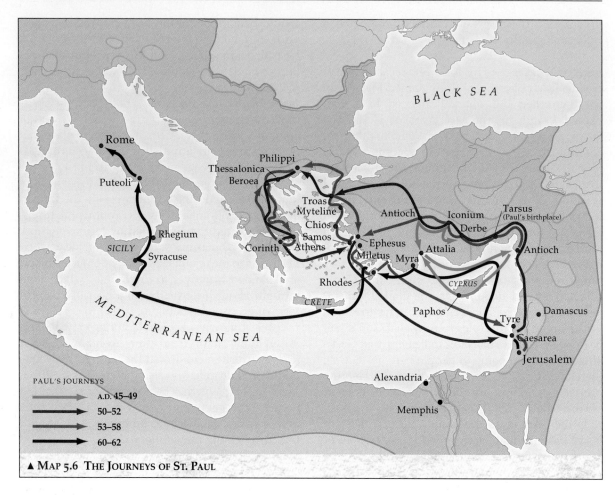

▲ MAP 5.6 THE JOURNEYS OF ST. PAUL

the Apostles to Paul's career as a courageous witness who fought with burning missionary fervor for his new lord.

***Paul and the Conversion of the Gentiles*** Above all, Paul rejected the policy of some early Jewish Christians who wanted to restrict membership in the new faith to Jews or to gentiles who had become Jews through circumcision. In one of his tautly argued letters in the Bible's Book of Romans he asked: "Is God the God of the Jews only? Is he not also the God of the Gentiles? Yes, of the Gentiles also." By rejecting circumcision as a condition of membership, Paul helped firmly establish the Christian church on the basis of personal faith, not limited by ethnic identity, bloodlines, or observation of the Mosaic law.

He and later Christian teachers saw themselves as the direct heirs of the Jewish tradition, from which they drew their concept of one God and their notions of creation and the early history of humanity. The first human beings, Adam and Eve, had disobeyed God, thus introducing sin and death into the world. By nature Adam was the founder of the human race; by grace—in Christian theory, that gift from God that redeems sinners and gives them life after death—Jesus was its second founder, restorer, and redeemer.

***Paul and Christian Communities*** Paul taught Christians to regard themselves as citizens of heaven and to begin living with one another in humility and love, in joyous expectation of their final destiny. Christians were sure that God would soon consign their world's system of honor and shame based on violence, pride, and class discrimination to the trash heap of history. Paul also redefined the notion of the Messiah. For Jews, this leader would someday arrive and create another kingdom on earth. For Paul, the messianic age had begun with Jesus, interrupting the age of violence and death as the sign and promise of what the future would bring.

Paul's vision of human freedom and a renewed human community characterized by mutual service is one of the most compelling social images in Western culture. Taking this message throughout the lands of the eastern Mediterranean, Paul and his successors brought converts by the thousands into the new church.

*Persecutions* The Roman government adopted a general policy of toleration toward the many religious sects of the Empire, seeking the blessings of all divine powers on the Empire. The Romans even paid for sacrifices to be performed on behalf of the Empire in the temple in Jerusalem. They asked only that veneration be shown on official occasions to the traditional gods and to the deceased and deified emperors—little more than public patriotism. But the Christians, like the Jews

▼ **The fourth-century sarcophagus of Junius Bassus, in classicizing style, showing Adam and Eve in Eden with the threatening serpent.**
Scala/Art Resource, NY

before them, refused even this apparently small compromise with polytheism.

Rome's attitude toward Christians wavered between lack of interest and cruel persecution. The first serious persecution took place under Nero in A.D. 64. A vast fire had ravaged the crowded areas in central Rome, and Nero had many Christians brutally killed as scapegoats. The historian Tacitus, in reporting the affair, declares that Christians were thought guilty of a wicked style of life, but he makes it clear that the persecution was based on a false charge (*Annals*, 15.44). From time to time other anti-Christian actions took place, but it is unlikely that the mild doctrines of Christians were the reason. Their main offense was, rather, their stubbornness or *contumacia*, which caused many in the Roman world to see them as enemies of society. The emperor Trajan, giving instructions to his civil servant Pliny, agreed that laws against Christians should be followed, but he warned against anonymous accusations, which he would not tolerate.

Occasional persecutions and long periods of peace marked the history of the Church—that is, the Christian community—into the fourth century. Then, in the period 303–313, came the Great Persecution under Diocletian and his successors, when the rulers sought to eliminate what they saw as a potential menace to the state. Their unsuccessful efforts testify to the widespread strength of Christianity. Moreover, the persecutions created a list of venerated Christian martyrs, which led to the cult of saints, thereafter an integral part of Christian piety.

*Female Martyrs* In Christian thought, women could receive God's favor just as men could. Therefore Roman officials persecuted women as well as men. Our sources (called Acts of the several martyrs) record many stories of horrific punishments inflicted on women. According to Christian sources, virgins were thrown into brothels and women were fastened naked to trees by one foot and left to perish as they hung downward. One woman of Alexandria boldly refused to abandon her faith and is said to have been tortured to death by having boiling pitch poured over her body.

A famous martyr was St. Perpetua, who was put to death in Carthage in 203. A narrative in

Latin records her fate. The emperor Septimius Severus had forbidden any subjects to become Christians, but Perpetua and five others fearlessly confessed their Christianity. Her mother was a Christian, but her father was a pagan. In vain he begged her to renounce her faith in order to spare his family the disgrace of having a Christian daughter. She was tried before a procurator, who also urged her to recant, but she refused the customary sacrifice for the emperor. Perpetua and her slave, who became St. Felicitas, welcomed their martyrdom; they and their fellow Christians were mauled by wild animals before being killed by the sword.

***St. Agnes and St. Cecilia***   The narratives of the martyrs are meant to show the steadfast courage of early Christians and the solace they found in their faith. Christian sources preserve, for example, the story of St. Agnes, in the time of Diocletian. She was exposed in the stadium of Domitian in Rome (now the Piazza Navona, where a church stands bearing her name), but her nakedness was covered by the miraculous growth of her hair. She was then tied to a stake to be burned, but the flames would not touch her and the emperor had her beheaded.

Again, St. Cecilia, the purported inventor of the organ and the patron saint of music, was according to tradition imprisoned in her own bath to be scalded. She emerged unscathed and was then beheaded (the date of her death is uncertain). A church to her memory stands on the spot of her house in Rome, where she lived with her husband, whom she converted.

***An Emperor Becomes the Church's Patron***   One of the most amazing changes of face in Roman history is the radical shift in the policy of the government toward the Christians initiated in 313 by the emperor Constantine. In the traditional story, first appearing around the period 318–320, Constantine had a dream on the evening before he was to fight a rival for supremacy over Italy in 312, at the Milvian Bridge near Rome. In the dream he was told to decorate the shields of his soldiers with the Greek letters *chi* and *ro*, the monogram of Christ: "In this sign you shall conquer." Constantine won the battle

▲ **The fourth-century emperor Valentinian I shown as Christian ruler in a colossal statue from Barletta in southeast Italy. In one hand, he holds an orb (restored) to signify his imperial power; in the other, the cross to show his devotion to the Church. The portrait thus unites the two forces that sustained the later Empire.**
Scala/Art Resource, NY

and thereafter recognized divine power in the name of Christ.

At what point Constantine himself converted to Christianity is debated. In any case, in 313, at a conference held at Milan, he ended the age of persecutions by extending complete freedom of worship to the Christians and ordering the return of their confiscated goods. As to Constantine himself, his conversion had certain political reasons, for there were now so many Christians that he naturally wanted to include them within the state. But his own letters and actions show a serious personal commitment to Christianity.

***The Victory of Christianity*** Just before his death in 337, Constantine received baptism from the bishop Eusebius of Nicomedia, but Christianity was not yet the official religion of the Empire. The emperor Julian, known as the Apostate, turned his back on the church and tried in the period 361–363 to restore the position of the traditional gods, but by then the wave of Christianity could not be stopped. In 391 and 392 Theodosius the Great forbade the practice of all religions except the form of Christianity recognized by the government, thus transforming in one move the character of both the Empire and Christianity. He reversed Rome's long-standing policy of religious toleration and changed the Church from a brave alternative society sharply critical of "this world" into a friend of worldly power; it thus began attracting some "converts" who sought personal gain rather than spiritual renewal.

***Christianity and Roman Law*** The law had been moving for many years toward more humane regulations, partly under the influence of philosophic conceptions of "natural" law that could apply to all mankind. For example, the old supreme power of the father had long since fallen away. Christianity moved this spirit forward. Constantine and his successors gave more and more privileges to the church. Christians became exempt from the much-resented burdens of civil service in local curiae. Churches could own property and enjoyed exemptions from certain taxes, and bishops were allowed to judge the legal disputes of the members of their congregations. The clergy had the power to preside over the freeing of slaves by their owners, and freed slaves became citizens at once. Thus the Church acquired a privileged juridical status that it would retain, in many Western lands, until the eighteenth and nineteenth centuries.

Constantine repealed the old laws of Augustus that regulated marriage and punished celibacy—a lifestyle now tolerated more easily because celibacy in priests was seen as a virtue. Emperors tried, though without great success, to discourage the ease with which people could be divorced (St. Jerome writes of a man living with his twenty-first wife, a woman who had already had twenty-two husbands), and cases in divorce could be heard by priests. Women were given greater protection with regard to dowries; husbands had less power over a dowry during marriage, and it became easier for a wife to recover it after divorce (Hammurabi of Babylon had long ago seen to similar rights for women).

## ◆ BATTLES WITHIN CHRISTIANITY

Usually the Christian community did not bother to define matters of dogma or discipline until disputes threatened its internal unity. The losers in these disputes, if they did not amend their beliefs, were regarded as heretics (from the Greek word *hairesis*, meaning "choice"—that is, a wrong choice). This word was used from the earliest days of Christianity.

***The Heresies of Marcion and Montanus*** A heresy that threatened the character of the Christian revelation was that of Marcion of Sinope in Asia Minor (ca. 150). He sought to reform Christianity by restricting it to the message of St. Paul alone. He therefore edited his version of the New Testament, which included and recognized as divine only the Gospel of Luke and the Epistles of Paul.

Another heresy was that of a bishop from Asia Minor, Montanus (ca. 170–200), who maintained that certain living believers were prophets who were continuously receiving direct inspiration from the Holy Spirit. Women were prominent among these prophets, and Montanus' ideas eventually won the allegiance of the great North African writer Tertullian. The movement forced Christians to ask: Who should rule the Christian congregations—teachers, who could only interpret texts from the past, or living prophets, who might expect continuing new revelations?

***Christian Responses to Heresy*** Christians who accepted the standard doctrines of the Church branded the ideas of Marcion and Montanus as heresy. Because such heresies have vanished over the centuries, one might ask: What is their historical importance? The answer is that they stimulated the early Church to redefine its positions. Out of the turmoil and disagreement, the Church emerged stronger, even though the price was sometimes the blunt suppression of sincerely held opinions.

Orthodox theologians of the second century answered Marcion by defining the canon of sacred writings to include, in effect, the modern Bible—the entire Old and New Testaments. And the Church answered Montanus by declaring that the age of divine inspiration had come to an end. All the truths needed for salvation, the Church now said, were complete with the work of St. John, the last inspired author (ca. 100), and no new revelations were needed. In the fourth century, too, the Church refused to accept as inspired certain other writings, calling them the Apocrypha (obscure or unclear writings).

***The Government of the Church*** Evidence from the first century indicates that James, a relative (perhaps a brother) of Jesus, was the recognized head of the Christians in Jerusalem. During this period, too, we meet the terms deacon (*diakonos*), bishop (*episkopos,* or "overseer"), and elder (*presbuteros*), which at first were nearly synonymous. Then, in the second century, the bishop became the elected leader of a group of elders (later called priests) and of deacons (both men and women), who became responsible for collecting donations, distributing charities, and managing the Church's material affairs.

Bishops gained the right to appoint priests, define doctrine, maintain discipline, and oversee morals. This political structure gave Christianity a stable administration and a hierarchy that no ancient mystery religion enjoyed. In the West, the number of bishops remained small; they thus obtained power over fairly large areas. Bishops in cities with the largest Christian communities—Rome, Alexandria, Antioch—became the most influential. Finally, the bishop of Rome became the head of the Church in the West. The general name for a bishop was *papa,* or father, but eventually the bishop of Rome was the only one who could so call himself (in English, *pope*).

***Women in the Church*** The role of women in early Christianity presents some contradictions to the historian. The figure of Mary, mother of Jesus, was of course universally revered, and Gospel accounts associate other women with Jesus: Mary Magdalene and another Mary are said to have been the first to see Jesus risen from his tomb. Paul names one Junia in the Book of Romans as "outstanding among the apostles." Other gifted women served as teachers and coworkers with Paul.

On the other hand, the Christian writer Tertullian says of women, "You give birth to suffering and anguish. You are Eve. The Devil is in you. You were the first to abandon God's law. You were the one who deceived man." Such a stern condemnation of women reminds us of the much milder words of Paul commanding women to be silent in church: "Let the woman learn in silence with all subjection. But I suffer not a woman to teach, nor to usurp authority over the man, but to be in silence" (1 Tim. 2).

***Widows and Virgins in the Church*** But as the church developed it made more and more use of the devotion and abilities of women. Widows, for example, had always inspired compassion as people in need of help, and special honor was paid to widows who had led a chaste life and could show that they had done good works. Their duty was to pray at home but also to visit the sick and pray at their bedsides. But, in accordance with Paul's words, they were not to teach the Gospel.

Later, in the third and fourth centuries, widows and virgins could become deaconesses and thus rise higher in status within the church. Though they were members of the clergy, they still could not teach or interpret the scriptures. Their main duty was to maintain order and assist the male clergy in performing duties such as baptism, especially for women. They continued to visit the sick and to pray at their bedsides; in doing so they confirmed the church's role as the loving protector of humankind.

***Powerful Christian Women*** If women could not perform the duties reserved for priests, they could still be powerful behind the scenes. St. John Chrysostom (345?–407), a priest at Antioch

▲ **Mosaic of the Three Magi, kings or wise men, Balthasar, Melchior and Gaspar in Saint Apollinare Nuovo, 6th century A.D. Ravenna.**
San Apollinaire Nuovo Ravenna/Dagli Orti (A)/The Art Archive

and later archbishop at Constantinople, complained that influential women could get their favorites chosen as priests. Among the women whom he accused of greed and immorality was the empress Eudoxia, wife of the emperor Arcadius (r. 383–408). In the end she got Chrysostom exiled to a remote place in Armenia.

Women, especially those in the court, could also contribute stupendous fortunes to the founding of churches. St. Helena, the mother of the emperor Constantine, founded churches in Palestine, and others are known to have endowed hospitals and monasteries. Above all, historians have pointed to the ability of women in the field of conversion as their most important contribution to the early church. Paul refers to the power of women to maintain and pass on the faith in a letter to his lieutenant Timothy: "Recalling your tears, I long to see you so that I may be filled with joy. I am reminded of your sincere faith, a faith that lived first in your grandmother Lois and your mother Eunice" (2 Tim. 1). Again, St. Helena was a Christian before her son Constantine became one and probably influenced his conversion. St. Monica, the mother of St. Augustine, was a Christian and lovingly worked for the conversion of her husband and for the salvation of her son.

*Donatists*   In 303, Diocletian issued an edict ordering that churches and sacred books should be destroyed throughout the Empire. Some Christians sought to escape punishment by surrendering their copies of the Scriptures. Those who did so were called *traditores* ("those who handed over" the Scriptures—thus our word *traitor*), and the more steadfast Christians hated them. When the persecutions ended in 313, a party of North African Christians led by a bishop named Donatus declared that the "traitors," even if repentant, had forever lost membership in the Church; all the sacraments they had ever administered—all baptisms, marriages, ordinations, and the like—were declared worthless. Because the traitors were many, acceptance of the Donatist program would have brought chaos to the North African church.

The result was violent schism, which mounted on occasion to civil war. Refusing to accept the rule of traitors, the Donatists established their own bishops and hierarchy. In response, the more forgiving orthodox Church declared that the sacraments conferred grace on the recipients *ex opere operato*, simply "from the work having been performed," and that the spiritual state of the priests at the time did not matter. This attitude remained the official Christian doctrine until challenged during the Protestant Reformation of the Middle Ages.

*Arius and Arianism*   The heresy of Donatus, which insisted on proper order in the church, partakes of the Roman heritage of law and discipline within the Western church. Another heresy reflects the Greek interest in theosophical and philosophical issues. This was the movement beginning about 311 when Arius, an Alexandrian priest, began to teach that Jesus was not coequal with God the Father but had been created by him at a moment in time. Arius stated, "There was a time when he [Jesus] was not." The teachings of Arius raised a furor in Egypt and soon throughout the Empire. To restore peace, Constantine summoned the first "ecumenical" council (that is, one representing the entire inhabited world) of the Church, which met at Nicaea in Asia Minor in May 325. The council condemned Arius in the "Nicene Creed," which declared that Jesus was coeternal with the Father and of one substance with God.

Arius was exiled but was later allowed to return to Alexandria. Arianism persisted in many places, and even Constantine gradually moved to a more tolerant policy toward it. A later council, meeting at Constantinople in 381 under the emperor Theodosius, restated the Nicene Creed. These declarations had behind them the full power of the state and could be enforced as a matter of law, although belief might waver with political currents. Finally, at the Council of Chalcedon of 451, Jesus was clearly defined as one person with two natures. As a human being, he was the son of Mary; as God, he was coequal with the Father and had reigned and would reign with him eternally. This definition has since remained the belief of Christians in general.

*The Church and Classical Culture* Christian writers, although they proclaimed themselves enemies of pagan culture, had no choice but to accept classical traditions. The basic grammars and texts, the authoritative models of argument and style, were all pagan. To defend the faith, Christian apologists had to master the art of rhetoric and use the arsenal of pagan learning. This Christian accommodation with pagan learning had decisive repercussions. Nearly all the texts of the great classical authors have reached us in copies made by Christians, who believed they were useful in education. Paradoxically, these outspoken enemies of pagan values actually preserved a rich cultural heritage that they sought to undermine.

#### ◆ THE FATHERS OF THE CHURCH

Christianity became the chief religion of Europe partly because it reached the people through the languages and thought of Greco-Roman civilization. Even before the birth of Jesus, Greek-speaking Jews in Alexandria had translated the Old Testament into Greek; this version, said to have been made by seventy-two scholars, is called the *Septuagint* (from the Latin *septuaginta*, meaning "70"), and the authors of the New Testament referred to it and wrote their own works in the common Greek of the day. On the basis of these sacred texts, there grew an ocean of commentary

and persuasion by the so-called Fathers of the Church, the leading theologians of the second to fifth centuries.

*Origen and Eusebius* The most learned Church father writing in Greek was Origen (185?–253?), a priest in Alexandria. Both the volume and the profound scholarship of his writings were a wonder of late antiquity. He worked especially on the text of the scriptures by comparing the original Hebrew and the Septuagint; he also wrote extensive commentaries on books of the Bible and a tract, *Against Celsus,* in which he answers the arguments of an elitist critic of the Christians. Another highly influential Greek father was Eusebius of Caesarea (260?–340?). His most original work was a history of the Church, which became the model for later such histories. The most learned man of his time, he also wrote a *Chronicle* of universal history, which is one of our most important sources for ancient history in general.

*The Latin Fathers: Ambrose and Jerome* Among the fathers who wrote in Latin was Ambrose, bishop of Milan from 374 to 397. His most important doctrine was that the Church must be independent of the emperor and that bishops should have the right to chastise rulers. In 390 Ambrose excommunicated the emperor Theodosius after he had massacred the rebellious citizens of Thessalonica, forbidding him to receive the eucharist and thus placing him outside the body of the Church. Theodosius admitted his guilt and repented, and the popes of later centuries who struggled with secular officials owed much of their power to the resolute example of Ambrose.

Jerome (340?–420) succeeded Eusebius as the most learned Church father of his time. His translation of both the Old and the New Testaments into Latin, usually called the Vulgate version of the Bible, is probably the most influential book ever written in the Latin language. It became the medium through which the Judeo-Christian writings permeated the Latin-speaking nations of Europe and was the biblical text most often used during the Middle Ages. It also assured that Latin would survive deeply into the Middle Ages as the medium of debate and would thus provide a necessary link to the classical past.

▲ An early mosaic (ca. 400) showing Christ holding a book and surrounded by apostles in Roman dress. Two women, perhaps saints, crown St. Peter and St. Paul, with the holy city of Jerusalem in the background. The commanding figure of Jesus resembles that of Jupiter in Roman art. From the church of Santa Pudenziana, Rome.

Scala/Art Resource, NY

*Augustine*   Augustine (354–430), the best known of the fathers, was born in North Africa of a pagan father and a Christian mother and accepted Christianity under the influence of Ambrose in 387 (see "Augustine Is Brought to His Faith," p. 172). He became bishop of Hippo in North Africa in 395 and spent the remaining years of his long life writing, preaching, and administering his see.

In his voluminous writings Augustine had something to say about almost every question of Christian theology. He profoundly influenced, for example, Christian teachings on sexual morality and marriage. Like some of his pagan contemporaries, he believed that the world was already filled with people. "The coming of Christ," he wrote, "is not served by the begetting of chil-

dren." He therefore urged all Christians to a life of celibacy, even though this would cause their number to decline: "Marriage is not expedient, except for those who do not have self-control." He banned all sexual activity for the unmarried. Within marriage, husband and wife should unite sexually only for procreation, and even the pleasure they took in this act, representing a triumph of libido over reason, was a small, though pardonable, sin.

*The Working of Grace*   Augustine was passionately interested in the operations of grace (see p. 172). He sought the work of grace in his own life, and the result was his *Confessions*, an intensely personal autobiography; it is both a record of his

## Augustine Is Brought to His Faith

◆

*St. Augustine describes how, after many struggles to overcome his lustful nature, he was inspired at age thirty-one to pick up and read in the New Testament; this was the critical moment in his conversion.*

"And, not indeed in these words, but to this effect I spoke often to you: 'But you, O Lord, how long? Will you be angry forever? Do not remember against us the guilt of past generations.' I sent up these sorrowful cries—'How long, how long? Tomorrow, and tomorrow? Why not now? Why is there now no end to my uncleanness?'

"I was saying these things and weeping in the most bitter contrition of my heart, when I heard the voice of a boy or girl, I do not know which, coming from a neighboring house, chanting, and often repeating, 'Take up and read; take up and read.' Immediately my face changed, and I began to consider whether it was usual for children in any kind of game to sing such words; nor could I remember ever hearing anything like this. So, restraining the torrent of my tears, I rose up, interpreting it as nothing but a command from heaven to open the Bible, and to read the first chapter I saw. So I returned to where I had put down the apostles. I grasped it, opened it, and in silence read the first paragraph I saw—'Not in rioting and drunkenness, not in debauchery and lust, not in strife and envy; but let Jesus Christ be your armor, and give no more thought to satisfying bodily appetites' [Romans 13–14]. I read no further, I did not need to; for instantly, as the sentence ended—by a light of security that poured into my heart—all the gloom of doubt vanished."

From *Confessions*, 8.12, J. G. Pilkington (tr.), in Whitney Oates (ed.), *The Basic Writings of Saint Augustine*, vol. 1 (Random House, 1948), p. 126, language modified.

early life, when he gave way to material and sexual temptations, and a celebration of the providence that had guided him in his struggle toward God. This masterpiece of introspective analysis is a type of literature virtually unknown in the classical tradition.

In theological matters, Augustine distinguished between God the creator (the author of nature) and God the redeemer (the source of grace), and insisted that these two figures not be confused. God as creator had given humanity certain powers, such as intelligence superior to that of beasts, but those powers, injured by the original fall of Adam and Eve, are insufficient to earn salvation. Only through grace, which Jesus' sacrifice had earned, could humanity hope to be saved. Moreover, God had already decided on whom he would bestow grace; hence, even before we are born, we are all predestined either to heaven or to hell.

*Augustine on Salvation* Augustine deeply pondered the problem of sin—the breaking of God's law—and quarreled with Pelagius, a British monk who argued that sin was only the result of a wrong choice and that people could achieve perfection, do good works, and thus attain salvation. For Augustine, sin descended from Adam into every human being, and doing good works, no matter how many, could not guarantee salvation, which was the gift of God alone through his grace. Humanity's salvation must await a glorious transformation at the end of time.

Augustine further believed that the power of grace might redeem the whole course of human history. In his greatest work, *The City of God*, he set out to show that there was order in history: Behind the manifold events of the past the hand of God was evident, directing people through his grace to their destiny. Into this immense panorama, Augustine brought the sacred history of the Jewish Testament, the history of his own times, and the Christian expectation of resurrection. He held that the grace of God united the chosen in a form of community or city that stood against the community of those joined by the love of earthly things. The city of God, in which live those chosen for salvation, was as yet invisible, and the elect who were its members should recognize that this present earth was not their true home. Augustine saw history as moving in a straight line toward humankind's salvation, as

▲ The cathedral in Syracuse, Sicily. The interior, in powerful historical symbolism, shows a Doric temple to Athena (fifth century B.C.) with its original columns, now supporting the walls and roof of a Christian church built in the seventh century A.D.

Art Resource, NY

compared with cyclical views among some Greeks. Therefore, to Christians of his own troubled age and to those of later ages, Augustine held out the beckoning vision of a heavenly city, a celestial Jerusalem, where at last they would be at home with God.

## SUMMARY

In the history of the Roman Empire, several great themes are seen. The body politic soon lost direct elections by the people, and the structure of society became constantly more monarchic. As success in war led to an established empire, a long period of peace nourished the economy and saw the development of urban centers throughout Europe. The Empire managed to avoid a near-collapse, and within its survival the Christian religion won the victory of faith. Christians felt able to ignore or transcend the "fall" of Rome—an event that the modern world sees as a possible model of its own fate. The transformation of the Empire, as it is better called, is a challenge and a warning to all who read history; it is also the recognized end of the ancient world and the beginning of a long period in which new nations would use the legacy of antiquity in their own development.

## QUESTION FOR FURTHER THOUGHT

1. It may well surprise the historian that the Roman Empire, which controlled almost all of Europe in its time, suffered a catastrophic decline. By what means, if any, might this decline have been mitigated or even prevented?

## RECOMMENDED READING

### Sources

*Early Christian Writings: The Apostolic Fathers.* M. Staniforth (tr.). 1968.

Suetonius. *Lives of the Caesars.* Robert Graves (tr.). 1972.

Tacitus. *Annals of Imperial Rome.* Michael Grant (tr.). 1978.

———. *The Histories.* Kenneth Wellesley (tr.). 1976. The two works give the history of the Empire in the first century A.D. by the leading Roman historian.

### Studies

Barnes, Timothy D. *The New Empire of Diocletian and Constantine.* 1982. Detailed study of the reigns of the two emperors who restored the power of Rome.

Birley, Anthony. *Marcus Aurelius: A Biography.* 1987. Study of the only philosopher-king in Roman history.

Bradley, Keith R. *Slaves and Masters in the Roman Empire: A Study in Social Control.* 1987. Modern treatment of slave families, freeing of slaves, rewards and punishments.

Brown, Peter. *Augustine of Hippo: A Biography.* 1986. Masterly treatment of the greatest of the church fathers.

———. *The World of Late Antiquity, AD 150–750.* 1971. One of many illuminating books by this great scholar. Brief, well illustrated.

Cameron, Averil. *The Mediterranean World in Late Antiquity, AD 395–600.* 1993. A brief, accessible modern survey.

Cross, Frank M. *The Ancient Library of Qumrân and Modern Biblical Studies.* 1976. Good introduction to the study of the Dead Sea Scrolls.

Frend, W. H. C. *The Rise of Christianity.* 1984. Most extensive one-volume history of the early church down to about A.D. 600.

Galinsky, Karl. *Augustan Culture.* 1996. Art, architecture, literature, and culture of the age.

Lieu, Judith, et al. (eds.). *The Jews among Pagans and Christians in the Roman Empire.* 1992. Essays on various aspects of Jewish life and society in the Empire.

MacMullen, Ramsay. *Christianizing the Roman Empire.* 1986. The spread of Christianity, with attention to conversion of Constantine and results.

————. *Constantine.* 1988. Biography of the emperor who pointed the Empire toward Christianity.

————. *Paganism in the Roman Empire.* 1981. Study of pagan beliefs, worshipers, and cults in the Empire.

Musurillo, Herbert (ed.). *The Acts of the Christian Martyrs.* 1979. Translations of accounts of torture and martyrdom in early Christianity.

Nicholas, Barry. *An Introduction to Roman Law.* 1988. Study of principles of the law, with attention to its influence in medieval and modern times.

Stambaugh, John E. *The Ancient Roman City.* 1988. Study of development of the city; comparisons with other ancient cities.

Wells, Colin. *The Roman Empire.* 2d ed. 1995. The best one-volume modern narrative.

Whittaker, C. R. *The Frontiers of the Roman Empire: A Social and Economic Study.* 1994. On the Germans and other neighbors of the Empire.

▲ The gilded copper relief of the Lombard king Agilulf, shown flanked by his warriors, shows Germanic adaptation of kingship in imitation of the Roman emperors. The Lombards conquered much of the Italian peninsula in 568. Agilulf became king shortly afterward.
Scala/Art Resource, NY

# Chapter 6

---

# THE MAKING OF WESTERN EUROPE

The "Dark Ages" is the popular conception of the period after the decline of the Roman Empire in Western Europe, but the period was one that saw continuities as well as radical changes. In the period of roughly the fifth through the eighth centuries A.D., the composition and customs of Western Europe's population changed with the invasion of various Germanic and Hunnish peoples. The former Celtic and Roman populations gradually intermarried with the invaders; classical Latin ceased to be the ordinary language of people and instead evolved into Spanish, Portuguese, French, and Italian. Roman law blended with the law of the invaders. Settlement patterns also changed. Those Romans wealthy enough to have country villas moved from the cities to the country. The invaders, who had lived in forests and practiced agriculture in villages, also preferred to live in the countryside. Roman cities fell into a decline, and aqueducts, roads, walls, baths, and the general infrastructure that made the cities comfortable were no longer maintained. But with all these changes, some semblance of the earlier glory of Rome remained, particularly among educated churchmen.

Christianity continued to gain widespread acceptance among the Roman population and among the invading tribes. Although most of the tribes initially converted from paganism to the heresy espoused by Arius (see chapter 5), eventually the population of Western Europe became Roman or Catholic Christians. Paganism lingered, and Jews continued to live in the West. Monasteries, religious communities for men and women, provided a refuge for those who wished to lead a life of prayer and scholarly pursuits. Heroic missionaries went among the tribes and brought them Christianity along with Roman civilization and writing. It was a period of major spiritual expansion.

For the ordinary people, both Roman and tribal, these centuries were ones of violence, danger, and movement. Waves of invasions made agriculture and even survival unpredictable, but eventually the movement stopped and kingdoms were established so that agriculture and trade resumed. Even during these political disruptions innovations were improving agriculture, including a better plow, a new system of crop rotation, the horse collar, and the stirrup.

| CHAPTER 6. THE MAKING OF WESTERN EUROPE | | | | | | | |
|---|---|---|---|---|---|---|---|
| | Social Structure | Body Politic | Changes in the Organization of Production and in the Impact of Technology | Evolution of Family and Changing Gender Roles | War | Religion | Cultural Expression |
| I. THE NEW COMMUNITY OF PEOPLE | | | | | | | |
| II. THE NEW POLITICAL STRUCTURES | | | | | | | |
| III. THE NEW ECONOMY | | | | | | | |
| IV. THE EXPANSION OF THE CHURCH | | | | | | | |

# I. The New Community of Peoples

The civilization that took root in the west and north of Europe after the decline of the Roman Empire was the direct ancestor of the modern Western world. Historians call the millennium between the fall of the Roman Empire and approximately 1500 the Middle Ages, or the medieval period of European history. The Early Middle Ages witnessed the emergence of new types of social and cultural organization from the shambles of the Roman Empire; this new civilization embraced both the former subjects of the Empire and peoples from beyond its borders. The Greeks and Romans called all these peoples *barbarians* because of their unintelligible languages and strange customs.[1] There was no single barbarian nation: These peoples were many and differed considerably in language and culture.

## ◆ THE GREAT MIGRATIONS

Among the barbarian peoples were the Celtic tribes in northern Scotland and in Ireland. (The common name for the Celtic Irish was, confusingly, Scots.) These Celts escaped the Roman domination that had befallen their cousins, the Britons and Gauls. The underlying culture of

France and Spain remained Celtic. Although Roman occupation imposed its government and civilization on the Celts, it did not destroy their own culture.

More numerous and more formidable than the Celts were the Germans, who were settled in a great arc that stretched from Scandinavia to the Black Sea. Historians have given these peoples the generic names of Germans or Goths, based loosely on their membership in the Germanic linguistic group to which their various dialects belonged. The term does not imply unity of culture, a self-designation by the people, or a relationship to modern Germans. Many of the Germanic tribes had long been exposed to Mediterranean influences and had some understanding of the Roman economy, warfare, and culture. From about 350, Christianity spread among the Germans north of the Danube, but in its Arian form. Beyond this Germanic cordon lived the still pagan Slavic tribes, also identifiable by their linguistic group, and the most numerous of the barbarians. When the tribes migrated, they traveled as family groups with their possessions, abandoning the land on which they had previously lived.

*Huns and Germanic Peoples* Germanic tribes had for centuries challenged the Roman frontiers because their primitive, unproductive economies forced them to search constantly for new lands to plunder or settle. The wealth and splendor of the Roman world attracted the Germans. The Romans

---

[1]The Greeks invented the word *barbaros* to imitate the strange sounds of unintelligible languages.

## *Chronology*
### THE GERMANIC INVASIONS

| | |
|---|---|
| ca. 310 | Goths and other Germans on the Danube. |
| ca. 350 | Huns invade Europe, destroy Ostrogoths, and drive Visigoths to seek settlement south of the Danube in Byzantine territory. |
| 378 | Battle of Adrianople: Visigothic defeat of Byzantine army. |
| ca. 400 | Franks, Alamans, Burgundians, Vandals, and others cross the Rhine into Gaul. |
| 410–412 | Visigoths sack Rome and move on into Gaul. |
| 429 | Visigoths in Spain and South Gaul. |
| ca. 430–500 | Anglo-Saxons in England, Vandals in Africa, Franks in Gaul, Alamans in Alsace and upper Danube, Burgundians in Rhone Valley. |
| (d. 461) | St. Patrick: Conversion of Ireland. |
| (r. 485–511) | Clovis: Conversion of Franks to Roman Christianity. |
| (r. 493–526) | Theodoric and the Ostrogothic kingdom of Italy: Boethius and Cassiodorus. |
| (r. 527–565) | Justinian: Conquest of Vandal kingdom of North Africa and part of Spain and Italy. |
| (r. 590–604) | Pope Gregory the Great: Mission of Augustine (597) to England. |
| (664) | Council of Whitby: United English Christians under the papacy. |
| (r. 714–741) | Charles Martel: Defeats the Arabs at Tours (Poitiers) in 732. |
| 751 | Pepin III: Becomes King of Franks with papal support, anointed by pope in 754. |

brought them into the Empire initially as slaves or prisoners of war, then as free peasants to settle on deserted lands, and finally as mercenary soldiers and officers. By the fourth century, however, the barbarian penetration of the Empire became more violent because the barbarians themselves were being invaded and forced southwestward by nomadic hordes from central Asia.

The nomads who sowed tumult in the barbarian world were the Huns, a people probably of Mongolian or Tatar origin. Perhaps in reaction to climatic changes that desiccated their pastures, the Huns swept out of their Asiatic homeland and terrorized Western Europe. Unlike the Germanic tribes, they had no previous contact with Rome or Christianity. Their great chief Attila (r. 433?–453), the "scourge of God" according to Christian writers, established his horde on the plain of the middle Danube and from there led the Huns on raids into both Gaul and Italy. With Attila's death in 453, the Hunnic empire disintegrated, but the Huns had already given impetus to the great movement of peoples that marks the beginning of the Middle Ages.

*Visigoths*  The Visigoths (or West Goths) were the first of the Germanic tribes that the Huns dislodged. Fleeing before the Huns, the Visigoths asked the Byzantine emperor to settle them in a depopulated area south of the Danube. In 376 the

▼ VISIGOTHIC FIBULAE
**Fibulae were decorative pins used to fasten clothes. These sixth-century Spanish examples are typical of the sophisticated metalwork practiced by medieval artisans. Gems set in gold and bronze reveal the outline of an eagle form, as well as a delight in pattern that was characteristic of the age.**
Walters Art Gallery, Baltimore

emperor Valens admitted them into the Empire. Although the Visigoths were willing to settle peacefully, the Byzantine officials treated them miserably, raping their women and forcing them to sell children into slavery in return for food. The starving Goths rebelled and Valens led an expedition against them. The triumph of the Visigothic cavalry over the Byzantine army at the battle of Adrianople in 378 showed the superiority of the Gothic mounted warrior (the prototype of the medieval knight) over the Roman foot soldier.

Continuing their westward movement, the Visigoths sacked Rome in 410, the first time in 800 years that a foreign army had occupied Rome. The Visigoths took gold and silver treasure, slaves, and movable property. The devastated Romans asked the Visigoth leader what he would leave for them, and he is reputed to have replied, "Your lives." Crossing the Alps into Gaul, the Visigoths established in 418 the first autonomous kingdom on Roman soil. At its height in the mid-fifth century, the kingdom of the Visigoths extended from Gibraltar to the Loire River. Another Germanic people, the Franks, conquered the Visigothic kingdom in Gaul in the sixth century and confined the Visigoths to Spain.

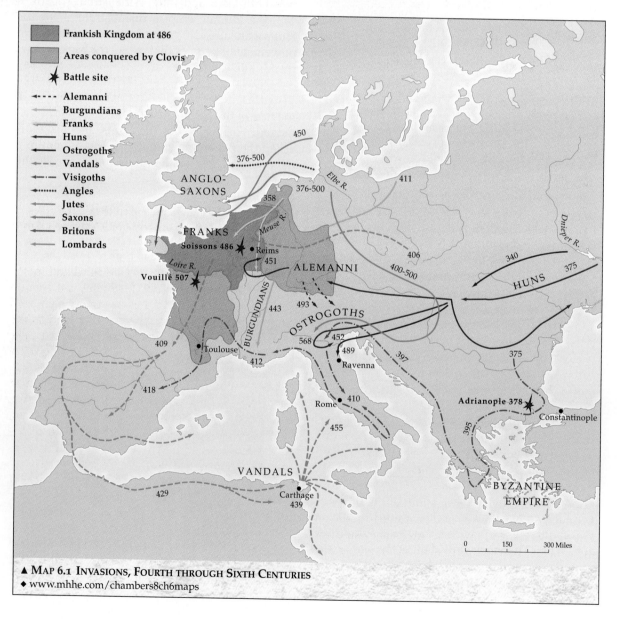

▲ MAP 6.1 INVASIONS, FOURTH THROUGH SIXTH CENTURIES
◆ www.mhhe.com/chambers8ch6maps

*Vandals and Burgundians* The Vandals were another Germanic people that the Huns forced out of their territory. Coming from eastern Germany, the Vandals crossed the Rhine River into Gaul in 406. Perhaps eighty thousand in number, they continued south through the Iberian Peninsula (Spain) and crossed to North Africa, where they established a permanent kingdom in 429. Like the Visigoths, the Vandals were Arians, and they persecuted orthodox Christians. They became so powerful on the Mediterranean Sea that in 455 they were able to plunder Rome. This act, the cruelty involved in their religious persecutions, and their piracy in the Mediterranean earned the Vandals a reputation for senseless violence, which the modern word *vandal* still reflects. The Vandal kingdom survived until the Byzantine emperor Justinian destroyed it in the sixth century.

The Burgundians, another Germanic tribe from eastern Europe, followed the Vandals into Gaul, probably in 411. These Germans established an independent kingdom in the valleys of the upper Rhône and Saône rivers in 443, which gave the region its permanent name, Burgundy (see map 6.1).

*Ostrogoths* The ease with which all these Germanic peoples invaded the Roman frontiers shows that the Empire had lost virtually all authority in the West by the middle of the fifth century. The emperor Valentinian III was the last Roman to exercise any real power in the West. A series of feeble emperors were raised to the throne and then deposed or murdered by German officials, who were the effective rulers. One of these rulers, Odovacar, deposed the last emperor in 476. Although no more than a palace mutiny, this coup marks the final passage of power from Roman to German hands in the West.

The Ostrogoths (eastern Goths) moved into the territory vacated by the Visigoths at the invitation of the Byzantine emperor. Young Theodoric, son of one of their kings, was sent as a hostage to Constantinople. There he learned at least something of Greek and Roman culture, although he continued to adhere to Arian Christianity. The emperor so favored him that he was even made a Roman citizen. When Theodoric united all of the Ostrogoths under his command, they became too dangerous to keep in the East and the emperor dispatched Theodoric and the Ostrogoths to deal with

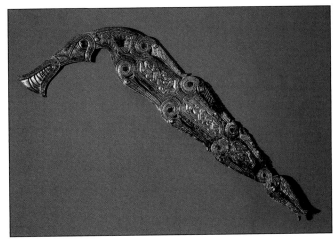

▲ SUTTON HOO DRAGON OF ANGLO-SAXON ENGLAND
There were many metallic buckles and pins found at Sutton Hoo, the ship burial site of the East Anglian king Anna, who died in 654. Shown here is a dragon, made of gilt bronze and garnet. The body, extending from the head—with its jaws, teeth, and garnet eye—to the tail, is embellished in a style common at the time, with intricate beasts intertwined in long ribbonlike patterns.
© British Museum (PS199015)

Odovacar. Theodoric led his troops into Italy in 489 and conquered it, overthrowing Odovacar in 493.

*Germanic Tribes in Gaul* In the third and fourth centuries the Germanic tribes living just beyond the Roman frontier in the Rhine valley coalesced into two large federations, the Alemanni in the upper valley and the Franks in the lower valley. The Alemanni pushed beyond the Rhine into the middle of Gaul and founded a kingdom in 420. They give to both modern French and Spanish their names for Germany (*Allemagne, Alemania*). The Franks slowly penetrated into northern Gaul, moving across the valley of the Seine up to the Loire River. By the fifth century they had separated into two peoples: the Salian, or "salty," Franks, who occupied the lands from the shores of the British Channel to the Loire valley (excluding only Brittany); and the Ripuarian, or "riverbank," Franks, whose history is wrapped in obscurity but who seem to have settled between the Rhine and Meuse rivers. The first-mentioned king of the Salians, a figure who stands on the dark margin between legend and history, was called Merovech, and he gave his name to the first dynasty of Frankish kings, the Merovingians.

***Anglo-Saxons in Britain***  The Romans had withdrawn their legions from Britain in 407 to defend Rome against the Visigoths, leaving the island open to invasion. The Germanic settlement of Britain differed from the conquests on the continent. Rather than traveling as family groups, the Angles, Saxons, Jutes, and even some Franks came in small bands under the authority of chiefs. These Germanic peoples did not settle and assimilate with the native peoples (the Britons) as they did in most other Roman provinces; they either exterminated the Britons or pushed them westward into Cornwall and Wales.

For a few decades in the early sixth century the Britons in Britain unsuccessfully rallied against the Germanic invaders under a king whom later sources call Arthur, but after 550 the invaders triumphed and imposed their language on the region. So sharp was the linguistic change thus enforced that modern English, apart from place names, shows little trace of the speech of the original Britons.

***The Early Slavs***  The Slavic tribes living to the east of the Germans embarked on their own extensive migrations. In the fifth and sixth centuries some Slavic tribes pushed their settlements as far west as the Elbe River and as far north as the Baltic Sea; they are the ancestors of the modern West Slavs—the Poles, Czechs, and Slovaks. During the same years, other Slavic tribes penetrated into the Balkan peninsula and Greece; their descendants are the modern South Slavs—the Serbs, Croats, Bulgarians, and Macedonians. Still other tribes moved east beyond the Dnieper River and north into the forest regions of Russia; they are the ancestors of the modern East Slavs—the Russians, Ukrainians, and Belarussians (or White Russians).

#### ◆ GERMANIC SOCIETY

Much of what we know about Germanic society comes from a Roman historian and writer, Cornelius Tacitus (ca. A.D. 56–120). While he lived before the period of the invasions, he knew of Germanic customs from talking to Germanic soldiers and slaves. In recent years archaeology has

done much to supplement his account of the these peoples.

***Social Structure***  Germanic society was composed of chiefs who distinguished themselves by success in battle, free warriors and their families, and some slaves. The Germanic free warrior owned land, and individual ownership existed as far back in their history as our knowledge goes. Individual ownership allowed some families to become richer than others. Germanic society was not egalitarian. Families with a common ancestry were linked together into kindreds (groups of near relatives). The kindred fought, migrated, settled, and held certain forms of property (forests and wastelands) in common.

The kindred also adjudicated disputes among its members and avenged injuries done to them. Compensation was defined in money for loss of a person's life. The amount of compensation, called a *Wergeld* (literally, "man money"), depended on the social rank of the individual. Offenders could also pay the family compensation for the loss of an arm, eye, teeth, or nose. The wergeld helped to prevent feuds.

Kindreds grouped together to form a tribe, a people, or a nation; members of a tribe always looked upon themselves, rightly or wrongly, as descendants from a common ancestor. Before the Germanic invasions of the Roman Empire, the tribes or peoples did not usually have kings; only the invasions, which required a continuing military command, made the king (who also served as chief priest) usual within Germanic society.

***The Valued Role of Women***  A sensitive indicator of social values in any society is the status of women. Tacitus praises the Germans for their chastity and fidelity. German women, Tacitus also tells us, were mature at first marriage, and their husbands were their equals in age. Women were so valued in marriage that the family of the groom paid a dower (or marriage gift) to the bride, which was hers to keep and pass on to her heirs. When Germanic laws were recorded in the sixth century, the value placed on killing a woman of marriageable age was among the highest wergelds a murderer could pay.

Women made essential contributions to the Germanic household at every social level. A free

German male who aspired to be a warrior needed a wife who would tend his fields and watch over his flocks and herds during his absences on campaigns. The chief or king similarly looked for a wife who could collect his dues, pay his retainers, and manage his lands. The social importance of Germanic women was not, however, an unmixed benefit. According to Tacitus, they worked harder than the men did. In addition to doing much of the agriculture, women brewed, spun cloth, and made clothing for their families. They were often the prized booty for raiding expeditions and constant targets of abduction. Their life expectancy seems to have been shorter than that of males, and their resulting smaller number added to their social value.

***Comitatus or Warrior Bands***   Warfare was a way of life and an integral part of the economy for the Germanic peoples. While herding, agriculture, and hunting provided much of their daily needs, the Germans also raided other peoples and eventually the Roman territory to get metals, slaves, and precious objects. The warriors were organized into bands under the leadership of a chief. Tacitus called this warrior band a *comitatus* ("following"), in which young warriors would join the retinue of an established chief, follow him to battle, and fight under his leadership in return for his protection and a share of his booty. Historians have traced the origins of feudalism to the comitatus (see Chapter 8).

***Law and Procedures***   Germanic laws were not written down until the sixth century, and reliance on oral tradition explains several peculiarities of Germanic institutions. To recall the ancient laws, the Germans consulted old, respected men of the community, who could remember past customs. One of the most distinctive features of tribal government was its reliance on large councils or assemblies. The chief or king had only limited power and never made decisions alone; he always acted in an assembly or council of free warriors who aided him in making his judgments.

To confirm the making of contracts within the community, Germans (and the medieval world after them) relied heavily on symbolic gestures publicly performed. In conveying property, for example, the former owner would hand over a twig or a clod of earth to the new owner in the presence of witnesses. But since the memory of witnesses was often unreliable as a record of such agreements, the Germans also determined truth or falsehood, guilt or innocence, in disputes by investigating the character of the litigants or by appealing to magic. In a practice known as *compurgation*, twelve good men would swear to the honest reputation and presumed innocence of the accused. Or the accused would undergo an *ordeal* (the word originally meant "judgment"), such as stepping barefoot over hot irons or immersing a hand in boiling water; if the feet or hand showed no severe burns, the accused was declared innocent. Sometimes two litigants would simply fight before the court (trial by combat) on the assumption that an innocent man could not be vanquished.

All these practices influenced the development of medieval law and government. The use of juries in trials, a common practice of Europe in the Middle Ages, was based on the assumption that the entire community, represented by sworn men, should determine when a law was violated. The medieval king, like his early Germanic predecessor, was also expected to make his major decisions with the advice of senior men, assembled in councils (see "Tacitus on the Early Germans," p. 184).

***The Literary Legacy of Germanic Poetry***   Since the Germans made little use of writing, their literature was preserved by oral transmission. They favored poetry, more easily memorized than prose, for literary expression. The earliest surviving examples of Germanic poetry were not written down until the ninth century, but they still provide an authentic reflection of Germanic culture, testifying to a violent age.

In the Anglo Saxon epic *Beowulf,* the king of the Danes, Hrothgar, is powerless against the terrible monster Grendel; his plight illustrates the weakness of tribal kingship. Hrothgar must appeal for help to the hero Beowulf, a great warrior who comes from a tribe in southern Sweden. Beowulf succeeds in defeating Grendel by tearing off his arm. Grendel flees and dies. When Grendel's mother, a sea-witch, comes seeking revenge, Beowulf chases her to her underwater cave, where he finds a giant's ancient sword and slays Grendel's mother. Beowulf becomes king and dies

## TACITUS ON THE EARLY GERMANS

◆

*The short book by Cornelius Tacitus,* Germania, *published in 98, is virtually the only surviving portrait of early Germanic society. In this passage Tacitus describes the customs of the Germans in government.*

"On matters of minor importance only the chiefs deliberate, on major affairs the whole community; but, even where the people have the power to decide, the case is carefully considered in advance by the chiefs. Except in case of accident or emergency they assemble on fixed days.... When the mass so decide, they take their seats fully armed. Silence is then demanded by the priests, who on that occasion have also power to enforce obedience.... If a proposal displeases them, the people roar out their dissent; if they approve, they clash their spears.

"One can launch an accusation before the Council or bring a capital charge. The punishment varies to suit the crime. The traitor and deserter are hanged on trees, the coward, the shirker and the unnaturally vicious are drowned in miry swamps under a cover of wattled hurdles. The distinction in the punishment implies that deeds of violence should be paid for in the full glare of publicity, but that deeds of shame should be suppressed. Even for lighter offences the punishment varies. The man who is found guilty is fined so and so many horses or cattle. Part of the fine is paid to the King or State, part to the injured man or his relatives."

From H. Mattingly (tr.), *The Germania* (Penguin Classics, 1970), pp. 11–12.

---

years later in his last major fight against a dragon. The poem is rich in descriptions of drinking halls, court intrigues, kingship, and personal loyalties of a follower to his leader. Other than Grendel's mother, women do not play a role in the poem. Christian elements appear in the earliest written version, indicating that the poem underwent transformation over the years it was recited.

*Religion and Superstition* Germanic religion displayed an abiding sense of pessimism. The Germans saw nature as a hostile force controlled by two sets of gods. Minor deities, both good and bad, dwelt in groves, streams, fields, and seas and directly affected human beings. Through incantations, spells, or charms, people tried to influence the actions of these spirits. Such practices strongly influenced popular religion and mixed with it a large element of superstition, which lasted through the Middle Ages and long beyond.

The higher gods lived in the sky and took a remote interest in human affairs. Chief among them was Woden, or Odin, god of magic and victory. Woden; his wife, Friia or Frig; Thor, the thunderer; Ti or Tyr, the god of war—all give their names to days of the week in all Germanic languages, including English.

*The Art of Metal Working* Because they changed their homes so frequently, the Germans developed no monumental art—no temples, palaces, or large statues—before settling within the Empire. Their finest art was jewelry made from precious metals, often embodying forms of animals (see photos on pages 179 and 181). This animal style, probably originating in the steppe region of eastern Europe and Asia, strongly influenced early medieval art; even the lettering and illuminations in the manuscripts of that epoch reflect some of its motifs.

### ◆ GERMANS AND ROMANS

Historians have estimated, although on flimsy evidence, that the Germans who settled within the Roman Empire constituted no more than 5 percent of the total population. The Germans did not exterminate the Romans; rather, through gradual settlement and intermarriage with Romans, the Germans adopted lives that made them almost indistinguishable from their Roman counterparts. Some historians have argued that both Romans and Germans came to resemble the indigenous Celts.

Historians no longer speak confidently, as they once did, of the Germans being responsible for the

## SIDONIUS APOLLINARIS ON LIVING WITH GERMANS

◆

*A Roman of patrician birth and training living in Gaul, Sidonius (ca. 431–ca. 480) wrote a series of letters to friends commenting on the loss of the Latin language, the wreck of the Roman Empire, and the crudity of the Germanic tribes.*

"Though you descend in the male line from an ancestor who was not only consul—that is immaterial—but also (and here is the real point) a poet . . . yet here we find you picking up a knowledge of the German tongue with the greatest ease; the feat fills me with indescribable amazement. . . . You can hardly conceive how amused we all are to hear that, when you are by, not a barbarian but fears to perpetrate a barbarism in his own language. Old Germans bowed with age are said to stand astounded when they see you interpreting their German letters; they actually choose you for arbiter and mediator in their disputes. You are a new Solon in the elucidation of Burgundian law. . . . You are popular on all sides; you are sought after; your society gives universal pleasure. You are chosen as adviser and judge; as

soon as you utter a decision it is received with respect. In body and mind alike these people are as stiff as stocks and very hard to form; yet they delight to find in you, and equally delight to learn a Burgundian eloquence and a Roman spirit.

"Let me end with a single caution to the cleverest of men. Do not allow these talents of yours to prevent you from devoting whatever time you can spare to reading. Let your critical taste determine you to preserve a balance between the two languages [Latin and German], holding fast to the one to prevent us making fun of you, and practicing the other that you may have the laugh of us."

From O. M. Dalton, *The Letters of Sidonius,* 2 volumes, V. v. To his friend Syagriius (Clarendon Press, 1915).

---

destruction of the Western Roman Empire. Even before entering the Empire, many Germans, particularly those settled near the frontiers, had achieved a cultural level that resembled that of Romans living in those areas. In the northern part of Gaul, Celtic influences had already reemerged, and Roman influence proved to be a rather thin veneer on the region and its peoples. Assimilation, however, was slow and had a definite impact on Roman society. In the course of time, the Germanic chiefs and armies obtained perhaps a third of the territory of the former Western Empire. Some of them paid Romans for the confiscation. One Roman in Gaul wrote to a friend that he had lost all his lands, but eventually the Visigoth who took them sent him a payment much lower than the value of the land. Even this amount was enough that he could hold up his head in Roman society again. The letters of Sidonius Apollinaris (431–480) are eloquent about the experiences of the Roman patricians (see "Sidonius Apollinaris on Living with Germans," above).

***Changes Following Settlement*** The settling tribes changed the landscape and language of the

areas they invaded. Before the invasions the tribes had lived in nucleated villages (houses in a central area and fields surrounding the housing area). When they moved into the Roman Empire, the Germanic tribes showed a preference for continuing this settlement pattern rather than living in cities. Since those Romans who had villas also preferred to live in the countryside, urban populations shrank and the infrastructure of the cities, such as aqueducts, disappeared. With education abandoned except in the Church and among some Romans, the Latin language was no longer commonly written or spoken, and vernacular languages (the romance languages, or languages derived from the Roman one) began to develop.

As the invaders settled and established states modeled as much as possible on their understanding of Roman government, they needed written law rather than oral tradition. The Germanic law codes, modeled on Roman law codes but codifying Germanic law, included the schedule of wergelds and the power of kings. The codes allowed Romans to continue under their own laws.

Intermarriage in the population was inevitable. The Roman middle class married with the invaders. Most of the humble Germanic free war-riors settled as cultivators on the land. If there were anxieties among Roman or Germanic parents about intermarriage or among free warriors becoming peasants, these anxieties are not expressed in written accounts.

*Christianity and the Tribes*   By the time many of the tribes entered Europe, they had already converted to Christianity. The conversion began with Ulfila (ca. 310–ca. 381), the son of Christian parents who lived in the land of the Goths. His parents had been captured by the Goths so that he grew up a Gothic-speaking Christian. He received a Christian education and was consecrated in 341 by the bishop of Constantinople, who was the leader of the Arian party. Ulfila brought the Arian version of Christianity to the Goths and translated the Bible into their language. From these early missionary activities Arian Christianity spread to the Visigoths, Vandals, and Ostrogoths.

The difference between the Arian Goths and the Roman Christians was one of the most serious barriers to peaceful settlement of the tribes. Most of the Arian kings persecuted the native Christian population. Only the Franks, under Clovis, converted to Roman Christianity. Because of this early conversion, the Frankish rulers developed a close relation with the Roman Church.

# II. The New Political Structures

By the beginning of the sixth century, the initial wave of tribal migrations into the West had eased and the tribes began to settle, forming monarchies and recording their law in imitation of the Romans. While the Western Empire was undergoing a major reconfiguration of its political landscape that only partially resembled its Roman past, the Eastern Empire continued to flourish.

## ◆ THE EARLY BYZANTINE EMPIRE

The name Byzantine is, strictly speaking, a historical misnomer. The inhabitants of the Eastern Empire recognized no break between their civilization and that of classical Rome. Throughout their history they called themselves *Romans*, even after Rome had slipped from their power and

they had adopted Greek as their official language. Indeed, modern Western historians sometimes forget that the Roman Empire did not fall in the East until 1453.

*Capital at Constantinople*   Byzantine history began when the emperor Constantine transferred the capital of the Roman Empire from the West to the East in 330. The emperor probably had many motives for moving the capital further east, including the larger Christian population in the east. It was also the wealthiest and most populous part of the Empire, and Constantine found, as had his predecessor, Diocletian, that it was easier to

▼ **This Byzantine gold cup, dating from the sixth or seventh century, was found at Durazzo in modern Albania. Four female figures in gold repoussé symbolize the cities of Rome, Cyprus, Alexandria, and Constantinople. The detail shows the figure of Constantinople. The representation of cities in allegorical form indicates the prominence of urban centers in Byzantine thought and society.** Metropolitan Museum of Art, Gift of J. Pierpont Morgan, 1917 (17.190.1710) Photograph © 2001 The Metropolitan Museum of Art, New York.

▲ EMPEROR JUSTINIAN, RAVENNA
**The mosaics—patterns made from small chips of tinted glass backed with gold leaf—that cover the wall of the church of San Vitale in Ravenna are one of the greatest achievements of the Byzantine era. Here, the emperor Justinian is surrounded by both priests and warriors, emphasizing his power over the religious as well as the secular domain.**
Scala / Art Resource, NY

raise both money and troops to defend the Empire. The most threatening of the external enemies were also on the eastern frontier, including the Persian Empire and various Germanic tribes.

Constantine chose as his new capital the site of the ancient Greek colony of Byzantium, located on a narrow peninsula that appears as a hand trying to connect Europe and Asia. The official name of the rebuilt city was New Rome; however, it soon came to be called the City of Constantine, or Constantinople, after its founder.

The location of this capital influenced the character of Byzantium and the course of its history. The city stood at the intersection of two heavily traveled trade routes: the overland highway from the Balkans to Asia Minor and the maritime route between the Black and Mediterranean seas. Moreover, the city at once acquired the aura of a Christian city, the capital of the Christian empire. Because of his close association with the emperor, the bishop of Constantinople enjoyed the high status of patriarch, and in the entire Church only the bishop of Rome ranked above him.

*Abandonment of the West* The successors of Constantine had no intention of abandoning the powers of the old Roman Empire in either the West or the East. However, the Eastern emperors lacked the resources to come to the aid of the Western emperors. They could only try to preserve the boundaries in the East by a combination of warfare against the barbarians and paying tribute to them to remain in peace within the borders. When the Visigoths and Ostrogoths became rebellious, the emperors paid them to go west. The idea of restoring the Empire to its former size, power, and glory was never lost. The emperor whose actions best illustrate this aim was Justinian.

## ◆ JUSTINIAN THE GREAT (R. 527–565) OF BYZANTIUM

Justinian pursued three principal goals in his reign: the restoration of the Western provinces to the empire, the reformation of laws and institutions, and an ambitious program of splendid public works.

*Justinian and Theodora*   Historians have much information, or at least many allegations, about Justinian from his court historian, Procopius. While the emperor lived, Procopius praised him in two official histories: *On the Wars* recounts Justinian's victorious campaigns, and *On Buildings* describes his architectural achievements. But after Justinian's death, Procopius also wrote one of the most vicious character assassinations in history. *The Secret History* paints Justinian, empress Theodora, and several high officials of the court as monsters of public and private vice. Historians still have not satisfactorily reconciled the contradictory portraits that the two-tongued Procopius has left to us.

Justinian's name is linked to that of his empress, Theodora, with whom he shared power. Born in about 500, Theodora became a famous actress and a celebrated courtesan before she was twenty. She traveled through the cities of the Empire, earning her way, according to Procopius, by skilled prostitution. In her early twenties she returned to Constantinople, where she mended her morals, but lost none of her charm, and married Justinian. She was, in sum, an outsider, with no roots in the social establishment of the capital and no inclinations to respect its conventions.

Theodora's influence on her husband was decisive from the start. In 532 the popular factions of Constantinople rose in a rebellion known as the Nike Revolt. The two parties at the chariot races at the hippodrome in Constantinople were known as the Blues and the Greens. In addition to supporting their own horses and drivers, they had taken different sides on religious and political divisions in the Empire. Uniting against Justinian and Theodora, they rebelled. Justinian panicked and planned to flee. But in a moving speech, as recorded by Procopius, Theodora urged her husband to choose death rather than exile. Justinian remained and crushed the uprising.

*Reconquest of the West*   To restore imperial rule over the lost Western provinces, Justinian attacked the kingdoms of the Vandals, Ostrogoths, and Visigoths and sought a precarious peace with the Persians beyond his eastern frontier. By 554 his troops had destroyed the Vandal kingdom in North Africa and established Byzantine rule there; had forced the Visigoths in Spain to cede the southern tip of the Iberian peninsula; and had triumphed, at least for a while, over the Ostrogothic kingdom in Italy (see map 6.2). Although Justinian finally controlled only Sicily and southern Italy, Ravenna became the glorious center of Byzantine conquest in Italy. The Greek presence remained strong in these places throughout the Middle Ages. Ravenna preserves churches with mosaics of Justinian and Theodora.

Justinian sought to reconcile the Eastern and Western branches of the Church, which were bitterly divided over a theological question concerning the nature of Christ.[2] He had the pope abducted from Rome and taken to Constantinople, where he bullied him into accepting an unwelcome compromise. Justinian's coercive tactics did not bring union and peace to the Church, and all the conflicting parties bitterly resented them.

*Codex Justinianus*   In 528 Justinian appointed a commission to prepare a systematic codification of Roman law. The result was the *Corpus Iuris Civilis* ("Body of Civil Law"), often called Justinian's Code. It consisted of four compilations: the *Codex*, an easily consulted arrangement of all imperial edicts according to topics; the *Digest*, or *Pandects*, a summary of legal opinions; the *Institutes*, a textbook to introduce students to the reformed legal system; and the *Novellae*, a collection of new imperial edicts issued after 534. These

---

[2]The Monophysite theory holds that Jesus has one nature, partly divine and partly human; he was not, in other words, simply true man. Condemned as heretical at the Council of Chalcedon (451), the belief remained strong in the East. The orthodox view is that Jesus has two natures, one human and one divine, and is both true God and true man.

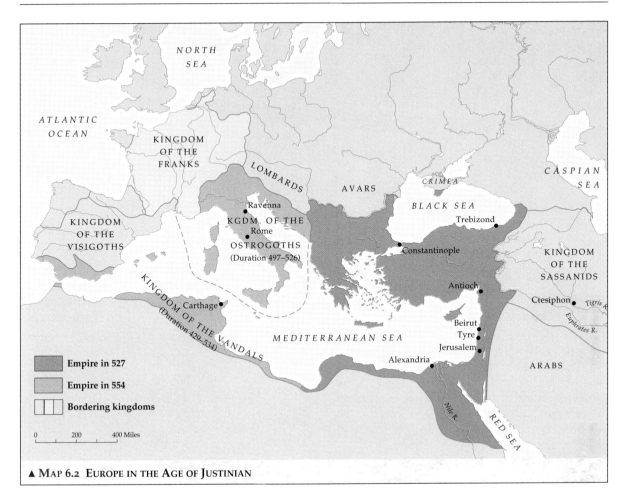

▲ MAP 6.2 EUROPE IN THE AGE OF JUSTINIAN

works are the last major ones written in Latin in the East; the language of the Empire was now Greek.

It would be hard to exaggerate the importance of the *Corpus Iuris Civilis*. It has remained for all subsequent generations the largest and richest source of information concerning the legal institutions and thought of Roman antiquity. In the Middle Ages international and commercial law were based on it, as was much of Church law. The modern legal systems of most Western countries incorporate the principles of Roman law as preserved in the Corpus.[3]

---

[3]The British Commonwealth and the United States (except Louisiana) follow common law, based on cases decided in medieval England; but common law too was strongly influenced by Roman legal concepts.

*Hagia Sophia*  The destruction that the Nike revolt caused in Constantinople gave Justinian an opportunity to start a rebuilding program. The most spectacular of his many new churches, palaces, and public works was the great church of Hagia Sophia, or Holy Wisdom. Begun in 532 and completed in 537, it became the model for churches all over the Empire. As Procopius described it, its great dome seemed to float in the air, as if suspended by a chain from heaven. Hagia Sophia is one of the acknowledged architectural masterpieces of the world. Like other Byzantine churches, it was decorated with brilliant mosaics, but most of these were destroyed by the iconoclasts (people who regarded the use of icons for worship as a form of idolatry) in the eighth and ninth centuries. Because of the iconoclastic movement, the richest examples of the early mosaics

▲ INTERIOR OF HAGIA SOPHIA
Hagia Sophia, the monumental project of the emperor Justinian, is a lasting reminder of the power of the Byzantine Empire. The saucerlike dome, which rises 180 feet, is carried on four pendentives (the wedge-shaped supports that allow a circular dome to rest on a square structure) and is a notable achievement of Byzantine engineering. The original mosaics were destroyed during the iconoclastic controversy, redone afterwards, and whitewashed by the Turks after the conquest of Constantinople in 1453.
© 1993 Tibor Bognár/Corbis Stock Market

are not to be found in Constantinople and Asia Minor but rather in areas that were no longer under Byzantine rule in those centuries. San Vitale and San Apollinare in Ravenna, Italy, are particularly noted for early Byzantine mosaics.

*Historical Assessment of the Reign*  Justinian was remarkably successful in all his ambitious policies until the last years of his reign. Beginning in 542, terrible plagues (the same type of plague as the Black Death in the fourteenth century) repeatedly struck the imperial lands. Justinian was waging a two-front war against the Persians to the

east and the resurgent Ostrogoths on the western frontier. The strains on human resources left the entire Empire on the defensive at his death.

Historians have viewed Justinian's policies as unrealistic, excessively ambitious, and ultimately disastrous. Memories of ancient Roman greatness blinded him to the inadequacy of his own resources. Yet Hagia Sophia and the *Corpus Iuris Civilis* ensure him a permanent reputation in both the East and the West.

In the years following Justinian's death, new invaders overwhelmed the frontiers and wrested from his successors most of the territorial acquisitions of his reign. These emperors could not recover the Western provinces of the old Roman Empire, and the Byzantine Empire, unable to remain a universal state, had to find its way as an Eastern, and exclusively Hellenic, Empire.

▼ BAPTISM OF CLOVIS I
**Although this depiction of Clovis comes from a fourteenth-century manuscript, it suggests the continuing power of his image and particularly the importance of his conversion and baptism, which is here commemorated some 800 years after the event. Even as the bishop performs the baptism, he is helped by an angel from above. Apart from its content, this miniature is a splendid example of the way the initial letters of chapters were decorated by medieval monks.**
The Huntington Library, San Marino, CA

## ◆ THE FRANKISH KINGDOM

*Unification under Clovis*  The founder of the kingdom of the Franks was Clovis (r. 485–511),[4] putative grandson of Merovech, king of the Salians. Clovis' great accomplishment was the political unification of nearly the whole of Gaul, corresponding roughly to most of modern France. Already king of the Salians, he had himself elected king of the Ripuarians and thus ruled a united Frankish people. According to the bishop and historian Gregory of Tours (538–594), one of the reasons Clovis succeeded in becoming the sole ruler was that he killed all his relatives who might challenge him. His sons added both Burgundy and Provence to the kingdom, nearly completing the conquest of Gaul.

No less important than military force for unification was Clovis' conversion, probably about 496, to Roman, rather than Arian, Christianity. Gregory of Tours tells us that Clovis' wife, Clotilda, urged him to convert and that he had promised to be baptized if he won a battle that he was losing. Winning it, he and all his troops were baptized. This step facilitated his conquests and made possible the peaceful assimilation of the diverse peoples he ruled. As the first barbarians to accept Roman Christianity, the Franks became the "eldest daughter" of the Western Church and soon its acknowledged sword and champion.

*The Later Merovingians*  Clovis had established a strong Frankish kingdom in Gaul, but his Merovingian successors, known traditionally as the "do-nothing kings," showed the weaknesses of tribal monarchy. Unable to conceive of the kingdom as anything but a private estate, they divided and redivided their lands among their heirs. Frankish custom dictated partible inheritance, that is, all surviving sons inherited the property equally. To resolve territorial disputes, the Merovingians relied primarily on violence to define their powers. The history of their reigns is largely a dismal story of intrigue and destructive feuds. Nevertheless, they enlarged their territory by subjugating the Burgundians and Alamans.

---

[4]His name is really a cognate of Louis; thus, by this historical oddity, all the long line of French kings named Louis are misnumbered.

Amid wars and rivalries among the Merovingians, the character of Frankish society was changing; the decisive shift was in the technique of making war. The introduction of the stirrup, probably in the early eighth century, gave a final advantage to the mounted warrior over the foot soldier: He could now strike a hard blow without falling from his horse. This improvement confirmed the superiority, which had been evident for several centuries, of cavalry over infantry. Since horses were expensive, war became a pre-eminently aristocratic occupation; therefore, a new functional and social division appeared in Frankish society. In the past most freemen had been both peasants and warriors. Now freemen who could not afford horses and arms—a majority of the population—became full-time peasants; those freemen who could afford the new implements of battle became full-time fighters and formed the new military aristocracy.

Because of the Merovingian kings' negligence, their chief household official, known as the mayor of the palace, gradually took over the real powers of government. The mayor's functions were to manage the palaces and supervise the royal lands; he was also able to distribute the lands largely as he saw fit. Using this privilege, some of the mayors began to supply the aristocracy with the estates they needed to maintain expensive animals and arms. The mayors thus built a following among the new military aristocracy. One mayor, Pepin of Heristal (d. 714), who already administered the eastern lands of the kingdom, gained control over the western lands in 687, thus unifying nearly the whole kingdom of Gaul under his administration.

*Charles Martel* Pepin's son and successor, Charles Martel, or "The Hammer" (r. 714–741), succeeded in defeating the Arab advance into Europe at the battle of Tours in 732 (see p. 223). This great victory saved the Frankish lands from invasion and stopped the advance of the Arabs in Europe. He cultivated the support of the warrior aristocracy by granting them land for their service. He encouraged Christian missionaries to convert newly conquered people. With the aid of these two groups, Charles began to extend Christianity and Frankish domination over the Germanic tribes settled beyond the Rhine River.

*Pepin the Short* Charles' son, Pepin the Short (r. 741–768) continued the policies of his father. The continuing support of the military aristocracy and the new sympathy of the ecclesiastical hierarchy enabled the mayor Pepin to effect a major constitutional change. In 751 an assembly of Frankish notables declared that the last Merovingian king, the feeble Childeric III, was not truly a king and recognized Pepin as their legitimate sovereign. Pepin had sent a delegation to the pope asking about the legitimacy of the change and had been assured that it was better that the person with the power of the king be actual king.

Threatened with attack on Rome by the Lombards, a Germanic people who had been harassing Italy, Pope Stephen visited King Pepin's court in 754 and anointed him king. The act left the implication that the Frankish king had a special tie to the papacy and to the Roman past. Twice Pepin came to Italy with troops and defeated the Lombards, confirming papal possession of the Patrimony of St. Peter (Rome and its environs). Later popes would repeatedly point to this Donation of Pepin as establishing the Papal States. By building strong Christian and Roman influences within his kingship, Pepin strengthened and transformed his reign. He bequeathed to his successors a monarchy founded on the support of great warriors and priests and dignified by association with the Christian and Roman past.

## ◆ KINGSHIP IN ITALY AND SPAIN

*Theodoric and the Ostrogothic Kingdom in Italy* After the Visigoths had left Italy for southern Gaul and Spain, the Ostrogoths, led by King Theodoric (r. 493–526), settled in Italy (see p. 181). A shrewd ruler, Theodoric founded a kingdom in Italy that provided more than thirty years of peace. The Roman Christian bishops had helped the Ostrogoths conquer Italy even though they were Arian heretics. Theodoric, like Clovis, understood the importance of the Church and practiced a policy of toleration, even hiring Roman Christians for his government.

Theodoric made no attempt to combine the Gothic state with the remnants of the Roman one. He allowed the Goths to continue with their laws and customs while the native population continued under Roman law. But in his own government, he imitated Roman rulers. Knowing Byzantine traditions well from his youth in Constantinople, he issued law codes and kept a court in Ravenna similar to that of Byzantium. All officials were Romans rather than Goths.

Theodoric was liberal to the Roman population, returning two-thirds of the taxes to them and taxing the Goths as well as the Romans to keep the treasury full. He even undertook to rebuild cities. Toward the end of his reign, perhaps in response to the Church's attempt to put down Arianism, he became more suspicious of the Romans in his administration (see p. 204). After Theodoric's death, Justinian's wars set off bloody fighting in Italy.

*Lombards*  A weakened Italy could not withstand the incursion of another Germanic tribe, the Lombards. Entering Italy in 568, they knew little about the Roman civilization or Christianity. Pope Gregory the Great bribed them not to attack Rome itself. After Pepin defeated them in the mid-eighth century, the Lombards settled in northern Italy (now called Lombardy).

*Visigothic Kingdom*  The Visigoths could not control the vast territory that they had initially taken in Gaul and Iberia; Clovis defeated them in 507 and drove them into Spain. United under King Leovigild (r. 569–586), they gained control over most of the Iberian peninsula. Like Theodoric in Italy, Leovigild realized that he could rule only with the cooperation of the Roman landlords and bishops. As in Ostrogothic Italy, the period of Visigothic rule allowed Roman/Christian culture to flourish.

The Visigoths remained Arian until the reign of Leovigild's son, Reccared (r. 586–601). When he converted to Roman Christianity, most of his bishops also became adherents of that Church. The close relationship between the bishops and kings in Spain became important for the course of Spanish politics. The bishop of Toledo anointed the Visigothic kings in a ceremony similar to the ordination of a priest. Attacks on the kings were equated with attacks on Christ. The Visigothic kingdom fell in 711 to Muslim invaders, who had only to kill the king to subdue the country.

## ◆ ANGLO-SAXON ENGLAND

The invasions in the fourth through sixth centuries divided England into more than twenty petty dynasties and kingdoms. Unlike invaders into other lands, the invaders of England did not find Roman populations or Christian bishops, and the invaders themselves were not yet Christian converts. The story of Christianity in the British Isles is told later in this chapter. The invaders retained the Germanic government of kings and chieftains and warrior bands. In addition to Beowulf, a number of other poems date from this period, including *The Wanderer* and *The Seafarer*, which describe the adventurous lives of warriors and the loss of a powerful chief and protector.

The numerous petty dynasties coalesced into seven fairly stable kingdoms, traditionally known as the heptarchy: Northumbria, Mercia, East Anglia, Essex, Sussex, Kent, and Wessex (see map 6.3). The first kings to exert a stable hegemony over England were the rulers of Northumbria in the seventh and eighth centuries. This was the golden age of Northumbrian culture; the monastery at Wearmouth-Jarrow then counted among its members Bede the Venerable (see p. 206), the greatest scholar of his day. But Northumbrian rule was short-lived, and by the late ninth

▲ MAP 6.3 Anglo–Saxon England

century leadership passed to Egbert of Wessex and his successors.

# III. The New Economy, 500–900

The great achievement of the Early Middle Ages was the emergence of the single-family peasant farm as the basic unit of agricultural production. There were three reasons for this development. First, many owners of villas found that they could not purchase new slaves and found it more economical to settle their slaves on family farms for which they paid rent to the estate owner. Second, changes in warfare, specifically the new supremacy of the mounted warrior, made fighting an expensive profession and converted many free warriors into full-time cultivators. Finally, a series of technological innovations in agriculture aided the peasant farmer in supporting himself, his family, and the new relationship between landlord and peasant farmer. As in the ancient world, most of the wealth came from agrarian pursuits, including the production of grains, wines, olive oil, and linen and woolen cloth.

## ◆ AGRICULTURAL INNOVATIONS

*The Heavy-Wheeled Plow*  The most fertile agricultural region of Europe is the great alluvial plain that stretches from southeast England and France to the Urals. The peoples of the ancient world had not been able to farm it efficiently. The light plow of antiquity only scratched the heavy soils of the north. The light plow was suitable enough for the thin soil and dry climate in the Mediterranean, where the best strategy was only to pulverize the surface in order to retain moisture. On the northern plain, however, the earth had to be cut deeply and turned to form the furrows needed to carry away excess water from the abundant rains. Thus, a heavier, more powerful plow was needed. Archaeological evidence has shown that such a plow emerged simultaneously among the Germans and the Slavs in the sixth century.

Other changes in farming techniques accompanied the development of the heavy plow. The Mediterranean plow required only two oxen to pull it, while the northern plow needed as many as eight. Thus, peasants in the north often kept

oxen collectively and therefore needed to live in communities rather than in isolated individual settlements. Since the Germanic peoples had been accustomed to living in villages before they settled in former Roman territory, their agricultural arrangements suited their living preferences.

*Efficient Use of Horses*  At the same time, new techniques allowed peasants to use horses in addition to oxen as draft animals. The Romans had harnessed the horse with almost incredible inefficiency. Pliant straps around the horse's throat and belly could strangle a heavily loaded horse. Horses could pull only light chariots with this harness. In the ninth century northern Europeans developed a collar and harness that rested the load on the horse's shoulders, making the horse efficient for pulling wagons and plows. At about the same time, the tandem harness appeared, which permitted teams of horses to be hitched one behind the other. The horseshoe, introduced at this time, gave the animal better traction and protected its sensitive hooves.

Horses were faster than oxen for plowing and carting, but they were also a more expensive investment. They cost more to buy and, unlike oxen, they could not live on grass alone but had to be fed grain as well. As a consequence, horses were not universally used in agriculture in the Middle Ages.

*The Three-Field System*  Northern Europeans also developed a new method of crop rotation: the three-field system. An estate's arable land was divided into three large fields of several hundred acres each, with two-thirds of the land cultivated each year on a rotating basis. The system was first documented in 763. A field was planted in winter wheat, then in a spring crop—oats, barley, peas, or beans—then permitted to lie fallow for a year. (See map 8.1 for an illustration of the three-field system.) The older two-field system, based on the yearly alternation of winter wheat and fallow, continued to be used in Mediterranean lands, where spring crops were difficult to raise because rain was scarce in the spring and summer. The north, however, had abundant year-round rainfall.

The three-field system kept a larger portion (two-thirds) of the soil in crops each year. The

▲ Bad and Good Regiment, ca. 1125
**This manuscript illustration shows a typical medieval plow team of oxen. The heavy plow used on the plains of Northern Europe included three indispensable parts: a colter, or knife, to cut the soil; a share, or wedge, to widen the breech and break up the clods; and a moldboard to lift the earth and turn the furrow.**
Photo, D. Pineider, Biblioteca Medicea Laurenziana, Florence

fallow became pasture for village animals, and their manure returned the soil to fertility. With only one-third rather than one-half of the land lying fallow, the other two-thirds produced grain and other crops. Yields from the new crop rotation show the increased productivity: In the Mediterranean system, one bushel of planted grain yielded only two or three bushels at harvest, while in the new system the yields might be as high as seven bushels harvested.

A spring crop of legumes restored fertility to the soil, provided a more varied diet for the people, and lessened the risk of total failure, because two crops were planted in one year. A spring crop of oats was used for fodder and thus helped support a larger number of animals, which in turn provided manure for more abundant crops. Barley was turned into beer.

The agricultural innovations spread through Europe at a glacial pace, but their eventual adoption profoundly affected the new Western civilization. They allowed northern Europe to support a denser population and established a tradition of

technical innovation that has remained alive and unbroken to the present.

*Peasant Life*   A glimpse of the life of peasants comes from the estate books of the great abbey of Saint-Germain-des-Prés near Paris. The list of peasants shows that remnants of the old Roman *latifundia* system were still present, since some of the inhabitants were called slaves and others were free. Both the status listings and the names show that there had been considerable intermarriage among the original population of the estate and the newly settled Franks. Thus, Maurisius (a Roman name), a half-free man, was married to Ermegardis (a Germanic name). The peasants paid rent for their farms and had to provide labor for their lords, such as carting, plowing, harvesting, and hay making on the estate. True manorialism did not develop until the eleventh century (see chapter 8).

The settlement of the Germanic peoples as peasants brought its own revolution in the roles of men and women. Women, children, and slaves

▲ FRENCH ILLUMINATIONS OF PEASANTS
**The division of labor by sex was a prominent part of the peasant economy. Men did the heavy field work including beating the grain of the stalk with a flail. Women did spinning and weaving. The symbol for the peasant man was the flail and for the woman the spindle.**
The Giraudon/Art Resource, NY

had done all the agriculture during the period before migration, but once settled, men became the farmers as had been true in the ancient world. Handling the heavy plow and the large oxen teams was considered men's work. Women, in addition to caring for children, tended to domestic animals, produced cheese, brewed beer and mead (a fermented honey drink), and took up the Mediterranean women's tasks of spinning and weaving. As in ancient Greece, a special house was set aside for young women to spend a few years spinning and making cloth for the estate. The medieval artistic symbols for men and women reflected this agricultural shift: Peasant women were depicted with a spindle, and peasant men were shown at the plow or with a flail for beating grain from sheaves.

### ◆ TRADE AND MANUFACTURE

One of the central issues that economic historians of the early Middle Ages have debated is the decline of trade and towns as the political power of the Roman Empire waned in the West. Henri Pirenne laid out his thesis in *Mohammed and Charlemagne* (1935), arguing that the Germanic invaders did not destroy the Roman political and cultural life but tried to preserve it where they

could. It was only the Arab conquest of land surrounding the Mediterranean in the eighth century that brought Roman trade patterns to an end. Modern archaeology indicates that Northern Europe was developing trade routes and commercial goods before the Arabs dominated the Mediterranean.

*Trade and Commerce* The Mediterranean had been a great commercial artery for the exchange of Western goods, for the spices and fine cloths of the Levant, and for papyrus and grain from Egypt. Trade in Eastern luxury items never disappeared, because the Church and wealthy individuals demanded such items as silk, dyes, perfumes, olive oil, wine, and papyrus. Jews and Syrians carried on the trade with the East. Slaves (the word *slave* derives from *Slav,* which were the people most often sold) were traded to the East to pay for the luxury goods. Evidence of trade in gold from sub-Saharan Africa (Sudan) existed from the sixth century and became important by the tenth century through the Iberian Peninsula. Salt, tin, and copper were exported to Africa. Archaeological evidence, however, indicates that this trade was of minimal importance to the Western economy and that the trade that had characterized the western Mediterranean in Roman times had all but disappeared with the Visigothic and Vandal invasions in the fifth century. The eastern Mediterranean continued to provide vital trade until well into the seventh century.

A northern trade was gaining in importance. The Frisians were the most active traders, relying on the Rhine River to export cloth and luxury items into the hinterland of Europe. Through ports on the North Sea, the Frisians also traded with England, the coast of France, Denmark, and other Baltic countries. The cloth they traded, which was valued for its thick, waterproof quality, probably was the surplus production of estates and monasteries in northern Europe.

*Towns and Production*   Some historians have argued on the basis of written evidence that Roman towns continued to flourish and to manufacture goods for the surrounding countryside. Again, archaeology shows that the inhabited area of those Roman towns that continued to exist had shrunk to little more than ecclesiastical buildings, inns, and some residences. The thriving Roman pottery centers were gone, and towns ceased to serve as administrative centers except for Church business. Craft production was done at the village and estate level. Little trade moved any of this production around the hinterland. Luxury objects were circulated only among elites, both in the Church and in lay society.

# IV. The Expansion of the Church

The Church in the early Middle Ages was both a dynamic leader, guiding the West in the period of the collapse of Roman authority, and the preserver of the classical educational traditions of literacy, rhetoric, and logic. The development of monasticism provided a new opportunity for pious men and women to live a life of prayer and service in a world in which much was changing. Within the walls of monasteries and nunneries as well as in bishops' residences, classical learning was preserved, copied, and taught. Missionaries went to frontier areas and converted to Christianity people who had never been exposed to the Roman civilization. The missionaries brought both Christian and Roman traditions to these peoples and incorporated into Christianity some of the traditions they found among these peoples as well. By the

beginning of the seventh century, all of Christian Western Europe had abandoned Arianism and adopted Roman Christianity. Concurrent with the monastic movements and missionary activities, the papacy developed as the religious and often the political leader in the West. Powerful popes filled the void left by the Roman state, carrying on diplomacy and legitimizing kings.

## ◆ ORIGINS OF THE PAPACY

The papacy—*pope* derives from *pappas,* a Greek word for *father*—had its origins in the bishopric of Rome. The pope's authority gradually grew in importance and power so that he became the head of the Roman Catholic Church.

*Doctrine of Petrine Succession*   According to the traditional Catholic (and medieval) view, Jesus himself endowed the apostle Peter with supreme responsibility for his church: "And I say unto thee, thou art Peter and upon this rock I will build my church, and the gates of hell shall not prevail against it" (Matt. 16:18). In the Aramaic language that Jesus spoke, as well as in Greek and Latin, *Peter* and *rock* are the same words, implying that the Church was to be founded upon Peter. This play on words has been called the most momentous pun in history. Medieval tradition further held that Peter became the first bishop of Rome and was martyred there about the year 60. Historical evidence does not conclusively establish Peter's presence in Rome.

*Growth of Papal Primacy*   Several factors led to the predominance of the Bishop of Rome and the subsequent growth of papal power. Rome was the city of the Caesars, the capital of the world, and the center of Latin culture; people were accustomed to seeking guidance from Rome. As the authority of the emperors waned and disappeared in the West, people still looked to Rome for leadership, and increasingly its bishop provided it. The emperors, eager to use the Church as an adjunct to their own imperial administration, favored the concentration of religious authority in the West in the Bishop of Rome's hands. During the invasions, the papacy represented the orthodox Christian practice as opposed to the Arian heresy of the Germanic invaders and so became the focal point of orthodox Christians in the West.

The idea of the primacy of the pope gained support in the fourth and fifth centuries, largely through the activities of powerful popes such as Pope Leo I (r. 440–461). It was he who sent a delegation to Attila the Hun to persuade him not to attack Rome. Leo I also addressed the issue of papal primacy in numerous letters and sermons, identifying the living pope as the successor of Peter and enjoying the same powers that Peter had as the chosen disciple. Although the popes were not exercising an autocracy over the Church, their prestige in the Western world was unrivaled. Some church leaders expressed doubts about the primacy of the pope, maintaining that all bishops were equal in authority. The patriarch of Constantinople, primate of the Eastern Christians, did not recognize the superior authority of the papacy.

*Gregory the Great* The popes increasingly assumed responsibility for the security of Italy and the defense of the Church. They negotiated with a sequence of invaders—Huns, Vandals, Ostrogoths, and Lombards—and repeatedly sought help from the distant and distracted Eastern emperors. The pope who best exemplifies the problems and accomplishments of the early medieval papacy is Gregory I (r. 590–604).

When Gregory became pope, the Lombards were plundering the Roman countryside and threatening Rome with destruction and starvation. Under these difficult conditions, Gregory maintained the productive capacity of the Church's estates, kept food coming to Rome, ransomed captives, aided widows and orphans, and organized the defense of the city. Gregory finally negotiated a truce with the Lombards in 598, although they continued to pose a threat to the security of Rome for more than a century.

Gregory was no less solicitous for the welfare of the entire Church. During his pontificate Gregory gave new momentum to missionary efforts and achieved some remarkable successes. The Spanish Visigoths were converted from Arian to Roman Christianity during Gregory's reign. By establishing a tradition of active involvement in the affairs of the world, to which most of his medieval successors would faithfully adhere, Gregory widened enormously the influence of the Roman see.

Like many of the early church leaders, Gregory came from a Roman patrician background and

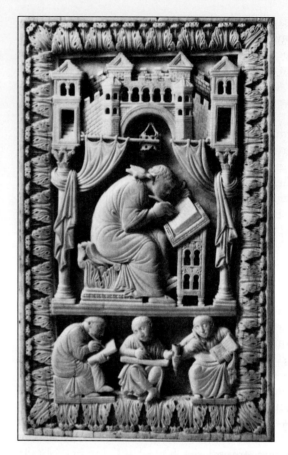

▲ Pope Gregory the Great was one of the key figures in the transition from the ancient world to the Middle Ages. He is regarded—along with Jerome, Ambrose, and Augustine—as one (and the last) of the four fathers of the Latin Church. His efforts to defend Rome against the Lombards and to advance missionary work gave added prestige to the papal see.
Art Resource, NY

had been educated to be an imperial administrator. Using the experience of his career in the civil administration of the declining Roman state, he organized the estates belonging to the papacy around Rome to provide a more solid financial base for the papacy. This action by Gregory is an example of the survival of Roman governmental genius in the service of the Church.

## ◆ MONASTICISM

Even more effective than the papacy in shaping medieval civilization were the monks. The ascetic ideal of fleeing the world in order to devote oneself to worship is common to many religions. Beginning in the third century, highly devout Christians who sought refuge in permanent prayer and isolation began to live apart from the daily world. The most renowned of these was St. Anthony, who lived a life of rigid asceticism in the desert of Egypt for more than twenty years (started ca. 285). Some of the early Syrian hermits, such as Simon Stylites, lived on a pillar for years, eating only millet seeds. The Church Father Jerome criticized hermitic excesses, commenting that if beards made a man holy, all goats were holy.

It became more common for people who wished to follow an ascetic life to live and work together in cenobitic ("living in common") monasticism. Even Anthony found that the numbers of people who flocked to his isolated retreat had to be organized and given rules for guidance. Egypt was the home of the first true monasteries and nunneries, with the days divided by work and prayer. St. Basil, the father of Greek monasticism, spent a year in Egypt before establishing a monastery (ca. 360) in Greece. The Basilian order, which is still in existence today, established the tradition of shared meals, sleeping quarters, and common prayers. It became the predominant order in the Eastern Empire. Double houses, monasteries and nunneries with communities of the opposite sex attached to them, were common in early monasticism in the East and in Gaul and Anglo-Saxon England.

*Benedict and the Benedictine Rule*   The man who designed the most common Western form of monasticism—St. Benedict, a Roman patrician—founded a community at Monte Cassino in ca. 520 and drew up a rule, or manual of conduct, for its members. The Benedictine rule dealt with all the main problems of monastic life, including food (the rule provided for an allotment of wine each day) and clothing, discipline, prayer, the work of monks, and sleeping arrangements. The rule was a flexible one, applicable to many individual communities. The abbot was to be elected for life, with full authority over the community, but he was to consult the elder and even the younger monks. One of the most famous regulations required some manual labor, lending to it a dignity that both the Greeks and Romans had denied. "Idleness," said the regulation, "is the enemy of the soul." The core vows for joining the Benedictine

order were poverty, chastity, and obedience (see "The Rule of St. Benedict on the Clothing of Monks," p. 200).

*Early Nunneries*   From the earliest days of monasticism, women joined communities of nuns. St. Jerome designed a rule for the women in his family and their friends. St. Basil's mother and sister were already living in a nunnery when he founded his monastic order. St. Scholastica, Benedict's sister, lived in a nunnery near Monte Cassino. In Anglo-Saxon England abbesses, such as Hilda of Whitby (657–680), headed double monasteries and had such prestige that princes and kings consulted them. Abbess Hilda encouraged learning at Whitby; five of its monks went on to become bishops.

*Relationship of Monasteries to Lay Society*   The monks exerted an extraordinary influence on every level of medieval civilization. They were the most successful agriculturists of the age, first as farmers in their own right and then, gradually, as

▼ ST. BENEDICT PRESENTING HIS RULE
**This fourteenth-century image depicts Saint Benedict presenting his rule to a group of nuns. His connection with female spirituality went back to his own lifetime, because his sister, Scholastica, was also devout and lived at a convent near Benedict's at Monte Cassino.**
Bibliotheca Seminario Vescovile/Photo, © P. Tosi/Index, Florence

## THE RULE OF ST. BENEDICT ON THE CLOTHING OF MONKS

◆

*The rule of St. Benedict (ca. 480–ca. 550) tried to anticipate all the needs of monks and all the problems that might arise in monastic communities in terms of regulation of work, prayers, relations among the monks, visitors to the monastery, travel, and monastic vows. This humane rule became the basis of monastic rules in Western Europe.*

"The clothing distributed to the brothers should vary according to local conditions and climate, because more is needed in the cold regions and less in warmer. This is left to the abbot's discretion. We believe that for each monk a cowl and tunic will suffice in temperate regions; in winter a woolen cowl is necessary, in summer a thinner or worn one; also a scapular for work, and footwear—both sandals and shoes.

"Monks must not complain about the color or coarseness of all these articles, but use what is available in the vicinity at a reasonable cost. However, the abbot ought to be concerned about the measurements of these garments that they not be too short but fitted to the wearers.

"Whenever new clothing is received, the old should be returned at once and stored in a wardrobe for the poor. To provide for laundering and night wear, every monk will need two cowls and two tunics, but anything more must be taken away as superfluous. When new articles are received, the worn ones—sandals or anything old—must be returned.

"Brothers going on a journey should get underclothing from the wardrobe. On their return they are to wash it and give it back. Their cowls and tunics, too, ought to be somewhat better than those they ordinarily wear. Let them get these from the wardrobe before departing, and on returning put them back.

"For bedding the monks will need a mat, a woolen blanket and a light covering as well as a pillow.

"The beds are to be inspected frequently by the abbot, lest private possessions are found there. A monk discovered with anything not given him by the abbot must be subjected to very severe punishment. In order that this vice of private ownership may be completely uprooted, the abbot is to provide all things necessary: that is, cowl, tunic, sandals, shoes, belt, knife, stylus, needle, handkerchief and writing tablets. In this way every excuse of lacking some necessity will be taken away."

From Timothy Fry (ed.), *The Rule of St. Benedict in Latin and English with Notes* (Liturgical Press, 1980), pp. 261–265.

---

managers of ever larger estates; thus, they set an example of good farming practices and estate management from which laypeople could benefit.

Monasteries and nunneries came to play a major role in early medieval society and government. Powerful families often established religious communities on their lands. The abbots and abbesses were often closely related to these prominent laypersons, and they administered the monastery's lands and resources in the interest of their lay relatives. Monasteries, in other words, became integrated into the structures of local power.

Kings, too, relied heavily on monastic farms to supply food for their administrations and armies and often appropriated part of the monks' income

to finance their own needs. Able abbots served as advisors and administrators for the kings.

***Education and Preservation of Learning***  Culturally, monks and nuns were almost the only people who were literate and learned. The Benedictine rule assumed that the monk could read; and the monasteries, although not expressly obliged to do so, maintained both libraries and schools for the training of young monks and nuns and, sometimes, lay children.

Monasteries organized *scriptoria*, or writing rooms, in which manuscripts that were needed for liturgy or education were copied. The great bulk of the surviving Latin literary works of both pagan and Christian antiquity were preserved in libraries, the monks were virtually the only intellectuals in society. Monastic scribes wrote nearly all the administrative records, lay and ecclesiastical, that have survived from the early Middle Ages.

*The Appeal of the Ascetic Life* Part of the monks' importance to society came from their communal organization, which enabled them to cope effectively with the problems of a turbulent

▼ **This Spanish manuscript illumination of daily life in the monastery shows that the writing of manuscripts was one of the monks' principal occupations. In addition, one of the monks is ringing the bells that marked the different services of the day and that also served to remind the surrounding countryside of the activities of the monastery.**
The Pierpont Morgan Library / Art Resource, NY

▲ Centula Abbey, after Eleventh-Century Manuscript
**Centula Abbey, in northwestern France, was founded in 790 by Angilbert, a poet-scholar in Charlemagne's circle. This seventeenth-century engraving after a lost eleventh-century manuscript depicts the heart of a vast complex that included three churches (all known) and seven villages and that housed more than three hundred monks.**
Bibliothèque Nationale de France, Paris

copies made in monasteries and nunneries. Sometimes monks decorated, or illuminated, the manuscript pages; manuscript illuminations are among the loveliest art forms that have come from the age. Because they maintained the schools and

age. Monasteries and nunneries provided a haven for people like Gregory the Great, St. Benedict, and St. Scholastica, to compensate for the disappearance of Roman intellectual life. At the same time, they extended charity to the poor and to pilgrims who stopped at their doors. Brothers and sisters with more practical skills were useful in monastic work and administration. In a turbulent age, the community provided a valued sense of continuity over generations.

Asceticism seems peculiarly suited to an age of transition. The ascetic, by his or her life, calls into question the accepted attitudes of the age. The monks rejected both the classical and barbarian systems of values and thus helped uproot or weaken attitudes such as the classical aversion to physical labor and the barbarian love of violence.

Finally, the monks and nuns were thought to ensure God's blessings for the world. Establishments of men and women who spent their life in prayer and charitable works were a hope and inspiration for those who did not have the opportunity to withdraw from the world. All ranks of society valued and made pious gifts to monasteries and nunneries.

## ◆ MISSIONARIES AND POPULAR RELIGION

One of the major achievements of the Church was to spread Christianity, including Roman culture, to parts of Europe that had never experienced extensive contacts with Rome. The missionary initiative was often made individually before the time of Gregory the Great. St. Patrick was a Briton who was captured and became a slave in Ireland. Escaping from his captors, he went to Gaul, where he was ordained a bishop. He returned to Ireland in 430 and converted the Irish, establishing monasteries there.

The Irish monks converted northern Anglo-Saxon England, establishing monasteries in northern England, including Lindisfarne and Whitby. These monasteries and nunneries became great centers of learning and religious crafts. They preserved many texts that were destroyed on the continent during the invasions. The illuminated manuscripts of these Celtic/Anglo-Saxon monasteries combined elements of Christianity with the indigenous designs of dragons, snakes, animals, and plants, as can be seen in the *Book of Kells* and the *Lindisfarne Gospel*.

***Benedictines as Missionaries***  Gregory the Great understood the potential of the Benedictines as missionaries. According to legend, he saw some fair-haired Anglo-Saxon children in the slave market and asked about their origins. Being told that they were Angles, he commented that they looked like angels. Further questions revealed that the Angles still worshiped trees and stones. Gregory sent a bishop, Augustine, to England with other priests in 597. Augustine found that the Kentish king's wife, Bertha, the great-granddaughter of Clovis and Clotilde, had been prevailing on the king to convert, and he eventually did convert to Roman Christianity.

The conversion of the Frisians and other groups to the east of the Rhine was more challenging. Anglo-Saxon Benedictines moved into this rough land with the blessings of the pope. Willibrord (later called Clement, 658–739) went to Frisia, and Winfrith (later Boniface, 675–754) went into Bavaria. They established churches where the pagans had formerly worshiped trees, sometimes even cutting down the sacred trees to build the church.

Elements of the former religion remained a part of Christianity, so that many of the days that had been pagan holidays were coordinated with saints' feasts. Conversion was gradual, and the new converts only partially understood the religion. Christianity brought the converts into contact with the wider world of the old Roman culture, including the Latin language and writings, and into potential trade and political contacts with other Christian peoples.

***Council of Whitby***  As the Roman variety of Christianity, brought by Augustine of Canterbury, spread in England, it came into conflict with the Irish and Anglo-Saxon versions. The two versions had differences in the date for the celebration of Easter and in some points about monasticism.[5] Finally, at the Council of Whitby in 664, the king of

---

[5]Irish Christians set the date of Easter later than the Romans (reflecting later springs in the north), applied the tonsure (the haircut symbolizing clerical status) in their own way, and conceived differently the role and powers of the bishop.

Northumbria questioned both sides about their belief in St. Peter. When both agreed on Peter's primacy, he concluded that his people should observe Roman practices.

*The Role of Miracles*  One of the convincing tools of conversion was miracles and stories of miracles. Stories of how saints cured sick people who worshiped at their tombs or how saints punished the ungodly when they stole sacred objects from churches conveyed a persuasive message about the power of the Christian God and his faithful followers. The miracle stories are historians' best source of popular culture during the early Middle Ages, because they record instances in daily life that were changed because of divine intervention.

◆ THE CHURCH AND CLASSICAL LEARNING

Christian writers had an ambiguous attitude toward classical texts: Many prominent Christian writers condemned classical literature as foolishness and an incitement to sin, and yet the classical authors provided both the language for study and philosophical texts that demanded reconciliation with Christian teachings. Christianity itself was a religion founded on a book, the Bible, and Christian theologians had to have the skill to read and interpret the sacred texts. Because the Church had not yet established its own schools, its scholars studied in secular schools, learning the techniques of philosophical argument and rhetorical expression that were traditional among pagan scholars.

*Preservation of Classical Texts*  Christian scholars preserved a tradition of literacy in the fifth and sixth centuries, but their output accurately reflects the difficult conditions of their times and the biases of their own mental outlook. An important part of their literary effort was devoted to the preparation of textbooks that would preserve a modicum of ancient learning and the ability to read the ancient authors. One of the most influential of these textbooks was *Introductions to Divine and Human Readings* by Cassiodorus, a sixth-century monk and official in

◄ PHILOSOPHY CONSOLING BOETHIUS, EARLY ELEVENTH CENTURY
In his *Consolation of Philosophy,* Boethius described the embodiment of philosophy as a mature woman who had grown as tall as the heavens and carried a scepter and books. This image, from an eleventh-century manuscript, depicts philosophy as equal in height to the building whose solid facade and row of small windows may be the prison in which Boethius wrote his famous work.
Bibliothèque Nationale de France, Paris

Theodoric's government. In it he listed the religious and secular books that he thought a monk should copy and read. This book is about as appealing to modern readers as a library catalog, but at the time it was carefully studied and used to determine the holdings of medieval libraries.

Another sixth-century Christian scholar in Theodoric's service, Boethius, translated portions of Aristotle's treatises on logic from Greek into Latin; these translations were the main source of early medieval writers' limited but significant familiarity with Aristotelian logic until the thirteenth century. Boethius wrote on many other subjects as well and is most famed now for his *Consolation of Philosophy,* a meditation on death that does not mention the Christian religion. Boethius wrote the *Consolation* while imprisoned by Theodoric at the end of his reign. The book helped preserve the dignity of learning by showing the role that reason and philosophy play in solving human problems. In Spain classical learning was preserved by Isidore, bishop of Seville, in his *Etymologies,* which were a vast encyclopedia of ancient learning, covering in twenty books subjects from theology to furniture and providing a rich source of classical lore and learning for medieval writers.

***Christian Writings*** Scholars also helped through original works to shape the character and interest of the age, especially by writing *exegeses,* or comments and interpretation, on the Bible. In this field the most important writer after St. Augustine was Pope Gregory. His commentary on the Book of Job made extravagant use of allegory in explaining the biblical text and set the style for biblical exegesis in the medieval world. Pope Gregory also taught readers, notably through his *Dialogues,* about the lives of the saints and the miracles that God wrought through them. Gregory had an ability to simplify works of theology and wrote the *Pastoral Care* as instruction for bishops.

Since Christians viewed history as a vast panorama illustrating and proclaiming God's miraculous providence, the study of history also evoked great interest among scholars. One of the most influential accounts was the *History of the Franks* by Gregory, bishop of Tours. Like many of

▲ CHI-RHO, *BOOK OF KELLS*
**The Greek letters *chi* and *rho*, the first two letters of Christ's name, were frequently used as symbols of Christianity by early believers. This page, from the late eighth-century Irish manuscript *The Book of Kells*, is an example of the complex interlacing that was characteristic of Anglo-Saxon manuscript illumination in this period.**
The Board of Trinity College Dublin

the early medieval historians, Gregory began with creation; he then recounted the history of the human race up to 591.

***Learning and Scholarship*** Scholarship on the continent sank to its lowest level in the seventh and early eighth centuries, but it flourished in Ireland in the seventh and in England in the early eighth century. Scholars there enjoyed the relative shelter of an insular home. They had the zeal of new converts and a strong monastic system that supported the schools. Since they did not speak a language derived from Latin, they could learn a correct Latin in schools without being confused by related vernacular forms. Thus, their Latin was closer to classical Latin than that used on the continent.

The finest English scholar was undoubtedly Bede the Venerable (673?–735), whose *Ecclesiastical History of the English People*, an account of the conversion of the English and the growth of their Church, established his fame even until today. His high sense of scholarship is evident in his excellent Latin and in the careful way he cites his sources: oral interviews with knowledgeable eyewitnesses, documents from local archives, and accounts written at his request. His book is the product of a medieval writer, not a modern one; Bede recounted miracles, and the principal theme of his history is the story of salvation. But his belief that history was the unfolding of God's plan did not lead him to distort the material in his sources. He is a man who in any age would be recognized as a scholar.

# SUMMARY

◆

By the close of the seventh century, Europe was much changed from the days of the Roman Empire. The new Visigothic kingdom controlled the territory that would become modern Spain, the Merovingians ruled over the former Roman province of Gaul, which had roughly the borders of modern France. Anglo-Saxon England under the Northumbrian hegemony included all of modern England. In Italy the pope had proved a powerful force not only in religion but also in politics. The people who moved into the old Roman Empire came as settlers. While their customs of governing were different from those of the Roman population, they soon blended their own practices with those of the Romans. Christianity proved one of the most powerful tools of assimilation because it taught both the Christian and Roman culture. Missionaries, drawn from the Benedictine monastic order, went beyond the borders of the old empire and converted those who had no exposure to the Roman world. The monastic orders provided a refuge for those who wanted to live a life of prayer and those who wanted to read classical philosophy and Christian theological texts. The preservation of texts was largely the work of monasteries. The medieval economy was based on agriculture, and the period of the sixth and seventh centuries saw the development of new technologies: stirrups for the better use of horses for fighting, the horse collar that allowed horses to replace oxen, the heavy-wheeled plow for cultivating the fields of northern Europe, and a crop rotation system that permitted two-thirds of the land to be cultivated each year. With increased agricultural production, Europe was on the verge of greater wealth, which would be concentrated in the north rather than on the Mediterranean. In Europe and the eastern Mediterranean major political changes were again on the horizon as the Franks continued to consolidate their power, the Byzantine Empire faced renewed invasions, and Islam inspired the Arabs to conquer the old Persian Empire and much of the Byzantine Empire.

## Questions for Further Thought

◆

1. What were the problems that the Germanic folk encountered in trying to assimilate with the Romans? What problems did the Romans have in living side by side with the tribesmen?

2. Historians have long argued that three elements went into the making of what we call "medieval civilization"—Roman government and culture, Germanic government and social customs, and Christianity. What elements did each of these contribute to the emerging medieval culture in the West?

3. What was the influence of the technological developments in the sixth and seventh centuries on warfare and on agriculture?

## Recommended Reading

◆

### Sources

Colgrave, B. (ed.). *The Life of Bishop Wilfrid . . . , Two Lives of Saint Cuthbert . . . , Felix's Life of Saint Guthlac, and The Earliest Life of Gregory the Great.* 1985. The hagiographies of the missionary saints.

Gregory of Tours, *History of the Franks,* trans. Ernest Brehaut, 1916.

*Herlihy, David (ed.). *Medieval Culture and Society.* 1968. A collection of primary sources that illustrate social and cultural aspects of the Middle Ages.

*Mattingly, H. (tr.). *Tacitus on Britain and Germany: A Translation of the "Agricola" and the "Germania."* 1967. A description of the life and culture of Germanic tribes including his experience living in Roman Britain.

*Peters, Edward. *Monks, Bishops, and Pagans: Christian Culture in Gaul and Italy, 500–700.* 1975. A collection of primary sources related to the early western church.

*Procopius. *Secret History.* Richard Atwater (tr.). 1964. A scandal-filled history of Justinian's reign.

### Studies

*Brown, Peter. *The Cult of the Saints: Its Rise and Function in Latin Christianity.* 1980. Locates the cult of the saints not in popular religion but in the power structures of late ancient society.

*Burns, Thomas S. *A History of the Ostrogoths.* 1984. Based on archaeological as well as literary evidence.

Carver, Marvin. *Sutton Hoo: Burial Grounds of Kings.* 1998.

*Duby, Georges. *The Early Growth of the European Economy: Warriors and Peasants from the Seventh to the Twelfth Century.* Howard B. Clark (tr.). 1974. The early medieval economy viewed in terms of "gift and pillage."

*Dunbabin, Jean. *France in the Making: 843–1180.* 1985. On the formation of the political structure of France and the growth of a strong monarchy.

*Fleckenstein, Josef. *Early Medieval Germany.* Bernard F. Smith (tr.). 1978. Germanic institutions from the migrations to the eleventh century.

Fossier, Robert (ed.). *The Cambridge Illustrated History of the Middle Ages. Vol. 1: 350–950.* Janet Sondheimer (tr.). 1989. Essays by French scholars, including four on Eastern Europe. Full bibliographies; lavishly illustrated.

*Geary, Patrick. *Before France and Germany: The Creation and Transformation of the Merovingian World.* 1988. A comprehensive summary of recent research, stressing the importance of the Roman heritage for the growth of Frankish institutions.

*Herrin, Judith. *The Formation of Christendom.* 1987. A survey of the development of the Christian world from Constantine to the mid-ninth century, with particular emphasis on the Western debt to Byzantium.

*Herwig, Wolfram. *History of the Goths.* Thomas J. Dunlap (tr.). 1988. Stresses the instability of Gothic tribal formations.

Hodges, Richard, and David Whitehouse. *Mohammad and Charlemagne: The Origins of Europe.* 1983. A reevaluation of the Pirenne thesis using archaeological evidence. The authors explore the shift of trade from the Mediterranean to northern Europe.

James, Edward. *The Franks*. 1988.

*Lawrence, C. H. *Medieval Monasticism: Forms of Religious Life in Western Europe in the Middle Ages*. 2d ed. 1989. On the Rule of Benedict, the rise of Cluny, and other topics.

*Lynch, Joseph. *The Medieval Church: A Brief History*. 1992. A very readable introduction to the history of the church.

*Moorhead, John. *Justinian*. 1994. A lively discussion of the reign of Justinian in the context of his times.

Pirenne, Henri. *Mohammed and Charlemagne*. 1935. A classic discussion of the effects of Islamic conquests on the rise of the Franks and the interruption of Mediterranian trade.

Stenton, Frank. *Anglo-Saxon England*. 1971. Basic introductory text.

*Straw, Carole. *Gregory the Great: Perfection in Imperfection*. 1988.

*Wallace-Hadrill, J. M. *The Barbarian West*. 1962. Brief and readable essays.

Wemple, Suzanne Fonay. *Women in Frankish Society: Marriage and the Cloister, 500 to 800*. 1981. An important study of a neglected topic.

Wickham, Chris. *Early Medieval Italy: Central Power and Local Society, 400–1100*. 1981. Mainly social history of the decline of unity within Italy after the fall of the Roman Empire.

*Available in paperback.

▲ This twelfth-century silver reliquary from Aachen represents Charlemagne as emperor, saint, and protector of the Church. After his death, through all the subsequent medieval centuries, Charlemagne was remembered and viewed as the ideal Christian emperor.

Scala/Art Resource, NY

# THE EMPIRES OF THE EARLY MIDDLE AGES (800–1000): CREATION AND EROSION

Europe's fate was inextricably bound with that of the old Roman world in the period of the seventh through the eleventh century. New conquests, the spread of Christianity to previously non-Christian peoples, and the rise of a new religion, Islam, had major impacts on the West. Combining conquest with missionary activity, the Frankish kings, like the Byzantine emperors, spread their power and Christianity to the Slavs of eastern Europe and previously unconverted Germanic tribes in the north of Europe. Islam influenced the course of history for both Western Europe and the Byzantine Empire. Muhammad, the founding prophet of Islam, enjoined his followers, the Muslims or, believers in Islam, to do battle for their faith. The leaders who followed Muhammad rapidly conquered Byzantine provinces but were turned back at Constantinople. They conquered the Persian Empire and moved west, conquering the Iberian Peninsula. The Byzantine Empire recovered from the Arab and other attacks to play an active role in the politics of Eastern Europe and the Arab world. In the West Pepin's son, Charlemagne, unified the Frankish lands under his control and conquered large portions of northern and eastern Europe to form the Carolingian Empire.

The old Roman world was now divided into three vast Empires: Charlemagne's empire was largely located in northwest Europe and the northern Mediterranean. The Byzantine Empire included parts of Turkey and the areas to the north and west of Constantinople. The Arabic Caliphate extended from Persia all along the southern Mediterranean and included the Iberian Peninsula. In addition there were the smaller political units of Anglo-Saxon England and the Kievan state.

The formation of large political units and the conversion of populations to new religions had widespread effects. The position of women changed with new religious laws. Intellectual revival occurred with the peace and patronage fostered by the regimes. And new military and political arrangements arose. But all these political units had inherent internal weaknesses that made them unable to withstand new invasions of Turkish peoples and war parties from Scandinavia. The empires broke up into smaller political units more capable of dealing with immediate problems of defense.

| CHAPTER 7. THE EMPIRES OF THE EARLY MIDDLE AGES | | | | | | | |
|---|---|---|---|---|---|---|---|
| | Social Structure | Body Politic | Changes in the Organization of Production and in the Impact of Technology | Evolution of Family and Changing Gender Roles | War | Religion | Cultural Expression |
| I. THE BYZANTINE EMPIRE | | | | | | | |
| II. ISLAM | | | | | | | |
| III. CAROLINGIAN OR FRANKISH EMPIRE | | | | | | | |
| IV. THE VIKINGS, KIEV, AND ENGLAND | | | | | | | |

# I. The Byzantine Empire (632–1071)

◆

The Byzantine Empire developed a decisively Eastern orientation. The characteristic was already observable in Justinian's reign. Although Justinian's great codification of Roman law was in Latin, he issued his own edicts in Greek, now the common language of the Empire. Court ceremonials resembled those of an Eastern ruler, in which the subjects were distanced from the ruler by space, dress, and submissive behavior. Social organization was also undergoing changes that made large estates look more like those in the West (see chapter 6) and forced a reorganization of the army that eventually created a rural elite and a subservient peasant class. Although Byzantium remained wealthy, aggressive in defending its borders, and expansive in its missionary activity, it was under constant attack and its physical territory shrank to an area in Europe and Asia surrounding Constantinople.

### ◆ STRAINS ON THE EMPIRE

***Heraclius and the Persian Wars***   Heraclius (r. 610–641) came to power amid repeated military disasters. The Avars, a nomadic tribe from Central Asia, and Slavs invaded the Balkans right up to the walls of Constantinople. While the Avars withdrew again to above the Danube River, the Slavs remained in the Balkans. The aggressive

Persians took Antioch, Jerusalem, and Alexandria. The Persians even removed from the Church of the Holy Sepulcher in Jerusalem the cross on which Jesus was crucified. Raising money through treasures donated by the churches, Heraclius strengthened the army and then boldly opened a successful war against the Persians in 622. The Persians agreed to a humiliating peace and returned the Holy Cross.

The Persian wars left Byzantium financially depleted and its army exhausted. The Empire was not in a position to defend itself immediately against a new menace on its borders. After the death of Muhammad in 632, his Muslim followers from the Arabic world embarked on a tidal wave of conquests, overrunning much of the Empire in scarcely more than ten years.

***Effects of Territorial Losses***   A century elapsed before the Byzantines were able to take the offensive against the Muslims. The Empire had lost Egypt and Syria, but the loss had positive as well as negative effects. Those regions had never become entirely Greco-Roman and had resisted Byzantine administration, taxation, and religion. These regions embraced the Arian (see chapter 5) and monophysite (see chapter 6) heresies. Their religious beliefs were closer to Islam, thus making the Arab conquest easier. Furthermore, the economic importance of Constantinople as the major trading city for the West increased after the Arab conquest of Egypt. Asia Minor, Antioch, and Jerusalem, however, had been of major importance to Byzantium, and the Empire tried to reconquer them (see maps 6.2 and 7.1).

***Military Revival***   The emperor Leo III (r. 717–741) beat back a Muslim attack on Constantinople in 717 and 718 and then began to reconquer Asia Minor. The military revival reached its height under the great warrior emperors of the ninth through eleventh centuries. Byzantine armies pushed the Muslims back into Syria and waged successful wars in southern Italy, the Balkan Peninsula, and the Caucasus. Their principal military accomplishment was in the Balkan Peninsula, where they defeated the nomadic people known as the Bulgars. The modern Bulgarians are entirely Slavic in language and culture and retain only the name of the original nomads. During

the late ninth and tenth centuries, Byzantium experienced once again a period of stability, wealth, and artistic glory.

***Leo III and Iconoclasm***   While Leo III's military campaigns marked the turn of the tide against the Arab expansion, his religious policies plunged the Empire into turmoil. Leo had grown up in Asia Minor, where he had contact with both Islam and heretical Christians, and he absorbed some of their suspicions that the use of holy images, or icons (from the Greek *eikon,* "image"), in worship was akin to idolatry. He introduced *iconoclasm* ("image-breaking") in the Empire in 726. Not only did he forbid the veneration of images within churches, he pursued a policy of actively destroying them. Iconoclasm was a drastic policy,

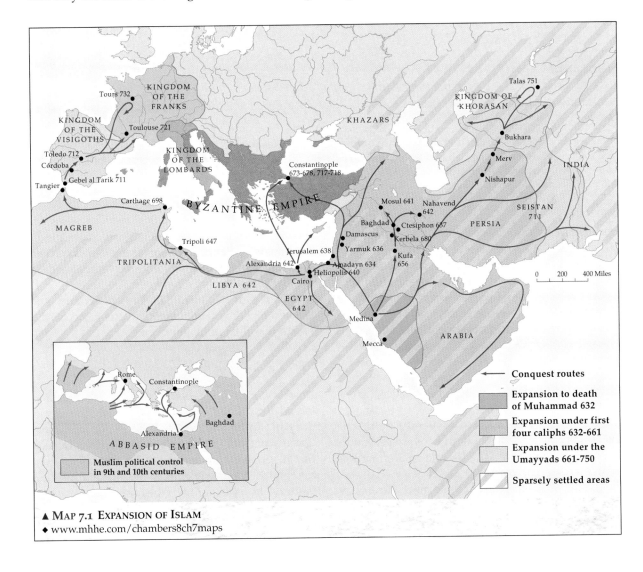

▲ **Map 7.1 Expansion of Islam**
◆ www.mhhe.com/chambers8ch7maps

▲ ICONOCLAST WHITEWASHING AN IMAGE OF CHRIST, CA. 900
**Byzantine iconoclasts, protesting the worship of images and the leadership of a Latin pope, destroyed the decorations of numerous churches. This page from a Psalter illuminated around 900 depicts the obliteration through whitewashing of an icon of Christ.**
Moscow, Historical Museum; photo, Ecole des Hautes Etudes, Paris.

because many of the worshipers had come to regard particular icons, images of Jesus, Mary, and the saints, as being efficacious as intercessors for divine help. Leo and the iconoclasts argued that people were worshiping pieces of wood and stone rather than God, Jesus, or Mary.

Historians still do not agree about Leo's motives. He may have used iconoclasm as a legal pretext for obtaining land to support the army. By seizing the holdings of the monasteries, which strongly advocated the worship of images, he enriched the treasury. Other historians argue that he was attempting to make Christianity more appealing to the Muslims, whom he was seeking to conquer, by emulating the Islamic condemnation of the worship of images.

Whatever the reasons, Leo's iconoclastic policy had a disastrous effect on relations with the West; it antagonized the popes and was a major factor in

their decision to seek out a Frankish champion in the person of Pepin the Short (see chapter 6). The veneration of images was restored temporarily in the Byzantine Empire between 784 and 813 and then permanently after 843. But the iconoclastic policy helped to widen the cleavage between the Western and Eastern churches.

## ◆ BYZANTINE GOVERNMENT

*Position of the Emperor*   The Byzantines believed that if the Empire performed the sacred duty of aiding the salvation of the human race, God would never permit its destruction, an idea that inspired Byzantines with the courage to resist for centuries a nearly continuous onslaught of invaders. The association of the sacred with the secular in the Empire meant that the emperor was a holy figure as the head of the state. A Christian emperor could not claim divinity (as pagan Roman emperors had), but the emperor lived surrounded by ceremony that imparted an aura of sanctity to his person; and the term *sacred*, used much as we use the word *public*, was liberally applied to his person, palace, and office.

Although the Byzantine emperor was head of both Church and state, recent historians have pointed out that his powers over the Church were restricted. He could not repeal the Nicene Creed or personally flout laws of Christian morality. Since he was not a priest, he could not say Mass or administer the sacraments. Yet the emperor exercised a wide authority over ecclesiastical matters. He supervised the discipline of the Church, set the qualifications for ordinations, created bishoprics and changed their boundaries, investigated the monasteries and reformed them when necessary, and appointed patriarchs and at times forced their resignation. Even dogma and practice were not beyond his influence, as Leo III demonstrated in his initiation of iconoclasm. The emperor summoned councils, supervised their proceedings, and enforced their decisions. Because of the emperor's extensive powers, the clergy was largely limited to performing the sacred liturgy and administering the sacraments.

***Elaborate Bureaucracy*** The emperor, like his predecessors in the old Roman Empire, enjoyed absolute authority and governed with the aid of an elaborate civil service. In Byzantium all justice flowed from the emperor, and he or his chief official could hear appeals from any local court in the Empire. The Byzantine government supported such refinements as an effective fiscal system, a state postal service, and even a secret police, ominously called the *agentes in rebus* ("those doing things"). Western governments had none of these innovations.

At a time when Western governments operated almost without a budget, the Byzantine government collected large revenues from the 10 percent tariff on trade and from the profit from the state monopolies. The government also employed skilled diplomats, whom contemporary observers celebrated for their ability to keep enemies divided and for their liberal use of bribes, tributes, and subsidies. In contrast to this elaborate bureaucracy, Western kingdoms functioned with a rudimentary administration and without a professional civil service.

Literate and trained laymen largely staffed the bureaucracy. Eunuchs (castrated men) were preferred for important positions in the government because it was believed that they would not be tempted by sexual intrigue and would have no wife or children to compete with the emperor for their loyalties. Eunuchs performed managerial functions that in the West were assumed by queens and women of the court.

## ◆ THE TWO CHURCHES

The contrasting experiences in the early Middle Ages deeply affected the character and spirit of the two major branches of Christianity. The differences between the two Churches clarify other contrasts in the history of the Eastern and Western peoples. The Eastern Church developed and functioned under the supervision of the emperor. In the West, on the other hand, the collapse of central authority in the Roman Empire gave the clergy a position of leadership in secular affairs.

***Theological Differences*** Both the Eastern Church and the Western Church considered themselves catholic (that is, universal) and orthodox (that is, holding true beliefs); the terms *Roman Catholic* and *Greek Orthodox* used to identify the Churches today are exclusively modern usages. The two Churches maintained nearly identical beliefs. Perhaps the principal, or at least the most famous, disagreement was and still is the *filioque* dispute (meaning "and from the son"), which concerns the relationship between members of the Trinity: the Father, Son, and Holy Spirit. The Eastern Church held, and still holds, that the Holy Spirit proceeds only from the Father, while the Western Church maintained that the Holy Spirit proceeds from the Father "and from the Son."

The Eastern Church permitted, as the Western Church did not, divorce for reasons of adultery and the ordination of married men to the priesthood, although bishops had to be celibate.

***Languages in Liturgy*** The most significant liturgical difference between the two Churches was that the Eastern Church allowed the use of vernacular languages—Greek, Coptic, Ethiopian,

Syriac, Armenian, Georgian, Slavonic, and others—in the liturgy. Liturgical usage added great dignity to these Eastern languages and stimulated their development. The East Slavs, for example, possessed a rich literature in Slavonic within a century after their conversion to Christianity. Western vernacular literature was much slower in developing. On the other hand, the toleration of many vernacular languages weakened the unity of the Eastern Church. An Eastern cleric using his own vernacular language could not easily communicate with clerics from other regions, whereas a Western cleric who used Latin could make himself understood anywhere in the West. Because of linguistic differences from their neighbors, Eastern churches tended to develop in isolation from one another. Moreover, the toleration of many vernacular languages made difficult the revival of classical learning. In learning Latin, a Western cleric also acquired the ability to read the great Latin classics, while an Eastern cleric who did not know Greek was blocked from the Greek classics. Eastern cultures were thus deprived of access to scholarship of the ancient world.

The Eastern Church remained thoroughly decentralized because of its diverse languages. It developed into a loose confederation of independent national churches that relied on secular authority (on the model of the emperor's control over the Greek church) to defend their temporal interests. In contrast, with the unity of Latin as its liturgical and literary language, the Western Church began to develop a centralized control over Christianity in the West under the papacy. The popes' power was often strong enough to defy secular rulers (see chapter 8).

*Missionary Activities* The two Churches came into direct conflict in the Balkans over the conversion of the Slavs. Two Christian brothers of Slavic descent, Cyril and Methodius, set out in about 862 as missionaries from the Byzantine Empire to preach to the Slavs. Cyril developed a Slavonic script based on Greek letters called the Cyrillic alphabet. The brothers used the Yugo-Slav or South Slav dialect, translating the Bible and the liturgy into Slavonic. With modifications, the Cyrillic alphabet remains in use in parts of Eastern Europe and Russia today.

Cyril and Methodius had their first success with the conversion of the Serbs. Then the Bulgar-

ians, now settled in a kingdom in the Balkans, requested missionaries. In their peace settlement with the Byzantine Empire, the Bulgarians had been allowed to settle in the Balkans in exchange for converting to Christianity. They too adopted the Cyrillic alphabet and adhered to the Eastern Church.

In the West the sword opened the way for missionaries. The papacy relied on the Frankish rulers to expand the boundaries of the Western Church through conquest. The struggles between Rome and Constantinople for conversion of the Slavic peoples brought about the area's religious configuration that still exists today. Croatia, Albania, and Moravia (the Czechs and Slovacs) came under the Roman Church, but the Serbs and the rest of the Balkan area adhered to the Greek Church. Russia was converted to the Eastern Church in the tenth century.

## ◆ BYZANTINE ECONOMY AND SOCIETY

*Urban and Rural Population* The outstanding feature of Byzantine civilization, compared with that of Western Europe, was the continuing vitality of its cities. At one time the Byzantine Empire included such great urban centers as Alexandria, Antioch, Beirut, Constantinople, Trebizond, and Tyre. At its peak under Justinian, Constantinople probably contained more than three hundred thousand inhabitants. The city had paved and illuminated streets and splendid churches and palaces. Urban society was, however, marked by a wide division between rich and poor. The rich lived among magnificent surroundings in huge palaces; the poor, in sprawling slums. Crimes committed in broad daylight were commonplace.

Rural society was organized on a theme system. The themes were administered by generals, who became the elite of the Empire. Soldiers and sailors were paid by granting them their own farms. They fought in their own theme army or navy to defend their land. These soldier/farmers made decisions concerning the use of uncultivated or common lands, assumed (or were required to assume) collective responsibility for the payment of taxes, and elected judges and other officials to supervise the village government. The village organization was similar to the one that developed in the West.

*Trade and Manufacture* The Byzantine Empire was wealthy compared with other states of the age. One great source of wealth came from the commerce that passed through the ports and gates of Constantinople. The Slavs from the north carried amber, fur, honey, slaves, wax, and wheat; Armenians and Syrians from the east brought clothing, fruit, glass, steel, and spices; merchants from the west contributed arms, iron, slaves, and wood. The vigorous commerce attracted large colonies of foreign merchants. The commercial importance of Byzantium is revealed in the prestige of its gold coin, the *bezant*. Its weight and purity were kept constant from the reign of Constantine to the late eleventh century; no other major system of coinage can match its record of stability.

Constantinople was also the producer of luxury items. When the Persian Empire blocked the trade in silk from China and India across the land routes (the Great Silk Road), Justinian tried to find other ways to import silk from China. He experimented with sending missionaries to Ethiopia and the Arabian peninsula to create a route through the Red Sea. Finally, two monks who had

▼ **AGRICULTURE**
**Cultivating their own plots was the principal work of Byzantine peasants. This manuscript illustration shows the various labors of digging, harvesting, and watering taking place in a fanciful landscape.**
Bibliothèque Nationale de France, Paris

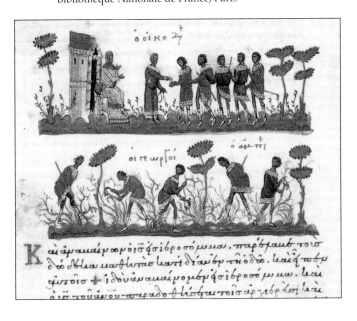

▲ **SILK TEXTILE**
**A splendid example of the quality of silk manufacture in Constantinople around the year 1000, this textile shows the eagle, an ancient symbol of power and victory, holding in its beak a ring while resting its claws on a row of pearls. This particular work of craftsmanship is said to have been used to transport the remains of St. Germain, who died in Ravenna in 448, back to Auxerre in France.**
Giraudon/Art Resource, NY

returned from northern India revealed to him the secret of silkworm cultivation and weaving, which the Chinese had known for at least two millennia. Justinian established silk production as a state monopoly; it enriched the state and meant that the emperor controlled the distribution of prestigious quality silk fabrics and dyes among aspiring tribal kings who wished to imitate the emperor. The best silk, rich purple-dyed cloth, was reserved for the imperial family. So significant was the symbolic value of purple silk that it became a particular distinction of legitimacy to "be born in the purple," indicating that the emperor's mother gave birth in a chamber hung with purple cloth. One emperor, Constantine Prophyrogenitus ("born in the purple," r. 913–957), took it as a name.

Byzantine artisans producing luxury goods such as silk were organized into *guilds* (organizations of craftsmen who trained skilled workers and organized artisans to ensure quality products). The *Book of the Prefect,* written in about 950 and describing the duties of a city's chief administrative officer, mentions twenty-one craft guilds; most of these made luxury products. The artisans were famed for gold work, glass objects, ivories, jewelry, icons, and reliquaries, all of which were shipped everywhere in the known world. The government closely regulated prices and movement of goods and maintained state monopolies.

***Limited Role of Women***   Women in the Byzantine Empire continued as they had in the ancient world. Their lives centered around the home, and their contact with men outside the family was strictly limited. They wore veils over their heads, but not their faces. Whereas in Western monasticism nuns performed charity work and ran schools, Byzantine nuns were strictly cloistered and performed none of these functions, which were reserved for monks. Only at the imperial and aristocratic level could women play an active role, including acting as regent and even becoming sole ruler, as did Empress Irene (r. 797–802) and Theodora (r. 1042, 1055–1056). It was another Theodora, a regent, who initiated the return to icon veneration in 843. Aristocratic women played a role in administering family lands.

The streets and fields were not devoid of women. Poor women had no recourse but to aid in family agriculture, to become street vendors of food and drink, or even enter into the theater and prostitution.

The law placed women and children under the protection of male relatives, so they could not act legally on their own. Nonetheless, the law afforded women the protection of their dowries—

▼ Women Weaving and Spinning

**Textile production was an important industry in Byzantine culture. This manuscript illustration depicts one woman weaving on a simple rectangular frame and another woman spinning.**
Bibliothèque Nationale de France, Paris

the goods, money, and land that the wife brought to the marriage. The dowry was an important economic asset to the family, and the husband could administer but not sell it during the marriage. On his death the wife regained it for her widowhood. Widowhood did not leave women legally free, as it did in the West, because the Eastern Church intervened and discouraged women from remarrying.

## ◆ BYZANTINE CULTURE

*Education*   Byzantine wealth supported a tradition of learning that benefited not only the clergy but also many laymen. There were three types of institutions of higher learning: a palace school, primarily for laymen, trained civil servants in language, law, and rhetoric; a patriarchal school instructed priests in rhetoric and theology; and monastic schools taught young monks the mystical writings of the past. With the demise of public grammar schools in the sixth and seventh centuries, the poor depended on their guild for what education they received. A general shift in education reflected the shifts connected with the medieval period of Byzantine history. In the past, boys, particularly sons of the elite, had been trained in the Greek and Latin classical authors. That became obsolete, and instead, they learned Greek from a Psalter (containing the biblical Psalms) and other devotional literature.

*Scholarship*   Scholars used the Greek rather than the Latin language almost exclusively after the sixth century. They composed school manuals, histories, saints' lives, biblical commentaries, and encyclopedias of ancient science and lore. With the revival of the Empire under the Macedonian dynasty (ca. 870–1025), interest in learning gained prestige once again. Constantine VII Porphyrogenitos wrote books on history and supported scholarship. On the whole, Byzantine scholars did not show the fascination with Aristotle and science that the Arabs and the Western scholars did, but concentrated instead on Plato and religious writers. Their greatest accomplishment was the preservation of classical Greek literature. With the exception of some few works preserved on papyri, virtually all that the Western world possesses of classical Greek authors has come down

through Byzantine copies, most of which date from the tenth to the twelfth centuries.

*Art and Architecture*   With the final rejection of iconoclasm in the middle of the ninth century, art and architecture flourished once again. Byzantine artisans designed and decorated many churches throughout the Empire. Their work is found in such places as Messina and Palermo in Sicily and Venice in Italy. Artists were summoned to such distant places as Kiev to aid in the design, construction, and decoration of churches.

The mosaics make vividly concrete the Byzantine concepts of empire, emperor, and church. The emperor is always presented as the august figure that Byzantine ideology made of him. Christ is never shown as suffering; he is, in other words, always God and never man. The reason for this seems to have been the close association that the figure of Christ bore to the living emperor. To show Christ as suffering would suggest that the emperor too might be a weak and vulnerable man. The mosaics have no sense of movement, admission of human frailty, or recognition of the reality of change. Operating within this picture of the world, the artists nevertheless portrayed their solemn figures with a rich variety of forms, garments, and colors. Byzantine mosaics may be static, but they are neither drab nor monotonous.

*Popular Culture*   Byzantine popular culture had both secular and spiritual sides. The population entered vigorously into the theological debates over the nature of Christ (divine or human or both in the same person) and the use of icons. One Byzantine theologian observed that, when he went to the marketplace and asked the price of bread, he received an argument on the nature of Christ. Theological debate was not confined to arguments in councils of churchmen. Instead, the laity's involvement could lead to riots.

The Hippodrome in Constantinople and similar sports centers in other cities continued some of the entertainments of the Roman coliseums. Chariot racing was the most popular sport, but animal shows, theater, and other spectacles also enjoyed considerable vogue. The spectators divided into rival fan groups called the "Blues" and the "Greens," whose members adopted strange haircuts and clothing, carried weapons, and generally acted as rowdy sports fans. These "clubs" could form more serious factions if they involved themselves in religious or political issues and were responsible for some of the more serious riots.

## ◆ DECLINE OF THE BYZANTINE EMPIRE

*Social Transformations*   The theme system that Heraclius had created to recruit an army and navy of free peasant-warriors began to collapse. From the early tenth century these free peasant-warriors, apparently to escape mounting fiscal and military burdens, began to abandon their farms to more powerful neighbors. In the eleventh century many of them became serfs; they gave up their freedom of movement and paid landlords a rent for their property. The disintegration of the theme system reduced the military manpower and led to a rural aristocracy of landlords, which in turn weakened the strength of the central government.

The emperors tried to limit the size and number of great estates, but by the late eleventh century, their weaker successors preferred to purchase the loyalty of the rural aristocracy by distributing imperial estates to them. The aristocracy was also gaining control over ecclesiastical lands, as the Church granted them entire monasteries to administer in the name of the Church. But, in fact, these concessions represented virtual gifts of monastic properties to lay lords. Byzantium was being transformed from a disciplined society of peasant-warriors under a strong central government to a society with a dependent peasantry, strong local landlords, and a weak central government.

*Defense of the Empire*   Without a pool of free peasants to recruit for the army and navy, the emperors had to seek outside help. To maintain control of the sea, essential to the security of Constantinople, they sought the support of the growing naval power of Venice. Emperors in 998 and 1082 gave generous trading concessions to the Venetians, which were major steps in the growth of Italian (and Western) naval strength in the waters of the eastern Mediterranean. The problem of land defense was even more pressing. A new people, the Seljuk Turks, had recently emerged from the steppes to threaten the Eastern frontiers.

*The Seljuk Turks*   The Byzantines gave the name *Turk* to a number of nomadic tribes that lived in the region east and north of the Caspian Sea (modern Turkestan). In the eleventh century, members of one tribe, the Seljuks, penetrated beyond the eastern borders of the Empire into Asia Minor. They shattered the largely mercenary army of the Byzantines and took the emperor captive at Manzikert in 1071.

As the Byzantine defenses broke down, Asia Minor lay open to the Seljuk forces. One Turkish chieftain, Suleiman, established himself and his warriors at Nicaea, only a few miles from Constantinople. The virtual loss of Asia Minor forced the Byzantine emperor to appeal to the West for help, a request that led to the First Crusade. This appeal signaled the end of the Byzantine Empire as a great power in the East.

*East-West Schism*   The second disaster of the eleventh century was the formal schism between the Eastern and Western branches of the Church in 1054. Major dogmatic differences were less important in the schism than were rivalry, disputes, and snobbery. Competition over the conversion of the Slavs and control over the churches in southern Italy contributed to the rancor. Furthermore, the Byzantines resented the papal claim to primacy within the Church. Rome by this time appeared to them as a provincial town without an empire or a subject territory; the Byzantines considered Constantinople, the seat of wealth and power, the more appropriate capital for the Church.[1]

Perhaps even more fundamental, the rupture of relations reflected the breakdown in communications between the East and the West. After Justinian's reign, the two halves of the Roman Empire and the two halves of the Church ceased to speak or understand a common language, making misunderstandings more difficult to resolve.

The schism of 1054 destroyed the hope for a united Christian Church. Even today, more than nine hundred years after the event, adherents of

---

[1]In the tenth century the Byzantines told Liutprand, bishop of Cremona, that they, and not the residents of Rome, were the true Romans and that Rome was a town inhabited exclusively by "vile slaves, fishermen, confectioners, poulterers, bastards, plebeians, underlings."

the Western and Eastern traditions are still trying to overcome the rift. Only in 1965 did the pope and the Greek patriarch formally remove the excommunications of 1054.

# II. Islam

◆

Sometime about 610 in the Arabian town of Mecca, a merchant's son named Muhammad began to preach to the people, summoning them to repentance and reform. Gradually, he brought his teachings together to form a new system of religious belief that he called Islam. The explosive impact of his preaching must be reckoned as one of the most extraordinary events of world history. Within a century after Muhammad's death his followers had conquered and partially converted territories larger than the old Roman Empire. Today Islam remains the faith of perhaps 800 million people, more than an eighth of the world's population.

## ◆ THE ARABS

The Arabian peninsula, the homeland of the Arabs, profoundly influenced their culture and history. Its vast interior and northern regions have steppes, wastelands, and some of the hottest and driest deserts of the world. The Arabs, however, adapted to this harsh environment. They supported themselves by raising sheep and camels that provided nearly all their necessities: meat, milk, wool, skins for clothes and tents, and fuel from dried camel dung. The Arabs were extremely proud of their family, race, language, skill, and way of life. The harsh environment and their fierce pride made them spirited, tenacious, and formidable warriors.

The Arabian peninsula was in a state of intense political and social ferment on the eve of Muhammad's appearance. The stronger political powers—the Persians, Byzantines, and Abyssinians across the Red Sea—tried repeatedly to subdue the Arabs but could not dominate them in their desert home. Religious ferment was no less explosive. Several prophets, preaching new religious beliefs, had gained followers in Arabia before Muhammad. Their success indicated a growing dissatisfaction among the Arabs with their tradi-

tional paganism, which gave no promise of an afterlife and offered no image of human destiny and the role of the Arabs in it. Both Christianity and Judaism had won numerous converts, but neither one was able to gain the adherence of most Arabs. The religious leader who by the force of his vision fused all these contending pagan, Christian, and Jewish ideas into a single, commanding, and authentically Arabian religion was Muhammad.

## ◆ MUHAMMAD

Historians have little certain information about the founder of Islam. Muhammad was born at Mecca about 570 or 571. His father died before his birth, and his mother died when he was 6. Raised by his uncle, Muhammad worked as a camel driver in caravans. He may have been illiterate and may have had no direct knowledge of the Jewish and Christian scriptures; but he did acquire a wide, if sometimes inaccurate, knowledge of the history and teaching of those two religions. At about the age of twenty-five Muhammad married the widow of a rich merchant. Freed from economic concerns, he gave himself to religious meditations in the desert outside Mecca.

*Preaching* In 610 Muhammad heard the voice of the angel Gabriel speaking to him, and he continued to receive such revelations in increasing frequency and length for the remainder of his life. After his first revelation from Gabriel, Muhammad began to preach publicly about personal moral reform, but only his wife and a small group of relatives initially accepted his teachings. The people of Mecca feared him because his strictures against paganism seemed to threaten the position of Mecca as a center of pilgrimages. Rejected in his native city, Muhammad accepted an invitation to expound his ideas in Medina, about 270 miles to the north.

*Hijra* Muhammad's emigration from Mecca to Medina is called the *hijra* and occurred in 622, which later became the year 1 of the Islamic calendar. The *hijra* was a turning point in Muhammad's career for two reasons: He became the political leader and governor of an important town, which gave him a base for the military expansion of the

Islamic community; and his responsibilities as head of an independent town affected the character of his religious message. More and more, his message was concerned with public law, administration, and the practical problems of government.

Muhammad was more successful in making converts at Medina than he was at Mecca. He told his followers that God ordered them to convert or conquer their neighbors. With the support of his followers, Muhammad marched against the Meccans, defeating them in battle in 624 and taking Mecca in 630. He destroyed all the pagan shrines, keeping only the Kaaba (Arabic for "square building"), which Muslim tradition says that Abraham built. By his death in 632, Muhammad had given his religion a firm foundation on Arabian soil.

### ◆ THE RELIGION OF ISLAM

Instructed by the angel Gabriel, Muhammad passed on to his followers the words or prophecies of Allah (from *al ilah*, meaning "the God").

The collection of prophecies is known as the *Koran;* and Allah, in Islamic theology, is its true author. The Koran was written down in its present version in 651 and 652. It imparts to the sympathetic reader a powerful mood, one of uncompromising monotheism, of repeated and impassioned emphasis upon the unity, power, and presence of Allah. The mood is sustained by constant reiterations of set formulas praising Allah, his power, knowledge, mercy, justice, and concern for his people.

The chief obligation that Muhammad imposed on his followers was submission (the literal meaning of *Islam*) to the will of Allah. Those who submit are Muslims. (*Muhammadan,* which suggests that Muhammad claimed divinity, is an inappropriate usage.) Muhammad was little concerned with the subtleties of theology; he was interested in defining for Muslims the ethical and legal requirements for an upright life. Unlike Christianity, Islam retained this practical emphasis; jurisprudence, even more than speculative theology, re-

▼ KORAN, NINTH THROUGH TENTH CENTURY

**The Koran, the sacred book of Islam, in a ninth- or tenth-century printing. From the ninth century the design of sacred books followed specific forms that remained standard in Islamic art. Color and gilding are added not only as ornament but also to separate verses; the leafy projection to the left signals the beginning of a new chapter.**
Courtesy of the Freer Gallery of Art, Smithsonian Institution, Washington, D.C.

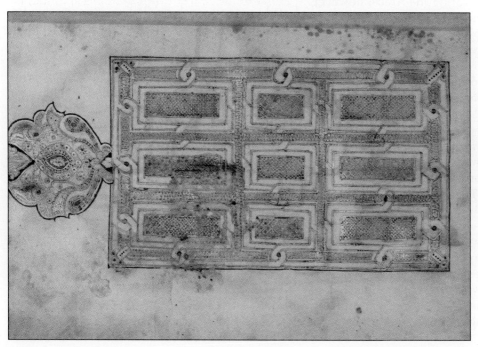

▲ PILGRIMAGE GUIDE
**This sixteenth-century illustration of a pilgrimage guide written around 900 shows the Kaaba at Mecca. The Kaaba, said to have been built by the Prophet Abraham, is the black rectangular building surrounded by domed arcades.**
Courtesy of The Arthur M. Sackler Museum, Harvard University Art Museums, The Edwin Binney, 3rd Collection of Turkish Art at the Harvard University Art Museums, © President and Fellows of Harvard College, Harvard University

mained the great intellectual interest of Muslim scholarship. Also in contrast to Christianity, Islam did not recognize a separate clergy and church, for there was no need for specialized intermediaries between Allah and his people. Allah was the direct ruler of the faithful on earth; he legislated for them in the Koran, which was administered through Muhammad, the Prophet, and his successors, the caliphs. Church and state were not separate entities, at least in theory. There was only the single, sacred community of Allah.

*Relationship to Other Religions*   The message of Islam exerted a powerful appeal to the Arabs. Compared with Christianity and Judaism, Islam was a starkly simple belief, easily explained and easily grasped. It was an effective fusion of religious ideas from Arabic paganism, Christianity, Judaism, and perhaps Zoroastrianism. Judaism influenced the legal code regulating diet and behavior. Judaism and Christianity provided the notion of prophecy, for Muhammad considered himself the last of a line of prophets that began with Abraham and included Jesus. More than that, the Bible tells that Abraham fathered Ishmael by Hagar, an Egyptian slave girl (Gen. 16–17), and Muslims believe that Ishmael was their ancestor and lies buried with Hagar in the Kaaba at Mecca. Christianity contributed the concepts of Last Judgment, personal salvation, heaven and hell, charity to the poor and weak, and a universal religion. Christianity, or perhaps Zoroastrianism, suggested the figures of Satan and evil demons. Paganism contributed the veneration of the Kaaba and the requirement of pilgrimage to the sacred city.

Islam was based on religious ideas already familiar to the Arabs. Perhaps more important, Islam appealed strongly to the intense racial and cultural pride of the Arabs. The Koran was written in their native language, Arabic, and only in Arabic could Allah be addressed. Islam was seen as the final revelation, completing the message that God had partially conveyed through the Hebrew prophets and Jesus. The Arabs, a people who had hitherto played a negligible role in history, were given an important mission in life: to carry to the world the ultimate saving message. The Arabs saw themselves as replacing the Jews as God's chosen people, with a sacred right to his holy places, including Jerusalem (see "The Koran on Christians and Jews," p. 222).

◆ EXPANSION OF ISLAM

*Conquests*   Several factors aided the extraordinary expansion of Islam in the first century of its existence. Islam fused the once contending Arab clans and tribes into a unified and dedicated force.

## THE KORAN ON CHRISTIANS AND JEWS

*In the Koran, Muhammad proclaims that the faith of Islam also welcomes "the people of the Book"—that is, Christians and Jews who have the Bible as their sacred book—and that Islam is the fulfillment of these earlier faiths.*

"Believers, Jews, Christians, and Sabaeans [of the kingdom of Saba in southwest Arabia]—whoever believes in Allah and the Last Day and does what is right—shall be rewarded by their Lord; they have nothing to fear or regret. To Moses We [that is, Allah] gave the Scriptures and after him We sent other apostles. We gave Jesus the son of Mary veritable signs and strengthened him with the Holy Spirit. And now that a Book [the Koran] confirming their Scriptures has been revealed to them by Allah, they deny it, although they know it to be the truth and have long prayed for help against the unbelievers.

"May Allah's curse be upon the infidels! Evil is that for which they have bartered away their souls. To deny Allah's own revelation, grudging that He should reveal His bounty to whom He chooses from His servants! They have incurred Allah's most inexorable wrath. An ignominious punishment awaits the unbelievers. The unbelievers among the People of the Book, and the pagans, resent that any blessings should have been sent down to you from your Lord. But Allah chooses whom He will for His mercy. His grace is infinite.

"Abraham enjoined the faith on his children, and so did Jacob, saying: 'My children, Allah has chosen for you the true faith. Do not depart this life except as men who have submitted to Him.' Say: 'We believe in Allah and that which is revealed to us; we believe in what was revealed to Abraham, Ishmael, Isaac, Jacob, and the tribes; to Moses and Jesus and the other prophets. We make no distinction between any of them, and to Allah we have surrendered ourselves. Your God is one God. There is no God but Him.' "

From *The Koran*, N. J. Dawood (tr.) (Penguin Books, 1968), condensed.

The Arabs, long familiar with camels, were masters of desert warfare. Their enemies, relying on horses, could not challenge them on desert terrain. Using the desert much as English imperialists later used the sea, the Arabs moved armies and supplies with facility across vast arid stretches, struck the enemy at places and times of their own choosing, and retreated to the safety of the desert when the odds turned against them. Moreover, the Arabs' immediate neighbors, the Byzantines and Persians, were mutually exhausted by their recurrent wars. Both the Byzantine and Persian empires included large Semitic populations that were linguistically and culturally related to the Arabs and could, therefore, comprehend the message of Islam.

The Arabs were able to make and hold their conquests through a unique combination of fanaticism and toleration. Warriors were inspired by the Prophet's promise of vast rewards to those who died in the Holy War against the nonbelievers and by the very real prospect of considerable booty if victorious. The Prophet, however, also enjoined a policy of partial toleration toward Christians and Jews, who were both known as the "people of the Book" (the Bible). Thus, Christians and Jews continued to live under their own laws, but they paid a special tax for the privilege. Many Persian, Greek, and Semitic people converted voluntarily because they found the religion close to their own beliefs. Finally, because the Arabs did not have the numbers and the skills to govern all the territories they conquered, they opened the ranks of government to men from the newly conquered peoples. This move added stability to Arabic rule.

Islam expanded most rapidly in the period following Muhammad's death in 632 and coinciding with the rule of the first four caliphs, as Muhammad's successors were called. Arabian forces seized the Byzantine provinces of Palestine and Syria, overran Persia, and conquered Egypt by the 640s. By 661 the Arabian Empire was firmly established as a world power.

**Umayyads**  Islamic conquests continued under the caliphs of the Umayyad family, who were the first line of hereditary rulers of the Arab Empire.

The Umayyads moved the capital from Mecca to Damascus. Under their rule the Muslims conquered North Africa and overran the kingdom of the Visigoths in Spain. After crossing the Pyrenees into the kingdom of the Franks, Muslim raiders were finally defeated by Charles Martel at Tours in 732. This battle, 100 years after Muhammad's death, marked the extent of the Arabs' western advance and stabilized the frontier of Islam for the next several centuries (see map 7.1).

*Sunni-Shiite Schism*   As the territory under Islamic control grew to enormous size, internal dissensions shattered Islamic unity. Relations among the various peoples who had accepted Islam became fractious, and religious divisions appeared. Islam had been an open and fluid religion at the death of Muhammad, but scholars and teachers gradually elaborated a theology that a majority of the believers accepted as orthodox. The scholars based the new orthodoxy not only on the Koran but also on the *Sunnas,* or traditions, which were writings that purported to describe how the first companions of Muhammad or how Muhammad himself dealt with various problems. Some Muslims, however, rejected the new orthodoxy of the *Sunnites,* as they came to be called. Those who opposed the Sunnites were called the *Shiites* ("party" or "faction" of Ali).

This earliest schism was more a political than a religious one. The Shiites maintained that only the descendants of Muhammad's son-in-law, Ali (r. 655–661), who was the fourth caliph, could lawfully rule the Islamic community; they rejected the Umayyads (and later the Abbasids) as usurpers. Shiism soon became a cloak for all sorts of antagonisms, protests, and revolts. It struck deep roots among the mixed populations, reflecting the dissatisfactions of non-Arabs with the Arab preponderance and channeling the antagonism between the poorer classes and their masters.

The growing social and religious dissensions finally destroyed the Umayyad caliphate. A descendant of Abbas, the uncle of Muhammad, revolted against the Umayyads, captured Damascus, and ruthlessly massacred the caliph's family in 750. This victor founded the Abbasid dynasty. Only one member of the Umayyads, Abdurrahman, escaped. He fled to Spain, where he set up an independent caliphate at Córdoba in 755. Other independent regimes soon arose: Morocco in 788,

Tunisia in 800, eastern Persia in 820, and Egypt in 868. All became virtually independent under their local dynasties. The new Abbasid caliph moved the capital from Damascus to a new city, Baghdad. The Abbasid dynasty, which endured until 1258, marked a high point in Islamic culture, but the political community of Islam was never again to be united.

## ◆ ISLAMIC ECONOMY AND SOCIETY

Despite disunity, medieval Islamic civilization reached its peak of prosperity, refinement, and learning in the ninth and tenth centuries. Arabic, the language of the Koran, served to unify literature, learning, and commerce across the Islamic lands.

*Diverse Economic Systems*   As Islam expanded, it embraced numerous economic systems. The Bedouins in the Arabian peninsula, the Berbers in North Africa, and the Turkish people of Eurasia continued to have a pastoral economy. The majority of those living in Egypt, Persia, Sicily, and Spain lived from settled agriculture. The inhabitants of cities, especially those along the caravan routes that tied the Middle East to India and central Asia, relied on commerce.

The universal language, Arabic, made commercial communications easy. Muhammad had been a merchant, and Islamic law favored commerce. Maritime commerce in the Mediterranean provided, until the sixteenth century, the chief commercial link among India, Egypt, and the West. A large collection of letters from Jewish merchants living in Cairo in the eleventh and twelfth centuries has survived and marvelously illuminates trade and many other aspects of social life in the medieval East.[2]

*Trade and Manufacture*   Commercial exchange stimulated agriculture within the Arabic world.

---

[2]These letters are called the *Geniza documents.* The *geniza* was a storeroom attached to a synagogue; records mentioning God's name (including merchants' letters) could not be destroyed and were stored in the geniza. The geniza of the Cairo synagogue was sealed up and not rediscovered until the nineteenth century. Its contents were then sold to collectors of Jewish documents and to libraries and thus dispersed throughout the world. For examples of these extraordinary records, see S. D. Goitein, *Letters of Medieval Jewish Traders,* 1973.

Cultivators in Sicily and Spain adopted new plants from Asia, such as rice, and new techniques of cultivation, such as irrigation. Muslims from Persia to Spain practiced an agriculture remarkably advanced for the age. Trade also stimulated urban artisans to improve the quality of their products. The steel of Damascus and Toledo, the leather of Córdoba, and the fine cotton, linen, and silk of many Eastern towns (damask, for instance, was named for the weaving of Damascus) were desired and imitated in the West. Merchants shipped these products to India and Indonesia, where they were traded for spices and other products.

**Cosmopolitan Cities**    A vigorous urban life, concentrated in the cities of Damascus, Baghdad, Cairo, and Córdoba, distinguished medieval Islamic society. According to travelers' reports, Damascus had 113,000 homes and 70 libraries. Baghdad surpassed all other cities in the number of palaces, libraries, and public baths. Products from almost all parts of the known world could be purchased at the markets, or bazaars, in all the major cities. The streets teemed with slaves, servants, artisans, merchants, administrators, and beggars. The aura of the Islamic cities was preeminently cosmopolitan.

**Advances in Technology**    The Arabs, often borrowing from China, India, and Byzantium, improved on what they found. Byzantium had used Greek fire, a compound based on naphtha, which could burn on water or be put in clay pots with a fuse and hurled across a wall, causing fires where it landed. Said to be a Syrian invention, the Byzantines kept it as a military secret, but the Arabs eventually got the formula. The Arabs also improved on siege weapons and fortress building that they learned from the Byzantines. Serving as a conduit to the West of inventions from China, they introduced the windmill and the spinning wheel as well as paper making, block printing, and specialized textile weaving.

**Law and Government**    Because Islam recognized no distinction between church and state, the caliph was the supreme religious and civil head of the Muslim world. He was not free, however, to change the laws at will, since Allah had already provided all the laws his people needed. The caliph's role was primarily a military chief and a judge. Administration at the local level was done by a judge whose task was to see that the faithful lived according to the law of the Koran.

**Mixed Role for Women**    In the early days of Islam, women played a major role in conversion. Muhammad's wife, Khadija, was his first convert. His second wife, daughter of a wealthy Meccan, was an early convert who shared the exile in Medina before Muhammad married her. The wives of two of the first caliphs were also early converts.

The Koran placed a high value on preserving and enhancing the family. It encouraged people to marry and enjoined men to support their wives. It allowed male Muslims to have as many as four legal wives, but only if they could support them and treat them all fairly. Divorce was difficult because the husband had to allow his divorced wife to keep gifts he had given her and support her and her children. Women could inherit from their male kin, but their portion was less than a male heir would receive: "A male child shall have the equivalent of two female children."

The position of women depended on their social class and on the period in which they lived. Islamic society became more restrictive of women in later centuries. Muhammad had urged his wives to live in seclusion, but eventually the harem (rooms reserved for women) was recommended for all women after puberty. But the strict seclusion of the harem was something that only the very wealthy could afford for their wives, daughters, and concubines. Peasant and artisan women would have to be in public. Women who left the seclusion of home did so with a veil covering the head and face.

### ◆ ISLAMIC CULTURE

The Islamic conquests brought the Arabs into contact with older and more accomplished civilizations than their own, particularly with the intellectual achievements of the Greeks, which they were eager to preserve. During the eighth and ninth centuries, scholars translated into Arabic many Greek authors: Aristotle, Euclid, Archimedes, Hippocrates, and Galen. Islamic scholars were especially interested in astronomy,

# WRITING MEDIEVAL WOMEN'S HISTORY

One of the most important new directions for historical writing has been the history of women. Books and articles on women from all time periods and all countries are now abundant, and courses on women's history are readily available. Writing the history of women in the Middle Ages, however, presents major interpretive problems.

Very few writings by women survive from the Middle Ages. Not very many women in the West were literate, and those who were knew vernacular languages rather than Latin, the language of learning. Still, learned nuns left devotional literature, plays, and histories. Arabic was the language of both literature and speech, and some women's poems in Arabic survive. Greek women wrote histories. Another source of women's own thoughts were accounts of their visions or of their lives that their priests recorded.

Most information about women, therefore, is filtered through sources written by men. Men wrote about women from a number of motives, and these biases must be taken into consideration when interpreting the sources. Religious sources, for instance, seek to organize society and instruct believers. To understand and interpret these sources, a historian needs to know a great deal about the context in which they were written. The strictures from the Koran, for example, could be read as being very repressive of women. When seen in the context of Muhammad's desire to preserve and strengthen the family, however, they take on a different meaning. Add the pre-Islamic context, and the Koran can be viewed as improving the position of women by protecting them against abuses they had previously experienced.

Other sources, such as laws, provide sparse information about the women they seek to regulate and protect. The researcher does not know whether the laws were actually applied. A variety of other sources help to elucidate this information. Court cases, of course, provide ready information when they are available. But historians have creatively used archaeological evidence and even place names. For example, the Anglo-Saxons had the custom that the husband presented the wife with a gift, the *morgangifu,* the day after the marriage. Present-day names such as Mayfield or Morgay Farm indicate that these were bridal gifts to women. The historian's craft is partly one of solving mysteries; the study of women's history provides rich opportunities for the historically minded sleuth. Both the subject itself and the problems of researching it contribute to the dynamics of the field.

---

astrology, mathematics, medicine, and optics, and in these areas their writings exerted a great influence on the Western world.

*Medical Education*   Al-Razi (known as Rhazes in the West) of Baghdad was director of the state hospital in Baghdad, and he had practical experience with medicine and medical education. He wrote some 140 medical treatises, including a description of smallpox. Among the accomplishments of the Abbasid caliphate were courses in pharmacy and licensing of all people practicing medicine.

*Mathematics and Astronomy*   Arabic mathematicians adopted their impressive numbering system from the Hindus, but made the critical addition of the zero, which is itself an Arabic word. The use of the zero allows figures to be arranged in columns and allows the use of a decimal system. Italian merchants became familiar with the Arabic numbers shortly before the year 1200 and carried them back to the West. Arabic mathematicians also developed algebra. Astronomers and astrologers invented an improved astrolabe (which measures the angular declination of heavenly bodies above the horizon) and were able to improve the astronomical tables of antiquity.

*Philosophy and Theology*   Scholars also wrote philosophical and theological treatises. The most important Islamic philosopher was the Spaniard ibn-Rushd, or Averroës (1126?–1198), who wrote commentaries on Aristotle and exerted a profound influence on Christian as well as Islamic philosophy in the Middle Ages. Islamic philosophical speculations nourished intellectual life in the West in two ways: Western philosophers

◄ ABU-ZAYD VISITING A MUSLIM VILLAGE
**This thirteenth-century illustration is a leaf from the *al-Hariri Magamat* (Assemblies of Entertaining Dialogues), a collection of tales set in various parts of the Muslim world. Here, the main character, Abu-Zayd, visits a lively village whose inhabitants carry on their daily tasks of spinning, agriculture, and worship.**
Bibliothèque Nationale de France, Paris

gained a much broader familiarity with the scientific and philosophical heritage of classical Greece through translations made from Arabic, chiefly in Spain; and Islamic philosophers explored issues central to religious philosophy much earlier than did Christian thinkers. What is the relation between faith and reason, between an all-powerful God and the freedom, dignity, and individuality of the human person? In posing these problems and in suggesting answers, the Muslims stimulated and enriched thought in the West.

***Centers of Culture*** Baghdad under the Abbasid dynasty was a great cultural center. Caliph Harun

al-Rashid's reign (r. 786–809) was the high point of Islamic culture. The *Arabian Nights* was first written in this period and put into its present form in the fourteenth century. The stories convey a glamorous and idealized, but not a false, picture of the luxurious life at Baghdad. Harun's son Al-Mamun (r. 813–833) reigned even more splendidly than his father did. He was also a patron of learning. Al-Mamun founded an observatory for the study of the heavens and established a "House of Wisdom" (sometimes referred to as the first Islamic institution of higher education), where translations were made and a library collected for the use of scholars.

▲ This thirteenth-century Arab commentary on the *Geometry* of Euclid illustrates the proof of the Pythagorean theorem. Mathematics was one science in which the Arabs surpassed the classical achievements.
© British Museum

embarked on the reconquest of the Iberian Peninsula, and Christian fleets broke the Islamic domination of the western Mediterranean islands. The Byzantine offensive gave rise to the First Crusade, which wrested Jerusalem from Islamic control in 1099. In the East, Turkish nomads infiltrated the Abbasid caliphate in considerable numbers, and the Seljuks (converts to Islam) seized Baghdad in 1055. Turkish rulers gained supremacy in all the eastern Islamic states over the next few centuries.

The Arabic economic base was changing. By the thirteenth century, maritime and commercial supremacy on the Mediterranean Sea passed

▼ FORMS OF THE FIXED STARS, CA. 1009–1010
One of the earliest examples of Islamic book illustration, this manuscript, written around 1009–1010, contains seventy-five drawings noting the forms of the fixed stars. Sagittarius, shown as an armed rider, is traced from the pattern of the constellation and indicates the sophistication of Muslim astronomy.
The Bodleian Library, University of Oxford. MS. Marsh 144, page 273

Spain was a notable center of medieval Islamic civilization. The brilliance of Islamic-Spanish civilization is best reflected in three great architectural monuments: the mosque (now a cathedral) at Córdoba, the Alhambra Palace in Granada, and the Alcazar at Seville. Jewish communities in Spain, the most creative of Jewish communities in the West, contributed to the high quality of intellectual life. It was also in Spain that Western Christians came into intimate contact with Islamic learning and drew from it the greatest benefits.

### ◆ DECLINE OF MEDIEVAL ISLAMIC CIVILIZATION

The earliest indication of decline was the growing military weakness of the various Islamic states in the face of new invasions in the middle of the eleventh century. In the West, Christian armies

▲ Mosque at Córdoba, 784 – 990
**Begun around 784, the Mosque at Córdoba was enlarged throughout the ninth and tenth centuries. The flexible plan of parallel aisles creates a complex visual forest of double-tiered arches that originally supported a wooden roof. This immense structure, with 850 columns and 19 aisles, was one of the largest buildings in the Islamic world.**
Fridmar Damm/Leo de Wys

to Italians and other Westerners. Arabian coins largely disappeared from circulation in the West, documenting a headlong retreat from commerce. Simultaneously, the Islamic states no longer supported their warriors with salaries but with grants of land, which weakened central authority. The growing importance of an aristocracy of rural warriors seems to have brought a new militarism and rigidity into society.

To be sure, Islamic civilization continued to support some great cultural centers and to inspire some great artists and thinkers; but after the eleventh century it began to lose the qualities of openness, flexibility, and intellectual daring that

had so distinguished it in the ninth and tenth centuries.

## III. The Carolingian, or Frankish, Empire

◆

The Frankish Empire was already strong when Charles the Great (r. 768–814) became its king. Charles Martel, Charlemagne's grandfather, had defeated the Arabs in a battle at Tours in 732, thus sparing Frankish lands the same fate that befell the Visigothic kingdom in Spain. Charles Martel's

▲ The remarkable series of rooms and courtyards that make up the Alhambra Palace in Granada are one of the supreme achievements of Islamic art. The delicate tracery, the elegant details, and the constant presence of running water create a mood of luxury and refinement that can still be experienced by the visitor today.
J. Messerschmidt/Leo de Wys

## EINHARD ON CHARLEMAGNE

*The most important Western ruler of the Early Middle Ages was Charles the Great, or Charlemagne. A member of his court, Einhard, wrote of his life and describes him as follows.*

"Charles was large and strong, and of lofty stature; his height was seven times the length of his foot. In accordance with the national custom, he took frequent exercise on horseback and in hunting. He often practiced swimming, in which he was so skilled that none could surpass him. He was temperate in eating, and particularly so in drinking, for he hated drunkenness in anybody, much more in himself and in members of his household. While dining, he listened to reading or music. The subjects of the readings were the stories and deeds of older times; he was fond, too, of St. Augustine's books, and especially of 'The City of God.'

"Charles had the gift of ready and fluent speech, and could express himself with the utmost clearness.

He was not satisfied with a command of only his native language, but studied foreign ones, and was such a master of Latin that he could speak it as well as his native tongue; but he could understand Greek better than he could speak it. He zealously cultivated the liberal arts, held those who taught them in great esteem, and conferred high honors on them. He also tried to write, and used to keep tablets under his pillow, so that in leisure hours he might train his hand to form the letters; but as he began his efforts late in life, he had poor success."

From Einhard, *Life of Charlemagne*, S. E. Turner (tr.) (University of Michigan Press, 1960).

---

son, Pepin the Short, had elevated the family role in government from that of mayor of the palace to that of king of the Franks. Forming an alliance with the Frankish aristocracy and the pope, he had deposed the last of the Merovingians and was crowned king (see p. 192). Through careful alliances with the aristocracy, continued warfare with neighbors, and good management, the Frankish kings established a large empire in the former Roman province of Gaul and extended their control beyond the Rhine River. Charles the Great was a worthy successor to his able ancestors.

### ◆ CHARLEMAGNE

Pepin's son Charles the Great, or Charlemagne, pursued the policies of his predecessors with unprecedented energy. His biographer, the court scholar Einhard, says that he was a large man, "seven times the length of his own foot," and that he delighted in physical exercise, particularly hunting, riding, bathing, and swimming. His taste for food and women seems to have been no less exuberant. Perhaps more remarkable in this man were his intellectual curiosity and alertness. He was probably illiterate; Einhard says that he kept tablets by his bed to practice forming letters at

night, though with "poor success." But Einhard also says that he spoke and understood Latin, comprehended Greek, and enjoyed the company of learned men (see "Einhard on Charlemagne," above). The vast empire that Charlemagne built (called the "Carolingian" Empire from "Carolus," his Latin name) was in large measure a personal accomplishment, a tribute to his abounding physical energy and intelligence.

*Victorious Wars* Charlemagne's success as king depended on his success in waging long wars on every frontier. He perceived that spreading Christianity along with conquest led to submission to Frankish authority among pagan peoples. Where permanent conquest and conversion were not possible, the expeditions would still weaken neighboring enemies and prevent them from striking into the Frankish domains. At the pope's request Charlemagne campaigned four times in Italy against the Lombards and against factions in Rome opposed to the pope. He suppressed the independent Bavarians and overcame the Saxons after thirty-three years of fighting, thus bringing them fully and finally into the community of Western peoples. His conversions could be brutal. When the Saxons resisted Christianity, he threatened to kill them if they did not convert. These victorious wars added new territories to his empire (see map 7.2).

*Imperial Title*   On Charlemagne's fourth visit to Italy in 800, when he was praying before St. Peter's altar on Christmas night, Pope Leo III crowned him emperor of the Romans. The coronation added nothing to his possessions but still was of great symbolic importance. It confirmed the alliance of the papacy and the Frankish monarchy. The coronation proclaimed the complete political and cultural autonomy of the Western community of peoples from Byzantine (Roman) control.

### ◆ CAROLINGIAN GOVERNMENT

*Imperial Ideology*   The coronation added much to Charlemagne's dignity, and a grandiose imperial ideology developed around his person. But the elevation at the hands of the pope also led to later conflicts between future emperors and popes over who had the right to grant imperial power. A cult developed around the emperor that played a vital role in preserving the unity of the Empire. In imperial propaganda Charlemagne became the new David (the ideal king of the Old Testament), the new Augustus (the greatest of the pagan emperors), and the new Constantine (the champion of the Church). By presenting the emperor as a figure of such sanctity and brilliance, the government hoped to make rebellion against him unthinkable. Idealization of the emperor might thus accomplish what armies could not do alone.

*Administering the Empire*   The emperor was the head of the government. He ruled with the aid of a small group of officials. The chaplain, head of the palace clergy, advised the emperor and the entire court in matters of conscience. The chaplain also supervised the chancery, or secretariat, where the official documents were written. The chief lay official, the count of the palace, supervised the administration, judged cases that the emperor did not personally handle, and acted as regent during the emperor's frequent absences. Other officials included the chamberlain, who looked after the royal bedroom and treasury; the seneschal, who kept the palace in food and servants; and the constable, who cared for the horses.

At the local level the fundamental administrative unit was the county, which resembled in its extent the Roman provinces. The count was the administrator, judge, and military leader of the county.

Charlemagne's chief administrative problem was to maintain an effective supervision and control over the local officials. He used three devices to resolve this problem. First, Charlemagne himself traveled widely to ascertain how the land was being administered and to hear appeals from the decisions of the counts. Second, he appointed special traveling inspectors, called *missi dominici* (or "emperor's emissaries"), to inspect a particular county every year. These men scrutinized the behavior of both the lay and the ecclesiastical officials, heard complaints, published imperial directives, and reported their findings to the emperor. Third, Charlemagne required that the important men of his realm, both laymen and ecclesiastics, attend a general assembly almost every year. There they reported on conditions in their local areas, advised the emperor on important matters, and heard his directives. Many of the imperial directives have survived. Divided into chapters (*capitula*), these informative records are known as *capitularies*.

*Currency*   To promote unity, Charlemagne also standardized weights, measures, and money throughout his Empire. The monetary system came to be based on a single minted coin, the silver *denarius*, or penny. Twelve of these made a *solidus*, or shilling (although such a coin was not actually minted), and twenty shillings made a pound.

### ◆ THE CAROLINGIAN RENAISSANCE

The Frankish rulers—Pepin, Charlemagne, and their successors—promoted learning within their domains in what is now called the Carolingian Renaissance. These rulers were interested in education for several reasons. In the sixth and seventh centuries, when the continent was divided among many small kingdoms, different styles of writing, known as *national hands* (Visigothic, Merovingian,

▲ Map 7.2 Carolingian Empire under Charlemagne
The dates indicate the years in which the regions were added to the Empire. Marches were the frontier provinces (except Brittany, which was a maritime province) specially organized for the military defense of the Empire. Magdeburg was the episcopal see that took the leadership in converting the Danes and Slavs to Christianity. Aix-la-Chapelle, also called Aachen, was the capital of the Empire. The tributary peoples were those beyond the frontiers of the Empire over whom the emperor exercised a loose authority. They owed allegiance to him but were never integrated administratively into the Empire.

Lombard, and so on), had developed; and numerous variant readings had slipped into such basic texts as the Bible and the Benedictine rule. The Latin grammar used by scholars had also absorbed many regional peculiarities.

Literate persons in one part of Europe had great difficulty recognizing or reading a text written in another. The widespread decline in education had left few persons who could read at all. Poorly educated priests could not properly perform the liturgy, on which God's blessings on the community were thought to depend; and variations in religious rituals were also growing. Both situations weakened the unity of the Church as well as the state.

***Carolingian Minuscule*** Pepin and Charlemagne sought to remedy the lack of literacy. One great achievement of this educational revival was a reform in handwriting. About the year 800, monks at the monasteries of Corbie and Tours devised a new type of formal literary writing, a "bookhand," using lowercase letters and known as the Carolingian minuscule. Previously, the bookhands had been based on various styles of capital letters only and were difficult to read rapidly. The Carolingian minuscule used capital letters for the beginning of sentences and smaller (or lowercase) letters for the text. Our modern printing is based on this Carolingian innovation. It was easier to read a page written in this way; also, more letters could be written on a page, and thus more books were produced at less expense. Use of this graceful new script eventually spread across Europe.

***Latin Language*** Another achievement of this educational revival was the development of a common scholarly language. Carolingian scholars perfected a distinctive language now known as medieval Latin, which largely retained the grammatical rules of classical Latin but was more flexible and open in its vocabulary, freely coining new words to express the new realities of the age. Medieval Latin was also clearly different from the vulgar, or Romance, Latin spoken by the people. The establishment of medieval Latin as a distinct language of learning thus freed the Romance vernaculars to develop on their own. One of these vernacular languages is Old French, whose oldest surviving text dates from 842.[3]

The Latin created by the Carolingian scholars enabled travelers, administrators, and scholars to make themselves understood in all parts of Europe; and it continued to serve this function until the modern era. Even when it disappeared as an international language, it helped promote

▼ **This ninth-century manuscript illumination from the first Bible of Charles the Bald displays the Carolingian minuscule, which is the model for the lowercase letters used today in what printers call Roman type.**
Bibliothèque Nationale de France, Paris

---

[3]At Strasbourg in 842, Charles the Bald and Louis the German, two of the sons of Louis the Pious, took an oath that was recorded in Latin, Old French, and German. The oath at Strasbourg not only preserves the oldest surviving text in Old French but also marks the first use of German in a formal legal document.

European unity. All the modern vernacular tongues of Europe developed under the strong influence of these scholars' Latin. One of the reasons why it is possible to translate quickly from one European language to another is that their learned vocabularies are in large measure based on common Latin models.

***Standardization of Texts*** A further achievement of the educational revival was the standardization of important texts. Pepin sought to standardize the liturgy on the basis of Roman practice and Charlemagne continued his policy. Charlemagne had Alcuin of York, an Anglo-Saxon scholar who served as a sort of minister of cultural affairs from about 783 until 794, prepare a new edition of Jerome's Vulgate translation of the Bible. This edition became the common biblical text for the entire Western Church. Charlemagne procured from Monte Cassino a copy of the Benedictine rule and

◄ EZRA RESTORING THE BIBLE
**The image of Ezra restoring the Bible, in this eighth-century English manuscript, gives the work of the medieval monk an exalted self-justification. Here we see a biblical figure doing exactly what monks did—namely, writing and copying. In this case, Ezra was purifying the text of the Bible, and the implication was that monks were engaged in the same task. The vivid depiction of the bookshelves, with their open doors, and the table and stool is clearly an attempt to bring to life a scene from a monastery of the time.**
Scala/Art Resource, NY

had it copied and distributed, so that monks everywhere would follow a standard code.

*Schools and Curriculum*  Expanding educational opportunities were essential for the success of Charlemagne's program. To increase the supply of locally trained scholars, he ordered all bishops and monasteries to establish schools to educate boys. Charlemagne himself set the example by founding a palace school for the sons of his own courtiers. Alcuin helped devise the standards for the school curriculum, based on the seven liberal arts. He divided the curriculum into the *trivium*, or verbal arts (grammar, rhetoric, and logic), and the *quadrivium*, or mathematical arts (arithmetic, astronomy, geometry, and music). In the twelfth century this curriculum would become the standard program of study for a bachelor of arts at universities.

*Court Scholars*  Charlemagne brought scholars from all around Europe to his court, including Anglo-Saxons and Italians. They formed an academy to discuss major intellectual issues in imitation of the classical world and used names drawn from the Bible or classics when they met together. Charlemagne was known as David and Alcuin as Horace.

Most of the scholars were grammarians and educators, engaged in producing teachers' manuals, textbooks, and school exercises; they went back to the Latin classics for models of correct grammar, usage, and vocabulary rather than for aesthetic satisfaction or philosophical insights. Their work was neither original nor possessed of rhetorical grace, but it was of the greatest importance for the intellectual growth of Europe. The revived mastery of correct Latin equipped scholars of later generations to return to the classical heritage and to recover from it philosophic and aesthetic values.

### ◆ CAROLINGIAN SOCIETY AND CULTURE

*Aristocratic Culture*  While Charlemagne was trying to raise the educational level of his people and the clergy, popular culture remained chiefly oral. The upper classes, including Charlemagne himself, enjoyed heroic poems of warfare, but only a fragment of this poetry remains. Fighting and hunting were the chief occupations of the aristocrats, and with the many wars and the large forests, they had much to occupy themselves. The aristocrats surrounded themselves with as much luxury as they could make on their estates or could purchase from traveling merchants. They bought goods whose origins were in Byzantium, and they had gold and silver objects made for them by local craftsmen.

*Economy and Society*  As described in chapter 6, the agricultural economy was gradually improving as new tools and farming techniques permitted cultivation of the fertile river-valley soils. Large landed estates, farmed by serfs, provided most of the food. Ordinary woolen and linen cloth was made on these estates, which also produced wine, cheeses, and other food. Aside from Venice and some Mediterranean port cities, the towns were small. Many of the artisans worked directly on estates rather than in towns, and long-distance trade was conducted by traveling merchants.

*Art and Architecture*  The increased prosperity is visible today in the number of fine churches and monasteries that date from this period. As Charlemagne conquered new territories, monks, nuns, and clergy moved into them and established new religious foundations. The period was one of major building. Byzantine architecture became the model for most of the churches, including the magnificent one that Charlemagne built at Aix-la-Chapelle (modern Aachen) and that still stands today.

Mosaics in imitation of Byzantine models graced many church walls, and if mosaics were too expensive, wall painting took their place. The clergy commissioned artisans to make ecclesiastical objects, especially reliquaries for the bones of saints, out of precious metals and precious gems and stones.

### ◆ DECLINE OF THE CAROLINGIAN EMPIRE

*Division of the Empire*  Charlemagne at his death left a united and apparently strong empire to his single surviving son, Louis the Pious. Louis, a weak and indecisive man, soon lost control over

▲ This small (8 5/8 inches) ivory depiction of the
Virgin was probably executed at Aachen, one of the
capitals of Charlemagne, in the ninth century. Note
that the Virgin holds spindles in her left hand;
spinning was typically woman's work. But
surprisingly, she also wears armor — gauntlets on
her wrists and what look to be shoulder pieces.
Though a woman doing woman's work, she is a
militant, imperious figure, strikingly different from
the motherly madonnas of later medieval art.
Metropolitan Museum of Art, Gift of J. Pierpont Morgan, 1917
(17.190.49) Photograph © 2001 The Metropolitan Museum of
Art, New York.

▲ Map 7.3 Partition of the Frankish Empire

the *missi dominici* on their circuits. The institutional and moral bonds tying their central governments to the peripheral territories were thus
broken or abandoned.

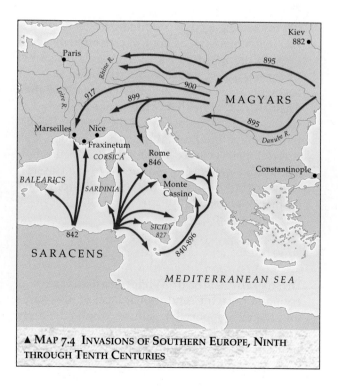

▲ Map 7.4 Invasions of Southern Europe, Ninth
through Tenth Centuries

his own family, and his sons rebelled against him.
After Louis' death, the three surviving sons parti-
tioned the Empire at the Treaty of Verdun in 843
and established their own kingdoms (see map 7.3;
see also footnote on p. 233).

As the family of Carolingian rulers divided
amid civil wars and partitions of territory, the loyalty of the military aristocracy also waned. The
new rulers conquered no new lands; so they had
no new offices or properties with which to buy the
loyalties of the aristocracy. The office of count, ap-
pointive under Charlemagne, became hereditary
under his successors. The Carolingian rulers no
longer summoned the great men of the realm to
the yearly assemblies and no longer dispatched

*New Invasions*   Under Charlemagne's weak successors, invasions of the Frankish Empire resumed, and centrifugal forces tore at the empire as well. To the south, Muslims from North Africa invaded Sicily and southern Italy in 827, attacked the valley of the Rhône in 842, and raided Rome in 846. Concurrently, from the east a new nomadic people, the Magyars, established themselves by about 895 in the valley of the Danube; from this base for the next fifty years, they struck repeatedly into the areas that are now France, Germany, and Italy (see map 7.4). Eventually they settled in modern-day Hungary. But none of these raids were as devastating to the Carolingian lands as those of the Scandinavians.

# IV. The Vikings, Kiev, and England

◆

For both Western and Eastern Europe, the migration and raids of the Vikings (Danes, Norwegians, and Swedes) altered the political map during a long period from the mid-eighth to the early tenth century. The Scandinavian migrations had a profound effect throughout the northern part of Europe, including the founding of the Kievan Rus principality and the invasion of Anglo-Saxon England and Carolingian France.

## ◆ THE VIKINGS

Scandinavia's sparse farmland could not support the populations that developed there. Parts of the population had migrated out in the fourth century and joined the Germanic invasions of Europe. The ninth and tenth centuries saw a resurgence of out-migration. Contemporary sources called them Northmen or Vikings (a name applied to all Scandinavians in the eighth century); the East Slavs called them Verangians.

*Viking Ships and Exploration*   One major factor in the migration of Northmen was their ships. These were shallow draft craft equally capable of traveling up rivers and on the high seas. A large square sail propelled the ship in winds and oarsmen propelled it in the calm. The ships were large enough to carry horses and provisions as well as men.

▲ **PICTURE-STONE**
This carving shows a Viking horseman at the top with his round shield and helmet. In the center section is a Viking boat. The prow was raised and cut into the shape of a dragon's head or some other ferocious beast. A rudder was used to guide the boat. The two occupants are shown wearing chain mail, the typical armor of the time.
Werner Forman/Art Resource, NY

The ships permitted both exploration and trade. As skilled and versatile seamen, the Vikings' explorations took them as far as a western territory they called Vinland, undoubtedly part of the North American continent. Iceland, settled as a result of these explorations, became a major center of medieval Scandinavian culture. The Vikings were constantly at war with one another because there was no stable kingdom; a defeated chief, rather than becoming a vassal under his conqueror, often preferred to seek out new land overseas.

*Eastern Expansion*   To the east the Vikings engaged in both trade and raiding. In about 830, Vikings from Scandinavia, known as the Rus,

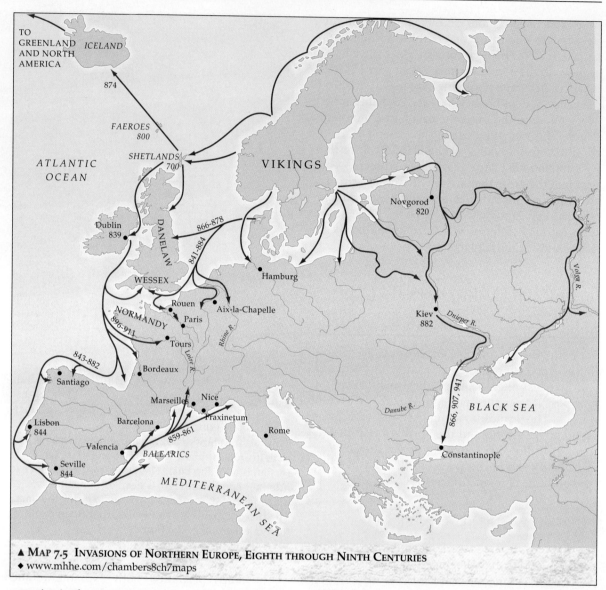

TO
GREENLAND
AND NORTH
AMERICA

ICELAND

874

FAEROES
800

ATLANTIC
OCEAN

SHETLANDS
700

VIKINGS

Novgorod
820

Dublin
839

DANELAW

866–878

841–884

WESSEX

Hamburg

Volga R.

NORMANDY

896–911

Rouen

Paris

Aix-la-Chapelle

Kiev
882

Dnieper R.

Rhine R.

Tours

843–882

Bordeaux

Loire R.

Santiago

Danube R.

866, 907, 941

BLACK SEA

Marseilles

Nice

Lisbon
844

Barcelona

Praxinetum

Rome

Valencia

859–861

BALEARICS

Seville
844

Constantinople

MEDITERRANEAN SEA

▲ **MAP 7.5** INVASIONS OF NORTHERN EUROPE, EIGHTH THROUGH NINTH CENTURIES
◆ www.mhhe.com/chambers8ch7maps

were invited to intervene in wars among the East Slavs. They staked out their own claims in Novgorod and Kiev, eventually establishing a principality composed largely of East Slavs (see more later in this chapter). The internal river systems of central Europe provided a conduit to Constantinople and the Black Sea. Some Vikings came to trade with Byzantium and Persia, but others made their wealth by hiring themselves out as mercenaries to the Byzantine emperor (see map 7.5).

*Western Expansion* In England and on the continent, the Vikings appeared first as merchants and

pirates, then as conquerors and colonists. Vikings, chiefly Danes, began raiding England in 787. One story tells of the attack on London: Unable to move up the Thames River because of London Bridge, the Vikings attached ropes to the pilings holding up the bridge and rowed downstream as the tide was going out; the pilings easily pulled out and the Vikings raided upstream. By 866 a Danish army landed in eastern England and established a permanent settlement. In Ireland and Scotland, Norwegians were the invaders and settlers. Dublin was a Norwegian settlement.

On the continent Danes began their attack along the western coast of France as early as 800, eventually penetrating far inland. Viking raiding parties even ventured around the Iberian Peninsula into the Mediterranean Sea and up the Rhône valley. In 911 the Viking Rollo secured from Charles the Simple, the king of France, the territory near the mouth of the Seine River, which became known as Normandy (from the name *Northmen*).

*Conversion to Christianity* Christianity only gradually made inroads in Scandinavia. Some Vikings converted in order to carry on trade in Western Europe. In the middle of the ninth century Anskar, a Dane trained in a Saxon monastery, made conversions in Denmark and southern Sweden, establishing churches and winning adherents among the nobility. The conversions, however, were often incomplete. Gravestones in the shape of a cross display carvings of the old gods as well. Burials continued to have grave goods (objects from daily life for use of the dead in afterlife), often with some Christian objects as well. Christianity did not have a strong enough hold to dissuade the Vikings from attacking and looting monasteries in England and France.

*Treatment of Women* The violent nature of Scandinavian society suggests that women were treated roughly. Polygamy was normal and concubines common. Other evidence, however, indicates that women were esteemed and played the role of advisers in politics. Archaeology has also indicated the value placed on women. For instance, one ship burial at Oseberg in Sweden is that of a noblewoman who was fifty years old. Her grave contained another woman, perhaps a servant (thirty years old), several beds with quilts and cushions, a chair, two lamps, tapestries, and spinning and weaving implements.

*Poetry and Sagas* The Edda are the legends of the Norse gods, telling their exploits and fights. They were recorded in the thirteenth century in both poetry and prose. According to the "Lay of Volund," warriors who died in battle joined the following of Odin in a great banquet hall, Valhalla. But the entire company of gods and heroes would be doomed to destruction by fire during a cosmic twilight when the ravaged earth would sink entirely into the sea. The myth

▲ Jewelry of Viking Handicraft and Plundered Coins
**The Viking artisans were skilled at stone and wood carving as well as making fine jewelry. They used their own designs, which included serpents, animals, and plants intertwined. They also incorporated plundered objects such as coins directly into their designs.**
© Universitetets Oldsaksamling, Oslo. Photo: Ove Holst/University Museum of National Antiquities Oslo, Norway

became the basis for Richard Wagner's opera *Götterdammerung*.

The sagas, although written down in Iceland during the thirteenth century, are prose stories that actually cover the Viking period to about 1000, when Iceland converted to Christianity. The sagas are adventure stories recounting a fierce sense of bravery and violence on the part of both men and women. In the Eddic poems Gudrun does not slay her brothers after they kill her husband, Sigurd, whereas in the *Gisla Saga* the widow has her brother killed after he kills her husband. *King Harald's Saga* recounts Harald's adventures traveling down the Eastern rivers to Constantinople and his exploits as a Verangian Guard (mercenary) in Constantinople. The saga describes his invasion of England in 1066 and his defeat.

### ◆ THE KIEVAN RUS PRINCIPALITY

The East Slavs invited the Vikings to aid them in their internal wars in the first half of the ninth century. The Vikings then became instrumental in establishing the first East Slavic state centered around Kiev on the Dnieper River and Novgorod on Lake Ilmen.

*Origins*   The *Primary Chronicle,* the most detailed and important source for the origin of the Rus state, recounts that the Rus (Vikings or Verangians) ruled Novgorod. Prince Oleg (r. 873?–913) united the two cities of Novgorod and Kiev under his rule. In 907 he led a fleet, allegedly containing two thousand ships, on a raid against Constantinople. The Byzantine emperor granted both tribute and trading concessions in order to purchase peace with the Rus. Oleg's successors completed the unification of the East Slavic tribes, bringing together an area that stretched from the Baltic to the Black Sea and from the Danube to the Volga rivers.

In 988 the Kievan ruler, Vladimir, converted to the Eastern form of Christianity and imposed baptism on his subjects. As was so often the case, the influence of a woman was important in the conversion. In exchange for military help in the defense of Byzantine territory, Vladimir demanded a Byzantine princess in marriage. The woman in question, Anna, sister of the emperor, would not marry Vladimir unless he converted to Christianity. He agreed, and she arrived with a group of missionaries. The missionaries translated the Bible and the liturgy by adapting the Cyrillic alphabet to East Slavic—the forerunner of modern Russian.

*Reign of Yaroslav the Wise*   The Principality of Kiev (see map 7.6) reached its height of power under Vladimir's son Yaroslav (r. 1015–1054). Yaroslav won self-government for the Rus Church from the patriarch of Constantinople in 1037. The head of the independent Church was called the *metropolitan* and lived in Kiev, which became the ecclesiastical as well as the political capital of the East Slavs.

During his reign Yaroslav had prepared the first written codification of East Slavic law, the *Russkaia Pravda.* He patronized church building, bringing in skilled Byzantine artisans to decorate them. The cathedral at Kiev was the masterpiece. Yaroslav, a writer himself, promoted learning in his principality and assembled many scribes to translate religious books from Greek into Slavic. Although located in the power axis of Byzantium, Kiev kept close ties to Western Europe. The family of Yaroslav had marriage connections with the ruling dynasties of Byzantium, England, France, Germany, Norway, Poland, and Hungary. Yaroslav's own daughter Anna married King Henry I of France. Charters with her signature survive, carefully inscribed with Cyrillic letters; she seems to have been the only layperson in the French court who could write.

*Agriculture and Trade*   Kiev was a leader in the agricultural revival of early medieval Europe; its fertile steppes produced abundant crops. The Rus peasants were plowing with horses at a time when oxen were still common in the West. Most of the population were free peasants, but there were some serfs and slaves.

The Rus traded with the Scandinavians, the steppe peoples, the Muslims at Baghdad, and especially the Byzantines. Every year a great fleet of boats, led by the princes themselves, assembled at Kiev and floated down the Dnieper River to the Black Sea and across to Constantinople. Amber, fur, honey, slaves, and wheat were exchanged for silks, spices, and other luxuries of the East. In recent years Russian archaeologists excavating at Novgorod have uncovered numerous commercial documents written on birch bark that documented this lively trade.

*Kievan Cities*   Trade supported the development of urban centers. Within the many towns, a wealthy aristocracy of princes, warriors, and great merchants rubbed shoulders with artisans, workers, and large numbers of destitute persons. Kiev in the eleventh century was one of the great cities of the age. A German chronicler, Thietmar of Merseburg, said it had 400 churches, 8 marketplaces, and unnumbered inhabitants. Kiev must have included 20,000 to 30,000 people—more people than any contemporary Western city.

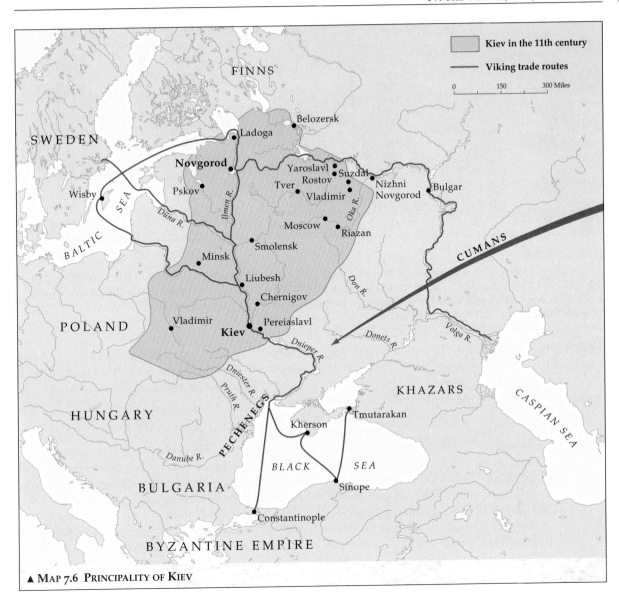

▲ MAP 7.6  PRINCIPALITY OF KIEV

***Kievan Government***  The head of the Kievan government was the prince, who selected nobles, called *boyars*, to aid him in governing. The towns had large citizen assemblies, called *veches*, that the prince also consulted for advice. The government was thus based on a balance of monarchic, aristocratic, and popular elements. The prince, unlike the Byzantine emperor, was not the fountain of justice. Most cases were settled in popular courts from which there was no organized system of appeal, features that brought Kievan justice closer to the Germanic system.

***Learning and Literature***  The clergy established a formal educational system primarily to train the clergy; but their schools were open to the sons of ruling families. A number of women, too, were educated in convents. Birch bark letters discovered by archaeologists show that women could read and perhaps write. Their letters are about business and love.

The *Primary Chronicle,* the literary masterpiece of the age, recounts the conversion of the Rus to Christianity and their battles against the pagan peoples who surrounded them. The poetry of

▲ YAROSLAV PRESENTING MODEL OF CHURCH
**Although now destroyed, a group of eleventh-century frescoes in St. Sophia Cathedral in Kiev once depicted the family of Prince Yaroslav. This re-creation of the frescoes in a drawing by the seventeenth-century Dutch artist A. V. Westvelt shows Yaroslav presenting a model of a church to Prince Vladimir.**
Courtesy, General Research Division, New York Public Library. Astor, Lenox, Tilden Foundations.

medieval Rus is represented by a short heroic epic titled *Song of Igor's Campaign,* which records an unsuccessful campaign that the Rus princes conducted in 1185 against the pagan Polovtsi, a people from the steppes.

*Art and Architecture*   Christianity had an immense influence on architectural and artistic development. The East Slavs built many churches based on Byzantine models. The familiar "onion" domes of Russian churches, for example, were a late effort to imitate in wood the domes on ecclesiastical structures at Constantinople. The Kievan principality appreciated magnificence and splendor in its churches and liturgical services. It hired Byzantines to train its artisans and to decorate its churches with icons.

*Decline of the Principality of Kiev*   As was true of the Byzantines, Arabs, and Carolingians, both internal and external troubles destroyed the peace of the land after Yaroslav's death. Like the Carolingians, Yaroslav divided his territory among all male heirs. The result was frequent bickering and civil wars. These internal struggles left the people unable to resist the renewed menace of the steppe nomads. In 1061 the Cumans, a nomadic Turkish people, began harassing the frontier, and they eventually cut off Kiev from contact with the Black Sea. This sundering of the trade route to

Constantinople was a disaster for commerce and culture because it deprived Kiev of contact with the Byzantine Empire and the Western world.

## ◆ ANGLO-SAXON ENGLAND

The Viking attacks on England had begun in the late eighth century, and by 793 the famous centers of Anglo-Saxon learning, Lindisfarne and Jarrow, were looted and destroyed. The Vikings successfully established themselves in the north of England and were pushing south when they encountered King Alfred of Wessex (r. 871–899).

*Alfred the Great*   King Alfred, after experiencing military defeats by the Danes in the early years of his reign, reorganized the defense of the kingdom. He reformed the militia to keep a larger and more mobile army in the field and built fortresses to defend the land and ships to defend the coast. His reforms proved successful. Before 880 several Danish chiefs received baptism as part of a treaty with Alfred, and in 886 the Danes agreed to confine themselves to a region in the north and east of England. This region, which the Danes continued to dominate for several generations, was later known as the *Danelaw,* in recognition of the fact that the Danish laws in force there differed from the English laws of other parts of the country.

## *Chronology*

## CHRONOLOGICAL CHART

| Byzantium | Islam | Frankish Empire | Vikings/England/Rus |
|---|---|---|---|
| Heraclius (r. 610–641) | Muhammad (d. 632) | Merovingians | |
| Defeat of Persia (622–629) | Hijra (622) | | |
| Loss of Egypt, Syria to Arabs | First four caliphs (632–666) | | Council of Whitby (664) |
| | Expansion into N. Africa | | |
| Leo III (r. 717–741) | Conquest of Visigoths | Charles Martel (714–741) | Bede (d. 735) |
| Iconoclasm | Defeat at Tours (732) | | |
| Siege of Constantinople (718) | | | |
| Bulgarian wars | Umayyads in Córdoba | Pepin becomes king (741) | |
| | | | Viking invasions |
| | Harun al-Rashid (r. 786–809) | Charlemagne (r. 768–814) | |
| | | Imperial coronation (800) | |
| | | Louis the Pious (r. 814–840) | |
| | Disintegration of Arab Empire | Division of Empire (843) | |
| Cyrillic alphabet | | | Alfred of Wessex (r. 871–899) |

*Intellectual Life*   Anglo-Saxon England was perhaps the most literate country of Europe at the time. Schools and tutors educated upper-class boys and girls in Old English. There was an audience for poetry and prose.

Alfred renewed intellectual life in England. He gathered a group of scholars and began a program of translating into Anglo-Saxon the works of such writers as Bede, Gregory the Great, and Boethius. During his reign, an unknown author compiled a history of England known as the *Anglo-Saxon Chronicle*. Continued thereafter by various authors and now extant in several versions, the *Chronicle* is an indispensable source for the later Anglo-Saxon period in English history.

## SUMMARY

The period from the seventh to the beginning of the eleventh century included the rise of a new religion, Islam, and an Arab conquest of the southern Mediterranean; a revival of the Byzantine Empire; the rise of Kiev; prosperity in Anglo-Saxon England; and the Carolingian Empire. But all these empires and kingdoms had internal weaknesses that left them too disorganized to resist fresh invasions. The Arabs, Byzantines, and Kievans lost territory to Turkish tribes. In the West Vikings, Magyars, and Muslim pirates disrupted peace. The Vikings plundered and eventually settled in large parts of Ireland, England, and France. The Carolingian Empire split into French-speaking and German-speaking halves.

Western Europe owed a debt to the Islamic civilization that came to influence almost every aspect of medieval Western life over the next few centuries. Western farmers imitated Muslim techniques of irrigation and learned to grow new plants, such as rice, citrus fruits, and peaches. Merchants adopted the Arabic numbers and probably some Islamic forms of business partnerships. Muslim mathematicians made enormous contributions to the development of algebra. These works provided the foundations for Islamic learning and preserved the thought of these writers through a period when Greek texts were not being widely copied in the West. Recovering from the latest invasions, Europe was on the threshold of a period of immense creativity in which Islamic contributions would play a large role.

## Questions for Further Thought

1. In both chapter 6 and chapter 7, one of the dominating themes was the migration of various peoples from Northern and Eastern Europe (Germanic tribes, Vikings, and Slavs), from Central Asia (Huns, Avars, Bulgarians), and from the Arabian Penninsula. Why were these people on the move? Speculate on both the conditions that might stimulate movement and those that attracted them to the West.

2. We have seen in chapter 6 that, aside from some outstanding figures such as Boethius and Bede, intellectual life suffered in the West during the invasions. What brought about the flourishing of Arabic, Carolingian, Anglo-Saxon, and Russian learning during the subsequent centuries? What political conditions give rise to intellectual advances?

3. The decline and fall of empires continues to challenge historians to look for causes. In this chapter we have seen the Byzantine, Arabic, Carolingian, and Kievan Empires go into decline after a period of expansion, consolidation, and brilliance. What influence does the personality of the emperor or ruler have, and what influence do internal and external events have on the fate of empires? Compare these empires to the Roman one.

## Recommended Reading

**Sources**

Cross, Samuel Hazard (ed.). *Russian Primary Chronicle: Laurentian Text.* O. P. Sherbowitz-Wetzor (tr.). 1968. The major primary source for early Russian history.

*Dmytryshyn, Basil. *Medieval Russia: A Source Book, 850–1700.* 3d ed. 1991. Primary sources for the period covered.

*Einhard, *The Life of Charlemagne.* 1962. Personal account by someone who lived in Charlemagne's court.

*Ibn, Khaldun. *The Mugaddimah: An Introduction to World History.* Franz Rosenthal (tr.). 1969. Reflections on societies and empires by a North African Muslim; written in the fourteenth century.

*The Meaning of the Glorious Koran.* M. Marmaduke Pickthall (tr.). 1948. Interpretation of Koran.

*Vernadsky, George (ed.). *Medieval Russian Laws.* 1964. Review of early Russian laws.

Zenkovsky, Serge A. (ed.). *Medieval Russia's Epics, Chronicles, and Tales.* 1974. Includes sermons and saints' lives.

**Studies**

Bulliet, Richard W. *The Camel and the Wheel*. 1990. On Arabic society and economy.

Fine, John V. A. *The Early Medieval Balkans: A Critical Survey from the Sixth to the Late Twelfth Century*. 1983. The only work of its kind in English.

*Geanakoplos, Deno J. *Byzantine East and Latin West: Two Worlds of Christendom in the Middle Ages and Renaissance*. 1966. The Western debt to Byzantium.

Hussey, J. M. *The Orthodox Church in the Byzantine Empire*. 1986. History of Orthodox Church in Byzantium.

Keddie, Nikki, and Beth Baron (eds.). *Women in Middle Eastern History: Shifting Boundaries in Sex and Gender*. 1991. Essays explaining the position of women in Islam.

Laiou, Angeliki E. *Gender, Society, and Economic Life in Byzantium*. 1992. A study of the lives of women, peasants, and more ordinary people in thirteenth- and fourteenth-century Byzantium.

Levin, Eve. *Sex and Society in the World of the Orthodox Slavs, 900–1700*. 1989. A study of the birch bark letters.

*Lewis, Bernard (ed.). *Islam from the Prophet Muhammad to the Capture of Constantinople*. Vol. 1: *Politics and War*. Vol. 2: *Religion and Society*. 1987. Collected essays.

Mango, Cyril. *Byzantium: The Empire of New Rome*. 1980. An introduction to the civilization of the Eastern Empire, with effective use of archaeological data.

*Martin, Janet. *Medieval Russia, 980–1584*. 1995. Short history of medieval Russia that also covers recent interpretations.

Meyendorff, John. *Imperial Unity and Christian Divisions: The Church 450–680*. 1989. An attempt to portray the divisions from the Eastern rather than the Western perspective.

*Ostrogorski, George. *History of the Byzantine State*. Joan Hussey (tr.). 1969. The basic reference for all matters of political history.

*Riché, Pierre. *Daily Life in the World of Charlemagne*. Jo Ann McNamara (tr.). 1975. A very good read on social and cultural history of the period.

Sawyer, P. H. *Kings and Vikings: Scandinavia and Europe A.D. 700–1100*. 1984. Excellent summary of recent research on the Vikings.

Stenton, Frank. *Anglo-Saxon England*. 1971. Basic introductory text.

Walther, Wiebke. *Women in Islam*. 1993.

---

*Available in paperback.

▲ URBAN GROWTH IN THE TWELFTH CENTURY

The economic prosperity and population growth of the twelfth century
permitted the development of urban centers for trade and commerce.
Urban centers continued to prosper throughout the Middle Ages. They all
had walls and defensive gates as well as town squares and houses
reaching three stories. Wealthy inhabitants came to enjoy considerable
comfort including barge parties.

© Victoria & Albert Museum, London/Art Resource, NY

# Chapter 8

# RESTORATION OF AN ORDERED SOCIETY

The year 1000 was greeted at the time with anxiety. It was the first millennium since the birth of Jesus of Nazareth, and people thought that the end of the world was at hand. To historians looking back at the period from 1000 to 1150, however, the outlines of medieval society, government, culture, and the economy have become clear. Although rudimentary castles, the origins of feudalism (a type of patron-client relationship between lords and vassals), and the economic and social arrangement of manors and serfs for agriculture had begun in the Carolingian period, it is after the year 1000 that these characteristics of medieval society were fully formed. Feudalism permitted a new order for the society. The society that evolved in the Middle Ages was very hierarchical, with a small elite group of nobles and a large peasant population that supported it through agriculture. Rulers used feudal ties as a basis for establishing their governments and extending their power. The geographical and political states of Europe formed during this period, and the rulers' governmental innovations laid the groundwork for late medieval states. With a restoration of order and an increase in agricultural productivity, trade once again prospered. Surpluses of grain supported an urban population, and towns once again grew in Europe. Reformed monasticism and the fear of the millennium kindled the spark of popular piety that had begun in the tenth century. Taking advantage of the enthusiasm for religion and reform, the papacy underwent a period of major change and consolidation of power that is recognizable in the Roman Catholic Church today. Europeans began to look from the local scenes of their own estates and towns to the larger world. Through both warfare and long-distance trade, they expanded to the east into Slavic lands and into the eastern Mediterranean in a series of campaigns called the crusades.

| Chapter 8. Restoration of an Ordered Society | | | | | | |
| --- | --- | --- | --- | --- | --- | --- |
| | Social Structure | Body Politic | Changes in the Organization of Production and in the Impact of Technology | Evolution of Family and Changing Gender Roles | War | Religion | Cultural Expression |
| I. Economic and Social Changes | | | | | | | |
| II. Governments of Europe | | | | | | | |
| III. Reform of the Western Church | | | | | | | |
| IV. The Crusades | | | | | | | |

# I. Economic and Social Changes

Historians use shorthand terms to refer to the period's major changes. *Manorialism* refers both to the economic organization of agricultural production and to the organization of the lives and labor of peasants who did the actual cultivating. Approximately 90 percent of the population were peasants. *Feudalism* refers to approximately the top 5 percent of the population. Feudalism governed relationships of the elite of society and consisted of a patron (lord) and clients (vassals). The lord offered his vassals protection and land in exchange for services from the vassals. Some historians favor the historical interpretation of Karl Marx and use *feudalism* to refer to both the social and economic organization of the manor and the personal, military, and governmental role of feudalism.

Europe experienced a period of growth and prosperity that began about 1050. A shift in weather to a warmer and dryer period, the release from the threat of external invasion, and the development of new agricultural practices discussed in chapter 6 all added to increased productivity. The new political order that feudalism began to offer brought at least a measure of peace and an expansion of trade. Economic and demographic growth led to a revival of cities and to internal and external colonization. The other roughly 5 percent of the population was made up of clergy and urban dwellers.

## ◆ FEUDALISM

The new stability in Europe altered the power structures and lives of the warrior class. Material comforts, housing, gender relations, and even the nature of warfare changed. But perhaps the most important factor for understanding the European Middle Ages was that the power relationships of the nobility to each other and to the monarch became more personal and private rather than being based on citizenship as in the Roman Empire.

*Definition*  Although historians debate the accuracy of using the term *feudalism* as shorthand for the personal bonds among the elite in the Middle Ages and as a descriptive term for the type of society and governments these bonds resulted in, the term is still a useful one. In its restricted meaning, *feudalism* refers to a patron/client relationship between two freemen (men who are not serfs), a lord and his vassal. *Vassal* derived from a Celtic word for servant, but in feudal terms *vassal* meant a free person who put himself under the protection of a lord and for whom he rendered loyal military aid. In practice, both lord and vassal came from the upper echelons of society, lay and clerical. Feudal arrangements did not include the serfs and the poorer freemen.

Historians have traced the development of feudalism to both the patron-client arrangements in the Roman Empire and to the chief-warrior relationship (*comitatus*) among the Germanic tribes. During the Carolingian period, changes in warfare made equipping and training warriors more expensive. The stirrup, unknown to the Romans, made it possible for a warrior to ride a horse without clasping it with his knees to stay in the saddle. The stirrup also permitted a more heavily armed warrior to fight, but this in turn required a bigger horse. Few warriors could afford the horse and new body armor, so the Carolingians began granting land to their warriors to support them. Charlemagne had a pyramidal plan for recruiting an army, with the king at the top, followed by counts and dukes, and under them the warriors. This simple plan proved unfeasible, and it took until about 1300 to work out the nuances of feudal relations.

*The Feudal Milieu*  To understand the growth of feudalism, we must first recall the chaotic conditions that marked the Viking invasion and the decline of the Carolingian Empire. In a milieu in which the kings could not protect their realm from raids and could not rein in local counts and freebooters, individuals sought security through their own efforts. The freeman in search of protection had little recourse but to appeal to a neighbor stronger than himself. If the neighbor accepted, the two men entered into a close, quasi-familial relationship. Like the bonds between father and son, the feudal relationship between the strong "lord" and the weak freeman was initially more ethical and emotional than legally binding. As feudalism matured as a tool of government and social organization, oaths sealed the agreement and the lords gave vassals estates or fiefs to alleviate the cost of their service.

The true homeland of Western feudalism was the region between the Loire and Rhine rivers. The institutions that developed there were subsequently exported to England in the Norman Conquest and to southern Italy. Gradually, the organization of government and society in southern France, Spain, and the Kingdom of Jerusalem copied the feudal model. Many parts of Germany did not develop full feudalism because of the continued importance of free land tenure. The Celtic areas (Ireland, Scotland, Wales, Brittany) did not develop classical feudalism, because powerful clans traditionally extended such protection.

Perhaps because of the early importance of towns in Northern Italy, the use of feudal ties was stunted but not suppressed.

*Vassalage*  Vassalage was an honorable personal bond between a lord and his man. An act of **homage** established the relationship. In this simple ceremony the prospective vassal placed his hands within those of his lord (sometimes they exchanged a kiss of peace) and swore to become his man. He might also swear **fealty** (swearing to be faithful to his oath of homage) on the Gospels or a saint's relic. The "joining of hands" was the central act in the ceremony of homage.

Vassalage imposed obligations on both the vassal and his lord. The vassal owed his lord material and military aid and counsel (advice). He had to perform military service in the lord's army and usually had to bring additional men in numbers proportionate to the wealth he derived from his land (fief). As military aid became more precisely defined, it was more a matter of contract than of emotional bonds. The contract could stipulate that the vassal serve, for example, forty days a year in a local war, less time if the lord intended to fight in foreign lands. The vassal could not refuse service, but if the lord asked for more than the customary time, the vassal could demand compensation or simply return home. The lord could demand other financial aids, such as paying the ransom if the lord was captured and paying for the ceremonies surrounding the knighting of his eldest son or the marriage of his eldest daughter.

The obligation of counsel required the vassal to give advice and to help the lord reach true judgments in legal cases that came before his court. Cases usually involved adjudication of disputes among the vassals and complaints brought by the lord against his men. By custom only a jury of his peers, that is, his fellow vassals, could judge a vassal.

The lord, in turn, owed his vassal protection and maintenance (military and material support). He had to come to his vassal's aid when requested, repel invaders from his vassal's land, and help a vassal being sued in another's court. In the formative period of feudalism, the lord's obligation of material support was provided in his own household, but as vassals became more

▲ INVESTITURE SCENE, FRESCO, FERRANDE TOWER, PERNES-LES-FONTAINES, FRANCE, CA. 1270
**Kneeling before his overlord the king, a vassal offers homage and receives in return investiture in a fief—the roll of parchment, which would have recorded the transaction in detail. As this thirteenth-century fresco from Pernes-les-Fontaines in France indicates, the ceremony takes place before witnesses.**
Giraudon/Art Resource, NY

numerous and more distantly located and as great princes came to be included among them, sheer logistics prevented the lord from feeding all his men. Because a lord often had no cash revenues for making monetary compensations, he would distribute land as a form of payment for the vassal's allegiance.

Disloyalty on the part of the vassal, such as refusing military service, gave the lord the right to terminate the bonds of homage and take back any property that he had given to the vassal.

***The Fief*** The lord's concession of land to his vassal was called a *fief* (rhymes with *leaf*). The granting of a fief superimposed on the personal relationship

of vassalage a second relationship, one involving property. The close union of personal and property ties was, in fact, the most characteristic feature of the Western feudal relationship.

The lord granted the fief to his vassal in a special ceremony called **investiture** (usually immediately following the act of homage). As a symbol of the land the vassal was receiving, the lord gave to his vassal a clod of earth or sprig of leaves. In a strict juridical sense the fief was a conditional, temporary, and nonhereditary grant of land or other income-producing property, such as an office, toll, or rent. At the vassal's death, disability, or refusal to serve his lord, the fief at once returned to the lord who granted it.

Although technically not inheritable, the fief gradually became hereditary. From the start, lords had found it convenient to grant a fief to the adult son of a deceased vassal, because the son could at once serve in his father's stead. The son had to make a special payment to the lord (the *relief*) to acquire the fief.

*Women and Minors*  Because women and young sons of vassals could not perform military service, their right to inherit initially was not guaranteed. But the advantages of orderly succession to valuable property led lords to recognize the right of a minor son to inherit. The lord retained the right of wardship, taking the heir and his property back into his hands or granting them to another noble until the heir reached the age of twenty-one.

Only reluctantly did feudal practice permit daughters to inherit a fief. Nevertheless, in most areas of Europe women could inherit. Their lord had the right to select their husbands for them, because their spouses assumed the obligations of service connected to the fief.

*Subinfeudation*  Initially, vassals were forbidden to sell the fief, grant it to the Church, or otherwise transfer it in whole or in part. Vassals, however, commonly sold or granted portions of their fiefs, but only with the lord's permission and usually accompanied by a money payment.

When lords regranted portions of their fiefs to other vassals, the process was called *subinfeudation*. Subinfeudation complicated the hierarchy that Charlemagne had initially envisioned. Instead of a neat pyramidal hierarchy, subinfeudation permitted vassals to have their own vassals. A vassal could acquire fiefs from several different lords, swearing homage and fealty to each. In case of conflict among his different lords, whom should he serve? To escape this dilemma, feudal custom required that the vassal select one of his lords as his *liege lord*, that is, the one whom he would serve against all others.

*Castles*  With the later invasions and breakdown of Carolingian government, those lords who could afford it invested in defensive fortress-homes, or castles. Initially these castles were a motte, a wooden tower built on a hill with an external courtyard, the bailey, surrounded by a wooden palisade. A castle-holder could offer weaker neighbors a place to shelter their animals and families in the event of attack. By the eleventh and twelfth centuries castles became more elaborate, with thick stone walls for the motte and larger stone-walled baileys that contained outbuildings such as stables, kitchens, and gardens. The moat, the ditch surrounding castles and sometimes filled with water, added to the defense. Castles were built throughout Europe and can still be seen today. The pace of castle building was rapid. In Florence and its surrounding countryside in Italy, for example, only two castles are mentioned in the sources before 900, 11 before 1000, 52 before 1050, 130 before 1100, and 205 before 1200.

The *castellan,* or owner of a castle, assumed many functions in addition to military ones. He acted as judge and tax collector and controlled the local church, including appointing the priest. The castellan was supported economically by a subject peasant population who cultivated the castle owner's land as well as giving him part of the crops they produced on their own plots. The castles with their lands constituted fairly stable, local governmental units.

*Feudal Government*  From about the year 1050, counts, dukes, and some kings were attempting to integrate these castles into centralized principalities, forcing the castellans to assume toward them the obligations of vassals and fief holders. The use of these feudal concepts and institutions to serve the interests of princely authority extended feudalism from bonds of personal loyalty and military service to a system of government.

In granting a fief, the lord gave his vassal all possible sources of revenue the land could produce. The primary source of wealth was from the work of the peasants, who were granted with the fief and cultivated the land. In addition, the lord gave the right to hold a manorial court and to profit from its fines and confiscations of livestock and goods. The manorial courts regulated the subject peasantry and were very lucrative. In addition, some vassals were granted the right to hear cases that were reserved for royal justice. This granting of royal judicial prerogatives contributed to another characteristic of feudal society, private justice (that is, the exercise of royal powers

## THE TERMINOLOGY OF FEUDALISM AND MANORIALISM

◆

**FEUDALISM**  An economic, political, and social organization of medieval Europe. Land was held by vassals from more powerful overlords in exchange for military and other services.

*Vassal*  A free warrior who places himself under a lord, accepting the terms of loyal service, fighting in time of war, and counsel in time of peace. As the system developed, women and minor sons also could become vassals, as could members of the clergy.

*Aid*  Aid was the military service that the vassal owed the lord.

*Fief (sometimes called benefice)*  Land given to a vassal from his lord in exchange for specified terms of service. A ceremonial presentation of a sheaf of grain often accompanied the grant of land.

*Homage*  An oath sworn by the vassal to the lord, acknowledging allegiance to the lord. The vassal took his oath by placing his hands within the hands of the lord.

*Fealty*  An oath, often accompanying the oath of homage, in which the vassal swears to uphold his homage. This oath was sworn on the Gospels or on a saint's relics.

*Relief*  An inheritance tax on the vassal at his death when the fief passed to his heir.

*Subinfeudation*  The grant of a fief by a vassal to a subordinate who becomes his vassal.

*Liege Lord*  That lord whom the vassal must serve even if he has conflicting oaths with subinfeudation.

**MANORIALISM**  An agricultural, legal, and social organization of land, including a nucleated village, large fields for agriculture, and serfs to work the land. The land and its inhabitants were called a manor and both belonged to the lord.

*Manor*  An estate held by the lord that included land, the people on the land, and a village, usually with a mill. A fief might contain a number of manors or sometimes just a part of one.

*Open Fields*  The agricultural area was divided up into three large fields (500 acres or more). The lord held land for his direct profit in these, and the serfs rented strips of land in all three fields for their profit and to pay their rent.

*Manorial Court*  The lord had the right to administer justice on his manor in order to regulate services and rents owed to him. Peasants also used manorial court for their own business and to keep peace within their village.

*Serf or Villein*  Peasant who was personally free, but bound to the lord of the manor and the land of the manor. Serfs rented land from the lord to cultivate to produce their own crops. In addition, they owed work for the lord and various gifts of produce.

*Week Work*  Work that the peasant owed to the lord every week.

*Boon Work*  Work that the peasant owed to the lord for special tasks such as plowing or harvesting.

*Demesne Land*  Land that the lord held for his own crops and profit. Serfs worked this land.

*Glebe Land*  Land held by the parish priest.

---

by private individuals as a right associated with their tenure of land). The idea that the king owned all the land and was the font of all justice did not disappear. In the twelfth and thirteenth centuries the kings began to use their position as pinnacle of the feudal hierarchy to assert the right to hear appeals from the courts of his chief vassals (as well as those "rear vassals" who stood lower on the feudal ladder). Monarchs also accepted directly cases that his vassals had traditionally heard. The exertion of these royal prerogatives brought about the gradual but unmistakable decline of private justice and led to the extension of royal justice throughout the realm.

### ◆ LIFE OF THE NOBILITY

Feudalism brought many changes to the elite's family arrangements, housing, fighting, and leisure activities. To proclaim their identity and distinctiveness from the rest of society, the nobles adopted family names, which usually recalled the name of the revered founder or of the ancestral castle. Other symbols also denoted elite status—coats of arms, mottoes, fanciful genealogies, and castles.

*Noble Families*  The appearance of a hereditary nobility in the eleventh and twelfth centuries

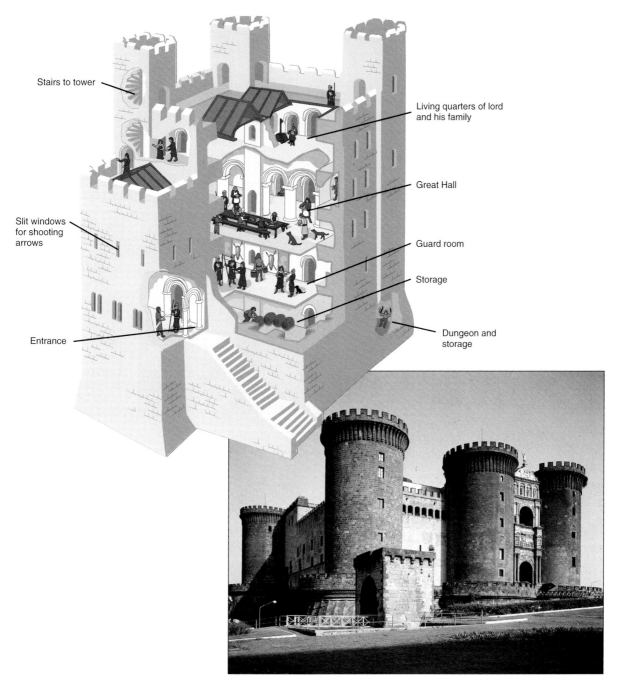

Stairs to tower

Living quarters of lord and his family

Great Hall

Slit windows for shooting arrows

Guard room

Storage

Entrance

Dungeon and storage

▲ **Castel Nuovo (new castle), 13th century, with triumphal arch, Naples, Campania, Italy. Castles developed from mounds of earth with a stockade on top. A major development in the twelfth century was the elaborate square keep shown in the diagram above. The keep included areas for storage of large quantities of food in the event of siege, a guard room, the great hall where meals were served and the guard slept, and finally, on the top, quarters for the family. Square keeps were vulnerable to attack so round towers were developed to protect the corners of the castle as seen in the photograph.**
Dagli Orti/The Art Archive

◀ A MEDIEVAL
KNIGHT IN ARMOR
The knight is fully
armed with chain
mail on his arms
and steel plates on
his shoulders and
legs. He is equipped
with spurs and a
sword, and he is
wearing a leather
cap. His wife holds
up his helmet and
lance, and a
daughter or court
lady holds his
shield. The surcoat
he wears, the horse
cover, and the
shield represent his
coat of arms. The
illustration is from
the fourteenth-
century English
*Lutteral Psalter.*
By Permission of The
British Library. Add.
42130. folio 202v

reflected a fundamental change in the structure of the elite families. In the Merovingian and Carolingian periods, families used partible inheritance; that is, all surviving sons inherited equally. In giving the fief, however, the lords endowed only one son and his immediate descendants. The custom came to be that the firstborn son would inherit the fief (primogeniture). If there were no sons, daughters inherited and the fief was divided equally among them.

Primogeniture had the advantage of keeping the estates intact, but it had implications for the younger sons and for the daughters. The great families provided their daughters with dowries, but otherwise excluded them from a full share in the inheritance. Anxious to attract a suitable husband for a daughter and settle her future early, noble fathers had to offer ever larger dowries and married their daughters off in their teens. Unmarried daughters usually became nuns. Younger sons had no lands unless they could win them in

war or marry an affluent heiress. With no lands, they could not support a family. As a consequence, unattached young warriors abounded. Some entered the Church and rose to high offices. Others drifted from court to court as warriors for hire. Some found new opportunities in the aggressive expansion of Europe in Spain, eastern Europe, and the Holy Land.

*Tancred de Hauteville's Sons*   Among such aggressive young nobles were the sons of Tancred de Hauteville, a minor Norman vassal. Three of the brothers—William Iron-Arm, Humphrey, and Drogo—sought their fortunes as warriors, sometimes acting as mercenaries and sometimes as brigands. On their way to pilgrimage in Jerusalem, they found that Sicily and southern Italy were fine places to practice their skills of warfare. The Arab and Greek factions, who were fighting each other, were both willing to hire mercenaries. Soon the Hauteville brothers were carving out their own estates rather than working for the local rulers. William's half-brother, Robert Guiscard ("the Sly" or "the Fox") managed to conquer southern Italy and receive papal recognition for the territory. Robert's brother, Roger, captured Sicily and held it with papal approval in 1072. The brothers established a Norman kingdom in these two areas.

*Knights and Armor*   Improvements in fighting equipment, including chain mail, long swords, stirrups, and lances, meant that a long period of training was necessary to become a skilled warrior. The equipment was so expensive that only the elite could afford to buy and maintain it.

A warrior cult that grew up surrounding the training was transformed into knighthood. Young sons of the elite started at an early age to learn to ride and use the weapons of war. Vassals might send their sons to the lord's household at age seven or eight to act as pages, becoming squires in their teenage years. Twenty-one was the age of majority and was usually accompanied by knighthood, which gave the person the honorific title of "sir." Knights had to be skilled in arms, brave, loyal to a leader, and conventionally pious.

*Song of Roland*   The heroic poems, or *chansons de geste*, of the eleventh and twelfth centuries underscore the values fostered by knighthood and the lord-vassal relationship. The oldest and best known of these poems is the *Song of Roland*, which was probably composed in the last quarter of the eleventh century. The subject of the poem is the ambush of the rear guard of Charlemagne's army under the command of Roland by the Basques at Roncesvalles in 778, but poetic imagination (or perhaps older legend) transformed this minor Frankish setback into a major event in the war against Islam.

With fine psychological discernment, the poem examines the character of Roland. The qualities that make him a heroic knight—his dauntless courage and uncompromising pride—are at war with the qualities required of a good vassal—obedience, loyalty, cooperation, and common sense. Roland is in serious danger but refuses for reasons of personal dignity to sound his horn in time for Charlemagne to return and save him and his men. By the time Roland's pride relents and he does blow the horn, his troops' deaths are ensured. The

▲ Making Coats of Chain Mail
**This depiction of a craftsman making chain mail suggests the high skills and hard labor that were needed to bend the metal into elaborate shapes. Armor made of chain mail allowed the knight far greater freedom of movement, but it could be penetrated by the sharp thrust of a sword or arrow. The expense of chain mail and of the other equipment associated with fighting, as well as the long training it took to become proficient in using the arms, meant that only the elite could afford the training and outfits for battle.**
Stadtsbibliothek Nuremberg (Ms.) Amb. 317.2°, f. 10r

sensitive examination of the conflict between Roland's thoughtless if heroic individualism and the demands of the new feudal order gives this poem its stature as the first masterpiece of French letters.

*Noblewomen*   While the young sons in a noble family were being trained for the battlefield, their sisters were taught to live in or travel between castles. The fathers, if still alive—and if not then the lord—arranged the marriages of these young women to men they might never have seen and

◄ MARRIAGE OF NOBLEWOMEN
Noblewomen had little control over their marriages, because their fathers or lords used their marriages to cement political alliances or ensure the transfer of land. Here Emma (Aelfgyfu in the Anglo-Saxon text of the picture) is shown with her husband, King Cnut, presenting a Cross at Winchester. Cnut, a Norwegian, became king of England in 1016. To make his foreign origin more acceptable to the Anglo-Saxon population, he married the deceased king's widow. After the Norman Conquest in 1066 some Normans, to reinforce their claim to the territory, married the widows or daughters of the Anglo-Saxon nobles whose land they had confiscated.
© British Museum

who might have been much older or younger than themselves. Even as widows, these women's lord could arrange for their remarriage. Noblewomen's chief functions were to cement alliances, transfer property, and produce children.

During periods of internal warfare in Europe and the Crusades, husband and wife often were separated for long periods of time. Noblewomen were called upon to administer the fief in their husbands' absence or to defend castles against siege.

Noblewomen were often knowledgeable in herbal cures, and they could care for the sick and wounded in their households. Like peasant women, they spun wool and flax. The elaborate embroideries for church vestments, wall and bed hangings, and personal adornment were often the work of noblewomen and their servants. Leisure activities included music, games, feasts, and stories.

Not all women who were married wanted to be; some would have preferred to become nuns. Christina of Markyate, daughter of a well-to-do family in England (d. after 1155) was forced into marriage by her parents but refused to consummate it. Her mother beat her and pulled her hair, and her father stripped her and threatened to force her out of the house. She fled and became a recluse, but finally became a nun. Some young women whose families forced them into nunneries were as miserable as those women forced into marriage. For a pious woman with a calling for monastic life, a nunnery offered an environment with educational opportunities, training in skilled crafts, and even the opportunity to administer nunnery property.

## ◆ MANORIALISM

Medieval Europe had a mix of cultivation strategies. Some areas were farmed by free peasants (those who owned their own land) who mixed cultivation with fishing or herding. Most of the grain, however, came from large manors with *serfs* (*villeins* was a term used in England and France) or unfree peasants working the land. As described in chapter 6, the major tool of agriculture was the heavy-wheeled plow with oxen or horses to draw it.

The manor, a community of serfs living under the authority of a lord, was the fundamental unit of economic, judicial, and social organization during the Middle Ages. The lord or his appointed officials regulated cultivation of the land as well as the rents, labor services, and fines that the peasants owed to the lord in return for the land they cultivated for themselves. Manors were characteristic of much of England, northern France, western Germany, and certain areas of the south, such as the Rhône and Po valleys. These areas were regions of fertile soil in which grains were cultivated intensively.

***Division of Land*** The lands of most manors were divided into two or three large fields (see map 8.1). Within these fields, the land was further divided into strips for cultivation. The lord owned all the land but he rented strips of land in all three fields to the peasants, who also had a house and garden area. A peasant's strips were not contiguous, but were scattered in each of the three fields. The strips and housing plots were protected by custom, and the right to rent them was passed on through inheritance. Peasants did not have equal holdings; some might have as many as thirty acres and others as little as two acres. These pieces of land formed the peasants' own farms to support their families and pay their rent.

Interspersed with the peasants' land was the *demesne* (rhymes with reign) land, or land that the lord reserved for his own use and that the peasants cultivated for him. In addition, a manor might have land reserved for the parish priest, called *glebe* land, which the priest either worked himself or hired laborers to work for him.

Many manors had extensive meadows, forests, and wastelands, where the lord hunted and the peasants grazed their animals, collected firewood, and procured timber for their houses. Peasants paid fees to use the forests and wastelands that were part of the lord's demesne. Peasants often had their own common, a collectively owned meadow in which each resident had the right to graze a fixed number of animals. Peasants who had too little land to support themselves worked as agricultural laborers or had an additional occupation on the manor such as blacksmith, carpenter, or baker.

***The Lord's Control*** The lord's control over his serfs was considerable. Serfs and their children were not chattel property, as were slaves, but they could not leave the manor without the lord's permission. The lord or his steward ran the manorial court, which was a way of regulating the serfs and an important source of profit from the manor. Peasants who did not pay their rent, who trespassed on the lord's property, or who otherwise broke the manorial rules paid fines in the court. The lord charged peasants for the use of his mill and winepress and required them to buy salt or iron from him. For many peasants, the manorial lord was the only government they ever directly confronted. Peasants paid to use the manorial court to settle their own disputes and to have a record kept of these transactions. The court also

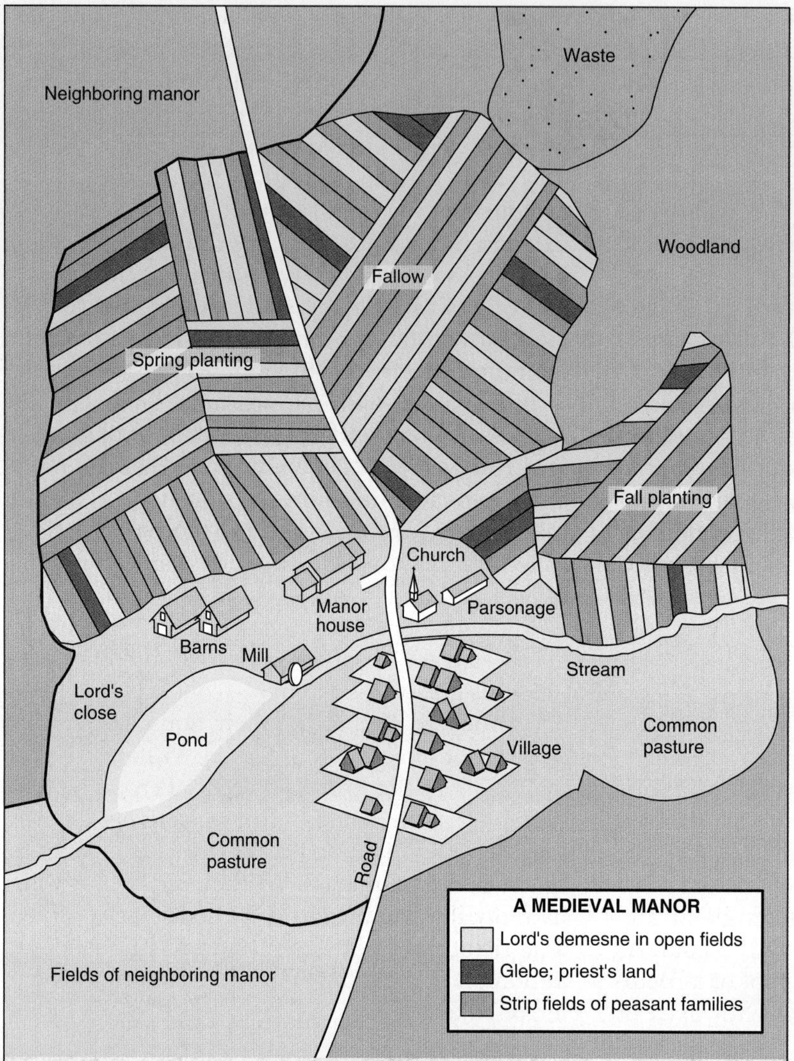

▲ MAP 8.1 IDEALIZED DIAGRAM OF MEDIEVAL MANOR
This diagram of a manor shows the nucleated village in which peasants
had their houses and gardens. The land was divided into strips, with
the peasants, lord, and priest holding strips next to each other in large,
unfenced fields. The three-field system of crop rotation, discussed in
chapter 6, is illustrated in the diagram.

regulated and punished disturbances of the peace
among villagers, including assaults, petty thefts,
and trespass.

*Serfdom* Most of the peasants inhabiting the
manor were serfs. Serfs were personally free, but
in addition to not having freedom of mobility,
they had to pay for the right to marry and had to
work for the lord a set number of days a week and

at intense periods of harvest and planting. Men
were usually obliged to work three days a week
on the lord's land, a service called **week work.**
The additional service at planting and harvest
was called **boon work.** The lord's fields had to be
plowed first and his crops brought in before those
of the serfs. The serfs also paid a yearly monetary
rent on their land. Lords received mandatory gifts
at holidays, such as eggs at Easter or a chicken at

Christmas—the origins of our holiday eating traditions. When a serf died and his farm passed to his son, or to a daughter if there were no sons, the family paid the lord an inheritance tax, either the best animal or money.

## ◆ PEASANT LIFE

While the life of the serf was one filled with heavy labor, the position had some security and advantages. Because serfs had a customary right to their land, they and their children could profit from the improvements they made on it. Moreover, the serfs' obligations and rents were traditional and fixed and could not be raised from year to year. Thus, in periods of economic prosperity, their rents remained fixed so that their profits increased.

*Housing and Food* Peasants lived in villages with large fields surrounding them. Housing varied from region to region. Where stone was plentiful, peasants built stone houses, often adding on to them so that parents, married children, and their children lived together as extended families in the same household. Other places had more rudimentary housing that resembled an A-frame of beams with the wall areas filled in with woven branches and covered with clay. These houses were cheap to build, and families living in them showed a preference for having only the conjugal couple and their children (in other words, the nuclear family) living in one house. Whatever the living arrangements, housing for the animals was connected to human housing, in part for warmth and in part because animals were the peasants' most valuable possessions.

◀ **The peasant house contained one or two rooms with a fire in the center of the room in the early Middle Ages, or in a fireplace at the side of the room by the late Middle Ages, as this illustration indicates. Stables were attached to the houses to protect the livestock, which were the peasants' most valuable possessions. Pegs and poles held clothing. Furniture was sparse. The beehives lining the fence in the garden area provided honey, the only sweetener available to peasants. Grain was valuable; in this picture a stone tower protects the grain.**
Giraudon/Art Resource, NY

▲ PEASANT WOMEN'S WORK
**Women's work included a number of cottage crafts in addition to rearing children and helping out in the fields during harvest. Women did shearing, washing, and spinning of wool thread. They also wove rough cloth of both wool and linen.**
Trinity College Library

Furnishings were rudimentary. They commonly included a straw pallet for a bed, a trestle table, benches, a cradle, sheets, towels, blankets, and pots and pans. Pegs held clothes, and rods suspended from the ceiling held hams, cheeses, and so on. Often the homes had a few luxury items, such as a piece of fine pottery or a crucifix.

Peasants largely ate a grain diet, with the addition of eggs, cheese, beans, and some meat for protein. Bread was made of a rough whole wheat or rye or a mixture of grains. Oats, peas, and beans were made into a gruel. For their ordinary drink, peasants made wine or beer, depending on the part of Europe in which they lived. Wine and olive oil were more typical of southern Europe, whereas beer and butter were more common in northern Europe.

*Sex Roles*  Sex roles were strongly differentiated on the manors. Men did the plowing and heavy field work, cutting of firewood, carting, and construction. Women tended the domestic animals, milking them, making butter and cheese, and collecting eggs. Women also raised the children, did the brewing, cooked the simple meals, and made thread from wool and flax. They also spun rough cloth. Harvest, done in August and September, took everyone out to the fields to cut the grain and bind it into sheaves to take back to the village.

It would be a mistake to assume that peasant households were like American pioneer households in which most things were made at home. In the eleventh century even peasants had access to a market economy, selling their surplus grain and animals and buying ready-made goods in market towns. Clothing, metal pots, fine ceramics, animals, and luxury items were all bought at markets. Markets stimulated the growth of cottage industries, especially in the vicinity of towns. Peasants produced grain, livestock, fruit and vegetables, and various craft items to sell to urban dwellers. Market production was consistent with the sex roles on the manor: women producing thread, beer, and butter and cheese and men making various handicraft objects.

*Popular Culture and Religion*  Popular entertainment included singing and dancing, wrestling and archery contests, and various ball games, including football. The peasant year, although filled with labor, was punctuated by festivals. Christmas celebrations lasted for twelve days, Mayday was a time for singing contests and maypoles, and Midsummer Eve was celebrated with bonfires.

Church councils repeatedly condemned dancing and singing in the churchyard, because they thought that such activities encouraged sin.

The rural church acquired new importance. Peasants contributed to building parish churches of stone. The parish priest was usually of peasant origin. Because he was frequently the only member of the community who could read, he aided the peasants in reading documents from merchants and government bureaucrats.

*Free and Unfree Peasants*   Manors had both free and unfree peasants. Freedom did not bring a substantially better standard of living, but it meant that the free peasant did not have to do week work or boon work. Economic conditions could increase the number of free peasants. During the period of expansion to which this chapter is devoted, lords had to offer generous terms, frequently guaranteed in a written charter, to encourage peasants to clear forest lands for settlement or to move to newly conquered territories. The peasant who settled in these new lands paid only a small fixed rent for the lands he cleared and did not have to work for the landlord. He could leave the new village at will, selling his lands and the house he had built at their market value. A runaway serf who resided in a free village or a town for one year and one day without being claimed by his owner was thenceforth free.

As Europe became even more of a market economy during the twelfth and thirteenth centuries, lords used their demesne lands to produce cash crops. They found it easier to have their peasants pay a money rent for the land and to commute the customary labor services into a monetary payment. With this revenue, the lords hired laborers drawn from the increasing surplus peasant population to cultivate the demesne. The distinction between free and unfree peasants became less meaningful as peasants commuted their serfdom or intermarried with free peasants.

## ◆ EXPANSION OF EUROPE

Europe's population in the early Middle Ages, to about the year 1050, was small in absolute numbers and was not distributed evenly across the countryside. The end of invasions, the relative sta-

bility that feudalism was bringing to government, the increased agricultural productivity, and new economic opportunities encouraged growth in family size. For the first time since the fall of the western Roman Empire, Europe experienced a sustained and substantial population growth. Europe became too densely populated for its existing cultivated land and began to expand both internally and externally. The expansion of Europe involved the clearing of forest and marsh areas for cultivation and habitation. But Europe also expanded to the east into Slavic lands, into Spain, and even to the Holy Land during the crusades.

*Internal Colonization*   In England, France, and Germany, the peasants cleared forests and drained marshes to expand agricultural space; in the Low Countries, they began building dikes and draining marshes by the sea. As we saw above, lords were willing to offer good terms to encourage peasants who would take up new land. This internal colonization can be seen in place names that indicate the home village, such as Great Horewood and the new settlement of Little Horewood. Other new settlements carry names such as Newcastle or Villenova (new town).

*Conquest of Frontiers*   German nobles pushed eastward beyond the former borders of the Frankish empire (see map 8.2) into territories that were thinly inhabited by Slavs, Prussians, Letts, and Lithuanians. Some Germans settled just beyond the Elbe River and established the Principality of Brandenburg. Other Germans advanced along the shores of the Baltic Sea at the same time that Swedes began to move across Finland. The Russian prince of Novgorod, Alexander Nevsky, defeated the Swedes on the Neva River close to the Baltic Sea in 1240 and repulsed the Germans in another victory in 1242. Although these defeats halted further advances in northeastern Europe, the Germans and Swedes retained control of the shores of the Baltic Sea. The Germans had by then pushed through the middle Danube valley and founded another principality: Austria. Offering land and low rents, the nobles advertised in the West for peasants to migrate and settle the newly opened territories. By the early fifteenth century the *drang nach Osten* ("drive to the east") had clearly spent its strength, but it had tripled the

▲ MAP 8.2  GERMAN MIGRATION EASTWARD

area of German settlement over what it had been in Carolingian times (see map 8.2).

Settlers also moved into the Iberian Peninsula (present-day Spain and Portugal). In the mid-eleventh century the Christian kings, whose kingdoms were confined to the extreme north of the peninsula, began an offensive against the Muslims, who ruled most of Iberia. The Christians pushed south over two centuries until they held most of the peninsula. The battle of Las Navas de Tolosa (in 1212), between an allied Christian army and an invading Muslim army from North Africa, confirmed this domination. By 1275 only the emirate of Granada remained under Muslim rule. The Christian kings actively recruited Christian settlers for the territories they reconquered and gave them land under favorable terms. The reconquest and resettlement of the peninsula, known as the *Reconquista*, proved lasting achievements; the Iberian frontier remained almost unchanged for the next 280 years, during which time Castile, Aragon, Portugal, and other states developed and flourished.

In Italy the Hauteville brothers, as we have seen, succeeded in defeating the Muslims and Byzantines in southern Italy and Sicily and united the two regions into the Kingdom of Naples and Sicily. This victory opened new areas for European settlement.

European power swept over the sea as well as the land. The leaders were the maritime cities of Venice, Pisa, and Genoa. In 1015 and 1016 fleets from Pisa and Genoa freed Sardinia from Islamic rule.

## ◆ COMMERCIAL EXPANSION

The European economy remained predominantly agricultural, although new forms of economic endeavor were emerging. Trade, which had dwindled in the Carolingian age, became more vigorous. Most of the trade was local, between rural areas or between city and countryside, but a dramatic rebirth of trade also took place with regions beyond the European frontiers. Three trading zones developed, based on the Mediterranean Sea in the south, the Baltic Sea in the north, and the overland routes that linked the two seas (see map 8.3).

***Mediterranean Trade***  Venice, Pisa, and Genoa led this commercial expansion. In 998 and again in 1082 the Venetians received from the Byzantine emperors charters that gave them complete freedom of Byzantine waters. In the twelfth century Pisans and Genoese negotiated formal treaties with Islamic rulers that allowed them to establish commercial colonies in the Middle East and North Africa. Marseilles and Barcelona soon began to participate in the profitable eastern trade.

In this Mediterranean exchange, the East shipped condiments, medicines, perfumes, dyes, paper, ivories, porcelain, pearls, precious stones, and rare metals such as mercury—all of which were known in the West under the generic name of *spices*. Eastern traders also sent a variety of fine linens and cottons (damask, muslin, organdy) as well as brocades and silks. Western North Africa supplied animal skins, leather, cheese, ivory, and gold. Europe shipped wood and iron and products made from them (including entire ships), as well as grain, wine, and other agricultural commodities. By the year 1200 manufactured goods, especially woolen cloth woven in Flanders and finished in Italy, began to play an increasingly important role in the Mediterranean exchange. This cloth gave European merchants a product valued in the Eastern markets; with it they were able not only to pay for Eastern imports but also to generate a flow of precious metals into Europe.

▲ **Map 8.3  Medieval Trade Routes**
◆ www.mhhe.com/chambers8ch8maps

*Baltic and Northern Trade*   Trade in northern Europe among the lands bordering the Baltic Sea linked the great ports of London, Bruges, Bergen, Cologne, Lübeck, and Novgorod with the many smaller maritime towns. The eastern Baltic regions sold grain, lumber and forest products, amber, and furs. Scandinavia supplied wood and fish. England provided raw wool and grains. Flanders, the great industrial area of the north, imported food stuffs and wool to support its cloth industry.

*Overland Trade*   The northern and Mediterranean trading zones were joined by numerous overland routes. After 1100 the most active ex-

change between north and south was concentrated at six great fairs, held at various times of the year in the province of Champagne in France. Merchants from all over Europe could find at least one fair open no matter what time of year they came. Trade included local products, but the fairs' chief importance was as redistribution points for spices, fine cloth, and other luxury goods. The fairs guaranteed the merchants personal security, low tariffs, fair monetary exchange, and quick and impartial justice. For two centuries the fairs remained the greatest markets in Europe.

Milan became a center for overland trade that funneled the luxury goods from the Mediterranean trade to the north into Germany and products from that region back to Venice, Genoa, and Pisa.

## ◆ REBIRTH OF URBAN LIFE

Although the towns in Western Europe were increasing in size and social complexity, their growth was very slow even in this age of economic expansion. Before 1200 probably no town in Western Europe included more than 30,000 inhabitants. These small towns, however, were assuming new functions.

In the early Middle Ages the towns had been chiefly administrative centers, serving as the residence of bishops—or, much more rarely, of counts—and as fortified enclosures to which the surrounding rural population fled when under attack. (The original sense of the English word *borough* and of the German word *Burg* is "fortress.") As the revival of trade made many of these towns centers of local or international exchange, permanent colonies of merchants grew up around the older fortresses. These merchant quarters were sometimes called a *faubourg* ("outside the fortress"). Many European towns, especially in the north, still show these two phases of their early history in their central fortress and surrounding settlements (see map 8.4).

***Urban Society*** Urban social organization was hierarchical, as was the rest of medieval society. At the top was a small elite group, usually referred to as *patricians*. In Italy the elite included nobles, merchants engaged in long-distance trade, and great landlords from the countryside, who lived for part or all of the year in the towns. In contrast, in Flanders and the rest of northern Europe the nobles and great landlords tended to keep to their rural estates, whence they viewed with disdain and fear the growing wealth of the towns. The powerful urban families in the north came chiefly from common origins, and most of them had founded their fortunes on commerce or the management of urban property. Social and cultural contrasts between town and countryside, then, were much sharper in the north than in Italy.

Below the patricians were shopkeepers and artisans. While the patricians had a single guild in most towns before 1200, after that date guilds multiplied, showing an ever greater diversifica-

tion in the commercial enterprises of the mercantile classes. Goldsmiths (also bankers), spice merchants, and those importing such items as salt fish and cloth, formed guilds. Artisans and less prominent merchants organized trade guilds to regulate their crafts, such as those of the shoemakers, bakers, saddlers, fishmongers, and so on. The craft guilds began disputing, often with violence and soon with some success, the political domination of the patricians. As urban economies became more developed in the thirteenth century and some industries, such as cloth making, became prominent, cities also supported a number of skilled laborers. Perhaps the most distinctive feature of urban society, even in the twelfth century, was the fluidity of class divisions. Vertical social mobility was easier in the city than in any other part of the medieval world, except possibly in the Church. The patrician class was always admitting new members, chiefly wealthy, recent immigrants from the countryside. The towns of the Middle Ages were more efficient than was rural society in recognizing, utilizing, and rewarding talent.

***Urban Life*** The urban milieu provided entirely different living conditions than did that of the castle or the manor. The houses were close together and faced streets that could be narrow and smelly, because they served for general rubbish disposal. The houses were of stone and contained a cellar for storage, a ground floor for a shop or workplace, a hall and perhaps a loft above for living space. The area behind the house might contain a garden, a courtyard, and work space. In some towns the house completely surrounded the courtyard. Higher structures of three and four floors were characteristic of larger cities. Patricians had full houses to themselves, but many people rented portions of houses for business and suites of rooms for residences. The poorer people rented one room on the upper floors or even shared the rent for such spaces.

Rather than growing their own food, urban dwellers relied on the surrounding countryside to provide their sustenance. Small towns had one market square, but cities had separate markets for fish, meat, grain, bread, and so on. The diet varied very much by the wealth of the inhabitant, but an idea of the variety of foods available can be seen

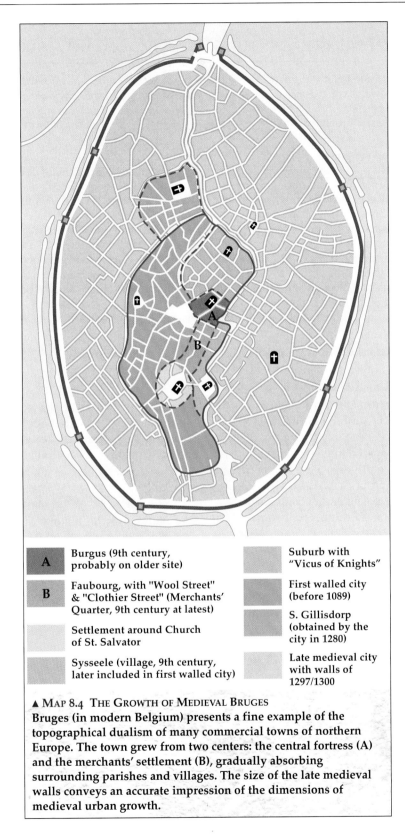

| A | Burgus (9th century, probably on older site) |
|---|---|
| B | Faubourg, with "Wool Street" & "Clothier Street" (Merchants' Quarter, 9th century at latest) |
| | Settlement around Church of St. Salvator |
| | Sysseele (village, 9th century, later included in first walled city) |

| | Suburb with "Vicus of Knights" |
|---|---|
| | First walled city (before 1089) |
| | S. Gillisdorp (obtained by the city in 1280) |
| | Late medieval city with walls of 1297/1300 |

▲ MAP 8.4  THE GROWTH OF MEDIEVAL BRUGES

Bruges (in modern Belgium) presents a fine example of the topographical dualism of many commercial towns of northern Europe. The town grew from two centers: the central fortress (A) and the merchants' settlement (B), gradually absorbing surrounding parishes and villages. The size of the late medieval walls conveys an accurate impression of the dimensions of medieval urban growth.

## A Twelfth-Century Description of London

◆

*William Fitz Stephen introduced his biography of Thomas Beckett (written in 1183) with a description of his beloved city of London. He describes a busy commercial town with vendors of food catering to those on limited budgets as well as to nobles. Prepared food is available to take home or eat at a tavern. Peasants participate in the market economy by bringing livestock and other wares.*

". . . there is in London upon the river's bank, amid the wine that is sold from ships and wine-cellars, a public cook shop. There daily, according to the season, you may find viands, dishes roast, fried and boiled, fish great and small, coarser flesh for the poor, the more delicate for the rich, such as venison and birds both big and little. If friends, weary with travel, should of a sudden come to any of the citizens, and it is not their pleasure to wait fasting till fresh food is bought and cooked and 'till servants bring water for hands and bread,' they hasten to the river bank, and there all things desirable are ready to their hand. However great the infinitude of knights or foreigners that enter the city or are about to leave it, at whatever hour of night or day, that the former may not fast too long nor the latter depart without their dinner, they turn aside thither . . . and refresh themselves. . . .

"In another place apart stand the wares of the country-folk, instruments of agriculture, long-flanked swine, cows with swollen udders and [sheep] 'woolly flocks.' Mares stand there, meet for plows, sledges and two-horsed carts."

From William Fitz Stephen, *Norman London* (Italica Press), pp. 52, 54.

---

in William Fitz Stephen's description of London (see "A Twelfth-Century Description of London").

Medieval cities were not the anonymous places that cities are now. People lived within a quarter of the city that provided them with their local courts and representatives to the larger urban government. Rich and poor lived side by side, often in the same house. The parish church served a very local population. London, for instance, had 104 churches for a city that included only a square mile of space within its walls.

Urban centers provided a rich variety of entertainment. Church feast days, civic celebrations, and visits of lords were all events calling for parades. Traveling entertainers—such as tumblers, animal trainers with their performing animals, players, and jugglers—offered diversion.

## II. Governments of Europe 1000–1150

◆

The expansion of Europe, growth of towns, increased prosperity, and framework of feudalism permitted larger governmental units (see map 9.3 for political developments and boundaries). The establishment of institutions characteristic of the Middle Ages included the formation of monarchies and principalities as well as the reform and strengthening of the papacy. The feudal customs that established bonds between lord and vassal became the basis for revitalizing lay governments.

### ◆ NORMAN ENGLAND

We could use the history of any one of several principalities—the Duchy of Normandy, the County of Flanders, the Kingdom of Naples and Sicily, among others—to illustrate the political reorganization characteristic of feudal government. But England offers the best example of feudal concepts in the service of princes. The growth of feudalism in England was intimately connected with the Norman Conquest of 1066, so that we can look at feudalism as a system of government imposed on England by William the Conqueror.

***The Norman Conquest*** Duke William of Normandy (1026–1087), the architect of the Conquest, is the epitome of the ambitious, energetic, and resourceful prince of the central Middle Ages. A bastard who had to fight 12 years to make good his claim over the Norman duchy, William early set his ambitions on the English crown. His claims were respectable, but not compelling. He was the first cousin of the last Saxon king, the childless Edward the Confessor, who allegedly had promised to make William heir to the throne. However, before his death, Edward selected the Saxon Harold Godwinson to succeed him, and his choice was supported by the Witan, the English royal council.

Edward died in 1066. William immediately recruited an army of vassals and adventurers to support his claim to the throne, but unfavorable winds kept his fleet bottled up in the Norman ports for six weeks. Meanwhile, Harold Hardrada, king of Norway, who also disputed Harold Godwinson's claim, invaded England with a Viking army, but the Saxons defeated his force near York on September 28, 1066. That same day, the channel winds shifted and William landed in England. Harold Godwinson foolishly rushed south to confront him. Although the Saxon army was not, as was once thought, technically inferior to the Norman army, it was tired and badly in need of rest and reinforcements after the victory over the Vikings. At the Battle of Hastings on October 14, fatigue seems eventually to have tipped the scales of an otherwise even struggle. The Normans carried the day and left Harold Godwinson dead upon the field. Duke William of Normandy had won his claim to be king of England.

*Impact of the Conquest*   The Norman Conquest provided areas of both continuity and change for the Anglo-Saxon population. Although local and central government remained similar, the society and economy underwent major reorientation.

The basic unit of local administration remained the shire, or county, under the supervision of the sheriff, who had primary responsibility for looking after the king's interests. The sheriff, chief official in the shire, administered the royal estates, collected the taxes, summoned and led contingents to the national militia, and presided over the shire court to enforce royal justice. William left all these institutions of local government intact.

The Conquest also brought major changes to Anglo-Saxon society. The Saxon *earls*, as the great nobles were called, and most of the lesser nobles, or *thanes*, lost their estates and fled. William redistributed the lands among his followers from the continent—his barons (a title of uncertain origin,

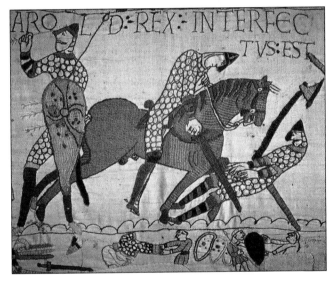

▲ THE BAYEUX TAPESTRY
**More of an embroidery than a true tapestry, the Bayeux Tapestry is a strip of linen 231 feet long and 20 inches wide depicting the Norman Conquest of England in 1066. The story is laid out as a running narrative, like a cartoon strip. The tapestry was commissioned by Odo, Bishop of Bayeux and half brother of William, and was embroidered by women. In the portion shown here, William arrives at Pevensey (top); King Harold fights in the Battle of Hastings and is shot in the eye by an arrow, killing him (bottom). The tapestry was completed toward the end of the eleventh century and is now housed in a museum connected with the Cathedral of Bayeux in Normandy in France.**
Erich Lessing / Art Resource, NY

now used to connote the immediate vassals of the king). He allotted land liberally but cautiously, creating each fief from several blocks of land in different parts of the island. This strategy gave his followers adequate support to serve him, but limited their autonomy and opportunity to rebel. William redefined the relations between the king and the great men of the realm on the basis of essentially feudal concepts. He now insisted that all English land be considered a fief held directly or indirectly (subinfeudated) from the king. The barons had to serve the king, and the knights had to serve the barons or risk losing their estates. In other words, he imposed a feudal hierarchy with the king as the recognized owner of all land and his vassals as recipients of fiefs from the king.

The peasant population, which had consisted of free peasants and slaves, was organized into manors on which most peasants became serfs.

*Domesday Book*   In 1086 William conducted a comprehensive survey of the lands of England, the report of which became known as the *Domesday Book*. In line with William's policy of maintaining control over his land and assets, he sent out royal officers to every shire. Assembling a jury of six Englishmen and six Normans to swear to the validity of the testimony of the local population, the royal officers questioned a gathering of shire representatives about the number of manors, plow teams, meadows, forests, animals, and people on the land. The taxes, tolls, markets, mints, and services owed the king were all recorded. The survey shows a population of about 1.1 million people. *The Domesday Book* also shows that the chief resistance to the Normans was in the north, where before the Conquest the land had been thriving with agriculture but was now waste. The Normans had brutally killed or evicted the resisters and adopted a scorched earth policy. The survey gave William a clear record of his own holdings and those of his barons, and it enabled him to know how much service the land could support.

*Curia Regis*   To maintain close contact with his barons and vassals, William adapted the Anglo-Saxon Witan to resemble the continental king's great council, or *curia regis*. Essentially, the great council was an assembly of bishops, abbots, and barons—in fact, anyone whom the king sum-

moned. The council fulfilled the feudal functions of giving the king advice and serving as his principal court in reaching judgments. It was a much larger assembly than the Saxon Witan. Because the great council could not be kept permanently in session, a small council, consisting of those persons in permanent attendance at the court whom the king wished to invite, carried on the functions of the great council between its sessions. The development of the great and small councils had major importance for English constitutional history. The great council was the direct ancestor of Parliament, whereas the small council was the source of the administrative bureaus of the royal government.

*Henry I*   William the Conqueror had three sons. The eldest became Duke of Normandy, the second, William Rufus, became king of England, and the youngest, Henry, was given a cash settlement. When William Rufus died of an arrow wound while hunting, Henry (r. 1100–1135) seized the royal treasure and became king. It was rumored at the time that Henry had a hand in his brother's death; the man who shot the arrow later received land grants from him. Henry I surrounded himself with able bishops who helped him organize the government. He also managed to take over the Duchy of Normandy when his eldest brother died, and once again united it with the kingdom of England.

Using the *curia regis* for settling feudal disputes, Henry began to make inroads in the autonomy of feudal lords by making his court one of appeal. He also began to reestablish the royal prerogative to try felonies, including homicide, robbery, arson, burglary, and larceny, which were offenses against the king's peace and punishable by death. The court business was profitable because the crown confiscated the goods from those convicted of crimes, but business was soon so brisk that the court was overwhelmed. The solution was to send itinerant justices, called *justices of eyre* (rhymes with tire), around to the counties to try cases in the shire courts and to investigate infringements of royal rights in the countryside.

*Exchequer*   To make the *curia regis* more efficient, Henry created separate departments. The financial department became known as the Exchequer—a name derived from a tablecloth marked out in squares like a checkerboard on which accounts were audited. The tablecloth was really a large abacus on which pennies were in one column, shillings in the next, and pounds and their multiples in the other columns. The Chancellor who headed the Exchequer audited the sheriffs' accounts and kept track of other revenues. The Chancellor of the Exchequer is still the financial officer in the British cabinet today. Because wealth was the basis of power for any medieval king, Henry had established an efficient way to collect revenue owed him and to control his barons. With able administrators in charge of his government, he was free to spend more time in Normandy putting down rebellions of his own vassals and fighting off attempts by neighboring counts and dukes to acquire parts of Normandy.

## ◆ CAPETIAN FRANCE

In France the pattern of feudal development was much different from that of England. Central government all but disappeared in the turmoil following the age of Charlemagne. What governmental functions could still be performed amid the chaos were carried out by counts, castellans, and other lords of small territorial units. These factors alone would have made rebuilding an effective national monarchy considerably more difficult in France than in England; but, in addition, France was a much larger country, and its regions preserved considerable cultural diversity.

The evolution of larger units of feudal government, however, can be discerned in several compact and effectively governed principalities, especially in the north—the Duchy of Normandy, the counties of Flanders and Champagne, the royal lands of the Ile-de-France, and others. French kings sought with some success to establish a lord-vassal relation with the great dukes and counts who governed these principalities. The kings did not envision, and could not have achieved, the unification of the entire realm under their own direct authority. The goal of monarchical policy was rather a kind of federation of principalities bound together by a common fealty to the king on the part of distant dukes and counts. Again, the theory that the king was at the pinnacle of the feudal hierarchy served to give the king a basis for increasing his power over the whole of the realm of France.

*The Capetians* In 987 the great nobles of France elected as their king Hugh Capet, whose descendants held the throne until 1792. Hugh was chosen primarily because his small possessions in the Ile-de-France, which included Paris and the surrounding region, made him no threat to the independence of the nobles. He and his successors for the next century made no dramatic efforts to enlarge their royal authority, but they carefully nursed what advantages they had: the central location of their lands; the title of king, which commanded a vague prestige; and a close association with the Church, which gave them an avenue of influence extending beyond their own territory. They also pursued a remarkably prudent policy of consolidating control over their own lands, and they had the good fortune to produce sons when the usual production of sons as heirs was only three generations. For three hundred years the kings crowned their sons during their own lifetime and thus built the tradition that the crown was theirs not by election but by hereditary right.

The Capetian policy first bore fruit under Louis VI, the Fat (r. 1108–1137). He achieved his goal of being master of his own possessions by successfully reducing to obedience the petty nobles and castellans who had been disturbing his lands and harassing travelers seeking to cross them (see "Louis VI Subdues a Violent Baron," p. 270). By the end of his reign, he had established effective control over the lands between the cities of Paris and Orléans. This move gave him a compact block of territory in the geographic heart of France. Louis VI promoted the colonization of forests and wastelands by establishing free villages, and he courted the support of the town communes. The king's encouragement of economic growth added to his own fiscal resources as he collected revenues from towns and trade.

## ◆ THE GERMAN EMPIRE

In the tenth and eleventh centuries the German lands east of the Rhine showed a pattern of political development very different from that of France or England. Whereas William forced central control over his territory in England by conquest and the Capetians established hereditary right to the French throne, Germany kept a strong tradition of elective kingship and a concentration of wealth and power in large territorial blocks—

# LOUIS VI SUBDUES A VIOLENT BARON

◆

*This selection describes the attempt of Louis VI (1108–1137), a strong monarch, to keep the peace in his realm. It comes from The Life of Louis VI, a chronicle by Suger, the head of a French monastery and a great admirer of the king. It is a good example of the chronicles that form one of the historian's basic sources for studying medieval history.*

"A king is obliged by virtue of his office to crush with his strong right hand the impudence of tyrants. For such men freely provoke wars, take pleasure in plunder, oppress the poor, destroy the churches, and give themselves free reign to do whatsoever they wish. . . .

"One such wicked man was Thomas of Marle. For while King Louis was busy fighting in the wars which we mentioned earlier, Thomas ravaged the regions around Laon, Reims, and Amiens. . . . Thomas devastated the region with the fury of a wolf. No fear of ecclesiastical penalty persuaded him to spare the clergy; no feeling of humility convinced him to spare the people. Everyone was slaughtered, everything destroyed. He snatched two prize estates from the nuns of Saint-John of Laon. And treating the two castles of Crècy-sur-Serre and Nouvion-Catillon as his own, he transformed them into a dragon's lair and a den of thieves, exposing the nearby inhabitants to the miseries of fire and plunder.

"Fed up with the intolerable afflictions of this man, the churchmen of France met together (on December 6, 1114) at a great council at Beauvais. . . . The venerable papal legate Cuno, bishop of Praeneste,

was particularly moved by the numerous pleas of the church and the cries of the orphans and the poor. He drew the sword of Saint Peter against Thomas of Marle, and with the unanimous assent of the council, declared him excommunicated, ripped from him in absentia the titles and honors of knighthood, branded him a criminal, and declared him unworthy of being called a Christian.

"Heeding the wishes of so great a council, King Louis moved quickly against Thomas. Accompanied by his army and the clergy, he turned at once against the heavily defended castle of Crècy. There, thanks to his men at arms, or should we say on account of divine aid, Louis achieved swift victory. He seized the new towers as if they were no more than the huts of peasants; he drove out the criminals; he piously slaughtered the impious; and as for those who had showed no pity, he in turn showed no pity towards them. . . . Flushed by the success of his decisive victory, the king moved quickly against the other illegally held castle, Nouvion."

From C. W. Hollister et al., *Medieval Europe: A Short Source Book* (New York: McGraw-Hill, 1992), pp. 207–208.

Saxony, Franconia, Swabia, and Bavaria. Originally districts of the Carolingian Empire, these territories became independent political entities under powerful dukes. Because these duchies were close to the hostile Eastern frontier, their inhabitants learned to appreciate the advantages of a unified leadership under territorial dukes. Paradoxically, the German populace also retained Charlemagne's Empire as the political ideal. The result of strong territorial allegiances and a desire for a larger political unit brought clashes between the nobles and their rulers throughout the Middle Ages.

***Otto I, the Great*** The last direct descendant of Charlemagne in Germany, a feeble ruler known as Louis the Child, died in 911. Recognizing the need

for a common leader, the German dukes in 919 elected as king one of their number, Henry of Saxony. His descendants held the German monarchy until 1024. The most powerful of this line of Saxon kings, and the true restorer of the German Empire, was Otto I, the Great (r. 936–973). Otto was primarily a warrior, and conquest was a principal foundation of his power. He routed the pagan Magyars near Augsburg in 955 and ended their menace to Christian Europe; he organized military provinces, or marches, along the Eastern frontier and actively promoted the work of German missionaries and settlers beyond the Elbe River; and in 951 he marched into Italy.

***Restoration of the Empire*** The immediate rationale for Otto's entrance into Italy was the appeal

▲ CROWN OF THE GERMAN EMPIRE, TENTH AND
ELEVENTH CENTURIES
The crown of the German Empire may originally
have been given to Otto I by Pope John, but
throughout the tenth and eleventh centuries various
pieces were added by different emperors. It eventually consisted of eight panels, decorated with cloi-
sonné enamels, which are hinged together with gold
filigree and surrounded with jewels and pearls.
Art Resource, NY

---

*Chronology*

## CHRONOLOGICAL CHART

Germany: Otto I, the Great (r. 936–973)
　　　　　Otto II (r. 973–983)
　　　　　Henry III (r. 1039–1056)
　　　　　Henry IV (r. 1056–1106)
France:　Hugh Capet (r. 987–996)
　　　　　Louis VI, the Fat (r. 1108–1137)
　　　　　Council of Clermont and preaching
　　　　　　of First Crusade (1095)
England:　Edward the Confessor (r. 1042–1066)
　　　　　Norman Conquest (1066)
　　　　　William I (r. 1066–1087)
　　　　　*Domesday Book* (1086)
　　　　　Henry I (r. 1100–1135)
Italy:　　Pope Sylvester II (999–1003)
　　　　　College of Cardinals (1059)
　　　　　Pope Gregory VII (1073–1085)
　　　　　Canossa (1077)
　　　　　Roger de Hauteville (d. 1101)
　　　　　　conquers Sicily (1072)
Crusades: First Crusade (1095–1099)
　　　　　Second Crusade (1147–1149)
　　　　　Third Crusade (1189–1192)

---

of Adelaid, widow of one of the Italian kings, who
was about to be forced into an undesirable marriage. He rescued the queen and married her himself. Historians have debated the real reasons Otto
wished to secure power in Italy. Perhaps, like
Charlemagne, he hoped to rescue the papacy from
the clutches of the tumultuous Roman nobility, to
which it had once again fallen victim. Apparently,
Otto conceived of himself not just as a German
king, but as the leader of all Western Christians.
He could not allow Italy, especially Rome, to remain in chaos or permit another prince to achieve
a strong position there. In 962, during Otto's

second campaign in Italy, Pope John XII crowned
him "Roman Emperor," a title with more prestige
than power.

The coronation of 962 confirmed the close relations between Germany and Italy that lasted
through the Middle Ages. Although the German
emperors claimed to be the successors of the Caesars and of Charlemagne and thus the titular leaders of all Western Christendom, their effective
power never extended beyond Germany and Italy
and the small provinces contiguous to them—
Provence, Burgundy, and Bohemia.

*Ecclesiastics as Administrators*　Otto's problems
of governing his far-flung territories were more
formidable than the problems that confronted the
English and French kings. Hoping to keep control

over the powerful duchies, Otto distributed the territories among his relatives. They proved to be disloyal to him. He found, as had the Carolingians, that bishops and abbots were more reliable and loyal as administrators of his realm. Otto could appoint loyal, educated, and clever administrators and invest them with the fiefs associated with their office without being concerned about hereditary claims from these celibate priests. Because he claimed the right to appoint bishops and abbots as well as controlling their fiefs, the emperor established enclaves of power in the duchies and in Italy that no potential rival could match.

*The Ottonian Renaissance*   The dynasty that Otto established fostered the revival of learning in Germany. The examples of two scholars indicate the intellectual activity that characterized the "Ottonian Renaissance."

Roswitha of Gandersheim (ca. 937–1004) came from a noble family of Saxony and was put into a Benedictine nunnery at an early age. A Saxon duke had founded Gandersheim in 852 with the intention that women of the Saxon dynasty would be its abbesses. Otto the Great's younger brother, a bishop, encouraged learning at the nunnery, and Roswitha had a series of learned nuns to teach her Latin. Her early writings were religious poetry, but, reading copies of Roman comedies that were in the nunnery library, she became fascinated by their language. Adapting the dramatic form, she wrote religious plays, the first plays to be written since Roman times. Toward the end of her life she wrote histories, including the *Deeds of Otto* about Otto the Great.

The other great figure was a monk, Gerbert of Aurillac in France (d. 1003). Gerbert came from a peasant family, but local monks recognized his genius and educated him. He was sent to Spain, where he came into contact with the great learning of Arab and Hebrew scholars in Barcelona. Although he studied with Christian scholars because he did not know Arabic, he learned something of Arab mathematics and astronomy. He had an abacus with Arabic numerals, but he did not use the zero as the Arabs did. His fame in France brought patronage from the Ottonians, who first made him tutor to the young Otto III and then appointed him pope in Rome, where

he served as Sylvester II. So great was his knowledge that people thought he was a necromancer or sorcerer. He was a man ahead of his time.

Artistic works flourished in the Ottonian period. The marriage of Otto II (r. 973–983) to a Byzantine princess formed an influential connection with Byzantine artistic expression. Otto III's ties were so close to Byzantium (his Greek mother acted as regent) that he learned Greek as a child. Soon German monastic workshops adapted the manuscript illuminations, ivory carving, and fine metal work of Byzantine craftsmen. The artistic style spread to the rest of Europe.

*Salian House*   The Ottonian line ended when Henry II died in 1024. The German nobles selected as emperor Henry III (r. 1039–1056), from another branch of the Saxon line. Some historians consider him to have been one of the strongest early medieval German emperors. Continuing the policy that was now well established in Germany, he relied on bishops and abbots that he had appointed as his administrators. But he also had a sincere interest in Church reform. In 1046 he crossed the Alps and called councils of clergy to reform the Church. He succeeded in nominating a series of able and educated popes to carry out reform programs such as promoting clerical celibacy, forbidding the sale of Church offices (simony), and restoring the Benedictine Rule in monasteries.

Henry III left a six-year-old son, Henry IV (r. 1056–1106). During Henry IV's minority, he had time to observe the weaknesses of the German monarchy. His father had designated his mother as regent, but civil war broke out and Henry became a pawn in power shifts, living with first one faction and then another. This unsettling childhood made him a ruler adept at dealing with adversity, but less sure of himself in dealing with success. On becoming emperor, Henry IV realized that he needed to consolidate the royal demesne as the English and French kings were doing. He also had to suppress the overpowerful dukes. Because the largest block of demesne land was on the borders of Saxony, he encroached on the Duke of Saxony's borders. Exercising his feudal position as liege lord, Henry IV used a fight between one of his vassals and the Duke of Saxony as an excuse to depose the Duke. The move alienated the nobles, who feared for their own estates.

Wanting to extend his authority through officials he could trust, Henry IV raised a number of lower born men to the rank of *ministeriales* (bureaucrats and soldiers), equipping them with horses and armor. Again, he offended the nobility because he required them to take orders from these lowly soldiers and bureaucrats rather than from fellow nobles. Henry's nobles rebelled over these innovations. At this point, Henry turned to the pope for help, but encountered a pope—Gregory VII—who was a strict reformer. Their clash is called the *Investiture Controversy*, as will be explained shortly.

# III. The Reform of the Western Church

The Church, like lay governments, was fundamentally transformed in the eleventh and twelfth centuries, acquiring characteristics that it was to retain in large measure to the present day. The reform of the Church resulted from a renewal of monastic discipline, an upsurge of popular piety among the laity, and a clerical revolt against the traditional system of lay domination over ecclesiastical offices and lands.

## ◆ THE CHURCH IN CRISIS

After the disintegration of the Carolingian Empire, a kind of moral chaos invaded the lives of the clergy. Since the fourth century, the Church had demanded that its clergy remain celibate, but this injunction was almost completely ignored in the post-Carolingian period. The sin of simony—the buying or selling of offices or sacraments—was also rampant. Many bishops and even some popes purchased their high positions, and parish priests frequently sold their sacramental services (baptisms, masses, absolutions of sins, marriages) to the people.

The traditional intervention of lay rulers in the affairs of the Church also led to the moral breakdown. On the highest level, the tradition of lay domination made the king or emperor effective head of the Church in their realms. At the local level, ecclesiastical offices and lands were largely under lay control. Landlords were considered to own churches and lands supporting them as their property. Thus, they could name the priests who served in those churches and profit from donations made to them, freely sell the offices they controlled, or distribute Church lands to their relatives and friends. The results were disastrous. The Church was flooded with unworthy men who were little concerned with their spiritual duties, and the pillaging of Church lands and revenues left many clerics without adequate livings.

*Early Attempts at Reform*    According to canon law, the bishops bore the chief responsibility for the clergy's moral conduct. A few reforming bishops in the tenth and eleventh centuries, some appointed by the German emperors, tried to suppress clerical marriage and the simony of their priests, but they could make little headway. The powers of a single bishop were perforce limited to his own diocese and to his own lifetime because he could not name his successor.

## ◆ MONASTIC REFORM

*Cluniac Monasteries*    Renewal of monastic discipline proved a more effective reform than the efforts of popes or bishops. The monastery of Cluny in Burgundy was the center of reform. Founded in 910, the monastery was placed directly under the pope (neither lay lords nor bishops could interfere in its affairs). The monastic community elected the abbot directly. He administered not only Cluny but also the many dependent monastic communities that his monks had founded or reformed. The abbot of Cluny could visit these communities at will and freely correct any abuses. The congregation of Cluny grew with extraordinary rapidity in the eleventh and twelfth centuries until it included no fewer than 1,184 houses, which were spread from the British Isles to Palestine.

The Cluniac monks advocated both a return to the strict observance of the Benedictine Rule (see chapter 6) and a new emphasis on the liturgy (services, songs, and prayers). The services were long, lasting most of the day and into the night. Rebuilding of the monastic church began around 1100. It became an example of a new architecture, Romanesque (discussed in chapter 9).

## ◆ PAPAL REFORM

The first of the reforming popes, Leo IX (r. 1049–1054), an appointee of the German emperor, traveled widely and presided at numerous councils, where he promulgated decrees ordering reforms in clerical marriage and simony, summoned bishops suspected of corruption, and deposed many of them. He was the first pope to make wide and regular use of papal *legates*, or emissaries, who, like Charlemagne's *missi dominici,* traveled through Europe, inspecting, reprimanding, and reforming. For the first time, lands distant from Rome were subject to the close supervision of the papacy.

Under Pope Nicholas II (r. 1058–1061) the movement toward ecclesiastical liberty took several forward strides. By allying himself with the Normans of southern Italy, Nicholas freed the papacy from military dependence on the German empire. He was the first pope who expressly, if vainly, condemned the practice of "lay investiture"—that is, receiving churches and Church offices from laymen. In 1059 a Roman council reformed papal elections and defined the principles and procedures by which popes to this day have been elected.

*College of Cardinals*   Tradition required that the clergy and people of the diocese elect all bishops and, by extension, the pope as bishop of Rome. In practice, however, either the emperor named the pope, or in the emperor's absence the powerful noble families and factions of Rome did. The council of 1059, however, set up the election procedures for the pope, conferring this prerogative on the cardinals, the chief clergymen associated with the Church at Rome. This procedure ensured that the College of Cardinals, and the reformers who controlled it, could maintain continuity of papal policy. (Even today, all cardinals, no matter where they live in the world, hold a titular appointment to a church within the archdiocese of Rome.) The College of Cardinals simultaneously deprived both the emperor and the Roman nobility of one of their strongest powers, the appointment of the pope.

*Gregory VII*   The climax of papal reform came with the pontificate of Pope Gregory VII (r. 1073–1085), a Cluniac monk named Hildebrand, who was instrumental in designing the College of Cardinals. Rather than being elected through the College of Cardinals, Gregory was proclaimed pope by the citizens and clergy of Rome. Gregory brought to the office a high regard for the papacy's powers and responsibilities and a burning desire for reform. With regard to Church matters, Gregory asserted that the pope wielded absolute authority—that he could, at will, overrule any local bishop in the exercise of his ordinary or usual jurisdiction.

Gregory's ideas on the relations of Church and state are less clear. According to some historians, he believed that all power on earth, including the imperial power, came from the papacy. According to others, Gregory held merely that the normal function of kings was far lower than the sacred authority of popes. This much at least is beyond dispute: Gregory believed that all Christian princes must answer to the pope in spiritual matters and that the pope himself had a weighty responsibility to guide those princes, including the rulers of the German Empire. Gregory's reforming ideals set up a direct conflict with the emperor Henry IV.

## ◆ INVESTITURE CONTROVERSY

As the name suggests, the principal issue in the Investiture Controversy was the practice of great laymen of "investing" bishops with their fiefs by using the spiritual symbols of office, the ring and staff (indicating their care of their flock of faithful), as secular indications of allegiance. At its root, the struggle revolved around the claims of these powerful laymen to dispose of ecclesiastical offices and revenues as fiefs by their authority as lords. Laymen felt that they had a right to select loyal churchmen as well as warriors for vassals. The giving of the ring and staff was, in their view, similar to giving a clod of earth in passing on the fief. For the German emperors, selecting the bishop meant selecting an imperial administrator. Kings and emperors also argued that they had a right to select and invest a bishop with his office because kings were anointed during their coronation ceremony, in imitation of David's coronation in the Old Testament, and consequently received spiritual and sacerdotal power. The pope, they argued, was not the only one with spiritual power.

▲ **Emperor Henry IV is shown at Canossa on his knees, begging Pope Gregory for readmission to the church. Countess Matilda of Tuscany, a powerful supporter of the pope, appears on the right.**
AKG London

*The Fight is Joined* When Henry IV sent a letter in 1075 to Pope Gregory VII asking for help against his rebellious German nobles, Gregory, convinced that Henry was in a weak position, took advantage of the situation to condemn lay investiture and excommunicate some of Henry's advisers. Henry, who in the interval had defeated the rebellious nobles, reacted with fury; he summoned a meeting of loyal imperial bishops and declared Gregory not the true pope but a "false monk" (a reference to his elevation by acclamation rather than election in the College of Cardinals.) His letter continued: "descend and relinquish the apostolic throne which thou hast usurped. . . . I Henry, king by the grace of God, do say unto thee, together with all my bishops: Down, down, to be damned through all the ages." Not one to pause in what he thought to be the work of God, Gregory excommunicated Henry, thereby freeing Henry's subjects from allegiance to him. These acts struck at the fundamental

theory of the Christian empire, according to which the emperor was supreme head of the Christian people, responsible only to God.

*Excommunication of Henry IV* The excommunication broke the feudal vows of loyalty since fealty was sworn to a Christian lord, and excommunication placed a Christian outside the Church. Henry's enemies demanded that he be judged, with Pope Gregory presiding, before an assembly of lords and prelates. Gregory readily accepted the invitation to meet at Augsburg in February 1077. Henry resolved to fight spiritual weapons with spiritual weapons. He slipped across the Alps and intercepted Gregory, then on his way to Germany, at the Apennine castle of Canossa near Modena. Henry came in the sackcloth of a penitent, radiating contrition, pleading for absolution. Gregory, who doubted the sincerity of the emperor's repentance, refused for three days to receive him, while Henry waited in the snow. Finally, in the face of such persistence, Gregory the suspicious pope had to give way to Gregory the priest, who, like all priests, was obliged to absolve a sinner professing sorrow (see "Gregory VII's Letter to the German Nobility after Canossa").

The incident at Canossa is one of the most dramatic events of medieval history. Henry was the immediate victor. He had divided his opponents and stripped his German enemies of their excuse for rebelling. They named a rival emperor anyway, Rudolf of Swabia, but he was killed in battle in what seemed a divine judgment in Henry's favor. Gregory appears to have become unsure of himself after Canossa. He finally excommunicated Henry a second time in 1080 but was forced to flee Rome at the approach of Henry's army. Gregory died at Salerno in 1085, in apparent bitterness, avowing that his love of justice had brought him only death in exile. But the popes' claim of authority over kings and emperors was not dead.

*Concordat of Worms* After years of argument and struggle, the papacy and lay rulers settled the Investiture Controversy through the Concordat of Worms in 1122. They agreed that the lay rulers, including the emperor, would no longer invest prelates with the symbols of their spiritual office. The pope would allow the elections of imperial

## Gregory VII's Letter to the German Nobility after Canossa

*Henry intercepted Gregory at a castle in Canossa in January of 1077, dressed as a penitent. Gregory explains why he gave in to Henry's contrition and removed the excommunication.*

"When, after long deferring . . . and holding frequent consultations, we had, through all the envoys who passed, severely taken him to task for his excesses: he came at length of his own accord, with a few followers, showing nothing of hostility or boldness. . . . And there, having laid aside all the belongings of royalty, wretchedly, with bare feet and clad in wool, he continued for three days to stand before the gate of the castle. Nor did he desist from imploring with many tears the aid and consolation of the apostolic mercy until he moved all those who were present there, and whom the report of it reached, to such pity and depth of compassion that, interceding for him with many prayers and tears, all wondered indeed at the unaccustomed hardness of our heart, while some actually cried out that we were exercising, not the gravity of apostolic severity, but the cruelty, as it were of a tyrannical ferocity.

"Finally, conquered by the persistence of his compunction and by the constant supplications of all those who were present, we loosed the chain of the anathema and at length received him into the favor of communion and into the lap of the holy mother church."

From Norman Downs, *Basic Documents in Medieval History* (Melborne, FL: Kreiger, 1959), pp. 64–65.

---

bishops and abbots to be held in the presence of the emperor or his representative, thus permitting the emperor to influence the outcome of elections. In addition, the emperor retained the right of investing prelates with their temporalities—that is, their imperial fiefs. Although a compromise, the Concordat was a real victory for the papacy because it gave the popes more control over their bishops throughout Europe than they had previously enjoyed. Ultimately, lay leaders accepted papal approval as essential to a valid choice of bishops.

### ◆ CONSOLIDATION OF PAPAL REFORM

In the twelfth century the popes continued to pursue and consolidate the Gregorian ideals of internal reform, freedom from lay domination, and centralization of papal authority over their bishops, abbots, and clergy. In their struggle to be free of lay authority, the reformers had insisted that members of the clergy, however minor their office, were to be tried in ecclesiastical courts, as were any cases touching on the sacraments and breaches of dogma: sacrilege, heresy, marriage, testaments, contracts, and the like. A complex system of ecclesiastical courts developed throughout

Europe to try people. The ecclesiastical courts paralleled and at times rivaled the courts of the kings. Judicial decisions from the ecclesiastical courts could be appealed to Rome.

*Canon Law*  Legal scholars at this time were compiling and clarifying the canons of the Church—the authoritative statements from the Bible, Church councils, Church fathers, and popes, which constituted the law of the Church. The compilation that was ultimately recognized as official and binding was the *Decretum*, put together by the Italian jurist Gratian in about 1142. With his systematic compilation came trained canon lawyers to comment on, interpret, and apply canon law.

*Papal Curia*  Like the monarchs of Europe, the popes experimented with creating a stronger central bureaucracy in a papal *curia* (council). Among the most important branches was a centralized financial administration, the *camera* or chamber. It handled moneys coming into the papacy from estates the papacy directly held around Rome, from the proceeds of administering justice in ecclesiastical courts, and from money bishops paid to the papacy. A judicial branch of the curia dealt with appeals on matters of canon law. Like monarchs, popes also had a chancery for sending out official letters to their clergy, legates, rulers, and laymen.

The reform of the Church in the eleventh and twelfth centuries left an indelible mark on both religious and secular life in the West. The Church became a powerful force not only in people's spiritual lives but also in the politics of Europe. No longer could lay rulers easily dominate the papacy or its bishops. The leadership of the Church, reinforced by the wave of popular piety that resulted from the Cluniac movement, led to the preaching of the First Crusade.

# IV. The Crusades

In the eleventh century Western Europeans launched a series of armed expeditions to the East in an effort to free the Holy Land from Islamic rule. Known as crusades, these expeditions stimulated trade, encouraged the growth of towns, and contributed to the establishment of a stable political order in the West. Seen from a different perspective, the crusades were costly failures: They drained resources for what proved to be a temporary foothold in Palestine; they worsened relations not only with the Muslims but also with Eastern Christians; and they set in motion one of Europe's grimmest traditions, in which crusading zeal stimulated dreadful riots and pogroms against those most accessible non-Christians, the Jews.

The appeal of the crusades was both religious and material. The Cluniac movement not only stimulated reform of the Church but also a revival of lay piety. The new prosperity and the expansion of trade had already opened markets in the East, and lay piety stimulated pilgrimage to the Holy Land and interest in freeing it from the Turks. As the growth of feudalism and the influence of more centralized governments became stronger, younger sons of nobles found fewer and fewer opportunities to carve out fiefs for themselves by conquest. The success of the Hautevilles in Sicily suggested the possibility of new lands to conquer. *The Song of Roland,* which was popular in Europe at the time, distorted the tenants of Islam and encouraged knights to fight the Muslims as infidels and polytheists.

## ◆ ORIGINS

The origins of the crusades must be sought in a double set of circumstances: social and religious movements in the West and the political situation in the East. Pilgrimage, a personal visit to a place made holy through the life of Christ or one of the saints or the presence of a sacred relic, was popular among Western Christians. Common since the fourth century, pilgrimages gained in popularity during the eleventh century. Bands of pilgrims, sometimes numbering in the thousands, set forth to visit sacred places; Palestine was the most holy.

*The Turks* The pilgrim traffic was threatened when the Seljuk Turks, Muslim nomads, overran much of the Middle East in the eleventh century. The Seljuks apparently did not consciously seek to prevent pilgrims from reaching Palestine, but they did impose numerous taxes and tolls on them, and many Christians became angry at the domination of the holy places of Palestine by a strong, aggressive Islamic power.

Even more daunting to the West was the possibility that the Turks would overrun the Christian empire of Byzantium. The Seljuks had crushed a Byzantine army at the Battle of Manzikert in 1071, and the road to Constantinople seemed wide open. The fall of Byzantium would remove the traditional barrier to Islamic advance toward the West and would be a major disaster for the Christian world. When, therefore, a delegation from the emperor of Byzantium requested the help of Pope Urban II in 1095, he resolved to appeal to the Western knights and princes to go to the aid of their fellow Christians in the East.

*The Byzantine Empire* Although severely threatened by the Turks, the Byzantine Empire was under able leadership once again with the Comnenus family. Alexius Comnenus (1081–1118) had some success against the Turks, but he needed mercenary soldiers to enlarge his army. Knowing of the Normans' successes in Sicily, he hoped to hire Norman mercenaries. When he wrote to Pope Urban II asking for assistance, he hoped to persuade the pope by suggesting that the schism between the Eastern and Western Churches, which had occurred in 1054, might be brought to an end.

## ◆ THE MOTIVES OF THE CRUSADERS

*Religious Fervor*   Christians viewed the crusades as acts of religious devotion. Even before Urban made his appeal, the idea had gained currency in the West that God would reward those who fought in a good cause, that is, that wars could be holy. The crusaders also shared the belief expressed in the movement for Church reform that the good ought not simply to endure the evils of the world but should attempt to correct them. This active, confident spirit contrasted strongly with the withdrawal from the world that most Christian writers recommended in the early Middle Ages.

*Economic Motives for Expansion*   Social and economic motivations also contributed to the expeditions. The age of mass pilgrimages and crusades, from about 1050 to 1250, corresponds to the period in medieval history during which the European population was growing rapidly. The crusades may be considered one further example of

▼ CHRIST LEADING CRUSADERS
**This fourteenth-century illustration from a manuscript on the Apocalypse captures an assumption that was common to all the crusaders—that their expedition was being led by Christ himself. On his magnificent charger, he leads into battle the troops carrying his symbol, the cross.**
By Permission of The British Library, London. Royal 19BXV, pages:Fol 37 min

the expansion of Europe, similar in motivation and character to the Spanish *Reconquista* or the German *Drang nach Osten*. Of course, the crusades differed in at least one significant way from these other ventures. The crusades were almost exclusively military expeditions of Europe's warrior classes; peasants did not settle in Palestine in significant numbers as they did in the lands of Eastern Europe and in the Iberian Peninsula.

*The Oversupply of Knights*   The younger sons of European knights were particularly aware of the pressures created by an expanding population. Trained for war, they used their skills to fight each other for land and castles. Pope Urban apparently observed the effects of land shortage, for he is reported to have told the knights of France: "This land which you inhabit is too narrow for your large population; nor does it abound in wealth; and it provides hardly enough food for those who farm it. This is the reason that you murder and consume one another." Urban urged them not to fight fellow Christians, but to go to the traditional land of milk and honey and fight Muslims instead for land.

War against the Muslims thus offered constructive employment for Europe's surplus knights. In the twelfth century St. Bernard of Clairvaux, whose preaching inspired thousands to join the Second Crusade, frankly affirmed that all but a few of the knights on the crusades were "criminals and sinners, ravishers and the sacrilegious, murderers, perjurers, and adulterers." Bernard observed the double benefit of having them out of Europe: "Their departure makes their own people happy, and their arrival cheers those whom they are hastening to help. They aid both groups, not only by protecting the one but also by not oppressing the other." The crusades were, in one respect, a violent means of draining the violence from Western medieval life.

## ◆ THE FIRST CRUSADE

In November 1095, Pope Urban II preached a sermon at Clermont in southern France, calling on the nobility to undertake an expedition to the Holy Land. The pope's sermon was intended for the upper classes, but its plea had sensational results at all levels of Western society.

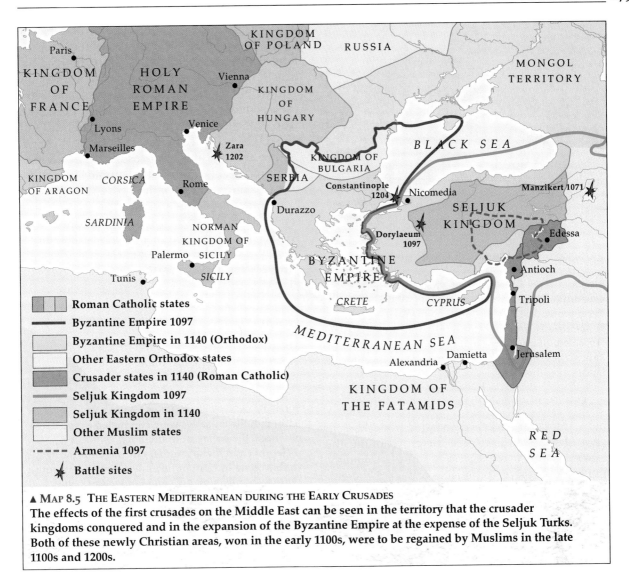

▲ MAP 8.5  THE EASTERN MEDITERRANEAN DURING THE EARLY CRUSADES
**The effects of the first crusades on the Middle East can be seen in the territory that the crusader kingdoms conquered and in the expansion of the Byzantine Empire at the expense of the Seljuk Turks. Both of these newly Christian areas, won in the early 1100s, were to be regained by Muslims in the late 1100s and 1200s.**

***The Popular Crusade***   In northern France and the Rhineland, influential preachers were soon rousing the people and organizing movements that historians now call the Popular Crusade. Bands of peasants and the poor (together with a few knights and clergy) set out for the East, miserably equipped and without competent leaders. They marched down the Rhine valley, attacking Jews as they went, and on through Hungary and Bulgaria to Constantinople. The emperor Alexius of Byzantium, who could only have been shocked at the sight of this hapless army, gave them transport across the Bosporus. The Turks at once cut them to pieces.

***The Crusading Army***   Far better organized was the official First Crusade, which was led by nobles. Robert of Normandy, son of William the Conqueror, headed a northern French army; Godfrey of Bouillon, his brother Baldwin, and Robert of Flanders commanded an army of Lotharingians and Flemings; Raymond of Toulouse led the men of Languedoc; and Bohemund of Taranto and his nephew Tancred marshaled the Normans of southern Italy. These four armies moved by various overland and sea routes to Constantinople (see map 8.5) and arrived there in 1096 and 1097.

Although the leaders of the First Crusade had intended to conquer lands in the East in their own

▲ **Godfrey Approaching the Gate at Constantinople**
This miniature illustration of a history of the expedition by one of its participants, William of Tyre, shows Godfrey of Bouillon, the leader of the First Crusade, entering Constantinople on his way to Jerusalem. In the lower half of the picture he approaches the city, and in the upper half he climbs a ladder over the walls.
Bibliothèque Nationale de France, Paris

name, Emperor Alexius demanded from them an oath of fealty in exchange for provisioning the armies as they marched to Palestine. Grudgingly, the leaders agreed, promising to regard the emperor as the overlord of any lands they might reconquer from the Turks. Subsequently, both the emperor and the Western leaders accused each other of violating the terms of the oath. The failure of the crusaders and the Byzantines to find a firm basis for cooperating ultimately weakened, although it did not defeat, the enterprise. *The Alexiad*, written by Anna Comnena, daughter of Alexius, reflects the Greek viewpoint: "there were among the Latins such men as Bohemund and his fellow counselors, who, eager to obtain the Roman Empire for themselves, had been looking with avarice upon it for a long time."

*Victories*  In 1097 the crusaders entered the Seljuk Sultanate of Rum, achieving their first major victory at Dorylaeum. Baldwin then separated his troops from the main body and conquered Edessa, where he established the first crusader state in the East. The decisive victory of the First Crusade came in the battle for the port city of

Antioch. After that, the road to Jerusalem was open. On July 15, 1099, the crusaders stormed Jerusalem and slaughtered its population of Muslims, Jews, and Eastern Christians.

Besides a high level of organizational skill and their own daring, the Westerners had the advantage of facing an enemy that was politically divided. The Seljuk Turks had only recently risen to power and had not yet consolidated their rule. They were still fighting the Fatimids, the ruling dynasty of Egypt, over the possession of Palestine. In addition, the ancient schisms among Islamic religious sects continued to divide and weaken the community. The Muslims' inability to present a united front against the crusaders was probably the decisive reason for the success of the First Crusade.

## ◆ THE KINGDOM OF JERUSALEM

The crusaders now faced the problem of organizing a government for their conquered territory and its population of Muslims, Jews, and Eastern

▼ **The Pillage of Jerusalem by Antiochus**
Although the crusades were conducted in the name of Christ, the behavior of their armies was no different from that of soldiers throughout the ages. In this scene in front of Jerusalem from a fifteenth-century manuscript, the commander Antiochus watches as his troops pile up the spoils they have looted from the Holy City.
Bibliothèque Nationale de France, Paris

▲ WOMEN ASSISTING KNIGHTS
**This manuscript illustration makes it clear that women took part in battles alongside the male crusaders. Here they wield picks and axes and throw stones in a siege. Moreover, it is clear that the woman in the foreground, just behind the ladder, who does not cower behind a shield like the man on the ladder, is about to be killed by an arrow.**
By Permission of The British Library, Ms Add. 15268 fol 101v

and Western Christians. They chose as ruler Godfrey of Bouillon, but he died in 1100, and his younger brother Baldwin, the conqueror of Edessa, succeeded him.

Baldwin organized his realm through the application of feudal concepts and institutions. He kept direct dominion over Jerusalem and its surroundings, including a stretch of coast extending from modern Gaza to Beirut. To the north, three fiefs—the County of Tripoli, the Principality of Antioch, and the County of Edessa—were made subject to his suzerainty (see map 8.6). Although King Baldwin and his successors were able to exert a respectable measure of authority over all these lands, profound weaknesses undermined their power. The kings were never able to push their frontiers to an easily defensible, strategic border, such as the Lebanese mountains. With only a small garrison, the Kingdom of Jerusalem

depended on a constant influx of men and money from Europe. Many knights and pilgrims came, but relatively few stayed as permanent settlers. The Westerners constituted a foreign aristocracy, small in number and set over a people of largely different faith, culture, and sympathies. The wonder is not that the crusader states ultimately fell but that some of their outposts survived on the mainland of Asia Minor for nearly 200 years, until 1291 when the port of Acre fell at last.

◆ THE LATER CRUSADES

Although historians have traditionally assigned numbers to the later crusades, these expeditions were merely momentary swells in the steady current of Western people and treasures to and from the Middle East. The recapture of the city of

enestoir semblant que nie sure li
adrestoir emaintenoit sauope.

son srere que voiant touf reconur
safolie e dist que il lauoit amende

Re auec op comr
rancres se conrenoir
en celisse. Li grant
ost qui les siuoit

se lon son plaisir atuiare. e encor
la mendroit se lon sa volente et
mst inra que il auoit sait plus por
aurcrui consisll que pa le sne porce

▲ Citizens of Edessa in Homage to Baldwin I
To emphasize the crusaders' triumph, this manuscript illustration shows Baldwin I, who captured Edessa in
1099, asserting his authority over the conquered Muslims. He sits on the left, with his knights next to him, and
receives the homage and tribute of his new subjects.
Bibliothèque Nationale de France, Paris

Edessa by the Muslims in 1144 gave rise to the Second Crusade (1147–1149). Two armies, led by King Louis VII of France and the Emperor Conrad III of Germany, set out to capture Damascus to give the Kingdom of Jerusalem a more defensible frontier. They were soon forced to retreat ignominiously before superior Muslim forces.

*The Third Crusade*   The unification of the Muslims under Saladin prompted the Third Crusade (1189–1192). Saladin already controlled Egypt and was able to conquer Syria as well so that the Latin Kingdom was surrounded. His capture of Jerusalem threatened to eliminate the Latin Kingdom of Jerusalem entirely. Emperor Frederick Barbarossa and kings Philip II of France and Richard I, the Lion-Hearted, of England all marched to the

East. (Frederick drowned while crossing through Asia Minor, and most of his forces turned back.) Philip II left the campaign early. Richard I fought on and the crusaders captured Acre. The Kingdom of Jerusalem remained limited to a narrow strip of the coast from Acre to Jaffa, but unarmed Christian pilgrims were given the right to visit Moslem-governed Jerusalem. These rights were paltry gains from so expensive a campaign.

*The Fourth Crusade*   Pope Innocent III preached the Fourth Crusade, but events soon took it out of his hands. The response was limited, so the leaders negotiated with Venice to take them by sea, rather than going overland, and to supply them with provisions for a year. In addition the Venetians were to provide their own troops and receive

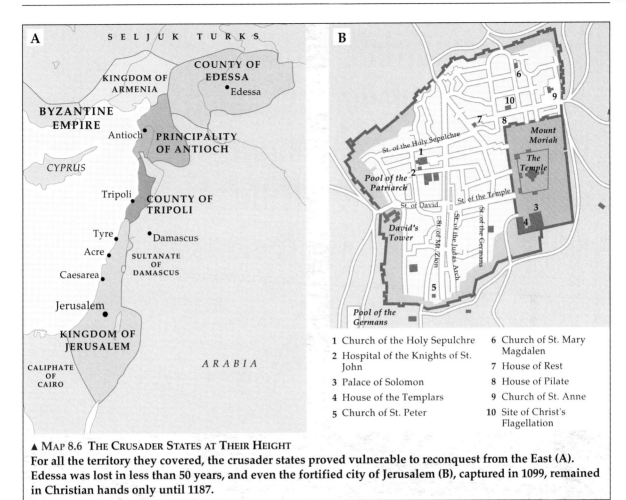

**A**

SELJUK TURKS

KINGDOM OF ARMENIA

COUNTY OF EDESSA
•Edessa

BYZANTINE EMPIRE

Antioch•  PRINCIPALITY OF ANTIOCH

*CYPRUS*

Tripoli•  COUNTY OF TRIPOLI

Tyre•
Acre•   SULTANATE OF DAMASCUS
Caesarea•
•Damascus

Jerusalem•

KINGDOM OF JERUSALEM

CALIPHATE OF CAIRO

*ARABIA*

**B**

6
10
9
7  8
St. of the Holy Sepulchre
1
Pool of the Patriarch   2
St. of David   St. of the Temple
David's Tower
5
Pool of the Germans

Mount Moriah
*The Temple*
3
4

St. of Mt. Zion
St. of the Judas Arch
St. of the Germans

1 Church of the Holy Sepulchre
2 Hospital of the Knights of St. John
3 Palace of Solomon
4 House of the Templars
5 Church of St. Peter
6 Church of St. Mary Magdalen
7 House of Rest
8 House of Pilate
9 Church of St. Anne
10 Site of Christ's Flagellation

▲ MAP 8.6  THE CRUSADER STATES AT THEIR HEIGHT
**For all the territory they covered, the crusader states proved vulnerable to reconquest from the East (A). Edessa was lost in less than 50 years, and even the fortified city of Jerusalem (B), captured in 1099, remained in Christian hands only until 1187.**

half the conquests. The Venetians proposed that the crusaders cancel their debt by aiding them in taking the trading port and Christian city of Zara, across the Adriatic from Venice. Although shocked at the proposal of attacking a Christian city, the crusaders were too far in debt to the Venetians to refuse. The Venetians and the crusade's leaders then persuaded the crusaders to attack Constantinople. The city, divided by factional strife, easily fell. Although Innocent III tried to stop the crusaders, they sacked the city and burned part of it. The Venetians and crusaders divided what remained of the Byzantine Empire into feudal principalities, but Western control lasted only until 1261.

*Further Crusades*  With the Muslims of Egypt in control of Jerusalem, later crusaders tried new tactics. Emperor Frederick II married the heiress of the Latin Kingdom of Jerusalem and negotiated directly with the Muslim leaders to regain Jerusalem; the treaty did not long outlast him. King Louis IX of France tried two disastrous expeditions to North Africa (sometimes called the Sixth and Seventh Crusades), but neither succeeded and Louis died in the last attempt in Tunisia.

◆ MILITARY-RELIGIOUS ORDERS

Soon after the First Crusade, a new kind of institution, the military-religious order, was founded. The military-religious orders combined the dedication, discipline, and organizational experience of monasticism with the military purposes of the crusade. The orders offered armed

▲ KNIGHTS IN COMBAT

**This contemporaneous manuscript illustration is a splendid depiction, full of motion and action, of two knights jousting. The figure on the left is thought to be Richard the Lion-Hearted, battling with Saladin himself.**

By permission of the British Library (1007628.011)

escorts and safe lodgings to pilgrims on their way to Palestine. The orders became indispensable for the Latin Kingdom, assuming a major role in supplying the settlers with services, goods, defense, and means of communication back to Europe.

*Templars*  The first of three great orders to emerge from the crusades was the Knights of the Temple, or Templars, founded sometime before 1120 by a group of French knights. The knights took the three monastic vows of poverty, chastity, and obedience and, like monks, lived together in their own convents or communities. The Templars assumed a major role in the maintenance of safe routes between Europe and the crusader states

and in the defense of the Kingdom of Jerusalem. The order also transported and guarded moneys in support of continued war, and thus became the most important banking institution of the age until its suppression by the pope in 1312.

*Hospitalers*  The Knights of the Hospital of St. John of Jerusalem, or Hospitalers, founded about 1130, enjoyed an even longer history. Never as numerous or as wealthy as the Templars, they still made a major contribution to the defense of the Kingdom of Jerusalem. With the fall of Acre in 1291 the knights moved their headquarters to Cyprus, then to Rhodes, and finally to Malta. As the Knights of Malta, they ruled the island until 1798. This "sovereign order" of the Knights of

Malta survives today as an exclusively philanthropic confraternity.

***Teutonic Knights***  About 1190, German pilgrims organized the Teutonic Knights as a hospital order. Reorganized as a military order at the end of the twelfth-century, the Teutonic Knights defended the eastern frontiers in Transylvania (in modern Romania) and, in 1229, in Prussia. There they became the armed vanguard of the German eastward expansion and conquered for themselves an extensive domain along the shores of the Baltic Sea. In 1525 the last grand master, Albert of Hohenzollern, adopted Lutheranism and secularized the order and its territories.

### ◆ RESULTS OF THE CRUSADES

Although the crusades did not produce a permanent Western political presence in Asia Minor, the whole experience of the campaigns and the contact with the East had a profound effect on Europe. When the Ottoman Turks, successors to the Seljuks, finally seized the islands of Cyprus and Crete, the Europeans had already found new routes to the Far East and were in the midst of a far broader overseas expansion.

***Warfare***  The crusades had a powerful influence on military technology. After their initial invasions, the crusaders waged a largely defensive war, becoming particularly skilled in the art of constructing castles. The numerous remains of crusader castles in nearly all the Eastern lands reflect these advances in such features as the overhanging tower parapets, from which oil or missiles could be rained down on attackers, and the angular castle entranceways that prevented the enemy from shooting directly at the gates. Islamic castles show a similar evolution toward a more advanced military design. Coincident with improvement of castle building was greater sophistication in siege engines to break down walls and gates. Battering rams, towers, mining under the walls (sapping), and catapults for throwing stones at walls all were used.

***Economy***  Historians still cannot draw up an exact balance sheet that registers accurately the economic gains and losses of the crusades. Although the campaigns were expensive, they also put a considerable amount of money in circulation by paying for weapons, provisions, shipping, and accommodations. Some of the money was drained to the East and only partially recovered in booty. Nevertheless, the crusades stimulated trade in

▼ HOSPITALERS IN RHODES

**This fifteenth-century manuscript depiction of the capture of the island of Rhodes commemorates an event in 1306, when the Hospitaler knights attacked this fortress from the neighboring island of Cyprus. Wearing their distinctive tunic with its white cross, the Hospitalers swarmed through Rhodes, which they were to control until it was conquered by the Ottomans in 1522.**

Bibliothèque Nationale de France, Paris

sugar, spices, and similar products from the East and encouraged the production of luxury goods, such as silk cloth, in Europe itself.

Since expenses for the crusades exhausted traditional sources of revenue, popes and princes began to impose direct taxes on their own lands and subjects. To finance the Third Crusade in 1188, for example, the pope authorized, and the princes collected, the so-called Saladin tithe, a direct tax of 10 percent imposed on all clerical and lay revenues. (Previously, European governments had made little use of direct taxes, because they were difficult to assess and collect.) The imposition of the Saladin tithe and subsequent direct taxes required new institutional methods for assessments, collecting of moneys, and transferring funds to where they were most needed. The crusades, in other words, encouraged Western princes to develop taxation for government expense.

*Explorations*   The crusades encouraged a curiosity about exotic cultures. Starting from the crusader principalities in the East, first missionaries and then merchants penetrated deep into central Asia, and by the early thirteenth century they had reached China. Their reports, especially the memoirs of the Venetian Marco Polo at the close of the thirteenth century, gave Europe abundant information about East Asia and helped inspire Western navigators in the late fifteenth and sixteenth centuries to seek new ways to trade with China directly. The desire to explore, conquer other cultures, and spread Christianity that was part of the crusades inspired later imperialism.

# SUMMARY

◆

The period from 1000 to 1150 was vigorously creative in every level of European life. Europe had changed substantially from what it was during the reign of Charlemagne. Its economy was more diversified and productive, its society more complex, its government more effective, its religion more organized. Europe had expanded its control into Spain, into the Slavic lands to the East, and even into Palestine. But the very innovations of the age posed severe problems for European society. How could the new forms of economic endeavor be reconciled with the older hostility and suspicion toward a life of buying and selling? How could the rising power of monarchs be reconciled with the self-consciousness and self-interest of the nobility, the reformed and independent Church, and the privileged towns? From about 1150 the West was trying to consolidate its recent advances and bring them into harmony with its older heritage. This effort at consolidation, reconciliation, and synthesis is the theme of Western history from 1150 to 1300.

# QUESTIONS FOR FURTHER THOUGHT

◆

**1. It is said that the invasions of the Vikings, Magyars, and Muslims created the conditions that gave rise to feudalism. Do you agree with this statement, or would you point to other factors in the development of feudalism?**

**2. In a modern democracy, it is hard to imagine a strictly hierarchical society, but to understand the Middle Ages it is necessary to do so. How would you explain the medieval hierarchy to a fellow student?**

**3. What factors made the crusades possible? Do you think that the crusades would have been less violent if Western Christians had a greater understanding of Islam?**

# RECOMMENDED READING

◆

## Sources

*Alexiad of Anna Comnena*. Elizabeth A. S. Dawes (tr.). 1978. A Greek version of the First Crusade.

*Benton, John F. (ed.). *Self and Society in Medieval France: The Memoirs of Abbot Guibert of Nogent (1064?–c. 1125)*. 1970. An autobiography.

*Fitz Stephen, William. *Norman London,* with an essay by Sir Frank Stenton and introduction by F. Donald Logan. 1990. A description of London.

*The Life of Christina of Markyate*. C. H. Talbot (tr.). 1987.

Peters, Edward (ed.). *The First Crusade: The Chronicle of Fulcher of Chartres and Other Source Materials*. 1971. Sources that detail the First Crusade.

*Shinners, John (ed.). *Medieval Popular Religion, 1000–1500, A Reader*. 1997.

*The Song of Roland*. D. P. R. Owen (tr.). 1990. Many translations are available.

Stenton, Frank (ed.). *The Bayeux Tapestry*. 1957.

*Tierney, Brian (ed.). *The Crisis of Church and State, 1050–1300*. 1964. A selection of primary resources illustrating disputes between Church and state.

Whitelock, Dorothy (ed.). *The Anglo-Saxon Chronicle*. 1961.

## Studies

*Arnold, Benjamin. *Medieval Germany, 500–1300: A Political Interpretation*. 1997.

Atiya, Azia S. *Crusade, Commerce, and Culture*. 1962. An evaluation of the results of the crusades in European history.

*Barraclough, Geoffrey. *The Origins of Modern Germany*. 1963. Classic interpretation of medieval German history.

*Bloch, Marc. *Feudal Society*. L. A. Manyon (tr.). 1961. A classic work on the social, economic, and cultural institutions in feudal society.

Chibnall, Marjorie. *Anglo-Norman England, 1066–1166*. 1987.

*Douglas, David C. *William the Conqueror: The Norman Impact upon England*. 1966. Outstanding among many biographies.

*Duby, Georges. *The Knight, the Lady, and the Priest: The Making of Modern Marriage in Medieval France*. 1983.

*———. *Rural Economy and Country Life in the Medieval West*. Cynthia Postan (tr.). 1968. A synthesis of rural life from 800 to 1400.

*Dunbabin, Jean. *France in the Making, 843–1100*. 1987. From Carolingian to Capetian France.

Ennen, Edith. *The Medieval Town*. Natalie Fryde (tr.). 1979. By a German historian; now the best introductory survey available in English.

*Ganshof, François. *Feudalism*. P. Grierson (tr.). 1961. Standard introduction to feudal institutions.

Gold, Penny Schine. *The Lady and the Virgin: Image, Attitude, and Experience in Twelfth-Century France*. 1985. A study based on literary and charter evidence exploring the role of women.

Green, Judith A. *The Government of England under Henry I*. 1986. Considers expansion of governmental institutions under Henry I.

*Herlihy, David. *Medieval Households*. 1985. Demography and family structure.

*Phillips, J. R. S. *The Medieval Expansion of Europe*. 1988. Crusades, but also other contacts with the Orient and the first explorations.

*Reuter, Timothy. *Germany in the Middle Ages, 800–1056*. 1991. This is a modern survey, brief and suited to students.

*Riley-Smith, Jonathan. *The First Crusade and the Idea of Crusading*. 1986. Examines the idea of the First Crusade and its reinterpretations.

*Southern, Richard W. *The Making of the Middle Ages*. 1955. Classic essay on twelfth-century culture.

*Swanson, R. N. *Religion and Devotion in Europe, c. 1215–c. 1515*. 1995. An emphasis on medieval religious experiences such as the mass and pilgrimages. Good book for students.

*Tellenbach, Gerd. *Church, State, and Christian Society at the Time of the Investiture Contest*. R. F. Bennett (tr.). 1970.

---

*Available in paperback.

▲ GOD AS ARCHITECT OF THE UNIVERSE
**The notion of God creating the universe as an architect was common during the
Middle Ages. In this manuscript illumination, God is depicted holding a compass
and literally measuring the structure of the physical world.**
Vienna, Austrian National Library

# THE FLOWERING OF MEDIEVAL CIVILIZATION

The period from 1150 to the beginning of the thirteenth century was one of creativity in Western Europe. The refinements in living that the nobility were beginning to experience led to the creation of an elaborate court culture and a French vernacular literature that accompanied it. Women had a profound influence on the themes of that literature and on court behavior. Intellectual revival, which far outstripped the Carolingian and Ottonian renaissances, led to new sophistication in philosophy and theology and to the establishment of universities. University-educated men found careers in the Church, with the increasingly powerful monarchies, and in urban centers. A unifying theme of the flowering of medieval civilization was the strong sense of community and class identity that was developing in universities, guilds, villages, and among the nobility.

Monarchies expanded their control over their populations through bureaucracy and law. In pursuing the unification of their governments, they formalized feudal principles into governmental ones. The Church also continued to press forward its control over its bishops, abbots, and the religious beliefs of all Christians. Its claim was not unchallenged during this period, because the Church was faced with two widespread heresies. However, with the help of two new mendicant orders, the Franciscans and Dominicans, the Church was able to suppress the heresies. The continued religious enthusiasm and devotions of the laity are dramatically evident in the great Romanesque and Gothic churches that they gave their money to build.

| | Social Structure | Body Politic | Changes in the Organization of Production and in the Impact of Technology | Evolution of Family and Changing Gender Roles | War | Religion | Cultural Expression |
|---|---|---|---|---|---|---|---|
| **CHAPTER 9. THE FLOWERING OF MEDIEVAL CIVILIZATION** | | | | | | | |
| I. CULTURAL DEVELOPMENTS | ▨ | | | ▨ | | ▨ | ■ |
| II. THE STATES OF EUROPE | | ▨ | | | ▨ | ▨ | |
| III. THE CHURCH | | ▨ | | | | ▨ | ■ |

# I. Cultural Developments

The changes that were going on in European society in the twelfth and early thirteenth centuries brought about an intellectual revival that revolutionized education. Universities developed that offered bachelor of arts degrees and advanced degrees in theology, law, medicine, and science. The increased bureaucratization of monarchies, the commercial transactions in cities, and the development of canon (Church) and civil law in general increased the demand for educated men with university degrees. As society became wealthier and more expansive, the austere Romanesque architecture inspired by the Cluniac reform gave way to Gothic architecture.

## ◆ THE RISE OF UNIVERSITIES

During the High Middle Ages, a new institution, the university, came to assume a role in intellectual life that it has not since relinquished. The university ranks as one of the most influential creations of the medieval world.

*Monastic Schools* Up to about 1050, monastic schools had dominated intellectual development in the West (see map 9.1). But the monastic devotion to prayer, self-denial, and mystical meditation was not especially favorable to original thought, while the isolation of monasteries restricted the experiences of the monastic scholar and made difficult the exchange of ideas that intellectual progress requires.

*Cathedral Schools* From about 1050 to 1200, the cathedral, or bishop's school, assumed the intel-

lectual leadership in Europe. These schools were at first very fluid in their structure. The bishop's secretary, the chancellor, was usually in charge of the school and was responsible for inviting learned men, or "masters," to lecture to the students. Both students and masters roamed from town to town, seeking either the best teachers or the brightest (or best-paying) students and the most congenial atmosphere for their work. The

▲ **MAP 9.1 GREAT MONASTIC CENTERS OF LEARNING**

twelfth century was the age of the wandering scholars, who have left us charming traces of their spirit or at least that of their more frivolous members in the form of "goliardic" verses,[1] largely concerned with such unclerical subjects as the joys of wine, women, and song.

Townspeople frequently protested to the bishops or the king against the students, whom they resented because of their boisterous ways and because their clerical status—all students automatically took minor orders of clergy—gave them immunity from the local courts. Students for their part resented the high prices that townspeople charged for rooms, food, and drink. Riots involving town and gown (as clerics, students wore ecclesiastical dress) were violent and commonplace. To impose some order on this flux and to protect young students from incompetent or unorthodox teachers, the twelfth-century cathedral schools gradually insisted that masters possess a certification of their learning. The chancellor awarded this "license to teach," the ancestor of all modern academic degrees.

*Universities*   The throngs of masters and students, many of them strangers to the city in which they lectured and studied, eventually grouped themselves into guilds to protect their common interests. It was out of these spontaneously formed guilds of masters and students that the medieval university grew (*universitas* was a widely used Latin word for "guild," as discussed in Chapter 10). The masters in Paris, for example, formed a guild and received a royal charter in about 1200 and sanction from the Pope in 1231. These documents confirmed the guild's autonomy and authority to license teachers. By contrast, the University of Bologna had a guild of students who ran the university.

*Italian Universities*   Even in the early Middle Ages professional schools for the training of notaries, lawyers, and doctors survived in some Italian cities. The Italian schools enjoyed rapid

growth from the late eleventh century, which led to the formation of guilds. In Italy the students were older and professionally motivated, desiring degrees in canon law for a career in the church or in civil law (Justinian's *Corpus Juris Civilis*). Wishing to guarantee the quality of their training, the students rather than the professors constituted the dominant "university." At the oldest of these schools, the University of Bologna, the students established the fees to be paid to the professors and determined the hours and even the content of the lectures. Thomas Becket and Innocent III, who are discussed in this chapter, attended Bologna.

*The University of Paris*   The University of Paris became the model for northern Europe as professors founded schools at Oxford, Cambridge, Prague, and other cities throughout Europe (see map 9.2). These universities were run by the masters and granted the baccalaureate, or bachelor of arts degree. The curriculum was the *trivium* and *quadrivium* that Alcuin had developed in the Carolingian period (see p. 228). A master's degree involved further work and licensed the holder to teach. Higher degrees in theology, law, and medicine took five to seven years to complete. A candidate for a theology degree had to be thirty years old; the degree took seven years.

Students matriculated at a university in their early teens. They were expected to know Latin already and to have money for tuition and living expenses. At the University of Paris classes were in rented halls on the left bank of the river, and since the language of the lecturers was Latin, the area came to be—and still is—known as the Latin Quarter. Because the students were young, often poor, and undisciplined, Robert de Sorbonne founded a college, the first, in 1275 in Paris. Colleges provided meals, housing, and libraries for the students. Masters resided in the colleges and supervised student behavior. The system still exists at Oxford and Cambridge.

### ◆ SCHOLASTICISM

Scholasticism was both a way of reasoning and a body of writings: Scholastics applied dialectic to Christian dogma. Dialectic is the art of analyzing the logical relationships among propositions in a

---

[1]The exact etymology of the word *goliardic* remains unknown. It possibly derives from Goliath the Philistine, who was honored as a kind of antisaint by the boisterous students.

Perth
St. Andrews 1412

*NORTH SEA*

Dublin 1312
York
Cambridge 1209
Oxford 12th cent.
Rostock 1419
Kulm 1366

*ATLANTIC
OCEAN*

Louvain 1425
Cologne 1388
Erfurt 1379
Leipzig 1409
Caen 1432
Paris 12th cent.
Heidelberg 1385
Bamberg
Würzburg 1402
Cracow 1364
Angers 1229
Orléans 1309
Prague 1348
Poitiers 1432
Gray 1291
Dôle 1422
Pavia 1361
Piacenza 1248
Vienna 1365
Mantua 1433
Verona 1339
Ofen 1389
Bordeaux 1441
Geneva 1365
Vercelli 1228
Vicenza 1204
Fünfkirchen 1367
Grenoble 1339
Cividale 1353
Cahors 1332
Orange 1365
Turin 1405
Treviso 1318
Palencia 1212
Toulouse 1229
Avignon 1303
Padua 1222
Valladolid 1346
Ramiers 1295
Montpellier 12th Cent.
Aix 1409
Reggio 12th cent.
Ferrara 1391
Bologna 12th cent.
Coimbra 1308
Huesca 1354
Lucca 1369
Florence 1349
Salamanca 1227
Calatayud 1415
Perpignan 1350
Gerona 1446
Pisa 1343
Arezzo 1215
Perugia 1308
Ragusa
Alcalá de Henares 1293
Lérida 1300
Barcelona 1430
Siena 1246
Fermo 1398
Lisbon 1290
Valencia 1245
Orvieto 1377
Rome 1303
Seville 1254
Naples 1224
Salerno 12th cent.

*MEDITERRANEAN SEA*

0    150    300 Miles

Catania 1444

▲ MAP 9.2 MEDIEVAL UNIVERSITIES

dialogue or discourse. The method of presenting an argument was to state a proposition and then dispute its validity either orally or in writing. Scholasticism represented a shift from the humanistic studies of the early twelfth century. Cathedral schools such as Chartres emphasized familiarity with the classical authors, particularly Plato, and the ability to appreciate and write good Latin. But dialectic won out in the late twelfth century, partly because Aristotle's complete logic became available to Western scholars.

*Anselm of Canterbury*    The first thinker to explore, although still not rigorously, the theological applications of dialectic was St. Anselm of Canterbury (1033–1109). Anselm defined his own intellectual interests as "faith seeking to understand"—in actuality, faith seeking to find logical

▶ The university as a community of scholars, teachers, and learners was a medieval innovation. Its structure was such that students exercised a degree of control that they rarely possess today. Since there were no salaries, professors relied on tuition fees for their daily bread, and students could starve out unpopular teachers merely by refusing to attend their classes. However, in other aspects, student life then was much the same as it is today. These scenes from a fifteenth-century manuscript show students gambling, opposing each other in disputations (class debates), and engaging in other activities of dormitory life.
University Library of Freiburg-im-Breisgau

consistency among its beliefs. He tried to show a necessary, logical connection between the traditional Judeo-Christian dogma that God is a perfect being and a logical proof that God exists. From the time of Anselm, Scholastic thought assumed that the human intellect was powerful enough to probe the logical and metaphysical patterns within which even God had to operate.

*Abelard* Peter Abelard (1079–1142) brought a new rigor and popularity to dialectical theology. We know a great deal about Peter Abelard because he wrote an autobiography later in his life called *Historia calamitatum* (*Story of My Calamities*). Eldest son of a petty noble from Brittany, Abelard was destined for warfare and lordship, but his intellectual interests overrode this career. As a wandering scholar, he came to Paris, entered into a decisive disputation with the leading theologian, and began to give lectures. His brilliance attracted the attention of a clergyman attached to Notre Dame Cathedral, who engaged Abelard to tutor his niece, Héloïse (ca. 1100–ca. 1163). Héloïse had a convent training and her uncle wanted to further her education by hiring the best instructor in Paris. Despite an age difference of twenty-four years, Abelard tells his readers, they fell in love and conceived a child. They had a clandestine marriage because Héloïse knew that it would ruin his career if he, as a member of the clergy, were married. He would have had to give up his lecturing, an activity only clergy could do. Her uncle, betrayed and angry, had thugs castrate Abelard to

▲ THE **Doorway of the Virgin at Chartres cathedral in France shows the seven liberal arts—arithmetic, astronomy, dialectic, geometry, grammar, music, and rhetoric—represented as female figures. These female figures each held a symbol of their discipline and they were used through Europe. The seven liberal arts formed the core subjects for the baccalaureate and the master's degrees.**
Mary Ann Sullivan

punish him. Abelard and Héloïse then entered separate monasteries.

The child of their marriage, Astrolabe, was born at Abelard's sister's home. Héloïse became a respected abbess, but in her letters to Abelard, it is apparent that she continued to care about him with undiminished love. Abelard's replies admonish her to pray and to administer the nunnery.

Abelard continued his writing, and in *Sic et Non* ("Yes and No") he used what became the standard Scholastic method of argumentation,

posing a formal question and citing authorities on both sides. Abelard assembled 150 theological questions and marshaled authorities from the Bible, Church councils, and Church fathers for arguments on either side. He made no effort to reconcile the discrepancies, but left the authorities standing in embarrassing juxtaposition (see "Abelard's *Sic et Non*," p. 295). *Sic et Non* implied that one must either enlist dialectic to reconcile the conflicts or concede that the faith was a tissue of contradictions. His book caused a furor of debate, and finally a Church council condemned it. To avoid charges of heresy, he was forced to throw it into the flames and submit to the Church. But the method of argument that he used, that of posing a question and then mustering arguments to support or refute it, became characteristic of medieval Scholasticism.

▼ **HÉLOÏSE AND ABELARD, FROM ROMAN DE LA ROSE**
**Already a famous professor in Paris, Abelard began a secret relationship with Héloïse, and in revenge her relatives had him castrated. The two were then separated for decades, and their correspondence remains one of the most powerful human documents of medieval times. Despite the conventions of the day, Héloïse was clearly an equal partner in the relationship, as is indicated in this fifteenth-century depiction of the pair engaged in intense discussion.**
Giraudon/Art Resource, NY

## ABELARD'S *SIC ET NON*

◆

*Completed in 1138, Peter Abelard's* Sic et Non *("Yes and No") explained the techniques for reconciling divergent opinions in theology and law. His approach reflects the ambition of Scholasticism to bolster faith through reason.*

"Among the many words of the holy fathers some seem not only to differ from one another but even to contradict one another. . . . Why should it seem surprising if we, lacking the guidance of the holy spirit, fail to understand them?

"Our achievement of understanding is impeded especially by unusual modes of expression and by the different significances that can be attached to one and the same word. We must also take special care that we are not deceived by corruptions of the text or by false attributions when sayings of the [Church] fathers are quoted that seem to differ from the truth or to be contrary to it; for many apocryphal writings are set down under names of saints to enhance their authority, and even the texts of the divine scripture are corrupted by the errors of scribes. If, in scripture, anything seems absurd, you are not permitted to say, 'The author of this book did not hold the truth,' but rather that the book is defective or that the interpreter erred or that you do not understand. But if anything seems contrary to truth in the works of later authors, the reader or auditor is free to judge, so that he may approve what is pleasing and reject what gives offense, unless the matter is established by certain reason or canonical authority.

"In view of these considerations we have undertaken to collect various sayings of the fathers that give rise to questioning because of their apparent contradictions. Assiduous and frequent questioning is indeed the first key to wisdom. For by doubting we come to inquiry; and through inquiring we perceive the truth."

From Brian Tierney, et al., *The Middle Ages: Sources of Medieval History*, 5th Ed. (McGraw-Hill Companies, 1992), pp. 172–175.

*Reception of Aristotle* By the end of the twelfth century, dialectical argument was supreme in Paris and elsewhere. One reason it predominated was that, after the middle of the twelfth century, translators working chiefly in Spain and Sicily introduced European scholars to hitherto unknown works of Aristotle as well as to the great commentary that the Muslim Averroës had written on them. Christian thinkers now had at their disposal the full Aristotelian corpus, and it confronted them with a philosophical system based solely on observation and human reason. Aristotle's logic drove Western scholars to examine his works and their own faith through Aristotelian logic. The difficult task of reconciling Aristotelian reason and nature with Christian revelation and divine grace remained the central philosophical problem of the thirteenth century.

*Thomas Aquinas* The most gifted representative of Scholastic philosophy, and the greatest Christian theologian since Augustine, was St. Thomas Aquinas (1225?–1274), whose career well illustrates the character of thirteenth-century intellectual life. At age seventeen Aquinas entered the new Dominican Order, perhaps attracted by its commitment to scholarship; he studied at Monte Cassino and Naples and later, as a Dominican, at Cologne and Paris (see map 9.2). His most influential teacher was another Dominican, Albertus Magnus, a German who wrote extensively on theology and natural science, especially biology. Aquinas was no intellectual recluse; he lectured at Paris and traveled widely across Europe. His was such an active mind that when he dined with King Louis IX of France, the king provided him with scribes to keep notes on his brilliant discourse.

Aquinas produced a prodigious amount of writing: commentaries on biblical books and Aristotelian works, short essays on philosophical problems, and the *Summa contra Gentiles*, which was probably intended for Dominican missionaries working to convert heretics and infidels. His most important work, however, was one he did not live to finish. Divided into three parts on God, Man, and Christ, the *Summa Theologica* was meant to provide a comprehensive introduction to Christian theology and to present a systematic view of the universe that would do justice to all truth, natural and revealed, pagan and Christian.

Aquinas brought to his task a subtle and perceptive intellect, and his system rests on several fundamental, delicate compromises. In regard to faith and reason, he taught that both are roads to a single truth. Reason is based ultimately on sense experience, as Aristotle argued. It is a powerful instrument, but insufficient to teach people all that God wishes them to know. Nature is good, and humans can achieve some partial, temporary happiness in this life. But nature alone cannot carry them to ultimate understanding of matters such as the Trinity. These matters must be accepted on the basis of faith, not reason. In the final analysis, God's mind is infinite, while human beings' minds are finite.

Building his proof for the existence of God on Aristotelian logic, Aquinas used *a posteriori* arguments, or arguments based on empirical observation. For instance: All motion is caused; we can observe motion; but there cannot be an infinite regress of movers, therefore, there must be a prime mover who is God.

The *Summa* shows certain characteristic weaknesses of Scholasticism. Aquinas affirmed that natural truth is ultimately grounded in observation, but in fact, he observed very little. He borrowed from Aristotle rather than doing his own observation or experimentation. Many later thinkers found his system too speculative, too elaborate. Nonetheless, the *Summa* remains an unquestioned masterpiece of Western theology. It offers comment on an enormous range of theological, philosophical, and ethical problems, and consistently demonstrates openness, insight, and wisdom.

*Duns Scotus*  Aquinas' system fell under critical scrutiny in the generation following his death. Among his early critics, the most influential was a Scottish Franciscan, John Duns Scotus (1265?–1308). Drawing inspiration from St. Augustine, Duns Scotus affirmed that faith was logically prior to reason. His arguments were based on *a priori* reasoning, a Platonic rather than Aristotelian concept that deduced arguments from concepts already held in the mind. To Duns Scotus the proof of God's existence was not based, as

with Aquinas, on the perception of change in the universe, for he did not trust the accuracy of sense observation; rather, it derived from an exclusively intellectual analysis of the concept of God as a necessary being, an argument closer to Anselm before him and Descartes in the seventeenth century.

## ◆ SPIRITUAL APPROACHES TO KNOWLEDGE

Many people who thought deeply about the nature of God and religion argued that the dialectic approach was not the best way to achieve knowledge. They argued that a spiritual approach based on prayer and humility would bring about a greater understanding of God. They emphasized the human side of the religion by encouraging worship of Mary.

*Worship of Mary*  Mary, mother of Jesus, became an important figure in the dedication of churches and in popular worship. Her presence added a humanizing touch to the religion and invited prayers of intercession with Jesus and God. In the early Middle Ages, a stern, mature Jesus was depicted as a lawgiver in churches, but in the late twelfth century Mary with an infant Jesus on her hip came to dominate church dedications and sculpture.

*Cistercians and St. Bernard*  The Cistercians took their name from their first house at Cîteau. Although founded in 1098, their prominence came with the arrival of Bernard of Clairvaux (ca. 1090–1153) with thirty companions in 1112. St. Bernard played a major role in European politics, including the condemnation of Abelard's *Sic et Non*. He preached the Second Crusade and served as adviser to the monarchs of Europe.

The Cistercians advocated a greater simplicity than the Cluniacs. Their robes were made of white, undyed wool; for that reason they were called the "white monks." They avoided the grand churches and elaborate ceremonies of the Cluniacs. Their emphasis, instead, was on emotional devotion to Christ's and Mary's humility. All of their churches were dedicated to Mary.

St. Bernard praised the human, nurturing quality of Mary in hymns as well as in devotional practices.

The Cistercian order spread rapidly both within the older borders of Europe and into frontier lands in northern England, along the newly reclaimed wasteland of Flanders, and in the newly conquered Slavic lands to the east. The order became identified with the expansion of Europe and the spread of efficient estate management and agriculture.

*Women's Spirituality*  Women could not attend universities in the Middle Ages, so their intellectual life centered in the nunnery or court. Perhaps because of the new emphasis on the worship of Mary, women became more prominent in the spiritual life of the Church. Hildegard of Bingen (d. 1179) was an abbess, musician, and writer. She wrote in Latin on scientific questions and revelations and corresponded with emperors and popes.

Other women became well known for their piety and their mystical visions. Marie D'Oignies (d. 1213), whose life was recorded by Jacques de Vitry, was a founding mother of the Beguines, a group of religious women to be discussed in chapter 10. Withdrawing to a cell connected to a monastery, she had a reputation as a healer and an ascetic. Women throughout the Middle Ages became anchorites, or holy women living in cells connected to churches or monasteries. Women who pursued a rigorous, individual asceticism inspired other women and men to lead a spiritual life.

### ◆ ROMANESQUE ARCHITECTURE

The increased prosperity and the revival of popular piety in the Early Middle Ages produced two major new developments in architecture, sculpture, painting, and illustration. The austerity of the Cluniac period led to the sober Romanesque style—a style that took the Roman, rounded arch as its model. The Cistercian movement and the greater social, cultural, and technological exuberance of the mid-twelfth century expressed its piety with sunlit churches of the Gothic style (see illustration on p. 298).

*The Romanesque Style*  The architectural and artistic style of *Romanesque* (meaning "of Roman origins") took some elements from earlier models, but not exclusively; it also drew on other artistic traditions, such as Germanic, Byzantine, and Arab. Thus, Romanesque buildings in different parts of western Europe had distinctive design features.

The most impressive artistic monuments left to us from the Romanesque period include churches, monasteries, and castles. One objective in the Romanesque style was to roof churches in stone rather than wooden beams and thatch roofs that were vulnerable to burning. Around the year 1000, small stone-roofed churches began to appear, especially in southern Europe. At first the builders used the simple barrel, or tunnel, vault. Because of the weight of the masonry roof, walls had to be thick and the windows had to be small. Engineers then developed and mastered the use of the groin vault, which is formed by the intersection of two barrel vaults. The area of intersection is called the bay, and the roof over the bay is supported at four points, not by the entire length of the lateral walls. Bays could be built next to bays, an entire church could be roofed with stone, windows could be enlarged, and the monotony of tunnel vaulting would be avoided.

*Romanesque Decoration*  Romanesque churches were decorated on the exterior with stone sculpture. Romanesque statues, which exist by the thousands, show a marked quality of antirealism, a refusal to allow visual accuracy to dominate portrayals. The artists were striving to present a world as seen by faith. Christ, for example, had to be shown larger than the other figures, in keeping with his dignity. Demons and monsters, many drawn from the popular imagination, abound in Romanesque sculpture. While similar to Byzantine portrayals in its antirealism, Romanesque style, unlike the Byzantine, overflows with movement, tension, excitement, and the spirit of mystical exhilaration. Romanesque statuary documents the exuberant spirit of this age of reform, when people seemed convinced that God was actively at work among them, setting right the world.

298

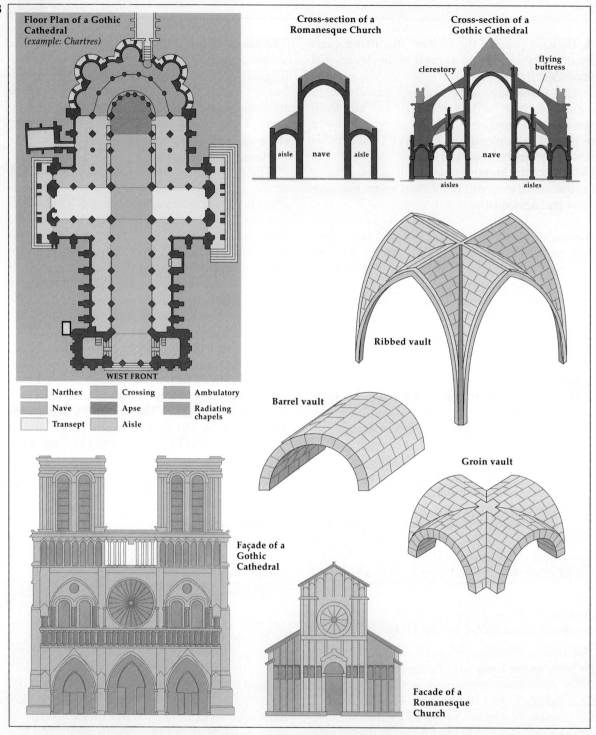

**Floor Plan of a Gothic Cathedral**
(*example: Chartres*)

WEST FRONT

| | Narthex | | Crossing | | Ambulatory |
| | Nave | | Apse | | Radiating chapels |
| | Transept | | Aisle | | |

**Cross-section of a Romanesque Church**

aisle    nave    aisle

**Cross-section of a Gothic Cathedral**

clerestory

flying buttress

nave

aisles    aisles

Ribbed vault

Barrel vault

Groin vault

Façade of a Gothic Cathedral

Facade of a Romanesque Church

▲ The Romanesque cathedral shown in cross-section in the middle top and as a façade in the bottom shows the simple nave and isle construction of the cathedral. The roof was either a barrel vault or a groin vault. The Gothic cathedral shown in the floor plan and the façade could be a more elaborate structure because of the use of flying buttresses, shown upper right, which formed an external skeleton supporting the walls. The buttresses permitted the walls to have great expanses of windows since they were not bearing all the weight of the stone roof. The ribbed vault permitted greater height in the Gothic cathedral.

▲ PISA CATHEDRAL, CA. 1063–1272
One of the finest architectural ensembles in the new Romanesque styles of the eleventh and twelfth centuries
is the cathedral and its surrounding buildings in Pisa, Italy. Although the famous leaning tower, which is now
restored to nearly vertical, is the best known of these buildings, the huge marble-clad cathedral was in fact
regarded as the supreme achievement of the Pisans and was widely influential in church building throughout
Italy.
Casimir/eStock Photo

***Other Characteristics of Romanesque Style***
Nobles became consumers of art and architecture
for building and furnishing their increasingly
elaborate castles, but art remained, in most of its
forms, the servant of the Church. The Cluniac
monastic reform in the eleventh century brought
with it a liturgical revival; the Cluniacs were especially devoted to (and occasionally criticized
for) sumptuous religious services. Liturgical
needs stimulated the art of metalwork (which
produced chalices and other sacred vessels),
glass making, and the weaving of fine fabrics for
priests' vestments.

The Gregorian chant (named for Pope Gregory
the Great, but in fact representing the traditional
plainsong of the Church of Rome) was established
as the common music of the Western Church in
the Carolingian epoch. The eleventh and twelfth
centuries witnessed the development of poly-
phonic music (part-singing). The coordination of
the vocal parts in choral music also required systems of musical notation. A monk named Guido

d'Arezzo is credited with giving the familiar
names to the notes.

#### ◆ THE GOTHIC STYLE

Artists as well as theologians were attempting to
present a systematic view of the universe that was
reflective of all truth. The artistic counterpart to
the Scholastic *Summas* was the Gothic cathedral.

***Gothic Architecture*** Sixteenth-century critics
coined the word *Gothic* as an expression of contempt for these supposedly barbarous medieval
buildings. In fact, the Goths had disappeared
some 500 years before any Gothic churches were
built. As used today, *Gothic* refers to the style of
architecture and art that initially developed in the
royal lands in France, including Paris and its surroundings, from about 1150. The abbey church of
Saint-Denis near Paris, built by the Abbot Suger in
1144, is usually taken as the first authentic example of the Gothic style. In the thirteenth century

▲ Tympanum of South Portal of St. Pierre, Moissac, ca. 1115–1135
**The revival of sculpture is one of the noteworthy achievements of Romanesque art. Integrating architecture and sculpture, this tympanum (the semicircular space above a church portal) shows the Second Coming of Christ, attended by symbols of the evangelists and the kings of the world seated in rows divided by stylized clouds.**
Giraudon/Art Resource, NY

the Gothic style spread widely through Europe and found special application in the large churches built by two new thirteenth-century religious orders, the Franciscan and Dominican orders.

Technically, three engineering devices helped stamp the Gothic style: the pointed rather than rounded arch; ribbed vaulting, which concentrated support around the lines of thrust and gave the buildings a visibly delineated skeleton; and the flying buttress, an external support that allowed the walls to be made higher and lighter. The flying buttress also freed sections of the walls from the function of supporting the roof and therefore permitted the use of large areas for windows. The windows were filled with stained glass that depicted scenes from the Bible or from saints' lives. Romanesque architects had pioneered all

three devices, but the Gothic engineers combined them and used them with unprecedented vigor and boldness.

The sculpture adorning buildings also represented innovation. Romanesque sculpture often conveyed great emotional power but did not reflect the natural world. Sculptors now wanted their works to emulate reality, or at least its handsomest parts (decorative foliage, for example, was carved with such accuracy that the botanical models can be identified). Their statues portray real and usually cheerful people, who subtly exert their own personalities without destroying the harmony of the whole.

*The Gothic Spirit*  These magnificent churches with their hundreds of statues took decades to construct and decorate, and many were never

▲ ST. ETIENNE, CAEN, VAULTS, CA. 1115–1120
St. Etienne, Caen, was begun by William the Conqueror in 1067 and is considered a superb example of
Norman Romanesque architecture. It was originally supposed to have a wooden roof, but it was vaulted
in stone between 1115 and 1120. Each section of the roof is held up by six ribs that meet at the center and
two arches, all of which rest on pillars at the side of the nave. The resultant pattern added to the sense of
height and drew the eye ever upward toward heaven.
Foto Marburg/Art Resource, NY

completed. The builders intended that the
churches provide a comprehensive view of the
universe and instruction in its sacred history. One

principal element of the Gothic aesthetic is a
strong sense of order. The naked ribs and buttresses and the intricate vaulting constitute a

▲ AMIENS CATHEDRAL, CA. 1220–1236
**Built between 1220 and 1236, Amiens Cathedral exemplifies the structure of a Gothic cathedral. The weight of the walls is supported by a system of buttresses and ribbed vaults, which allowed medieval builders to break up the walls with luminous areas of stained glass. The colored light that poured into these massive structures gave them an otherworldly majesty never before achieved.**
Scala/Art Resource, NY

◄ In contrast to Romanesque sculpture, which overflows with great displays of emotion, Gothic sculpture evokes a sense of calm and orderly reality, as can be seen in the jamb figures on the central portal of Chartres Cathedral.
Foto Marburg/Art Resource, NY

spectacular geometry that instills in the viewer a vivid impression of intelligence and logical relationships. The churches, reflecting the structure of the universe, taught that God, the master builder, created and still governs the natural world with similar logic.

The most distinctive aspect of the Gothic style is its use of light in a manner unique in the history of architecture. Once within the church, the visitor has entered a realm defined and infused by a warm, colored glow. In Christian worship light is one of the most ancient, common, and versatile symbols. It suggests to the worshiper mystical illumination, spiritual beauty, grace, and divinity itself.

The thirteenth century was a great age of cathedral building. Gothic architecture reached its highest point with cathedrals in France, including those of Chartres, Paris, Amiens, and Rheims. England and Germany also produced fine Gothic cathedrals, such as Salisbury, Lincoln, and Cologne. As the style was perfected, more height and light could be added to the cathedrals. The most extreme example is Sainte-Chapelle in Paris, where the walls were replaced entirely with windows. Enhancing the style perfected in the thirteenth century, later additions came to be more elaborate, and by the fifteenth century the encrustation of the cathedrals with carvings and the height of the naves and towers have led historians to call them "wedding-cake Gothic."

### ◆ COURT CULTURE

At the same time that universities were being established and Gothic cathedrals were being built, the nobility was developing its own distinctive culture. Wealth, leisure, and refinements in living learned from the Arabs and Greeks influenced the culture. A new code of behavior that included

◄ Sainte-Chapelle, Paris, Interior, 1243–1248
Sainte-Chapelle, the private chapel attached to the French royal palace in Paris, was built between 1243 and 1248 to house relics brought back from the crusades by Louis IX. The building was deliberately intended to resemble a reliquary, and the enormous jewel-colored stained-glass windows make up three-quarters of its wall surface.
Giraudon/Art Resource, NY

chivalry and courtly love became standard for all European nobility and was widely imitated by the urban elite as well.

*Chivalry*  A new code of behavior refined the manners of knights. Added to bravery and loyalty, exemplified in *The Song of Roland* (see p. 255), were devotion to the Church, polite behavior, and rules for behavior at the table and in the lord's court. *Courtesy* means the manners appropriate to the noble court. The knight no longer was simply dubbed with a sword when he reached the age of twenty-one, but instead went through a religious ceremony that included a vigil and the blessing of his arms, a ritual cleansing, and an oath to protect women and the Church. In addition to using weapons, training for knighthood included learn-

ing to sing or play an instrument, to carve a roast and serve it to a lord and lady, to dance, and to dress appropriately. The etiquette of tournaments was elaborately established and taught to knights when they were young.

*Courtly Love*  Courtly love, or the polite relations between men and women, developed at the court of Eleanor of Aquitaine, of whom we shall speak presently. While married to Henry II of England, she and her sons and daughters spent much of their time at the seat of her duchy in Poitiers. One of the writers they patronized, Andreas Capellanus, updated Ovid's writings on love in a book called *The Art of Courtly Love*. The book instructs men on how to please and seduce women of different ranks, although when he refers to the love of a noble for a peasant he sanctions rape: "Do not hesitate to take what you seek and to embrace her by force." According to Andreas, Eleanor and her daughters set up a court to correct men who erred or to set tasks, such as fighting in a number of tournaments, for those wishing to win the love of a particular lady.

In an age of arranged marriages, in which love might or might not be present between the couples, courtly love permitted an atmosphere for flirtation. Historians debate whether adultery was widespread in these courts. Historians are also undecided about the influence courtly love had on the position of noblewomen in society: Did it trivialize them by making them mere objects of sexual desire, or did it make them more valued and respected?

▼ **The most popular subject for courtly romance was the legends surrounding King Arthur. In the first picture, King Arthur is surrounded by his knights. His queen, Guinevere, is in the doorway. Below the induction of a knight to the Round Table is shown. The altar in the background indicates the religious nature of the knighting ceremony. Above is the romance of Tristan and below is the Holy Grail.**
Musée Condé Chantilly/Dagli Orti/The Art Archive

*Noblewomen* As in the early Middle Ages, women in the twelfth century spent much of their time in and around their castles. The castles had become much more comfortable, with pleasant quarters attached to gardens reserved for the women. Although noblewomen still faced the tasks of household and estate management in the absence of their husbands, the new luxury goods available and courtly manners provided more entertainment for them in their leisure hours. For noblewomen, as for knights, acquiring skill in singing, dancing, and playing musical instruments was important. With luxurious silks more available since the crusades, dress became more elaborate and noblewomen undertook embroidery with silk as well as woolen thread. Noblewomen learned to read and write vernacular poetry and prose, which was undergoing a great vogue in the twelfth century.

*Vernacular Literature* Acting as patrons, the nobility encouraged the development of vernacular literature. Scholars believe that this literature, or some oral version of it, was appreciated well beyond aristocratic circles. Townspeople and even peasants seem to have delighted in hearing of the adventures of knights and ladies.

Of the vernacular literatures of Europe, only Anglo-Saxon possesses a substantial number of surviving writings that antedate the year 1000. In forming the literary tastes of Europe, the Romance tongues (the vernacular languages descended from Latin) achieved prominence, particularly French by the eleventh and twelfth centuries. Castilian was slightly later than French in producing an important literature in Spain, and Italian did not emerge as a major literary language until the late thirteenth century.

There were three principal genres of vernacular literature: the heroic epic, of which *The Song of Roland* is the best example; troubadour lyric poetry; and the courtly romance.

*The Troubadours* Very different from the heroic epic is troubadour lyric poetry. The novelty of this complex poetry is its celebration of women and of love, as opposed to heroic epics, which were written for the masculine society of the battle camp. The troubadours sang at courts, in which women exerted a powerful influence. In a mobile age, when knights and nobles would be away for long periods on crusades and wars, their mothers, wives, and daughters influenced the literature that was heard within the castle walls.

The troubadour usually addressed a lady of superior social station, almost always someone else's wife, whom he had little chance of winning. Courtly love (at least as the troubadours present it) was not a dalliance but quite literally a means of rescuing the lover from despondency and introducing him into an earthly paradise of his imagination. This discovery and intensive exploration of the emotion of love represents one of the most influential creations of the medieval mind.

***The Courtly Romance***  The courtly romance, which entered its great age after 1150, combines traits of both heroic epics and troubadour lyric poetry. It is narrative in form, like the epic, but like lyrical love poetry, it allots a major role to women and love. Taking her stories from Celtic tales, Marie de France (d. 1210) wrote in the vernacular, composing *lais,* or brief romance narratives of love and adventure. Chrétien de Troyes wrote romances about King Arthur of Britain and his coterie of knights. Many of these tales are concerned with the tensions between adulterous love for a lord's wife and loyalty to the lord.

***Popular Literature***  At a less elevated level were a range of ballads, songs, and stories. The goliardic poems of students have already been mentioned. The *fabliaux* were often stories of adulterous love in which the wife outsmarts the husband and sleeps with a student or a priest. The setting for these stories often reflects urban life in which the husband is a merchant absent on business. Fables, with animals as their protagonists, taught moral lessons, just as they did in the ancient world. And miracle stories, particularly miracles of the Virgin Mary, taught religious devotion.

## II. The States of Europe

Governments in the eleventh and early twelfth centuries had taken tentative steps toward expanding their control over their subjects and extending royal justice, as opposed to feudal justice,

to everyone. The growth of universities and the use of academically trained lawyers helped define governmental and legal procedures. The monarchs and their university-trained lawyers began the long process of implanting in the West the assumption that people should be governed by fixed and known procedures. Subjects valued the more uniform law that royal justice provided. It meant that merchants could travel from place to place under the rule of the same laws rather than the arbitrary administration of law that a feudal lord might apply. Lesser landholders appreciated a central court of appeal that could overcome the might of local overlords.

### ◆ ENGLAND

In England the kings were particularly aggressive in extending their control over the English countryside and their subjects by making royal justice the most important arbitrator in England. In doing so the kings clashed with the papacy and the English clergy, who claimed to be exempt from royal justice. Royal justice also undermined the prerogatives of the nobility and led to the rebellion that produced the *Magna Carta*.

***Angevin Kingship***  Henry I had numerous bastard children, but the only legitimate child to survive him was a daughter, Matilda. Her first marriage was to the emperor of Germany, giving her the title of "Matilda Empress." Her second marriage was to the Count Geoffrey of Anjou. Rather than selecting a woman—and one who was married to a hostile and aggressive neighbor of the duchy of Normandy—the English nobility selected another descendent of William I's line, Stephen of Blois (r. 1135–1152), to be king. Civil war ensued, which was resolved with the compromise that the son of Matilda and the Count of Anjou would succeed to the throne at Stephen's death. In 1154 Henry of Anjou, grandson of Henry I, became the first Angevin king of England.

***Henry II***  Through combined inheritances from his father and mother and his marriage to Eleanor of Aquitaine in 1152, Henry II ruled over a sprawling assemblage of territories that included, besides England, nearly the entire west of France from the English Channel to the Pyrenees Moun-

▲ **This enameled plate shows Count Geoffrey of Anjou, who died in 1151, holding a shield that depicts his family's new coat of arms.**
Giraudon/Art Resource, NY

tains (see map 9.3). A man of great energy who carried to completion many of the reforms of Henry I, Henry II ranks among the most gifted statesmen of the twelfth century and among the greatest kings of England.

***Itinerant Justices*** Henry II left a permanent mark on English government and law. He resurrected the "justices in eyre" (that is, on journey, or itinerant), who were endowed with all the author-

ity of the king himself. The itinerant justice traveled regularly to the county courts, investigating and punishing crimes. Upon his arrival, the justice would impanel a jury of at least twelve "good men" and inquire of them under oath what crimes they had heard about since his last visit and whom they suspected of guilt. (This sworn inquest is the direct ancestor of the modern grand jury.) Those indicted by the twelve "good men" were still tried by the ancient ordeals of fire and water. After the Church condemned these procedures in 1215, a small, or petty (*petite* in French), jury was used, as it is today, to judge the guilt or innocence of the alleged felon.

The itinerant justices did not forcibly interfere in civil disputes, but they did offer the services of the royal court in settling them. Barons receiving fiefs from the king had also been given the right to hold a court and judge the disputes of their own knights and dependents. Normally, therefore, litigants in a civil dispute appeared before a baronial court. As a result of Henry's reforms, a litigant could purchase a royal writ, which ordered the sheriff to bring the case under the scrutiny of the royal court presided over by the justice in eyre. Sworn inquest juries were composed of "good men" from the neighborhood who were likely to know the facts at issue and were able to judge the truth or falsity of claims. They were put on oath to tell the truth of the case. While Henry made no effort to suppress baronial courts, the royal courts left them with a shrinking role in English justice.

***Common Law*** In time the justices built up a considerable body of decisions, which then served as precedents in similar cases. The result was the development of "common law"—common in that it applied to the entire kingdom and was thus distinct from the local customs. It differed from Roman law in that it represented not the edict of an emperor but the principles, based on precedents set in earlier cases, that were followed in deciding similar ones. Precedent cases mark the beginning of the common law tradition under which most of the English-speaking world continues to live.

***Thomas Becket*** The judicial reforms of Henry II led him into a bitter conflict with the English Church, which maintained its own ecclesiastical courts. Henry did not want a whole group of his

▲ ELEANOR OF AQUITAINE EFFIGY

Eleanor of Aquitaine bears comparison with other forceful female rulers of European history, such as Elizabeth I of England. Eleanor was a worthy consort for Henry II, one of the most powerful and innovative rulers of the Middle Ages, and is buried next to him. The site, a splendid French abbey, lies within the territories that Eleanor had inherited and added to the English kingdom. The crown and book in the effigy on her tomb are perfect symbols of the intelligence and power that characterized her life.

Giraudon/Art Resource, NY

subjects, members of the clergy, to fall outside his judicial system. Furthermore, the Church courts required only prayers or pilgrimages from those who committed felonies, while the king's court required hanging and confiscation of property. In 1164 Henry claimed the right to retry clerics accused of crime in his royal courts. The archbishop of Canterbury, Thomas Becket, rejected this claim. He argued that both the Bible and canon law forbade what we now call "double jeopardy"—that is, a second trial and punishment for one crime.

Becket had been a personal friend of Henry and had served him ably and faithfully as Chancellor of the Exchequer, the chief official of the realm. Royal friendship and favor had brought him his election as archbishop of Canterbury in 1162. After becoming archbishop, Becket seems to have undergone a conversion that made him devoted to the Church. When Henry tried to force Becket to agree to a document, the Constitutions of Clarendon, outlining the king's view of the relations of the church to the crown, Becket fled to France. He was reconciled with Henry once more

in 1170, but a few months later he excommunicated the bishops who had supported the king. Henry, then in France, demanded in fateful rhetoric, whether no man would free him of this pestilential priest. Four of the king's knights took the words to heart, journeyed to England, found Becket in his cathedral, and cut him down before the high altar on December 29, 1170. By popular acclaim Becket was regarded as a martyr and a saint. Canterbury became his shrine and a popular pilgrimage site. Henry had no choice but to revoke the objectionable reforms and perform an arduous personal penance for his unwise words, including a beating.

A compromise was reached in which clerics suspected of crimes were tried first in the royal courts and, if convicted, surrendered their wealth to the king. They were then tried in ecclesiastical court, in which punishment was a penance rather than hanging.

At the death of Henry II in 1189, the English monarchy wielded exceptional authority, but neither in practice nor in theory was it clearly established within what limits, if any, royal powers

▲ This depiction of the murder of Thomas Becket in Canterbury in 1170 was completed within a few years of the event. That it should have appeared as a wall painting in the church of Sts. Giovanni and Paolo in Spoleto, Italy, hundreds of miles away from Canterbury, suggests the intensity of the European reaction to the assassination.
André Held

should operate, or how, if at all, the great men of the realm might participate in government.

*Richard I* Henry's son and successor was Richard I, the Lion-Hearted. Growing up in Eleanor's court in Aquitaine, Richard acquired all the virtues of a model knight—boldness, military skill, stately bearing, even a flair for composing troubadour lyrics. He spent little time administering his realm, preferring fighting to ruling. In 1191 and 1192 he was fighting in the Holy Land on the Third Crusade. He died in 1199 from a neglected wound received while besieging a castle in a minor war in southern France. Richard spent less than ten months in England, but the English government continued to function efficiently even in the absence of its king—testimony to its fundamental strength.

*John I* Richard was succeeded by his younger brother John, who, rightly or wrongly, is considered a wicked king. His reign is largely a record of humiliations suffered at the hands of the pope, King Philip II of France, and his own barons.

Early in his reign he married Isabelle of Angoulême, who was already engaged to a vassal of King Philip II of France. Philip, upholding his feudal obligation to defend his vassal, used the incident as a pretext to seize the duchy of Normandy. John's wars to recapture Normandy were expensive. To pay for them, John abused the feudal contract by demanding payments rather than military service, marrying off heiresses to the highest bidder, selling off wardships, and even extorting money from his subjects.

In 1206 John defied Pope Innocent III by rejecting Stephen Langton as archbishop of Canterbury. Innocent retaliated and put England under interdict in 1208. An interdict meant that the English clergy were not to baptize babies, marry couples, or bury the dead in public ceremony. When the interdict did not sway John, Innocent threatened to encourage Philip to invade. In 1213 John accepted Stephen Langton as archbishop of Canterbury.

*Magna Carta*  Already angry with John's abuses of the feudal contract and taxation, his enraged barons turned on him after a humiliating defeat at the Battle of Bouvines in 1214. Encouraged by Stephen Langton, they took to arms, and in June 1215 at Runnymede the barons forced John to grant them the "Great Charter." Archbishop Langton probably inspired, if not largely composed, the Magna Carta (so called because it was a large piece of parchment). The Magna Carta resembled oaths that English kings since Henry I had taken upon their coronation; it obligated the king to respect certain rights of his subjects. But no previous royal charter of liberties equaled it in length, explicitness, and influence (see "Excerpts from the Magna Carta," p. 312).

The Magna Carta disappoints most modern readers. Unlike the American Declaration of Independence, it offers no grand generalizations about human dignity and rights. Its sixty-three clauses, arranged without apparent order, are largely concerned with technical problems of feudal law—rights of inheritance, feudal relief, wardship, and widow's rights. But it did establish, more clearly than any previous document, that the king ought not to disturb the estates of the realm—Church, barons, and all free subjects—in the peaceful exercise of their customary liberties. It thus guaranteed to the clergy the freedom to elect bishops and to make appeals to Rome; it protected the barons against arbitrary exactions of traditional feudal dues; and it confirmed for the men of London and other towns "all their liberties and free customs." To all freemen it promised access to justice and judgment by known procedures. Finally, the king could impose new taxes only with the common consent of the realm. While these concessions were certainly significant, the Magna Carta addressed the concerns of only the elite. The rights of the unfree classes, the serfs and villeins who constituted 80 percent of the population at the time, are hardly mentioned.

The Magna Carta marked a major step toward government by recognized procedures that could be changed only with the consent of the realm. Of course, the barons and the bishops never anticipated that subjects other than themselves might be called on to give consent, but this limitation in no way compromises the importance of the principle established. Future generations of English were to interpret the provisions of the Magna Carta in a much broader sense than its authors had intended. The document is important not only for what it said but also for what it allowed future generations to believe about the traditional relationship in England between authority and liberty.

John immediately renounced the Magna Carta as an oath sworn under duress, and the pope upheld this position. Fighting continued, but John died suddenly, leaving his son Henry, a nine-year-old boy, as heir. The barons reissued the Magna Carta and formed a council to rule in Henry's name.

## ◆ FRANCE

In France the problems of consolidation were greater than they were in England. Unlike the English kings, who controlled the whole country, the Capetian kings of France held as their direct demesne (land they inherited) only the area around Paris (the Ile-de-France). Powerful dukes and counts controlled large provinces and were only nominally vassals to the kings of France. Marriage alliances and conquests seemed at first to be the only solution to unifying the territory that theoretically constituted France. Gradually, however, the French kings also used law as a means of making inroads into their powerful vassals' territory.

*Louis VII*  The able advisor to Louis VI, Abbot Suger (also patron of the first Gothic church), arranged the marriage of Louis VII (r. 1137–1180) to Eleanor of Aquitaine, heiress to the extensive lands of the Duchy of Aquitaine. This was Eleanor's first marriage; she later married Henry

▲ MAGNA CARTA
Originally agreed to in 1215 by King John, the Magna Carta (or Great Charter) was
intended to settle disputes over the rights and privileges of England's nobility. The
document itself was issued in sealed copies and sent throughout England, but it was
successively modified during the thirteenth century. This example, which is one of only
four that have survived, dates from 1297, when the charter was confirmed in final form.
Corbis

## EXCERPTS FROM THE "MAGNA CARTA"

"John, by the grace of God, king of England, lord of Ireland, duke of Normandy and Aquitaine, and count of Anjou, to the archbishops, bishops, abbots, earls, barons, justiciars, foresters, sheriffs, stewards, servants, and to all his bailiffs and faithful subjects, greetings. Know that we, out of reverence for God and for the salvation of our soul and those of all our ancestors and heirs, for the honour of God and the exaltation of the holy church, and for the reform of our realm . . . :

"[6] Heirs may marry without disparagement; so nevertheless, that, before the marriage is contracted, it shall be announced to the relations by blood by the heir himself.

"[7] A widow, after the death of her husband, shall straightway, and without difficulty, have her marriage portion and her inheritance, nor shall she give anything in return for her dower, her marriage portion, or the inheritance which belonged to her. . . . And she may remain in the house of her husband, after his death, for forty days.

"[12] No scutage or aid shall be imposed in our kingdom unless by common counsel of our kingdom, except for ransoming our person, for making our eldest son a knight, and for once marrying our eldest daughter; and for these only a reasonable aid shall be levied. Be it done in like manner concerning aids from the city of London.

"[13] And the city of London shall have all its ancient liberties and free customs as well by land as by water. Furthermore, we will and grant that all other cities, boroughs, towns, and ports shall have all their liberties and free customs.

"[20] A free man shall not be amerced [fined] for a trivial offense except in accordance with the degree of the offense, and for a grave offense he shall be amerced in accordance with its gravity, yet saving his way of living; and a merchant in the same way, saving his stock-in-trade; and a villein shall be amerced in the same way, saving his means of livelihood—and none of the aforesaid amercements shall be imposed except by the oath of good men of the neighborhood.

"[21] Earls and barons shall not be amerced except by their peers, and only in accordance with the degree of the offense.

"[38] No bailiff shall in future put anyone to trial upon his own bare word, without reliable witnesses produced for this purpose.

"[39] No free man shall be arrested or imprisoned or disseised or outlawed or exiled or in any way victimized, neither will we attack him or send anyone to attack him, except by the lawful judgment of his peers or by the law of the land.

"[40] To no one will we sell, to no one will we refuse or delay right or justice.

"[52] If anyone has been disseised of or kept out of his lands, castles, franchises or his right by us without the legal judgment of his peers, we will immediately restore them to him: and if a dispute arises over this, then let it be decided by the judgment of the twenty-five barons who are mentioned below in the clause for securing the peace.

"[61] . . . the barons shall choose any twenty-five barons of the kingdom they wish, who must with all their might observe, hold and cause to be observed, the peace and liberties which we have granted and confirmed to them by this present charter of ours, so that if we, or our justiciar, or our bailiffs or any one of our servants offend in any way against anyone or transgress any of the articles of the peace or the security, and the offense be notified to four of the aforesaid twenty-five barons, those four barons shall come to us, or to our justiciar if we are out of the kingdom, and, laying the transgression before us, shall petition us to have that transgression corrected without delay. And if we do not correct the transgression . . . within forty days . . . , the aforesaid four barons shall refer that case to the rest of the twenty-five barons. And those twenty-five barons together with the community of the whole land shall distrain and distress us in every way they can . . . until, in their opinion, amends have been made; and when amends have been made, they shall obey us as they did before."

II of England. Her marriage to Louis more than doubled the lands under direct royal control, but the couple's incompatibility soon became clear. Louis had been raised for a career in the Church

and became king only when his older brother died. He retained a monkish character that clashed with Eleanor's upbringing in Aquitaine, where her grandfather had been one of the first to write troubadour poetry. Having failed to produce a male heir, Eleanor accompanied Louis on the Second Crusade hoping for better luck. She and her ladies dressed as Amazons and thoroughly enjoyed the jaunt. It was even rumored that she had an affair with her relative, Raymond of Antioch, while in the Holy Land. When the couple returned to France without a male heir, they agreed to have the Church annul their marriage on the grounds that they were too closely related. The dissolution of the marriage in 1152 meant that Eleanor resumed her duchy. In two months Henry II of England married her, although he was her junior by some ten years, and added the duchy of Aquitaine to his vast holdings in France (see map 9.3). Eleanor bore Henry four sons, two of whom (Richard and John) became kings of England.

*Philip II Augustus* Louis VII's son by a later marriage, Philip II Augustus (r. 1180–1223), was not a great warrior, but he was an aggressive politician and an able administrator. Forced to go on the Third Crusade with Richard the Lion-Hearted and Frederick I Barbarossa, he left the battle to Richard and returned home to harass Richard's possessions in France. It was Philip's intervention on behalf of his vassal that permitted him to confiscate Normandy from John I (see map 9.3). The victory over King John at Bouvines confirmed England's loss of Normandy and brought new prestige to the Capetian throne.

Under Philip, royal influence began to penetrate to the south of France. In 1208 Pope Innocent III declared a crusade against the Albigensian heretics of the south (discussed later in this chapter), who enjoyed the protection of many powerful nobles. Philip's vassals flocked to the pope's call, overwhelmed the counts of Toulouse and other prominent nobles, and seized much of their lands. The defeat of the southern nobility left a vacuum of power that the king's authority soon filled.

*Strengthening the Administration* In addition to increasing his lands, Philip strengthened the administration of his own properties, the royal demesne, although he still made no effort to interfere directly in the governments of the kingdom's fiefs. On the local level the representative of the king—the French counterpart of the English

| *Chronology* | |
| :-- | :-- |
| **POLITICAL EVENTS** | |
| **(d. 1106)** | Henry VI of Germany |
| **(1100–1135)** | Henry I of England |
| **(1108–1137)** | Louis VI of France |
| **(1137–1180)** | Louis VII of France |
| **(divorced 1152)** | Eleanor of Aquitaine |
| **(1154–1189)** | Henry II of England |
| **(married 1152)** | Eleanor of Aquitaine |
| **(1152–1190)** | Frederick I Barbarossa |
| **(1180–1223)** | Philip II Augustus of France |
| **(1189–1199)** | Richard I of England |
| **(1198–1216)** | Pope Innocent III |
| **(1199–1216)** | John I of England |
| **(1215)** | Magna Carta |
| **(1197–1250)** | Frederick II Hohenstaufen of Sicily |
| **(1227–1141)** | Pope Gregory IX Inquisition |
| **(1216–1172)** | Henry III of England |
| **(1226–1270)** | Louis IX of France |

sheriff—was the prévôt. About 1190, apparently in imitation of the English itinerant justices, Philip began to appoint a new official, the *bailli*, to oversee the work of the prévôt. The *bailli* supervised the collection of rents and taxes, the administration of justice, and all the king's interests within a certain prescribed circuit or area, but he never assumed the full range of functions and powers that the English justice in eyre had acquired. The baillinage system had some advantages, however, because the *bailli* was a paid official, increasingly university trained, and was moved from one place to another so that he could not build up local loyalties.

The central administration was also developing specialized bureaus, although less advanced than the English; the Chambre de Comptes, a special financial office, equivalent to the English Exchequer, gradually assumed responsibility for the royal finances.

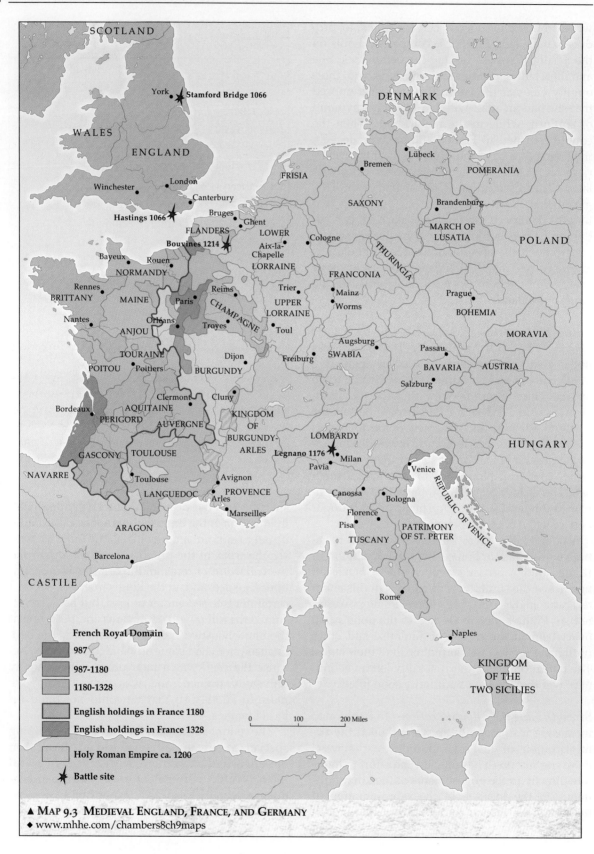

SCOTLAND

York  ✶ Stamford Bridge 1066

WALES

ENGLAND

Winchester  •  London •

• Canterbury

Hastings 1066 ✶

Bruges •

Ghent •

FLANDERS

Bouvines 1214 ✶

LOWER
LORRAINE

Aix-la-
Chapelle

Bayeux •  Rouen •

NORMANDY

Rennes •

BRITTANY    MAINE

Paris •

CHAMPAGNE

Reims •

Trier •

UPPER
LORRAINE

Mainz •
Worms •

Nantes •

ANJOU

Orléans •

Troyes •

Toul •

TOURAINE

POITOU   Poitiers •

Dijon •

BURGUNDY

Freiburg •

Augsburg •

SWABIA

Bordeaux •

AQUITAINE

PERIGORD

Clermont •

AUVERGNE

Cluny •

KINGDOM
OF
BURGUNDY-
ARLES

LOMBARDY

Salzburg •

GASCONY

TOULOUSE

Legnano 1176 ✶

Milan •

NAVARRE

Toulouse •

LANGUEDOC

Avignon •

PROVENCE

Pavia •

Arles •

Marseilles •

Canossa •

Bologna •

ARAGON

Florence •

Pisa •

TUSCANY

Barcelona •

PATRIMONY
OF ST. PETER

REPUBLIC OF VENICE

Venice •

CASTILE

Rome •

Naples •

KINGDOM
OF THE
TWO SICILIES

DENMARK

Lübeck •

Bremen •

POMERANIA

FRISIA

SAXONY

Brandenburg •

MARCH OF
LUSATIA

POLAND

Cologne •

THURINGIA

FRANCONIA

Prague •

BOHEMIA

MORAVIA

Passau •

BAVARIA

AUSTRIA

HUNGARY

**French Royal Domain**

987

987-1180

1180-1328

English holdings in France 1180

English holdings in France 1328

Holy Roman Empire ca. 1200

✶ Battle site

0   100   200 Miles

▲ **MAP 9.3  MEDIEVAL ENGLAND, FRANCE, AND GERMANY**
◆ www.mhhe.com/chambers8ch9maps

◄ In this fourteenth-century manuscript illumination, St. Louis hears the pleas of his humble and defenseless subjects, chiefly women and a monk. Note the hanged felons in the left panel. The picture illustrates the abiding reputation for justice that St. Louis earned for the French monarchy.
New York Public Library

Philip Augustus' reign made the French monarchy the unquestioned master in the Ile-de-France, greatly enlarged the royal demesne, and began the process of extending royal justice into the feudal principalities.

***St. Louis*** The successor of Philip Augustus, Louis VIII, ruled for only three years (r. 1223–1226). At Louis' death in 1226 the throne passed to Louis IX, St. Louis (r. 1226–1270), one of the great figures of the thirteenth century. Even during his life, Louis was considered saintly. He attended at least two masses a day, was sternly abstemious in food and drink, often washed the feet of the poor and the wounds of lepers, and was scrupulously faithful to his wife, Margaret of Provence, who, like her husband, bore an aura of sanctity. His personal asceticism did not preclude a grand conception of royal authority. He added new pomp to court ceremonies and freely acted against the pope's wishes whenever the interests of the monarchy or his people seemed to require it.

***Legal Reforms*** In his own realm Louis made no attempt to extend the royal power at the expense of his nobles or to deprive them of their traditional powers and jurisdictions, but he did expect them to be good vassals. He forbade wars among them, arbitrated their disputes, and insisted that

his ordinances be respected; he was the first king to legislate for the whole of France. Although Louis did not suppress the courts of the great nobles, he and his judges listened to appeals from their decisions, so that royal justice would be available to all his subjects. The king liked to sit in the open under a great oak at Vincennes near Paris to receive personally the petitions of the humble.

During Louis' reign, jurists began to clarify and codify the laws and customs of France. The most important of these compilations was the *Establishments of St. Louis*, drawn up before 1273. It contained, besides royal ordinances, the civil and feudal customs of several northern provinces and seems to have been intended for the guidance of judges and lawyers. It was not an authoritative code, but it and other compilations helped bring a new clarity and system to French law. Louis also confirmed the Parlement of Paris—a tribunal rather than a representative assembly like the English Parliament—as the highest court in France, a position it retained until 1789.

## ◆ THE IBERIAN KINGDOMS

The Christian *Reconquista* had achieved all but final victory by 1236, with only Granada still in Muslim hands. The principal challenge now was the consolidation of the earlier conquests under

▲ DEATH OF LOUIS IX
**Louis IX of France died of the plague in Tunis during his last Crusade. Attending his death bed in this manuscript illustration are his wife, Margaret of Provence, an unidentified bishop, and a mourner.**
Master and Fellows of Corpus Christi College, Cambridge

Christian rule and the achievement of a stable governing order.

The three major Christian kingdoms that emerged from the Christian offensive were Portugal, Castile (including Leon), and Aragon (including Catalonia and Valencia), but they were not really united within their own territories. The Christian kings had purchased the support of both old and new subjects through generous concessions during the course of the *Reconquista.* Large communities of Jews and Muslims gained the right to live under their own laws and elect their own officials, and favored towns were granted special royal charters that permitted them to maintain their own court or forum. Barcelona and Valencia in the kingdom of Aragon and Burgos, Toledo, Valladolid, and Seville in the kingdom of Castile were virtually self-governing republics in the thirteenth century. Because women were scarce in the military society of the *Reconquista,* town laws gave them particular protection and property rights to encourage them to marry and have families. The military aristocracy, particularly in Castile, the largest of the Iberian kingdoms, held much of their lands not as fiefs but as properties in full, free title, which reinforced their independent spirit.

***Strengthening the Monarchies***   To hold all these elements together under a common government was a formidable task, but the kings also retained real advantages. The tradition of war against the Muslims gave kings a special prestige. And their rivals were too diverse and too eager to fight one another to be able to present a united challenge.

In order to impose a stronger, essentially feudal sovereignty over their subjects, the Iberian kings set about systematizing the laws and customs of their realms, thus clarifying both their own prerogatives and their subjects' obligations. Alfonso X of Castile (r. 1252–1284) issued an encyclopedia of legal institutions, meant to instruct lawyers and guide judges. This code, known as the *Siete Partidas* ("Seven Divisions"), was thoroughly imbued with the spirit of Roman law and presented the king as the source of all justice. The code did serve to educate the people to the high dignity of kingship, even if the kings could not enforce it. Even more than in England and France, feudal government in the Iberian kingdoms rested on a delicate compromise between royal authority and private privilege, and this apparently fragile system worked tolerably well.

*Cortes*   Sooner than other Western monarchs, the Iberian kings recognized the practical value of securing the consent of their powerful subjects to major governmental decisions, particularly regarding taxes. By the end of the twelfth century the kings were frequently calling representative assemblies, called *Cortes*. Although they never achieved the constitutional position of the English Parliament because there were too many of them, the Cortes were the most powerful representative assemblies in Europe during the thirteenth century.

## ◆ GERMANY: THE HOLY ROMAN EMPIRE

For the German Empire, called the Holy Roman Empire in the late twelfth and early thirteenth centuries, the problems of unity as opposed to expansion remained unresolved. The lure of Italy and imperial aspirations diverted the attention of monarchs from unification of Germany. Meanwhile, the German dukes, unlike those of France, proceeded to establish independent authority. Unlike France with Paris or England with London, Germany did not have a capital city, nor did the German emperor have a unified demesne of his own. Furthermore, the German kingship remained elective for much of the Middle Ages, rather than being based on hereditary claim as was true in England and France.

*Frederick I Barbarossa*   The ruler who came closest to building a lasting foundation for the German Empire was Frederick I (r. 1152–1190) of the House of Hohenstaufen. He was called *Barbarossa*, meaning "red beard." Large, handsome, gallant, and courageous, Frederick, like Charlemagne before him, gained a permanent place in the memories and myths of his people. He much resembles in his policies, if not quite in his achievements, the other great statesmen of the twelfth century— Henry II of England and Philip II of France. Frederick showed a broad eclecticism in his political philosophy. He claimed to be the special protector of the Church and therefore a holy figure. He called his empire the Holy Empire; the later title,

*Holy Roman Empire,* was used after 1254 and until Napoleon abolished this German Empire in 1806.

Frederick pursued three principal goals. First, he hoped to consolidate a strong imperial demesne consisting of Swabia, which he inherited; Burgundy, which he acquired by marriage; and Lombardy, which he hoped to subdue. These three contiguous territories would give him a central base of power that he could use for his second goal—to force the great German princes in the north and east to become his vassals. Finally, in Italy, he claimed, as successor of the Caesars, to enjoy the sovereignty that Roman law attributed to the emperors.

*Italy and the Lombard League*   Frederick's Italian ambitions disturbed the popes and the town communes, which from about 1100 had become the chief powers in the northern half of the peninsula. Both feared that a strong emperor would cost them their independence. With active papal support, the northern Italian towns, led by Milan, formed a coalition known as the Lombard League that defeated the imperial forces at Legnano in 1176. The Battle of Legnano not only marked the failure of Frederick's efforts to establish full sovereignty over the Lombard cities but also was the first time in European history that an army of townsmen had bested the forces of an army under noble leadership. At the Peace of Constance in 1183, Frederick conceded to the towns almost full authority within their walls; the towns, in turn, recognized that their powers came from him, and they conceded to him sovereignty in the countryside. Frederick did not gain all that he had wished in Italy, but his position remained a strong one.

*Germany*   Forced to turn his attention to Germany, Frederick made effective use of feudal custom to try his vassals, particularly Henry the Lion, who married a daughter of Henry II and Eleanor. Frederick summoned Henry in 1180 to face trial for refusing to fight in Italy. The court condemned Henry and confiscated his Saxon fief. With Henry humiliated and deprived of his lands, Frederick seemed to be the unchallenged master in Germany (see map 9.3).

Frederick now wanted to advance the empire's prestige in Europe and sought out a position of leadership in the Third Crusade. But the aged emperor drowned while trying to ford a small stream in Asia Minor, bringing to a pathetic end a crowded and brilliant career.

*Henry VI (r. 1190–1197)*  Barbarossa's son Henry VI married Constance, heiress to the Norman Kingdom of the Two Sicilies, so that their son would have a legal claim to southern Italy and to the German throne. The prospect of Italian unification under German auspices disturbed both the papacy and the free cities of Lombardy. The towns and the pope feared that the direct domination of the emperor would curtail their liberty. In his brief reign of seven years, however, Henry VI had little chance to unify Sicily, northern Italy, and Ger-

▼ FREDERICK II'S TREATISE ON FALCONRY
**Frederick II was not only the dominant political leader of his age but also one of its most learned minds. He was an avid reader of classical texts and apparently used Aristotle's *Historia Animalium* as a guide in one of his favorite pursuits, a study of birds. Illustrated here is a page from his own copy of the treatise he wrote on falconry.**
Città del Vaticano, Biblioteca Apostolica

many. He did come up with an unscrupulous way of raising money: by imprisoning Richard I on his way home from the Third Crusade and holding him for ransom.

*Frederick II Hohenstaufen*  Frederick II (r. 1212–1250), son of Henry and Constance, is one of the most fascinating personalities of the Middle Ages. A contemporary called him *stupor mundi* ("wonder of the world"). Later historians have hailed him as the first modern ruler, the prototype of the cold and calculating statesman. Frederick spoke six languages, loved learning, patronized poets and translators, founded a university, and, after a fashion, conducted scientific experiments. He also corrected Aristotle by writing on the margins of his works in several places, "It isn't so."

The pope crowned Frederick emperor in 1219 on the double promise that he would renounce his mother's inheritance of southern Italy and lead a crusade to Palestine. Frederick procrastinated on both agreements.

*Fragmentation of Germany*  Frederick's policy toward Germany was to take as much profit as he could and devote his attention to Italy. To stabilize the political situation in Germany, he established on the empire's eastern frontier a military-religious order, the Teutonic Knights, who eventually created the Prussian state; he recognized Bohemia as a hereditary kingdom and Lübeck as a free imperial city; and he issued the earliest charter of liberties to the Swiss cantons. (Later in the century, in 1291, the cantons entered into a "Perpetual Compact," or alliance, which marks the formal beginnings of the Swiss Confederation.) His most important policy, however, was to confer upon the German ecclesiastical princes and the lay nobles virtual sovereignty within their own territories. The emperor retained only the right to set the foreign policy of the empire, make war and peace, and adjudicate disputes between princes or subjects of different principalities. All other powers of government passed to the princes, and no later emperor could regain what Frederick gave away.

*Attempt to Control Italy*  In Italy Frederick pursued a much different policy. For the government of the Kingdom of the Two Sicilies, he relied on a trained lay bureaucracy. He rigorously centralized

▲ Emperor Frederick II, in the ship showing the imperial eagles, watches his soldiers assaulting prelates on their way to a council summoned by Pope Gregory IX in 1241. This contemporary illustration of the emperor's sacrilegious behavior, taken from a manuscript, is a good example of the war of propaganda by which both pope and emperor sought to win public sympathy.
The Granger Collection, New York

his administration, suppressed local privileges, imposed a universal tax in money on his subjects, recruited his army from all classes and from Muslims as well as Christians, and issued a constitution that, in the spirit of Roman law, interpreted all jurisdiction as stemming from the emperor. He encouraged trade and stabilized the currency, bringing prosperity to the port cities.

Frederick had to face the increasingly bitter opposition of the popes and the free cities of the north, because it was apparent he planned to pursue the old policies toward them. Pope Gregory IX excommunicated him in 1227 because of his failure to lead an Eastern crusade. Frederick then departed on the crusade, but he preferred to negotiate rather than fight and made a treaty with the Muslims that guaranteed unarmed Christian pilgrims access to Jerusalem. The more militant among the Western Christians believed that this treaty was dishonorable. Frederick returned to Italy in 1229 and came to terms with Pope Gregory a year later.

The Lombard towns remained fearful of his designs and finally formed a league against him. He defeated them in 1237, but his success once more awakened Gregory's fears of encirclement. Gregory again excommunicated Frederick. Both sides struggled to win the European public sympathy, but the tide of history began to turn against Frederick. To break the power of the Lombard towns, he unsuccessfully besieged Parma in 1248. In 1250 death cut short his efforts to unify Italy under imperial auspices.

***Sicily and Germany after 1250*** Frederick II had reinforced a political fragmentation in Germany that had become ever more pronounced since the eleventh century. Wishing to keep the fragmentation, Germany elected a weak emperor who would not interfere with the independent princes.

In southern Italy Frederick II had completed the constitutional reorganization that the Norman kings, his forebears, had begun. With Frederick dead, the pope saw an opportunity to remove

Sicily from German hands. With the pope's cooperation, in 1262 the brother of Louis IX, Charles of Anjou, defeated Manfred, Frederick's son, and won Sicily. Later, the native population rebelled in an incident known as the Sicilian Vespers. On Easter Monday 1282, while the church bells were ringing to call people for vespers, a massive insurrection occurred and the French were massacred. The forces loyal to Manfred's daughter had contacted her husband, the king of Aragon, and his fleet was already close at hand. The king of Aragon ousted the Angevins, but the continued war over the claims of Aragon and Anjou left the Kingdom of the Two Sicilies impoverished.

# III. The Church

Since the time of the Gregorian reform of the eleventh century, the papacy had sought to build in Europe a unified Christian commonwealth, one based on faith and on obedience to the pope. In the early thirteenth century the Church came close to achieving this grand design, but it still had to face powerful challenges to both Christian unity and its own deficiencies in leadership. At the same time, the continued involvement of the papacy in political affairs, the moral laxity of the clergy, and the wealth of bishops, abbots, and popes offended the laity.

## ◆ THE GROWTH OF HERESY

The spread of heresy (adherence to religious views contrary to church dogma) in the eleventh and twelfth centuries can be traced to both discontent with the clergy and to new intellectual and spiritual demands on the part of the laity. The expansion of Europe meant that the population was more mobile and exposed to new ideas. Pilgrimage, crusade, and trade brought people into contact with the Greek church, with Islam, and with Eastern heretical groups. The movement into new territories, the growth of towns, the appearance of new trades and industries—all created strong psychological tensions, which often found an outlet in heretical movements. The Church's position was that the popes had the true interpretation of Christianity since their power derived from Peter through the Doctrine of the Petrine Succession (see chapter 6). The Church's charge

was to save all Christian souls; those who became heretics were, in the Church's view, condemned to damnation. Heretics must be returned to the doctrines of the Church.

*Appeal of Heresies* Corruption in the Church played a role in the spread of heresy. Satirists poked fun at the money needed to get a case tried in ecclesiastical courts. Nobles envied the property and power of the Church; to them, heresy offered a justification for seizing the wealth of a corrupt Church for themselves.

Among the urban poor, heresy became a form of social protest against elite government. It held potential for rich townsmen, too, inasmuch as traditional Christianity had been highly suspicious of wealth, particularly when earned in the marketplace, and gave the rich merchant little assurance of reaching heaven.

Heresy had a particular appeal to women. Many women could not marry because of the large dowry demanded and could not enter a religious order because this also required a monetary contribution. The Church would not allow women to preach, to enter universities, or to have an active role in pastoral care. Church law upheld the legal subordination of women to men. Heretical groups welcomed women, teaching them to read the Scriptures and offering a spiritual equality that the established Church did not.

This was an age of spiritual and intellectual tension. Some laypersons wanted a more mystical and emotional reward from religion, and those with an education wanted a better educated clergy. Both wanted the Bible translated into vernacular languages so that they could read the word of God for themselves. The clergy resisted, maintaining that the laity would draw false conclusions from the Bible and that only trained readers should interpret it for the laity.

*Waldensians* Around 1170 a rich merchant of Lyons, Peter Waldo, adopted a life of absolute poverty and began preaching. He soon attracted followers, who came to be known as "the poor men of Lyons," or Waldensians. The Waldensians attacked the moral laxness of the clergy and denounced the sacraments they administered. Women in the Waldensian movement could preach on a par with men. The group was declared heretical by the Lateran Council of 1215,

▲ GREGORY IX DECRETALS
One of the principal accomplishments of Pope Gregory IX was his sponsorship of an effort
to bring together and update the basic decisions and rulings of the Church. The resulting
collection is known as the decretals of Gregory IX, and it became the main source of canon
law. In this miniature from a fourteenth-century manuscript of the decretals, Gregory sits at
the center holding the book and surrounded by monks.
The Pierpont Morgan Library/Art Resource, NY

but the Church never succeeded in suppressing the movement.

***Albigensians or Cathari*** Far more powerful in their own day, though not destined to survive the Middle Ages, were the Cathari (Greek *katharos,* "pure"), or Albigensians, named for the town of Albi in Languedoc. The Albigensians' religious beliefs in purification of the body of material things developed from Manicheanism, an early dualist sect. The Albigensians, like the Manicheans, believed that two principles, or deities, a god of light and a god of darkness, were fighting for supremacy in the universe. They identified the god of darkness with the Old Testament and the creation of the material world, and the god of light with the New Testament and spiritual salvation. The good person must help the god of light vanquish the evil god of darkness, who had created and ruled the material world.

The true Albigensians led lives of rigorous asceticism. They abstained from sexual intercourse, since procreation replenished the earth, the domain of the god of darkness. Marriage they regarded as hypocrisy, and intercourse within it worse than any other sexual sin. They abstained from meat, since it was sexually reproduced. Because a sect that preached against marriage and procreation risked bringing about its own extinction, the Albigensians reached a practical compromise: Those who abided by these stringent regulations, both women and men, were the "Perfects"(they formed the priesthood); those who did not live by this stern code were the believers. Women who became Perfects had a higher sacerdotal status than did an abbess.

The Albigensians, like the Waldensians, denied all value to the sacraments and priesthood with the established Church. A person's affiliation to the sect rested on the agreement to accept the *consolamentum* before death. The Perfect came to the death bed and performed a laying on of hands as a spiritual baptism. The person then spent the last few days before death fasting to preserve the spiritual state for salvation. Many otherwise orthodox Christians found spiritual reassurance from the *consolamentum,* admired the Perfects, and appreciated the Albigensians' willingness to preach in the vernacular. The Albigensians developed a strong organization, with councils and a hierarchy of Perfects that resembled that of bishops.

## ◆ THE SUPPRESSION OF HERESY

The Church believed that the souls of Albigensians would be condemned to hell and that it was the responsibility of the Church, in its role as shepherd to its flock, to reclaim the Albigensians for the faith.

***St. Dominic and the Mendicants*** A priest from Castile named Dominic began to preach among the Albigensians of Languedoc in about 1205. Dominic insisted that his followers—whose mission was to preach—live in poverty and support themselves by begging; they thus constituted a *mendicant,* or begging, order. Mendicant orders were known as friars rather than monks, because they were to live with the laity rather than in the seclusion of the monastery and did not follow the Benedictine Rule. Dominic's instruction to his followers was: "The world henceforth is your home. . . . Go you therefore into the whole world and teach all nations."

The new Order of Preachers grew with amazing rapidity; the bishop of Toulouse approved the order in Toulouse in 1215 and papal approval followed shortly afterward. To prepare its members for their work, the Dominican Order stressed education. Their preachers were all university trained and many became masters at the universities. They became the intellectual arm of the medieval Church, counting among the order Albertus Magnus, Thomas Aquinas, and many other important religious thinkers of the thirteenth century. Dominicans responded to the demands of educated laity for intellectually stimulating sermons and to the needs of the Church for missionaries to the Turks and Mongols in the East.

***Crusade against Albigensians*** Reconversion through preaching, persuasion, and example remained a slow and uncertain process. While a bishop had the right to try a suspected heretic before his own court, a heretic who was protected by important men in the community was virtually immune to prosecution. Since the nobility of Toulouse, including the count of Toulouse, was sympathetic to the Albigensians, protection was easy to find.

By the early thirteenth century, the Church began to suppress the Albigensians by force. Pope Innocent III, of whom more will be said later, favored peaceful solutions to heresy until his legate, who had excommunicated the count of Toulouse

# THE TECHNIQUES OF THE INQUISITION

◆

*To combat heresy the Inquisition tried above all to get suspects to confess, repent, and thus save their souls. Bernard Gui, inquisitor at Toulouse in southern France between 1307 and 1323, left a vivid account of the psychological techniques used in interrogations.*

"When a heretic is first brought up for examination, he assumes a confident air, as though secure in his innocence. I ask him why he has been brought before me. He replies, smiling and courteous, 'Sir, I would be glad to learn the cause from you.'

"I [Inquisitor]. You are accused as a heretic, and that you believe and teach otherwise than Holy Church believes.

"A [Answer]. (Raising his eyes to heaven, with an air of the greatest faith) Lord, thou knowest that I am innocent of this, and that I have never held any faith other than that of true Christianity. . . .

"I. I know your tricks. What the members of your sect believe you hold to be that which a Christian should believe. But we waste time in this fencing. Say simply, Do you believe in one God the Father, and the Son, and the Holy Ghost?

"A. I believe.

"I. Do you believe in Christ born of the Virgin, suffered, risen, and ascended to heaven?

"A. (Briskly) I believe.

"I. Do you believe the bread and wine in the mass performed by the priests to be changed into the body and blood of Christ by divine virtue?

"A. Ought I not to believe this?

"I. I don't ask if you ought to believe, but if you do believe.

"A. I believe whatever you and other good doctors order me to believe. . . .

"I. Will you then swear that you have never learned anything contrary to the faith which we hold to be true?

"A. (Growing pale) If I ought to swear, I will willingly swear.

"I. I don't ask you whether you ought, but whether you will swear.

"A. If you order me to swear, I will swear.

"I. I don't force you to swear, because as you believe oaths to be unlawful, you will transfer the sin to me who forced you; but if you will swear, I will hear it.

"A. Why should I swear if you do not order me to?

"I. So that you may remove the suspicion of being a heretic.

"A. Sir, I do not know how unless you teach me.

"I. If I had to swear, I would raise my hand and spread my fingers and say, 'So help me God, I have never learned heresy or believed what is contrary to the true faith.'

"Then trembling as if he cannot repeat the form, he will stumble along as though speaking for himself or for another, so that there is not an absolute form of oath, and yet he may be thought to have sworn. . . . Or he converts the oath into a form of prayer. . . . [And when further hard pressed he will appeal, saying] 'Sir, if I have done amiss in aught, I will willingly bear the penance, only help me to avoid the infamy of which I am accused.' But a vigorous inquisitor might not allow himself to be worked upon in this way, but proceed firmly until he makes these people confess their error, or at least publicly abjure heresy, so that if they are subsequently found to have sworn falsely, he can, without further hearing, abandon them to the secular arm."

H. C. Lea, *A History of the Inquisition of the Middle Ages*, Vol. 1 (1887), pp. 411–414.

for tolerating heresy, was murdered. Innocent proclaimed a crusade (1208–1229) against the Albigensians and the nobles who supported them. Knights from the north of France responded with zeal, but more out of greed for plunder than concern for orthodoxy. They defeated the nobles of Toulouse, but the problem of suppressing heresy remained.

***Beginnings of Inquisition*** In 1231 Pope Gregory IX instituted a special papal court to investigate

and punish heresy. This was the famous papal *Inquisition*, which was to play a large and unhappy role in European history for the next several centuries. Like the English justices in eyre, the inquisitors were itinerant justices who visited the towns within their circuit at regular intervals. Strangers to the locale, they were not subject to pressures from the important men of the region. They accepted secret denunciations and, to protect the accusers, would not reveal their names to those denounced; at times they used evidence that was not even revealed to the accused. The accused had no right of counsel and could be tortured. The suspected heretics were, in fact, considered guilty before even being summoned to the Inquisition. They could confess and repent, with the likely consequence of a heavy penance and usually the confiscation of their property. But they had little chance to prove their innocence. As an ecclesiastical court, the Inquisition was forbidden to shed blood, but here too its procedures were novel: It delivered relapsed or unrepentant heretics to the secular authority with full knowledge that they would be put to death (see "The Techniques of the Inquisition," p. 323).

The weaknesses of the inquisitorial process soon became apparent. Secret procedures protected incompetent and even demented judges, who shocked and disgusted their contemporaries with their savage zeal. In addition, the Inquisition could function only where it had the close cooperation of the secular authority. It was never established in areas (for example, England) in which strong kings considered themselves fully competent to control heresy. (Kings characteristically equated religious and civil rebellion and considered heresy to be identical with treason.)

The number of heretics who were executed is not known exactly, but it was probably several hundred. Fines, confiscation of property, and imprisonment were the usual punishments for all but the most obstinate heretics. The Inquisition had a terrible effect upon the medieval Church because it associated the papacy with persecution and bloodshed.

### ◆ THE FRANCISCANS

Crusade and Inquisition could not alone preserve the unity of the medieval Church. A spiritual regeneration was needed; the Church had to reach lay people, especially those living in towns, and provide them with a spiritual message they could comprehend. The mendicant orders, or friars, met the needs of the laity. Dominicans spoke to those who wanted more intellectual content, while the Franciscans, the order founded by St. Francis of Assisi, responded to those who wanted a more spiritual, mystical approach.

***Francis of Assisi*** Francis (1182?–1226) is probably the greatest saint of the Middle Ages and pos-

sibly the most sensitive poet of religious emotion. He succeeded in developing a style of piety that was both faithful to orthodoxy and abounding in new mystical insights. Since most of Francis' life is screened by legend, it is nearly impossible to reconstruct the exact course of his spiritual development. His father was a wealthy merchant in Assisi, but Francis as a young man fancied the life of a knight and the pleasures of courtly love and troubadour poetry. He tried the rowdy amusements of the city and the life of a knight. A severe illness after one of his nightlong parties led to a conversion. He turned to religion and adopted a life of poverty.

▼ **This fresco from the basilica of St. Francis at Assisi, traditionally attributed to the Florentine painter Giotto, shows the saint preaching to the birds. He congratulates them on their bright plumage and bids them sing in praise of God. The implication is that if people too recognize God's providence over them, they will respond with gratitude and joy.** Scala/Art Resource, NY

*Franciscan Order* Disciples began to gather almost at once around the "little poor man" of Assisi. In 1215 Francis obtained papal approval for a new religious order. The papacy had some hesitation, since Francis' order resembled Peter Waldo's Poor Men of Lyons, but Francis recognized papal authority and the Church now realized the need for this sort of spiritual mission. His Order of Friars Minor (Lesser Brothers) grew with extraordinary rapidity: within ten years it included some five thousand members and spread from Europe to Palestine; before the end of the century it was the largest order in the Church. Although the problems of administering a huge order did not command Francis' deepest interests, he did write a brief rule for the Friars in which he stressed the importance of poverty and simplicity.

The success of the Friars Minor was an authentic triumph for the Church. Giving themselves to poverty and preaching, the Friars Minor came to include not only a second order of nuns but a third order of lay people. Francis and his followers opened orthodox religion to delight in the natural world, to mystical and emotional experience, and to joy, which all people, they believed, including the ascetic and the pious, should be seeking.

## ◆ PAPAL GOVERNMENT

The papacy recognized that in a period of social change and religious crisis they would have to clean their own house as well as address the problems of heresy. The pope whose reign best illustrates the aspirations and the problems of the medieval Church is Innocent III (r. 1198–1216).

*Innocent III* Innocent was the product of the twelfth-century papacy. He had a liberal arts degree from Paris and studied canon law at Bologna. Entering the papal government, he became a cardinal at age twenty-nine. As pope he sought with vigor and with remarkable, if always partial, success to achieve three major goals: the eradication of heresy, the hegemony of the papacy over Europe, and the clarification of Christian discipline and belief.

Within Europe, heresy was the greatest threat to Christian unity, and though he ordered the crusade against the Albigensians, Innocent primarily looked to the new mendicant orders, the Domini-

cans and Franciscans, to counter the appeal of the heretics.

The pope sought to exert his leadership over the princes of Europe in all spiritually significant affairs. Some of his efforts to bend kings to his will have already been mentioned, such as his struggle with King John to install Stephen Langton as archbishop of Canterbury. He also excommunicated Philip II of France for discarding his queen in order to cohabit with another woman. Innocent had occasion to reprimand the kings of Aragon, Portugal, Poland, and Norway. No prior pope had scrutinized princely behavior with so keen an eye.

*The Fourth Lateran Council* Innocent realized that problems and ambiguities within the Church were partly responsible for the problems it faced with heresy and dissent. In 1215 he summoned some 1,500 prelates to attend the Fourth Lateran Council. The Council identified the sacraments as exactly seven and reaffirmed that they are essential to salvation; imposed an obligation of yearly confession and communion on the faithful; and defined the dogma of transubstantiation, according to which the priest, in uttering the words of consecration at Mass, transforms the substance of bread and wine into the body and blood of Christ. Transubstantiation unambiguously affirmed the Mass as miracle and thus conferred a unique power on the Catholic priesthood. The Council also pronounced on a wide variety of disciplinary matters: the qualifications for the priesthood, the nature of priestly education, the character of monastic life, the veneration of relics, and other devotional exercises.

The Council's actions had implications for the broader population of Europe. Since it forbade priests to officiate at ordeals and trials by battle, these judicial tools were no longer valid for determining guilt or innocence of a person accused of crime. England adapted by extending the jury system to a trial, or petty jury, and France established panels of magistrates to examine the evidence in imitation of the Inquisition.

With marriage established as a sacrament, it came under greater Church scrutiny. Previously, people had made private contracts of marriage. Now these private contracts were to be read at the church door and bans announced the three Sundays preceding marriage to be sure the parties had no prior marriages. The new rules also insisted that the couples must freely consent to the marriage. Historians have argued about the extent to which free consent made it easier for women to refuse undesirable, arranged marriages. Where property and titles were involved, free consent seems to have had little effect during the Middle Ages, but it did influence practice later. Clandestine marriages were still common and still binding on the couples.

## SUMMARY
◆

The achievements in architecture and art, in intellectual life, in vernacular culture, in the improved standard of living, and in government have led historians to give the period of the twelfth and early thirteenth century the title of "The High Middle Ages." The growing consolidation of power by monarchs in France, England, and Germany, in addition to the strengthening of the papacy produced a demand for more educated men. Universities trained both theologians and those who would staff the growing bureaucracies of monarchies and the papacy. Urban governments developed along lines that are still familiar, and they too began to hire university-trained lawyers and notaries. The continued agricultural prosperity permitted the building of fine cathedrals throughout Europe. The Romanesque style that was typical of the Cluniac reform movement was replaced in the twelfth century with the Gothic style. The Gothic arches and the increased emphasis on windows were much in tune with the expansive feeling of the period. The Church, threatened by heresies, licensed two new orders, the Dominicans and Franciscans, who responded to the needs of the laity. The next hundred years, however, began to see an unraveling of the success of the papacy, while monarchies and ideas of governing lay society by a rule of law continued to develop.

## QUESTIONS FOR FURTHER THOUGHT
◆

**1. To what extent are contemporary universities similar to and different from medieval universities?**

**2. How did the Magna Carta reflect both continuity and change?**

**3. As you look at the buildings on your campus or in your town, what influences can you see of the Romanesque and Gothic architectural styles?**

## RECOMMENDED READING
◆

**Sources**

Aquinas, Thomas. *Basic Writings*. Anton C. Pegis (ed.). 1945.

Anselm of Canterbury. *Basic Writings: Proslogium, Monologium, Gaunilon's On Behalf of the Fool, Cur Deus Homo*. S. W. Deane (tr.). 1962.

*Brown, Raphael (ed. and tr.). *The Little Flowers of St. Francis*. 1971. Legends collected in the early fourteenth century exemplifying the style of Franciscan piety.

*Chrétien de Troyes. *Yvain, The Knight of the Lion*. Burton Raffel (tr.). 1987. Recent translation of a great French romance.

*De Villehardouin, Geoffrey, and Jean De Joinville. *Chronicles of the Crusades*. Margaret R. Shaw (tr.). 1963. The Fourth Crusade to Constantinople and the crusades of Louis IX.

*Frisch, Teresa G. *Gothic Art, 1140–1450: Sources and Documents*. 1987.

Goldin, Frederick. *Lyrics of the Troubadours and Trouvères: Original Texts, with Translations.* 1973. Troubadour works in both the original and translated versions.

*Marie de France. *The Lais of Marie de France.* Glyn S. Burgess and Keith Busby (trs.). 1986.

**The Letters of Abelard and Héloïse.* Betty Radice (tr.). 1974. A translation of their correspondence along with a short history of their lives.

*Otto of Freising. *The Deeds of Frederick Barbarossa.* Charles C. Mierow (tr.). 1953. Primary source regarding Frederick Barbarossa's life.

Paris, Matthew. *Chronicles: Monastic Life in the Thirteenth Century.* Richard Vaughan (ed.). 1984. Excerpts from an English chronicler with a superb perspective on medieval monastic mentalities.

*Peters, Edward (ed. and tr.). *Heresy and Authority in Medieval Europe.* 1980. Contains sources regarding medieval heresies and the response.

**Studies**

*Abulafia, David. *Frederick II: A Medieval Emperor.* 1988.

Barlow, Frank. *Thomas Becket.* 1986. Balanced biography of the martyred archbishop.

*Boswell, John. *Christianity, Social Tolerance, and Homosexuality in Western Europe from the Beginning of the Christian Era to the Fourteenth Century.* 1980. A learned survey of the treatment of homosexuals in medieval Europe.

Bouchard, Constance Brittain. *"Strong of Body, Brave and Noble": Chivalry and Society in Medieval France.* Cornell, 1998. Readable narrative of aristocracy aimed at general readers.

Calkins, Robert G. *Medieval Architecture in Western Europe: From A.D. 300 to 1500.* Oxford, 1998. Accompanied by an IBM-PC compatible CD-ROM. Calkins provides explanations of the transition from Romanesque buildings to Gothic.

Clanchy, M. T. *Abelard: A Medieval Life.* Blackwell, 1997. Abelard is placed within a medieval context with an emphasis on Héloïse's influence on him.

*Dillard, Heath. *Women of the Reconquest: Women in Castilian Town Society, 1100–1300.* 1984. Status of women on the Spanish frontier based on legal sources.

*Duby, Georges. *The Age of the Cathedrals: Art and Society, 980–1420.* Survey of the period, stressing the importance of artistic expression.

Fletcher, Richard. *Moorish Spain.* 1992. A concise survey of the Iberian Peninsula from the Muslim invasion to the fall of Granada.

*Furman, Horst. *Germany in the High Middle Ages, c. 1050–1200.* 1986. Readable survey of period.

Hallam, Elizabeth M. *Capetian France, 987–1328.* 1980. Survey of the period.

*Haskins, Charles H. *The Renaissance of the Twelfth Century.* 1927. A classic study.

———. *The Rise of Universities.* 1957.

*Holt, J. C. *Magna Carta.* 1965. Gives useful guidance to an extensive literature.

Lambert, Malcolm. *Medieval Heresy: Popular Movements from the Gregorian Reform to the Reformation.* 1992. Valuable summary of the heretical movements and the Church's response.

*LeRoy Ladurie, Emmanuel. *Montaillou: The Promised Land of Error.* Barbara Bray (tr.). 1978. Analysis of the inquisition records of one town's experience with Albigensianism. An engaging book.

*Moore, R. I. *The Formation of a Persecuting Society: Power and Deviance in Western Europe, 950–1250.* 1987. Examines the reasons for persecution in the Middle Ages.

*Morris, Colin. *The Discovery of the Individual, 1050–1200.* 1987. Looks not only at the intellectual movements of the twelfth century but also at the concept of the individual.

Munz, Peter. *Frederick Barbarossa: A Study in Medieval Politics.* 1969. A political biography.

*O'Callaghan, Joseph F. *A History of Medieval Spain.* 1975. Surveys medieval Spain.

*Panofsky, Erwin. *Gothic Architecture and Scholasticism.* 1951. Surveys the connections between Gothic architecture and Scholastic theory.

*Peters, Edward M. *Inquisition.* 1988. The Inquisition in fact and imagination.

*Sayers, Jane. *Innocent III: Leader of Europe 1198–1216.* 1994. Readable account of Innocent and his historical context.

*Southern, R. W. *The Making of the Middle Ages.* 1993. A standard book on medieval thought.

*Turner, Ralph V. *King John.* 1994. A political biography.

Wakefield, Walter L. *Heresy, Crusade, and Inquisition in Southern France, 1100–1250.* 1974. Narrative of events concerning the Albigensian crusade.

*Warren, William L. *Henry II.* 1973. Biography of this English king.

---

*Available in paperback.

▲ THE ENGLISH PARLIAMENT

A meeting of the English Parliament before Edward I. To the left are the bishops and to the right are the barons. The judges are seated on wool sacks between them. The wool sacks are an indication of the importance of England's export trade in wool. To further enhance Edward's position, his chief vassals — the king of Scotland and the Prince of Wales — sit on either side of him. The two archbishops are on the extreme right and left.

---

# THE URBAN ECONOMY AND THE CONSOLIDATION OF STATES

T he period from roughly 1250 to the arrival of the Black Death in Europe in 1348 was one of urban development and intensified trade. New instruments of trade added a sophistication to business endeavors, and the demand for goods produced in cities brought prosperity to urban centers. Towns rebelled against the control of local lords and bishops, favoring instead self-government and charters of independence from the monarchs of Europe. Urban life entered into every aspect of medieval Europe: Major cathedrals were located in cities, middle-class urban dwellers made careers in government and represented the interests of their cities with the monarchs, urban bankers played an important role in international politics.

Monarchs in Europe continued to consolidate control over their subjects, but they began to do so in consultation with representatives of their subjects in such bodies as the Parliament in England, the Estates General in France, and the Cortes in Spain. But while Western monarchies flourished, Eastern Europe and the Byzantine Empire went through another grim period of invasions, this time from the Mongols of central Asia. Ultimately the Byzantine Empire revived, and Moscow became the center of a newly reconstituted state of Russia.

With their power on the rise, monarchs' conflicts with the papacy intensified. The papacy continued its policy of trying to control the actions of the monarchs, but increasingly it did not have the resources to compete with secular states. Corruption of the Church's fiscal policies resulted in the laity's increased criticism of the papacy. But the laity, particularly laywomen, found spiritual comfort and even distinction in society through individual spiritual journeys. The greatest synthesis of medieval culture, Dante's *Divine Comedy,* is itself a poem of personal spiritual exploration.

| | Social Structure | Body Politic | Changes in the Organization of Production and in the Impact of Technology | Evolution of Family and Changing Gender Roles | War | Religion | Cultural Expression |
|---|---|---|---|---|---|---|---|
| **CHAPTER 10. THE URBAN ECONOMY AND THE CONSOLIDATION OF STATES** | | | | | | | |
| I. CITIES, TRADE, AND COMMERCE | | | | | | | |
| II. MONARCHIES AND REPRESENTATIVE INSTITUTIONS | | | | | | | |
| III. GOVERNMENT IN THE EAST | | | | | | | |
| IV. PAPACY AND THE CHURCH | | | | | | | |
| V. LEARNING AND LITERATURE | | | | | | | |

# I. Cities, Trade, and Commerce

Urban development continued with the prosperity and population growth of the twelfth and thirteenth centuries. As urban centers became more populous and engaged in more sophisticated artisanal trades and long-distance import-export business, they increasingly wanted independence to govern their own affairs. People who flocked into urban centers were a free population who did not fit easily into the old social divisions: peasants, or those who tilled the soil; nobility, or those who fought; and clergy, or those who prayed. The urban population also worked with their hands, but many made money in banking and trade. Increasingly the urban population felt that nobles and bishops, who were their overlords, were a hindrance to economic prosperity. Townsmen needed laws of commerce and contract and freedom from taxes. Thus, urban dwellers encouraged the revival of Roman law, including the *Codex Justinianus*, and sent their sons to Bologna for at least a year or two of legal studies.

Major economic changes occurred in cities as large-scale production, extensive trade, complex commercial and banking institutions, and the amassing of great fortunes became commonplace features of cities. These urban centers show much of the spirit of modern business enterprises.

## ◆ URBAN GOVERNMENT

*Town Independence*  The route to independent town government could be peaceful or violent. Some lords were eager to establish free towns in order to bring in wealth. In St. Omer's charter, dating from 1127, the count of Flanders granted the town freedom from taxes and the right of self-government. London won a similar charter from Richard I when its citizens agreed to pay a substantial portion of his ransom from imprisonment in Germany. In France, Philip II Augustus found that granting royal charters to towns was a way of securing their loyalty to the crown rather than to the counts and dukes, thus extending royal authority into the provinces.

At other times towns resorted to violence to free themselves of bishops and feudal lords. One of the most famous revolts was in Laon, where the bishop was found hiding in a wine cask. The finder "lifting his battle ax brutally dashed out the brains of that sacred, though sinner's head." The mob cut off his legs and one man, seeing the bishop's ring on the dead man, cut the finger off and took the ring. Milan and the Lombard towns managed to free themselves of the local bishops, but they continually fought the German emperors to preserve their freedom.

*Communes, Oligarchs, and Consuls*  One instrument by which medieval townsmen sought to

▲ YPRES GUILD HALL, CA. 1260–1380
The Flemish towns were renowned for their textiles, and the economic importance of this manufacture is reflected by the size of the thirteenth-century cloth hall at Ypres (destroyed in World War I). Rows of arched windows and a central tower puncture the massive square edifice that functioned as the headquarters of the guild as well as the place in which goods were marketed.
© Collection Roger-Viollet/Getty Images

govern themselves was the *commune,* a permanent association created by the oath of its members and under the authority of several elected officials. Communes first appeared in the eleventh century in northern Italy and Flanders, the two most heavily urbanized areas of Europe.

Few towns kept a communal form of government. For the most part, the wealthier elements, the long-distance merchants and knights, took control of town offices. Although revolts continued, the type of government that gradually evolved in urban centers was the oligarchy, in which the elite men of the city controlled the city government and its offices.

In Milan in 1097 the city set up a government of consuls, drawn from the city elite. Their function was both political and judicial. In order to control Milan after defeating it, Frederick I placed a city manager in Milan. The new official was an outsider with no local ties and so proved to be more even-handed in justice than the consuls had

been. The institution became popular in northern Italy, and university-trained men entered the profession.

In northern Europe the model of a mayor and councilors or aldermen developed. The city wards elected them from the wealthier members of the city elite. They administered both the city and the judicial system.

*Urban Population*  Everywhere the European urban population remained small compared to the rural population. In 1377 only 10 percent of the people in England lived in urban centers with a population greater than 3,200—a typical percentage for most of northern Europe—whereas in Tuscany and Flanders about a quarter of the population lived in urban centers.

The largest medieval city was Paris, with a population of perhaps 210,000 in 1328. Venice probably had 120,000 inhabitants in 1338. Few cities surpassed 40,000.

*Urban Regulation*    Growing towns needed considerable organization to regulate their concentrated populations. The total area of London within its walls was only a square mile; therefore its population of 60,000 was densely settled, with people living in rented rooms in houses three to four stories high. The crowding in cities led to settlement outside the city walls in what became known as suburbs, from the Latin *sub urbs,* or "below or under the city."

One of the first concerns of mayors and their councils was the protection of the city. The walls of European cities protected them against possible external attack; the gates could be closed at night, keeping out undesirable criminal elements. Cities developed militias or at the least had guards to watch the gates and patrol the streets. To ensure order, many cities had curfews, rules about carrying weapons after dark, and ordinances on noise and nuisance (foul smells, obstruction of streets, and throwing slops out the window).

Sanitary measures included street cleaning, provision for public latrines, wells and conduits to provide clean water, and segregation of the most noisome businesses, such as butchering, to places that were not upwind of the city.

Civic pride motivated a number of urban amenities. Guilds and citizens contributed money to performances of plays, processions, and tournaments. Hospitals were a frequent charity, as were foundling homes, free grammar schools, gardens, and chapels. In addition to a cathedral or large church, cities built a guildhall (town hall) where city officials held urban courts, private citizens met to transact business, and archives preserved records of both official business and private contracts.

*Moral Regulation*    Urban governments regulated the honesty and morality of their population. They maintained standard weights and measures and required those trading to use them. Prostitution was also regulated. While neither the Church nor urban governments condemned prostitution (they felt that it was better for men to seek sex with a prostitute than in adultery), they did not want its moral pollution in every part of the city. Some cities, such as London, limited the places that prostitutes could solicit. Other cities, such as Florence and Montpellier, set up official houses of prostitution, usually bathhouses, in which the city could regulate the trade and the health of the women practicing prostitution. People who used false weights, sold putrid food, or pimped or practiced prostitution outside the prescribed areas were fined and could be expelled from the cities for continuing offenses.

## ◆ THE ORGANIZATION OF CRAFTS

With the exception of mines, construction sites, and such enterprises as the arsenal in Venice, most work was performed in the home or in small shops. Increased efficiency was achieved through finely dividing the process of production and through developing highly specialized skills. A merchant or manufacturer acquired raw materials, gave (or "put") it out in sequence to specialized artisans, and then sold the finished product. Usually called the putting-out system, this method of production remained characteristic of the Western economy until the Industrial Revolution of the late eighteenth century.

*Wool Cloth Production*    The making of woolen cloth, the largest industry of the medieval town, well illustrates the complex character of thirteenth-century manufacturing. The raw wool—often coming from England, Spain, or North Africa—was first prepared by sorters, beaters, and washers. The cleaned and graded wool was then carded, or combed.

The next task, the spinning, was usually done by women who worked in their own homes with a distaff, a small stick to hold the wool, and a spindle, a weight to spin and twist the strands into thread. The spinning wheel, apparently first invented in India, adopted by the Arabs, and brought to Italy in the late thirteenth century, added speed and better quality to thread making. Since antiquity, women had been the primary weavers in society, but the invention of a larger, more expensive loom meant that the investment was beyond that of ordinary households. The weavers established guilds, purchased looms for their shops, and trained men to do the heavy work of manipulating the looms and large cloths they produced.

▲ ITALIAN GRAIN MERCHANTS
**This manuscript illustration shows Florentine grain merchants engaged in their trade and keeping their records in their shops. The manuscript itself noted the prices for grain between 1320 and 1335 that were set in the Or San Michele, the grain warehouse and market hall in Florence.**
Scala / Art Resource, NY

Weavers worked on large looms in shops and wove the thread into broadcloths that were 30 yards in length. The cloth was then fulled—that is, washed and worked with special earths that caused the wool to mat. This was arduous work and was often done at a water-driven fulling mill. The giant cloth was then stretched on a frame to dry properly and shrink evenly. Next, the dry cloth was rubbed with teasels to raise the nap, and the nap was then carefully cut. Several times repeated, this last operation gave the cloth a smooth, almost silky finish, but it was extremely delicate work; one slip of the scissors could ruin the cloth and the large investment it represented.

At various stages in this process the wool could be dyed—whether as unspun wool, thread, or woven cloth. Medieval people loved bright colors, and dyers used a great variety of animal, vegetable, and mineral dyes and special earths, such as alum, to fix the colors.

The medieval woolen industry came to employ a large, diversified labor force, which worked materials brought from all corners of the known world. Capital and labor were sharply divided; a few great entrepreneurs controlled huge masses of capital. In Florence in about 1300, wool shops numbered between two hundred and three hundred; they produced between 80,000 and 100,000 big broadcloths with a value surpassing 1.2 million gold florins. More than thirty thousand persons earned their living from this industry.

People took their surnames from their occupations. In England, *Weber* denoted a weaver, *Fuller* the one who fulled the cloth, *Shearer* the one who cut the nap, and *Dyer* and *Tailor* the obvious.[1]

◆ THE GUILDS

To defend and promote their interests, the merchants and master artisans formed associations known as *guilds*. (In chapter 9 we saw that university masters and students had also formed guilds.) Merchant guilds appeared in European cities in about 1000. From the twelfth century both master artisans (weavers, bakers, shoemakers) and merchants in special trades (dealers in wool,

---

[1]Surnames gradually became fixed in the late Middle Ages, and many reflect occupations. *Brewster,* for instance, indicates a female brewer. Trade names as surnames were common, but so too were place names of towns or places in towns, such as *Townsend.* Physical characteristics also became surnames, such as *Squint* and *Blond.*

▲ CLOTH MARKET IN BOLOGNA

**The manufacture and marketing of textiles was one of the main sources of wealth for the cities of northern Italy. This scene, from a manuscript dated 1411, gives us a sense of what the cloth market in Bologna must have been like as merchants examined, bought, and sold various fabrics.**

Alinari/Art Resource, NY

spices, or silk) had organized their own independent guilds to ensure the quality of the goods they produced and sold and to maintain a monopoly over their craft or trade. A large industrial town such as Florence had more than fifty professional guilds.

*Guild Functions*   Once a year the guild members met to elect permanent officials, called consuls or wardens. The consuls regulated methods of production and examined the finished product to maintain quality. To this end they restricted the number of working hours and the number of employees that could be hired by any single master. Guild members who produced bad quality goods were fined and sometimes even publicly humiliated: A vintner who sold bad wine had to stand at the public stocks, drink a gallon of his worst, and have the rest poured over his head. The consuls enforced the statutes, adjudicated disputes among the members, administered the properties of the guild, and supervised its expenditures. To protect the members from external competition, cities required all those who practiced a trade or craft within their walls to belong to the appropriate guild. Guilds reserved the right to examine and admit members (see "The Craft of Weavers of Silk Kerchiefs at Paris," p. 335).

Guilds provided their members with a strong sense of identity and fellowship. Often they aided members who lost goods through fire or flood and supported the widows and educated the orphaned children of deceased members. Banquets, public processions, and religious ceremonies enriched the social life of the membership. Many guilds were among the principal donors to charities and city beautification.

*Apprenticeship*   One of the chief features of the guilds was the apprenticeship system. Guilds stipulated what the apprentices had to be taught and what proof of skill they had to present to be admitted into the guild, how long they had to work and learn in the master's shop, and what the master had to give them by way of lodging, food, and pocket money. To enter an apprenticeship, candidates or their family had to pay the master and the guild an entrance fee; the training was, therefore, not available to everyone. If, after finishing their training, they were too poor to open their own shop, they worked as paid laborers, or journeymen, in the shop of an established master. Apprentices with family capital or loans from their master could eventually become masters in a guild and have a shop.

For boys, the age of entry into apprenticeship ranged from about fourteen to eighteen years of age. By the late Middle Ages masters required apprentices to be able to read, write, and cast

I: CITIES, TRADE, AND COMMERCE 335

# THE CRAFT OF WEAVERS OF SILK KERCHIEFS AT PARIS

*In about 1270 Etienne de Goileau compiled a Book of Crafts recording guild regulations for Parisian guilds. Although the regulations here are for a woman's guild, the regulations were similar to those for other craft guilds.*

"1. Any woman who wishes to weave silk kerchiefs in Paris may do so provided she knows how to practice the craft well and truly, according to the following usage and customs.

"2. First: it is ordered that no journeywoman of the craft may work on a feast day which the commune of the city celebrates and which is commanded by the Church.

"3. No one may work at night, because one cannot do as good work at night as during the day.

"4. It is ordered that no one may have more than one apprentice in the craft who is not related to her and one who is a relative; and she may not take an apprentice for fewer than seven years with a fee of twenty sous, or eight years without a fee. And if it happens that any mistress sells her apprentice for her need, she may not take another before her term is up; and if it happens that the apprentice buys her own freedom, the mistress may not take another

apprentice before the term of the one who bought her freedom is up.

"5. It is ordered that no mistress or journeywoman of the craft may buy silk from Jews, from spinsters or from any others, but only from the proper merchants.

"6. No woman may work on the premises of a man or woman if she does not know the craft.

"7. Whoever infringes any of these regulations, she must pay six sous as a fine for each time she is found at fault. . . .

"10. The aforesaid craft has three good women and true who will oversee the craft on behalf of the king, sworn and pledged at Chastelet, who will make known all the infringements against the craft, whenever they discover them."

From Emilie Amt, *Women's Lives in Medieval Europe: A Sourcebook* (Routledge, 1993), pp. 195–196.

accounts before becoming apprentices. Apprentices lived in the master's home, a relationship that could be quasi-familial or terribly abusive. The term of apprenticeship varied from seven to ten or more years; young men were in their twenties before they completed their training.

For girls, apprenticeship served different purposes, and their contracts were often shorter and not formally drawn up. Some girls entered into apprenticeships that would lead to independent careers, usually in dressmaking, embroidery, or silk working. Paris, for instance, had five guilds composed exclusively or predominantly of women. Many of the girls, however, learned a craft, such as gold thread making, that could be a useful supplement to their husbands and fathers in their labors. A young woman who had learned a trade would be a desirable marriage partner. Many widows continued in their own name the trade of their deceased husbands. Other widows remarried, bringing their skills and capital to establish another household.

## ◆ COMMERCIAL INSTITUTIONS

The growth of trade and manufacturing stimulated the development of sophisticated commercial institutions, though the pace of transactions and economic exchange was slow by our standards. The quickest a person or a letter could travel on land was between twenty and thirty miles per day: To get to Bruges by sea from Genoa took thirty days; from Venice, forty days.

**Banks** Since each monarch, independent city, bishop, and lord minted their own coinage, specialists were needed to assay coins for their precious metal content. Florence in 1252 began issuing gold florins—the first successful gold coinage in the West since ancient times. England maintained a stable silver currency, in contrast to Philip IV of France, who debased French currency so often that his subjects called him "the counterfeiter." Banks (from the Old French *banc*, or bench) set up at the great European trade fairs in St.

▲ COLLECTING SILKWORMS AND PREPARING SILK
One of the new industries that appeared in Europe in the fourteenth century was the raising of silkworms. Since the spinning of silk was a craft usually associated with women, this scene, from a fifteenth-century manuscript, shows a woman gathering silk cocoons from the mulberry bushes on which the worms lived, and from those cocoons the silk threads were unwound.
By Permission of The British Library, London. Ms. Royal. 16GV, Fol. 54v

Denis, Champagne, St. Ives, and elsewhere to assay money for a fee. Gradually bankers offered more sophisticated services. By the late 1300s "book transfers" had become commonplace; that is, a depositor could pay a debt without using coin by ordering the bank to transfer credit from his own account to his creditor's. At first the

depositor had to give the order orally, but by 1400 it was commonly written, making it an immediate ancestor of the modern check.

*Loans and Usury*  The Church condemned the practice of usury, which at the time meant any interest or profit on a loan, however tiny. In the Church's view, the only honest way to gain money was in exchange for work. Peasants and artisans worked with their hands, clergy prayed, and the nobility protected and governed society. Money could not make money, which is how the Church perceived the activity of bankers and merchants.

Because usury was prohibited, Christian merchants developed a variety of instruments of credit that disguised their profit. Most important for commercial purposes was the bill of exchange, in essence a loan, but one that required repayment at a specified time in another place with a higher valued currency. Thus, a Flemish merchant might borrow 100 pounds in Ghent and agree to repay the loan three months later in local money at a Champagne fair. He then bought goods in Ghent, sold them in Champagne, and repaid the bill in the highly valued florins. The rate of exchange thus concealed a substantial profit for the investor,

▼ EARLY BANKERS
This illustration from a printed Italian handbook, which gives instructions to merchants and is dated ca. 1496, shows the interior of a bank, or accounting house.
New York Public Library

who technically earned it for changing money, not for making the loan.

*Partnerships*  Business was risky, especially that which relied on sea trade, because a boat and its cargo could sink. Partnerships and business associations were an important hedge against disaster. At Venice, Genoa, and Pisa, overseas ventures were most often financed through temporary partnerships, in which an investor gave a sum of money to a merchant traveling abroad in return for a share (usually three-quarters) of the eventual profits; the investor bore the entire loss if the ship sank or the venture failed.

In the inland Italian towns a more permanent kind of partnership developed, known as the *compagnia* (literally, "bread together," a sharing of bread). These earliest companies seem to have been partnerships among brothers. By the thirteenth century such companies commonly included as partners persons who were not blood relatives but who could contribute capital and services, and they also accepted deposits from nonpartners in return for fixed yearly payments of interest that were called "gifts," lest they be considered usurious.

These companies performed a wide variety of functions and grew in size. They traded in any product that promised a profit, wrote bills of exchange, and fulfilled other banking services. From the late twelfth century, they served the Roman curia as papal bankers. They were also drawn into the risky business of extending loans to princes for wars. In 1338 the Bardi and Peruzzi companies loaned a total of 1,500,000 florins to England; in 1342 the English king defaulted, leaving both companies bankrupt.

*Medici Bank*  Merchant houses in the late fourteenth and fifteenth centuries were considerably smaller than those of the thirteenth century, but they were more flexible. The Medici bank of Florence, which functioned from 1397 until 1498, for example, was not a single monolithic structure; rather, it rested on separate partnerships, which established branches at Florence, Venice, Rome, Avignon, Bruges, and London. Central control and unified management were ensured by having the senior partners—members of the Medici family—

in all the contracts; but the branches had autonomy, and most important, the collapse of one did not threaten others. This system of interlocked partnerships resembled a modern holding company.

*Jewish Lenders*  Jewish bankers, who were not under Church restrictions on usury, usually handled loans at high interest rates or rates above market value. Nobles going to war or paying a dowry for their daughters or financing the knighting of their sons mortgaged portions of their fiefs to Jews in return for loans. Since these loans were consumer rather than business loans and the nobles could not hope to raise the money to repay them, they lost the land to Jewish money lenders. Western European laws forbid Jews from actually having title to these lands, and the Jews sold the lands to other Christians at a profit. Some minor nobility overextended themselves on these loans and were ruined.

*Accounting and Insurance*  Although double-entry bookkeeping was known in the ancient world, it was not widely practiced in the West until the 1300s. In single-entry bookkeeping, only the debts owed were recorded, so that a person did not know whether the year represented a profit or loss until all debts and receipts were tallied at the end of the year. Double-entry bookkeeping recorded both output in terms of goods and services and the profits that these outputs earned or lost. Thus, an individual, company, or government knew where it stood immediately with each transaction and any arithmetical mistakes were corrected with each entry.

Maritime insurance decreased the risk of losing everything if a ship went down. As early as 1318 insurance appeared in major Italian ports; a broker bought the ship and cargo at the port of embarkation and agreed to sell them back at a higher price once the ship reached its destination. If the ship sank, it was legally the broker's and he assumed the loss. By 1400 maritime insurance had become a regular item of the shipping business, and it was to play a major role in the opening of the Atlantic.

Insurance for land transport developed in the 1400s but was never common. The first life insurance contracts appeared in fifteenth-century Italy and were limited to particular periods (the duration of a voyage) or particular persons (a wife during pregnancy).

### ◆ SEA TRAFFIC

*Ships*  Before about 1325 there was still no regular sea traffic between northern and southern Europe by way of the Atlantic, but it grew rapidly thereafter. New, bigger ships increased profits because they carried more cargo with relatively smaller crews. Large ships were safer at sea, they could sail in uncertain weather when smaller vessels had to stay in port, they could remain at sea longer, and they did not have to sail close to the coastline in order to replenish their supplies.

The larger vessels required more sophisticated means of steering and navigation. Before 1300, ships were turned by trailing an oar over the side. This method provided poor control. Sometime during the fourteenth century the stern rudder was developed, which enabled a captain to tack effectively against the wind and control the ship closely when entering or leaving ports. Voyages became quicker and safer, and the costs of maritime transport declined.

*Navigational Instruments*  Ocean navigation also required a reliable means for estimating course and position, and here notable progress had been made in the late thirteenth century. Scholars at the court of King Alfonso X of Castile compiled the Alfonsine Tables, which showed with unprecedented accuracy the position and movements of the heavenly bodies. Using such tables, captains could take the elevation of the sun or stars with an astrolabe and calculate a ship's latitude, or position on a north-south coordinate. (They could not tell their longitude, or position on an east-west coordinate, until they could carry accurate clocks that could compare their time with that of a basic reference meridian, such as Greenwich in England. Until the 1700s, when the first accurate clocks immune to a ship's swaying were developed, navigators who sailed across the Atlantic could not tell how far they had traveled.) The compass, whose origin is unclear, was common on Mediterranean ships by the thirteenth century. By 1300 Mediterranean navigators had remarkably accurate maps and port descrip-

▲ View of Venice
**This elaborate depiction of Venice in a fourteenth-century manuscript shows the buying and selling that was characteristic of the citizens of this commercial and maritime center. Particularly notable at the upper left are the four bronze horses that the Venetians brought back to the city after the capture and looting of Constantinople in 1204 during the Fourth Crusade. The horses were placed on the facade of the cathedral of St. Mark's, and they have remained there ever since.**
The Bodleian Library, University of Oxford. MS. BODL. 264. fol., 218r.

tions that minutely described harbors, coastlines, and hazards. All these technical developments gave European mariners a mastery of Atlantic coastal waters and helped prepare the way for the voyages of discovery in the fifteenth century.

### ◆ URBAN LIFE

Life in an urban environment was quite different from life in a village or a castle. Housing could be palatial, as evidenced by the surviving grand houses of Venice and Florence, but most people lived in cramped and overcrowded quarters. Without space to cook or relax, many people bought their food from street vendors (the fast food of the Middle Ages) or in taverns. Because so many people crowded into urban centers, cities

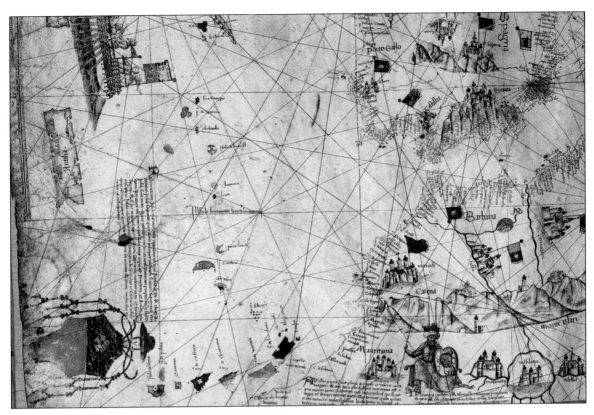

▲ An Early Map of the Western Mediterranean
Cartography benefited as sea voyages multiplied, as Europeans gained increased knowledge of the world, and
as they improved their skill in illustration. This map by the Italian cartographer Giovanni Benincasa
describes in great detail the coasts of Portugal, Spain, and North Africa.
Scala/Art Resource, NY

were dirty and their populations prone to disease. Medieval and early modern urban populations did not replace themselves, but had to be augmented with immigration from the countryside. Thus, cities had to assimilate fresh groups of young people who came from the hinterland to be servants or apprentices.

*Marital and Household Customs* Cities were populous, but urban households tended to be small and unstable. The average household size in Florence in 1427 was only 3.8 persons, and in some other cities it was even smaller. The low numbers reflected the numerous deaths in a time of plagues, but marital customs also had an effect. Urban males who practiced crafts or were merchants were generally older than their brides. Because these men went through apprenticeships

and started a business to accumulate capital, they postponed marriage. When they married, they tended to marry younger women: Florentine women were, on the average, less than eighteen years old when they married for the first time; women in London were more likely to be in their early twenties. Many young people, both men and women, came to the cities as servants and returned to their rural homes when they had enough money to marry. These young people did not form marriages in the urban centers at all.

Marriage customs varied in European cities. In northern Europe the marriage contract included dowry (the gift of the wife to the husband at marriage) and dower (a portion of the husband's property set aside for the widow's life use). Since women tended to outlive their husbands, they usually collected their dowers. Custom varied from town to town and from rural village to village, but widows usually had a third to half of their former husband's property for their lifetime. Widows were attractive marriage partners because the new husband could use the property as long as he returned it to the heirs when his wife died. Since widows frequently had family agricultural lands or businesses as well as young children, they preferred to remarry so that their new husbands could take over the farm or the trade.

▼ WOMAN SELLING POULTRY

**Women worked at many trades during the Middle Ages. They contributed significantly to luxury crafts such as silk spinning and weaving, but they were also a major presence in the marketplace, selling such items as bread, beer, and poultry.**
Bibliothèque Nationale de France, Paris

In Italy the dower had been abolished, and the dowry took on an increased importance in the formation of marriage. Florentine husbands typically tried to discourage their spouses from remarrying because widows, once remarried, might neglect the offspring of earlier unions and take their dowries to a new family. Thus, the wills of Florentine husbands often gave their widows special concessions that would be lost on remarriage: use of the family home, the right to serve as guardians over their children, sometimes a pension. In 1427 more than one-half of Florence's female population over forty were widows.

Urban wives had considerable influence within their families. Merchants relied on their wives to run both the household and business in their absence. Artisans' wives helped with their craft. Some wives had occupations or businesses that they could do along with running the house and rearing children. Silk weaving, running an inn or tavern, selling prepared foods, dressmaking, and other such occupations added considerably to family incomes or could support a single woman who chose not to marry.

# II. Monarchies and the Development of Representative Institutions

Monarchs in England and France in the late thirteenth century tried to concentrate more power and control over their subjects. The continual warfare between the two countries, however, was very expensive, and the kings could not finance these wars without their subjects' financial and moral support. In trying to raise money to achieve their goals, monarchs enlisted the cooperation of the nobles, knights, and urban dwellers through representative institutions. In England, after the Magna Carta, these representatives often saw their role as a check on the monarchy. In France the monarch saw the representative institutions as bodies he could manipulate to achieve his own ends. The spread of royal justice and monarchical power meant increased bureaucracy. Middle-class, university-trained lawyers became justices and filled royal administrative posts.

▲ MAP 10.1 EUROPE, CA. 1250
◆ www.mhhe.com/chambers8ch10maps

## ◆ ENGLAND AND THE DEVELOPMENT OF PARLIAMENT

The death of John I so soon after the signing of the Magna Carta and the long minority of his son, Henry III, increased the power of the nobles and the free population of England and their demand for a role in government. In the late thirteenth century, their protests resulted in the development of Parliament. The kings of the fourteenth century had such heavy expenditures for warfare in Wales, Scotland, and France that they continued to rely on Parliament to provide taxes to support their wars.

*Origins of Parliament* Henry III (r. 1216–1272) had an uneasy relationship with his barons from the beginning. During his minority, the barons

forced him to reissue the Magna Carta and appointed a regent who was to act on his behalf in consultation with a select council of barons.

Even after his majority in 1227, Henry III could only raise taxes through a grant from the Great Council of the barons and clergy. The meetings of the Great Council came to be called *parliaments*. (The word means "conversation" and, derivatively, an assembly in which discussion occurs.) Henry continued his father's policies of trying to regain Normandy. His wars and diplomatic efforts were expensive and unsuccessful, leading the barons to revolt against him under the leadership of Simon de Montfort (1208–1265). Simon de Montfort was the son of a French nobleman who came to England to pursue a claim to his English grandmother's estate. Henry befriended him, and de Montfort married Eleanor, Henry's sister. Like the other barons, however, de Montfort found Henry's ineptitude and expenditures too great. In 1258 the barons took control of the government, but dissensions within their own ranks rendered them unable to administer the realm. Henry regained power, but the barons under the leadership of de Montfort defeated him in 1264 at the battle of Lewes.

Because of continued divisions within the baronial ranks, Simon de Montfort sought to enlarge his power base by calling on the other constituents who had been at the signing of the Magna Carta, the knights and townsmen. In 1265 he summoned a parliament that included two knights elected from every shire and two townsmen from every town as well as the more powerful nobles, bishops, and abbots. Simon did not call the enlarged Great Council or a parliament to advise him, but rather sought to secure the loyalty of the countryside and the towns for his policies. The representatives were to go back to their shires and towns and inform the population of the baronial policies. De Montfort was slain in battle in 1265, but kings continued to call parliaments. In 1295, Henry III's son and successor, Edward I (r. 1272–1307), called the "Model Parliament," in which the two knights of the shire and two representatives from the towns became the customary practice.

*Two Houses of Parliament*   Historians cannot assign an exact date for the division of Parliament into separate houses: the House of Lords included the tenants-in-chief (the immediate vassals of the king, the upper-rank nobility), bishops, and the most powerful abbots, while the House of Commons was composed of two knights from each shire and two representatives of the towns. The meetings were officially called "Parliaments." Two unique features of the English Parliament helped enhance the influence of Commons. First, the knights and lower-ranked nobility sat with the burgesses and learned to act together in their mutual interests. Second, though the bishops continued to sit in the House of Lords, they gradually became less interested in using Parliament as a vehicle for political representation. The bishops preferred to hold their own convocations to discuss Church affairs and to approve grants of money to

the king. The functions of the House of Lords were thus reduced, a fact that benefited the House of Commons.

*Representation*   Parliament's role in levying taxes led to the development of a true system of representation. Feudal custom, the Magna Carta, and prudence had required that the English king seek the consent of his subjects for new taxes. He could not ask all freeholders of the realm individually. He might seek the consent of the separate shires and the towns, but this process was slow and awkward. Edward I ingeniously simplified the procedure of consent. Through special writs, he ordered the shires and the towns to elect representatives and to grant them "full power" to allow him to tax. These representatives, gathered in Parliament, thus had authority to consent to taxes that would be applicable to members of their shire and town. Paradoxically, the unique powers of the English king laid the basis for the eventual, unique powers of Parliament.

*Parliament as a Judicial Court*   As the supreme feudal council, Parliament was also England's highest court (an honor the House of Lords retains today). The members attending its sessions would carry petitions or appeals from decisions made in lower courts. At the shire level, a sheriff might have been subject to local intimidation, but Parliament, as a countrywide body, would not be. By welcoming petitions, the king thus made his justice better known and respected throughout the realm. As with the U.S. Supreme Court, the decisions of Parliament determined the future policies of all English courts. The decisions were thus nearly the equivalent of legislation, and from them there was no appeal.

*Edward I*   Henry III's son Edward I (r. 1272–1307) took over governing the realm even before the death of his father. Edward was the sort of king that the English nobility respected. He was a bold fighter, a crusader, and a success in wars. His interest in effective administration left a strong mark on English law and institutions. In 1284 he defeated the Welsh, killed their king, and later gave their land as an appanage (a province intended to provide "bread," or support) to his eldest son. (Since 1301 the heir presumptive to the English throne has borne the title Prince of Wales.) He also pursued a war with Scotland in an effort to control the entire island. His victory was short lived; Scotland regained independence under his son Edward II. He pursued a costly diplomatic war with France, which led to a breach with the Church and the growth of importance of Parliament.

*Legal Reforms*  The powers and procedures of the royal government received a still clearer definition under Edward I. Edward produced no systematic codification of English law, like Justinian, but he sought to correct, codify, and enlarge the common law in certain critical areas and to give the system a new flexibility. He issued the first *Statutes of the Realm*, thereby setting a precedent for changing law only by legislation rather than by administrative decision. Edward's statutes required the barons to show by what warrant, or royal license, they exercised jurisdiction in their own courts, marking an important step in the decline of baronial justice. While he did not eliminate their courts, Edward kept the courts from growing and changing. They became increasingly obsolete. His laws limited Church courts as well. Religious houses could not acquire more land without royal permission, nor could they send money to Rome. The statutes were especially important in determining the property law of England, regulating inheritance, and defining the rights of lords, vassals, and the king when land changed hands through inheritance or purchase. Edward laid the foundations upon which the English (and eventually American) law of real estate rested for centuries. In enacting these statutes and in governing the kingdom, Edward also placed a new emphasis on securing the consent of his subjects through Parliament.

At Edward's death in 1307 the English constitution had acquired certain distinctive features. The constitution was not contained in a single written document, but was defined by both custom and statute law. The king was the chief of the state, but it was recognized that the nobility and the representatives from the shires and towns should have some participation in the decision-making processes, especially regarding taxes. The

extraordinary continuity of these arrangements over centuries to come is testimony to the sound construction that the medieval English kings, lords, and commoners gave to their government.

## ◆ FRANCE AND THE CONSOLIDATION OF RULE

In France as well as England, representative institutions became a tool in the aid of royal government. As the French kings extended their power over the various provinces, meetings of representatives of their free subjects became valuable venues in which to announce policies. The turbulent struggles with England and with the papacy dominated Capetian policy in the late thirteenth and fourteenth centuries.

*Philip IV*  Louis IX's successors preserved the strength, but not the serenity, of his reign. His grandson Philip IV, the Fair (r. 1285–1314), is perhaps the most enigmatic of the medieval French kings; neither contemporaries nor later historians have agreed on his abilities. To some, Philip has seemed capable and cunning; to others, phlegmatic and uninterested, content to leave the business of government almost entirely to his ministers. If Philip lacked the personal ability to rule, he at least had the capacity to select strong ministers as his principal advisers. They were usually laymen trained in Roman law and possessing a high opinion of royal authority. They considered the king to be not merely a feudal monarch who ruled in agreement with the magnates of his realm but rather an "emperor in his own land" whose authority was free from all restrictions (the root sense of an absolute monarch) and subject to no higher power on earth.

The greatest obstacle to the advance of Philip's power was Edward I of England, master of the extensive fief of Aquitaine. Philip's resolve to drive England from the continent resulted in intermittent wars from 1294 to 1302. The woolen cloth weavers of the French county of Flanders relied on English wool. When Philip tried to block the importation of English wool into Flanders in order to hurt the English economy, the Flemish towns revolted against him. Philip's military campaign against them ended when the

*Chronology*

### POLITICAL EVENTS

| | |
|---|---|
| 1198–1250 | Frederick II of Germany and Sicily |
| r. 1226–1270 | Louis IX of France |
| 1216–1272 | Henry III of England |
| r. 1264–1265 | Baronial wars of Simon de Montfort |
| r. 1272–1307 | Edward I of England |
| r. 1273–1291 | Rudolf of Habsburg, Germany |
| r. 1261–1282 | Michael VIII Palaeologus, Byzantine Empire |
| 1259–1294 | Mongols |
| r. 1285–1314 | Philip IV of France |
| 1291 | Origin of Swiss Confederation |
| r. 1294–1303 | Boniface VIII |
| r. 1305–1314 | Pope Clement V |
| 1346–1378 | Beginning of Avignon papacy Charles IV Luxemburg of Germany |
| 1356 | Golden Bull |

Flemish towns' militias defeated him at Courtrai in 1302.

These costly wars had placed a heavy burden on the royal finances. Philip pursued a number of unscrupulous tactics to replenish the treasury. Following the lead of Edward I, who had confiscated Jewish property in England and expelled the Jews in 1290, Philip confiscated Jewish property in France and expelled them in 1306. He imprisoned foreign merchants to extort money from them. And he encouraged the pope to declare the wealthy Knights Templars heretics so that he could confiscate their property and treasure in France. Finally, Philip insisted on his right to demand from the Church "free gifts," which were actually taxes. The issue led to a protracted dispute with Pope Boniface VIII (see later in this chapter). In seeking to dominate these international powers—the Knights Templars and the Church itself—Philip showed his determination to become truly sovereign in his own lands.

*Estates General*   Seeking funds in his struggle against England and the pope, Philip used his royal bureaucrats to meet with provincial representative councils, the *estates*, to grant taxation. The estates were composed of three houses: representatives of the nobility (including the upper and lower nobility), of the clergy, and of the commoners (mostly urban middle class). The provincial estates usually granted the taxes and did not dispute the king's policies.

Philip called the first meeting of the *Estates General*, with representatives of nobility, clergy, and commoners from all provinces, in 1302 and again in 1308. He used these meetings very much as Edward I used the Parliament. He informed delegates about the insults that he and France had

▼ BATTLE OF THE GOLDEN SPURS
In 1302, Flemish peasants, who had rebelled because Philip IV of France attempted to block the importation of wool from England, defeated the king at the battle of Courtrai. It was said that after the battle, seven hundred pairs of spurs were collected and displayed in the local cathedral. Some sense of the brutality of the fighting is conveyed by this illustration, with King Philip brandishing his sword at the center and the pile of bodies at the lower right. Chroniques de France, fol. 333r. Copyright Bibliothèque royale Albert 1er, Bruxelles.

suffered at the hands of Pope Boniface VIII and his reasons for confiscating the property of the Templars. The Estates General met for Philip's propaganda purposes, not to deliberate on his policies.

In trying to achieve a powerful, centralized monarchy, Philip left France in a deeply disturbed condition. The Flemish towns remained defiant, and the king of England threatened to go to war. With the outbreak of the Hundred Years' War in the mid-fourteenth century, France under Philip's successors entered one of the darkest periods of its history.

◆ THE HOLY ROMAN EMPIRE AND THE FRAGMENTATION OF RULE

Frederick II's policy of granting away imperial rights in Germany left the vast territory a conglomeration of independent cities, bishoprics, dukedoms, and principalities. The king of Aragon's conquest of Sicily separated it from imperial ambitions. The German territory went through a period of interregnum until 1273, when the German nobles met and elected Rudolph Habsburg (r. 1273–1291) emperor. In the late Middle Ages the locus of power of the Holy Roman Empire shifted to the east, away from the Rhine and into central Europe.

*The Habsburgs*   Rudolph Habsburg was selected in part because he was a minor noble with isolated lands near the Alps and into Alsace. He took some initiatives that limited the outlawry of minor knights who were acting as tyrants over their territory, but he could not take on the more powerful nobles. He managed to take Austria by conquest from the king of Bohemia and add this territory to the family estates. The Habsburg's successes in acquiring territory alarmed the German nobles and bishops. In 1308 the German nobles and bishops elected a member of the house of Luxemburg in place of the Habsburgs.

*The Luxemburgs*   Like the Habsburgs, the Luxemburgs used the position of emperor to increase their personal holdings. Charles IV (r. 1346–1378) centered his power in Bohemia, a new acquisition

of the Luxemburgs. To stabilize the process of electing the emperor, Charles promulgated the so-called Golden Bull of 1356, which fixed the number of electors at seven. The choice represented a balance of traditional parties: Three were ecclesiastics (the archbishops of Mainz, Trier, and Cologne) and four were powerful nobles (the king of Bohemia, the count palatine of the Rhine, the duke of Saxony, and the margrave of Brandenburg). The electors were to meet a month after the death of the king and elect a new one. The plan eliminated the papacy from the deliberations and future emperors broke the custom of having the pope bestow the imperial title. The Habsburgs once again gained control with the extinction of the Luxemburg line in 1437, thus joining Bohemia and Hungary with Austria and the Tyrol, which were already under Habsburg control.

*Swiss Cantons*   While Rudolph Habsburg was successfully adding to his territories, he lost three of the Swiss cantons that were part of his original patrimony. The cantons argued that they were granted independence under Frederick II. It was not until 1315 that the Habsburgs, with a large feudal force, tried to retake them. Swiss patriots rolled stones and tree trunks down on them as they marched through a mountain pass and then descended on them with their axes. Their success led other cantons to join them in a loose federation of independent cantons. The Swiss confederation was a new form of government for Europe—neither a monarchy nor a feudal principality. While retaining independence, they formed militias that cooperated in defending their territory.

## III. Government in the East

While the West was secure from external invasions and able to continue its political, economic, and cultural development, the East was threatened by invasion from Asia once again. The East's defense against the new invaders meant that the West was sheltered, once again, from attack. The new threat came from the Mongols in the thirteenth century, followed by the Ottoman Turks in the fourteenth century.

## ◆ THE BYZANTINE EMPIRE

When Greece and Constantinople fell in the Fourth Crusade in 1204, the Greeks rallied under descendants from the imperial line and established several principalities in Asia Minor and along the southern shore of the Black Sea. But it was the territory in Asia Minor, with its capital in Nicaea, that eventually dominated the political scene.

*Michael VIII Palaeologus*   Under the leadership of Michael VIII Palaeologus (r. 1261–1282), the Nicaean empire managed to recapture Constantinople. By this time the Western attempt to establish an empire at Constantinople collapsed: The Venetians had taken the major trading islands and ports; the Western nobility had divided the Balkans into independent feudalities; and the Western emperors proved to be short lived and weak. Michael's general found the city unprotected and plundered of many of its treasures, which the crusaders had shipped back to Europe. The Greek population welcomed the return of Greek rule.

Michael VIII was an adept player in international politics and diplomacy. He needed to subdue a strong Bulgarian empire and the remaining Western feudal principalities in Greece and negotiate with the rising Serb state.

*The Balkans*   In the twentieth century we used the term "Balkanization" to refer to the splintering of a territory into a number of different states. Although the Byzantine emperors had settled various tribes in the Balkans, after the Fourth Crusade fights among these peoples became irreversible and are the root of modern tensions in the Balkans. The Bulgarians, taking advantage of the chaos after the Fourth Crusade, had established an empire (their leaders had taken the title of czar in imitation of the Roman "caesar") and threatened to invade Constantinople. Michael VIII managed to neutralize them through warfare and marriage with his female relatives. The Serbs had converted to Eastern Christianity in 1219. By Michael VIII's reign, they were beginning an ascendancy in the Balkans that allowed them to push into Byzantine territory.

Michael VIII left an empire that was again the Byzantine Empire, but warfare and taxation to defend the borders left it weak. Weakened as it was, it was still a major player, and the Palaeologus dynasty remained on the throne to the final fall in 1453.

## ◆ THE MONGOLS

The Mongols (of Turkic origin and sometimes called Tartars in medieval sources) threatened Europe much as other groups from central Asia, such as the Huns, had. They were composed of nomadic tribes organized under a chief, who took

▼ COURT OF A MONGOL KING
**The courts of the Mongol kings, as this illustration from a Persian manuscript suggests, were dazzlingly opulent. When Louis IX of France sent presents of liturgical objects (chalices and books), the Mongol king rejected the gift and suggested that a tribute of gold and silver would be more appropriate.**
Bibliothèque Nationale de France, Paris

the title of Genghis Khan, "Inflexible Emperor," in 1206. He turned eastward and took Beijing in 1216. Leaving his trusted lieutenants to subdue the rest of China, Genghis Khan turned his attention to the west and amassed the largest empire the world has ever known. Meeting little resistance from the Turks, his empire had expanded by 1225 to include central Asia, parts of Afghanistan, Persia, and the Caucasus.

*The Golden Horde*   In 1223 a Mongol army penetrated Eastern Europe in what seems to have been a reconnoitering expedition. The Mongols defeated the allied princes of Rus, and from 1237 to 1241 a Mongol army under the leadership of Batu, grandson of Genghis Khan, conducted raids throughout Eastern Europe, including Russia, Poland, and Hungary. The Mongols abandoned Poland and Hungary, but established the capital of a division of the Mongol empire, called "the Golden Horde," at Sarai, on the lower Volga River.

The khans, or rulers, of the Golden Horde maintained suzerainty over the lands of what are now Ukraine and Belarus until the mid-1300s and over eastern Russia until the mid-1400s. The princes who were subject to the Golden Horde had to pay tribute to the khans, but otherwise they could rule their own people. As a result, despite the power they exercised over the East Slavs for centuries, the Mongols' influence on Slavic languages and cultures remained relatively slight.

*Resettlement of the East Slavs*   The devastation of the Mongol invasions and the formation of the Golden Horde led a chronicler to lament that Kiev, once proudly known as the "mother of Rus cities," had only two hundred houses left standing in the 1200s. Rus population dispersed. Some colonists moved west into the upper Dniester River and became the ancestors of the modern Ukrainians and the Belorussians, or White Russians. After a short period of submission to the Mongols, these colonies fell under the political domination first of the grand dukes of Lithuania and then of the Polish kings. With a large Ukrainian population, these people developed their own literary languages and cultural traditions and remained under Polish or Austrian rule until 1944.

Other colonists moved north into a region ruled by the city of Novgorod, but it was too poor to either attract the Mongols or to support a dense population. The lands between the upper Volga and Oka rivers, the Russian "Mesopotamia," became the most important sites of Slavic resettlement, as the dense forests offered both relative security from the nomads and a productive soil. The Novgorod and Russian Mesopotamia immigrants were the ancestors of the modern Russians, forming the largest group of East Slavic peoples.

## ◆ MUSCOVITE RUSSIA

Historians call the period between the twelfth and fifteenth centuries the age of feudal Russia—the time during which Russia was divided into many princely domains. Nearly all the small towns within Russian Mesopotamia had their own princes, their own citadels, or *kremlins*, and their own territories. All the princes were subject to the khan of the Golden Horde.

Moscow gained preeminence primarily through the talents of its early princes. Abandoning the Kievan practice of dividing lands among surviving male heirs, the princes pursued a policy of primogeniture. They acquired new territories through wars, marriages, and purchases, and they sought to make Moscow the symbol and embodiment of Russian unity. Unlike Western Christians, they early on established a distinct Russian national and cultural identity.

*Ivan I of Muscovy*   Ivan I (r. 1328–1341) was the first Muscovite prince to raise Moscow to prominence. He extended his possessions along the entire course of the Moskva River and won enclaves of territory north of the Volga River. Ivan courted the favor of the still-powerful Mongol khan of the Golden Horde. In return for his loyalty and gifts, the khan made Ivan the chief representative of Mongol authority in Russia (the "grand duke"), with the right to collect the Mongol tribute from all Russian lands. Ivan increased his own treasury while collecting tribute for the Mongols.

With Ivan's encouragement the primate (or chief bishop) of the Russian Church often visited Moscow, finally making the city his permanent

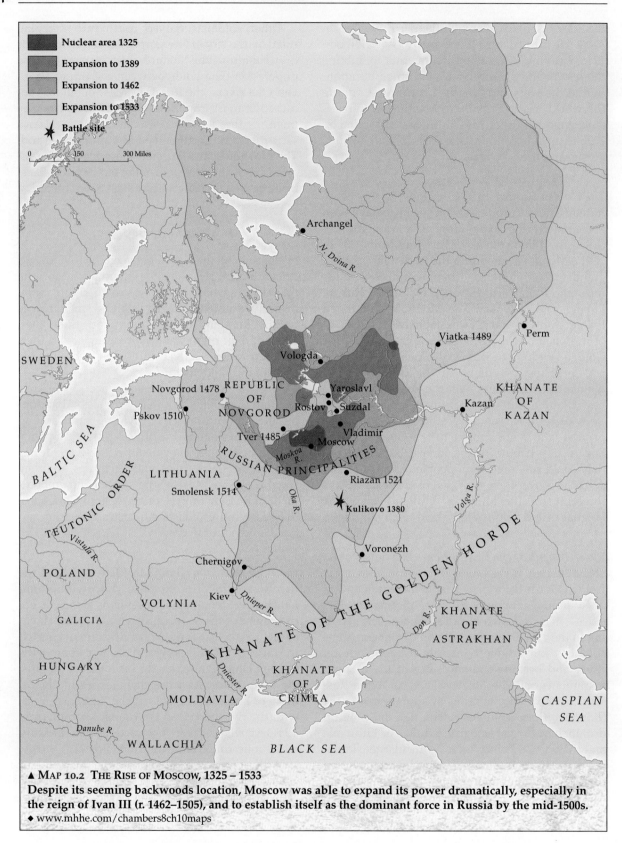

**Nuclear area 1325**

**Expansion to 1389**

**Expansion to 1462**

**Expansion to 1533**

✶ **Battle site**

0      150      300 Miles

SWEDEN

Archangel

*N. Dvina R.*

Viatka 1489        Perm

Vologda

REPUBLIC        Yaroslavl        KHANATE
Novgorod 1478        OF                                              OF
                NOVGOROD        Rostov   Suzdal        Kazan   KAZAN
Pskov 1510

                                Vladimir
Tver 1485        Moscow

        *Moskva*        Riazan 1521
BALTIC SEA        RUSSIAN PRINCIPALITIES
                *R.*

LITHUANIA

TEUTONIC ORDER        Smolensk 1514        *Oka R.*

        ✶ **Kulikovo 1380**        *Volga R.*

*Vistula R.*

POLAND        Voronezh

        Chernigov

VOLYNIA        Kiev   *Dnieper R.*        KHANATE OF THE GOLDEN HORDE

GALICIA        *Don R.*   KHANATE
                OF
                ASTRAKHAN

HUNGARY        *Dniester R.*        KHANATE
                OF        CASPIAN
MOLDAVIA        CRIMEA        SEA

*Danube R.*

WALLACHIA        BLACK SEA

▲ **Map 10.2   The Rise of Moscow, 1325 – 1533**
**Despite its seeming backwoods location, Moscow was able to expand its power dramatically, especially in
the reign of Ivan III (r. 1462–1505), and to establish itself as the dominant force in Russia by the mid-1500s.**
◆ www.mhhe.com/chambers8ch10maps

residence. This move made Moscow the head-quarters of the Russian Church even before it became the capital of the Russian people.

By the late 1300s the Mongols' power was declining, largely because of internal dissension. With the Mongols weakened, the princes of Moscow began to present themselves as leaders of the growing national opposition to Mongol rule.

***Ivan III***   Ivan III (r. 1462–1505) completed the unification of Russian land and laid the constitutional foundations for modern Russia. He acquired the prosperous city of Novgorod, which had developed strong trading and cultural links with Western Europe. The Novgorod merchant oligarchy favored its neighboring Catholic Lithuanians, but the populace was Orthodox in religion and preferred the prince of Moscow. Ivan demanded and received the submission of the city and incorporated Novgorod and its territories into the Muscovite state in 1478. Continuing his territorial expansion, he eventually ended two centuries of Mongol rule of Russia at the Oka River in 1480. No battle occurred, because neither side dared cross the river that separated them.

***Tsar***   Seeking to depict himself as the successor of the Byzantine emperors (Constantinople had fallen to the Ottoman Turks in 1453), Ivan adopted the title *tsar,* the Slavic equivalent of the Latin term *caesar.* Married to Sophia Palaeologus, who was the niece of the last Byzantine emperor and had been educated in Italy, Ivan added elaborate Byzantine pomp and etiquette to his court and adopted the Byzantine double-headed eagle as the seal and symbol of the new Russian empire. Under the influence of his wife, he invited Italian artists and architects to Moscow to help rebuild the Kremlin and make the city an impressive capital. In imitation of the Byzantine emperors, in 1497, Ivan promulgated a new code of laws known as the *Sudebnik.*

***The Third Rome***   The new strength and splendor of the tsar inspired several monastic scholars to propose the idea that Moscow was the third Rome. The first Rome, they said, had fallen into heresy, and the second, Constantinople, had been taken by the infidel. Moscow alone, the capital of the one Orthodox ruler, preserved the true religion.

Ivan's reforms were not completed until the reign of his grandson, Ivan IV, the Terrible (r. 1530–1584)—a tsar who brutally destroyed the old nobility of *boyars* (hereditary nobility) and imposed on all landowners the status of servant to the tsar. Nonetheless, Ivan III can be seen as the founder of the Russian state. He finished the task of unifying the Russian land and its people, and he declared himself to be the autocrat of Russia. Ivan III bequeathed to his successors one of the most characteristic institutions of modern Russia: its centralized, autocratic government.

# IV. The Papacy and the Church

◆

While the monarchs of France and England were continuing to consolidate their rule over their subjects and while Russia was beginning to form a national identity around Moscow, papal administration also continued to expand. Often desperate for funds to carry on their ambitious political involvement in European affairs, the popes by the late thirteenth century exploited their spiritual powers to raise money for their political endeavors. In the past centuries new or reformed monastic orders had brought the Church back to its spiritual mission, but no new orders developed and existing ones had become increasingly corrupt.

## ◆ THE PAPACY

***Boniface VIII***   The papal curia and the college of cardinals were aware that the papacy was losing its prestige, and they sought to remedy the situation by electing as pope a famous hermit, who took the name Celestine V (1294). They assumed that he would be a pious figurehead and that they could carry on business as usual. Celestine, however, observed the corruption and feared that his soul would be endangered if he continued as pope; he resigned in five months. His successor, Boniface VIII (r. 1294–1303), was rumored to have rigged up a speaking tube to the papal sleeping chamber through which he intoned that it was the will of God that Celestine resign.

***Clash with Philip IV of France***   By the late thirteenth century the papacy was facing a rising

▲ Andrei Rublev Old Testament Trinity, 1410–1420
**Andrei Rublev, one of the most influential Russian artists of the fifteenth century, worked within a Byzantine tradition of wall painting. His *Old Testament Trinity*, originally from a monastery, shows a reinterpretation of the standard Christian iconography: The three angels positioned around a dish represent God the Father, the Son, and the Holy Ghost.**
Scala/Art Resource, NY

challenge from lay lords, who sought to tax the clergy within their own territories. Both Philip IV of France and Edward I of England had been taxing the clergy through the fiction of asking for, and always receiving, gifts or money for specific royal enterprises. In 1296, in the bull *Clericis laicos* (all solemn papal letters were called *bulls* because they were closed with a lead seal, or *bulla*, and they are usually identified by their first two words), Boniface forbade all clergy to make

▲ ONION DOMES AT KIZHI
**Constructed entirely of wood, the remarkable churches of northern Russia, such as this eighteenth-century example from Kizhi, were made into magnificently elaborate structures even though they often served only small settlements. The onion domes were the characteristic symbol of the Russian Orthodox Church, and they were multiplied across the roofs of Russian churches.**
Magnum Photos, Inc.

payments without papal permission. Such a restriction would have given the pope a powerful, if not controlling, voice in royal finances that no king could tolerate. The English simply ignored the order, but Philip retaliated by forbidding all exports of coin from his realm to Rome. Boniface issued another bull condemning Philip directly. Philip called a meeting of the Estates General in 1302 (the first such meeting) and presented the three estates with an exaggerated description of Boniface's insults to the French king and people and revived the rumors surrounding the resignation of Celestine.

With both his personal character and the papal authority threatened, Boniface issued the bull *Unam Sanctam,* which declared that Philip must submit to his authority or risk the damnation of his immortal soul (see *"Unam Sanctam,"* p. 352). Philip accused the pope of shocking crimes and demanded his arrest and trial at a general church council. To enforce his accusations, Philip sent one of his principal advisers to Italy. With the aid of a small army of Boniface's enemies, the French adviser broke into the papal palace at Anagni and arrested the pope in 1303. The citizens of Anagni rescued Boniface shortly afterward, but he died in Rome only a few months later.

***Origin of the Avignon Papacy*** Succeeding popes capitulated to the French king and revoked *Unam Sanctam.* Philip's victory was complete when a Frenchman, Clement V, was elected pope in 1305. Clement V postponed going to Rome, preferring instead to settle in 1309 in the French-speaking

# Unam Sanctam

◆

*This statement of papal monarchy was issued by Pope Boniface VIII in 1302 to combat assertions of royal power by the kings of England and France against the authority of the universal Church. It did little, however, to deter the claims of such rulers to a growing sphere of authority.*

"That there is one holy, Catholic and apostolic Church we are bound to believe and to hold, our faith urging us, and this we do firmly believe and simply confess; and that outside this Church there is no salvation or remission of sins. . . .

"We are taught by the words of the Gospel that in this Church and in her power there are two swords, a spiritual one and a temporal one. For when the apostles said 'Here are two swords' (Luke 22:38), meaning in the Church since it was the apostles who spoke, the Lord did not reply that it was too many but enough. Certainly anyone who denies that the temporal sword is in the power of Peter has not paid heed to the words of the Lord when he said, 'Put up thy sword into its sheath' (Matthew 26:52). Both then are in the power of the Church, the material sword and the spiritual. But the one is exercised for the Church, the other by the Church, the one by the hand of the priest, the other by the hand of kings and soldiers, though at the will and sufferance of the priest. One sword ought to be under the other and the temporal authority subject to the spiritual power. For, while the apostle says, 'There is no power but from God and those that are ordained of God'

(Romans 13:1), they would not be ordained unless one sword was under the other and, being inferior, was led by the other to the highest things. . . . But that the spiritual power excels any earthly one in dignity and nobility we ought the more openly to confess in proportion as spiritual things excel temporal ones. Moreover we clearly perceive this from the giving of tithes, from benediction and sanctification, from the acceptance of this power and from the very government of things. For the truth bearing witness, the spiritual power has to institute the earthly power and to judge if it has not been good. . . .

"Therefore, if the earthly power errs, it shall be judged by the spiritual power, if a lesser spiritual power errs it shall be judged by its superior, but if the supreme spiritual power errs it can be judged only by God not by man. . . . Therefore we declare, state, define and pronounce that it is altogether necessary to salvation for every human creature to be subject to the Roman Pontiff."

From Warren Hollister et al., *Medieval Europe: A Short Sourcebook* (McGraw-Hill Companies, 1992), pp. 215–216.

---

city of Avignon (the city was in Burgundy, a German, not French, territory). Selecting a series of French cardinals, Clement V and his successors found Avignon congenial. For the next sixty-eight years the popes lived within the shadow of the French monarchy, executing its policies. In Rome revenues from the papal estates fell into the hands of competing factions of nobility. These nobles were so hostile to the French popes that return became impossible.

***Papal Corruption***   Separated from the normal income derived from papal estates around Rome, the popes sought to finance their extravagant living in Avignon and the extensive church bureaucracy from other sources. The popes sold bishoprics (simony) and then extracted substantial payments from the first year that the bishop

held his office; they imposed tithes (a tenth of income) on the clergy; and they sold to laypersons and clergy exemptions and dispensations from the regulations of canon law. Divorce or penances for sins could be purchased from the pope's representatives for a fee. The Dominicans and Franciscans, wandering through the world as they did, proved to be ideal agents for selling release from the strictures of canon law.

***Monastic Orders***   In the past when the papacy had faced criticism and spiritual crisis, reforming monastic orders had come to its rescue. In the late thirteenth and fourteenth centuries, however, the monastic orders contributed to the Church's poor image. The Dominicans had become deeply implicated with the Inquisition, a role that cost them the trust of the laity. Rather than maintain their mendicant roots, both the Franciscans and Dominicans had become wealthy monastic orders. Within the Franciscans, a bitter fight developed between the Spiritual Franciscans, who wanted to return to the order as St. Francis had founded it, and the Conventual Franciscans, who favored monasteries and continued involvement in Church politics. The Conventuals won the fight, and the pope renounced the Spiritual Franciscans.

### ◆ LAY RELIGIOUS OBSERVANCE

Whatever their discontent with the papacy, the laity were devoted to the Christian religion and found renewed spiritual commitments in their parish churches, their individual salvation, and in lay organizations centered around religious observance.

*Beguines and Beghars* Already in the twelfth century, pious groups of laity had formed quasi-monastic groups. The Beguines and their male counterparts, the Beghards, were popular in northern European cities. They lived together in houses or with families. While Beguines did not take vows of chastity and did not live by orders, they lived pious lives devoted to simple tasks such as spinning and caring for the sick, the old, and the bodies of the dead (see "The Benguinage of Saint Elizabeth in Ghent [1328]," p. 354). They might spend their whole lives in this work or they might eventually marry. They were regarded with general suspicion by the Church, who tried to force them to become extensions of the Dominican order. The Franciscans and Dominicans had associated other laypersons, called the Third Order, or tertiaries to their orders. Tertiaries included widows or married people who worked in the world but spent time and money on charity and pious works. Many women found the tertiaries a refuge from household cares and an outlet for their spiritual drive.

*Parish Guilds and Religious Practice* Married laypersons formed social-religious guilds within their parishes. The guilds celebrated the feast of their patron saint, helped maintain the parish church and perhaps even built a chapel within the church for their own use, provided candles for worship, and performed religious plays. In the early fourteenth century, a new theological emphasis on purgatory (the state in which the soul remained until it expiated the sins committed during life) encouraged the growth of guilds. The guild members prayed for the souls of dead brethren and sisters to release their souls from purgatory into heaven. Guilds also provided fellowship, including feasts, burial processions for members, and charity for those who had suffered illness.

Another theological and liturgical change influenced the practice of lay piety in the later Middle Ages. The emphasis of the Fourth Lateran Council on transubstantiation (the miraculous conversion of the bread and wine to the body and blood of Christ) and the requirement that the laity take Holy Communion (Eucharist) at least once a year, elevated the importance of this liturgical practice. To aid the laity in understanding the importance of the Eucharist, a special day was set aside, Corpus Christi Day, on which the communion wafer, in a special box, was carried by the priest in religious procession. The procession won lay devotion, and popular religious plays were performed on Corpus Christi Day.

*Antisemitism* Many of the Corpus Christi plays represented Jews dishonoring the Communion wafer by boiling it or nailing it to a piece of wood and being subsequently converted. Thus, an unintended result of the emphasis on the Eucharist was increased antisemitism in thirteenth-century Europe. The Fourth Lateran Council had also mandated that Jews wear special signs, the Star of David, on their dress to indicate their religion. While these rules were not immediately enforced, they gradually became part of urban law. The participation of Jews in money lending led to feelings of competition and hostility on the part of the urban Christian population and the nobles and monasteries who had mortgaged their lands to borrow money from Jews. The hostility led to sporadic pogroms throughout Europe, such as the massacre of the Jews in London in 1264. The growing antisemitism in the thirteenth century was in marked contrast to the twelfth century, when Jewish and Christian scholars exchanged their theological ideas. The increased suspicion and hatred explains why Edward I and Philip IV

## The Beguinage of Saint Elizabeth in Ghent (1328)

*The Beguines were religious women who chose to live not in nunneries but in communities such as that of Saint Elizabeth or in homes of their own family or others. They supported themselves with manual labor and tended to the poor and sick. Some became preachers, writers, and mystics.*

"The Beguinage of Saint Elizabeth . . . is encircled by ditches and walls. In the middle of it is a church, and next to the church a cemetery and a hospital, which the aforesaid ladies endowed for the weak and infirm of that same Beguinage. Many houses were also built there for habitation of the said women, each of whom has her own garden, separated from the next by ditches or hedges; and two chaplains were established in this place by the same ladies.

"In these houses, indeed, many dwell together communally and are very poor, having nothing but their clothing, a bed and a chest, nor are they a burden to anyone, but by manual work, washing the wool and cleaning the pieces of cloth sent to them from the town, they earn enough money daily that, making thereby a simple living, they also pay their dues to the church and give a modest amount in alms. And in each convent there is one who is called the mistress of work, whose duty is to supervise the work and the workers, so that all things are faithfully carried through according to God's will.

"We shall not say much of their abstinence from food and drink but this: that many of them are satisfied for the whole day with the coarse bread and pottage which they have in common in each convent, and with a drink of cold water they lessen their thirst rather than increase their appetite. And many among them are accustomed to fast frequently on bread and water, and many of them do not wear linen on their bodies, and they use straw pallets instead of beds."

From Emilie Amt, *Women's Lives in Medieval Europe: A Sourcebook* (Routledge, 1993), pp. 264–265.

were able to expel the Jews without public condemnation.

***Individual Spiritualism***   A combination of the emphasis on the Eucharist and the Franciscans' encouragement of spiritual exercises that involved imaginative participation in scenes such as the Crucifixion led to individual quests for spiritual satisfaction. Women in particular took to this form of religious experience, imagining that they were at the Crucifixion and that the wounds of Christ could nourish them. These pious women might be nuns or Beguines, but many were laywomen who were wives, mothers, and daughters. They led lives of extreme abstinence, giving their food to the poor and refusing to eat themselves or trying to live only on the Communion wafers. In addition to fasting, some women performed extreme asceticism, beating themselves with whips and wearing hair shirts. Some became saints, and some died from starvation.

The most famous among the saints was Catherine of Siena (1347–1380), the daughter of a wool-dyer and his wife. She began fasting early in life and refused to marry. Her good works took her among the sick, where she tried to drink puss from the ulcers of a cancerous woman. Her biographer says that he saw her stuff twigs down her throat to bring up food, but he says that even when she seemed emaciated, she would rise up if there was work to be done among the poor. Although closely associated with the Dominicans all her life, she remained a laywoman.

While men dominated the ecclesiastical institutions of the Church, women were able to gain prestige through their individual spirituality, visions, and work among the poor. Much of their spiritual prestige came through manipulating food. Women were closely associated with preparing and serving food, and the shared meal was the basis of much of medieval life. When a daughter defied her parents by fasting or giving away their food to the poor, she defied basic assumptions about female behavior and could often use this advantage to manipulate her family into canceling marriage plans. Many clergymen found the women's fasting and asceticism a valuable tool for instructing both the laity and other clergy on the strength of these women's devotion. Women could overcome the constraints society put on

▲ WOMEN MYSTICS

During the fourteenth and fifteenth centuries, individuals sought salvation through meditation. Women were among the most famous mystics. Birgitta of Sweden (ca. 1302–1373) came from a noble family, married, and served in the royal household. Widowed in 1344, she retreated to a house near a Cistercian monastery and led a life of prayer and penance. She experienced a series of revelations, one of which is pictured here, which she recorded in Swedish. She was famous throughout Europe for her writings.

The Pierpont Morgan Library / Art Resource, NY

them, both as participants in family and Church, through their own spiritual quests.

# V. Learning and Literature

◆

The thirteenth- and early fourteenth-century developments in learning and literature brought new trends in Scholasticism. Just as the Franciscans profoundly influenced individual spirituality, so too they influenced philosophy. Although some of the radical new philosophers had their works condemned in their lifetimes, their think-

ing laid the foundation for modern scientific inquiry. In vernacular literature, Dante (1265–1321) made the greatest syntheses of medieval culture in *The Divine Comedy,* in which he included Scholasticism, courtly romance, spiritual journey, classical learning, and contemporary politics.

## ◆ PHILOSOPHY

*St. Bonaventure (1221–1274)* Born in central Italy, Bonaventure was cured of a childhood illness through the intercession of St. Francis of Assisi. He went on to become a leading member of the Franciscan order and a contemporary of Thomas Aquinas at the University of Paris. Rather than advocating the rigorous logic for proof of the existence of God that Aquinas advocated, Bonaventure's proof was based on intuited principles (as was Duns Scotus'). To help humans understand the existence of God, Bonaventure emphasized spiritual exercises that began with looking at God's creations on Earth and seeing God in them. Contemplation would lead the believer to the revelation of God's existence. Bonaventure's theology and personal beliefs made him one of the great medieval mystics.

*English Scholastics*  Under the influence of two English Franciscans, Roger Bacon (1214–1294) and William of Ockham (ca. 1285–ca. 1349), philosophy began to investigate problems of natural laws. Both men were attracted to the emphasis in Aristotle's logic on empirical observation, and both are often considered the founders of Western scientific writing. Bacon's writings are in the medieval intellectual and Franciscan traditions, in that he emphasized revelation and the interior illumination of the soul through seven states of "internal experience." The new element in his writing is his argument that knowledge can only be verified through "experimental science," that is, he suggested establishing empirical hypotheses and developing ways of testing them. He did not specify whether he was advocating a new methodology for approaching knowledge or just a special subject matter that was different from established sciences and authorities. He was imprisoned for his unorthodox views in 1278.

William of Ockham did not attack Thomas Aquinas, but he did point out Aquinas' limitations. He argued that the articles of Christian faith could not be proved with logic and that they should be left to belief. Observation could be applied to nature, including the heavenly bodies and Earth. His guiding principle in logical argument is called Ockham's razor: "What can be explained on fewer principles is explained needlessly by more." Simplicity, or elegance of argument, became the basis for scientific explanation to the present day.

*Medieval Science*  Bacon and Ockham were medieval thinkers, but their students began to take their lessons to levels that we consider to be the beginnings of scientific thinking. Nicholas of Oresme (1320–1382), a student of Ockham, suggested that the movement of the planets could be better explained if Earth was in motion, like the planets, rather than stationary, which was the accepted view of the day. John Buridan (ca. 1300–ca. 1358) argued, following Ockham's razor, that there was no reason to assume that the celestial bodies were composed of a matter different from Earth. The work of Oresme later influenced Galileo's description of the uniform acceleration of falling bodies and Descartes' development of analytical geometry.

## ◆ DANTE

Literary output in most vernacular languages was abundant during the thirteenth century except in English, which was retarded in its development by the continued dominance of a French-speaking aristocracy. The masterpiece that best summarizes the culture of the age is the *Comedy* of Dante Alighieri.

Dante was born in Florence in 1265. Little is known of his education, but he seems to have been immersed in scholarship. The *Comedy* is one of the most learned, and hence most difficult, poems of world literature.

Two experiences in Dante's life profoundly influenced his attitudes and are reflected in his works. In 1274, when he was only nine years old, he fell deeply in love with a young girl named Beatrice. Much mystery surrounds her, but she seems to have been Beatrice Portinari, who later married into a prominent family and died in 1290. Dante could have seen her only rarely; we do not know if she ever returned his love. Still, in his youthful adoration of Beatrice he seems to have attained that sense of harmony and joy that the troubadours considered to be the great reward of lovers.

In 1302 an experience of a much different sort shattered his life. For political reasons Dante was exiled from Florence. He spent the remaining years of his life wandering from city to city, a disillusioned, even bitter man. He died in 1321 and was buried at Ravenna.

*The Comedy*  Dante composed his masterpiece from 1313 to 1321. He called it a *commedia* in conformity with the classical notion that a happy

Nel uano tutti sua cor guizaua.
torcendo in su la uenenosa forcha.
cha guisa di scorpion la punta armaua
Lo duca disse or conuien che si torcha.
la nostra uia un poco in fina quella.
bestia maluagia che colla si torcha.
Pero scendemmo a la destra mamella.
e diece passi femmo in su lostremo.
per ben cessar la rena ela fiamella.

▲ A detail from a fourteenth-century manuscript copy of Dante's *Divine Comedy* illustrates the section of hell reserved for usurers. The Church regarded usury as one of the many earthly sins that condemn people in the eyes of God. Dante appears three times in this scene, on two occasions accompanied by his bearded guide, Virgil.

By permission of the British Library

ending made any story, no matter how serious, a comedy; the adjective *divine* was added to its title only after his death. The poem is divided into three parts, which describe the poet's journey through hell, purgatory, and heaven.

The poem opens with Dante "in the middle of the way of this our life." An aging man, he has grown confused and disillusioned; he is lost in a "dark forest" of doubt, harassed by wild animals, symbols of his own untamed passions. The theme of the poem is Dante's rediscovery of a former sense of harmony and joy. Leading him back to his lost peace are two guides. The first, Virgil, who represents human reason, conducts Dante through hell and then up the seven-storied mountain of purgatory to the earthly paradise, the vanished Eden, at its summit. In hell Dante encounters people who have chosen as their supreme goal in life something other than the love of God—riches, pleasure, fame, or power. Virgil shows Dante that

the good life cannot be built on such selfish choices. Reason, in other words, can enable humans to avoid the pitfalls of egoistic, material existence. In fact, reason can accomplish even more than that, for as embodied by Virgil, it guides Dante through purgatory and shows him how to acquire the natural virtues that are the foundations of the earthly paradise—a full and peaceful earthly existence.

In the dignity and power given to Virgil, Dante shares the high regard for human reason characteristic of the thirteenth century. However, reason can take humans only so far. To enter heaven, Dante needs a new guide—Beatrice herself, representative of supernatural revelation and grace. She takes the poet through the heavenly spheres into the presence of God, "in Whom is our peace." The peace and joy of the heavenly court set the dominant mood at the poem's conclusion, in contrast to the confusion and violence of the dark forest with which it opens.

The poem reflects the great cultural issues that challenged Dante's contemporaries—the relations between reason and faith, nature and grace, human power and the divine will. Dante, like Aquinas, was trying to combine two opposed views of human nature and its ability to shape its own destiny. One, rooted in the optimism of the twelfth and thirteenth centuries and in the more distant classical heritage, affirmed that human beings were masters of themselves and the world. The other, grounded in the Judeo-Christian tradition, saw them, fundamentally, as lost children in a vale of tears. Dante's majestic panorama summarizes not only the medieval vision of the universe but also his estimation of what it meant to live a truly wise, truly happy, truly human life.

# SUMMARY

Medieval civilization attained a new stability in the thirteenth and early fourteenth centuries. Large-scale woolen cloth production, long-range commercial exchanges, and sophisticated business practices gave the economy a dynamic aura. In political life, feudal governments consolidated and clarified their constitutional procedures, and parliaments and representative assemblies came to play a recognized role in the processes of government. Urban institutions and the middle class became part of the political, economic, and social life of medieval Europe. The papacy energetically sought to lead the Western monarchs as their guide and conscience, but secular entanglements and fiscal problems threatened and gradually diluted its moral authority. While the papacy went into a serious decline, as did the Dominican and Franciscan orders, the laity remained deeply pious and increasingly sought communal or individual routes to salvation. Philosophy began to turn its attention to empirical science, and literature developed a new sophistication with the *Comedy* of Dante. The East, by contrast, suffered continual warfare and a devastating new invasion by the Mongols. Out of the ashes of this conquest, however, emerged a new state of Russia centered on Moscow. The fourteenth and fifteenth centuries, however, brought radical new challenges to the stability achieved in the thirteenth century. Famines became common in the early fourteenth century, Philip IV and Edward I had sown the seeds of the Hundred Years' War, and the Byzantine Empire was so weakened by protracted warfare that the arrival of the Ottoman Turks would finally spell its doom.

## QUESTIONS FOR FURTHER THOUGHT

**1. In many ways the development of Parliament was a direct outgrowth of the Magna Carta. Who were the chief beneficiaries of the Magna Carta and of Parliament? How do these beneficiaries indicate a shift in the social class structure?**

**2. If you think of Dante's *Divine Comedy* as having intellectual roots in both medieval thought and the new "humanistic" thought, what elements of his writing would you use to make an argument that he was a bridge between the two?**

**3. Commerce assumed a larger and larger role in the European economy. What factors contributed to the success of trade and commerce? Think back to the early development of towns as well as the current chapter.**

# RECOMMENDED READING

## Sources

*Alighieri, Dante. *The Divine Comedy.* Mark Musa (tr.). 1996.

*Amt, Emilie (ed.). *Women's Lives in Medieval Europe: A Sourcebook.* 1993.

*The Chronicle of Novgorod.* Robert Mitchell and Neville Forbes (trs.). 1914. Portrays social and political life of the principal commercial town of medieval Russia.

*Geary, Patrick J. (ed.). *Readings in Medieval History.* 1997. Collection of documents and texts covering the whole of the Middle Ages. Selections are long and representative of the writings of historical figures.

Howes, Robert Craig (ed. and tr.). *The Testaments of the Grand Princes of Moscow.* 1967.

*Shinners, John (ed.). *Medieval Popular Religion, 1000–1500.* 1997. Valuable collection with generous selections from texts.

## Studies

Boase, T. S. R. *Boniface VIII.* 1933. Standard biography of the controversial pope.

*Bynum, Caroline Walker. *Holy Feast and Holy Fast: The Religious Significance of Food to Medieval Women.* 1987. Discussion of female mystics in the later Middle Ages and their abstinence.

*Duby, Georges. *William Marshal: The Flower of Chivalry.* 1985. Sensitive biography of an Anglo-Norman lord.

Durham, Thomas. *Serbia: The Rise and Fall of a Medieval Empire.* 1989.

Fernández-Armesto, Felipe. *Before Columbus: Exploration and Colonization from the Mediterranean to the Atlantic, 1229–1492.* 1987. Discusses medieval exploration before Columbus, illustrating that later exploration grew out of the earlier tradition of navigating along the Atlantic coast.

*Geremek, Bronislaw. *The Margins of Society in Late Medieval Paris.* 1987. Examines the Parisian underworld.

*Hanawalt, Barbara. *Growing Up in Medieval London: The Experience of Childhood in History.* 1993. Childhood and adolescence in medieval London.

*Herlihy, David. *Opera Muliebria: Women and Work in Medieval Europe.* 1990. A survey of women's work with very good information on Paris.

*Jones, W. T. *A History of Western Philosophy: The Medieval Mind.* 1969. Very good survey with selections from the writings of major thinkers.

*Klapisch-Zuber, Christiane. *Women, Family, and Ritual in Renaissance Italy.* 1985. Collection of essays by Klapisch-Zuber concerning her work on women and the family.

Leuschner, Joachim. *Germany in the Late Middle Ages.* 1980. Survey of the period.

*Martin, Janet. *Medieval Russia 980–1584.* 1995. An accessible account of the development of medieval Russia.

*Miskimin, Harry A. *The Economy of Early Renaissance Europe, 1300–1460.* 1975. Synthesis of economic situation in Europe during this period.

Morgan, David. *The Mongols.* 1986. Emphasizes the impact of the Mongol conquests and empire on Eastern Europe.

Otis, Leah. *Prostitution in Medieval Society: The History of an Urban Institution in Languedoc.* 1985. Examination of prostitution in southern France.

Ozment, Steven. *The Age of Reform, 1250–1550: An Intellectual and Religious History of Late Medieval and Reformation Europe.* 1980. Survey of intellectual history for the period.

Strayer, Joseph R. *The Reign of Philip the Fair.* 1980. Biography of Philip with emphasis on his administration.

*Ward, Jennifer. *English Noble Women in the Later Middle Ages.* 1992. A valuable study of noble households and women in them.

*Wood, Charles T. *Philip the Fair and Boniface VIII: State vs. Papacy.* 2d ed. 1971. Presents historiography of this conflict.

*Available in paperback.

▲ King Henry V of England crosses the Somme while French Marshal
Bouciquaut holds the ford at Blanchetaque before the Battle of Agincourt.
Bibliothèque Nationale Paris/The Art Archive

# Breakdown and Renewal in an Age of Plague

The vigorous expansion that marked European history from the eleventh to the thirteenth centuries came to an end in the 1300s. Plague, famine, and recurrent wars decimated populations and snuffed out former prosperity. At the same time, feudal governments as well as the papacy struggled against mounting institutional chaos. But for all the signs of crisis, the fourteenth and fifteenth centuries were not merely an age of breakdown. The failures of the medieval economy and its governments drove the Western peoples to repair their institutions. By the late fifteenth century the outlines of a new equilibrium were emerging. In 1500 Europeans were fewer in number than they had been in 1300, but they had developed a more productive economy and a more powerful technology than they had possessed two hundred years before. These achievements were to equip them for their great expansion throughout the world in the early modern period.

Some historians refer to the fourteenth and fifteenth centuries as the "autumn of the Middle Ages," emphasizing the decline and death of a formerly great civilization. People living at the time tended to think in terms of the Biblical passage in Revelations referring to the Four Horsemen of the Apocalypse—famine, disease, war, and the white horse of salvation. Constantinople, the last remnant of the Byzantine Empire, fell to the Ottoman Turks, providing a powerful symbol of decay. But the study of any past epoch requires an effort to balance the work of death and renewal. In few periods of history do death and renewal confront each other so dramatically as in the years between 1300 and 1500.

| CHAPTER 11. BREAKDOWN AND RENEWAL IN AN AGE OF PLAGUE | | | | | | | |
|---|---|---|---|---|---|---|---|
| | Social Structure | Body Politic | Changes in the Organization of Production and in the Impact of Technology | Evolution of Family and Changing Gender Roles | War | Religion | Cultural Expression |
| I. POPULATION CATASTROPHES | ▨ | | | ▨ | | | |
| II. ECONOMIC DEPRESSION AND RECOVERY | ▨ | ▨ | ▨ | ▨ | | | ■ |
| III. POPULAR UNREST | ▨ | ▨ | | | | | |
| IV. GOVERNMENTS OF EUROPE | ▨ | | ▨ | | ▨ | ▨ | |
| V. FALL OF BYZANTIUM AND THE OTTOMAN EMPIRE | | ▨ | | | | ▨ | |

## I. Population Catastrophes

◆

The famines and plagues that struck European society in the fourteenth and fifteenth centuries profoundly affected economic life. Initially, they disrupted the established patterns of producing and exchanging goods and led directly to widespread hardship. As Europeans recovered and reorganized the economy to greatly changed demographic conditions, they were able to significantly increase the efficiency of economic production. To understand this paradox, we must see how the disasters affected the population of Europe.

### ◆ DEMOGRAPHIC DECLINE

A few censuses and other statistical records give us an insight into the size and structure of the European population in the 1300s. Nearly all these records were drawn up for purposes of taxation, and usually they survey only limited geographical areas—a city or a province. They are rarely complete even in limited areas and give us no reliable totals, but they still enable us to perceive with some confidence how the population was changing.

*Population Losses*    Almost every region of Europe from which we possess records shows an appalling decline of population between approxi-

mately 1300 and 1450. In Provence in southern France, the population seems to have shrunk after 1310 from between 350,000 and 400,000 to roughly one-third, or at most one-half, of its earlier size; only after 1470 did it again begin to increase. The city and countryside of Pistoia, near Florence, fell from about 43,000 people in the mid-thirteenth century to 14,000 by the early fifteenth. The nearby city and countryside of San Gimignano has not regained to this day the approximately 13,000 residents it had in 1332.

For the larger kingdoms of Europe, the figures are less reliable, but they show a similar pattern. England had a population of about 3.7 million in 1347 and 2.2 million by 1377. By 1550 it had no more people than it had had in the thirteenth century. France by 1328 may have reached 15 million; it, too, was not again to attain this size for two hundred years. In Germany, of some 170,000 inhabited localities named in sources before 1300, about 40,000 disappeared during the 1300s and 1400s. Since many of the surviving towns were also shrinking in size, the population loss was greater.

Certain favored regions of Europe—the fertile lands surrounding Paris and the Po valley in Italy—did continue to attract settlers and maintain fairly stable populations, but they owed their good fortune more to immigration than to high birthrates or immunity from disease. It can safely be estimated that all of Europe in 1450 had no more than one-half, and probably only one-third, of the population it had had around 1300. Population did not begin to recover until the end of the fifteenth century.

***Famine and Hunger*** The first demographic catastrophe in late medieval Europe was famine and general food scarcities. In 1315, 1316, and 1317 a severe famine swept the north of Europe. Chroniclers described the incessant rainfall that rotted crops in the fields and prevented harvests; they spoke of people dying in the city streets and country lanes; cannibalism is another theme. In 1339 and 1340 a famine struck southern Europe. During famines, the starving people ate not only their reserves of grain but also most of the seed they had set aside for planting. Medieval Europe lacked a system that could handle such massive crop failures. When harvests failed, the monasteries and charitable institutions also lost their crops and could not aid the starving. The king of England tried to import several shiploads of grain for distribution in those years, but these loads fell into the hands of pirates before they reached England.

Why was hunger so widespread in the early fourteenth century? Some historians see the root of trouble in the sheer number of people the lands had to support by 1300. The medieval population had been growing rapidly since about 1000, and by 1300 Europe, so this analysis suggests, was becoming the victim of its own success. Parts of the continent were crowded, even glutted, with people. Some areas of Normandy, for example, had a population in the early fourteenth century not much below what they supported six hundred years later. Thousands, millions even, had to be fed without chemical fertilizers, power tools, and fast transport. Masses of people had come to depend for their livelihood on infertile soils, and even in good years they were surviving on the margins of existence.

Although hunger did not always result in starvation, malnutrition raised the death rate from respiratory infections and intestinal ailments, which also reached epidemic proportions in the fourteenth century. While some parts of Europe returned to prosperity and good diets before the next disaster—plague—the experience of others demonstrated the dual impact of famine and plague. Barcelona and its province of Catalonia experienced famine in 1333; plague in 1347–1351; famine in 1358–1359; and plague in 1362–1363, 1371, and 1397.

## ◆ PLAGUE

The great plague of the fourteenth century, known as the Black Death, provides a dramatic, but not a complete, explanation for the huge human losses. Plague is endemic (always present) in several parts of the world, including southwestern United States, and occasionally spreads to become a pandemic. In the mid-fourteenth century it spread along caravan routes of central Asia and arrived at the Black Sea ports. Europe's active trade in luxury items from the East gave plague a route to Europe. In 1347 a merchant ship sailing from Caffa in the Crimea to Messina in Sicily seems to have carried rats infected with the plague. A plague broke out at Messina, and from there it spread rapidly throughout Europe (see map 11.1).

***Nature of the Disease*** The plague took several forms in Europe. The most identifiable one—the one that contemporary sources describe (see "Boccaccio on the Black Death," p. 365)—is the bubonic form. The pathogenic agent (not discovered until the late nineteenth century) is *Bacillus pestis*. While normally a disease of rodents, particularly house rats, it can spread to humans by fleas that carry the infection from rodents to humans through a flea bite. Bubonic plague has an incubation period of about two to ten days; its symptoms are chills, high fever, headache, and vomiting. The next symptoms are swellings (bubos) in lymph nodes of the groin and clotting blood under the skin, hence the name "Black Death." Death is likely in 90 percent of the cases. Plague also spreads through a pneumonic variety in which the droplets containing the infection can spread directly from human to human. Infection is very rapid and bubos may not form before the bacillus travels through the bloodstream to the lungs, causing pneumonia and death within three or four days. The real killer in the 1300s seems to have been pneumonic plague; it probably was spread through coughing and was almost always fatal.

In spite of the virulence of pneumonic plague, it is hard to believe that medical factors alone explain the awesome mortality. Europeans had maintained close contact with the East, where the

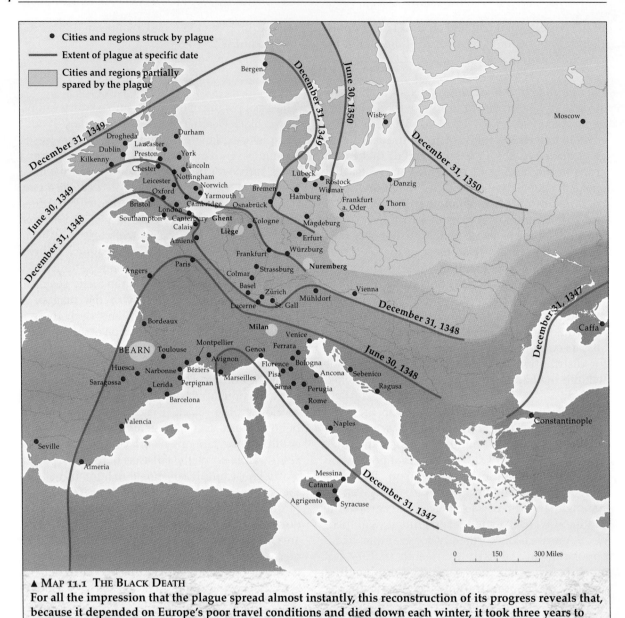

▲ **MAP 11.1  THE BLACK DEATH**
**For all the impression that the plague spread almost instantly, this reconstruction of its progress reveals that, because it depended on Europe's poor travel conditions and died down each winter, it took three years to move from Sicily to Sweden.**

plague had been endemic, since the eleventh century, but not until 1347 and 1348 did it make serious inroads in Europe. In addition, pneumonic plague is a disease of the winter months, but the plagues of the 1300s characteristically raged during the summer and declined in the cooler weather of autumn. Some scholars think the weather, which had become colder and wetter, brought famines and created a favorable environment for plague.

What made plague so much more terrifying than famine was that it struck the rich and poor; young and old, women and men; urban dwellers, nobles, peasants, monks, and clergy. Not knowing the cause of plague, physicians could do no more than lance the bubos to bring comfort, and many refused to treat plague patients at all. Those members of the clergy who went among the dying usually became infected themselves. Not knowing the true cause of the disease, people blamed the Jews

# BOCCACCIO ON THE BLACK DEATH

◆

*The following eyewitness description of the ravages of the Black Death in Florence was written by one of its most famous citizens, the writer Giovanni Boccaccio. This passage comes from his masterpiece,* The Decameron, *written during the three years following the plague.*

"In the year of our Lord 1348, there happened at Florence a most terrible plague, which had broken out some years before in the Levant, and after making incredible havoc all the way, had now reached the west. There, in spite of all the means that art and human foresight could suggest, such as keeping the city clear from filth and the publication of copious instructions for preservation of health, it began to show itself in the spring. Unlike what had been seen in the east, where bleeding from the nose is the fatal prognostic, here there appeared certain tumors in the groin or under the arm-pits, some as big as a small apple, others as an egg, and afterwards purple spots in most parts of the body—messengers of death. To the cure of this malady neither medical knowledge nor the power of drugs was of any effect; whether because the disease was in its own nature mortal, or that the physicians (the number of whom, taking quacks and women pretenders into account, was grown very great) could form no just idea of the cause. Whichever was the reason, few escaped; but nearly all died the third day from the first appearance of the symptoms, some sooner, some later, without any fever or other symptoms. What gave the more virulence to this plague was that it spread daily, like fire when it comes in contact with combustibles. Nor was it caught only by coming near the sick, but even by touching their clothes. One instance of this kind I took particular notice of: the rags of a poor man just dead had been thrown into the street. Two hogs came up, and after rooting amongst the rags, in less than an hour they both turned around and died on the spot."

From Warren Hollister et al., *Medieval Europe: A Short Source Book* (McGraw-Hill Companies, 1992), pp. 248–249.

for poisoning the wells; others (the Flagelants) thought it was the wrath of God and walked in procession beating themselves. Eventually, cities formed a contagion theory of the disease and refused admittance within their walls of anyone who came from a city in which the plague was prevalent.

*Pandemic* The Black Death was not so much an epidemic as a pandemic (universal disease), striking an entire continent. The plague was the same one that had visited the Mediterranean and Western Europe in 542, during the reign of Justinian (see chapter 7). The plague struck not just once but repeatedly, until the last great outbreak in 1665, the Great Plague in London. A city was lucky if more than ten years went by without an onslaught; the plague was raging in some part of Europe almost every year.

Some of the horror of the plague can be glimpsed in this account by an anonymous cleric who visited the French city of Avignon in 1348: "To put the matter shortly, one-half, or more than a half, of the people at Avignon are already dead.

Within the walls of the city there are now more than 7,000 houses shut up; in these no one is living, and all who have inhabited them are departed. . . . On account of this great mortality there is such a fear of death that people do not dare even to speak with anyone whose relative has died, because it is frequently remarked that in a family where one dies nearly all the relations follow him."[1]

# II. Economic Depression and Recovery

◆

A continent does not lose a third to a half of its population without feeling the effects immediately. After burying the dead, often in mass graves outside city walls, the survivors took stock of their economic position. According to contemporaries, survivors of the plague often gave up toiling in

---

[1]*Breve Chronicon clerici anonymi,* quoted in Francis Aidan Gasquet, *The Black Death of 1348 and 1349,* 1908, p. 46.

◄ THE *TRIUMPH OF DEATH*
The great social disaster of the Black Death left few traces in the visual arts; perhaps people did not wish to be reminded of its horrors. One exception was the *Triumph of Death,* a mural painted shortly after 1348 in the Camposanto (cemetery) of Pisa in Italy. In this detail of the mural, an elegant party of hunters happens upon corpses prepared for burial. Note the rider who holds a handkerchief — scented, undoubtedly — to his nose, to ward off the foul odors.
Art Resource, NY

the fields or looking after their shops; presumably, they saw no point in working for the future when it was so uncertain. But in the long run Europeans adapted to the new conditions. In agriculture, for example, the contraction of the population enabled the survivors to concentrate their efforts on better soils. In both agriculture and industry, the shortage of laborers was a challenge to landlords and entrepreneurs to save costs either by adopting productive measures that were less labor intensive or by increasing investment in labor-saving devices. Thus, the decline in population eventually encouraged Europeans to find better techniques for making the most of available resources.

### ◆ AGRICULTURAL SPECIALIZATION

Perhaps the best indication of the changes in the European economy comes from the history of prices. This evidence is scattered and rarely precise, but it does reveal roughly similar patterns in prices all over Europe. The cost of most agricultural products—cereals, wine, beer, oil, and meat—shot up immediately after the Black Death and stayed high until approximately 1375 in the north and 1395 in Italy. High food prices in a time

of declining population suggests that production was falling even more rapidly than the number of consumers. But high food prices mask the shift in agricultural production that led to greater specialization and improved diets.

*Impact on the Peasantry*   Some historians have called the period following the depletion of population a golden age for peasantry. Conditions did change for the peasants, but these changes were not uniformly for the better across Europe. The peasantry quickly realized that with labor in short supply they could demand higher wages for their labor, and that they could even break the bonds of their serfdom and move around the countryside to follow higher wages. The nobles and landlords were swift in their reaction to such gains.

In England the peasants had, as elsewhere in Europe, enjoyed a period of relative freedom from the labor demands of serfdom, but in the late thirteenth century landlords reimposed serfdom to take advantage of the money they could make from their crops in the period of high population and high demand for grain. With the sudden drop in population and demand for higher wages, Parliament passed the Statute of Laborers in 1351, which fixed prices and wages at what they were in 1347, the year before the plague. Like any law against supply and demand, the statute was hard to enforce, and during the course of the fifteenth century serfdom gradually disappeared in England, as the population moved away from the old manors or simply refused to pay any dues other than their rent.

*Serfdom Revisited*   England's experience of a gradual decline in serfdom was by no means the pattern for Europe as a whole. In some parts of Europe, serfdom was reimposed or newly imposed in response to the decrease in laborers. In the eleventh and twelfth centuries, lords in the newly opened lands of Prussia and Poland offered peasants freedom to come and settle. By the late fifteenth century peasants began to lose their freedom in Poland, and by the early sixteenth century peasants in Hungary, Bohemia, Silesia, and Poland were serfs. By the early thirteenth century serfdom had almost disappeared in France, Italy, and western Germany. Following the Black Death, however, lords moved to reinstate it, and vestiges of it were to remain in those countries through the eighteenth century. In Catalonia, the thirteenth century saw a rise in serfdom and it was not until the late fifteenth century that serfs were freed.

*Agricultural Specialization*   One branch of agriculture that enjoyed a remarkable period of growth in the fifteenth century was sheep raising. Since the prices for wool, skins, mutton, and cheese remained high, English landlords sought to take advantage of the market by fencing large fields and converting them from plowland into sheep pastures and expelling the peasants or small herders who had formerly lived there. This process, called enclosure, continued for centuries and played an important role in English economic and social history. Other countries as well began to have agricultural specialization. Netherlands did cheese and dairy while Spain developed Merino wool.

By the middle of the fifteenth century, agricultural prices stabilized, suggesting that production had become more dependable. Farms enjoyed the advantages of larger size, better location on more profitable soil, and increased capital investments in tools and animals. Agriculture was now more diversified, which benefited the soil, lowered the risk of famine from the failure of a single staple crop, and provided more nourishment for the people.

*Gentry*   The specialized agriculture brought prosperity to the land-owning nobility, but also to a new rural middle class. The middle-class urban dwellers, lawyers, bureaucrats, and wealthy peasants began to invest in land in the countryside. With capital to invest in either the purchase or lease of land, these people made considerable profits. New fortunes gave rise to a country middle class called the gentry.

## ◆ PROTECTIONISM

The movement of prices created serious problems for employers in cities. As the labor force contracted, wages in most towns surged to levels as much as four times higher than they had been before 1348. Although the prices of manufactured goods also increased, they did not rise as much as wages, and this trend reduced profit margins. To offset these unfavorable tendencies, the employers sought government intervention. Between 1349 and 1351, England, France, Aragon, Castile, and other governments tried to fix prices and wages at levels favorable to employers. The typical policy was to forbid employers to pay more than customary wages and to require laborers to accept jobs at those wages. Such early experiments in a controlled economy failed.

*Guilds on the Defensive*   A related problem for businesses was that competition grew as population fell and markets contracted. Traders tried to protect themselves by creating restricted markets and establishing monopolies. Guilds limited their membership, and some admitted only the sons of established masters. To keep prices high, some guilds prohibited their members from hiring any women as workers because their wages were low. Only wives and daughters of the household could work in the shops.

*The Hanseatic League*   Probably the best example of the monopolizing trend is the association of northern European trading cities, the Hanseatic League. Formed in the late thirteenth century as a defensive association, by the early fourteenth

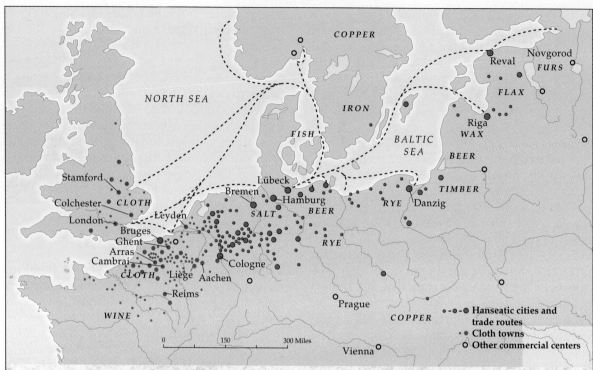

▲ MAP 11.2  THE HANSEATIC LEAGUE AND THE GOODS IT TRADED IN THE FOURTEENTH CENTURY
**Even in the age of the Black Death, international trade remained vigorous in northern Europe. Its leaders were the cities of the Hanseatic League, which shipped a variety of commodities across the continent, though the most sought-after commodity was the cloth produced in England, the Netherlands, and northern France.**

century it imposed a monopoly on cities trading in the Baltic and North seas. It excluded foreigners from the Baltic trade and could expel member cities who broke trade agreements. At its height, the Hanseatic League included seventy or eighty cities, stretching from Bruges to Novgorod and led by Bremen, Cologne, Hamburg, and especially Lübeck (see map 11.2). Maintaining its own treasury and fleet, the league supervised commercial exchange, policed the waters of the Baltic Sea, and negotiated with foreign princes. By the late fifteenth century, however, it began to decline and was unable to meet growing competition from the Dutch in northern commerce. Never formally abolished, the Hanseatic League continued to meet—at lengthening intervals—until 1669.

### ◆ TECHNOLOGICAL ADVANCES

Attempts to raise the efficiency of workers proved to be far more effective than wage and price regulation in laying the basis for recovery. Employers

were able to counteract high wages by adopting more rational methods of production and substituting capital for labor—that is, providing workers with better tools. Although hard times and labor shortages inspired most technical advances of the 1300s and 1400s, increased efficiency helped to make Europe a richer community.

*Metallurgy*  Mining and metallurgy benefited from a series of inventions after 1460 that lowered the cost of metals and extended their use. Better techniques of digging, shoring, ventilating, and draining allowed mine shafts to be sunk several hundred feet into the earth, permitting the large-scale exploitation of the deep, rich mineral deposits of central Europe. Some historians estimate that the output from the mines of Hungary, the Tyrol, Bohemia, and Saxony grew as much as five times between 1460 and 1530. During this period, miners in Saxony discovered a method for extracting pure silver from the lead alloy in which it was often found—an invention that was of major and iron wares; such products found wide application in construction work and shipbuilding. Skill in metalworking contributed to two other inventions: firearms and movable metal type.

*Firearms and Weapons* Europeans were constantly trying to improve the arts of war in the Middle Ages. The crossbow was cranked up and shot with a trigger; it was so powerful that it could penetrate conventional armor. The long bow came into widespread use during the Welsh wars of Edward I. It was light, accurate, and could be shot rapidly. In response to these two weapons, armor became more elaborate, with exaggerated convex surfaces designed to deflect arrows from the chest, arms, and knees.

Siege weapons that hurled projectiles with great force and accuracy were also important. Adapting a Chinese invention for fireworks consisting of an explosive mixture of carbon, sulfur, and saltpeter, the Europeans developed gunpowder and cannons to hurl boulders at an enemy. Firearms are first mentioned in 1328, and cannons were used in the early battles of the Hundred Years' War. At first, their effect was chiefly psychological: The thunderous roar, merely by frightening the enemy's horses, did far more damage than the usually inaccurate shots. Still, a breakthrough had been made, and cannons gained in military importance. They played a major role in the fall of Constantinople in 1453. Their development depended primarily on stronger, more precise casting, on proper granulation of the powder to ensure that the charge burned at the right speed and put its full force behind the projectile, and on an understanding of the trajectory of the cannon ball when fired. With firearms, fewer soldiers could fight more effectively; capital, in the form of an efficient though expensive tool, was being substituted for labor.

*Military Engineering* Medieval architects and artists had long been interested in military engineering as well as building. Konrad Kyeser wrote and illustrated a book of weapons of war between 1395 and 1405. His work included cannons, siphons and wheels for raising water, pontoon bridges, hot-air balloons, and a device to pull horses across streams. He also made drawings of multiple guns arranged like a revolver. A Bohemian engineer's sketchbook shows the

▲ MINING, 1389
One does not normally associate miners with elegant decoration, but in this fourteenth-century manuscript, a miner provides the subject for the ornamentation of the capital *M* that starts the word *metalla* (metals). That the artist even considered such a subject is an indication of the growing importance of the industry in this period.
Index, © Giancarlo Costa

importance for the later massive development of silver mines in America. Larger furnaces came into use, and huge bellows and trip-hammers, driven by waterpower, aided the smelting and working of metals. Simultaneously, the masters of the trade were acquiring a new precision in the difficult art of casting.

By the late fifteenth century, European mines were providing an abundance of silver bullion for coinage. Money became more plentiful, which stimulated the economy. Exploitation also began in the rich coal deposits of northern Europe. Expanding iron production meant more and stronger pumps, gears and machine parts, tools,

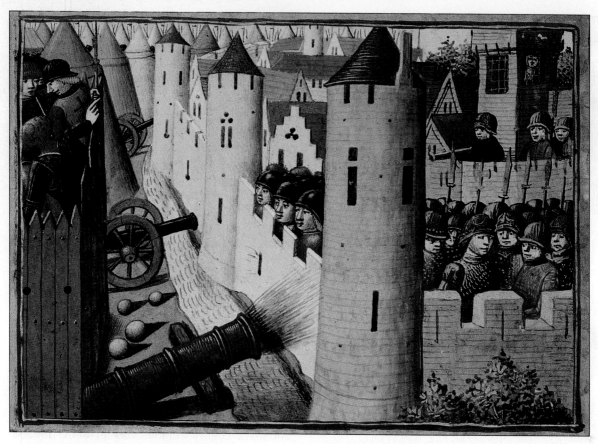

▲ The *English Siege of Orléans* (1428–1429) shows the English soldiers behind a siege wall (left) firing cannons across the Loire River. The cannons at this stage were more frightening for their noise than for their destructive power because of design problems. The siege of Orléans was brought to an end by a French relief force led by Joan of Arc.
Bibliothèque Nationale de France, Paris

development of the use of cannon over fifty years; his book also has drawings of a primitive tank and a diving suit complete with a tube for getting air. Iacopo Mariano of Siena drew all sorts of mechanical counterbalances, that helped to operate cranes, bridges, and wells.

*Mechanical Clocks*   Telling time in the Middle Ages was imprecise, based as it was on the position of the sun and the canonical hours for prayer at about three-hour intervals during the day. Times of meetings, for instance, were set within vague parameters of "at vesper," "at sunrise," or even within a few days. But in 1360 Henry De Vick designed the first mechanical clock with an hour hand for King Charles V of France, which

was placed in the royal palace in Paris. Other clocks had been alluded to in sources, but De Vick's marked the start of mechanical clocks in municipal buildings and large churches. Large astronomical clocks that showed the signs of the zodiac were the precursors of clocks that kept time and tolled the hours. Milan had a clock that struck a bell at every hour of the day. The regular ringing of the hours brought a new regularity to life, work, and markets and gave time itself a new value. Even if the clocks were inaccurate, they gave a focus to time and to the possibility of hours kept distinct from the seasonal position of the sun. Pocket watches, although cumbersome, had appeared by 1550 with the invention of the spring for running clocks.

▲ The mechanical clock, a medieval invention, was installed in major buildings. The Wells Cathedral clock was built in England. The face was decorated with the four winds and angels. The clock told the hours twenty-four hours a day and told the days in the lunar month. Bells tolled the hours.
(Top) Derek Bayes/Aspect Picture Library Ltd.
(Bottom) Science Museum, London

*Printing* The extension of literacy among laypeople and the greater reliance of governments and businesses on records created a demand for a cheap method of reproducing the written word. The introduction of paper from the East was a major step in reducing costs, for paper is far cheaper than parchment to produce. A substitute for the time-consuming labor of writing by hand was also necessary: Scribes and copiers were skilled artisans who commanded high salaries. To cut costs, printers first tried to press woodcuts—inked blocks with letters or designs carved on them—onto paper or parchment. But these "block books" represented only a small advance over handwriting, since a separate woodcut had to be carved for each page, and they tended to split after being pressed a number of times.

By the middle of the fifteenth century several masters were on the verge of perfecting the technique of printing with movable metal type. The first to prove this practicable was Johannes Gutenberg of Mainz, a former jeweler and stonecutter. Gutenberg devised an alloy of lead, tin, and antimony that would melt at a low temperature, cast well in the die, and be durable in the press; this alloy is still the basis of the printer's art. His Bible, printed in 1455, is the first major work reproduced through printing.

The technique spread rapidly. By 1500 some 250 European cities had presses. German masters held an early leadership, but Italians soon challenged their preeminence. The Venetian printer Aldus Manutius and his fellow Italians rejected the elaborate Gothic typeface used in the north and developed their own *italic* type, modeled on the clear script they found in old manuscripts. They believed this was the style of writing used in ancient Rome, but in fact they were imitating the Carolingian minuscule script.

*The Information Revolution* The immediate effect of the printing press was to multiply the output and cut the costs of books (see map 11.3). It made information available to a much broader segment of the population, and libraries could store more information at lower cost. Printing helped disseminate and preserve knowledge in standardized form—a major contribution to the advance of technology and scholarship. Printing produced a revolution in what we would call information

◄ **Gutenberg's Bible**
A page from Johannes Gutenberg's Bible marks one of the most significant technical and cultural advances of the fifteenth century: printing with movable type, a process that made possible a wider dissemination of literature and thought.
E. Harold Hugo

technology, and indeed it resembles in many ways the profound changes that computers are making in our own lives. Finally, printing could spread new ideas with unprecedented speed—a fact that was not fully appreciated, however, until the 1500s, when print became essential to the propaganda of religious reformers in the Protestant Reformation.

## ◆ THE STANDARD OF LIVING

For those who survived the famine, plagues, and wars, the standard of living became better as the economy began to grow again in the late fifteenth century; but the pall of death and disease hung over the survivors.

▲ **MAP 11.3 THE SPREAD OF PRINTING BEFORE 1500**
After its invention in the Rhineland, printing first spread along the rivers that were Europe's main highways. By 1500 it was concentrated mainly in southern Germany, the Netherlands, and northern Italy.

*Reduced Life Expectancy* The family memoirs of Florentine merchants, which recorded births and deaths, suggest that life expectancy from birth for these relatively affluent persons was forty years in about 1300, dropping to only eighteen years in the generation of the Black Death, and rising to thirty years in the fifteenth century as the plagues declined in virulence. (Today in the United States a newborn may be expected to survive for more than 76 years.) The principal victims were the very young. In many periods, between a half and a third of the babies born never reached age fifteen. Society swarmed with little children, but their deaths were common occurrences in almost every family.

The plague took a greater toll among young adults than among the aged. In effect, a person who survived one or more major epidemics had a good chance of living through the next onslaught. A mild attack of plague brought immunity rather than death as the population built up resistance to the disease; a favored few thus did reach extreme old age. The young adults always faced high risks of dying, perhaps because of their first exposure to plague or from other diseases. Friars who entered the convent of Sta. Maria Novella at Florence in the last half of the fourteenth century, for example, lived an average of only twenty years after entering their order (which they usually did in their late teens). The death toll of people in their child-bearing years slowed the demographic recovery.

*Female Survival*    Women seemed to be more robust than men in resisting or recovering from plague and the other diseases, and they became a

▼ CHRISTINE DE PISAN PRESENTS POEMS TO ISABEAU OF BAVARIA
**Christine de Pisan (1364–1439) was the author of several important historical and literary works including a biography of King Charles V of France and *The Book of the Three Virtues*, a manual for the education of women. She is here depicted presenting a volume of her poems to the queen of France, who is surrounded by ladies-in-waiting and the symbol of the French royal family, the fleur-de-lis. It is significant that there were such scenes of elegance and intellectual life even amidst the chaos and destruction of the Hundred Years' War.**
By Permission of The British Library. Harly Ms. 4431 fol 3

disproportionately larger part of the population. Historians have interpreted this fact in a number of ways. Some have argued that women took a greater role in urban and rural life and that this was a golden age for women. As historians find more evidence about women during this period, however, it appears that while more women found employment in urban centers, their roles were limited to household servants and unskilled labor. Women did not move into positions of power in government or guilds. Indeed, female guilds that had women as guild officers were forced to elect men.

*Misogyny or the Debate over Women's Nature*
Witchcraft charges against women were rare in the Middle Ages, but some historians have argued that the greater preponderance of women in the population contributed to the witch hunts of the sixteenth centuries. By the Late Middle Ages the intellectual debate about women's nature had become more pointed (see chapter 16). Both the ancient and the medieval world had relegated women to inferior positions, and some of the ancient and Christian authors had added strong negative invectives against women. The Church offered two images of women—Eve, the sinner who led Adam astray in the Garden of Eden, and the Virgin Mary, mother of Jesus. Neither image fit ordinary women's lives very well. As we saw in the last chapter, some very pious women commanded the respect of the Church through their asceticism.

The debate over women's nature came to the forefront early in the fourteenth century when Jean de Meun, an educated layman, revised a thirteenth-century poem, *The Romance of the Rose.* His additions became a satire on human follies, particularly those of the clergy and of women. Relying on ancient authors, theologians, and contemporary folklore, de Meun outlined the depravity, vanity, fickleness, and weaknesses of women.

A number of famous authors replied to his poem in the late fourteenth century, including Christine de Pisan. Christine's father was an Italian who had come to France as court astronomer to the French king. Her father oversaw her education in Latin and French. She married a French

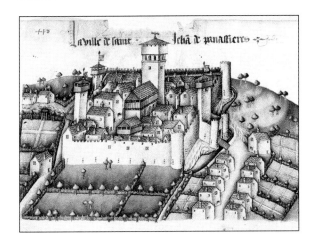

▲ VIEW OF PANISSIÈRES, FROM A FIFTEENTH-CENTURY ARMORIAL
As the population of Europe began to recover from the Black Death, signs of expansion and prosperity became evident in its most fertile regions. This fifteenth-century view of the town of Panissières, in the rich Loire valley in France, indicates that houses were again springing up and fields were being cultivated outside the walls of the fortified heart of the town.
Bibliothèque Nationale de France, Paris

nobleman, but when he died, leaving her a widow with young children, she turned to writing and translating to make a living. Among her books was *The City of Ladies,* a refutation of Jean de Meun. She pointed to all the heroic women in history as examples of women's superior qualities, describing virtue in the most trying circumstances, heroism, self-sacrifice, wisdom, and leadership (see "The Status of Women in the Middle Ages: Historiographical Debate," p. 376).

*Knowledge of the Human Body*   During the Late Middle Ages, some modest advances were made in medicine. Eyeglasses, invented in the thirteenth century, were perfected in the fourteenth century. For the most part they were designed for reading rather than distance vision.

Until the later part of the Middle Ages, religious prohibitions against dissecting the human cadaver meant that medicine had not advanced much beyond the Hellenistic and Arabic contributions. By the end of the thirteenth century, a teacher of medicine at the University of Bologna

wrote a textbook on dissections with illustrations of human anatomy. With a superior knowledge of the human body, physicians' ability to diagnose ills advanced, but their knowledge of cures did not. Surgery remained the practice of barber-surgeons, guildsmen whose sharp knives could shave beards and perform surgery and whose supply of leeches could draw blood. Such men remained more important for immediate cures than did university-trained physicians.

*Housing and Diets*   The revitalized economy brought improvements in housing, dress, and diet and increased spending on art and decorative objects. Housing was generally improving for most people in the Late Middle Ages. The increasing use of brick and tile meant that buildings were more substantial and more spacious. Changes in warfare meant that only kings could afford to build castles that would withstand a siege of cannons. The nobility, gentry, and wealthy urban dwellers built large town houses and country houses with gardens and large windows rather than defensive walls. The fireplace on the wall replaced the hearth in the center of the room even in peasant houses.

The European diet had been largely based on cereal products, and when population was dense, all land had to be devoted to raising grain, even if the land was not particularly well suited for it. Reduced population meant that land could be devoted to other crops or to animal rearing. Diet generally improved, with more meat, cheese, oil, butter, fruit, wine, and beer.

*Courtesy and Dress*   Refinements in living brought a new emphasis on polite behavior, particularly at the table. Guild ordinances began to include instructions about manners at the annual feast, and books of advice for young people moving up in social station proliferated in every language. Silver forks replaced fingers as a tool for polite dining among the upper class.

Dress for the upper classes became very grand, with the tall pointed caps and the long pointed shoes that we associate with medieval Europe. That the fine dress was not limited to the upper classes is obvious from the sumptuary legislation that cities and kingdoms passed, which tried to

# The Status of Women in the Middle Ages: Historiographical Debate

*The study of medieval women has become a major area of historical research in the past thirty years. Scholars have raised a number of unresolved questions about women's lives and their experiences. The questions discussed here suggest ongoing areas of research.*

1. Does the periodization of political history apply to women's history or to the history of ordinary people? Historians have used watersheds in political history such as the Battle of Bosworth Field in 1485 to define the end of medieval England and the beginning of early modern England. But did women or peasants wake up after the battle and declare that a new era had begun and life was going to change for them? Intellectual movements, since they largely involved men, may have had little influence on women's lives, as Joan Kelly asked in her famous essay, "Did Women Have a Renaissance?"*

2. To what extent did the Church's misogyny influence the way women lived? In Church writings, women were either saintly like the Virgin Mary or sinners like Eve. The Church blessed women's roles only as virgins or as wives and mothers. The general misogyny was also prevalent in medieval lay society and appeared in jokes, in literary pieces such as the *Romance of the Rose*, and in various regulations regarding women. But did women consciously take these strictures to heart when they lived their everyday lives? Some women did move into positions of power as regents and queens; powerful female saints and mystics became a part of late medieval religious life; women joined the tertiaries and the Beguinages. Individual peasant and urban women farmed their plots or ran their own businesses. Many other women moved into business and administrative capacities when their husbands were away or when they became widows. But women who took these initiatives generally worked within a framework of acceptable female behavior. Joan of Arc, on the other hand, offended the Church perhaps more because she adopted male dress and role than because of the heresy and witchcraft charges the Inquisitors brought.

3. Understanding the role of patriarchy is important for understanding women's freedom in marriage and widowhood. Customs varied greatly depending on the availability of women for marriage, on local laws covering dower and dowry, and on economic necessity. Some marriage arrangements, particularly among the peasantry, assumed that the household was the unit of economic production and that the sex roles were equally important for the survival of the family. In urban Florence the age differences between spouses seemed to preclude a strong voice for a young bride. Other studies will, no doubt, show other patterns.

4. Women's participation in intellectual and political life continues to be researched. Women could not attend universities, be ordained as priests, or participate in legal and magisterial roles. On the other hand, nunneries, courts, and individual experiences did permit them to write, engage in intellectual debate, and contribute to the cultural enrichment of the Middle Ages. Much women's writing and artistic work has been lost, but enough survives to indicate the ways women participated in the cultural life of the Middle Ages. Christine de Pisan is an example of a writer who was so well-known that Richard II of England offered to be her patron.

*Joan Kelly, *Women, History, and Theory: The Essays of Joan Kelly* (University of Chicago Press, 1984), pp. 19–50.

regulate who was allowed to wear fine cloth with furs and who was prohibited from doing so.

***Art for the Lay Consumer*** Consumption of art for domestic residences changed. In the past the chief patrons of the arts had been churches and nobility, and the major artistic themes had been religious. With more disposable wealth and a larger middle class, consumption patterns changed. While laypeople still gave heavily to the Church, they tended to give for the building of parish churches rather than cathedrals. But they also bought fine silver and gold objects, jewelry, furniture, and paintings, including portraits of themselves and their families. Oil paint was the favored new medium for pictures.

▲ **Dress became very elaborate, with tall headdresses for women and pointed shoes and tights for men. The most elaborate court was that of the Duke of Burgundy, which is pictured here with courtiers dancing.**
Bibliothèque Nationale de France, Paris

# III. Popular Unrest

The demographic collapse and economic troubles of the fourteenth century deeply disturbed the social peace of Europe. European society had been remarkably stable and mostly peaceful from the Early Middle Ages until around 1300, and there is little evidence of uprisings or social warfare. The fourteenth and fifteenth centuries, however, witnessed numerous revolts of peasants and artisans against what they believed to be the oppression of the propertied classes.

## ◆ RURAL REVOLTS

One of the most spectacular fourteenth-century rural uprisings was the English Peasants' Revolt of 1381. This revolt originated in popular resentment against both the policies of the royal government and the practices of the great landlords. Although the Statute of Laborers (1351), which

tried to fix prices and wages at the preplague level, had little practical success, the mere effort to implement it aggravated social tensions, especially in the countryside, where it would have reimposed serfdom on the peasants. Concurrent attempts to collect poll taxes (a flat tax on each member of the population), which by their nature demanded less from the prosperous than the humble, crystallized resentment against the government.

Under leaders of uncertain background—Wat Tyler, Jack Straw, and a priest named John Ball—peasant bands, enraged by the latest poll tax, marched on London in 1381. They called for the abolition of serfdom, labor services, and tithes and demanded an end to the poll taxes. The workers of London, St. Albans, York, and other cities who had similar grievances rose in support of the peasants. After mobs killed the king's advisers and burned the houses of prominent lawyers and royal officials, King Richard II, then age fifteen, bravely met with the peasants in person at Mile End, outside the walls of London. One of his followers killed Wat Tyler as he negotiated with the king. Thinking quickly, Richard told the peasants that he was their leader and promised to give them charters of freedom. But as the peasants dispersed, the great landlords reorganized their forces and violently suppressed the last vestiges of unrest in the countryside; the young king also reneged on his promises and declared the charters invalid.

The peasant uprising in England was only one of many rural disturbances between 1350 and 1450, including revolts near Paris, called the Jacquerie, and in Languedoc, Catalonia, and Sweden. Germany also experienced such disturbances in the fifteenth century and a major peasant revolt in 1524, which was to feed into the tensions of the early days of the Protestant Reformation.

## ◆ URBAN REVOLTS

The causes of social unrest within the cities were similar to those in the countryside—wages and taxes. In the 1300s and early 1400s, Strasburg, Metz, Ghent, Liège, and Paris were all scenes of riots. Though not entirely typical, one of the most interesting of these urban revolts was the Ciompi uprising at Florence in 1378.

▲ THE ENGLISH PEASANTS' REVOLT OF 1381
One of the leaders of the peasant revolt was a preacher, John Ball, who is shown on the horse.
One of his messages was a simple egalitarian rhyme: "When Adam delved and Eve span, where
then were all the gentlemen?" Wat Tyler, another leader, is in the foreground holding a banner with
the English coat of arms. Rather than a rabble with pitchforks, many peasants had trained in the
militia that defended the English coast against French raids. Loyal to the king, the peasants did
not want to kill him, but rather to get rid of his bad advisers.
British Library, London/Bridgeman Art Library

*The Ciompi*  Florence was one of the wool manufacturing centers of Europe; the industry employed probably one-third of the working
population of the city, which shortly before the
Black Death may have risen to 120,000 people.
The wool industry, like most, entered bad times
immediately after the plague. To protect themselves, employers cut production, thereby spreading unemployment. Since many of the employers
were also members of the ruling oligarchy, they
passed laws limiting wages and manipulating
taxation and monetary policy to benefit the rich.
The poorest workers were denied their own guild
and had no collective voice that could influence
the government. In all disputes they were subject
to the employers' laws and judges.

The poorest workers—mainly the wool
carders, known as *Ciompi*—rose in revolt. They
demanded, and for a short time got, several reforms: The employers would produce at least
enough cloth to ensure work, they would refrain
from monetary manipulations considered harm-
ful to the workers, and they would allow the
workers their own guild and representation in
communal government. These concessions did
not offer any power for the workers, but they
were nevertheless intolerable to the ruling oligarchy. Because the Ciompi did not have the leaders to maintain a steady influence on government
policy, the great families regained full authority in
the city by 1382 and quickly ended the democratic
concessions. Although the Ciompi revolt was

short-lived and ultimately unsuccessful, the incident is one of the first signs of the urban class tensions that would be a regular disturbance in future centuries.

### ◆ THE SEEDS OF DISCONTENT

While local and unique circumstances shaped each of the social disturbances of the 1300s and 1400s, the social movements had common elements. With the standard of living generally rising after the Black Death, misery was not the main cause of unrest. Rather, the peasants and workers, now reduced in number, were better able to bargain for lower rents, higher wages, and a fairer distribution of social benefits.

With the possible exception of the Ciompi, the people who revolted were rarely the desperately poor. In England, for example, the centers of the peasant uprising of 1381 were in the lower Thames valley—a region with more fertility, more prosperity, less oppression, and less serfdom than other parts of the kingdom had. Also, the immediate provocation for the revolt was the imposition of a poll tax, and poll taxes (or any taxes) do not alarm the truly destitute who cannot be forced to pay what they do not have, but they do anger people who have recently made financial gains and are anxious to hold on to them.

The principal goad to revolt in both town and country, therefore, seems to have been the effort of the propertied classes to retain their old advantages and deny the workers their new ones. Peasants and workers felt that their improving social and economic status was being threatened.

The impulse to revolt also drew strength from the psychological tensions of this age of devastating plagues, famines, and wars. The nervous temper of the times predisposed people to take action against real or imagined enemies. When needed, justifications for revolt could be found in Christian belief, for the Christian fathers had taught that neither the concept of private property nor social inequality had been intended by God. In John Ball's words: "When Adam delved and Eve span, where then were all the gentlemen?" The emotional climate of the period turned many of these uprisings into efforts to attain the millennium, to reach that age of justice and equality that Christ-ian belief saw in the past, expected in the future, and put off for the present.

# IV. Challenges to the Governments of Europe

◆

War, the third horseman of the Apocalypse, joined famine and disease. War was frequent throughout the Middle Ages but was never so widespread or long lasting as in the conflicts of the 1300s and 1400s. The Hundred Years' War between England and France is the most famous of these struggles, but there was fighting in every corner of Europe. The inbred violence of the age indicated a partial breakdown in governmental systems, which failed to maintain stability at home and peace with foreign powers.

The governmental systems of Europe were founded on multiple partnerships: feudal ties with vassals, relations with the Church, representative institutions, and subjects in general. The king enjoyed supreme dignity and even a recognized sacred character, but he was far from being an absolute ruler. In return for loyalty and service, he conceded a large share of the responsibility for government to a wide range of privileged persons and institutions: the great secular and ecclesiastical princes, the nobles, religious congregations, free cities or communes, and even favored guilds such as the universities. Out of the crises of the fourteenth and fifteenth centuries many of the new governments that came to dominate the European political scene in the late 1400s conceded far more power to a king, prince, despot, or oligarchy.

### ◆ ROOTS OF POLITICAL UNREST

*Dynastic Instability*   In a period of demographic instability, dynasties suffered, as did the population as a whole. The Hundred Years' War, or at least the excuse for it, arose from the failure of the Capetian kings of France, for the first time since the tenth century, to produce a male heir. The English War of the Roses resulted from the uncertain succession to the crown of England and the claims of the two rival houses of Lancaster and York. In Portugal, Castile, France, England, Naples,

Hungary, Poland, and the Scandinavian countries, the reigning monarchs of 1450 were not the direct, male, legitimate descendants of those reigning in 1300. Most of the founders of new lines had to fight for their positions.

*Changes in Warfare*   The same powerful economic forces that were creating new patterns of agriculture and trade were also reshaping the fiscal policies and financial machinery of feudal governments. War grew more expensive as well as more frequent. Better-trained armies were needed to fight for longer periods of time and with more complex weaponry. Above all, the increasing use of firearms added to the costs of war. To replace the traditional, undisciplined, unpaid, and poorly equipped feudal armies, governments came to rely on mercenaries, who were better trained and better armed than the vassals who fought to fulfill their feudal obligations. The major battles of the Hundred Years' War—those of Crécy, Poitiers, and Agincourt—showed the advantage of well-trained foot soldiers over knights. Many mercenaries were organized into associations known as companies of adventure, whose leaders were both good commanders and good businessmen. They took their enterprise where the market was most favorable, sold their services to the highest bidder, and turned substantial profits. Money increasingly determined who could hire mercenaries and thereby win battles.

*Seeking Revenue*   While war went up in price, the traditional revenues on which governments depended sank. Until the fourteenth century, the king or prince met most of the expenses of government from ordinary revenues, chiefly rents from his properties; but his rents, like everyone else's, were falling in the late Middle Ages. Governments of all types—monarchies, the papacy, cities—desperately sought to develop new sources of revenue. For example, the Avignon papacy, because it could not rely on the meager receipts from its lands, built a huge financial apparatus that sold ecclesiastical appointments, favors, and dispensations from normal canonical requirements; imposed tithes on ecclesiastical revenues; and sold remissions of sin known as indulgences. In France the monarchy established a monopoly over the sale of salt. In England the

king at various times imposed taxes on movable goods and on individuals (the poll tax), plus a host of smaller levies. The Italian cities taxed a whole range of items from windows to prostitutes. Under acute fiscal pressures, governments scrutinized the necessities, pleasures, and sins of society to find sources of revenue. Surviving fiscal records indicate that governments managed to increase their incomes hugely through taxes. For example, the English monarchy never collected or spent more than £30,000 per year before 1336; thereafter, the budget rarely sank below £100,000 and at times reached £250,000 in the late fourteenth century.

*Representative Institutions*   This new reliance on extraordinary taxes had important political consequences. The most lucrative taxes were not limited to the ruler's own lands but extended over all of the realm. Since he had no established right to these demands, the king had to seek the consent of his subjects. Therefore, he had to summon territorial or national assemblies of estates, such as Parliament in England or the Estates General in France, to grant new taxes. But these assemblies, in turn, often balked at the demands or offered taxes only in return for political concessions. Even in the Church, many reformers maintained that a general council should have ultimate control over papal finances. The extraordinary expansion of governmental revenues thus raised profound constitutional questions in both secular and ecclesiastical governments.

## ◆ THE NOBILITY AND FACTIONAL STRIFE

*The Nobility*   The nobility that had developed nearly everywhere in Europe also entered a period of instability in the Late Middle Ages. Birth was the main means of access to this class, and membership offered legal and social privileges such as exemption from most taxes, immunity from certain juridical procedures (such as torture), and hunting privileges. The nobles saw themselves as the chief counselors of the king and his principal partners in the conduct of government.

By the 1300s, however, the nobles began to experience economic instability. Their wealth was chiefly in land, and they, like all landlords, faced

▲ FAMILY TOWERS AT LUCCA
**This fourteenth-century view of the Italian city of Lucca testifies to the violence of factional conflict within these cities. Each major family and its leading supporters built a defensible structure, topped by an identifiable tower. Here, in a large building that surrounded a central courtyard and had its own chapel, they could find refuge from rival families and factions.**
Scala/Art Resource, NY

the problem of declining rents. Unlike the gentry, they often lacked the funds needed for the new agricultural investments, and they continued to have the problem of finding income and careers for their younger sons. In short, the nobles were not immune from the acute economic dislocations of the times, and their class included men who lived on the brink of poverty as well as holders of enormous estates.

*Factional Politics*  To maintain their position, some of the nobles joined the mercenary companies. Others hoped to buttress their sinking fortunes through marriage or by winning offices, lands, pensions, or other favors from governments. But as the social uncertainties intensified, the nobles tended to coalesce into factions that disputed with one another over the control of government and the distribution of its favors. From England to Italy, factional warfare constantly disturbed the peace. A divided and grasping nobility added to the tensions of the age and to its violence.

Characteristically, a faction was led by a great noble house and included people of varying social

station—great nobles in alliance with the leading royal house, poor knights, retainers, servants, sometimes even artisans and peasants. Some of the factions encompassed scores of families and hundreds of men and could almost be considered little states within a state, with their own small armies, loyalties, and symbols of allegiance in the colors or distinctive costumes (livery) worn by their members.

*The Pastons*  A good example of liveried retainers of these great nobles are the Pastons of England. The family originated from wealthy peasant stock who prospered in the agricultural opportunities of the fifteenth century. The founder of the family fortune, William, managed to marry up socially, taking a knight's daughter as wife. He educated his sons in law because land could be gained by legal maneuverings as well as through advantageous marriages. He was also careful about the local patronage system and placed his eldest son, John, in the Duke of Norfolk's household. John was part of the duke's retinue on ceremonial occasions. Sir John Fastolf, a soldier who made a fortune in the Hundred Years' War and was the model for Shakespeare's Falstaff, relied on John for legal advice and eventually made him his heir. The Pastons continually defended their lands either in court or in actual sieges. At one point John's wife, Margaret, organized the defense of one of their manors from armed attack. The people trying to obtain their property had the support of other great lords in the district, particularly the Duke of Suffolk. The family managed to survive the War of the Roses to emerge in the sixteenth century as nobility.

### ◆ ENGLAND, FRANCE, AND THE HUNDRED YEARS' WAR

All the factors that upset the equilibrium of feudal governments—dynastic instability, fiscal pressures, and factional rivalries—helped to provoke the greatest struggle of the epoch, the Hundred Years' War. The war had distinctive characteristics. It was not fought continually for one hundred years, but in different phases. The great battles were of less significance for determining the outcome than was the war of attrition against the population. Economic embargo and interruption of trade became weapons of states in winning wars.

*Causes*  The issue that is alleged to have started the Hundred Years' War was a dispute over the French royal succession. While most noble families had direct father-to-son succession for only three generations, the Capetians had produced male heirs for three hundred years. The last three Capetian kings (the sons of Philip IV, the Fair), all died without male heirs. In 1328, when the last Capetian died, the nearest surviving male relative was King Edward III of England, son of Philip's daughter Isabella. The Parlement of Paris—the supreme court of France—discovered that the laws of the Salian Franks precluded women from inheriting or transmitting a claim to the crown. Philip of Valois, a first cousin of the previous kings, became king. Edward did not at first dispute this decision, and, as holder of the French fiefs of Aquitaine and Ponthieu, he did homage to Philip VI.

More important than the dynastic issue was the clash of French and English interests in Flanders, an area whose cloth-making industry relied on

▼ *Ambrogio Lorenzetti*
THE *PEACEFUL CITY* (DETAIL FROM *GOOD GOVERNMENT*), 1338–1341
**The effects of good government, seen in this idealized representation of the *Peaceful City* by Ambrogio Lorenzetti, include flourishing commerce, dancing maidens, and lavish residences, as opposed to the protective towers of feudal warfare. This fresco in the city hall of Siena was a constant reminder to the citizens of the advantages of living in their city.**
Scala/Art Resource, NY

England for wool. In 1302 the Flemings had rebelled against their count, a vassal of the French king, and had remained virtually independent until 1328, when Philip VI defeated their troops and restored the count. At Philip's insistence, the count ordered the arrest of all English merchants in Flanders; Edward retaliated by cutting off the export of wool, which spread unemployment in the Flemish towns. The Flemings revolted once more and drove out the count. To give legal sanction to their revolt, they persuaded Edward to assert his claim to the French crown, which held suzerainty over Flanders.

The most serious point of friction, however, was the status of Aquitaine and Ponthieu. Edward had willingly performed ordinary homage for them, but Philip then insisted on liege homage, which would have obligated Edward to support Philip against all enemies. Edward did not believe that, as a king, he could undertake the obligations of liege homage to any man, and refused. Philip began harassing the frontiers of Aquitaine and declared Edward's fiefs forfeit in 1337. The attack on Aquitaine pushed Edward into supporting the Flemish revolt and was thus the main provocation for the Hundred Years' War.

Economic maneuvers by both sides aggravated tensions. The French king encouraged French pirates and shippers to interfere with the wine trade from English Gascony. Edward began to tax wool leaving England and encouraged the Flemish weavers to come to England under his special protection to set up workshops with their superior craftsmanship. Incidentally, this move was the beginning of the woolen cloth weaving tradition in England.

◆ THE TIDES OF BATTLE

The French seemed to have a decisive superiority over the English at the outset of the war. The population of France was perhaps 15 million; England had between 4 and 7 million. But the war was hardly ever a national confrontation, because French subjects (Flemings, Gascons, Burgundians) fought alongside the English against other French subjects. The confused struggle may, however, be divided into three periods: initial English victories from 1338 to 1360; French resurgence, then stalemate, from 1369 to 1415; and a wild denouement

with tides rapidly shifting from 1415 to 1453 (see map 11.4).

*First Period*  The English never fully exploited their early victories, nor did the French ever manage to undo them. An English naval victory at Sluys in 1340 ensured English communications across the channel and determined that France would be the scene of the fighting. Six years later Edward landed in France on what was more a marauding expedition than a campaign of conquest. Philip pursued the English and finally overtook them at Crécy. The English were on a hill, and Edward positioned his troops so that the longbowmen could shoot into the advancing French line. The French knights had arrived after a long journey, but decided to attack without waiting for their crossbowmen, who were coming on foot. Charging up the hill, the French knights met a rain of arrows that cut their horses from under them. The English knights came down to finish the fight. The victory ensured the English possession of Calais, which they took in 1347.

The scenario was repeated in 1356 at Poitiers when John II, who had succeeded Philip, attacked an English army led by Edward's son, the Black Prince, and suffered an even more crushing defeat. John was captured and died, unransomed by his son and vassals. English victories, the Black Death, and mutual exhaustion led to the Peace of Brétigny in 1360. The English were granted Calais and an enlarged Aquitaine, and Edward, in turn, renounced his claim to the French crown.

*Second Period*  The French were not willing to allow so large a part of their kingdom to remain in English hands. In 1369, under John's successor, Charles V, the French opened a second phase of the war. Their strategy was to avoid full-scale battles and instead wear down the English forces, and they succeeded. By 1380 they had pushed the English nearly into the sea, confining them to Calais and a narrow strip of the Atlantic coast from Bordeaux to Bayonne. Fighting was sporadic from 1380 until 1415, with both sides content with a stalemate. During this war of attrition, mercenaries on both sides devastated the countryside, plundering villages, ruining crops and vineyards, and driving the population to seek refuge. It was

**Kingdom of France in 1339**

**English areas in 1339**

**English controlled areas in 1429**

**Burgundian areas in 1441**

**Battle site**

NORTH SEA

HOLY ROMAN EMPIRE

*Rhine R.*

London

ENGLAND

Sluys 1340

Bruges

Antwerp

Calais

COUNTY OF

Cassel

FLANDERS

Agincourt 1415

Arras

DUCHY OF BRABANT

NAMUR

COUNTY OF HAINAUT

*Moselle R.*

Crécy 1346

ENGLISH CHANNEL

*Meuse R.*

ALSACE

Rouen

*Seine R.*

Compiègne

Reims

*Marne R.*

NORMANDY

BRITTANY

Rennes

MAINE

Paris

CHAMPAGNE

Troyes

DUCHY OF LORRAINE

Domremy

Brétigny

Orléans 1429

Angers

ANJOU

*Loire R.*

Chinon

DUCHY OF BURGUNDY
*(Supporting English Claim)*

Dijon

COUNTY OF BURGUNDY

POITOU

Bourges

Poitiers 1356

AUVERGNE

HOLY ROMAN EMPIRE

BAY OF BISCAY

Bordeaux

*Dordogne R.*

AQUITAINE

*Garonne R.*

*Durance R.*

Avignon

GUIENNE

ARMAGNAC

PROVENCE

Bayonne

GASCONY

Aix

NAVARRE

0    50    100 Miles

MEDITERRANEAN SEA

ARAGON

▲ MAP 11.4  THE HUNDRED YEARS' WAR
Because of their closeness to the continent and their naval power, the English were able to dominate northern France, the area that traditionally had been that kingdom's heartland. As a result, Joan of Arc's decisive victory came not in Paris but in Orléans on the Loire River — which proved to be a crucial boundary between the two sides.
◆ www.mhhe.com/chambers8ch11maps

*Chronology*

◆

## THE HUNDRED YEARS' WAR

| | |
|---|---|
| **1328** | Charles IV, last Capetian king in direct line, dies; Philip of Valois is elected king of France as Philip VI; Philip defeats Flemings at Cassel; unrest continues in Flemish towns. |
| **1329** | Edward III of England does simple homage to Philip for continental possessions but refuses liege homage. |
| **1336** | Edward embargoes wool exports to Flanders. |
| **1338** | Philip's troops harass English Guienne; Edward, urged on by the Flemings, claims French crown; war begins. |
| **1346** | Major English victory at Crécy. |
| **1347–1351** | Black Death ravages Europe. |
| **1356** | Black Prince defeats French at Poitiers. |
| **1358** | Peasants' uprising near Paris. |
| **1360** | Peace of Brétigny; English gain major territorial concessions but abandon claim to French crown. |
| **1369** | Fighting renewed in France. |
| **1370** | Bertrand du Guesclin, constable of France, leads French resurgence. |
| **1381** | Peasants' Revolt in England. |
| **1392** | Charles VI of France suffers first attack of insanity; Burgundians and Armagnacs contend for power over king; fighting wanes as both sides are exhausted. |
| **1399** | Henry IV of Lancaster takes English throne, deposing Richard II. |
| **1415** | Henry V wins major victory at Agincourt. |
| **1420** | Treaty of Troyes; Charles VI recognizes Henry V as legitimate heir to French crown; high-water mark of English fortunes. |
| **1429** | Joan of Arc relieves Orléans from English siege; Dauphin is crowned king at Reims as Charles VII. |
| **1431** | Joan is burned at the stake at Rouen. |
| **1435** | Peace of Arras; Burgundy abandons English side. |
| **1436** | Charles retakes Paris. |
| **1453** | Bordeaux falls to French; English retain only Calais on continent; effective end of war, though no treaty is signed. |

a type of warfare that reappeared in the Thirty Years' War and in World War II.

***Third Period*** The last period of the war, from 1415 to 1453, was one of high drama and rapidly shifting fortunes. Henry V of England invaded France and shattered the French army at Agincourt in 1415. The battle was a replay of Crécy and Poitiers. The English longbowmen shot at the French knights in full armor as they charged downhill into a marshy area. Henry's success was confirmed by the Treaty of Troyes in 1420, an almost total French capitulation. King Charles VI of France declared his son the Dauphin (the future Charles VII) illegitimate, named Henry his successor and regent of France, and gave him direct rule over all French lands as far south as the Loire River (see map 11.4). Charles also gave Henry his daughter Catherine in marriage, with the agreement that their son would become the next king of France.

The Dauphin could not accept this forced abdication, and from his capital at Bourges he led an expedition across the Loire River. The English drove his forces back and systematically took the towns and fortresses north of the river that were loyal to him. In 1428 they finally laid siege to Orléans, a city whose fall would have given them a commanding position in the Loire valley and would have made the Dauphin's cause desperate.

***Joan of Arc*** The intervention of a young peasant girl, Joan of Arc, saved the Valois dynasty. Convinced that heavenly voices were ordering her to rescue France, Joan persuaded several royal officials, and finally the Dauphin himself, of the authenticity of her mission and was given command of an army. In 1429 she marched to Orléans and forced the English to raise the siege. She then escorted the Dauphin to Reims, the historic coronation city of France, where his coronation

▲ JOAN OF ARC, 1484
**Surrounded by the clerics who had condemned her, Joan of Arc is bound to the stake in this scene from a manuscript that was prepared half a century after she was executed in 1431. Despite Joan's own preference for short hair and manly costume, she is shown here as a conventionally idealized female figure.**
Bibliothèque Nationale de France, Paris

confirmed his legitimacy and won him broad support as the embodiment of French royalist sentiment. The tide had turned.

Joan passed from history as quickly and as dramatically as she had arrived. The Burgundians, allies of the English, captured her in 1430 and sold her to the English, who put her on trial for witchcraft and heresy (see "The Trial of Joan of Arc," p. 387). She was burned at the stake at Rouen in 1431. Yet Joan's commitment was one sign of an increasingly powerful feeling among the people. They had grown impatient with continuing destruction and had come to identify their own security with the expulsion of the English and the establishment of a strong Valois monarchy. This growing loyalty to the king finally saved France from its long agony. A series of French successes followed Joan's death, and by 1453 only Calais was left in English hands. No formal treaty ended the war, but both sides accepted the outcome: England was no longer a continental power.

◆ THE EFFECTS OF THE HUNDRED YEARS' WAR

Like all the disasters of the era, the Hundred Years' War accelerated change. It stimulated the development of firearms and the technologies needed to manufacture them, and it helped establish the infantry—armed with longbow, crossbow, pike, or gun—as superior in battle to mounted knights. It also introduced wars of attrition in which the countryside was devastated in an effort to bring the enemy to submission. The war had a major effect on government institutions in England and France.

*Parliament*  The expense of fighting forced the English king to request more revenue through taxation. In England the king willingly gave Parliament a larger political role in return for grants of new taxes. The tradition became firmly established that Parliament had the right to grant or refuse new taxes, to agree to legislation, to channel appeals to the king, and to offer advice on important decisions such as peace and war. The House of Commons gained the right to introduce all tax legislation, since the Commons, unlike the Lords, were representatives of shires and boroughs. Parliament also named a committee to audit tax records and supervise payments. Equally important, the Commons could impeach high royal officials, a crucial step in establishing the principle that a king's ministers were responsible to Parliament as well as to their royal master. By the end of the Hundred Years' War, Parliament had been notably strengthened at the expense of royal power.

*French Government*  The need for new taxes had a rather different outcome in France, where it enhanced the power of the monarchs while weakening the Estates General, the national representative assembly. In 1343 Philip VI established a monopoly over the sale of salt, fixing in many areas of France its cost and the amount each family could have to consume. The tax on salt, called the *gabelle,* was to be essential to French royal finance until 1789. In gaining support for this and other taxes, Philip and his successors sought the agreement of regional assemblies of estates as well as the national Estates General. The kings' reliance on the local estates hindered the rise of a centralized assembly that could speak for the entire kingdom. By the reign of Charles VII, during the last stages of the war, the monarchy obtained the right to impose national taxes (notably the *taille,* a direct tax from which nobles and clerics were exempt) without the consent of the Estates General. By

# THE TRIAL OF JOAN OF ARC

◆

*The records of the trial of Joan of Arc in Rouen in 1431 give us a rare opportunity to hear her directly, or at least the words a secretary heard. Whether recorded accurately or not, her testimony does give us a glimpse of her extraordinary spirit and determination.*

"When she had taken the oath the said Jeanne was questioned by us about her name and her surname. To which she replied that in her own country she was called Jeannette. She was questioned about the district from which she came.

"She said she was born in the village of Domrémy. Asked if in her youth she had learned any craft, she says yes, to sew and spin; and in sewing and spinning she feared no woman in Rouen.

"Afterwards she declared that at the age of 13 she had a voice from God to help her and guide her. And the first time she was much afraid. And this voice came towards noon, in summer, in her father's garden. Asked what instruction this voice gave her for the salvation of her soul, she said it taught her to be good and to go to church often; and the voice told her that she should raise the siege of the city of Orléans.

"Asked whether, when she saw the voice coming to her, there was a light, she answered that there was a great deal of light on all sides. She added to the examiner that not all the light came to him alone!

"Asked whether she thought she had committed a sin when she left her father and mother, she answered that since God commanded, it was right to do so. She added that since God commanded, if she had had a hundred parents, she would have gone nevertheless.

"Jeanne was admonished to speak the truth. Many of the points were read and explained to her, and she was told that if she did not confess them truthfully she would be put to the torture, the instruments of which were shown to her.

"To which Jeanne answered in this manner: 'Truly if you were to tear me limb from limb and separate my soul from my body, I would not tell you anything more; and if I did say anything, I should afterwards declare that you had compelled me to say it by force.'"

From G. G. Coulton and Eileen Power (eds.), *The Trial of Jeanne d' Arc*, W. P. Barrett (trans.) (Routledge, 1931).

---

then, too, the royal government was served by a standing professional army—the first in any European country since the fall of the Roman Empire.

***The War of the Roses*** Both England and France experienced internal dissension during the Hundred Years' War. Both countries experienced a brutalization of life, with groups of former fighters and thugs pillaging the countryside. After the death of Edward III in 1377, England faced more than a century of turmoil, with nobles striving to maintain their economic fortunes through factional conflicts. The powerful magnates and their liveried followers used law and brute force to gain lands of competitors, as we have seen in the case of the Pastons. The son of Henry V and Catherine of France, Henry VI, went through periods of insanity, which led to a civil war for succession to the throne. Two factions, the Lancastrians and the Yorkists, laid claim to the throne, and the English nobles aligned themselves on one side or the other. The civil war that followed is known to historians as the War of the Roses (the Lancastrians' emblem was a red rose, the Yorkists' a white rose).

The civil war lasted some thirty-five years. While not bloody for the population as a whole, the war did decimate the ranks of the nobility. It also gave rise to the allegations that Richard III, a Yorkist, killed his two young nephews in the Tower of London because they had a clearer title to the kingship than he had. Finally, the Lancastrian Henry Tudor defeated Richard III at Bosworth Field in 1485. Henry VII married Elizabeth of York to heal the breech between the factions. By the end of the fifteenth century, prosperity had relieved the pressures on the English nobles, and the people in general, weary of war, welcomed the strong and orderly regime that Henry established.

***Burgundy*** In France, too, the power of the monarchy was threatened by rival factions of nobles, the Armagnacs and the Burgundians. The Armagnacs wanted the war with England vigorously pursued, while the Burgundians favored accommodation. The territorial ambitions of the Burgundians also posed a threat to the French monarchy. King John II of France had granted the huge Duchy of Burgundy to his younger son, Philip the Bold, in 1363. Philip and his successors greatly enlarged their possessions in eastern France, the Rhône and Rhine valleys, and the Low Countries (see map 11.3). They were generous patrons of literature and the arts, and they made their court at Dijon the most brilliant in Europe.

The dukes seem to have sought to establish a Burgundian "middle kingdom" between France and the Holy Roman Empire; such a state would have affected the political geography of Europe permanently and undermined the position of the French monarch. But the threat vanished in 1477 when the last duke, Charles the Bold, was killed in battle with the Swiss at Nancy. His daughter and heir, Mary of Burgundy, could not hold her scattered inheritance together, and a large part of it came under French control.

***The English and French States*** With the loss of most of its continental possessions, England emerged from the war geographically more consolidated. It was also homogeneous in its language (English gradually replaced French and Latin as the language of the law courts and administration) and more conscious of its cultural distinctiveness and national identity. Although the French had made some incursions in coastal areas, England had not been invaded, and the woolen industry began to be very profitable. Freed from its continental entanglements, England was ready for its expansion beyond the seas and for a surge in national pride and self-consciousness.

France did not immediately achieve quite the territorial consolidation of England, but the expulsion of the English from French lands and the disintegration of the Duchy of Burgundy left the French king without a major rival among his feudal princes. The monarchy emerged from the war with a permanent army, a rich tax system, and no clear constitutional restrictions on its exercise of power. Most significantly, the war gave the French king high prestige and confirmed him as the chief protector and patron of the people. Although rav-

aged by warfare, the land was so rich that, when the peasants returned and began cultivating, the French economy quickly recovered.

In both France and England, government at the end of the Middle Ages was still decentralized and "feudal," meaning here that certain privileged persons and institutions (nobles, the Church, towns, and the like) continued to hold and to exercise some form of private jurisdiction. They retained, for example, their own courts. But the king had unmistakably emerged as the dominant partner in the feudal relationship. Moreover, he was prepared to press his advantages in the sixteenth century.

## ◆ THE STATES OF ITALY

Free cities, or communes, dominated the political life of central and northern Italy in the early fourteenth century. The Holy Roman Empire claimed a loose sovereignty over much of the peninsula north of Rome, and the papacy governed the area around Rome; but most of the principal cities, and many small ones too, had gained the status of self-governing city-states.

The new economic and social conditions of the 1300s, however, worked against the survival of the smaller communes. Economic contraction made it increasingly difficult for industries and merchant houses in the smaller cities to compete with their rivals in the larger ones. And the rising costs of war made it hard for small communes to defend their independence. Factional strife made political order difficult in both small and large towns leading to despotisms. Regional states, dominated politically and economically by a single metropolis, replaced the numerous, free, and highly competitive communes.

***Milan*** Perhaps the most effective Italian despot was the ruler of Milan, Gian Galeazzo Visconti (r. 1378–1402), who set about enlarging the Visconti inheritance of twenty-one cities in the Po valley. Through shrewd negotiations and opportune attacks, he secured the submission of cities to his east, which gave him an outlet to the Adriatic Sea. He then seized Bologna, purchased Pisa, and through a variety of methods was accepted as ruler of Siena, Perugia, Spoleto, Nocera, and Assisi. In the course of this advance deep into

◄ INVESTITURE OF GIAN GALEAZZO VISCONTI, CA. 1395 This contemporary depiction of the investiture of Gian Galeazzo Visconti as duke of Milan is from a manuscript he commissioned to commemorate the occasion. The picture on top shows Visconti in a white cape seated next to the emperor's representative, who in the picture below places the diadem on the kneeling Visconti's head. The spectators, coming from all walks of life, include bishops and soldiers carrying cannons, but the ceremony itself takes place in front of an altar. The margins contain such Visconti family symbols as the eagle, the cheetah, and various fruit trees, and the entire manuscript leaf is a rich and colorful glorification of a central event in Visconti's life.

Index, © Giancarlo Costa

central Italy, Gian Galeazzo kept his chief ene-mies, the Florentines and the Venetians, divided, and he seemed ready to create a united Italian kingdom.

To establish a legal basis for his power, Gian Galeazzo secured from the emperor an appoint-ment as imperial vicar in 1380 and then as heredi-tary duke in 1395. This move made him the only duke in all Italy, which seemed a step closer to a royal title. He revised the laws of Milan, but the chief administrative foundation of his success was his ability to wring enormous tax revenues from his subjects. Gian Galeazzo was also a generous patron of the new learning of his day; with his conquests, wealth, and brilliance, he seemed to be awaiting only the submission of the Florentines before adopting the title of king. But he died unexpectedly in 1402, leaving two minor sons who were incapable of defending their inheritance.

*Florence* Florence by the mid-1300s was the principal banking center in Europe and one of the most important producers of luxury goods. Its silks, textiles, fine leather, and silver and gold objects were much prized, and the training its guilds offered in design and craftsmanship was a major reason for the high skills of its artists. The florin, the city's gold coin, had international standing as one of the most reliable currencies of the time, and the broad contacts of its merchants gave Florence a cosmopolitan air.

By the 1300s Florence had been a self-governing commune for two centuries, but it had rarely enjoyed political stability. It was ruled by a series of councils, whose members were drawn from the leading families. From time to time, however, as movements for wider representation arose, such as the Ciompi revolt of 1378, seats on the councils were opened to a broader segment of the citizenry—at times, as many as 20 percent of adult males may have been eligible for office.

The volatile fortunes of the different groups did not give way to a more stable regime until the rich Medici banking family gained control of the city's government in 1434 and made sure that only people they favored were defined as eligible for government positions. While retaining a facade of republican government, Cosimo de Medici established a form of boss rule over the city. His tax policies favored the lower and middle classes, and he also gained the support of the middle classes by appointments to office and other forms of political patronage. He secured peace for Florence and started his family's brilliant tradition of patronage of learning and the arts.

This tradition was enhanced by Cosimo's grandson, Lorenzo the Magnificent (r. 1469–1492), who beat back the plots of other powerful Florentine families and strengthened centralized control over the city. Lorenzo's Florence came to set the style for Italy, and eventually for Europe, in the splendor of its festivals, the elegance of its social life, the beauty of its buildings, and the lavish support it extended to scholars and artists.

*Venice* Already independent for more than five hundred years, the city of Venice by 1400 controlled a far-flung empire in northern Italy and the eastern Mediterranean and kept a large army and navy. Venice's wealth came from its dominance of the import of goods from Asia, notably spices like black pepper and cloves, which were probably the most expensive commodities, per ounce, sold in Europe. Its wealthiest citizens also controlled its government; unlike Florence, Venice was ruled by a cohesive, rather than faction-ridden, oligarchy of some 150 families who inherited this dominance from generation to generation. From among their number they elected the *doge,* the head of the government, who held that position for life. (To increase turnover, older men were usually elected.)

Venice enjoyed remarkable political stability. There were occasional outbursts of discontent, but usually the patricians—who stayed united, relied on informers, made decisions in secret, and were ready to punish troublemakers severely—were able to maintain an image of orderliness and justice in government. They were also careful to show a concern for public welfare. The chief support of the navy, for instance—an essential asset for a city that, though containing more than 100,000 people, was built on a collection of islands in a lagoon—was a unique ship-building and arms manufacturing facility, the Arsenal. This gigantic complex, which employed more than 5 percent of the city's adult population, was not only the largest industrial enterprise in Europe but also a crucial source of employment. The Arsenal could build a fully equipped warship, starting from scratch, in just one day, and the skills it required helped maintain Venice's reputation as a haven for the finest artisans of the day. Not only men but entire families came to work there; one visitor described a "hall where about fifty women were making sails for ships" and another where one hundred women were "spinning and making ropes and doing other work related to ropes."

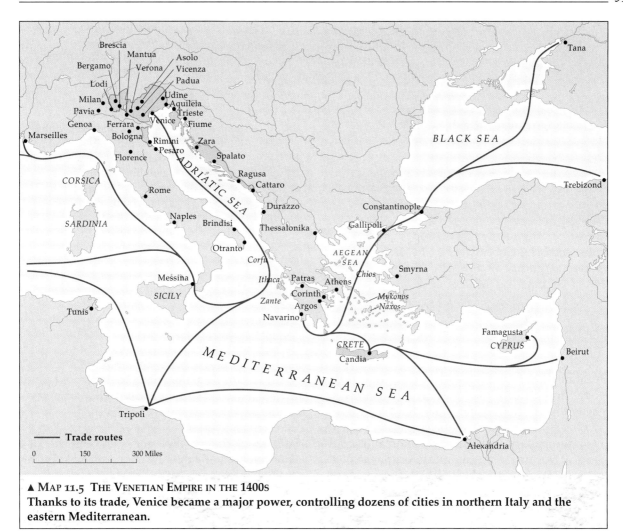

▲ MAP 11.5  THE VENETIAN EMPIRE IN THE 1400S
**Thanks to its trade, Venice became a major power, controlling dozens of cities in northern Italy and the eastern Mediterranean.**

An institution like the Arsenal promoted economic and social stability by offering so many jobs and also helped improve the craftsmanship and skills of the city's artisans. In addition, because of its location and its easy openness to all who wished to trade, Venice was a meeting ground for Slavs, Turks, Germans, Jews, Muslims, Greeks, and other Italians. It was a favorite tourist spot for travelers and for pilgrims on the way to the Holy Land, a major center for the new international art of printing, and famous for its shops and entertainments. By the mid-1400s, its coin, the ducat, was replacing the florin as a standard for all Europe; and its patrons, often interested in more earthy themes than the Florentines, were promoting a flowering of literature, learning, and the arts that made Venice a focus of Renaissance culture.

From the early fifteenth century onward, Venice initiated a policy of territorial expansion on the mainland. By 1405, Padua, Verona, and Vicenza had become Venetian dependencies (see map 11.5).

*Papal States*   The popes, like the leaders of the city-states, worked to consolidate their rule over their possessions in central Italy, but they faced formidable obstacles because the papacy was now located in Avignon in southern France. The difficult terrain of the Italian Papal States—dotted with castles and fortified towns—enabled communes, petty lords, and brigands to defy papal

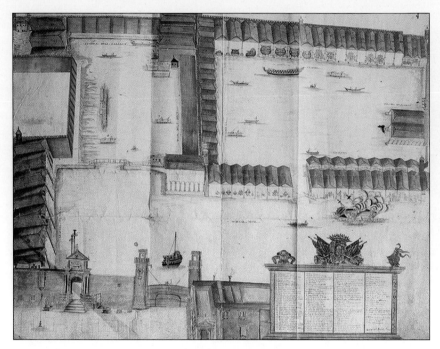

◄ *Antonio Natale*
VENICE ARSENAL
**This eighteenth-century depiction of the huge complex that made up the Arsenal in Venice indicates some of the specialized buildings that formed the production line around the pools in which the ships were built. At the back, hulls are being laid, and in the foreground, a ship is being scuttled. At the very front are the two towers that flanked the entrance gate to the Arsenal.**
Index, © Giancarlo Costa

authority. Continuing disorders discouraged the popes from returning to Rome, and their efforts to pacify their tumultuous lands were a major drain on papal finances. Even after its return to Rome in 1378, the papacy had difficulty maintaining authority. Not until the pontificate of Martin V (r. 1417–1431) was a stable administration established, and Martin's successors still faced frequent revolts throughout the fifteenth century.

***Kingdom of Naples and Sicily*** The political situation was equally confused in the Kingdom of Naples and Sicily. Following the Sicilian Vespers in 1282, Sicily and Naples became a battleground for the competing ambitions of the Aragonese and the Angevins (descendants of Charles of Anjou). In 1435 the king of Aragon, Alfonso V, the Magnanimous, reunited Sicily and southern Italy and made the kingdom the center of an Aragonese empire in the Mediterranean. Alfonso sought to suppress the factions of lawless nobles and to reform taxes and strengthen administration. His efforts were not completely successful, for southern Italy and Sicily were rugged, poor lands and difficult to subdue; but he was at least able to overcome the chaos that had prevailed earlier. Alfonso thus extended to the Mediterranean the strengthening of central governments that took place else-

where in Europe in the 1400s. The court he created at Naples was one of the most brilliant centers of art and literature of the age.

***Balance of Power*** Relations between the city-states on the Italian peninsula were tense as they clashed over trade and the acquisition of surrounding territory. The Peace of Lodi in 1454 ended a war among Milan, Florence, and Venice. Cosimo de Medici sought to make the peace a lasting one by creating an alliance system between Milan, Naples, and Florence on one side and Venice and the Papal States on the other (see map 11.6). During the next forty years, until the French invaded the peninsula in 1494, the balance was occasionally rocked but never overturned. This system represents one of the earliest appearances in European history of a diplomatic balance of power for maintaining peace.

# V. The Fall of Byzantium and the Ottoman Empire

◆

Although the Byzantine Empire revived under Michael VIII Palaeologus, by the mid-fifteenth century the empire's control was effective only in

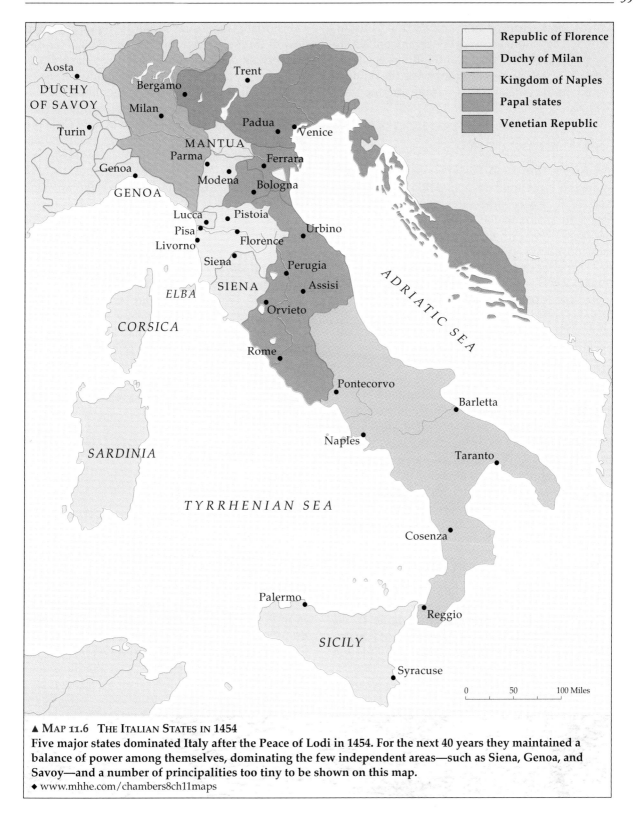

▲ MAP 11.6   THE ITALIAN STATES IN 1454

Five major states dominated Italy after the Peace of Lodi in 1454. For the next 40 years they maintained a balance of power among themselves, dominating the few independent areas—such as Siena, Genoa, and Savoy—and a number of principalities too tiny to be shown on this map.

◆ www.mhhe.com/chambers8ch11maps

Greece, the Aegean, and the area around Constantinople. The Ottoman Turks eventually fell heir to Byzantium's former power and influence, and by the early sixteenth century they were the unquestioned masters of southeast Europe and the Middle East.

## ◆ THE FALL OF CONSTANTINOPLE

***The Rising Threat***   Turkish peoples had been assuming a large military and political role in the Middle East since the late tenth century. The Seljuk Turks dominated western Asia Minor since the late 1000s. Although Turks survived the attacks of Western crusaders, they were defeated by the Mongols in the thirteenth century. The Ottoman Turks, who had converted to Islam, followed the Mongol invasions and took over Asia Minor. They took their name from Osman, or Othman (r. 1290–1326), who founded a dynasty of sultans that survived for six centuries.

Establishing themselves at Gallipoli on the European side of the Straits in 1354, the Ottomans completely surrounded the Byzantine territory. The Byzantine emperors, fearing the worst for their small and isolated realm, tried desperately but unsuccessfully to persuade the West to send military help. At the council of Florence in 1439, Emperor John VII even accepted reunion with Rome, largely on Roman terms, in return for aid, but he had no power to impose the reunion of the churches on his people; in fact, many Eastern Christians preferred Turkish rule to submission to the hated Westerners.

***The Capture of the City***   The Ottomans were unable to mount a major campaign against Constantinople until 1453, when Sultan Mehmet II, the Conqueror, finally attacked by land and water. The city fell after a heroic resistance, and Emperor Constantine XI Palaeologus, whose imperial lineage stretched back more than 1,400 years to Augustus Caesar, died in this final agony of the Byzantine Empire.

The fall of Constantinople had little military or economic effect on Europe and the Middle East. The Byzantine Empire had not been an effective barrier to Ottoman expansion for years, and Constantinople had dwindled commercially as well as politically. The shift to Turkish dominion did not,

as historians once believed, substantially affect the flow of trade between the East and West. Nor did the Turkish conquest of the city provoke an exodus of Byzantine scholars and manuscripts to Italy. Scholars from the East, recognizing the decline and seemingly inevitable fall of the Byzantine Empire, had been emigrating to Italy since the late fourteenth century; the revival of Greek letters was well under way in the West by 1453.

***The End of an Era***   The impact of the fall was largely psychological; although hardly unexpected, it shocked the Christian world. The end of the Byzantine Empire had great symbolic importance for contemporaries and, perhaps even more, for later historians. In selecting Byzantium as his capital in 324, Constantine had founded a Christian Roman empire that could be considered the first authentically medieval state. For more than 1,000 years this Christian Roman empire played a major political and cultural role in the history of both Eastern and Western peoples. In some respects, the years of its existence mark the span of the Middle Ages, and its passing symbolizes the end of an era.

## ◆ THE OTTOMAN EMPIRE

***Expansion***   Under Mehmet II (r. 1451–1481), who from the start of his reign committed his government to a policy of conquest, the Ottomans began a century of expansion (see "The Sultan Mehmet II," p. 395). After the fall of Constantinople, which became his capital under the name of Istanbul (though the name was not officially adopted until 1930), Mehmet subjugated Morea, Serbia, Bosnia, and parts of Herzegovina. He drove the Genoese from their Black Sea colonies, forced the khan of the Crimea to become his vassal, and fought a lengthy naval war with the Venetians. At his death the Ottomans were a power on land and sea, and the Black Sea had become a Turkish lake (see map 11. 7).

Early in the following century Turkish domination was extended over the heart of the Arab lands through the conquest of Syria, Egypt, and the western coast of the Arabian peninsula. (The Arabs did not again enjoy autonomy until the twentieth century.) With the conquest of the sacred cities of Mecca and Medina, the sultan

# The Sultan Mehmet II

◆

*One of the first histories of the Ottomans by a Westerner was written by an English schoolmaster named Richard Knolles and published in 1603. It is obvious that a great deal of research went into his work, which is marked by vivid portraits such as this one of the Sultan Mehmet II, known as the Conqueror because of his capture of Constantinople, who had lived a century before Knolles wrote.*

"He was of stature but low, square set, and strongly limbed; his complexion sallow and melancholy; his look and countenance stern, with his eyes piercing, and his nose so high and crooked that it almost touched his upper lip. He was of a very sharp and apprehending wit, learned especially in astronomy, and could speak the Greek, Latin, Arabic, Chaldee, and Persian tongues. He delighted much in reading of histories, and the lives of worthy men, especially the lives of Alexander the Great and Julius Caesar, whom he proposed to himself as examples to follow. He was of an exceeding courage, and a severe punisher of injustice. Men that excelled in any quality, he greatly favored and honorably entertained, as he did Gentile Bellini, a painter of Venice, whom he purposely caused to come from thence to Constantinople, to draw the lively counterfeit of himself for which he most bountifully rewarded him. He so severely punished theft, as that in his time all the ways were safe. He was altogether irreligious, and most perfidious, ambitious above measure, and in nothing more delighted than in blood: insomuch that he was responsible for the death of 800,000 men; craft, covetousness and dissimulation were in him accounted tolerable, in comparison of his greater vices. In his love was no assurance, and his least displeasure was death; so that he lived feared of all men, and died lamented of none."

From Richard Knolles, in John J. Saunders (ed.), *The Muslim World on the Eve of Europe's Expansion* (Prentice-Hall, 1966), adapted by T. K. Rabb.

▼ *Gentile Bellini*
**Mehmet II**
**Mehmet II, here shown in a painting attributed to the Venetian artist Gentile Bellini, was the conqueror of Constantinople in 1453.**
The Granger Collection, New York

assumed the title of caliph, "successor of the Prophet," claiming to be Islam's supreme religious head as well as its mightiest sword.

*Suleiman II* Suleiman II, the Magnificent (r. 1520–1566), brought the Ottoman Empire to its height of power. In 1521 he took the citadel of Belgrade, which had hitherto blocked Turkish advance up the Balkan Peninsula toward Hungary, and the next year he forced the Hospitalers, after a six-month siege, to surrender the island of Rhodes, a loss that was a crippling blow to Western naval strength in the eastern Mediterranean.

Suleiman achieved his greatest victory in 1526 with the defeat of the king of Hungary's army at Mohacs and the occupation of Hungary. He then launched his most ambitious campaign, directed against Austria, the Christian state that now assumed chief responsibility for defending Europe's eastern frontiers. This effort, the high-water mark of Ottoman expansion into Europe, failed when Suleiman was unable to capture Vienna in 1529. The frustrated sultan returned home and turned his attention toward the East. His armies overran Mesopotamia and completed the conquest of

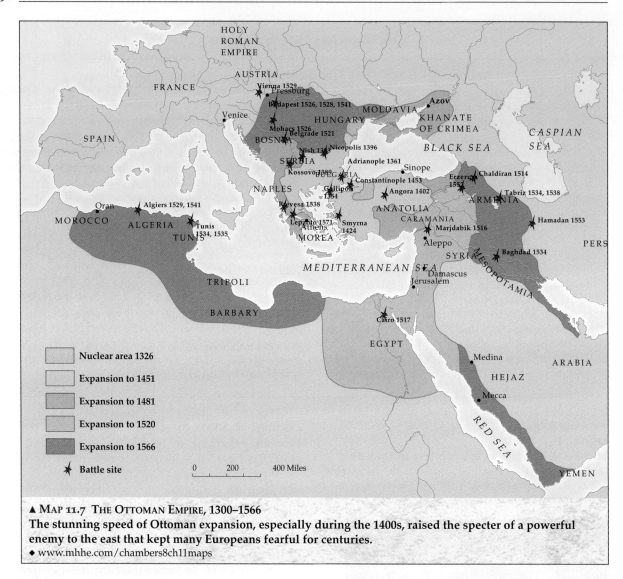

▲ **MAP 11.7  THE OTTOMAN EMPIRE, 1300–1566**
**The stunning speed of Ottoman expansion, especially during the 1400s, raised the specter of a powerful enemy to the east that kept many Europeans fearful for centuries.**
◆ www.mhhe.com/chambers8ch11maps

southern Arabia, and for the next two centuries the Ottoman Empire included all of southeastern Europe as well as the Middle East, Egypt, and Arabia.

*Reasons for Success*   The intense rivalries among the Christian faiths facilitated Ottoman expansion. Some Balkan Christians accepted papal supremacy, others adhered to the Eastern Orthodox traditions, and still others were regarded as heretics by both the Roman Catholics and the Orthodox. Often a Christian sect preferred the rule of the tolerant Ottomans to that of a rival Christian sect. In preserving peace among these dissident Christians, the Ottomans could serve as

impartial referees, while Christians obviously could not.

The Ottomans gained the loyalty of subject populations by allowing them to live by their own laws under their own officials, requiring them only to pay taxes and supply men for the Ottoman army and administration. Trade, for example, which remained vigorous in the Black Sea and the eastern Mediterranean Sea, was still largely in the hands of Greeks, Armenians, and Jews. The Ottomans themselves remained aloof from commercial undertakings and confined their careers to government service and the army.

Set on the frontier between the Islamic and Christian worlds, the Ottomans became a power in the political struggles of both Europe and the Middle East and were able to take advantage of favorable opportunities in both regions, even enlisting allies in one area to wage war in the other.

*Power of the Sultan* Influenced by Byzantine views of imperial authority, the sultan united in his own person supreme civil, military, and religious authority. Court ceremony contributed to the aura of sanctity that surrounded him as it had the emperor. Still more influential were Islamic traditions concerning governmental power, particularly the notion that the sultan was the successor of Muhammad, the legitimate ruler of all true believers. In a strict sense, the sultan could not be an absolute ruler, for he was, like every member of the Islamic community, subject to the sacred law. But he was also the supreme judge of that law; only revolution could challenge his authority.

The early sultans devised a striking solution to a problem common to most medieval states: the peaceful transfer of power from a ruler to his successor. From the fifteenth to the seventeenth century, the Ottomans followed what has come to be called the law of fratricide. The sultan cohabited with numerous slave girls of the harem, and usually he fathered numerous progeny. He then picked one of the boys to be his successor. At the sultan's death, the designated heir had the right and obligation to put his brothers and half-brothers to death. (They were strangled with a silken bowstring to avoid the shedding of their imperial blood.) The religious judges allowed such massacres because an uncontested succession was essential to the welfare of the empire.

*The Sultan's Advisers* Like all other medieval rulers, the sultan originally governed with the aid of a council of chosen advisers, which was called the *divan*. The function of presiding over the meetings of the divan fell to the grand *vizier*, who became the chief administrative official of the Ottoman state. The divan administered the civil and the military branches, including the collection of taxes and tribute, the conscription of soldiers, and the conduct of foreign affairs. It acted as a court of justice except in religious affairs, which were handled by judges trained in Islamic law.

*The Sultan's Army* The army had two principal divisions: unpaid holders of fiefs granted by the sultan in exchange for military service; and paid soldiers, technically considered slaves, who remained permanently in the sultan's service. As in the West, the fief holder was required to provide the military with armed men, the number being set in strict proportion to the revenue deriving

▼ Suleiman
**This portrait of Suleiman the Magnificent from a sixteenth-century Turkish manuscript suggests the ornate splendor that was associated with the awesome figure of the sultan. His court was famous for its lavish festivities and splendid costumes and decorations.**
By Permission of The British Library. Ms. Add. 7880 fol. 53v

from his estates. Among the paid soldiers, the most important were those belonging to the highly trained, thoroughly professional, but legally unfree corps of the *Janissaries*, meaning "new troops."

Slave armies had been common in Islamic states, but the Ottomans did not adopt the practice until the fifteenth century. According to the accounts of the earliest chronicles, Sultan Murad learned from a theologian in about 1430 that the Koran assigned him one-fifth of the booty captured by his army, including prisoners. Murad decided to convert his prisoners to Islam, teach them Turkish, and train them as a tough, well-disciplined military contingent, the Janissaries. The Ottomans continued to demand a tribute of young boys from the Christian parts of their vast empire as slaves for their elite corps. The Janissaries, dedicated to Islam, soon became a powerful force in Ottoman politics.

# SUMMARY

◆

While the fall of Constantinople had a strong psychological effect on Europe, the threat of the Ottoman invasion initially meant little except to the Austrians, Hungarians, Balkan states, and the Knights Hospitalers. The West was preoccupied with the reality of the Four Horsemen of the Apocalypse. Early fourteenth-century famines, recurrent plague, and wars, including the Hundred Years' War, diverted their attention. By the end of the fifteenth century, peace was generally restored. England emerged as a government that would come to be described as a constitutional monarchy, the French king was on his way to a control over his subjects that would be called absolutism, and Italy had established a balance-of-power politics. The economy was strengthened by new inventions, such as the printing press, that would change the way people spread and received information to the present day. Europe was on the verge of new expansions. The explorations of the late fifteenth century introduced new concepts of power and wealth to the competing countries; the problems of the Church intensified with major splits; and the economy, although plagued with problems of overpopulation once again, was expanding in new directions and with new products from the conquests in America.

# QUESTIONS FOR FURTHER THOUGHT

◆

1. What made the Hundred Years' War different from the other wars that you have studied in the Middle Ages?

2. Compare Europe in 800 to Europe in 1450. What new political boundaries had been established? How had society changed? How was the economy different?

3. What influence has epidemic disease and famine had on the history of Europe and the world in general?

# RECOMMENDED READING

◆

## Sources

*Brucker, Gene A. (ed.) *The Society of Renaissance Florence: A Documentary Study.* 1971. Collection of primary sources.

*Dobson, R. B. (ed.). *The Peasant's Revolt of 1381.* 1983. Primary sources related to the revolt.

*Froissart, Jean. *The Chronicles of England, France, Spain and Other Places Adjoining.* 1961. Chronicles of the Hundred Years' War.

*Horrox, Rosemary. *The Black Death.* 1994. Primary sources on the Black Death.

*The Pastons: The Letters of a Family in the War of the Roses.* Richard Barber (ed.). 1981.

Pernoud, Régine (ed.). *Joan of Arc: By Herself and Her Witnesses.* 1966. Documents relating to Joan's life and trial.

*Pizan, Christine de. *The Book of the City of Ladies.* Earl Jeffrey Richards (tr.). 1982. The author was a court writer who wrote this book on women's virtues in response to the debate of the time on women.

## Studies

*Allmand, Christopher. *The Hundred Years' War: England and France at War, c. 1300–1450.* 1988. An account of the military aspects.

*Bennett, Judith M. *Women in the Medieval English Countryside.* 1987. An assessment of peasant women's status.

*Brucker, Gene A. *Giovanni and Lusanna: Love and Marriage in Renaissance Florence.* 1986.

Eisenstein, Elizabeth L. *The Printing Press as an Agent of Change in Early-Modern Europe.* 2 vols. 1979. Provocative interpretation of the place of printing in European history.

*Erler, Mary, and Maryanne Kowaleski (eds.). *Women and Power in the Middle Ages.* 1988. A collection of essays on women's access to and use of power.

Gillingham, John. *The Wars of the Roses: Peace and Conflict in Fifteenth-Century England.* 1981. Readable political and military history.

Gimpel, Jean. *The Medieval Machine.* Penguin, 1976. Useful analysis of mechanical innovations in the Middle Ages.

*Hanawalt, Barbara. *The Ties That Bound: Peasant Families in Medieval England.* 1986. Peasant life in England sympathetically viewed.

*——— (ed.). *Women and Work in Preindustrial Europe.* 1986. Collection of essays covering the issues of working women in Europe.

Harvey, L. P. *Islamic Spain 1250–1500.* 1990. A survey of the one non-Christian territory in Western Europe and its steady decline.

*Hilton, Rodney. *Bond Men Made Free.* 1979. A study of peasant unrest in the Late Middle Ages.

Kaeuper, Richard W. *War, Justice, and Public Order: England and France in the Late Middle Ages.* 1988. Assessment of the intersection of war and justice in two countries.

Martin, Henri-Jean, and Lucien Febvre. *The Coming of the Book: The Impact of Printing 1450–1800.* 1976. Survey.

Merriman, Roger B. *Suleiman the Magnificent, 1520–1566.* 1966.

Oakley, Francis. *The Western Church in the Later Middle Ages.* 1979.

*Perroy, Edouard. *The Hundred Years' War.* 1965. Classic; excellent survey.

Richmond, Colin. *The Paston Family in the Fifteenth Century: The First Phase.* 1990. The experiences of one family as seen through their letters during the War of the Roses.

Unger, Richard W. *The Ship in the Medieval Economy.* 1980. The evolution of medieval ship design.

Warner, Marina. *Joan of Arc: The Image of Female Heroism.* 1981. Examination of Joan's life and legend.

Wittek, Paul. *The Rise of the Ottoman Empire.* 1971.

*Ziegler, Philip. *The Black Death.* 1970. Synthesis of plague studies.

---

*Available in paperback.

▲ *Jan Van Eyck*
*PORTRAIT OF GIOVANNI ARNOLFINI AND HIS WIFE*, **1434**
**The symbolism that permeates this depiction of a husband and wife has led to the suggestion that it is a wedding picture. The bed and seeming pregnancy are symbols of marriage, and the husband blesses his wife as he bestows the sacrament of marriage (for which the Church did not yet require a priest). On the back wall, the mirror reflects the witnesses attending the wedding. Van Eyck's use of the new medium of oil paint allowed him to reproduce vividly the texture of the fur-edged robe and the glimmer of the mirror's glass.**

# TRADITION AND CHANGE IN EUROPEAN CULTURE, 1300–1500

By 1300 the civilization of Europe appeared to have settled into stable and self-assured patterns. Society as a whole shared assumptions about religious beliefs, about the appropriate way to integrate faith with the heritage of the ancient world, about the purposes of scholarship, and about the forms of literature and art. These shared assumptions have led historians to describe the outlook of the age as "the medieval synthesis." But such moments of apparent stability rarely last long. Within a few generations, profound doubts had arisen on such fundamental questions as the nature of religious faith, the authority of the Church, the aims of scholarship, the source of moral ideals, and the standards of beauty in the arts. As challenges to old ideas arose, especially in the worlds of religion and cultural expression, there was an outpouring of creativity that has dazzled us ever since. Because those who sought new answers tended to look for guidance to what they considered a better past—the ancient world, or the early days of Christianity—and sought to revive long-lost values, their efforts, and the times in which they lived, have been called an age of rebirth, or Renaissance.[1]

---

[1]The creator of the modern view of the Renaissance as one of the formative periods of Western history, and the single most influential historian of the subject, was Jacob Burckhardt (see Recommended Reading).

| | | | | | | | |
|---|---|---|---|---|---|---|---|
| **Chapter 12. Tradition and Change in European Culture** | | | | | | | |
| | Social Structure | Body Politic | Changes in the Organization of Production and in the Impact of Technology | Evolution of Family and Changing Gender Roles | War | Religion | Cultural Expression |
| I. The New Learning | | | | | | | |
| II. Art and Artists in the Italian Renaissance | | | | | | | |
| III. The Culture of the North | | | | | | | |
| IV. Scholastic Philosophy, Religious Thought, and Piety | | | | | | | |
| The State of Christendom | | | | | | | |

# I. The New Learning

Although traditional forms of learning remained vital in the fourteenth and fifteenth centuries, medieval Scholasticism, with its highly refined forms of reasoning, had little to offer Europe's small but important literate lay population. The curriculum was designed mainly to train teachers and theologians, whereas the demand was increasingly for practical and useful training, especially in the arts of persuasion and communication: good speaking and good writing. For many, the Scholastics also failed to offer moral guidance. As Petrarch emphasized, education was meant to help people lead a wise, pious, and happy life. A central aim of the Renaissance was to develop new models of virtue and a system of education that would do exactly that.

## ◆ THE FOUNDING OF HUMANISM

One minor branch of the medieval educational curriculum, rhetoric, was concerned with the art of good speaking and writing. More and more, its practitioners in Italy began to turn to the Latin classics for models of good writing. Their interest in the Classical authors was helped by the close relationship between the Italian language and Latin, by the availability of manuscripts, and by the presence in Italy of countless Classical monuments. It was rhetoricians who first began to argue, in the late thirteenth century, that education should be reformed to give more attention to the classics and to help people lead more moral lives.

These rhetoricians were to found an intellectual movement known as Humanism. The term *Humanism* was not coined until the nineteenth century. In fifteenth-century Italy, *humanista* signified a professor of humane studies or a Classical scholar, but eventually *Humanism* came to mean Classical scholarship—the ability to read, understand, and appreciate the writings of the ancient world. Humanist education helped its students master the classics, so they could learn both the wisdom they needed to choose the right way in life and the eloquence that could persuade others to follow that same way. The modern use of the word *humanism* to denote a secular philosophy that denies an afterlife has no basis in the Renaissance. Most Renaissance humanists read the Church fathers as avidly as they read pagan authors and believed that the highest virtues were rooted in piety. Humanism sought far more to enrich than to undermine traditional religious attitudes.

**Petrarch** The most influential early advocate of Humanism was Francesco Petrarca, known as Petrarch (1304–1374). He was a lawyer and cleric who practiced neither of those professions but rather devoted his life to writing poetry, scholarly and moral treatises, and letters. He became famous for his Italian verse—his sonnets inspired poets for centuries—but he sought above all to emulate Virgil by writing a Latin epic poem. A master of self-promotion, he used that work as the occasion for reviving the ancient title of "poet laureate" and having himself crowned in Rome in 1341. But he was also capable of profound self-examination. In a remarkable work, which he called *My Secret*—a dialogue with one of his heroes, St. Augustine—he laid bare his struggles to achieve spiritual peace despite the temptations of fame and love. Increasingly, he became concerned that nowhere in the world around him could he find a model of virtuous behavior that he could respect. The leaders of the Church he considered poor examples, for they seemed worldly and materialistic. Convinced that no guide from his own times or the immediate past would serve, Petrarch concluded that he had to turn to the Church fathers and the ancient Romans to find worthy examples of the moral life (see "Petrarch on Ancient Rome," p. 404).

How could one be a good person? By imitating figures from antiquity, such as Cicero and Augustine, who knew what proper values were and pursued them in their own lives, despite temptations and the distractions of public affairs. The period between their time and his own—which Petrarch regarded as the "middle" ages—he considered contemptible. His own world, he felt, would improve only if it tried to emulate the ancients, and he believed that education ought to teach what they had done and said. In particular, like the good rhetorician he was, he believed that only by restoring the mastery of the written and spoken word that had distinguished the great Romans—an imitation of their style, of the way they had conveyed their ideas—could his contemporaries learn to behave like the ancients.

**Boccaccio** The program Petrarch laid out soon caught fire in Florence, the city from which his family had come and in which he found influential friends and disciples. The most important was the poet and writer Giovanni Boccaccio (1313–1375). He became famous in Florence for a collection of short stories known as *The Decameron*, written between 1348 and 1351. It recounts how a group of young Florentines—seven women and three men—fled during the Black Death of 1348 to a secluded villa, where for ten days each told a story. The first prose masterpiece in Italian, *The Decameron*'s frank treatment of sex and its vivid creation of ordinary characters make it one of the first major works in Western letters intended to divert and amuse rather than edify. But in his later years Boccaccio grew increasingly concerned with the teaching of moral values, and he became a powerful supporter of Petrarch's ideas.

**The Spread of Humanism** In the generation after Petrarch and Boccaccio, Humanism became a rallying cry for the intellectual leaders of Florence. They argued that, by associating their city with the revival of antiquity, Florentines would be identified with a distinctive vision that would become the envy of their rivals elsewhere in Italy. And that was indeed what happened. The campaign for a return to the classics started a revolution in education that soon took hold throughout Italy; the writing and speaking skills the humanists emphasized came to be in demand at every princely court (including that of the papacy); and the crusade to study and imitate the ancients transformed art, literature, and even political and social values.

Led by the chancellor of Florence, Coluccio Salutati (whose position, as the official who prepared the city's official communications, required training in rhetoric), a group of humanists began to collect ancient manuscripts and form libraries, so as to make accessible virtually all the surviving writings of Classical Latin authors. These Florentines also wanted to regain command of the Greek language, and in 1396 they invited a Byzantine scholar to lecture at the University of Florence. In the following decades—troubled years for the Byzantine Empire—other Eastern scholars joined the exodus to the West, and they and Western visitors returning from the East brought with them hundreds of Greek manuscripts. By the middle of the fifteenth century, Western scholars had both the philological skill and the manuscripts to

## PETRARCH ON ANCIENT ROME

*Petrarch was so determined to relive the experience of antiquity that he wrote letters to famous Roman authors as if they were acquaintances. In one letter, he even described Cicero coming to visit him. While he was passing through Padua in February 1350, he recalled that the city was the birthplace of the Roman historian Livy, and he promptly wrote to him.*

"I only wish, either that I had been born in your time or you in ours. If the latter, our age would have benefited; if the former, I myself would have been the better for it. I would surely have visited you. As it is, I can merely see you reflected in your works. It is over those works that I labor whenever I want to forget the places, times, and customs around me. I am often filled with anger at today's morals, when people value only gold and silver, and want nothing but physical pleasures.

"I have to thank you for many things, but especially because you have so often helped me forget the evils of today, and have transported me to happier times. As I read you, I seem to be living with Scipio, Brutus, Cato, and many others. It is with

them that I live, and not with the ruffians of today, among whom an evil star had me born. Oh, the great names that comfort me in my wretchedness, and make me forget this wicked age! Please greet for me those older historians like Polybius, and those younger than you like Pliny.

"Farewell forever, you unequalled historian!

"Written in the land of the living, in that part of Italy where you were born and buried, in sight of your own tombstone, on the 22nd of February in the 1350th year after the birth of Him whom you would have seen had you lived longer."

Petrarch, *Epistolae Familiares*, 24.8. Passages selected and translated by Theodore K. Rabb.

establish direct contact with the most original minds of the Classical world, and they were making numerous Latin and Italian translations of Greek works. Histories, tragedies, lyric poetry, the dialogues of Plato, many mathematical treatises, and the most important works of the Greek fathers of the Church fully entered Western culture for the first time.

*Civic Humanism* Salutati and his contemporaries and successors in Florence are often called civic humanists because they stressed that participation in public affairs is essential for full human development. Petrarch had wondered whether individuals should cut themselves off from the larger world, with its corruptions and compromises, and focus only on what he called the contemplative life, or try to improve that world through an active life. Petrarch's models had offered no clear answer. Cicero had suggested the need for both lives, but Augustine had been fearful of outside temptations. In the generations following Petrarch, however, the doubts declined, and the humanists argued that only by participating in public life, seeking higher ends for one's so-

ciety as well as oneself, could an individual be truly virtuous. Republican government was the best form, they argued, because unless educated citizens made use of their wisdom for the benefit of all, their moral understanding would not benefit their societies. These were lessons exemplified by the ancient classics, and thus in one connected argument the civic humanists defended the necessity of studying the ancients, the superiority of the active life, and the value of Florentine republican institutions.

## ◆ HUMANISM IN THE FIFTEENTH CENTURY

As the humanist movement gained in prestige, it captured all of Italy. Pope Nicholas V (1447–1455), for example, founded a library in the Vatican that was to become the greatest repository of ancient manuscripts in Italy. And princely courts, such as those of the Gonzaga family at Mantua and the Montefeltro family at Urbino, gained fame because of their patronage of humanists. Moreover, the influence of antiquity was felt in all areas of learning and writing. Literature was profoundly influenced by the ancients, as a new interest in Classical models reshaped the form and content of both poetry and drama, from the epic to the bawdy comedy. Purely secular themes, without religious purpose, became more common. And works of history grew increasingly analytic, openly acknowledging inspiration from ancient writers such as Livy.

*Education*   Perhaps the most direct effect was on education itself. Two scholars from the north of Italy, Guarino da Verona and Vittorino da Feltre, succeeded in turning the diffuse educational ideas of the humanists into a practical curriculum. Guarino argued for a reform of traditional methods of education, and Vittorino brought the new methods to their fullest development in the various schools he founded, especially his Casa Giocosa ("Happy House") at Mantua. The pupils included boys and girls, both rich and poor (the latter on scholarships). All the students learned Latin and Greek, mathematics, music, and philosophy; in addition—because Vittorino believed that education should aid physical, moral, and social development—they were taught social graces, such as dancing and courteous manners, and received instruction in physical exercises like riding and fencing. Vittorino's school attracted pupils from all over Italy, and his methods were widely imitated.

Ultimately, a humanist education was to give the elite throughout Europe a new way of measuring social distinction. It soon became apparent that the ability to quote Virgil or some other ancient writer was not so much a sign of moral seriousness as a badge of superiority. What differentiated people was whether they could use or recognize the quotations, and that was why the new curriculum was so popular—even though it seemed to consist, more and more, of endless memorizations and repetitions of Latin texts.

*New Standards of Behavior*   The growing admiration for the humanists and their teachings also gave an important boost to the patronage of arts and letters. In the age of gunpowder, it was no longer easy to claim that physical bravery was the supreme quality of noblemen. Instead, nobles began to set themselves apart not just by seeking a humanist education but also by pa-

▲ *Raphael*
Baldassare Castiglione
**Raphael painted this portrait of his friend, the count Baldassare Castiglione, around 1514. Castiglione's solemn pose and thoughtful expression exude the dignity and cultivation that were described as essential attributes of the courtier in Castiglione's famous book on courtly behavior.**
Giraudon/Art Resource, NY

tronizing artists and writers whose praise made them famous. Thus, a new image of fine behavior, which included the qualities that Guarino fostered—a commitment to taste and elegance as well as to courage—became widely accepted. This new lifestyle was promoted in a book, *The Courtier*, written in 1516 by Baldassare Castiglione, which took the form of a conversation among the sophisticated men and women at the court of Duke Federigo Montefeltro of Urbino, Castiglione's patron. *The Courtier* became a manual of proper behavior for gentlemen and ladies for centuries.

▲ **MAP 12.1 THE SPREAD OF UNIVERSITIES IN THE RENAISSANCE**
A significant indication of the rising status accorded to learning, and the growing importance of education in general during the Renaissance, is the opening of major new universities. Even where earlier universities existed, as at Oxford, many new colleges were founded, and the number of graduates increased rapidly in the fifteenth and sixteenth centuries.
◆ www.mhhe.com/chambers8ch12maps

*Humanism Triumphant* By the mid-1400s Humanism dominated intellectual life in much of Italy, and by 1500 it was sweeping all of Europe, transmitted by its devotees and also by a recent invention, printing, which made the texts of both humanists and ancients far more easily available. Dozens of new schools and universities were founded, and no court of any significance was without its roster of artists and writers familiar with the latest ideas. Even legal systems were affected, as the principles of Roman law (which tended to endorse the power of the ruler) were adopted in many countries. But in the late fifteenth century the revival of antiquity took a direction that modified the commitment to the active life that had been the mark of the civic humanists. A new movement, Neoplatonism, emphasized the interest in spiritual values that was the heart of the contemplative life.

#### ◆ THE FLORENTINE NEOPLATONISTS

The turn away from the practical concerns of the civic humanists toward a renewed exploration of grand ideals of truth and perfection was a result of the growing interest in Greek as well as Roman antiquity—especially the works of Plato. A group of Florentine philosophers, active in the last decades of the fifteenth century and equally at home in Greek and Latin, led the way. They were known as "Neoplatonists," or "new" followers of Plato.

*Ficino*   The most gifted of these Neoplatonists was the physician Marsilio Ficino. His career is a tribute to the cultural patronage of the Medici family, which spotted his talents as a child and gave him the use of a villa and library near Florence. In this lovely setting, a group of scholars and statesmen met frequently to discuss philosophical questions. Drawn to the idealism of Plato, Ficino and his colleagues argued that Platonic ideas demonstrated the dignity and immortality of the human soul. To spread these views among a larger audience, Ficino translated into Latin all of Plato's dialogues and the writings of Plato's chief followers. In his *Theologica Platonica* (1469), he made an ambitious effort to reconcile Platonic philosophy and the Christian religion.

*Pico*   Another member of the group was Count Giovanni Pico della Mirandola, who thought he could reconcile all philosophies in order to show that there was a single truth that lay behind every quest for the ideal. In 1486 Pico sought to defend publicly, in Rome, some nine hundred theses that would show the essential unity of all philosophies. The pope, fearful that the theses contained several heretical propositions, forbade the disputation, but Pico's introductory "Oration on the Dignity of Man" remains one of the supreme examples of the humanists' optimism about the potential of the individual.

*The Philosophy of Neoplatonism*   Both Ficino and Pico started from two essential assumptions. First, the entire universe is arranged in a hierarchy of excellence, with God at the summit. Second, each being in the universe, with the exception only of God, is impelled by "natural appetite" to seek perfection; one is impelled, in other words, to achieve—or at least to contemplate—the beautiful. As Pico expressed it, humans are unique in that they are placed in the middle of the universe, linked with both the spiritual world above and the material world below. Their free will enables them to seek perfection in either direction; they are free to become all things. A clear ethic emerges from this scheme: The good life should be an effort to achieve personal perfection, and the highest human value is the contemplation of the beautiful.

These writers believed that Plato had been divinely illumined and, therefore, that Platonic philosophy and Christian belief were two wholly reconcilable faces of a single truth. Because of this synthesis, and also its passionate idealism, Neoplatonic philosophy was to be a major influence on artists and thinkers for the next two centuries.

#### ◆ THE HERITAGE OF THE NEW LEARNING

Although its scholarship was often arid and difficult, fifteenth-century Italian Humanism left a deep imprint on European thought and education. The humanists greatly improved the command of Latin; they restored a large part of the Greek cultural inheritance to Western civilization; their investigations led to a mastery of other languages associated with great cultural traditions, most notably Hebrew; and they laid the basis of modern textual criticism. They also developed new ways of examining the ancient world—through archaeology, numismatics (the study of coins), and epigraphy (the study of inscriptions on buildings, statues, and the like), as well as through the study of literary texts. As for the study of history, while medieval chroniclers had looked to the past for evidence of God's providence, the humanists used the past to illustrate human behavior and provide moral examples. They also helped standardize spelling and grammar in vernacular languages; and the Classical ideals of simplicity, restraint, and elegance of style that they promoted helped reshape Western literature.

No less important was the role of the humanists as educational reformers. The curriculum they devised spread throughout Europe in the sixteenth century, and until the twentieth century it continued to define the standards by which the lay leaders of Western society were trained. The fact that men and women throughout Europe came to be steeped in the same classics meant that they thought and communicated in similar ways. Despite Europe's divisions and conflicts, this common humanistic education helped preserve the fundamental cultural unity of the West.

# II. Art and Artists in the Italian Renaissance

The most visible effect of Humanism and its admiration for the ancients was on the arts. Because the movement first took hold in Florence, it is not surprising that its first artistic disciples appeared among the Florentines. They had other advantages. First, the city was already famous throughout Italy for its art, because the greatest painters of the late 1200s and 1300s, Cimabue (1240–1302) and his pupil Giotto (1276–1336), were identified with Florence. Giotto, in particular, had decorated buildings from Padua to Naples and thus gained a wide audience for the sense of realism, powerful emotion, and immediacy that he created (in contrast to the formal, restrained styles of earlier artists). Second, Florence's newly wealthy citizens were ready to patronize art; and third, the city had a tradition of excellence in the design of luxury goods such as silks and gold objects. Many leading artists of the 1400s and 1500s started their careers as apprentices to goldsmiths, in whose workshops they mastered creative techniques as well as aesthetic principles that informed their painting, sculpture, and architecture.

## ◆ THREE FRIENDS

The revolution in these three disciplines was started by three friends, who were united by a determination to apply the humanists' lessons to art. They wanted to break with the styles of the immediate past and create paintings, statues, and buildings that would not merely imitate the glories of Rome but actually bring them back to life. All three went to Rome in the 1420s, hoping by direct observation and study of ancient masterpieces to

▲ *Giotto*
*LAMENTATION*
**The Florentine Giotto di Bondone (1267?–1337) was the most celebrated painter of his age. He painted fresco cycles in a number of Italian cities, and this segment from one of them indicates the qualities that made him famous: the solid bodies, the expression of human emotion, and the suggestion of landscape, all of which created an impact that was without precedent in medieval art.**
Alinari/Art Resource, NY

re-create their qualities and thus fulfill the humanists' goal of reviving the spirit of Classical times. The locals thought the three very strange, for they went around measuring, taking notes, and calculating sizes and proportions. But the lessons they learned enabled them to transform the styles and purposes of art.

*Masaccio* Among the three friends, the painter Masaccio (1401–1428) used the inspiration of the ancients to put a new emphasis on nature, on three-dimensional human bodies, and on perspective. In showing Adam and Eve, he not only depicted the first nudes since antiquity but showed them coming through a rounded arch that was the mark of Roman architecture, as opposed to the pointed arch of the Middle Ages. The chapel he decorated in a Florentine church, the Carmine, became a place of pilgrimage for painters, because here the values of ancient art—especially its emphasis on the individual human figure—were reborn.

***Donatello*** Masaccio's friend Donatello (1386–1466) was primarily a sculptor, and his three-dimensional figures had the same qualities as Masaccio's in paint. Once again the focus was

▲ *Masaccio*
*The Expulsion of Adam and Eve*, ca. **1425**
Masaccio shows Adam and Eve expelled from paradise through a rounded archway that recalls ancient architecture. Also indicative of the influence of Roman art is the attempt to create what we would consider realistic (rather than stylized) human beings and to portray them nude, displaying powerful, recognizable emotions. This was one of the paintings that made the Brancacci Chapel an inspiration to generations of artists.
Erich Lessing/Art Resource, NY

▲ *Donatello*
*David*, ca. **1430–1432**
Like Masaccio, Donatello imitated the Romans by creating idealized nude bodies. His David has just killed and decapitated Goliath, whose head lies at his feet. Goliath's helmet recalls those worn by Florence's enemies, which makes this sculpture a work of patriotism as well as art. It happens also to have been the first life-size bronze figure cast since antiquity.
Alinari/Art Resource, NY

on the beauty of the body itself, because that had been a notable and distinctive concern of the ancients. The interest in the nude, accurately displayed, transformed the very purpose of art, for it led to an idealized representation of the human form that had not been seen in centuries. Because the biblical David—shown by Donatello in contemplation after his triumph over Goliath—symbolized vigor, youth, and the weak defeating the strong, he became a favorite hero for the Florentines.

*Brunelleschi*   The most spectacular of these three pioneers was the architect Brunelleschi (1377?–1446). For decades, his fellow citizens had been building a new cathedral, which, as a sign of their artistic superiority, was going to be the largest in Italy. Seen from above, it was shaped—as was traditional—like a cross. The basic structure was in place, but the huge space at which the horizontal and vertical met, the crossing, had not

▼ *Brunelleschi*
**DOME OF FLORENCE CATHEDRAL, 1420–1436**
**Brunelleschi's famous dome—the first built in Italy since the fall of the Roman Empire—embodied the revival of classical forms in architecture. The contrast with the bell tower designed a century earlier by Giotto, with its suggestion of pointed Gothic arches, is unmistakable. The dome was a feat of engineering as well as design: Its 135-foot diameter was spanned without scaffolding, and Brunelleschi himself invented the machines that made the construction possible.**
© David Ball/Corbis Stock Market

yet been covered. In response to a competition for a design to complete the building, Brunelleschi, inspired by what he had learned in Rome, proposed covering the crossing with the largest dome built in Europe since antiquity. Although the first reaction was that it was impossible, eventually he got the commission. In an extraordinary feat of engineering, which required that he build the dome in rings, without using scaffolding, he erected a structure that became not only a fitting climax to the cathedral but also the hallmark of Renaissance Florence and an inspiration for all architects. The symmetrical simplicity of his other buildings shaped a new aesthetic of harmony and balance that matched what Masaccio and Donatello accomplished in painting and sculpture. In all three, the imitation of ancient Rome inspired subjects and styles that broke decisively with their immediate medieval past.

*New Creativity*   During the remaining years of the 1400s, a succession of artists, not just in Florence but increasingly in other parts of Italy as well, built on the achievements of the pioneer generation. They experimented with perspective and the modeling of bodies and drapery, so as to recapture the ancients' mastery of depth, and they made close observations of nature. Sculptors created monumental figures, some on horseback, in imitation of Roman models. And architects perfected the use of the rounded arches and symmetrical forms they saw in antique buildings. Subject matter also changed, as artists produced increasing numbers of portraits of their contemporaries and depicted stories out of Roman and Greek myths as well as traditional religious scenes. By the end of the 1400s, the leading Florentine painter of the day, Botticelli (1444?–1510), was presenting ancient subjects like the *Birth of Venus*, goddess of love, in exactly the way a Roman might have fashioned them.

## ◆ THE HIGH RENAISSANCE

The artists at work in the early years of the 1500s are often referred to as the generation of the High Renaissance. Four, in particular—Leonardo, Raphael, Michelangelo, and Titian—are thought of as bringing the new movement that had begun a hundred years before to a climax.

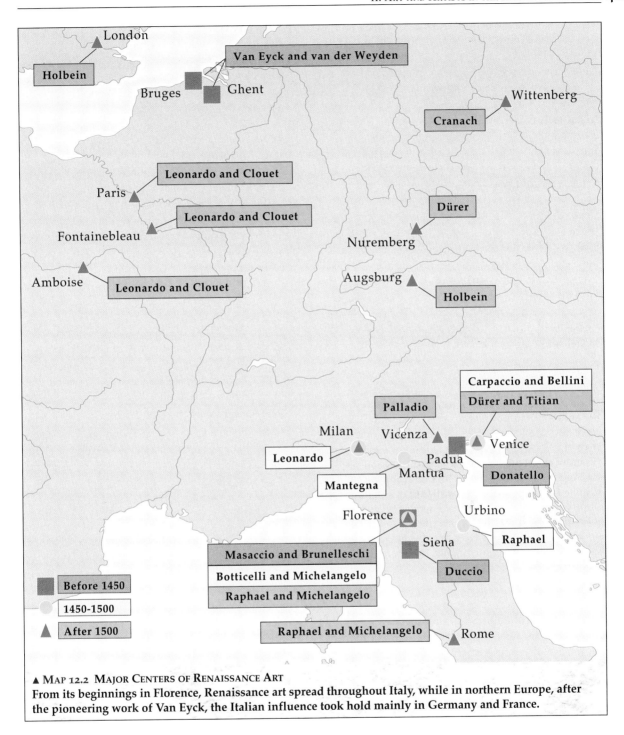

▲ MAP 12.2  MAJOR CENTERS OF RENAISSANCE ART
**From its beginnings in Florence, Renaissance art spread throughout Italy, while in northern Europe, after the pioneering work of Van Eyck, the Italian influence took hold mainly in Germany and France.**

*Leonardo*  The oldest, Leonardo (1452–1519), was the epitome of the experimental tradition. Always seeking new ways of doing things, whether in observing anatomy or designing fortifications, he was unable to resist the challenge of solving practical problems, even in his paintings. They are marvels of technical virtuosity, which make difficult angles, tricks of perspective, and bizarre geological formations look easy. His portrait of the *Mona Lisa*, for example, is famous not only for her

▲ *Leonardo da Vinci*
Mona Lisa, ca. 1503–1505
This is probably the most celebrated image in
Renaissance art. The famous hint of a smile and the
calm and solid pose are so familiar that we all too
easily forget how striking it seemed at the time and
how often it inspired later portraits. As in his *Last
Supper*, however, Leonardo was experimenting with
his materials, and the picture has therefore faded
over the years.
Giraudon/Art Resource, NY

## Chronology
### A Century and a Half of Renaissance Art

**1420s** Masaccio, Donatello, and Brunelleschi visit Rome and begin transforming painting, sculpture, and architecture

**1430s** Donatello's *David;* completion of Brunelleschi's dome; Van Eyck's *Arnolfini Marriage*

**1440s** Botticelli born; death of Brunelleschi

**1450s** Leonardo da Vinci born

**1460s** Death of Donatello

**1470s** Dürer, Michelangelo, and Titian born

**1480s** Raphael born; Botticelli's *Birth of Venus*

**1490s** Dürer's *Apocalypse*

**1500s** Leonardo's *Mona Lisa;* Michelangelo's *David;* Cellini born

**1510s** Raphael and Michelangelo decorate the Vatican; Titian's *Bacchanal*

**1520s** Deaths of Raphael and Dürer

**1530s** Michelangelo's *Last Judgement* in the Sistine Chapel

**1540s** Cellini's *Salt Cellar;* Titian's *Charles V at Mühlberg*

**1550s** Vasari begins publishing his *Lives of the Artists*

**1560s** Death of Michelangelo

**1570s** Deaths of Cellini and Titian

mysterious smile but for the incredible rocky landscape in the background. Unfortunately, Leonardo also experimented with methods of painting; as a result, one of his masterpieces, the *Last Supper*, has almost completely disintegrated.

***Raphael***  By contrast, Raphael (1483–1520) used the mastery of perspective and ancient styles that had been achieved in the 1400s to produce works of perfect harmony, beauty, and serenity. His paintings give an impression of utter relaxation, of an artist in complete command of his materials and therefore able to create sunny scenes that are

balanced and at peace. His tribute to the ancient world, *The School of Athens*, places in a Classical architectural setting the great philosophers of Greece, many of whom are portraits of the artists of the day: Aristotle, for instance, has Leonardo's face. If the philosophers were the chief glory of Athens, Raphael seems to be saying, then the artists are the crowning glory of the Renaissance.

***Michelangelo***  For Michelangelo (1475–1564), painting was but one means of expression. Equally at home in poetry, architecture, and sculpture, he often seems the ultimate embodiment of the achievements of his age. Constantly seeking

▲ *Raphael*
*SCHOOL OF ATHENS*
**Painted in 1510 and 1511, this fresco celebrating the glories of Greek philosophy represents the triumph of the Renaissance campaign to revive antiquity. That the classical setting and theme could have been accepted as appropriate for a wall of the Vatican suggests how completely humanism had captured intellectual life. A number of the figures are portraits of artists whom Raphael knew: Plato, pointing to heaven at the back, has the face of Leonardo, and the notoriously moody Michelangelo broods, with his head on his arm, at the front.**
Scala / Art Resource, NY

new effects, he once said that no two of the thousands of figures he depicted were the same, and one might add that just about every one of them conveys the sense of latent strength, of striving, that was Michelangelo's signature. In *The Creation of Man* Adam, shown at the moment of his creation, has not yet received the gift of life from God, but he already displays the vigor that Michelangelo gave to every human body. The same is true of Michelangelo's version of David, seemingly tranquil but showing his potential power in his massive, oversized hand. The human

being is shown in full majesty, as an independent and potent individual.

*Titian*   In Venice, developments in art took a slightly different form. This was also a rich trading city, sophisticated, with broad international connections. But here Humanism was not so central, and the art—as befitted this most down-to-earth and cosmopolitan of Europe's cities—was more sensuous. The most famous Venetian painter, Titian (1482?–1576), depicted rich velvets, lush nudes, stormy skies, and dogs with wagging

◄ *Michelangelo*

*THE CREATION OF MAN*

**Michelangelo worked on the ceiling of the Sistine Chapel in the Vatican from 1508 to 1512 and painted hundreds of figures. None has come to symbolize the rebirth associated with the Renaissance and the power of creative genius so forcefully as the portrayal of God extending a finger to bring the vigorous body of Adam to life. Tucked under God's other arm is the figure of Eve, ready to join Adam in giving birth to humankind.**

Scala/Art Resource, NY

◄ *Titian*

*BACCHANAL*, CA. 1518

**The earthy realism of Venice contrasted sharply with the idealization common in Florentine art. The setting and even the sky seem more tangible, and Titian's lush nude in the foreground (who was to be much copied) is the essence of sensuality. It has been suggested that the painting represents the different stages of life, from the incontinent child through the vigorous youths and adults to the old man who has collapsed in the back.**

Scala/Art Resource, NY

tails with a directness and immediacy that enable the viewer almost to feel them. His friend Aretino said of one of his pictures: "I can say nothing of the crimson of the garment nor of its lynx lining, for in comparison real crimson and real lynx seem painted, and these seem real." Titian was Europe's most sought-after portraitist, and to this day we can recognize the leading figures of his time, and sense their character, because of the mastery of his depictions.

### ◆ STATUS AND PERCEPTION

*Art as Craft*    To the generation of Masaccio, a painter was merely one of the many people engaged in a craft, not inherently more admired than a skilled leather finisher or mason. Like them, he was a member of a guild, he had to pass a carefully

regulated apprenticeship, and he was subject to the rules that controlled his trade. Both Donatello and Brunelleschi were trained as goldsmiths, and the latter was even briefly imprisoned by his guild for not paying his dues while he was working on the cathedral dome—as an independent person, so he thought, and thus outside the guild structure. Given the Florentines' interest in gaining fame by beautifying their city, it was not surprising that the work of these artists should have attracted considerable attention. But it rarely occurred to anyone in the early 1400s—as Brunelleschi discovered from his guild—that they might deserve special respect or be considered more elevated than tradesmen. It was true that some of them were becoming famous throughout Italy, but would that lead to a change in their social status?

*Humanism and the Change in Status*    The answer was that it did, and again the impetus came from the humanist movement. Three consequences of the revival of antiquity, in particular, began to alter the position of the artist. First was the recognition that the most vivid and convincing re-creations of the achievements of the ancient world were being produced in the visual arts. No letter written like Cicero's could compare with a painting, a statue, or a building as a means of bringing Rome back to life for all to see—as an open and public display of the virtues of Classical times.

A second influence was the humanists' new interest in personal fame. This had been an acceptable aspiration in antiquity, but during the Middle Ages spiritual concerns encouraged a disdain for worldly matters. It was still a problem for Petrarch to admit that, like the ancients he admired, he wanted to be famous. Among later humanists, the doubts receded, and the princes who valued their ideas eagerly accepted the notion that they should devote their lives to attaining fame. That was what nobles previously had won as warriors, but now there was a more reliable way to ensure that one's name lived forever.

*The New Patrons*    That way was provided by the third of the humanists' lessons: that the truly moral person had to combine the contemplative with the active life. A prince, therefore, ought to cultivate the fine as well as the martial arts. No

aristocratic court could be complete without its poets and painters, who sang their patron's praises while fashioning the masterpieces that not only brought prestige but also endured forever. As a result, if an aristocrat wanted immortality, it was no longer enough to be a famous warrior; now it became essential to build a splendid new palace or have one's portrait done by a famous painter. To be most like the virtuous heroes of Rome who were the society's ideal, vigorous leadership had to be linked to patronage of culture, and this outlook was not confined to noblemen. Noblewomen, whose chief role had long been to offer an idealized object of chivalric devotion and who continued to struggle to gain access to education, occasionally won that struggle, and the result was a refined patronage that could be crucial in fashioning a princely image. Without Isabella d'Este, for example, the court in Mantua would not have achieved its fame as a center of painting, architecture, and music. That both Leonardo and Titian did her portrait was a reflection not of her husband's importance but of her own independent contribution to the arts. Her rooms, surrounding a lovely garden, remain one of the wonders of the palace at Mantua and a worthy testimony to her fame as a patroness (see box, p. 417).

The effect of this new attitude was to transform the status of artists. They became highly prized at the courts of aristocrats, who saw them as extraordinarily effective image makers. Perhaps the most famous family of patrons in Italy, the Medici of Florence, were envied throughout Europe mainly because, for generations, they seemed always to be surrounded by the finest painters, sculptors, and architects of the age. And soon the richest princes in Italy, the popes, followed suit. The Church had been the main sponsor of art in the Middle Ages, but now it was the papacy in particular that promoted and inspired artistic production. In their determination to rebuild and beautify Rome as a worthy capital of Christendom, the popes gave such artists as Raphael and Michelangelo their most famous commissions—notably Michelangelo's Sistine Chapel within the Vatican. It was thus as a result of shifting patterns in the commissioning and buying of art that, as honored members of papal as well as princely courts, Renaissance artists created both a new aesthetic and a new social identity.

# ISABELLA D'ESTE'S QUEST FOR ART

◆

*As the passion for art took hold, the great patrons of the Renaissance became relentless in their search for new works. None was more avid than Isabella d'Este (1474–1539), who became the wife of the Gonzaga prince of Mantua at the age of sixteen and made her private suite of rooms (which she called her studio) a gathering place for artists, musicians, and poets for nearly fifty years. Her passion for art shines through her letters; in these extracts, she is pursuing both the Venetian painter Bellini and Leonardo da Vinci.*

"To an agent, 1502: 'You may remember that many months ago we gave Giovanni Bellini a commission to paint a picture for the decoration of our studio, and when it ought to have been finished we found it was not yet begun. We told him to abandon the work, and give you back the 25 ducats, but now he begs us to leave him the work and promises to finish it soon. As till now he has given us nothing but words, tell him that we no longer care to have the picture, but if instead he would paint a Nativity, we should be well content, as long as he does not keep us waiting any longer.'

"Two months later: 'As Bellini is resolved on doing a picture of the Madonna and Child and St. John the Baptist in place of the Nativity scene, I should be glad if he would also include a St. Jerome; and about the price of 50 ducats we are content, but above all urge him to serve us quickly and well.'

"Three years later, to Bellini himself: 'You will remember very well how great our desire was for a picture painted by your hand, to put in our studio. We appealed to you for this in the past, but you could not do it on account of your many other commitments. (We recently heard you might be free,) but we have been ill with fever and unable to attend to such things. Now that we are feeling better it has occurred to us to write begging you to consent to painting a picture, and we will leave the poetic invention for you to make up if you do not want us to give it to you. As well as the proper payment, we shall be under an eternal obligation to you. When we hear of your agreement, we will send you the measurements of the canvas and an initial payment.'

"In the meantime, in May 1504, she wrote to Leonardo da Vinci: 'Hearing that you are staying in Florence, we have conceived the hope that something we have long desired might come true: to have something by your hand. When you were here and drew our portrait in charcoal, you promised one day to do it in color. Since it would be inconvenient for you to move here, we beg you to keep your good faith with us by substituting for our portrait a youthful Christ of about twelve years old, executed with that sweetness and soft ethereal charm which is the peculiar excellence of your art.'

"Five months later she wrote again: 'Some months ago we wrote to you that we wanted to have a young Christ, about twelve years old, by your hand. You replied that you would do this gladly, but owing to the many commissioned works you have on your hands, we doubt whether you remembered ours. Wherefore it has occurred to us to send you these few lines, begging you that you will turn to doing this little figure for us by way of recreation, which will be doing us a very gracious service and of benefit to yourself.'"

From D. S. Chambers (ed.), *Patrons and Artists in the Italian Renaissance* (London: Macmillan, 1970), pp. 128–130 and 147–148.

***Vasari*** In the mid-1500s, a leading protégé of the Medici, an architect and painter named Giorgio Vasari (1511–1574), sought to figure out how and why he and other artists were being showered with privileges. He himself had designed, built, and decorated a large new government office building in the center of the city—in Italian, *Uffizi* (now the main museum of Renaissance art in Florence). He had been knighted for his services, and to understand his good fortune, he looked to the past and wrote the first major work of what became a new field of study: the history of art.

Vasari suggested that certain artists were filled with a special spirit, which he called genius, that set them apart from—and above—other people. The status that artists had achieved was, in Vasari's account, richly deserved. Their genius and fame entitled them to high status, and it was appropriate that Titian, for example, lived in splendor, like the finest families of Venice. The

▲ *Sandro Botticelli*
*Birth of Venus*, ca. 1480
Sandro Botticelli was a member of the intellectual circle of Lorenzo de Medici, and this painting is evidence of the growing interest in Neoplatonism at the Medici court. The wistful, ethereal look on Venus' face reflects the otherworldliness that was emphasized by the Neoplatonists; moreover, their belief in the analogies that link all ideas suggests that Botticelli may have been implying that Venus resembled the Virgin Mary as a source of divine love. In depicting an ancient myth as ancient painters would have shown it, Botticelli represents the triumph of Renaissance ambitions, and the idealized beauty of his work helped shape an aesthetic standard that has been admired ever since.
Erich Lessing/Art Resource, NY

acceptance of artists into the uppermost levels of society was one of the most remarkable transformations produced by the Italian Renaissance.

## III. The Culture of the North

North of the Alps the transformations of the 1300s and 1400s were not as dramatic as in Italy, but they had consequences after 1500 that were no less dramatic than the effects of Humanism, Neoplatonism, and the other changes in the south. This area of Europe did not have the many large cities and the high percentages of urban dwellers that were crucial to the humanist movement in Italy. Nor did the physical monuments and lan-

guages of northern Europe offer ready reminders of the Classical heritage. Humanism and the revival of classical learning—with its literate, trained laity—did not come to the north until the last decade of the fifteenth century. But in these territories, where cultural life was dominated by the princely court rather than the city, and by the knight rather than the merchant, there were other vital shifts in outlook.

### ◆ CHIVALRY AND DECAY

In 1919 a Dutch historian, Johan Huizinga, described northern European culture in the 1400s and 1500s not as a renaissance but as the decline of medieval civilization. His stimulating book, *The*

▲ *Benozzo Gozzoli*
*PROCESSION OF THE THREE KINGS TO BETHLEHEM* (DETAIL)
This enormous fresco in the Medici palace in Florence, completed in 1459, gives place of honor in the biblical scene of the procession of the Magi to the future ruler of Florence, the ten-year-old Lorenzo de Medici, riding a white horse, and to his grandfather Cosimo de Medici, the founder of the dynasty's power, who is behind Lorenzo, also on a white horse.
Erich Lessing/Art Resource, NY

*Waning of the Middle Ages,* focused primarily on the court of the dukes of Burgundy, who were among the wealthiest and most powerful princes of the north. Huizinga found tension and frequent violence in this society, with little of the serenity that had marked the thirteenth century. Writers and artists seemed to have little grasp on reality and displayed deep emotional instability. Although Huizinga's interpretation may have been exaggerated, his analysis did contain much that is accurate.

A good example of the poor grasp of reality was the extravagant cultivation of the notion of chivalry. Militarily, the knight was becoming less important than the foot soldier armed with longbow, pike, or firearms. But the noble classes of the north continued to pretend that knightly virtues governed all questions of state and society; they discounted such lowly considerations as money, arms, recruitment, supplies, and the total resources of countries in deciding the outcome of wars. For example, before the Battle of Agincourt, one knight told the French King Charles that he should not use contingents from the Parisian townsfolk because that would give his army an unfair numerical advantage; the

▲ *Benvenuto Cellini*
*SALT CELLAR FOR FRANCIS I*
**Benvenuto Cellini, a Florentine goldsmith who challenged Giorgio Vasari's distinction between artisan and artist in his lively *Autobiography* (1562), executed this work for the French king Francis I in 1543. Juxtaposing allegorical images of the Earth and the Sea, which he presented as opposing forces, Cellini created figures as elegant as any sculpture and set them on a fantastic base of gold and enamel. His extraordinary skills indicate why so many Renaissance artists began their careers in goldsmiths' workshops.**
Erich Lessing/Art Resource, NY

battle should be decided strictly on the basis of chivalrous valor.

*Bravery and Display*   This was the age of the perfect knight and the "grand gesture." King John of Bohemia insisted that his soldiers lead him to the front rank of battle, so that he could strike at the enemy even though he was blind. The feats of renowned knights won the admiration of chroniclers but hardly affected the outcome of battle. And the reason for the foundation of new orders of chivalry—notably the Knights of the Garter in England and the Burgundian Knights of the Golden Fleece—was that these orders would reform the world by cultivating knightly virtues.

Princes rivaled one another in the sheer glitter of their arms and the splendor of their tournaments. They waged wars of dazzlement, seeking to confound rivals with spectacular displays of gold, silks, and tapestries. Court ceremony was marked by excess, as were the chivalric arts of love. A special order was founded for the defense of women, and knights frequently took lunatic oaths to honor their ladies, such as keeping one eye closed for weeks. Obviously, people rarely made love or war in this artificial way. But they still drew satisfaction in dreaming about the possibilities for love and war if this sad world were only a perfect place.

*The Cult of Decay*   Huizinga called the extravagant lifestyle of the northern courts the "cult of the sublime," or the impossibly beautiful. But he also noted that both knights and commoners showed a morbid fascination with death and its ravages. Reminders of the ultimate victory of death and treatments of decay are frequent in both literature and art. One popular artistic motif was the *danse macabre,* or dance of death, depicting people from all walks of life—rich and poor, clergy and laity, good and bad—dancing with a skeleton. Another melancholy theme favored by artists across Europe was the *Pietà*—the Virgin weeping over her dead son.

This morbid interest in death and decay in an age of plague was not the result of lofty religious sentiment. The obsession with the fleetingness of material beauty in fact indicated how attached people were to earthly pleasures; it was a kind of inverse materialism. Above all, the gloom reflected a growing religious dissatisfaction. In the 1200s Francis of Assisi addressed death as a sister; in the fourteenth and fifteenth centuries people apparently regarded it as a ravaging, indomitable fiend. Clearly (as Petrarch, too, had noted) the Church was failing to provide consolation to many of its members, and a religion that fails to console is a religion in crisis.

*Devils and Witches*   Still another sign of the unsettled religious spirit of the age was a fascination with the devil, demonology, and witchcraft. The most enlightened scholars of the day wondered whether witches could ride through the air on sticks. One of the more notable witch trials of Western history was held at Arras in 1460, when scores of people were accused of participating in a witches' sabbath, giving homage to the devil, and having sexual intercourse with him. In 1486 two inquisitors who had been authorized by the pope to prosecute witches published the *Malleus Maleficarum* ("hammer of witches"), which defined witchcraft as heresy and became the standard handbook for prosecutors. Linked to the fear of the devil was a fear of women. They were the most frequent victims of witchcraft accusations, easy scapegoats in an age of social upheaval. Any hint of change in their traditional subordination to men, such as learning to read, combined with their vulnerability to make them targets of denunciation.

***Relics*** There was also a growing fascination with concrete religious images. The need to have immediate, physical contact with the objects of religious devotion added to the popularity of pilgrimages and stimulated the obsession with the relics of saints. These were usually fake, but they became a major commodity in international trade. Some princes accumulated collections of relics numbering in the tens of thousands.

Huizinga saw these aspects of northern culture as signaling the disintegration of the cultural synthesis of the Middle Ages. Without a disciplined and unified view of the world, attitudes toward war, love, and religion lost balance, and disordered behavior followed. The culture was not young and vigorous but old and dying. Yet the concept of decadence must be used with caution. Certainly this was a psychologically disturbed world that had lost the self-confidence of the thirteenth century; but these supposedly decadent people, though dissatisfied, were also passionately anxious to find solutions to the tensions that unsettled them. We need to recall that passion when trying to understand the appeal and the power behind other cultural movements—lay piety and efforts of religious reform.

### ◆ CONTEMPORARY VIEWS OF NORTHERN SOCIETY

***Froissart and Langland*** Huizinga wrote about chivalric society from the perspective of the twentieth century. Among contemporary observers was Jean Froissart (1333?–1400?) of Flanders, who traveled widely across England and the continent, recording the exploits of valiant men. His chronicles have no equal for colorful, dramatic narration, but he seemed overly preoccupied with chivalric society, treating peasants and townspeople with contempt or indifference. His contemporary, a poet known as William Langland, offered the viewpoint of the humbler classes. His *Vision of Piers Plowman,* a poem describing eleven visions, probably written about 1360, is one of the most remarkable works of the age. Each vision is crowded with allegorical figures and filled with spirited comment about the various classes of people, the impact of plague and war on society, and the failings of the Church.

***Chaucer*** The greatest work of imaginative literature of the late fourteenth century was written by the son of a London vintner, Geoffrey Chaucer (1340?–1400), who was a soldier, diplomat, and government official. His *Canterbury Tales,* written in the 1390s, recounts the pilgrimage of some thirty men and women to the tomb of St. Thomas Becket at Canterbury. For entertainment on the road, each pilgrim agrees to tell two stories. Chaucer's lively portraits are a rich tapestry of English society, especially in its middle ranges. The stories also sum up the moral and social ills of the day. His robust monk, for example, ignores the Benedictine rule; his friar is more interested in donations than in the cure of souls; his pardoner knowingly hawks fraudulent relics; and the wife of Bath complains of prejudice against women. But Chaucer's picture remains good humored; he also praises the student of Oxford, who would gladly learn and gladly teach, and the rural parson, who cares for his flock while others neglect the faithful. Apart from the grace of his poetry, Chaucer had the ability to delineate character and spin a lively narrative. The *Canterbury Tales* is a masterly portrayal of human personalities and human behavior that can delight readers in any age.

### ◆ ART AND MUSIC

The leaders of the transformation in both the style and the status of artists in the 1400s were mainly Italians. But there were also major advances in northern Europe. Indeed, oil painting—on wood or canvas—was invented in the Netherlands, and its first great exponent, Jan Van Eyck, a contemporary of Donatello, revealed both the similarities and the differences between north and south. Van

Eyck was less interested in idealization than were the Florentines and more fascinated with the details of the physical world. One sees almost every thread in a carpet. But his portrait of an Italian couple, the Arnolfinis, is shot through with religious symbolism as well as a sly sense of humor about sex and marriage. The dog is a sign of fidelity, and the carving on the bedpost is of St. Margaret, the patron saint of childbirth; but the single candle is what newlyweds are supposed to keep burning on their wedding night, and the grinning carved figures behind their clasped hands are a wry comment on their marriage. The picture displays a combination of earthiness and piety that places it in a tradition unlike any in the Italy of this time (see p. 400).

*Dürer*  The leading northern artist of the period of the High Renaissance was a German, Albrecht Dürer, who deliberately sought to blend southern and northern styles. He made two trips to Venice, and the results were clear in a self-portrait that shows him as a fine gentleman, painted in the Italian style. But he continued, especially in the engravings that made him famous, to emphasize the detailed depiction of nature and the religious purposes that were characteristic of northern art.

Dürer refused to break completely with the craft origins of his vocation. He knew, from his visits to Venice, that Italian painters could live like lords, and he was invited by the Holy Roman Emperor to join his court. But he preferred to remain in his home city of Nuremberg, earning his living more through the sale of his prints than from the stipends he was offered by patrons. Eventually he became a highly successful entrepreneur, creating different kinds of prints for different markets—the elite liked elegant and expensive copper engravings, while others preferred cruder but cheaper woodcuts—and producing a best seller in a book of illustrations of the Apocalypse. His wife was a highly effective seller of his prints, and she preferred running her stall in the marketplace to fine entertainments by city fathers. Indeed, the couple can be seen as pioneers in the business of art.

*Developments in Music*  The process that was at work in the visual arts had similar effects in music, which again had developed primarily for liturgical purposes in the Middle Ages. In the Renaissance,

▲ *Albrecht Dürer*
*The Four Horsemen of the Apocalypse*
**The bestseller that Dürer published in 1498, *The Apocalypse*, has the text of the biblical account of the apocalypse on one side and full-page woodcuts on the other. The four horsemen who will wreak vengeance on the damned during the final Day of Judgment are Conquest holding a bow, War holding a sword, Famine, or Justice, holding scales, and Death, or Plague, riding a pale horse and trampling a bishop.**
A. Dürer, "The Riders on the Four Horses from the Apocalypse," c. 1496. Woodcut. The Metropolitan Museum of Art, Gift of Junius S. Morgan, 1919. (19.73.209). Photograph © 2002 The Metropolitan Museum of Art, New York

musicians became as prized as artists at princely courts, and their growing professionalism was demonstrated by the organists and choir singers hired by churches, the trumpeters employed by cities for official occasions, and the composers and performers who joined the households of the wealthy. Musical notation became standardized, and instruments became more diverse as old ones were improved and new ones—such as the viol, the oboe, and the clavichord—were invented. Moreover, unlike the practice of art, which usually required apprenticeship to guilds that were closed to women, musical performance, whose patron saint was St. Cecilia, relied on the talents of both men and women.

Unlike the visual arts, the chief musical center of Europe around 1500 was in the Low Countries, not Italy. The choirmasters of cathedral towns like Bruges employed professional singers who brought to new levels the traditional choral form of four-part polyphony (that is, four different lines playing against one another). This complex vocal harmony had no need of instrumental accompaniment; as a result, freed from their usual subservience to the voice, instruments could be developed in new ways. The greatest masters of the time, Guillaume Dufay and Josquin des Prez, excelled in secular as well as religious music, and theirs was one field of creativity in which new techniques and ideas flowed mainly from the north to Italy, not the other way around.

# IV. Scholastic Philosophy and Religious Thought

In theology, Scholasticism retained its hold even as Humanism swept the literary world. But it was not the thirteenth-century Scholasticism of Thomas Aquinas, which asserted that human reason could fashion a universal philosophy that embraced all truths and reconciled all apparent conflicts. Nor did the traditional acceptance of ecclesiastical law continue, with its definition of the Christian life in terms of precise rules of behavior rather than interior spirit. The style of thinking changed as the Scholastics of the 1400s and 1500s were drawn to analysis (breaking apart) rather than synthesis (putting together) as they examined philosophical and theological statements. Many of them no longer shared Aquinas' confidence in human reason, and they hoped to repair his synthesis or to replace it with new systems that, though less comprehensive, could at least be more easily defended in an age growing doubtful

about reason. Discussions of faith changed too, as more and more Christian leaders sought ways to deepen the interior, sometimes mystical, experience of God.

## ◆ THE "MODERN WAY"

The followers of Aquinas remained active in the schools, but the most original of the Scholastics in the fourteenth century took a different approach to their studies. They were known as nominalists, because they focused on the way we describe the world—the names (in Latin, *nomina*) that we give to things—rather than on its reality. The nominalists denied the existence, or at least the knowability, of the universal forms that make up the world—"manness," "dogness," and the like. The greatest among them was the English Franciscan William of Ockham (1300?–1349?), and his fundamental principle came to be called Ockham's razor. It can be stated in various ways, but essentially it says that, between alternative explanations for the same phenomenon, the simpler is always to be preferred.

*Ockham* On the basis of this "principle of parsimony," Ockham attacked the traditional focus of philosophy on the universal, ideal forms. These concepts had led Aquinas to argue, for instance, that all individual beings must be understood as reflections of their universal forms. By contrast, Ockham argued that the simplest way to explain the existence of any specific object is just to say it exists. The mind can find resemblances among objects and make generalizations about them, which can then be examined in coherent and logical ways. But these offer no certainty of the actual existence of Aquinas' ideal forms—the universal principles like "manness" that all beings and objects reflect.

The area of reality that the mind can grasp is thus severely limited. The universe, as far as human reason can detect, is a collection of separate beings and objects, not a hierarchy of ideal forms. The proper way to deal with this universe is by direct experience, not by speculating about abstract natures. Such a theology, based on observation and reason, was obviously rather limited. Ockham believed that one could still prove the existence of some necessary principles in the universe, but he thought human beings could know very little about the ultimate necessary principle, God.

*Nominalist Theology*   Ockham and many of his contemporaries insisted on the total power of God and humanity's absolute dependence on him. If he chose, God could reward vice, punish virtue, and act erratically; which raised the question, how could there be a stable system of theology or ethics? The nominalists' answer was that, instead of using his absolute power, God relied on his ordained power: through a covenant, or agreement, God assures people that he will act in consistent and predictable ways. Thus, theology becomes the study not of metaphysics but of God's will and covenant with the human race.

Nominalists rejected Aquinas' high assessment of human powers and his confident belief in the ordered and knowable structure of the natural world. Living in a disturbed, pessimistic age, they reflected the crisis of confidence in natural reason and human capability that is a major feature of the cultural history of the north in these years. Nominalists were popular in the universities, and Ockhamite philosophy, in particular, came to be known as the *via moderna* ("modern way"). Although nominalists and humanists were frequently at odds, they did share a dissatisfaction with aspects of the medieval intellectual tradition, especially the speculative abstractions of medieval thought; and both advocated approaches to reality that concentrated on the concrete and the present and demanded a strict awareness of method.

◆ SOCIAL AND SCIENTIFIC THOUGHT

*Marsilius*   The belief of the nominalists that reality was to be found not in abstract forms but in concrete objects had important implications for social thought. The most remarkable of these social thinkers was Marsilius of Padua, an Italian lawyer who served at the French royal court. In 1324 he wrote a book, *Defender of Peace,* which attacked papal authority and supported lay sovereignty within the Church. His purpose was obviously to endorse the independent authority of his patron, the king of France, who pursued a running battle with the pope. But his work had wider impli-

cations. Using nominalist principles, Marsilius argued that the reality of the Christian community, like the reality of the universe, consists of the sum of all its parts. The sovereignty of the Church thus belongs to its members, who alone can define the collective will of the community.

Marsilius was one of the first theorists of the modern concept of sovereignty. Emphasizing secular authority, he maintained that only regulations supported by force are true law and that, therefore, the enactments of the Church do not bind because they are not supported by coercive force. The Church has no right to power or to property and is entirely subject to the sovereign will of the state, which is indivisible, absolute, and unlimited. *Defender of Peace* is noteworthy not only for its radical ideas but also for its reflection of deep dissatisfactions. Marsilius and others revealed a hostile impatience with the papal and clerical domination of Western political life. They wanted laypersons to guide the Church and the Christian community. In this respect at least, the book was a prophecy of things to come.

*New Explanations of Nature*   In studies of nature, a few nominalists at Paris and Oxford in the fourteenth century took the first hesitant steps toward a criticism of the Aristotelian world system that had dominated European studies of physics since antiquity. At the University of Paris, for example, Jean Buridan proposed an important revision in Aristotle's theory of motion. If, as Aristotle had said, all objects are at rest in their natural state, what keeps an arrow flying after it leaves the bow? Aristotle had reasoned rather lamely that the arrow disturbs the air through which it passes and that it is this disturbance that keeps pushing the arrow forward. Buridan suggested, instead, that the movement of the bow lends the arrow a special quality of motion, an "impetus," that stays with it permanently unless removed by the resistance of the air. In addition, Buridan and other fourteenth-century nominalists theorized about the acceleration of falling objects and made some attempt to describe this phenomenon in mathematical terms. Although they were often inadequate or inaccurate, these attempts at new explanations started the shift away from an unquestioned acceptance of ancient systems (such as

Aristotle's) that was to climax, three hundred years later, in the scientific revolution.

***Humanism and Science*** Humanists also helped prepare the way for scientific advance. They rediscovered important ancient writers whose works had been forgotten, and their skills in textual and literary criticism taught people to look with greater precision at works inherited from the past. As more of the classics became available, it became apparent that ancient authors did not always agree. Could they, therefore, always be correct? Furthermore, the idealism of Plato and the number mysticism of Pythagoras suggested that unifying forms and harmonies lay behind the disparate data of experience and observation. Once this assumption took hold, it was soon being argued that perhaps the cosmic harmonies might be described in mathematical terms.

# V. The State of Christendom

The Church as an institution also experienced major transformations in the 1300s and 1400s. It continued to seek a peaceful Christendom united in faith and obedience to Rome. But the international Christian community was in fact beset by powerful forces (reflected by Marsilius) that undermined its cohesiveness and weakened papal authority and influence. Although the culmination of these disruptions did not come until the Reformation in the 1500s, the history of the previous two centuries made it clear that the institution was profoundly troubled.

***The Avignon Exile*** The humiliation of Pope Boniface VIII by the agents of Philip IV of France at Anagni in 1303 opened the doors to French influence at the Curia. In 1305 the College of Cardinals elected a French pope, Clement V, who because of the political disorders in the Papal States eventually settled at Avignon (1309). Though technically a part of the Holy Roman Empire, Avignon was in language and culture a French city. The popes who followed Clement hoped to return to Rome but remained at Avignon, claiming that the continuing turmoil of central Italy would not permit papal government to function effectively. These popes

were skilled administrators who expanded the papal bureaucracy enormously—especially its fiscal machinery—but the long absence from Rome clearly harmed papal prestige.

***Fiscal Crisis*** Like many secular governments, the papacy at Avignon faced an acute fiscal crisis. But unlike the major powers of Europe, its territorial base could not supply it with the funds it needed, because controlling the Papal States usually cost more money than they produced. As a result, the papacy was drawn into the unfortunate practice of exploiting its ecclesiastical powers for financial gain. Thus, the popes insisted that candidates appointed to high ecclesiastical offices pay a special tax, which usually amounted to a third or a half of the first year's revenues. The popes also claimed the income from vacant offices and even sold future appointments to office when the incumbents were still alive. Dispensations, which were also sold, released a petitioner from the normal requirements of canon law. A monastery or religious house, for example, might purchase an exemption from visitation and inspection by the local bishop. The pope received in tithes one-tenth of the revenues of ecclesiastical benefices or offices throughout Christendom. And the Church offered indulgences, remissions of the temporal punishment for sin, in return for monetary contributions to the papacy.

These fiscal practices enlarged the popes' revenues, but they had deplorable results. Prelates who paid huge sums to Avignon tended to pass on the costs to the lower clergy. Parish priests, hardly able to live from their incomes, were more easily tempted to lower their moral standards. The flow of money to Avignon angered rulers and prompted demands for a halt to such payments and even for the confiscation of Church property. Dispensations gravely injured the authority of the bishops, since an exempt person or house all but escaped their supervision. The bishops were frequently too weak, and the pope too distant, to deal effectively with abuses on the local level. The fiscal measures thus helped sow chaos in many parts of the Western Church.

***The Great Schism*** The end of the seventy-year Avignon exile led to a controversy that almost split the Western Church. In 1377 Pope Gregory XI returned reluctantly to Rome and died there a short time later. The Roman people, fearing that Gregory's successor would once more remove the court to Avignon and thereby deprive Rome of desperately needed revenues, agitated for the election of an Italian pope. Responding to this pressure, the College of Cardinals found a compromise candidate who satisfied both French and Italian interests, but the new pope, Urban VI (1378–1389), soon antagonized the French cardinals by trying to limit their privileges and by threatening to pack the College with his own appointments. Seven months after choosing Urban, a majority of the cardinals declared that his election had taken place under duress and was invalid; they then named a new pope, who returned to Avignon. Thus began the Great Schism of the West (1378–1417), the period when two, and later three, popes fought over the rule of the Church.

Christendom now had two pretenders to the throne of Peter, one in Rome and one in Avignon. Princes and peoples quickly took sides (see map 12.3), and the troubles of the papacy multiplied. Each pope had his own court and needed yet more funds, both to meet ordinary expenses and to pay for policies that he hoped would defeat his rival. And since each pope excommunicated the other and those who supported him, everyone in Christendom was at least technically excommunicated.

***The Conciliar Movement***   Theologians and jurists had long speculated on who should rule the Church if the pope were to become heretical or incompetent; some concluded that it should be the College of Cardinals or a general council of Church officials. Since the College of Cardinals had split into two factions, each backing one of the rival popes, many prominent thinkers supported the theory that a general council should rule the Church. These conciliarists, as they were called, went further. They wanted the Church to have a new constitution to confirm the supremacy of a general council. Such a step would have reduced the pope's role to that of a limited monarch, but the need to correct numerous abuses strengthened the idea that a general council should rule and reform the Church.

***Pisa and Constance***   The first test of the conciliarists' position was the Council of Pisa (1409), convened by cardinals of both Rome and Avignon. This council asserted its supremacy within the Church by deposing the two popes and electing another. But this act merely added to the confusion, for it left Christendom with three rivals claiming to be the lawful pope. A second council finally resolved the situation. Some four hundred ecclesiastics assembled at the Council of Constance (1414–1418), the greatest international gathering of the Middle Ages. The council was organized in a new way, with the delegates voting as nations to offset the power of the Italians, who made up nearly half the attendance. This procedure reflected the new importance of national and territorial churches. It enabled the delegates to depose both the Pisan pope and the Avignon pope and persuade the Roman pope to resign. In his stead they elected a Roman cardinal, who took the name Martin V. Thus, the Great Schism was ended, and the Western Church was once again united under a single pope.

As the meetings continued, the views of the conciliarists prevailed. The delegates formally declared that a general council was supreme within the Church. To ensure continuity in Church government, they also directed that new councils be summoned periodically.

## ◆ THE REVIVAL OF THE PAPACY

In spite of this assertion of supremacy, the council made little headway in reforming the Church. The delegates, mostly great prelates, were the chief beneficiaries of the fiscal system and were reluctant to touch their own privileges and advantages. The real victims of the fiscal abuses, the lower clergy, were poorly represented. As a result, the council could not agree on a general program of reform, because it was too large, too cumbersome, and too divided to maintain effective ecclesiastical government. The restored papacy soon reclaimed its position as supreme head of the Western Church.

The practical weaknesses of the conciliar movement were revealed at the Council of Basel (1431–1449). Because disputes broke out almost at once with the pope, the council deposed him and elected another, Felix V. The conciliar movement,

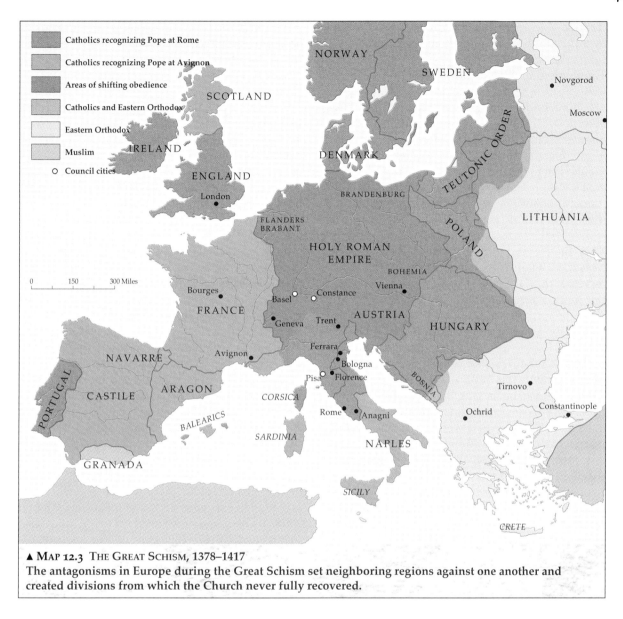

▲ MAP 12.3 THE GREAT SCHISM, 1378–1417
The antagonisms in Europe during the Great Schism set neighboring regions against one another and created divisions from which the Church never fully recovered.

designed to heal the schism, now seemed responsible for renewing it. Recognizing the futility of its actions, the council tried to rescue its dignity when Felix died by endorsing the cardinals' election of a new pope, Nicholas V, in 1449 and then disbanding. This action ended efforts to give supreme authority to councils. But the idea of government by representation that they advanced was to have an important influence on later political developments in Europe.

*Territorial Independence* Although the popes remained suspicious of councils, they had much more serious rivals to their authority in the powerful lay princes, who were exerting ever tighter control over territorial churches. Both England and France issued decrees that limited papal powers within their kingdoms, and this policy was soon imitated in Spain and the stronger principalities of the Holy Roman Empire. Although such decrees did not establish national or territorial churches, they do document the decline of papal control over the international Christian community.

***The Revival of Rome***   When Martin V returned to Rome in 1417, the popes faced the monumental task of rebuilding their office and their prestige as both political and cultural leaders of Europe. They wanted Rome to be a major capital, a worthy home for the papacy, and not dependent on French rulers or culture, as they had been for the past century. To this end, they adopted the new literary and artistic ideas of the Renaissance, and the result was a huge rebuilding program that symbolized the restored authority of the popes. They sought, as one contemporary put it, "by the construction of grand and lasting buildings to increase the honor of the Roman Church and the glory of the Apostolic see, and widen and strengthen the devotion of all Christian people." One of the popes even proclaimed that if any city "ought to shine by its cleanliness and beauty, it is above all that which bears the title of capital of the universe." The building of a new St. Peter's Church in the 1400s was but the climax of this campaign of beautification, designed to assert a cultural supremacy that went along with the supremacy of the Pope's authority. At the same time, vigorous military campaigns in the Papal States subdued that difficult territory and established the papacy as a major Italian power.

It could be argued, however, that in identifying itself so closely with Rome and with Italian politics, the papacy became less universal. For all its splendor and its renewed control over the institution of the Church, it was failing to retain the spiritual allegiance of Europe, especially in the north. The popes may have succeeded in reshaping the Church into a powerful and centralized body, and in making Rome once again a cultural capital of the Western world, but the new cultural and intellectual forces that were at work in the 1400s ultimately undermined the centrality of the papacy to the life of Europe.

◆ STYLES OF PIETY

Partly in response to the disorder of the Church as an institution, new forms of piety and religious practice began to appear. Whereas praying for the salvation of the community had once been considered the clergy's responsibility, many now felt that it was up to each individual to seek the favor of God.

***Lay Mysticism and Piety***   One consequence was that mysticism—an interior sense of the direct presence and love of God—which previously had been seen only in monastic life, began to move out of the monasteries in the thirteenth century. The prime mission of the Franciscans and the Dominicans was preaching to the laity, and they were now communicating some of the satisfactions of mystical religion. Laypersons wishing to remain in the outside world could join special branches of the Franciscans or Dominicans known as third orders. Confraternities, which were religious guilds founded largely for laypersons, grew up in the cities and, through common religious services and programs of charitable activities, tried to deepen the spiritual lives of their members. Humanism had strong overtones of a movement for lay piety. And hundreds of devotional and mystical works were written to teach laypersons how to feel repentance, not just how to define it. Translations of the Scriptures into vernacular languages also appeared, though the Church disapproved of such efforts, and the high cost of manuscripts before the age of printing severely limited their circulation.

This growth of lay piety was, in essence, an effort to give everyone access to forms of faith that hitherto had been restricted to a spiritual elite. Frightened by the disasters of the age, people hungered for emotional reassurance, for evidence of God's love and redeeming grace within themselves. Also, the spread of education among the laity, at least in the cities, made people discontented with empty forms of religious ritual.

***Female Piety***   The commitment to personal piety among the laity was particularly apparent among women. It is significant that in the years between 1000 and 1150 male saints outnumbered females by 12 to 1, but in the years 1348 to 1500 the ratio dropped to 2.74 to 1. Moreover, the typical female saints of the later Middle Ages were no longer queens, princesses, and abbesses. They were mystics and visionaries, ordinary yet charismatic people who gained the attention of the Church and the world by the power of their message and the force of their own personalities. Catherine of Siena (1347–1380), for example, was the youngest of the twenty-five children of a humble Italian dyer. Her reputation for holiness attracted a company of followers from as far away as England, and she wrote (or dictated, for she probably couldn't write) devotional tracts that are monuments of Italian literature. Similar charismatic qualities made a simple Englishwoman, Margery Kempe, famous for her visions and her piety.

Women who out of poverty or preference lived a religious life outside convents became numerous, especially in towns. Some lived with their families, and others eked out a living on the margins of society. Still others lived in spontaneously organized religious houses—called *Beguines* in northern Europe—where they shared all tasks and property. The Church was suspicious of these women professing a religious life outside convents, without an approved rule. But the movement was too large for the Church to suppress or control. And many of them came to be particularly identified with one of the most powerful forms of lay piety in this period, mysticism.

*The Mystics*  Among the most active centers of the new lay piety was the Rhine valley, a region that was especially noted for its remarkable mystics. The most famous was the Dominican Meister Eckhart (1260?–1327?), a spellbinding preacher and a devoted student of Aquinas, who sought to bring his largely lay listeners into a mystical confrontation with God. Believers, he maintained, should cultivate the "divine spark" that is in every soul. To achieve this, they had to banish all thought from their minds and seek to attain a state of pure passivity. If they succeeded, God would come and dwell within them. Eckhart stressed the futility of dogma and, implicitly, traditional acts of piety. God is too great for such categories, he taught, and cannot be moved by conventional piety.

*Brethren of the Common Life*  Just as the nominalists argued for philosophical reasons that God is unknowable, so the mystics dismissed the value of formal knowledge and stressed the need for love and an emotional commitment to God and

▲ *Pisan Artist of XIV Century*
*THE MYSTIC MARRIAGE OF CATHERINE OF SIENA*
**Catherine of Siena was a nun who was known for her efforts to return the papacy to Rome. Part of the reason for her sainthood was that, like Joan of Arc, she experienced visions from an early age. She is shown here with her symbol, the lily, in a scene from one of her visions. About to enter into a mystic marriage with Christ, she is accepting the wedding ring directly from him. Note that in the Renaissance, wedding rings were often placed on the middle finger of the right hand.**
Soprintendenza B.A.A.A.S., Pisa, Museo Nazionale di S. Matteo

his attributes. Perhaps the most influential of the mystics was Gerhard Groote of Holland. Groote wrote sparingly, exerting his influence over his followers largely through his personality. After his death in 1384, his disciples formed a religious congregation known as the Brethren of the Common Life. Taking education as their principal task, they founded schools in Germany and the Low Countries that imparted a style of lay piety known as the *devotio moderna* ("modern devotion"). Later reformers, such as Erasmus of Rotterdam and Martin Luther, were to be among their pupils.

***Thomas à Kempis*** The richest statement of the *devotio moderna* appeared about 1425 in *The Imitation of Christ*, a small devotional manual attributed to Thomas à Kempis, a member of the Brethren of the Common Life. *The Imitation of Christ* says almost nothing about fasting, pilgrimages, or other traditional acts of private piety. Instead, it emphasizes interior experience as essential to religious life. The believer, it argued, needed only to emulate the life of Jesus. The book's ethical and social consciousness is also unusual. Powerful interior faith leads not to extreme acts of personal expiation but to highly ethical behavior: "First, keep yourself in peace, and then you shall be able to bring peace to others."

***Features of Lay Piety*** The new lay piety was by no means a revolutionary break with the medieval Church, but it implicitly discounted the importance of many traditional institutions and practices. In this personal approach to God, there was no special value in the monastic vocation. As Erasmus would later argue, what was good in monasticism should be practiced by every Christian. Stressing simplicity and humility, the new lay piety was reacting against the pomp and splendor that had come to surround popes and prelates and to mark religious ceremonies. Likewise, the detailed rules for fasts, abstinences, and devotional exercises; the cult of the saints and their relics; and the traffic in indulgences and pardons all seemed peripheral to true religious needs. Without the proper state of soul, these traditional acts of piety were meaningless; with the proper state, every act was worship. This new lay piety, emerging as it did out of medieval religious traditions, was clearly a preparation for the reformations of faith that took place in the sixteenth century among both Protestants and Catholics. It helped produce a more penetrating faith at a time when the formal beliefs of the Middle Ages, for all their grandeur and logical intricacies, no longer fully satisfied the religious spirit and were leaving hollows in the human heart.

Although the *devotio moderna* was a religious movement with little regard for humanist learning, it shared the humanists' distaste for the abstractions and intellectual arrogance of Scholasticism, and their belief that a wise and good person will cultivate humility and will maintain a "learned ignorance" toward the profound questions of religion. Moreover, both movements directed their message primarily to laypersons, in order to help them lead a higher moral life. The humanists, of course, drew their chief inspiration from the works of pagan and Christian antiquity, whereas the advocates of the new lay piety looked almost exclusively to Scripture. But the resemblances were close enough for scholars like Erasmus and Thomas More, writing in the early 1500s, to combine elements from both in the movement known as Christian Humanism.

◆ MOVEMENTS OF DOCTRINAL REFORM

The effort to reform the traditions of medieval Christianity also led to open attacks on the religious establishment—fueled, of course, by antagonism toward the papacy and Church corruption and by the larger tensions of this troubled epoch. Above all, these attacks gained support because the Church remained reluctant to adapt its organization and teachings to the demands of a changing world. In two prominent cases, moreover, the critiques arose at a university, where the basic method of instruction, the disputation, encouraged the discussion of unorthodox ideas. At disputations, students learned by listening to arguments for and against standard views. It was not impossible for someone taking the "wrong" side in such a debate to be carried away and cross the line between a theoretical discussion and open dissent.

***Wycliffe*** Whatever its origins, the most prominent of the assaults of the 1300s was launched by an Englishman, John Wycliffe (1320?–1384), who taught at Oxford University. Wycliffe argued that the Church had become too remote from the people, and he wanted its doctrines simplified. To this end, he sought less power for priests and a more direct reliance on the Bible, which he hoped would be translated into English to make it easier to understand. Beyond his unease over the Church's remoteness from ordinary believers, he may have had political reasons (and thus support) for his stand. He was close to members of the royal court, who were increasingly resistant to papal demands and who were troubled that, in the midst of England's war with France, the papacy should have come under French influence when it moved from Rome to Avignon. In 1365 Wycliffe denounced the payment of Peter's pence, the annual tax given by English people to the papacy, and shortly thereafter he publicly denounced the papal Curia, monks, and friars for their vices.

Wycliffe argued that the Scriptures alone declared the will of God and that neither the pope and the cardinals nor the Scholastic theologians could tell Christians what they should believe. In particular, he questioned one of the central dogmas of the Church that emphasized the special power of the priest: transubstantiation, which asserts that priests at the Mass work a miracle when they change the substance of bread and wine into the substance of Christ's body and blood. Besides attacking the exalted position and privileges of the priesthood in such rites as transubstantiation, Wycliffe denied the authority of the pope and the hierarchy to exercise jurisdiction or to hold property. He claimed that the true Church was that of the predestined—that is, those whom God would save and were thus in a state of grace. Only these elect could rule the elect; therefore, popes and bishops who had no grace could have their properties removed and had no right to rule. Responsibility for ecclesiastical reform rested with the prince, and the pope could exercise only as much authority as the prince allowed.

*The Lollards* Many of Wycliffe's views were branded heretical, but even though he was forced to leave Oxford when he offended his protectors at the royal court, they did keep him unharmed until he died. His followers, mostly ordinary people known as Lollards—a name apparently derived from *lollar* ("idler")—were not so lucky. They managed to survive as an underground movement in the countryside until the Protestant Reformation exploded more than a century later, but they were constantly hounded, and in 1428 the Church had Wycliffe's remains dug up, burned, and thrown into a river.

*Hus* An even harsher fate awaited Wycliffe's most famous admirer, a Bohemian priest named

Jan Hus (1369–1415), who started a broad and even more defiant movement in his homeland. Hus was a distinguished churchman and scholar. He served as rector (the equivalent of president) of the Charles University in Prague, one of Europe's best-known institutions, and he was the main preacher at a fashionable chapel in Prague. Like Wycliffe, whose ideas he had first heard expounded at a disputation, he argued that priests were not a holy and privileged group, set apart from laypersons, but that the Church was made up of all the faithful. To emphasize this equality, he rejected the division that allowed the congregation at a Mass to consume the wafer that symbolized Christ's body but not the wine that symbolized his blood, which only the priest could drink. In a dramatic gesture, Hus shared the cup of wine with all worshipers, thus reducing the distinctiveness of the priest. His followers adopted a chalice, or cup, as the symbol of their movement.

Hus was not hesitant about defying the leadership of the Church. Denounced for the positions he had taken, he replied by questioning the authority of the pope himself: "If a Pope is wicked, then like Judas he is a devil and a son of perdition and not the head of the Church militant. If he lives in a manner contrary to Christ, he has entered the papacy by another way than through Christ." In 1415 Hus was summoned to defend his views before the Church Council at Constance. Although he had been guaranteed safe passage if he came to answer accusations of heresy, the promise was broken. He was condemned, handed over to the secular authorities, and executed (see "Hus at Constance," p. 432). But his followers, unlike the Lollards who stayed out of sight in England, refused to retreat in the face of persecution.

*The Hussites* A new leader, Jan Žižka, known as John of the Chalice, raised an army and led a successful campaign against the emperor, who was also king of Bohemia and the head of the crusade that was now mounted against the Hussites. The resistance lasted twenty years, outliving Žižka, but sustained by Bohemian nobles, and eventually the Hussites were allowed to establish a special church, the Utraquist Church, in which both cup and wafer were shared by all worshipers at Mass. But Hus's other demands, such as the

## Hus at Constance

◆

*A few weeks before he was executed, Jan Hus wrote to his Czech followers to tell them how he had responded to his accusers at the Council of Constance:*

"Master Jan Hus, in hope a servant of God, to all faithful Czechs who love God: I call to your attention that the proud and avaricious Council, full of all abomination, condemned my Czech books having neither heard nor seen them; even if it had heard them, it would not have understood them. O, had you seen that Council which calls itself the most holy, and that cannot err, you would have seen the greatest abomination! I have heard it commonly said that Constance would not for thirty years rid itself of the sins which that Council has committed. That Council has done more harm than good.

"Therefore, faithful Christians, do not allow yourselves to be terrified by their decrees, which will profit them nothing. They will fly away like butterflies, and their decrees will turn into a spiderweb.

They wanted to frighten me, but could not overcome God's power in me. They did not dare to oppose me with Scripture.

"I am writing this to you that you may know that they did not defeat me by any Scripture or any proof, but that they sought to seduce me by deceits and threats to recant and abjure. But the merciful Lord God, whose law I have extolled, has been and is with me, and I hope that He will be with me to the end and will preserve me in His grace until death.

"This letter was written in chains, in the expectation of death."

From Matthew Spinka (ed.), *The Letters of John Hus* (Manchester: University Press, 1972), pp. 195–197.

surrender of all personal possessions by the clergy (an echo of St. Francis), were rejected. Those who tried to fight on for these causes were defeated in battle, and after a long struggle the resistance came to an end, having made only a minor dent in the unity of the Church.

## Summary

◆

The popular appeal of Wycliffe and Hus reflected widespread dissatisfaction with official teachings in the late 1300s and 1400s—a dissatisfaction that Petrarch, too, had shared, though he did not challenge traditional doctrine but simply looked elsewhere for moral guidance. The movement that he launched, Humanism, transformed education and the arts, but others were determined to bring change to Europe's spiritual leadership as well. When, in pursuit of this ideal, Wycliffe and Hus chose to risk open confrontation, they demonstrated that reform ideas, advanced by charismatic leaders, could find a following among those who resented the authoritarian and materialistic outlook of the Church. At the same time, however, it became clear that such dissent could not survive without support from nobles, princes, or other leaders of society. Even with such help, the Hussites had to limit their demands; without it, they would have gained nothing. It was one hundred years after Hus's death before a new reformer arose who had learned these lessons, and he was to transform Western Christianity beyond recognition.

# QUESTIONS FOR FURTHER THOUGHT

1. Why is it, when we think of the "golden ages" of history, that it is not just new ideas, but great art, that makes them seem such special times?

2. How do dominant cultural institutions like the medieval Church lose their hold over peoples' loyalty and respect?

# RECOMMENDED READING

## Sources

*Brucker, Gene A. (ed.). The Society of Renaissance Florence: A Documentary Study. 1971.

*Cassirer, Ernst, P. O. Kristeller, and J. H. Randall, Jr. (eds.). The Renaissance Philosophy of Man. 1953. Selections from Petrarch, Ficino, Pico, and others.

*Chambers, David, and Brian Pullan (eds.). Venice: A Documentary History, 1450–1630. 1992.

Kempe, Margery. The Book of Margery Kempe (1436). B. A. Windeatt (tr.). 1985. The autobiography of an extraordinary woman.

*Kohl, Benjamin G., and Ronald G. Witt (eds.). The Earthly Republic: Italian Humanists on Government and Society. 1978.

*Marsilius of Padua. Defender of Peace. Alan Gerwith (tr.). 1986.

## Studies

*Baron, Hans. The Crisis of the Early Italian Renaissance: Civic Humanism and Republican Liberty in the Age of Classicism and Tyranny. 1966. Fundamental analysis of Florentine "civic humanism."

*Berenson, Bernard. The Italian Painters of the Renaissance. 1968. Classic essays on the history of art.

*Burckhardt, Jacob. The Civilization of the Renaissance in Italy. 1958. One of the pioneering works of European history, first published in 1860.

Cole, Bruce. The Renaissance Artist at Work: From Pisano to Titian. 1983.

*Hale, John. The Civilization of Europe in the Renaissance. 1993. The best overview.

*Hollingsworth, Mary. Patronage in Renaissance Italy from 1400 to the Early Sixteenth Century. 1994.

*Huizinga, Johan. The Waning of the Middle Ages. 1954.

Klapisch-Zuber, Christiane. Women, Family, and Ritual in Renaissance Italy. 1985. Collected essays.

*Kristeller, Paul O. Renaissance Thought and Its Sources. 1979. By a leading historian of Renaissance thought.

*Rabb, Theodore K. Renaissance Lives. 1993.

## Web Sites

http://www.kfki.hu/%7Earthp/artist/html

http://www.hermitagemuseum.org

http://www.learner.org/exhibits/renaissance

http://www.mega.it/eng/egui/hogui.htm

*Available in paperback.

# Appendix

## RECOMMENDED FILMS

### Chapter 1

*Ancient Civilizations.* Color. 1978. National Geographic Society. Looks at archaeology of Mesopotamia, Egypt, Greece, Rome, and China.

*\*Ancient Egypt.* 51 min. Color. 1971. Time-Life Video. Kenneth Clark on Egyptian culture and society.

*Ascent of Man: Lower Than the Angels.* 52 min. Color. 1974. BBC. Explores the evolutionary changes of humankind at the dawn of civilization.

*Yesterday's Worlds: The Missing City Gates.* 29 min. Color. National Educational Television. A description of the Assyrians and their civilization.

*Yesterday's Worlds: Treasures from the Land of the Bible.* 29 min. Color. National Educational Television. The Dead Sea Scrolls and ancient Palestine.

### Chapter 2

*Minoan Civilization.* 53 min. Films for the Humanities and Sciences (BDU3289).

*Greek Epic.* 40 min. Films for the Humanities and Sciences. Explores *The Iliad* and *The Odyssey* and examines the nature of the epic.

*The Glory That Was Greece: The Age of Civil War.* 36 min. B/W. Time-Life Films. The revolt against Persia and the Greek victories in the Persian Wars.

### Chapter 3

*The Classical Age.* 57 min. Films for the Humanities and Sciences.

*The Athenian Trireme.* 55 min. Films for the Humanities and Sciences.

*Antigone.* 88 min. B/W. 1962. Fleetwood. Sophocles' play with English subtitles.

*Art of the Western World.* Vol. 1, 1. *The Classical Ideal*, Part I. 28 min. Color. 1989. Educational Broadcasting Corporation, funded by Annenberg/CPB Project. Presents art and architecture within the context of history.

*Plato's Apology: The Life and Teachings of Socrates.* 29 min. Color. 1962. Encyclopedia Britannica Educational Corporation. The teachings of Socrates as presented in Plato's famous dialogue.

### Chapter 4

*The Etruscans.* 27 min. Films for the Humanities and Sciences (BDU132).

*Pompeii: Daily Life of the Ancient Romans.* 45 min. Color. Films for the Humanities and Sciences. Uses artifacts from Pompeii to recreate Roman life.

*I, Claudius.* 780 min. Color. 1976. Series depicting the history of the Roman Empire from Emperors Augustus to Claudius.

*Julius Caesar: The Rise of the Roman Empire.* 22 min. Color. 1962. Encyclopedia Britannica Educational Corporation. Examines the successes of Julius Caesar.

### Chapter 5

*Cyber Rome.* 39 min. Films for the Humanities and Sciences. A tour of Rome, about A.D. 200, in virtual reality.

*Intimate Details of Roman Life.* 27 min. Color. Films for the Humanities. Everyday life in the early Empire.

*Testament: Thine Is the Kingdom.* 52 min. Color. Films for the Humanities. Christianity under Diocletian and Constantine.

## Chapter 6

*Beowolf.* 38 min. Color. Films for the Humanities. Detailed contextual survey of the epic.

*The Book of Kells.* 26 min. Color. Films for the Humanities and Sciences. Identifies the faces and figures in the drawings of the book and explains the symbolism.

*The City of God.* 39 min. Color. Film for the Humanities and Sciences. Surveys the resurgence of the Church, development of the Vulgate Bible, Pope Gregory the Great, Romanesque architecture, and the significance of pilgrimages.

*The Lindisfarne Gospels: A Masterpiece of Anglo-Saxon Book Painting.* 35 min. Color. Films for the Humanities and Sciences. Explains the creation of the gospels.

*Medieval Manuscripts.* 30 min. Color. Films for the Humanities and Sciences. Surveys the work behind the making of manuscripts and the key role that monasteries played in the preservation of Western culture.

## Chapter 7

*Charlemagne.* 240 min. 1995. British miniseries.

*Constantinople: City in the Middle Ages.* 17 min. Color. 1992. Britannica Films.

*Islam: The Prophet and the People.* 34 min. Color. 1975. Texture. A biography of Muhammed and a history of the Islamic people.

*The Vikings.* Ten 30-min. episodes. Color. 1980. Films for the Humanities. Surveys the life and culture of the Vikings.

*The World of Islam: Islamic Art and Islamic Science and Technology.* 30-min. episodes. Color. Films for the Humanities. Surveys Islamic artistic and scientific contributions in the Middle Ages.

## Chapter 8

*Castle.* 60 min. Color. 1983. Unicorn Projects. Study of castle construction in Wales.

*The Crusades.* 200 min., 5-part series. Color. 1995. A&E Home Video. Terry Jones explores the subject of the crusades during the eleventh and twelfth centuries.

*The Crusades: Saints and Sinners.* 25 min. Color. 1967. Learning Corporation of America. Examines the First Crusade based on contemporary accounts.

*Medieval London: 1066–1500.* 20 min. Color. Films for the Humanities and Sciences. Traces some major events in London from 1066 to 1500, including the rebuilding of Westminster Abbey in the Gothic style, the first stone bridge across the Thames, and the occurrence of the Black Death.

*The Middle Ages: The Rise of Feudalism.* 20 min. Color. Encyclopedia Britannica Educational Corporation. Surveys the development of feudalism using contemporary documents.

## Chapter 9

*Acts of Faith: Jewish Civilization in Spain.* 52 min. Color. Films for the Humanities and Sciences. Examines the Jewish civilization in Spain and its remnants.

*Art of the Western World.* Vol. 1, *1. A White Garment of Churches—Romanesque and Gothic*, Part II. 28 min. Color. 1989. Educational Broadcasting Corporation, funded by Annenberg/CPB Project. Presents art and architecture within the context of history.

*Becket.* 149 min. Color. Paramount. Tells the story of Henry II's conflict with Thomas Becket.

*Cathedral.* 60 min. Color. 1985. Unicorn Projects. Account of the building of a thirteenth-century cathedral.

*Hildegard of Bingen.* 52 min. Color. 1997. Oblate Media and Communication Corporation. Explores the life of this famous medieval woman.

*Illuminated Lives: A Brief History of Women's Work in the Middle Ages.* Color. 1982. National Film Board of Canada.

*Lion in Winter.* 1968. Color. Portrays the conflict between Henry II and his family at their Christmas court.

## Chapter 10

*Mongols: Storm from the East.* 200 min., 4-part series. Color. Films for the Humanities and Sciences.

*Medieval Realms. Britain from 1066–1500: From the Collections of the British Library.* CD-ROM. Films for the Humanities and Sciences. Includes manuscripts; historical documents and maps; pictures of buildings and artifacts; extracts from wills, chronicles, letters, and charters; music; and spoken word recordings.

*The Trinity Apocalypse.* Films for the Humanities and Sciences. Illustrations from this thirteenth-century manuscript with transliteration of the original text.

## Chapter 11

*Civilization: Romance and Reality.* 50 min. Color. 1969. BBC. Kenneth Clark on the achievements of the later Middle Ages in France and Italy.

*Faith and Fear.* 40 min. Color. 1976. McGraw-Hill. Examines religion in the period of the Black Death.

*The Fall of Constantinople.* 34 min. Color. 1970. Time-Life Films. Examination of Constantinople's demise; filmed on location.

*Henry V.* 138 min. Color. 1989. Portrayal of Shakespeare's classic telling of the battle of Agincourt.

*Joan of Arc.* 26 min. Color. 1976. Learning Corporation of America. Recreates the era and personality of Joan of Arc using modern interview techniques.

*York Mystery Plays: The Annunciation and Joseph's Trouble About Mary.* 25 min. Color. Films for the Humanities and Sciences. Reconstruction of two fifteenth-century mystery plays.

## Chapter 12

*Renaissance: The Artist.* 55 min. Color. 1994. PBS.

*The Seventh Seal.* 96 min. B/W. 1956. Allegorical film portraying a "man, his eternal search for God, with death his only certainty."

*Civilization: The Hero as Artist.* 52 min. Color. 1970. Time-Life Films. Kenneth Clark on the High Renaissance.

*I, Leonardo da Vinci.* 52 min. Color. 1965. McGraw-Hill. Uses his journals and writings.

*Tradesmen and Treasures: Gothic and Renaissance Nuremberg.* 60 min. Color. Bayerischer Fund with the Metropolitan Museum of Art. Uses art and artifacts to explore fourteenth-, fifteenth-, and sixteenth-century Nuremberg.

# Text Credits

## Chapter 1

**(13)** Reprinted from *The Code of Hammurabi*, Robert F. Harper, trans., Gordon Press, 1904, 1991. Reprinted with permission. **(26)** Scripture quotations from Exodus, 15, are from the *Revised Standard Version of the Bible*. Copyright © 1946, 1952, 1971 by the Division of Christian Education of the National Council of the Churches of Christ in the USA. Used by permission. **(27)** Scripture quotations from Jeremiah, 11, are from the *Revised Standard Version of the Bible*. Copyright © 1946, 1952, 1971 by the Division of Christian Education of the National Council of the Churches of Christ in the USA. Used by permission.

## Chapter 2

**(48)** From *Black Athena* by Martin Bernal, Rutgers University Press, 1987, pp. 17–23, abridged. Reprinted by permission. **(48)** Excerpt from *Black Athena Revisited* edited by Mary R. Lefkowitz and Guy MacLean Rogers. Copyright © 1996 by the University of North Carolina Press. Used by permission of the publisher. **(53)** From Guy Davenport, *7 Greeks*. Copyright © 1995 by Guy Davenport. Reprinted by permission of New Directions Publishing Corp. **(65)** From *Herodotus, Book VII*, M. H. Chambers, trans., pp. 101–104. Copied with permission from Ayer Co. Publishers, Inc., N. Stratford, NH 03590.

## Chapter 3

**(78)** From *The Last Days of Socrates* by Plato, translated by Hugh Tredennick, Penguin Classics 1954, Second revised edition 1969. Copyright © 1954, 1959, 1969 by Hugh Tredennick. Reproduced by permission of Penguin Books Ltd. **(86)** Abridged from *The Peloponnesian War* by Thucydides, translated by Rex Warner, Penguin Classics, 1954. Copyright © 1954 Rex Warner. Reproduced by permission of Penguin Books Ltd.

## Chapter 6

**(200)** Excerpt from *The Rule of St. Benedict in Latin and English with Notes* edited by Timothy Fry, Liturgical Press, 1980, pp. 261–265. Reprinted with permission.

## Chapter 8

**(266)** From William Fitz Stephen, *Norman London*, Italica Press, pp. 52, 54. Used by permission of Italica Press, in cooperation with The Historical Association, London. **(270)** C. W. Hollister et al., *Medieval Europe: A Short Sourcebook*. Copyright © 1992 by McGraw-Hill. Reprinted by permission of The McGraw-Hill Companies. **(276)** From *Basic Documents in Medieval History* by Norman Downs. Copyright © 1959 by Krieger Publishing Company. Reprinted with permission.

## Chapter 9

**(295)** From *The Middle Ages: Sources of Medieval History*, Fifth Edition, by Brian Tierney et al., pp. 172–175. Copyright © 1992 by McGraw-Hill. Reprinted with permission from The McGraw-Hill Companies.

## Chapter 10

**(335, 354)** From *Women's Lives in Medieval Europe: A Source Book* by Emilie Amt, pp. 195–196, 264–265. Reprinted with permission from Routledge. **(352)** From *Medieval Europe: A Short Source Book* by Warren Hollister et al., pp. 215–216. Copyright © 1994 McGraw-Hill. Reprinted with permission from The McGraw-Hill Companies.

## Chapter 11

**(365)** From *Medieval Europe: A Short Source Book* by Warren Hollister et al., pp. 215–216. Copyright © 1994 McGraw-Hill. Reprinted with permission from The McGraw-Hill Companies. **(376)** Excerpted from "Did Women Have A

# *Volume of Index*

*Index notes: Main themes are indicated in **bold type.** Page numbers in *italics* indicate illustrations and their captions; page numbers followed by *m* indicate maps; page numbers followed by *t* indicate tables; page numbers followed by *n* indicate notes.